The Beautiful, the True & the Good

Studies in Philosophy and the
History of Philosophy

General Editor: Jude P. Dougherty

Volume 58

The Beautiful, the True & the Good

Studies in the History of Thought

Robert E. Wood

The Catholic University of America Press
Washington, D.C.

Library of Congress Cataloging-in-Publication Data

Wood, Robert E., 1934–

[Essays. Selections]

The beautiful, the true, and the good : studies in the history of thought /
Robert E. Wood.

pages cm. — (Studies in philosophy and the history of philosophy ;
Volume 58)

Includes bibliographical references and index.

ISBN 978-0-8132-2747-4 (cloth : alk. paper)

1. Phenomenology.   2. Philosophy—History.   I. Title.

B829.5.W66 2015

190—dc23   2015001339

To my grandchildren and great grandchildren—
the hope for the future

Contents

Acknowledgments

The chapters collected in this volume have appeared in the following sources: "Nature, Culture, and the Dialogical Imperative," in *History: Essays in Honor of Kenneth Schmitz*, ed. M. Baur and R. Wood (Washington, D.C.: The Catholic University of America Press, 2011), 325–39; "Reflections on Heraclitus," *Existentia* XIV, fasc. 3–4 (2004): 177–85; "Parmenides," based on a chapter in *A Path into Metaphysics* (Albany: State University of New York Press, 1991), 125–132. "Plato's Line Revisited: The Pedagogy of Complete Reflection," *The Review of Metaphysics* XLIV (March 1991): 525–47; "Phenomenology and the Perennial Task of Philosophy: A Study of Plato and Aristotle," *Existentia* XII, fasc. 3–4 (2002): 253–63; "Two Banquets: Plato's and Kierkegaard's," *Stages on Life's Way* in International Kierkegaard Commentary (Atlanta: Mercer University Press, 2000), 49–68; "Plato, Descartes, Heidegger: An Inquiry into the Paths of Inquiry," *Existentia* XIII, fasc. 3–4 (2003): 161–78; "Art and Truth: Plato, Nietzsche, Heidegger," in *On Truth: A Robust Presence*, ed. K. Pritzl (Washington, D.C.: The Catholic University of America Press, 2010); "The Self and the Other: Towards a Re-interpretation of Aquinas' List of the Transcendentals," *Philosophy Today* X (Spring 1966): 43–63; "Kant's Antinomic Aesthetics," in *Immanuel Kant*, ed. Philip Rossi and John Treloar, Special Issue of the *American Catholic Philosophical Quarterly* (Spring 2001): 271–95; "Hegel: From Misunderstanding to a Beginning of Understanding," *Epoché* (2011): 337–49; "Hegel on the Heart," *International Philosophical Quarterly* (June 2001): 133–44; "The Free Spirit: Spinoza, Hegel, Nietzsche," *International Philosophical Quarterly* (2011); "Monasticism, Eternity, and the Heart: Hegel, Nietzsche, Dostoevsky," *Philosophy and Theology* 13, no. 2 (2001): 193–211; "High and Low in Nietzsche's *Zarathustra*," in *Friedrich Nietzsche*, ed. Charles Bambach, Special Edition of *American Catholic Philosophical Quarterly*, 2010, 357–82; "Five Bodies and a Sixth: On the Place of Awareness in an Evolutionary

x   Acknowledgments

Universe," *American Catholic Philosophical Quarterly* 83 (Winter 2009): 95–105; "Six Heideggerian Figures," in *Martin Heidegger*, ed. John Caputo, Special Issue of the *American Catholic Philosophical Quarterly* 49 (Spring 1995): 311–33; "The Phenomenologists," in *Philosophy for the XXIst Century*, ed. George McLean (New York: University Press of America, 1989), 131–60; "Weiss on Adumbration," *Philosophy Today* 22 (Winter 1984): 339–48; "Buber's Use of Oriental Themes," in *Martin Buber: A Centenary Volume*, ed. H. Gordon and J. Bloch (New York: Ktav, 1984), 325–49; "The Dialogical Principle and the Mystery of Being: The Enduring Relevance of Buber and Marcel," *International Journal for the Philosophy of Religion*, 1999, 83–97; "Silence, Being, and the Between: Picard, Heidegger, Buber," *Man and World* 27 (1994): 121–34.

Preface

> What is acquired is truly acquired only if it is taken up again
> in a fresh momentum of thought.
>
> — Maurice Merleau-Ponty,
> *Phenomenology of Perception*

The text before you is a selection of papers published over a period of more than four decades. Each is grounded in the regular teaching of graduate and undergraduate courses and based on the reading of select classic texts from Heraclitus and Parmenides to Nietzsche and Heidegger. Some of them consist in a reading of a single text, some in a wide variety of texts from a single thinker, and others are comparisons of the works of two or three figures on a single theme or set of related themes.

The title of the present work, *The Beautiful, the True, and the Good*, focuses on the fundamental themes that operated throughout my career: thinking, Being, and the heart. The human being is the thinking being who thinks with both intellect and heart, and what is thought most basically is presented through the notion of Being. I am particularly concerned with the notion of the heart as the zone of radical subjectivity and its relation to the encompassing, indicated by the notion of Being that includes everything in its scope. It is linked to the matter of aesthetics, as indicated by my book *Placing Aesthetics* and its completed sequel, *Nature, Artforms, and the World Around Us*, as well as by several pieces in the present work.

The basic method I employ throughout this book is "descriptive phenomenology," which attends to how things present themselves in the field of experience. The basic structure of this field calls for the interpretation of what is described directly, especially as present in the texts of the philosophic tradition. That same structure orients us beyond current understanding and calls for dialogue.

The central idea of this book is the notion of Being, which in principle covers all that is by way of intention. It is an empty notion—having the erotic structure that Plato describes as always empty but as having designs on fullness. Placing us beyond the here-and-now of sensory awareness, the notion of Being grounds our ability to recognize forms that are repeatable any time and any place their instances are met. Oriented toward the Whole, we are detached from any part of the whole, including our own lives, and are thus given over to ourselves to do what we will, grounding our responsibility. Intellect and will are grounded in the notion of Being, but Being covers both the level of the universal *and* the level of the individual.

The emptiness of the notion of Being solicits understanding and choice, through the notions of the True and the Good, to fill the empty space of meaning between the sensory and the totality. Thus arise differing cultures and differing epochs within a culture. The interplay in the individual between genetic endowment and cultural shaping opens the space for individual choice, which leads to the establishment of character. Central here is the notion of the heart, the locus of radical individuality, and the default mode for one's spontaneous preferences. Central to my work is art: the artist, rendered sensitive to beauty by nature, produces artworks that arise from the heart and address themselves to the heart.

This work involves two different modes of thinking: what Heidegger has called *representative-calculative thinking* and *meditative thinking*, conquestive thinking that masters and orders what is known by that part of oneself we have come to call "intellect," and letting oneself be taken by that upon which one meditates or what I call "thinking with the heart" or "thinking with the whole of oneself." The former operates in abstraction and absence; the latter operates in presence. Thus, the work involves both modes of thinking in which the notion of Being is central.

The first and enduring influence on my thought is my study of Plato, especially in his *Republic* where the philosopher is first introduced as "the lover of the vision of Beauty Itself," set off from the lovers of beautiful things as the highest achievement of education in the purged city. The Line of Knowledge follows (to which I have devoted what might be considered the grounding move in my own thought), filling in the space of meaning between beautiful things and Beauty Itself. The Line is the first phenomenological inventory of the field of experience and is absolutely central to my own thought. The love of Beauty Itself grounds the pursuit of the True that appears in light of the Good as the term of aspiration—hence the title of this work. The exposition of Plato's Line—chapter 3, one of the most important chapters in this volume—lays the foundation, as it were, of the Western philosophical tradition as it lays the foundation for my own thought. I return to its themes several times in this collection of essays.

My approach is also guided by Heidegger's focus on the ground of metaphysics, dwelling in the world that underpins metaphysics and yields the "sense of Being." For Heidegger, this leads to an inquiry into the history of Western thought from its "first beginning" in Plato, and its culmination in Hegel and Nietzsche, to a "second beginning," working from the ground of metaphysics to conduct a fugal *Zuspiel*, playing counterpoint with the tradition and listening for the "echoes" that sound out of the tradition. While the tradition is governed by "representative-calculative" thinking, the second beginning is conducted through "meditative thinking," appreciative thinking that allows things to draw near and become significant presences.[1] It is the notion of indwelling, coming to presence, drawing near playing counterpoint to conceptualization, that has been and is my constant preoccupation. And just as Heidegger turned toward the arts in following his way back into the ground of metaphysics so have I paid special attention to the arts as the work of the heart.

Heidegger appears four times in the following essays: comparing him with Plato and Descartes on the notion of method ("An Inquiry into the Paths of Inquiry"), comparing him with Plato and Nietzsche ("Art and Truth"), giving an exposition of his thought by focusing upon six different human forms of life ("Six Heideggerian Figures"), and comparing him with Martin Buber and Max Picard on the link between "Silence, Being, and the Between" that concludes this book.

1. See *Heidegger's Contributions to Philosophy: On Enowning*, trans. P. Emad and K. Maly (Bloomington: Indiana University Press, 1999), 3–7. For a sketch, see my "The Fugal Lines of Heidegger's *Beiträge*," *Existentia* 11, fasc. 3–4 (2001). The two types of thinking are introduced in his "Memorial Address," in *Discourse on Thinking*, trans. J. Anderson and E. Freund (New York: Harper, 1966), 46–47. I am aware of Heidegger's not-too-exemplary life, but I do not believe that negatively affects what he has written. I am *also* aware of John Caputo's *Demythologizing Heidegger* (Bloomington: Indiana University Press, 1993), much of which I accept: the later Heidegger's presentation of a *Judenrein* story of the continuity between the Greeks and the Germans, obliterating the other origin of Western culture, Judaism carried forward by Christianity, and his lack of attention to the other person, especially those who are more "other": the poor, the sick, the outcast, the focus of Christian *kardia*.

The approach through Heidegger has a special connection with the meditative mode of thought and its relation to the lifeworld. In Heidegger's terms, it is the mode sensitive to the "aletheic" level of truth that founds the "orthotic." Coming out of concealment (*a-letheia*) and preserving the relation to the concealed mystery of Being (the *Lethe*) founds the space of lived meaning and makes possible our re-presentations and the formulation of propositions whose correspondence to what is given can be checked. This concept appears in different forms in Martin Buber and Gabriel Marcel ("The Dialogical Principle and the Mystery of Being"), the subjects of the penultimate paper in this collection.

Hegel is the third major figure anchoring my own thought. I focus attention upon Hegel in three chapters. The first is "Hegel: From Misunderstanding to the Beginning of Understanding," which heads off the widespread ways in which Hegel is misread and therefore summarily rejected. I follow that with "Hegel on the Heart," heading off a misinterpretation involved in Kierkegaard's critique. I also deal with Hegel in comparison with Spinoza and Nietzsche in "The Free Spirit: Spinoza, Hegel, and Nietzsche." This chapter shows three different systematic frameworks within which one can consider the free spirit as one involving the recognition of necessity. My claim is that Hegel provides the most adequate framework for doing justice to our experience of freedom; however, the other two thinkers have also contributed much to that understanding.[2]

The introductory piece to the current volume ("Nature, Culture, and the Dialogical Imperative") is directed to the contemporary context.[3] It deals, phenomenologically, with the basic structure of the field of human experience that grounds the requirement to step out of one's own basic orientation in order to—as Nietzsche put it—"develop as many eyes as possible." The task is to see things from a diversity of points of view, to establish a set of epicenters from one's own proclivities, in order to see things more richly, more broadly, more profoundly so as to be able to conduct fruitful dialogue. This sets up the study of the history of thought centered upon classic texts from a variety of different thinkers: ancient

2. I have published several other articles on Plato, Hegel, and Heidegger that I am gathering for a volume called *Three Paths of Thinking*.

3. This essay appeared originally in *Person, Being, and History: Essays in Honor of Kenneth Schmitz* (Washington D.C.: The Catholic University of America Press, 2011), which I edited with Michael Baur.

Greeks, Latin medievals, moderns, and contemporaries. But the overriding interest is not historical, not directed toward what they *used* to think, but to what they have to say to us *now* about "the Things Themselves." Both that orientation and the introductory chapter have their roots in the practice of phenomenology.

As the first historically oriented piece ("Reflections on Heraclitus") states, these chapters exhibit an attempt at what Gadamer has called a *Horizontverschmelzung*, a "fusion of horizons" between a contemporary state of mind and the figure studied—in this case Heraclitus—a principle that is uppermost in my own practice. In this chapter, I focus attention not only upon Heraclitus's familiar teaching of universal flux; it highlights the fact that the flux occurs according to fixed measures that are provided by the cosmic Logos that, in turn, is instantiated by various languages that draw its speakers out of their privacy and into a public space of meaning. Among other things, the first chapter draws upon evolutionary theory that is picked up again later in "Five Bodies and a Sixth."

Heraclitus and Parmenides are the deepest of the pre-Socratics. Plato's Line of Knowledge assimilates central aspects from each of these thinkers, and they lead into Aristotle's concepts as well. And, as a lead into Plato and Aristotle, the chapter on Heraclitus is followed by one developed from a chapter on Parmenides that appeared in my *Path into Metaphysics: Phenomenological, Hermeneutical, and Dialogical Studies.*[4] It is both a commentary on Parmenides and a discussion of Heidegger's interpretation. I show how Parmenides's introduction of the notion of Being shorn of all nonbeing provides what might be called a "negative onto-theo-logy," to use Heidegger's expression.

Continuing the treatment of Plato's Line of Knowledge, in "The Phenomenologists" I sketch the linkage between Plato's Cave and Line and various early phenomenologists: Husserl, Scheler, Heidegger, Sartre, and Merleau-Ponty. In "Recollection and Two Banquets: Plato's and Kierkegaard's," I show the parallels and differences between the *Symposium* and *In Vino Veritas*. This chapter focuses on the theme of beauty in Plato and that of the aesthete in Kierkegaard. In "Plato, Descartes, Heidegger: An Inquiry into the Paths of Inquiry," the methods Plato employs in his var-

4. This appeared in 1991 through the State University of New York in Albany, New York.

ious works, especially in his *Statesman* (aimed, as he said, not so much at understanding the statesman as at understanding how to think about *all* things), are compared with the narrowing of methodology in Descartes and the questioning of the full adequacy of method by Heidegger. In the most ample piece in this volume, "Art and Truth," I have also compared Plato with Nietzsche and Heidegger on the notions in question.

Following upon inquiries that begin with Plato, we move forward historically to Aristotle, attempting to show works of both thinkers as proto-phenomenology. Together, they provide an inventory of the basic features of the field of awareness within which all inquiry and, indeed, all human life takes place. Aristotle's thought is to a large extent an explanatory resituating of what is provided in the field of experience to which Plato attended.

Then follow treatments of the pillars of Latin Medieval thought: Augustine and Aquinas. I consider Augustine's *Confessions* and Aquinas's reflections on the transcendentals. My treatment of Aquinas here was my first published piece. It puts Aquinas in relation to Jean-Paul Sartre and focuses upon *aliquid* or otherness as a key to understanding the hierarchy of being. Though it was written over forty years ago, I find that I can still, for the most part, stand by it today; indeed, I find it contains the basic orientation that has governed my thought ever since. It foreshadows my increasing interest in the thought of Hegel, whose central insight is identity-in-difference realized for him in the Incarnation and the Trinity. I assimilated this text on Aquinas as the climax to my treatment of the antecedent metaphysical tradition in my exposition of Aquinas's metaphysics in a chapter in my *A Path into Metaphysics*. It was this early work focusing upon the Other that led me to my first book, *Martin Buber's Ontology: An Interpretation of I and Thou*, which centers upon relationality.[5] Though by no means trying to be a Thomist, I have found that the central themes of Aquinas remain central to my own thought.

The treatment of the *Confessions* in "The Heart in/of Augustine's *Confessions*" focuses upon the notion of the heart, which has been one of the dominant themes in my own thought and is the locus of human dwelling as it is the ground of meditative thinking.[6] The heart was also

5. Published in 1969 by Northwestern University Press.
6. I translated and provided an extensive introduction to Stephan Strasser's *Phenomenology of Feeling: An Essay on the Phenomena of the Heart* (1977).

the central theme of my book *Placing Aesthetics: Reflections on the Philosophical Tradition*.[7] The same theme, the notion of the heart, also appears, to the astonishment of many, as central to understanding Hegel's view of human existence, setting the place of "passion and inwardness" (that Kierkegaard falsely claims Hegel forgot "in world-historical absent-mindedness") within the general structures of human experience ("Hegel on the Heart"). A related piece compares Hegel, Nietzsche, and Dostoyevsky on the notions of "Monasticism, Eternity, and the Heart."

"Kant's 'Antinomic' Aesthetics" picks up on one of my dominant interests: aesthetics. It focuses upon the contrarian character of the properties of the beautiful as Kant presents them. It is linked to the discussion of Plato, Nietzsche, and Heidegger in "Art and Truth."[8]

Nietzsche appeared in conjunction with Plato and Heidegger in my treatment of the just mentioned article and also in conjunction with Hegel and Dostoyevsky in my treatment of the themes of monasticism, eternity, and the heart. I also give exclusive consideration to Nietzsche's central work, *Thus Spoke Zarathustra*, in "High and Low in Nietzsche's *Zarathustra*." Here, I not only give an exposition but also attempt to defend his hierarchy of values. I do so by appealing to the notion that Nietzsche regarded as "the last trailing cloud of evaporating reality" but which is central to my own thought and the speculative tradition generally: the notion of Being.[9]

"Five Bodies and a Sixth" sketches the positions of Hobbes, Berkeley, Descartes, Plato, and Aristotle and then argues for the superiority of a Leibnizian–Whiteheadian view that can come to terms with an evolutionary worldview and deal more adequately with the phenomena highlighted in each of the first five views. The approach is guided by Nietzsche's notion of "fidelity to the earth," stressing the essential incarnate character of human experience.

---

7. Published in 1999 by Ohio University Press in Athens, Ohio, this book was the recipient of an American Library Association's Choice Outstanding Academic Title Award for 2000.

8. I followed the idea of aesthetics from Plato to Heidegger in *Placing Aesthetics*. Here, I placed aesthetics phenomenologically in the field of human experience, claiming its locus lies in the human heart; I placed it in the history of thought through the treatment of thirteen focal figures; and I placed it in each of the figures within the general conceptual framework of his thought, lying at the center, I claim, rather than on the periphery of the speculative tradition.

9. This *pia interpretatio* is not unaware of many outrageous things Nietzsche has said in his posthumous papers. Walter Kaufmann has largely defanged many criticisms in his *Nietzsche: Philosopher, Psychologist, Antichrist* (New York: Meridian Books, 1956). I prefer to harvest what I find suitable for thought trained primarily upon "the Things Themselves."

Three chapters deal with the nature of *indwelling* or inhabiting the life-world. "Six Heideggerian Figures" gathers together Heidegger's thoughts on indwelling in relation to the poet, the peasant, the philosopher, the scientist, the contemporary man on the street, and the thinker.

The chapter "Weiss on Adumbration" attempts to assimilate Paul Weiss's key notion to understanding his *Modes of Being* and the expansion involved in *Beyond All Appearances*. The notion of adumbration points to a peculiar experience of encompassment, a kind of indwelling in each of the regional modes of Being that leads on the attempts at conceptual elaboration. This relation has parallels with Heidegger's two notions of truth, *aletheia*, a mode of indwelling that founds *orthotes*, the level of conceptual formulation. Weiss is an unduly neglected thinker whom Mortimer Adler called "the wisest man of the twentieth century."

Along the same lines, and, indeed, giving the first and enduring orientation to my thought through Buber, in "Buber's Use of Oriental Themes" I focus upon the turn toward the East that developed from my book *Martin Buber's Ontology*. Its central theme is *Lehre* (teaching), whose aim is the transformation of human life. The felt sense of indwelling in Heidegger, Weiss, and Buber runs throughout my work and also appears in the penultimate chapter on Marcel and Buber, "The Dialogical Principle and the Mystery of Being." It hearkens back to the introductory chapter on the dialogical principle.

I end the collection with "Silence, Being, and the Between: Picard, Heidegger, and Buber," which brings into focus two notions central to human reflection, Being and the Between (the space limned by the relations of I to Persons, Nature, and God), and the disposition required for dwelling in them. I think it appropriate to end on silence.

Throughout this work, I have attempted to think with the various philosophers about the issues with which they have wrestled. Such an attempt is always guided by the practice of phenomenological description, whose essential points I sketch in the introductory chapter.[10]

---

10. There is some duplication in the papers, owing to the way they were written. But I have decided to keep each paper intact. In each case, recalling the main points is essential to the argument. Further, recalling a topic treated previously will serve to reinforce the earlier treatment and keep it in the mind of the reader as he/she continues through the work.

Introduction

Human Nature, Culture, and the Dialogical Imperative

THE CONTEMPORARY SITUATION

The horizon of contemporary discussion includes a rejection of human nature that stands in tension with attempts to revive the notion within the context of dialogue. Lyotard considers the notion of human nature as a construct of the Enlightenment, a blanched, one-leveled notion that destroys the plurality of cultural experiences. He reaffirms the plurality of Wittgensteinian language games and rejects the Habermasian search for consensus by calling attention to the dissension from dominant paradigms that leads to scientific expansion.[1] Habermas claims that the structure of language implies a decentered subjectivity in a community underpinned by language and aimed at an ideal consensus to be sought through dialogue governed by the power of the stronger argument.[2] Heidegger lays the grounds for that possibility through his questioning of Being as the ground for the emergence of collective worlds of meaning.[3] Derrida also argues for the priority of the notion of Being as opening up fields of discourse[4] but argues against a logocentric understanding of it. By "logocentrism," he understands both the dominance of logic, which presupposes translogical starting points for its machinery to work upon, and the *logos*-centrism of Heidegger's reading of Heraclitean

1. Jean-François Lyotard, *The Postmodern Condition: A Report on Knowledge*, trans. G. Bennington and B. Massumi (Minneapolis: University of Minnesota Press, 1984), 503.
2. Jürgen Habermas, "Discourse Ethics: Notes on a Program of Philosophical Justification," in *Moral Consciousness and Communicative Action*, trans. C. Lenhardt and S. Nicholsen (Cambridge, Mass.: The MIT Press, 1990), 43–115.
3. Martin Heidegger, *Being and Time*, trans. J. Maquarrie and E. Robinson (New York: Harper and Row, 1962), 2–35.
4. Jacques Derrida, "The Supplement of the Copula: Philosophy before Linguistics," in *Margins of Philosophy*, trans. A. Bass (Chicago: The University of Chicago Press, 1982), 194–205.

gathering.[5] For Derrida, the *logos* is disseminated and *différance* takes center stage as metaphysics is "sent packing."[6] Derrida in effect rejected a proposed dialogue with Gadamer, who, following Heideggerian *Logos-Being*, seeks a *Horizont-verschmelzung* with other thinkers.[7]

Conversely, Levinas, like Kierkegaard, claims that there is a basic totalitarianism implicit in the notion of Being, whether given a Hegelian or a Heideggerian reading. He favors an infinity "beyond Being" that transcends the enclosed universe of Being and leaves its trace in the face of the human Other. Levinas would replace ontology, understood as a comprehensive "physics," with metaphysics as a disciplined attention to what is "*meta*," beyond.[8]

In relation to this situation, I will argue, against Lyotard, that there is a human nature that has a peculiar bipolar character: it is biologically grounded and ontologically referred, via the notion of Being, to the whole of what is. The ontological reference is shared in different ways by Heidegger and Derrida, the latter of whom attempts to occupy a ground between Heidegger and Levinas.[9] I would claim that the grounding in ontological reference is precisely the basis for openness to the mystery of the Beyond, which is both revealed and concealed in the present epiphany of the face of the human Other upon which Levinas is focused. I consider talk of something "beyond Being" as nonsense since by claiming that "there is" something beyond Being, it is positioned within Being. I would claim that, by reason of its bipolarity, human nature is culture-creating, establishing a second nature on top of the first. Its bipolar character gives human activity its unitary ground; its culture-creating consequence gives that activity its diversity and concreteness. But that unitary

5. Jacques Derrida, *Of Grammatology*, trans. G. Spivak (Baltimore: Johns Hopkins University Press, 1976), 3, 23, 74.

6. Jacques Derrida, "Différance," in *Speech and Phenomena and Other Essays*, trans. D. Allison (Evanston, Ill.: Northwestern University Press, 1973), 129–60; *Of Spirit: Heidegger and the Question*, trans. G. Bennington and R. Bowlby (Chicago: The University of Chicago Press, 1989), 75.

7. See also D. Michelfelder and R. Palmer, eds., *Dialogue and Deconstruction: The Gadamer-Derrida Encounter* (Albany: State University of New York Press, 1989); Hans-Georg Gadamer, *Truth and Method* (New York: Crossroad, 1975), 273ff and 337ff.

8. Emmanuel Levinas, *Totality and Infinity*, trans. A. Lingis (Pittsburgh: Duquesne University Press, 1969), 33–52.

9. Jacques Derrida, "Violence and Metaphysics," in *Writing and Difference*, trans. Alan Bass (Chicago: The University of Chicago Press, 1978), 79–153.

ground entails several positive and negative imperatives that center upon inquiry and freedom and impel us to dialogue, thus furnishing the grounds for the Habermasian and Gadamerian projects.

HUMAN BIPOLARITY

Attend then to the bipolarity of human nature.[10] At one pole, human nature is set on an animal base. It is the locus of a field of awareness that is a synesthetic-orectic-kinesthetic circle displaying relational features of an environment of goods, threats, and neutralities in relation to the achievement of the immanent goals of the organism for growth, sustenance, reproduction, and fostering of offspring as well as for defense against predators. At the other pole, peculiar humanness is open to the whole scheme of things via the notion of Being, which includes everything; but, as given by our nature, the notion of Being is, as Hegel claimed, only empty reference.[11] It begins as Nietzsche's "last trailing cloud of evaporating reality."[12] That sets up the human being as the locus of the question of Being. This being open means that the Whole is pregiven as a question: What is it all about? What is "the scheme of things"? How does humanness fit within that scheme? Religions (as inspired and proclamatory pronouncements about the Whole) and philosophies (as critical and systematic claims about the Whole) attempt to fill in what is an initially empty reference to that totality.

"Scheme of things" suggests an outline. How is that possible? Granted, it is a human construct, but is it only a human construct? Scheme is already entailed in the character of the animal base. The appetites and sensory powers involved are concrete universals, oriented toward specific kinds of achievement in relation to aspects and types of environmen-

10. I have previously treated this in slightly different ways: in *A Path into Metaphysics: Phenomenological, Hermeneutic, and Dialogical Studies* (Albany: State University of New York Press, 1991), I provided an approach parallel to Plato's Cave by using the model of multidimensional space provided by Edwin Abbott's *Flatland*; in *Placing Aesthetics: Reflections on the Philosophic Tradition* (Athens: Ohio University Press, 1999), I explored the structure of the field of experience as a way into the study of select highpoints in the history of thought on matters aesthetic.

11. G. W. F. Hegel, *Hegel's Science of Logic*, trans. A. Miller (London: George Allen and Unwin, 1969), 82.

12. Friedrich Nietzsche, *Twilight of the Idols*, trans. R. Hollingdale (Baltimore: Penguin, 1968), III, 4.

tally given entities. Native powers are both *individual* aspects of *individual* things and *universal* orientations toward the *kinds* of individuals in the environment that could activate them. As concrete universals, they sublate the distinction between individual and universal. An animal that cannot distinguish instances of the type (*eidos*) "food" or "enemy" will perish—perishing being a *type* of event overtaking the *type* called living.[13]

The concretely available scheme of things is present in the food chain. Humans sit at the top of a hierarchy as omnivores who subsume carnivores, herbivores, plants, and aspects of the nonliving environment. Carnivores subsume herbivores, who, in turn, consume plant life. And plant life subsumes aspects of the nonliving environment. The nonliving forms each consist of determinate powers of acting and being acted upon that link them together in various systems. One could say, with Plato's Eleatic Stranger, that the definition of being is "the power of acting and being acted upon."[14]

Now what that involves is that each individual, manifest in the environment as individual and actual, contains underlying powers as universal orientations toward the kind of things correlative to it: those things upon which it can act and which can act upon it. So individuals are not simply other than the universals we use to describe them; they are themselves the loci of concrete, that is, *individual* powers that themselves are *universal* orientations. They mesh with their kind of environment and, ultimately, with the cosmos itself.

What throws us off is that sensory appearance is misleading theoretically. It misleads us into thinking that all-that-is is individual and actual. But reflection shows that individuals are the loci of powers as *universal* orientations. They each contain concrete universals peculiar in their interrelation to a given type of individual. And that the individuals are instances of types is not only something we add to them by abstraction and classification. At least in the case of living things, by way of reproduction each organism is an instance of the type of its progenitors and offspring.

The distance from the environmentally and intraorganically manifest afforded by orientation toward the Whole makes possible reflection

---

13. See my "Potentiality, Creativity, and Relationality: Creative Power as a 'New' Transcendental?," *The Review of Metaphysics* 59, no. 2 (2005): 379–401. This paper was originally delivered at the John Paul II Institute at a symposium in honor of Kenneth Schmitz.

14. Plato, *Sophist*, 247e.

upon those concrete universals, grasping their repeatability any time and any place the conditions for their activation are met. Reference to the Whole solicits the attempt to link them together in systematic ways, paralleling, in the distinctively human in relation to its world, the systematicity that is involved in the organism in itself and in its relation to its environment.

Reference to the Whole as reference to Being sets up a tension between organ-based appearance, a selective filter in relation to the whole of what appears in service of biological needs, and the encompassing Whole—in such a way, however, that the appearance *expresses* for us the character of that Whole. This calls for interpretation that may stay at the level of reading how the given affords occasions for identifying supportive, threatening, or neutral aspects of the manifest environment. Conversely, guided by the notion of Being, it might advance, in a purely theoretical way, through inference and the invention of appropriate methods and instruments, into the character of what underlies the initial appearance.

That same reference that solicits interpretation also, as Sartre put it, *condemns* us to choose from among the possibilities for action demanded by our animal nature and opened up by the interplay of sensory manifestness and historically situated interpretation.[15] Referred to the Whole, we are pried loose at the deepest level of ourselves from the partially manifest and are thus able and even required to choose among the options as we come to understand them. As in our case, sexuality drives males and females together but also poses problems not solved by sheer natural drive, namely, "How shall we care for the offspring that emerge from that togetherness?" And subsequently, "How shall we conceive of the relation of our freedom to choose and that natural drive?" Nature addresses humankind in terms of problems not solved by nature; nature presses human freedom for decisions. The cluster of decisions provided by humankind in response to these questions as they pass on to others constitutes the history of the institutions of marriage and child-rearing. Feelings of possessiveness and power, grounded in nature but focused by the sedimentation of decisions we call institutions, cluster about mates and offspring to furnish a second level, beyond natural organic feelings, of felt reverberations in the presence of *sensa*.

15. Jean-Paul Sartre, "Existentialism is a Humanism," in *Existentialism from Dostoyevsky to Sartre*, trans. and ed. W. Kaufmann (New York: Meridian, 1956), 287ff.

The togetherness of the family makes collective the first problem posed by nature, namely, "How do I get enough to eat and drink?" and "How do I protect myself against the threats posed by the environment, natural and human?" Actually, because human beings are not born even relatively self-sufficient but require years of care, these questions might actually originate from the questions "How do *we* get enough to eat?" and "How do *we* protect ourselves against the environment?" As larger conglomerations of humans form, the sedimentation of decisions in this realm gives rise to the history of institutions of production and exchange. The plurality of humans poses the problem of how we relate to others in and beyond those relations of mate and offspring grounded in sexuality, and eventuates in determinate social practices.

Of course, involved in all of this is the problem of authority: Who makes the decisions? And how do we pass on the results of these processes to those who follow us? This introduces not only the dialectic between individuals and groups who are coexistent but, perhaps even more powerfully, that between the live community and the tradition of folkways, the sedimented set of decisions, now become second nature, that have allowed the community to survive against the more or less frequent hostility of the environment, natural and social. The answers we give to the questions posed by nature and by our sedimented responses to nature are not just *ad hoc* solutions but involve the establishment of anticipated possible regularities of response that could apply anywhere and any time we meet the same situations. By our decisions, we help establish or disestablish both individual and collective principles for action.

But the questions posed to our freedom by our nature in relation to the natural and social environment are not the only questions. Our nature as oriented toward the Whole of being poses to us the basic question of *the meaning of the Whole* as an object of our deepest human desire.[16] It may not be the most immediately overpowering desire, but the latter ultimately pales into insignificance without some sense of its relation to the Whole. After the height of orgasm, one could readily ask if it "means" anything. And meaning, we suggest, is a matter of seeing and indwelling in the belonging together of humans and other entities within the Whole. So we not only have to make fundamental decisions

---

16. See also Heidegger's notion of *Dasein* in *Being and Time*, 27.

as to how we are to respond to the basic questions posed by nature in the realm of practice, but we also stand under the requirement of certain interpretative decisions regarding the meaning of each entity within the Whole. That they are, in a sense, decisions seems clear from the fact that there is a plurality of them. Yet neither type of decision—interpretive or practical—can be simply arbitrary and unconstrained, since they will not hold over time unless they are in some way compatible with the totality of what is given, both in terms of the encountered and in terms of our own needs, individual and collective. They are deeply tied to the sedimented history of decisions of those long dead that constitute the institutions within which a *we* exists. Fundamental decisions are responses to directions we are invited to walk, presented by the concrete situation in which we find ourselves, insofar as such decisions involve our place in the whole scheme of things.[17]

It is out of the ground of this question about the Whole that the most powerful and sophisticated of all institutions emerges, namely the institution of language. In the first place, that structure makes possible the functioning of each individual entity given in the sensory field as an icon of the Whole. Further, the factual reoccurrence, spatially and temporally, of *types*, of *kinds* of entities as necessary correlates to our native powers, mediates the mode of manifestation in the individual's relation to the Whole. It is language that allows us to retain our awareness of types. And in its mediation, language functions fundamentally in opening up the space from which decisions come, the space of meaning that emerges from the wedding between immersion in the problems posed by the sensory now and our fundamental reference to the encompassing Whole of being. Focus upon the rude artifacts from prehistorical times that archaeologists discover often makes us forget that so-called primitive peoples for millennia were developing that most sophisticated of instruments to which we are still necessarily beholden: language.[18] Language, initially incarnated in the flow of sound generated by our lips, gathers about the immediately given *sensa* the Whole as known, as inferred, and as imagined. It endows the objects presented with emotional reverbera-

17. On "decision" in this regard, see Heidegger, *Contributions to Philosophy: From Enowning* (Bloomington: Indiana University Press, 2000), 66–69.

18. See also Lewis Mumford, *The Myth of the Machine: Technics and Human Development* (New York: Harcourt, Brace, and World: 1976), 79.

tions of extreme depth and subtlety, upon which the arts play in their reconstruction of the sensory. Language binds together a people over space
and time, but at the same time it separates those people from all others.

This binding is made possible by the extraction of an interrelated set
of vowels, consonants, and phonemes that play in relation to one another, from the indeterminate number of sounds made possible by the structure of the human oral cavity. Such units are eidetic constants, humanly
constructed identities over against the plurality of their sensory instances. For example, it is the same "a" that is repeated again and again in the
differing spaces of this page and generated during different aspects of the
time span within which I am writing. But it would be the same eidetic
"a" if it is written as A or as a/A, *a/A* and the like. The intelligible/sensible
distinction is present in the formation of words as sensibly present individuals—abstracting from the fact that the words so formed incarnate
the apprehension of universal terms. The components of words are themselves exhibitions of a culturally formed eidetic alphabet.

The accumulation of observations, interpretations, and choices sedi-
ments into a habituated world that is shared by others and passed on to
offspring. It fills the initially empty space of meaning between the animal
now and our empty, founding orientation toward the Whole. It stamps
those who enter into it as "the way things are." As the Latins would have
it, *cultura fit secunda natura*, culture becomes second nature. On top of
the spontaneities afforded by the two poles constituting human nature,
another set of spontaneities is added: habituation, culturally stamped
and individually chosen.

It is not until people confront the differently sedimented worlds of
interpretation and action coming out of different traditions or out of the
past of their own tradition that they are forced to come to terms with
real human otherness. Prior to that, the stamp of tradition is so strong
that individual otherness is a minor variation on a cultural theme. One
traditional way of coming to terms with otherness is condemnation of
the others and exaltation of one's own— until one begins to understand
something of the origins and sedimented character of one's own. Then
we first meet the conditions for genuine dialogue. This is especially the
case in religion that develops a system of legitimation so powerful that
the individual fears—and is strongly encouraged to fear—even to raise
questions with regard to that religion. It is only relatively recently that re-

ligions have dared to enter into real dialogue, to question their own legitimation structures. This occurs against the background of the emergence of religious freedom through the separation of religious understanding and political power and with the common threat to irrelevance posed by the developing secular world of science, technology, economics, and democratic government.

INDIVIDUAL, CULTURE, AND THE HEART

Once again, it is our contention that the natural human structure, what Hegel calls the structure of "Subjective Spirit," consists of ontological reference as founding an empty intention of the totality playing in tandem with the ever-manifest sensory emergence from the organic pole.[19] This structure places the human being on the level of ontological reference at an infinite distance from biological givenness and makes descriptive eidetic inventory, interpretation, and choice possible. Out of those possibilities built into human structure emerge the multiplicity of cultural traditions, the plurality of the works of Hegelian "Objective Spirit" that stamp the individuals raised within them. This sets up a tension between nature and culture. But ontological distance also creates another tension: that between the individual on the one hand and the nature-culture tension on the other.

At the individual level, the founding structure of "Subjective Spirit" makes possible the distinction between I and Me. The Me is everything about myself from which I, as the conscious and initiating center, can gain distance. It includes the genetically grounded set of individual possibilities and the cultural opening and closure of those possibilities by the stamp I have received from my primary caregivers and from the impact of those who have surrounded and continue to surround me. Like the founding structure of human nature, both the genetic and the initial cultural stamp are features about which I have no choice. But when I initially came into the capacity to stand at an inward distance from those factors and determine myself by choosing from among the options they

19. On the notion of "Objective Spirit," see G. W. F. Hegel, *Hegel's Philosophy of Mind*, trans. W. Wallace (Oxford: Clarendon Press, 1971). For a fuller treatment, see G. W. F. Hegel, *Elements of the Philosophy of Right*, trans. H. Nisbet (Cambridge: Cambridge University Press, 1991). I develop this further in the chapter "Rationality and Actuality."

afforded, I began to determine the Me for which I am increasingly responsible. At any given moment of lucid wakeful awareness, I have to decide what to do with Me, with the sedimented resultant of genetic, cultural, and personal-historical factors that afford me my real possibilities for choice now. We would have, then, within the Me a series of zones of greater and lesser proximity to the I. At the outermost zone, setting the framework for all achievements, would be the genetic. Closer to the I would be the cultural stamping one has received and continues to receive, and closer still the habit structure one has cooperated in forming on the basis of the other two. The biological pole provides a given set of proclivities for action. The way I come finally to take them up and set them in relation to the other features of my experience establishes that multiple set of proclivities that sediment into what a long tradition calls "the heart." The heart is the unique center formed by the meeting of my given and chosen proclivities. It sets close to me the things and persons and the lines of action I am spontaneously inclined to take in relation to those things and persons; it sets other things and persons and lines of action further from me. The heart determines significant presences that solicit my action. But as a creature of ontological distance, I am still remote from that which spontaneously solicits my attention and action. Consequently, I still have to ask myself, "Where is my heart? And is it where it should be?" The founding ontological reference has its own natural proclivity, leading to that curious expression "in my heart of hearts" as a center of desire beyond the center constituted by my past history of passive stampings and active choices.[20]

Just as sexual desire is an expression, as Plato's Diotima would have it, of "the desire of the mortal for the immortal,"[21] even though such underlying desire is not that to which the one experiencing that desire usually attends, so there is a natural "desire for the Totality" following from the all-encompassing notion of Being that leads us to ask how what we do fits within the largest possible Whole, even though such underlying desire is also not something to which one usually attends. It is interpret-

20. On the notion of the heart, see my "Hegel on the Heart," *International Philosophical Quarterly* 41, no. 2 (2001): 131–44, reproduced in this volume. See also Stephan Strasser, *Phenomenology of Feeling: An Essay on the Phenomena of the Heart*, trans. and introduced by R. Wood, preface to the English edition by Paul Ricoeur (New York: Humanities Press, 1977); and Paul Ricoeur, *Fallible Man*, trans. C. Kelbley (Chicago: Regnery, 1965), 122–202.

21. Plato, *Symposium* 206c–208b.

ed religiously as the thirst for the presence of God as all-encompassing. Augustine would say: our hearts are restless until they rest in God.[22]

CULTURAL PLURALISM

The structure of the human individual sets the conditions for the possibility for different developments. The structure of the human race, whose basic features we have presented in the first part, sets the general frame of distinctively human possibilities. The genetic structure of each individual specifies the general limits for that individual's possibility of development within that more generalized structure. And the type and level of the culture further sets the concrete institutional parameters within which the most general and the most genetically specific can operate.

The history of the race necessarily ramifies into the history of different cultures with their own ways of understanding and acting, within which, collectively, the possibilities of humanness can be discovered and the understanding of our place in the scheme of things expanded. At a certain level, the contacts between cultures led to comparisons and attempts at synthesis, with the search for standards of comparison and evaluation. The founding level of human nature affords the basis for understanding the necessity of the plurality of cultures and of individual lifestyles within cultures, but it also affords the basis for evaluation of the resultant ways of understanding and differentiation of practices as it affords us the drive toward synthesis.

At an earlier stage, realization of the fact that a culture provides the concrete possibilities for human thought and action led to the priority of the disposition of *pietas*, a sense of unpayable indebtedness to one's parents for life and upbringing, to the culture for the way of life, and to the divine for the whole context of existence.[23] And the three tended to bond together in the projection of the notion of the father from the family to the head of the group and on to the ground of Being itself. Fathers determined the occupation and the marriage partners of their children, and the king-father commanded the group while the Father in heaven backed up the institutional arrangement.

---

22. Aurelius Augustine, *Confessions*, I, 1.
23. Thomas Aquinas, *Summa theologica*, II-II, q. 103, a. 3, ad 1.

With the emergence of the study of comparative cultures and the search for measures that transcend cultures, one measure of a culture became the degree to which it fosters such inquiry. Inquiry takes place by means of individuals standing at the level of ontological reference, pried loose from both biology and culture, and taking their measure from what emerges through inquiry. This establishes a certain dignity to the individual human being. Although at one level that dignity was deeply ingrained in the religious tradition of the West, at the same time freedom of choice and inquiry were severely restricted by the alliance of that tradition with political power. A first step was the separation of religion from political power and thus freedom of choice in religion, which, when it emerged, was viewed as an extreme act of impiety.[24] Thomas Aquinas held that one is obliged to follow one's conscience, but, on the other hand, he held that the civil power is responsible to see to it that the true faith rules the realm and that heretics are to be persuaded if possible but excised if necessary.[25] After the fracturing of political unity under the legitimation structure of religion, freedom of inquiry was followed by freedom of dissemination of the results of inquiry, freedom of assembly, free election of leaders, and free enterprise.[26] This was allied with what were viewed as acts of impiety toward the family through free choice of marriage partners and occupations. The fathers no longer dominated the marriages and lifework of their children; the father-king was subject to his subjects' elective choice and no longer determined enterprise; and the Father in heaven no longer directly supported the paternal regime.

"Freedom" is the watchword of the modern world, its one absolute, in spite of, indeed as a major cause of, the claim to ethical and cognitive relativism. The advancement of freedom to the center of human existence is perhaps *the* achievement, the true glory of modernity but also its central problem.[27] It emerged at the expense of that *pietas* which held the pre-

24. See Pius IX, *Quanta Cura and the Syllabus of Errors*, esp. 17, 24, 77; and John Locke, "An Essay Concerning Toleration," 184–209, and "A Letter Concerning Toleration," 390–435, in *Political Writings of John Locke*, ed. D. Wooton (London: Penguin, 1993).

25. Aquinas, *Summa Theologiae*, II-II, q. 10, a. 8 and q. 11, a. 3.

26. Grounding such rights is at the center of Hegel's Philosophy of Right on love, conscience, and inquiry, *Elements of the Philosophy of Right* §124, 151–52; on conscience, §137/201–2; on choice of marriage partners §162/201–2; on religion §270/291ff; on speech and the press §319/355–58; on property §41ff; on occupation §254/272.

27. On Hegel's notion of freedom, see *Hegel's Philosophy of Mind*, 481–82, 238–40, and *Lec-*

modern world together. Is there any possibility of a rapprochement between these two views?

Earlier, Martin Buber wrote on "the dialogical principle" and claimed that our epoch afforded the situation for a real dialogue between religions rather than polemically speaking past one another as they always have. The dialogue must be rooted in a real meeting with the Other, a dialogue first of all of life-to-life with deepest respect and the capacity to respond from the depths of one's being, with the possibility of a move from communication to communion. Traditions necessarily degenerate from original presence to morality and religion as objectifications and hardenings, and "just as nothing can hide from us the face of our fellow man as morality can, so nothing can hide from us the face of God so much as religion can."[28]

THE DIALOGICAL IMPERATIVE

The bipolar structure of human nature grounds cultural and individual diversity and calls forth intelligence and creativity, but it also grounds critique of individual and cultural understanding and practice. It imposes a dialogical imperative: to seek the other, to understand the other, to let the self and the other be measured by what emerges from the dialogue. It aims at an ideal consensus open to its own correction through *dissensus*, which, contrary to Lyotard, only makes sense in terms of an aim at a richer *consensus*. Difference is not a final aim except as a contribution to identity. The difference of cultures is their contribution to humanity.

Reference to the Whole sets us at a distance from all putative claims to theoretical and practical completion. Human nature at its deepest level generates and transcends the second natures we have produced on its basis. It raises in principle questions with regards to the final adequacy of given ways of understanding and consequent ways of life. In fact, it poses the demand that questioning go forward.[29] Rather than letting us

---

tures on the Philosophy of World History, trans. H. Nisbet (Cambridge: Cambridge University Press, 1975), 47–55 *passim*.

28. Martin Buber, "Dialogue," in *Between Man and Man*, trans. R. Smith (Boston: Beacon Press, 1955), 1–39, esp. 54.

29. See Charles Peirce's imperative: "Do not block the way of inquiry." "The Scientific Attitude and Fallibilism," in *Philosophical Writings of Peirce*, ed. J. Buchler (New York: Dover, 1955), 54.

rest complacently with our individual and cultural proclivities, it puts them all into question. Indeed, as the condition for the possibility for all responsible questioning, it puts oneself into question first of all. Where should my heart be? Ultimately, it should be in that place where it is respectful of all beings, most respectful of all humans, founded upon respect for oneself as responsible openness to the Whole.

And though one's first measures for that self-questioning are culturally provided, the power of the questioning can then be focused upon the cultural measures themselves. If humility consists in letting oneself be measured, a deeper humility lets one's measures be measured. In fact, the claim to having the final measures too often tends to make one arrogant and closed. The vehicle of such questioning is dialogue: the opening out of oneself to the other for mutual testing and consequently mutual refutation and/or confirmation. The dialogical imperative is rooted in the sense of our own individual and collective questionability on the one hand and an appreciation for one's own and one's culture's achievements on the other: freedom of inquiry—and the imperative of inquiry—on the one hand and *pietas* toward one's tradition on the other. We can understand and act and question the adequacy of our ways of understanding and acting, not only because of our common human nature but also because we are the recipients of specific ways of understanding and acting, including the tradition of questioning the adequacy of our ways of understanding and acting.[30] In dialogue, we "bear witness" to ourselves and our traditions as well as submit them and ourselves with them to a questioning that is not only self-generating but which comes from the testimony of the other, inside and outside our specific tradition. In virtue of our common human nature, oriented toward a totality that we do not and cannot fully possess, we are essentially "on the way," in the tension between the past and the future, between *pietas* and freedom, in the tension between the self and the other, in the tension between bearing witness and questioning, both individually and collectively. Human nature generates culture, transcends any given culture, and imposes the dialogical imperative involved in the plurality of cultural modes and modes of transcendence.

30. This moves in the direction of Alasdair MacIntyre's notion of tradition-bound inquiry but gives it a ground. See "The Rationality of Traditions," in *Whose Justice, Which Rationality?* (Notre Dame: University of Notre Dame Press, 1988), 349–69.

The Beautiful, the True & the Good

1 ∽ Reflections on Heraclitus

The work of Heraclitus, unlike the work of Plato or Aristotle, has come down to us only in fragments preserved in various ancient sources that cited his work. As Charles Kahn has pointed out, every age has "projected its own meaning and its own preoccupations onto the text of Heraclitus."[1] His fragments have had a peculiar attraction in modern times. Hegel said that there was not a single fragment (or "proposition") that had not found a place in his System.[2] Nietzsche drew deeply from them. He claimed that "what he (Heraclitus) saw, the teaching of *law in becoming* and of *play in necessity*, must be seen from now on in eternity."[3] Heidegger treated Heraclitus at some length in *Introduction to Metaphysics* and elsewhere, as well as co-teaching a semester's seminar with Eugen Fink given to the interpretation of the fragments.[4]

Fragments have a certain beguiling character. Having been torn from their context, they call for interpretation. Perhaps influenced by Heraclitus, Nietzsche's own thought is expressed largely in aphorisms, inviting interpretation. But it is not only that Heraclitus's fragments, like Nietzsche's aphorisms, might tempt the curious to interpret them—much like a crossword puzzle that calls out for solution—it is more the case that they provide flashes of comprehensive insight. In this chapter, I will join this recent tradition, ferreting out those insights interpretively in or-

1. Charles Kahn, *The Art and Thought of Heraclitus* (Cambridge: Cambridge University Press, 1979), 87.

2. G. W. F. Hegel, *Lectures on the History of Philosophy*, trans. E. Haldane (Lincoln: University of Nebraska Press, 1995), 279.

3. Friedrich Nietzsche, *Philosophy in the Tragic Age of the Greeks*, trans. M. Cowan (Chicago: Regnery, 1962), 68.

4. Martin Heidegger, *Introduction to Metaphysics*, trans. G. Fried and R. Polt (New Haven, Conn.: Yale University Press, 2000), 133–43; "Logos," in *Early Greek Thinking*, trans. D. Krell and F. Capuzzi (San Francisco: Harper, 1975), 59–78; with Eugen Fink, *Heraclitus Seminar*, trans. C. Seibert (Evanston, Ill.: Northwestern University Press, 1993).

der to achieve a *Horizontverschmelzung*, a "fusion of horizons," bringing them into the contemporary world to contribute to a way of orienting ourselves in a most fundamental way.[5]

Heraclitus said, "The lord whose oracle is at Delphi neither reveals nor conceals but gives a sign" (93).[6] He himself spoke oracularly and was thus known as "the Obscure."[7] The uncomprehending would be able to memorize what he said and thus give the appearance of understanding. One who understands therefore gives a sign that speaks only to those who have the capacity to understand and are willing to work. Plato understood this and thus said that a real thinker never writes down his deepest thoughts.[8] He also invented the dialogical form as a proleptic protreptic, containing anticipatory hints as a philosophic propaideutic for one who is capable of the comprehensive reflectiveness that is philosophy itself. In his study of Socrates, Kierkegaard learned the same lesson and thus wrote through pseudonyms.[9]

Through Plato's own underscoring of the thesis of becoming, Heraclitus is best known for the claim attributed to him that all things flow, *panta rhei*: you cannot step into the same river twice (91). In the *Theaetetus*, Plato has focused the attention of subsequent tradition upon that notion.[10] In the *Cratylus*, named after Heraclitus's alleged disciple, this comprehensive feature raised for Plato the question of language. If all things flow, there is no enduring sameness that could ground language.[11] Underlying the apparent distribution of motion and rest in the things of experience, even apparent rest is a slower motion relative to our awareness: all things flow and nothing is at rest. You cannot step into the same river twice because it is not the same: different waters are flowing. The appar-

---

5. On the notion of *Horizontverschmelzung*, see Hans-Georg Gadamer, *Truth and Method*, trans. G. Barden and J. Cumming (New York: Crossroad, 1982), 269–74.

6. References to Heraclitus will be to the Diels-Kranz fragment number as found in a bilingual Greek and English form in Kahn, *The Art and Thought of Heraclitus*, 28–85.

7. Cicero, *De finibus*, trans. H. Rackham, (Cambridge, Mass.: Harvard University Press, 1931), II, 5, 15.

8. Plato, *Seventh Letter*, trans. J. Bury (Cambridge, Mass.: Harvard University Press, 1929), 344c.

9. I consider this as following from his study of irony, providing a certain distance from any immediate claims. See Søren Kierkegaard, *The Concept of Irony*, trans. L. Capel (Bloomington: Indiana University Press, 1965).

10. Plato, *Theaetetus*, 152e ff.

11. Plato, *Cratylus*, 402a.

ently stable things are more like the apparently stable form of a candle flame in still air (or, in a more modern example, like the unaltered shape of a Bunsen burner flame): what is really there is an incredible flow of energy being consumed, though what appears is a fixed shape. A tree on a calm day appears still, but there is constant growth going on underneath the placid surface. Even more so, the surface of our bodies at rest actually covers an ever-flowing process of anabolism and catabolism, a buildup and breakdown of cells such that some fifty million are destroyed each minute, and some fifty million are generated at the same time. The mountains themselves arise and crumble over the long haul, towering up from the pressure of underlying geological plates and wearing down through erosion. Modern physics underscores this further: the elements are not so much stable "things" as processes, pulsating centers of energy irradiating their light spectra. And if we attend to our own awareness, we see that it is a continual stream of different contents: changing perceptions brought about by the changes both in the things perceived and in our own bodies and their position relative to the things encountered—sensations, imaginings, remembrances, desires, pleasures and pains, thoughts, choices—all tumbling together, some rising focally, some sinking back into the periphery, and then into oblivion, only to rise again. Plato speaks of the region of focal attention and organic grounding as the realm of *genesis*, of coming into being and passing out of being. Aristotle says that if you want to understand what the Greeks mean by *phusis* or nature, emphasize the *phu-*, the *"ou"* as a straining to emerge.[12] *Phusis* is the realm of constant process. Thus, all things share in common the fact that they are processes and not "things." Even Aristotle's physical "substances" are processes.

Conversely, according to Heraclitus, processive things occur according to fixed measures and in different kinds (1, 5, 30, 112).[13] So, although all things flow, their measures do not. Indeed, things rest by changing (84), that is, by developing and sustaining their selves according to their kinds. Plato picked this up in his *Theaetetus*, where it is only through change that things develop and retain what they have been.[14] And al-

12. Aristotle, *Metaphysics*, V, 4, 1014b 16.

13. Heraclitus speaks in 230 of the world order as "kindling in measures (*metra*) and going out in measures," in 229 of the sun not overstepping its measures, and in 235 of the soul as having its measure. In 197 he claims to distinguish each thing according to its nature (*kata phusin*).

14. Plato, *Theaetetus*, 153a-c. See also Plato, *Symposium*, 207d.

though what flows are individual things, their kinds do not flow. This points in the direction Plato will designate as that of the forms (*eide*). Plato followed this up in the *Sophist* with the inclusion of motion as one of the five genera found in everything (along with rest, sameness, and difference, under the overarching notion of Being).[15] Though all things are in motion, the notion of motion is not in motion, nor are the *types* of things in motion. Such encompassing notions ground *logos* as the interweaving of notions applied to things and expressed in the flowing sonority of speech.[16]

Here, Plato is only following Heraclitus, whose central insight lies in the notion of the *Logos* as that which is common to all (50). One who would speak with understanding, *sun noo*, should follow that which gathers together, which is *xunos* (114). *Logos* means many things, but they center upon language as word, sentence, account, or even scroll. It also means ratio or proportion or ground and thus reason, which grasps the proportionate relations and presents the ground or gives an account. *Logos* is linked to the verb *legein*, which means to gather and also to read.

If we begin with the notion of *word*, we underscore the notion of *the common*: the word gathers together the many divergent instances of a meaning. Thus, the word "red" gathers all instances of all the different shades, but it is involved in further gatherings. Red is understood as a color, something it shares with other visible things and under which at the same time it is differentiated from them. And color in its turn is understood as a feature of a visible thing that it shares with other sensory features from which it is distinguished. Sensory features are identified with and distinguished from other features such as *intelligent* or *good* under the more general heading of quality, itself a subdivision of features that are co-yoked with (*symbebekota*) but distinguished from the things whose features they are. The features cluster differently about different kinds and instances of things to reveal a logical hierarchy that articulates the cosmic Whole in relation to which the flow of human experience occurs. The word gathers together this differentiated and interrelated set of meanings. It thus corresponds to the gathering that is the cosmos and which Heraclitus names the *Logos* that is common to all.

At the same time as it gathers together meanings, and things under

15. Plato, *Sophist*, 254d.
16. Plato, *Theaetetus*, 206d; *Sophist*, 264e.

meanings, *logos* as language gathers together a community that has learned to associate a common sound with a common meaning. The sounds themselves are part of a phonic system composed of identical units, culturally created eidetic types set over against the plurality of their instantiation in different times and places with different vocal timbres and both local and personal accents. Such a system is invented from out of the indeterminate plurality of sounds capable of being generated by the human oral cavity. Through the linguistic system, individual members of the community are taken out of their pure privacy into the common world of communication, linked together by commonly accessible things. Privacy plays in relation to the community established by common language just as the dream world plays in relation to the wakeful world (89, 34). Privatized individuals fail to see that their private lives feed off of the public (198).

I remember once hearing a psychologist proclaim the apparent truth that we are all locked within our own privacy. I thought: I understand perfectly what he means, since I understand well all the common terms of his claim and their interrelation as well as the sentences expressing the evidence he brought to bear upon the claim in our common discussion. We cannot think in any sustained and comprehensive way unless we have language, and we cannot have language without having entered into a prior community formed centuries and even millennia ago and focused upon common objects. We are always outside our private inside, within the space of common linguistic meanings. Language is the first institution making possible the coexistence of large numbers of people over long periods of time, developing and passing on their ways of understanding and modes of practice that constitute their culture. It is for this reason that Aristotle defined the human being as *zoion politikon*, which subsequent Aristotelians, focusing upon language, further narrowed to *zoion logon echon*, the animal that has the *logos*.[17] The medieval translation as *animal rationale* retained something basic but lost the whole communal character of Aristotle's insight. Heidegger's notion of *Dasein* as Being-in-the-World recovers this Aristotelian dimension.[18] But Aristotle was only developing what Heraclitus initiated. The human being is the linguistic animal.

17. Aristotle, *Nicomachean Ethics*, 1097b, 12.
18. Martin Heidegger, *Being and Time*, trans. J. Macquarrie and E. Robinson (New York: Harper and Row, 1962), 27 and 67ff.

Further, for Heraclitus the gathering of the community through language allows for the possibility of establishing the protective walls of laws and customs that fix the measures of the community against the incursions of barbarian privacy as the physical walls protect against external barbarians (252). Conversely, as language gathers a community together regarding the gathering of a world of meaning, it separates a community so gathered from other linguistic communities. We see in the case of Ontario in Canada and the Basques in Spain how difference of language continually initiates a demand for separate governments. So just as the waking are separated from the dreaming and, within the waking, the public from the private, so also the various publics are separated from each other by the way a public is established linguistically. This is the basis for one instance of Heraclitus's more general axiom that "War is king" (214, 215).

However, the deeper notion of the Heraclitean *Logos* lies in the ground in which all language and human law is rooted: the cosmic *Logos*, nature itself (197, 198). According to that *logos*, "All things are one," *hen panta*, the grounding formula of German idealism (199).[19] The plurality of experiences and languages hides a deeper unity so that there is not simply the apparent pluriverse of different things moving in different directions but an underlying universe, the turning of the plurality toward unity to constitute a cosmos, an ordered totality. All languages and customs are rooted in the cosmic *Logos*.

Now all this *logos*-reflection plays in tandem with another notion that would seemingly have to be left behind in any contemporary *Horizontverschmelzung*. That is the notion of fire as *phusis*. Fire is not only an *example* of cosmic flux; Heraclitus identifies it as the *principle* of the flux (220, 222). First of all, we have to keep in mind here the general hylozoism of the early philosophers. Thales had proposed water as the principle of life, Anaximenes air, linked in much early language usage to soul as Greek *psyche*, Latin *spiritus*, Hebrew *ruah*. Without water, without air, without fire (heat and light), there is no life. No one chose earth as the principle of *phusis* because earth is essentially plural: matter individuates, form integrates. One or the other of the elements, thought of as principles of life, are what were thereby thought to unify that plurality,

---

19. Terry Pinkard, *Hegel: A Biography* (Cambridge: Cambridge University Press, 2000), 31–32.

to be the one of the essentially many. Now life not only gathers the plurality of elements into the unity of a single life process in individual organisms, but it also gathers generations together in the unity of a single species or, through the transformation of species, into the possible unity of life itself.

These thinkers were not "materialists," as is often claimed, since the very term is based upon a distinction—and in modern times since Descartes, a separation—of matter from mind, combined with a view of the forms of organic life as mechanical combinations of, in effect, "dead stuff."[20] As Hans Jonas observed: the problem of the ancients was death, since everything is in some way alive; the problem of the moderns is life, for everything living is thought to be but an external combination of the essentially nonliving.[21] For these early thinkers, what we experience outside ourselves through sensation is identical to what we discover in ourselves when we reflect upon the experience: sensations, feelings, desires, thoughts. This would fit into contemporary discussion with an emergentist understanding of evolution in accordance with which we have to understand the earlier, less complex state of the cosmos in terms of the later, more complex stage that includes the inwardness of observing and theorizing awareness. What we observe externally has a potential inwardness that emerges into actuality only through specific relations between externally related earlier forms. Those specific relations unlock the latent powers of supervening, controlling wholes or life-forms that, in turn, ground conscious and then reflectively conscious inwardness.[22]

For Heraclitus, the principle of life is simultaneously the principle of thought. The opposite of fire, that which quenches it, is water. Translated mentally, drunkenness makes the soul "wet" and thus extinguishes the "fire" of awareness (233, 234). Fire is all-consuming flux, but it also generates both light and warmth; translated "inwardly," the cosmic fire produces both insight and corresponding desire. Plato will later take the fiery sun not only as the source of life and sight but also as symbol for

---

20. I have attempted to situate this view within the history of reflection on the nature of body in the following essay: "Five Bodies and a Sixth: On the Place of Awareness in the Cosmos," *American Catholic Philosophical Quarterly* 83, no. 1 (2009): 95–105.

21. Hans Jonas, *The Phenomenon of Life: Toward a Philosophical Biology* (New York: Delta, 1966), 7–8.

22. I have attempted a fuller grounding of this position in "Potentiality, Creativity, and Relationality," *The Review of Metaphysics* 59, no. 2 (2005): 379–401.

the Good, "the sun of the intelligible world."[23] However, once again, the sensible-intelligible distinction has not as yet been made explicit, much less separate, in Heraclitus. What we experience from within when we understand and not simply see is the same fire that we see with our eyes from without.

Seeing and hearing are crucial for understanding (200), but eyes are better witnesses than ears because one can see for oneself what one otherwise only takes on the word of others (101A). Furthermore, something more than eyes and ears is needed because they are poor witnesses to the *Logos* for those with barbarian souls (201). There are two ways of reading this. First, the barbarian is one for whom a given language is babble. As Socrates noted in his refutation of the thesis that knowledge is sensation, one who does not know the language only hears an incoherent multiplicity of sounds coming from the mouth of the speaker.[24] On another reading, the barbarian soul is one that is sunk in privacy. In Plato's discussion of the tyrant, he lives through within the wakeful world the delirious dreams arising in sleep.[25] The tyrant does not have the inner alertness to read the language of the cosmos presented through sensation. Being present, he is still absent in relation to what is going on at the deeper levels (34).

Beyond barbarism there is polymathy, the deliberate accumulation of information (55). Though a necessary condition, it is also insufficient for deeper understanding (40). As in prospecting for gold, one has to dig up and sift through much dirt (22). Facts do not show their meaning on their faces; they have to be interpreted by fitting them into the larger framework that gathers a world of meaning. Along these lines, Heraclitus further claims that the underlying *phusis* is what loves to hide, in the sense that hiddenness is, as it were, the default mode (123). We have to move beyond the surface to reach the depth. It is the depth that contains the hidden harmony that is the best (54/210).

Now, harmony is not placidity. On the contrary, as we noted, Heraclitus stoutly proclaims that war is king—the flux is comprised of the struggle of opposites: night and day, waking and sleeping, male and female, sickness and health, life and death. We might add items like hot-cold,

23. Plato, *Republic*, VI, 506e ff.   24. Plato, *Theaetetus*, 163b.
25. Plato, *Republic*, IX, 274d.

dry-moist—in fact, all the sets of continua between opposite poles comprising sensory experience in general. But the pulling apart is the coming together, as in the case of the bow where the flight of the arrow is the unitary result of the pulling of the bow in opposite directions or in the case of the lyre strung according to opposite tensions (8). Once again, we find in the struggle the notion of fixed measures.

It is the struggle with the threats of the environment that produces the unity of mature organisms. It is the struggle between contending ways of life that binds together those under each of the ways. Hegel incorporated this insight into his argument against a single world government. Unless a nation contends with others, the individuals that comprise the nation tend to sink into their own private affairs and lose sight of their belonging to the civic or national whole.[26] That is why Hegel said that war is not a wholly bad thing and one of the reasons Heraclitus said that war is king.

Consider here the World Trade Center attack. It had bound together the American people as strongly as the threat of the Axis powers in World War II. Initially, it had further bound together the nations of the civilized world in reaction to the threat to civilization itself posed by the terrorists who perpetrated the act. The terrorist war revealed the otherwise hidden harmony of interests in the civilized world. (Unfortunately, the tightness of the bond was loosened with the clash of interests over the Iraq war.)

In the line of the hidden harmony that is proclaimed best, Heraclitus found the depth of the *logos* in the soul. Here is a primary instance of what Bruno Snell termed "the discovery of mind."[27] Heraclitus tells us, "I searched myself" (101/249), and he declares that he found no limits to the soul, so deep is its *logos* (45/235). We might think of the depth of the soul's *logos* in two directions, that of intensity and that of extensity. The former is suggested by Heraclitus's claim that it is by sickness that we know health, by hunger and thirst satiety, and by weariness rest (111). Now the "knowing" involved is a matter of appreciation or realization. When we are healthy, well fed, and rested, these factors disappear from attention;

---

26. G. W. F. Hegel, *Elements of the Philosophy of Right*, trans. H. Nisbet (Cambridge: Cambridge University Press, 1991), §324.

27. Bruno Snell, *The Discovery of the Mind*, trans. T. Rosenmeyer (Cambridge, Mass.: Harvard University Press, 1953).

they go without saying. It is when they are lacking and then return that they take on a new presence. Pushing the unity of opposites in relation to life and death, we might say that it is by death that we "know," that is, realize, appreciate, and are more deeply present to life. Being gripped by our own certain death, letting it become a presence, rebounds upon our sense of living now, giving it a kind of depth it would not otherwise have. In this realization, death as a matter of objective knowing touches us most intimately and moves us at the level of the heart, the most personal, intimate zone of the individual.

Conversely, the depth of the *Logos* can be considered in terms of its extensity, for the limits of the soul's reach lie in the all-encompassing *Logos* that draws the whole into unity. As Aristotle will later say, "The human soul is, in a way, all things."[28] "The way" is the way of reference, of openness toward the Whole. In the Fink-Heidegger seminar, Heraclitus is interpreted in terms of "the basic experience of the outbreak of the Whole. . . ." Echoing Heidegger, Fink says, "A human has the possibility of letting become explicit that implicit relationship to the whole as which relationship he always already exists. He exists essentially as a relationship to being, to the whole."[29]

But in either case, considering both the intensity and extensity of the soul's *logos*, Hegel remarked on the requirement of authentic existence as the unity of intellect and heart, of the extensity and intensity of the depth of the spirit. Inauthentic existence consists of intellect without heart, intellectual extensity without personal assimilation into the depth of the heart or heart without intellect.[30] For Heidegger, the realization of one's Being-toward-death pries one loose from everydayness, gathers one's life together as a whole, and simultaneously discloses the encompassing Whole in the mode of dwelling.[31] In this way, there is created that "world space" out of which poetry speaks and in which even the ordinary appears extraordinary.[32]

It is this openness to the Whole that grounds the reflective ability to lay hold of the two general characteristics of all experience and its ob-

28. Aristotle, *On the Soul*, III, 425b 27.

29. Heidegger and Fink, *Heraclitus Seminar*, 88.

30. G. W. F. Hegel, *Hegel's Philosophy of Mind*, trans. W. Wallace (Oxford: Clarendon Press, 1971).

31. Heidegger, *Being and Time*, 278–311.

32. Heidegger, *Introduction to Metaphysics*, 28.

jects: flux and plurality. These are the same two overarching features noted by Parmenides as constituting the realm of *doxa* within which we live,
oblivious of the absolute unity and changelessness of Being itself apart
from beings.[33] Anticipating Plato, Heraclitus sees the unity as unifying
the plurality and fixing the kinds and measures of the flux.

Furthermore, Heraclitus found that the soul is a self-augmenting *logos* (115). One might link this with the famous *ethos anthropo daimon*,
translating it in a traditional manner as "a man's character is his destiny"
(199).[34] Human beings are not playthings of the gods; they are each their
own *daimon* through the establishment of the fixed disposition. But
the most fundamental disposition is the turn to the depth. As the soul
turns within and discovers the secret harmony between this within and
the hidden *phusis* underlying observed things without, it is able to ex-
pand its horizon under its own power. As it expands, it grows in wisdom:
"Wisdom is one thing, to be skilled in true judgment, how all things are
steered through all things" (41).

The features of the underlying *Logos* connect it with the religious tradition. If humans can continue to grow in wisdom, the underlying *Logos*
is wisdom itself. "The wise is one alone; it is unwilling and willing to be
called by the name of Zeus" (32). It is willing because it is, like humans,
aware and, like the wise, aware of the cosmic *Logos*—though in a fuller
way—because it *is* the cosmic *Logos* present to itself. It is unwilling to be
called Zeus because the divine, which is set apart from all, is not some
anthropomorphic divinity. It steers all things by its lightning flashes, the
conventional weapon of Zeus: "Thunderbolt steers all things" (64).[35] Hip-
polytus, from whom we have this fragment, comments that "by 'thunderbolt' he means the eternal fire . . . intelligent and cause of the universe" (65). Here it seems to mean the flashes of insight we receive that
display their awesome power to illuminate and move. And the fire of the
underlying *Logos* not only gathers as an impersonal principle, it also sees
and is thus, like the mythical Zeus, personal. Heraclitus asks, "How can

33. "Parmenides," in *The Presocratic Philosophers*, ed. G. Kirk, and J. E. Raven (Cambridge:
Cambridge University Press, 1966), §374, DK Fragment 8. This indicates the opposite regarding Being itself.

34. Heidegger translates it: "Ethics for man consists in relation to the divine." "Letter on
Humanism," in Martin Heidegger, *Basic Writings*, ed. D. Krell (New York: Harper and Row,
1977), 233.

35. Heidegger had this aphorism placed above the entrance to his mountain retreat.

one fail to be seen by that which never sets?" (102). The manifest source of light does set; the hidden source of "interior light" never sets. It not only shows, it itself sees. And yet, it loves to hide!

But again, the divine is also presented as something like a perfume base which receives whatever fragrance is applied to it (67). All things are "made out of" the divine substance that is thus both apart from all things, as all-seeing and steering, and immanent within things, as that in which everything shares. This prefigures Spinoza's single Substance— *deus sive natura*—rendered Subject by Hegel. In Hegel, the Trinitarian God "others" itself in creation and returns to itself through the developed self-consciousness of humankind.[36]

For Heraclitus, the divine point of view is situated "beyond good and evil." "To god all things are beautiful and good and just, but men have supposed some things to be unjust, others just" (102). It depends on the kind of creature how things are judged: water that sustains fish drowns men; donkeys prefer chaff to gold (61, 9). But for humans, deep fulfillment lies in following the ways of the cosmic *Logos* as it steers all things into a hidden harmony. Out of the many it establishes oneness, and from the one it establishes many (10).

Reflection oriented around the fragments of Heraclitus drives us back to think comprehensively about the necessities involved in our own experience. So driven, we can see why Hegel, Nietzsche, and Heidegger drew inspiration from this oracular ancient. Twenty-five centuries after he was consumed in the cosmic flux, Heraclitus continues to speak to us today. He speaks in the fixity of his fragments, rescued from the flux by the works of succeeding generations who were so sufficiently impressed by the fixed truth of what the fragments say that they copied his words when the media that carried them to that point were themselves consumed. And so we have access to them still today as we flow through life to our own inevitable dissolution—all according to the *Logos*.

---

36. Hegel, *Lectures on the History of Philosophy*, 154–65; *Phenomenology of Spirit*, §17; *Hegel's Science of Logic*, trans. A. Miller (London: George Allen and Unwin, 1969), 536–39, 580–83; *Lectures on the Philosophy of Religion*, trans. R. Brown, J. Stewart, and H. Harris (Berkeley: University of California Press, 1988); Charles Kahn, *The Art and Thought of Heraclitus*, 87.

2 ∽ Parmenides

"HEART" AS STARTING POINT

Parmenides is traditionally approached in terms of his basic distinction between the "Way of Truth" and the "Way of Seeming." We prefer to begin with a distinction implicated in the very first line, a distinction little attended to by interpreters of Parmenides, but a distinction of pivotal importance both for the understanding of our relation to Being and for a rapprochement between Eastern and Western thought: "The steeds that carry me took me as far as my heart could desire?"[1] Heart and the limits of its desire initiate Western metaphysics. Not thought, not logic or reason, but "the heart" with its desire is first. And not the heart's desire in any one of its moments, but the heart at its outermost limits is what opens that metaphysics. We are thus installed from the very onset in relation to Being as the plenitude.

The correlation between the deep center of the self and its total object pushes us to the limits within and without. What a contrast to the "here, now, red spot" of those who would construct all from bare *sensa* without consideration of what animates such desire. What a contrast even to the ordinary language of "the cat is on the mat" of contemporary language analysis or the early phenomenologists' attempts at such things as the phenomenology of a mailbox. But sooner or later, sensist language reconstruction gives way to attention to ordinary language and phenomenology to the lifeworld. And sooner or later, our ordinary language runs up against religious language and phenomenology against religious phenomena.[2] Then a revisioning is called for, a reconfiguration of the ordi-

1. G. S. Kirk and J. E. Raven, *The Presocratic Philosophers* (Cambridge: Cambridge University Press, 1966), frag. 342, 266. (All unnamed references in this chapter are to Parmenides.)
2. For a history of the analytic movement, see James Cornman, "Philosophical Analysis and the Future of Metaphysics," in *The Future of Metaphysics*, ed. Robert E. Wood (Chicago:

nary world in terms of those extraordinary experiences that situate the immediate in relation to what it ultimately reveals and conceals.

"Heart" is a cross-cultural constant expressed in the ordinary language of many different peoples. It has four basic levels of meaning: (1) the literal meaning, the organic pump in the center of the chest, which is an abstraction from (2) the metaphorical meaning of a psychological center between *Bios* and *Logos*, the center of vitality, will, memory, and thought; (3) an extension from the subject to the object, indicating the binding tie of the heart's desire, used primarily in song (e.g., "dear heart" or "heart of my heart" but also commonly, though a bit mawkishly, as in "sweetheart"); and (4) a "transcendental" level, extending to all things the notion of center and functioning as equivalent to "essence" in expressions like "the heart of the matter."[3]

The proem to Parmenides's solitary extant work, the exceedingly short *On Nature*, expresses in terms appropriate to the heart, that is, in metaphorical terms, the movement of the heart. Metaphors function appropriately here since heart is the medium between the too-often dichotomized literalism of a mechanized body and a logicized reason.[4] Drawn in a singing chariot and led by the daughters of the sun past the gates of the ways of night and day opened by avenging Justice, the aspirant is greeted by "the goddess" who teaches him the momentous truth.[5] Corresponding to the heart, which one does not give oneself (whence the liturgical prayer, "Create in us a new heart, O Lord"), the truth involved is not wrested from things as a conquest but is given as a gift, a grace from the goddess, hence the contention of many commentators that Parmenidean metaphysics is rooted in a kind of mystical experience, a revelation.[6] Consequently, Heidegger in commenting speaks of Parmenides's use here of *noein* (Greek "to know" from which the English "noetic" is

Quadrangle, 1970), 32–49; for a history of the phenomenological movement, see Herbert Spiegelberg, *The Phenomenological Movement: A Historical Introduction*, Phenomenologica 6 (The Hague: Martinus Nijhoff, 1960).

3. See my introduction to Stephen Strasser, *Phenomenology of Feeling: An Essay on the Phenomena of the Heart*, trans. Robert E. Wood, preface for this translation by Paul Ricoeur (Pittsburgh: Duquesne University Press, 1977), 3–14.

4. The father of this approach is, of course, René Descartes.

5. Kirk and Raven, *The Presocratic Philosophers*, frag. 342, 267.

6. Werner Jaeger suggests the same in *Theology of the Early Greeks* (Oxford: Clarendon Press, 1960), 10ff; see esp. 98.

derived), the activity of *nous* (the "faculty" of "knowing"), as "an event which has man," to be distinguished from a mode of apprehension that is something man has.[7] *Nous* is the capacity of being apprehended by things, a being-taken that is the condition for "letting them be" (i.e., be manifest to us). The "whole person" is involved, "grasped," and "touched" to his very heart. Given such an interpretation, Heidegger surprisingly fails to take into consideration the first line of the proem.

THE LOGIC OF BEING

But what is this astonishing revelation? "It is and It-is-not is not." Or there is Being, but no nonbeing.[8] A revelation? What could be more obvious? In order to get some insight into the content of the revelation aspect, Parmenides asks us, in effect, to work out the logical consequences of this compound proposition. He asks us to "test by *logos* the truth of what I say."[9] (*Logos*, basically "word," is used here for the first time in history as "logical deduction.")[10]

Try to think of change in terms of "Being." In order to change, a thing must *be*, but it must also *not be* what it will be. In other words, to think change, we must think that *not being in some way is*. But to think Being by itself (i.e., apart from all nonbeing), we must think changeless Being.

Or come at it another way, lest the above appear a mere verbal trick. Consider that which is most deeply implicated in the changing world, either as its measure or in some way as its inner reality: consider time. Time must be thought of in terms of its three dimensions: past, present, and future. But what is the ontological mode or mode of being of each of these dimensions? The past is not: it is what is no longer; the future is not either: it is what is not yet. But what of the present, that which is between the no-longer and the not-yet, which are themselves distinguishable both from each other, from absolute nonbeing, and from the present? Just what further is the present or the now? Can we be more precise as to its function between the no-longer and the not-yet? We tend to use it with more or less

---

7. Heidegger, *Introduction to Metaphysics*, 141.

8. Kirk and Raven, *The Presocratic Philosophers*, frag. 2 (344), 269.

9. Ibid., frag. 7 (346), 271.

10. Jaeger, *Theology of the Early Greeks*, 102ff. See also his *Paideia: The Ideals of Greek Culture*, trans. G. Highet (New York: Oxford, 1945), vol. 1, 174–76.

stringency (e.g., *now*, in the era since man appeared on the planet; or *now*, since the appearance of Christ; or *now*, in the twentieth century; or *now*, in 2014; or *now*, in March; or *now*, Friday; or *now*, at the tenth hour; or *now*, at 10:08, etc.). For everyday purposes, that is usually as far as we precise the now. But in the case of an Olympic swimmer, we go to the hundredth of a second to determine the now of his or her finish; and in the case of the measurement of subatomic events, to micro-milliseconds, and so forth. As we attempt in this way to make the now precise, it tends to disappear, or rather to be viewed in its "reality" as a nontemporally extended divider moving from the no-longer to the not-yet: a not-being between two not-beings! Well then, ordinary experience and its objects have to be thought of as in some way both being and nonbeing. But then we have to think the seemingly impossible: that nonbeing *is*!

Parmenides attempts to "think" Being itself, apart from all nonbeing. Being itself thus shows itself to "logic" as changeless, though things in experience and our experience of them do indeed change. But "logic" for Parmenides is only a kind of exterior test for what is essentially a matter of direct revelation: an experience that fills the heart, an experience out of the ordinary "flowing now" (*nunc fluens*), an experience of the "stand-ing now" (*nunc stans*, as the medieval, who knew these things so much better than we, expressed it).[11] So we must distinguish between the now as one moment, the pivotal moment, of temporality and the eternal now standing beyond time burdened with nonbeing.

Consider a second approach Parmenides used. Think, in terms of Be-ing, the multiplicity of and in the things of experience and in our experi-ence of them. For each member of this multiplicity to *be*, it must *not be* the other things that are. And each of the things that are is itself an inter-nal multiplicity composed of parts, each one of which *is not* the others, and each one of which is, in its turn, composed of an internal multiplic-ity: from organism to organs, to cells, to molecules to atoms, to subatomic particles, to . . . ? Press that to its logical limit, and you see that any item of spatial extensity, even of a supposedly homogeneous (i.e., finally noncom-posed) body (in Greek noncomposition was expressed in the term *atomos* which meant "un-cuttable"),[12] is such that its center is not its periphery

11. Aquinas, *Summa Theologiae*, I, 10, 5, and 2.
12. A. van Melsen, *From Atomos to Atom* (New York: Harper, 1960). See esp. 17–23.

and any point on its surface is not any other point either on the surface or between the surface and the center.[13] Theoretically, there can be no *atomos* because one can always think its in-principle divisibility ad infinitum. The concept of the *atomos is* rooted in a decision to stop analysis and to flee (as later Leibniz and Kant were not to flee) from the paradox of infinity involved in the notion of spatial extensity. Parmenides's conclusion is that Being itself must be absolutely one: not a one-of-many. It is absolute plenitude, full, with no cracks of division or negation. Parmenides's follower Melissus concluded, following these lines, that it could not be material because it could not be spatial.[14]

One obvious problem is that an absolute unity considered apart from the multiple also has to be thought of as *not being* among the multiple—and thus, paradoxically, as included in the multiple, being part of the total system comprised of itself and the others. This is a move Spinoza and Hegel will make. Parmenides would undoubtedly seek for a distinction, since "logic" is only an outside test for the "noetic" experience of absolute plenitude apart from things. The One is "wholly other," with no internal multiplicity, and including in itself in absolute simplicity what the many contain in scattered fashion. This is essentially the classical position taken up by Plato, Aristotle, Plotinus,[43] and the Judaeo-Christian tradition.

Melissus also concluded—in a peculiarly un-Greek fashion—that it must be infinite, for what is there to limit it?[15] I say "un-Greek" because the Greeks tended to view the infinite (Greek *a-peiron*) as indeterminate: as lacking *fines*, or boundaries, and thus lacking definition, having no termination and thus being indeterminate. Hence, the infinite was conceived of as chaotic, imperfect.[16] In spite of this, Parmenides's logic led Melissus to conceive of that which filled the heart's desire as beyond finitude, thus introducing the notion of the finite (and therefore also of definition) as itself a limitation, the negation of the plenitude of the infinite which we now express negatively as a negation of negation (of which Hegel makes much).

13. Cf. Joseph Owens, *A History of Ancient Western Philosophy* (New York: Appleton-Century-Crofts, 1959), 96.

14. Melissus, cited in Aristotle, *Sophistical Refutations,* trans. E. Forster (Cambridge: Oxford University Press, 1955), 167n13.

15. Kirk and Raven, *The Presocratic Philosophers*, frags. 3–6 (288–385), 299.

16. Ibid., frag. 3 (344).

Logic thus tests the truth of the heart: the experience in question is not only an experience of the *nunc stans* but an experience of perfect plenitude, absolute fulfillment. Parmenides says in the proemium, through the mouth of the goddess (or, Parmenides would probably say, the goddess says through the mouth—or stylus—of Parmenides), that "thought and Being are one."[17] This could be read in several different ways, conceiving it first of all in terms of ourselves as subjects thinking, then in terms of Being as object of such thought. Our thinking at this level could be related to pure Being either by way of identity or union. The former is the tendency in the Hindu tradition: Atman is Brahman, the Self is the All. The "I" for which everything, even its own structures, is an object is not simply the I viewing itself as correlated with empirical objects or with intelligible relations, for all this is *maya*, the web of illusion wherein we misconstrue both Being and ourselves. Beyond all the distinctions provided at the empirical and rational levels, the I and the All are nondistinct, identical.[18]

Conversely, the way of union is the dominant tradition of the West, rooted in the doctrine of God as Absolute Other.[19] But on Parmenidean grounds, the union could be conceived as Being linked either to a nonconscious *principle* or with thought that is itself pure Being. In the latter case, Being as a nature would thus not only be the unchanging one, a pure principle, dead, dull, unaware, but it would be self-presence without the distinction of subject and object, pure *noein*. This is a reading that developed, through Plato and Aristotle, into the Hebrew-Christian tradition as classical monotheism.

But with the Parmenidean thrust immediately locating itself at the outermost limit of the heart's desire, experience is cleft in two: our experience of the ordinary world of "unthinkable" (but experienceable and imaginable) multiplicity and change, and the extraordinary experience of eternal fullness. The hardheaded, tough-minded, no-nonsense, red-blooded objector will ask: "But what of the 'real world' in front of us now?" One who has experienced eternal fullness might reply, "What of it? It's not a world that can fill the outermost limits of the heart's desire.

---

17. Ibid., frag. 2 (344), 269.

18. Ranakrishna, "Mundaka Upanishad," in *A Sourcebook in Indian Philosophy*, ed. S. Radhakrishnan and C. Moore (Princeton, N.J.: Princeton University Press, 1957), 52–53.

19. Kirk and Raven, *The Presocratic Philosophers*, frag. 1 (342), 267.

And there is something that can." But Parmenides insists that one who would walk the way of truth (*aletheia*) must also know "the wandering opinion of mortals" on the way of seeming (*doxa*).[20] And on this way of seeming, Parmenides himself positions Eros in the center, "first of all the gods."[21] One who walks the way of truth must come to see "how the things that seem, as they pass through everything, must gain the semblance of Being."[22] The semblance of Being shows by virtue of Eros as desire for the fullness. Such Eros is symbolized by the moon, wandering about the earth with borrowed light, looking always to the sun.[23] The plurality of changing things, "unthinkable" (i.e., nonidentical, in their plurality and change, with the changeless One with which thought is identified), nonetheless shows the absolute fullness to Eros, which is man who reflects "the light of Being" upon things.

Heidegger offers a different interpretation. He moves away entirely from the standard interpretation that I largely share. Being, in Heidegger's view, is indeed other than the multiplicity of beings. It abides, one and permanent, the imperishable, but not apart from things. Being is the light that gathers beings together and allows them to make their appearance to us. Being provides the meaning field within which we dwell and within which our relation to other beings (and to ourselves) is realized.[24] The way of *doxa* is simultaneously appearance and opinion: the way beings show themselves is a function of the modes of meaning through which we take them. Acquaintance with the realm of seeming is thus "needful," as Parmenides says. But so, for Heidegger, is the unthinkable way of nonbeing, struggle with which provides the contrast in terms of which Being itself grips us. As with Heraclitus, through death we "know" life, so here, through nonbeing, we know Being. Beings manifest themselves in deepening presence as we are drawn away from them through the realization of the otherness of Being itself and impelled more deeply to them in a way analogous to the way we are impelled more deeply to the realization of life through the realization of death.[25]

20. Ibid., frag. 12 (358), 283.

21. Ibid., frag. 1 (342), 267.

22. Frag. 15 in Philip Wheelwright, *The Presocratics* (New York: Odyssey, 1966), 100.

23. Ibid.

24. Martin Heidegger, *Introduction to Metaphysics*, 110–12, 136–9; *What Is Called Thinking?* trans. F. Wieck and J. Gray (New York: Harper and Row, 1968), 170ff.

25. Martin Heidegger, *Being and Time*, 279ff.

As richly suggestive as that analysis is, it does not necessarily have to be (as Heidegger thinks) incompatible with the standard interpretation of Parmenides's Being as transcendent, existing eternally in itself apart from the multiplicity of changing beings. Heidegger's understanding highlights the "being-apprehended" aspect of our relation to Being and draws a tighter link between the realm of seeming and the realm of Being. But there is room for an otherness of Being as a nature linked to beings through the light of the human being's openness to the transcendent.

One could read Parmenides as presenting the first negative ontotheology, a term Heidegger coined for Hegel's thought of God. It involves the unfolding of the *logic* of the notion of *Being* (*to on*) as a representation of God (*theos*). Being appears as unchanging, indivisible, beyond space and time, unlimited, completely other than all encounterable entities and ourselves as encountering. Anticipating Augustine, one could read it through the first line of *On Nature* as the term of the outmost limit of the heart's desire.

3 ❦ Plato's Line Revisited

The Pedagogy of Complete Reflection

The Platonic dialogues are not treatises in disguise. They are protreptic and proleptic instruments, positioning the reader dispositionally and providing hints for the work of completing the direction of thought by attending to "the things themselves," the phenomena to which human beings, properly attuned, have native access. Plato, I would contend, is a proto-phenomenologist whose dialogues yield significant coherent results when approached from that point of view.

In this chapter, I will focus on the center of one dialogue, the Line of Knowledge in the middle of the *Republic*. It contains a set of assertions, or "poetic proclamations," and is embedded in a context of what seem to be even more arbitrary assertions concerning the Good as the object of philosophic study. Paul Shorey goes so far as to say that they belong "to rhetoric rather than to systematic metaphysics."[1] Properly understood (and, of course, that means understood in the way this chapter will attempt to clarify), the Line allows us to cash in on the proclamations. It is a pedagogical device that not only invites reflection but leads us to a connected sequence of ever more comprehensive levels of reflection, culminating in what the medievals called a *reditio completa subiecti in seipso*,[2] an anticipatory catching up with the fundamental orientation of human being as directed toward the Whole, an orientation that is completely hidden in Socrates's purged city. Everything is contained within such complete reflection, including an awareness of the initial situation where one is not aware of the fundamental orientation of human existence. The Line lays out the eidetic field of conscious human operation and discerns

---

1. Plato, *Republic*, trans. Paul Shorey (Cambridge, Mass.: Harvard University Press, 1969), vol. 2, 104, note c.
2. Aquinas, *Summa Theologiae*, I, q. 84, a. 6.

its fundamental teleology. It contains the art of the *periagoge*, the turning around of the soul.[3]

Let us begin by laying out the relevant preliminary assertions:

Well, then, I said, say that the sun is the offspring of the good, I mean—an offspring the good begot in a proportion with itself: as the good is in the intelligible region with respect to intelligence and what is intellected, so the sun is in the visible region with respect to sight and what is seen. . . .

Say that what provides the truth to things known and gives the power to one who knows is the idea of the good. And as the cause of the knowledge and truth, you can understand it to be a thing known; but, as fair as these two are— knowledge and truth—if you believe that it is something different from them and still fairer than they, your belief will be right. . . .

I suppose you'll say the sun not only provides what is seen with the power of being seen, but also with generation, growth, and nourishment although it itself isn't generation. . . .

Therefore, say that not only being known is present in things known as a consequence of the good, but also existence and being are in them besides as a result of it, although the good isn't essence but is still beyond essence, exceeding it in dignity and power.[4]

What Socrates provides us with here is a set of initially poetic proclamations, visionary pronouncements to which we may or may not respond favorably, depending upon the character of our basic disposition, our fundamental attunement to this poetic word. But Socrates is a philosopher, and for a philosopher (to employ a later expression), *quod gratis assertur, gratis negatur* ("what is gratuitously asserted may be gratuitously denied"). Socrates the philosopher-pedagogue ought to lead us to ground such assertions and thus test their claims. It will be my contention that this is precisely what he attempts to do with the development of the Line of Knowledge. The Line is an introductory delineation of the fundamental structures of the field of experience as a hierarchy of ever more encompassing reflections, culminating in the *reditio completa subiecti in seipso*, the complete return of the subject to itself. The structure of

3. Plato, *Republic*, VI, 518c. Henceforth, reference to this work will be made only by book and line numbers, with the exception of my rendering *epekeina tes ousias* as "beyond essence" and not "beyond being" to which I strongly object. All translations are from *The Republic of Plato*, trans. Allan Bloom (New York: Basic Books, 1968).

4. Ibid., VI, 508c–509c.

this field in its hierarchical character provides the grounds for testing the character of all poetic proclamations in terms of how adequately they do justice to that field.

Let us first of all list the various claims involved in the aforementioned citations and then indicate their basis as that which is brought to light in the course of our exposition of the Line:

1. The sun is created by the Good as an analogy of itself.

2. The Good provides truth (*aletheia*) to things known and the power (to know) to the knower.

3. The Good is fairer than knowledge and truth.

4. Existence (*einai*) and being (*ousia*) are in things because of the Good.

5. The Good is beyond essence (*epekeina tes ousias*).

Socrates's task is to ground these assertions.

Let us first attend to the initial delineation of the space of Socrates's inquiry by backing up in the text of the *Republic*. Socrates introduced the notion of the Good when he attempted to define "philosopher" and "the object of philosophic study." He initially approached the two concepts together by saying that, in contrast to the lovers of beautiful things that had been cultivated in the preceding books, the philosopher is a lover of the vision of Beauty itself.[5] Hence, we have an anticipatory drawing of the Line. When Socrates goes further and designates the study of the Good as the object of philosophic inquiry, he further articulates the space carved out by drawing a line between beautiful things and Beauty itself according to the following parallel:

FIGURE 3-1

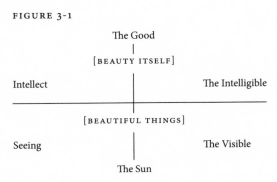

5. Ibid., V, 509d.

That space is further articulated by the actual Line—and here begins the grounding of all these assertions. Socrates says, "Take a line cut in two unequal segments, one for the class that is seen, the other for the class that is intellected—and go on and cut each segment in the same proportion."[6] So, draw a vertical line, AE (see fig. 3-2). Divide the line into four equal units (numbering the divisions and ends 1–5), and, assuming the proportion of 3 to 1, put the first cut (C) at the top of the first unit (1 and 2) from the bottom, so that we have a bottom segment (AC) of one and a top segment (CE) of three units—an example of the unequal segmentation with which Socrates asks us to begin. To secure the required proportionate segmentation of the two segments, begin with the bottom (AC). Divide it into four equal subunits and cut the line in turn after the first unit (AB) from the bottom of that segment, giving us another 3-to-1 ratio. The bottom subunit (AB) is then one-quarter of the original unit, making the next division (BC) three-quarters. Considering the line from the bottom, we have a one-quarter subunit (AB) followed by a three-quarters subunit (BC).

FIGURE 3-2

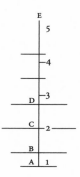

Next, consider the line (CE) above the first original unit. It is composed of three original units: 2 and 3, 3 and 4, and 4 and 5. To divide it by a ratio of 3 to 1, divide the three original units by four, yielding .75 or three-quarters as the subunit for this whole section (CE). Draw a line (D) at the top of the bottom unit of CE. That gives us three subunits of three-quarters or a total of 2.25 for DE. The four segments in order, then, from

6. Ibid., V, 476b–c; VI, 508c.

bottom to top are .25, .75, .75 and 2.25. What is pertinent to see is that the two central segments are thus equal.

Let us try again, using a nine-unit line (again, AE) divided by a 2-to-1 ratio (see fig. 3-3). The first division (AC) will then be between the third and fourth units, leaving six units for CE and three for AC. The bottom segment of three units will divide into segments of two (BC) and one (AB) units. The six-unit top (CE) will divide, according to the chosen 2-to-1 ratio, into segments of four (DE) and two (CD) units. So we have our four segments, reading from bottom to top as 1 (AB), 2 (BC), 2 (CD) and 4 (DE). Again, the central segments are equal.

FIGURE 3-3

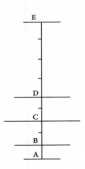

One could make several other attempts at it, continuing the process of geometrical induction. What emerges is that the line Plato asks us to construct, once we reflect upon it, shows itself as a visible instance of a geometric theorem: any line, divided by any given proportion and sub-divided by the same proportion, will yield four segments so related that the two central segments are always equal. (Incidentally, we could make a similar observation about each of our examples: any line, of a given length, divided by the chosen ratios, will always yield the same subdivisions as we indicated in each example.) Now, "any" and "always" seem to be extreme claims. We really have what Plato calls in the *Meno alethe doxa*, or "manifest appearance," direct insight into universal relations, as distinguished from *orthe doxa*, or "correct appearance," on the one hand and false opinion on the other. *Orthe doxa*, from the point of view of the one holding it without insight, only *happens* to be correct—

perhaps he memorized the answer without any insight whatsoever, like a tape recorder. In both cases, one must ultimately go further, "tethering" or "chaining down" the *doxa* by reasoning to and from the axioms of (Euclidean) geometry.[7] One proceeds to demonstrate what induction has suggested, thus grounding the unrestricted generality referred to by the suspect terms "any" and "always."[8] These considerations initially fill in for us what Plato means by the *noeta*, or the intelligibles.

The peculiar relations between the various segments of the visible line led us first to a mode of reflection that we term "geometrical induction." The suggestions of unrestricted generality pointed further to "geometrical deduction" or demonstration in the strict sense of the term. Reflection in both cases terminated in rendering explicit what was only implicit in the visibility of the proportionally drawn line. But it is important to see that the very character of the visible invited reflection upon the universal relations it exhibited.

The proximate reason why the line was introduced (to lead us to understanding something of the Good on analogy with the sun) leads us further still to a third level of even more encompassing reflection, rendering explicit a more comprehensive level of what is implicit in our mode of access to the visible. Through metaphoric (poetic) reflection, Plato employs the line further as a device for indicating more encompassing types of reflection by arbitrarily letting its four segments represent the nonarbitrary relations involved in what the line itself represents literally and nonarbitrarily. (When referring to the line in its symbolic employment, we will henceforth capitalize it.) Socrates lets the bottom two segments together represent the visible (*horaton*) or the changing realm of particulars and their relations, while the top two segments represent the intelligible (*noeton*) or the changeless realm of universal relations.[9]

Let us contrast now the character of the visible as such and the *noeta* to which the visible led us by giving rise to reflection. Here, we are not dealing with the particular visible line but with visibility as such—indeed, ultimately with the "as such" as such, with universality. The lines we drew according to prescription could have been, in principle, of any

7. Plato, *Meno*, 98a.

8. For the deductive proof, see Jacob Klein, *Commentary on Plato's Meno* (Chapel Hill: University of North Carolina Press, 1965), 119n27.

9. Plato, *Republic*, VI, 509d; cf. VII, 524c.

length. And any particular length chosen could be replicated any number of times and in many different places. This is so because the line illustrates a *principle*, the authentic *noeton*, object of *noesis*, translated into Latin as *intellectus*, from *intus legere*, to "read within" the sensible its intelligibility.[10] Any of these lines likewise illustrates visibility or the visible as such. Any visible object is a particular thing, appearing under the limitations of a biologically conditioned perception, at a particular region in space and at a particular moment of time. Again, it came into being at a particular moment in time and will pass out of being. Finally, it only approaches the absolutely exact character of the metric relations it represents, since the character of our instruments for drawing it are exact only relative to our purposes.

By contrast, the intelligible relations, though they came into and will eventually pass out of my awareness, nonetheless present themselves as independent of my or any individual awareness, having an unalterable character in themselves. Even if no one ever thought of them and even if everyone were to forget them once they are thought of, the relations would still hold. They would do so because, contrasted with visible relations, the intelligible relations stand beyond the here and now of this particular line as present in this particular act of awareness: they apply to space and time as a whole and for any intellect in principle because they are transspatial and transtemporal—or maybe omnispatial and omnitemporal—and thus transsubjective. Plato calls the region of intelligible relation the realm of *ousia*, of essence or beingness.[11] An object in this realm is an *eidos* or *idea*,[12] literally something seen but only in "the mind's eye." Now, by contrast, Socrates presents the realm of *genesis*,[13] which can be spoken of as a synthesis of being and nonbeing (*on* and *me on*).[14] The being of this realm is the presence of intelligible form; its nonbeing is its temporality, caught in the flow from the no-longer to the not-yet, and its spatiality, caught in the otherness of one visible instance to another of an intelligible relation.

---

10. Aquinas, *Summa Contra Gentiles*, IV, c. 11.VI, 509b.

11. Plato, *Republic*, VI, 509b. Heidegger translates *ousia* as *Seiendheit*, the beingness of beings, their forms. "Plato's Doctrine of Truth," in *Pathmarks*, ed. William McNeill (Cambridge: Cambridge University Press, 1998), 155–82.

12. Ibid., VI, 507d and 511c.   13. Ibid., VI, 525b.

14. Plato, *Sophist*, 237a.

Taken now symbolically, the Line divides into two parts at C, so that AC represents the visible and CE the intelligible. Socrates thus returns to the earlier opening of the field of inquiry as the region of the intelligible governed by the Good and the region of the visible governed by the sun. The visible is literally divided into visible things and their images or shadows.[15] (We will see that this, too, has a metaphoric usage, giving rise to a double metaphor or a metaphor reflected back upon itself.) The first level of the intelligible is said to represent mathematics, while the second represents Forms. Reflection upon the visible line led us into mathematics by geometrical induction and pointed further to the possibility of deduction, placing us at the third level. But the aim of that reflection is to lead us to metareflection upon the eidetic features, the contrasting characteristic Forms of the visible and the intelligible. When we see that, we are no longer in the geometrical realm but already in the metarealm of those Forms that constitute the framework of geometry, and indeed of human experience as such. So, we are following the movement from the third (CD) to the fourth (DE) level of the Line now taken figuratively. So taken, the line folds back upon itself like a sardine can. The literal line, reflected upon geometrically, leads us to the third level of the Line taken metaphorically, and reflection upon the framework of geometry leads us to the fourth metaphoric level or philosophy as examination of the frameworks presupposed in all our dealings.

We might add here that the equality of the middle segments may also have a metaphoric point, as suggested by *Timaeus*: the intelligibility of physical things lies in mathematical relations.[16]

But let us look at the context more carefully. We are not concerned here simply with the differing ontological status of geometric objects and their empirical instantiations. We are ultimately, within the overall context of the *Republic*, concerned with the good life, with what justice itself might be, with whether justice is better than injustice, and with the final Good. We are concerned with the fundaments of human existence. At this point, we can link the original metaphoric triplet, comparing the Good with the sun, to the Line. Hence, there is a twofold division of the Line: a horizontal division and a vertical division.

15. Plato, *Republic*, VI, 510a.
16. Plato, *Timaeus*, 53ff.

FIGURE 3-4

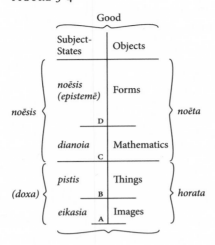

The horizontal division represents the two great ontological regions of the visible and the intelligible. The vertical division represents the division between states of mind (*pathemata*) and types of objects.[17] The two represent the visible-intelligible relation and the subject-object relation respectively, and together they represent the fundamental structure of the field of human experience. Hence, there is another type of reflection called for here. What we have carried on thus far might be called "object reflection," with its three strata of induction, deduction, and metareflection upon the contrasting characteristics of the objects involved in the move from the given visible line to geometry. The further type of reflection might be termed, by contrast, "subject reflection," or reflection upon various mental acts correlated with differing object-types. Socrates lists the various mental states that ground the four levels of appearance of objects as (from bottom to top) *eikasia* correlated with images and shadows, *pistis* with things, *dianoia* with mathematics, and *noesis* with Forms.[18] The voyage of discovery here is a voyage of self-discovery—though not in any subjectivistic sense. It is the discovery of the structure of the human subject as subject of awareness that comes to its own fuller self-awareness

17. Plato, *Republic*, VI, 511d.
18. Ibid.

as it uncovers ever more encompassing regions of objects and reflects further upon itself as the locus of the manifestness of those regions.

Apprehension of the immanent Forms of vision and intellection leads us to grasp the distinction and relation between seeing and intellection as immanent in and transcendent of the here-and-now, respectively. Our human mode of being present to the here-and-now sensorily given is simultaneously a transcendence of the here-and-now of our own bodiliness by being present to the overarching intelligibility that situates the sensorily given within the Whole of what is and that thereby allows us to attend to the sensorily given as what it is. The play of this fourfold set of relations constitutes the unalterable frame of human existence and is implicit in all our wakeful life, underpinning both the ordinary life-world and the various realms of scientific endeavor. Plato provides a fundamental phenomenological inventory of the basic framework of the field of experience. It is an initial opening up of a field for reflective exploration in its fuller complexity, but it sets up fundamental distinctions that are not theoretical in the modern sense of tentative but are theoretical in the ancient sense of directly intuitable and invariantly given.

Socrates does not directly fill in the fourth level of the Line except by indicating that it is the region of operation of *noesis* whose vehicle is dialectic.[19] He also has precious little to say about dialectic here except that it starts from the assumptions of the other sciences and moves toward their ultimate presuppositions;[20] it grasps the reason for being of each thing (*ton logon tes ousias*);[21] and it involves an overview (*synopsis*) of relations between various regions.[22] But when we reflect upon what Socrates has been doing throughout the dialogue, we are able to anchor these three rather bald assertions in actual procedure.

Socrates began the dialogue with an examination of common opinions on the nature of justice (giving what is due, giving benefits to allies and harm to enemies, and obeying the laws that are made in the self-interest of the stronger).[23] Dialectic here consisted in placing each of these definitions in a broader context to see how they worked in that expanded framework.[24] It consisted further in showing that what a given defini-

19. Ibid., VI, 511b.   20. Ibid.
21. Ibid., VII, 534b.   22. Ibid., VII, 537c.
23. Ibid., I, 351c.

24. For example, the context of the criteria for determining real friends and enemies (I, 334c), real benefit and harm (I, 339d).

tion excluded was presupposed in its own operation (the self-interest of the crime syndicate boss required that he be fair to those who worked for him as partners in crime).[25] It also consisted in making explicit what was implicit in the interlocutor's understanding of the proffered definition.[26] Broader contextualization, explicitation, and self-inclusion are all ways of rendering more comprehensive the context within which understanding occurs, thus permitting intelligent criticism of any claim. Now, that is just what the Line is calculated to achieve: to establish the basic, all-encompassing context out of which human beings necessarily operate, but which for the most part remains only implicit in what they do and which, rendered explicit, shows that what they do often contradicts the basic structures involved in that context. The Line awakens *noesis* to a reflective explicitation of its own eidetic features and leads it to discover its own immanent teleology. The fourth level is at least partially filled in by grasping the eidetic features presented in the Line. The Line as drawn exists in the cave of the visible; the Line's exposition repeated without a grasp of its necessity exists in the cave of opinion; the Line itself as understood in its necessity exists at its own fourth level.

It is, however, also important to note that when Socrates recapitulates the Line at the end of his exposition of the levels of education in explaining the parable of the Cave, he speaks only of the states of mind along with the great regions of *ousia* and *genesis*. About the particular regions of objects he is silent, claiming that that would involve us in too long an exposition.[27] I suggest this is so because the exposition of the objects is the history of *philosophia* itself, the enduring quest for the manifestness of the Whole to which we are directed by the ever-manifest but usually only implicitly given character of our own immanent structure. The object of our natural quest is manifest as a whole and will always remain so manifest "only to God."[28] The irremovable, ever-enduring character of the field of awareness sets the conditions for dialogical life.

Plato has Socrates carry further the two forms of reflection we have called object-reflection and subject-reflection. On the object side, Socrates reflects upon the grounds for the possibility of geometric knowledge,

25. Plato, *Republic*, I, 351c.
26. For example, that which is due is not something which harms the one to whom it is *prima facie* due (I, 332b).
27. Plato, *Republic*, VI, 537e.
28. Plato, *Apology*, 23a.

which proceeds "downward" from the relative fewness of axioms to the increasing plurality of theorems demonstrated in terms of their coherence within the geometric network generated by deduction and perhaps also suggested by induction. Now, we are asked to focus not upon the presupposed framework of geometry but upon geometry's internal mode of procedure. Socrates has us consider the possibility of moving in the other logical direction, "upward" from the relatively few, but still multiple, principles of geometry, toward an even more basic region of principles.[29] A concept gathers individuals and classes of things together into an intelligible unity; a geometrical system gathers a region of classes together into a deductive unity; reflection upon the framework of experience laid out in the Line unifies the field of experience. But all these forms of unity, gathered together in evermore simple principles, point toward that which is simply one. Elsewhere Plato calls it the One.[30] If it were known, one might deduce all intelligibility from it, and not only the quantitative aspects considered in (Euclidean) geometry. Geometry itself results from a search for the mirroring of the One in the many, for that high type of unity compatible with multiplicity that we call intelligible coherence. "In the light of" the One that is not directly known but to which *nous* aspires, we come to understand anything that we understand, for understanding in general, whether in the life-world or in the various sciences, is the grasping of coherence in what might otherwise appear as a meaningless plurality, like these words on the page to one who does not know how to read.

Keeping in mind the level of reflection that moved from describing the contrasting features of the visible and the intelligible to laying bare the structural features of awareness, namely, seeing and understanding, what is at stake in the upward movement to the One is an aspiration toward a unification not simply of the world of objects but of the total field of operation of the subject-object relation. The notion of the One as intelligible light is thus not the notion of another intelligible object; it is rather the notion of the ground of the subject-object relation in its all-encompassing character. Hence, it is "beyond *ousia*" (claim 5), though it is at the same time also designated as *tou ontos phanotaton*, the brightest region of *being*.[31] It is beyond *ousia* but not beyond *to on*. Hence, we have

29. Plato, *Republic*, VI, 510b–c; cf. 525d.
30. Ibid., VI, 524d.
31. Ibid., VI, 518c. *Ousia* is perhaps best translated as "essence" since *to on* (neuter participial

rendered *epeikein tes ousias* as "beyond essence." The Good, Socrates says, provides manifestness (*aletheia*) to things and enables the mind to be the locus of that manifestness, of the uncovering of the intelligible-visible relation implicit in all things encountered (claim 2) because the Good is for all things the source of existence (*to einai*)—that they are at all—and of essence (*ousia*) (claim 4)—what or how they are. The ground of mind and things is a common ground that lets things lie open to mind, that makes it such that mind is no stranger to things and things to mind, as if the mind were observing some foreign region where it had no real place. Observation is part of the same system as the observed. Mind and things belong together; they are grounded in their mutual referentiality that neither of them establishes on its own. According to the old adage of Parmenides that began Western metaphysics, "Thought and Being are one."[32] The One/Good is neither subject nor object but the ground of their relation of manifestness, their *aletheia*, their "truth," by being the ground of their being. The One/Good is ground of the play of the fourfold of vision and object of vision, of intelligible and power of understanding. It is indeed truth in this originary sense of *aletheia* to which Heidegger repeatedly called attention. *Aletheia* is "un-concealment," the coming out of concealment as that which makes possible truth in the secondary, derived sense of *orthotes*, or correctness of propositions, by which we come to correspond intellectually to the lineaments of what is.[33] Thought that moves in the direction of the ground of objective truth involves even more comprehensive reflection than reflection upon the fourfold framework of human experience, since it surmounts that framework to attend to the ground of the possibility of the comprehensive region of intelligible manifestness.

The question "Why?" leads first to an indication of empirical regularities in the visible realm, and then to an indication of motives in the realm of everyday human relations. Pressed further under the impetus of a purely theoretical interest, it leads to demonstration in terms of fundamental principles in a given region and further still into the conditions

---

form of *to einai*, "to be") is used here as a generic term covering *ousia* and the Good (*agathon*). The correlate to essence is intellect (*nous*), while the correlate to *agathon* is *eros*.

32. Kirk and Raven, *The Presocratic Philosophers*, frag. 3 (344), 269.

33. Martin Heidegger, "On the Essence of Truth," in *Martin Heidegger: Basic Writings*, ed. D. Krell (New York: Harper and Row, 1971), 117ff.

for the possibility of that region, both ontological and epistemological, both on the object and on the subject side. Ultimately, one is led to the ultimate Why? Why are things such as to be manifest? The One/Good is the putative answer, but the term indicates a direction rather than a direct seeing, for what is that which is neither subject nor object? Socrates refers to the seeing of the Good as "[his] dream"[34] and elsewhere in the dialogue says that a dream, whether in sleep or in wakeful life, is an image of reality taken as reality.[35] Elsewhere he says, "Let us not create darkness at noon by attempting to stare at the sun. Let us rather contemplate it in its images."[36] The Good as the sun of the intelligible world is only indirectly apprehensible in terms of the whole hierarchy of "images" that it illuminates by making understanding possible.

Here we are at the limits of inquiry. What are we to do with such an ultimate nonobject? Perhaps we must learn not to do something with it but to allow the power of its ultimacy to take hold of us, to learn to sense the strangeness of that ultimate otherness that makes everything strange by prying us loose from the self-evidence of everydayness and the temptation to settle into regional satisfactions. But we are still not at an end of our exposition of the Line.

Book VII of the *Republic* introduces us to the allegory of the Cave as our own image and as an image of our education. We are, says Socrates, like men chained from birth in a deep cave so we cannot turn our heads around. All we ever saw were shadows on a wall projected by a set of puppets manipulated by puppeteers behind whom is enkindled a great fire. One of the prisoners was unchained, turned around, and then dragged out of the cave where he gradually got accustomed to seeing the originals after which the puppets had been modeled and the sun which shines upon those originals. He then went back to the cave to attempt to persuade the incredulous prisoners.[37]

By the time we are finished with Socrates's explication of the meaning of the parable, the bottom two levels of the Line have undergone a metaphorical shift. Earlier, Socrates had designated the objects on the bottom two levels as visible things (the second level from the bottom) and their images or reflections or shadows (the bottom level). The corresponding states

34. Plato, *Republic*, VII, 517b.
36. Plato, *Laws*, X, 897d.
35. Ibid., V, 476d.
37. Plato, *Republic*, VII, 514a–517a.

of mind are *pistis*, or trust, and *eikasia*, or image-thinking, which were earlier simply labeled and not discussed. In discussing the Cave, Socrates indicates that that to which we are initially chained are not literally shadows or images but things like "images of justice in the lawcourts"[38]—the very things with which the dialogue began. "Images" in this sense are the socially conditioned interpretations, the stereotypical judgments that constitute what "they say." Their range extends to the whole of our ordinary experience, to the life-world that is always the world of culture in the broadest sense of the term. It is the world of a people as a kind of second womb without which we cannot grow up mentally but from which we should eventually be "born again." And the most fundamental aspect of our enchainment is the realm of judgments about value and final reality.

In his rehearsal of the levels of the Line at the end of his discussion of the Cave, the lower two levels are now levels of *doxa*, not simply levels of seeing but of judging.[39] *Doxa*, I suggest, is not simply a matter of free-floating opinions but modes of presence. Things appear in function of how they are taken up in judgments. Then why focus on the visible if judgments are what is involved here in the Cave? The sun as the principle of the visible rules in this realm metaphorically because vision is our primary sense. As Augustine noted, visual metaphors govern all our cognitive vocabulary: "see" how this food tastes, how this cloth feels, how this food tastes, how this perfume smells—and not smell how this looks, or listen to how this smells, or hear how this feels.[40] The sun is now taken to stand for the principle of sense-perceptibility as the proximate criterion ("Unless I see for myself . . ."). And as far as value is concerned, the proximate principle is, indeed, the sensorily gratifying: food, drink, sex, relaxation, and the like. The chaining to common opinions tends to be at the same time a chaining to the sense-perceptible and the sensorily gratifying as the criteria of reality and value, respectively. Neither of these

38. Ibid., VI, 493a.

39. Ibid., VI, 534a; cf. 476d on *doxa* as belonging to the lover of beautiful things. At 534a, *episteme* takes the place of *noesis* on the earlier list of levels of the Line (511e). *Noesis* is then assigned the generic place corresponding to *ousia*. (Cf. the terms in parentheses in fig. 3–4.) Both *dianoia* as operative in mathematics and *episteme* involve eidetic intuition (*noesis*) into rational structures, but *episteme* transcends the "hypotheses" of mathematics (511b) to stand upon (*episteme*) the firmer ground of the framework presupposed by mathematics. Both have to be seen in the light of the Good/One which grounds our distinctively human life.

40 Augustine, *Confessions*, X, 54.

work as ultimate criteria because the sensa need to be taken up into interpretation, and the sensorily gratifying needs to be made coherent with the whole of our lives, especially with that dimension of our lives given to the interpretation of the place of the *sensa* in the whole—that is, both have to be seen in the light of the Good/One that grounds our distinctively human life.

The second level of the Line, the level of *pistis* or trust, has to do with the reliability of both the empirical world and the repetitive behavioral forms of the community that constitute the factual adjustments of people to one another and to the natural environment, the regularities of which impose themselves upon us and demand and permit our adjustment.

So, there is a further step. Just when we thought we had performed the ultimate comprehensive reflection on the Good as the most basic and thus the most comprehensive theme, we are led to consider further: that to which the mind is referred in the mode of manifestness is not just the intelligible region, it is the Whole. The Good, Socrates says, is the *arche tou pantos*, the principle of the whole.[41] It is *epekeina tes ousias*, not only in the sense of transcending the subject-object relation but also in the sense that it grounds the relation between the realm of *ousia*, of changeless eidetic principles, and the realm of *genesis*, of becoming.

Hence, aspiration toward the Good does not only lead us, by a first series of acts of abstractive reflection, out of the Cave of culturally supported and/or privately sustained opinions and proclamations, but it also leads us back, by a set of acts of recuperative, concrete reflection, into the Cave of everydayness as part of the whole.[42] The *reditio completa subiecti in seipso*, the complete return of the subject into itself, is not the involution of an abstractive intellect but the return of the mind, mediated by the body, to the concrete presence of things in the visible world. The Good, Socrates says, creates for itself an image of itself in the visible (claim 1), namely, the sun which is the source not only of visibility but of the realm of becoming itself. The *aletheia* of the whole is not simply the manifestness of intelligible relations, of *ousia* as essence, but it is the manifestness of the play between the visible and the intelligible. In fact, that is why we were able, in attending to the relations on the visible line,

41. Plato, *Republic*, VI, 511b.
42. Cf. Gabriel Marcel, *The Mystery of Being* (Chicago: Regnery, 1960), vol. I, 95–126 and 260.

to move to the intelligible theorem that it instantiated. The return to the Cave involves the understanding that the Beyond is already here in the intelligible depths, carved out through and beyond the sensory surface by a process of reflection of an increasingly more comprehensive nature. To that reflection, the pedagogy of the Line has led us. Its visible relations invite reflection and indicate that the visible "is" the image of the intelligible.

The visible line, reflected upon literally, leads us to the intelligible theorem that it embodies. Reflected upon metaphorically, it folds back upon its own third level, that of *ta mathemata*. This third level, in turn, understood as involving the interplay of the fourfold of the subject-states (*pathemata*) of *dianoia* and *aisthesis* on the one hand and their co-given visible and intelligible objects on the other, folds back upon its own fourth level, that of *noesis* and its eidetic objects (here the *eide* of the interplay of the fourfold). Reflected upon in terms of the ground of the whole field of manifestness (*aletheia*), this subject-object interplay points to the Good as the final encompassment of the whole region of manifestness as the Whole. As such, the Line could be viewed as a circle that curves back from the "height" of the Good to the "depth" of the lowest level (sunk in the Cave of biology and culture), now not simply dwelt-in unreflectively but understood in its fuller cosmic context.

The initial *periagoge*, the turning about of the soul, involves a turning away from secondhand opinions that may or may not be *orthai doxai*, or correct but indirect showings of what-is, attending, as we did, to clear relational features on the surface of things in order to arrive at *alethai doxai*, or manifest and thus direct insights into rational possibilities. But the point of that turning is to move us beyond culturally induced and personally sustained values and claims to ultimate reality that affect our whole sense of being, in order to bring us out of the Cave of *doxa* and into the realm of evermore comprehensive reflection upon the rational constitution that underpins our life-world. Hence, it is that Socrates speaks of a turning around of the "whole" soul, a "conversion."[43] The employment of geometry is a device to bring us to the more comprehensive reflection that corresponds to the fundamental desire of the whole soul as geometry does not.

43. Plato, *Republic*, VI, 518c.

This brings us to the real animating principle of the Platonic vision, the fundamental ground of that kind of manifestness that draws the soul upward and inward: the link between *eros* and beauty, for *eros* is the ground of the soul. Natural desire sets everything else in motion. Everything living is, as Socrates reports Diotima's teaching in the *Symposium*, the desire of the mortal for the immortal, the drive of living process, destined to die, for that which endures. Brought to the level of an awareness aimed at the whole of being, *eros* in us seeks identity with the undying Whole. As an object of *eros*, the Whole is manifest in its beauty.[44]

The *Republic* subtly nourishes the sense of beauty in its ascent from the first city dedicated to health up to the introduction of the philosopher-king and thus of the notion of the Good. The luxurious city emerges out of the healthy city through Glaucon's desire for luxuries.[45] Luxury is a surplus that testifies to a distinctively human need, the need for beauty. Luxury is, however, a confusion of the character of that need, locating it more in the sensory thrills that beauty provokes rather than in the character of beauty itself. Hence, the purged city focuses its education upon the appreciation of beautiful "things," turning the soul about from its tendency to wallow in fine feelings. Glaucon is the interlocutor, and not the more stolid Adeimantus, when Socrates turns from a consideration of the civic exemplarity of the referents of poetry to its pure aesthetic features, its meters, accompanying melodic forms and instrumental timbres.[46] But even this initial conversion is insufficient to satisfy the true direction of the desire Socrates is nourishing. He introduces the philosopher, in contrast to those who love beautiful things, as one who loves the vision of Beauty itself in which beautiful things share. Beauty itself is no mere concept: it is the real presence in beautiful things of an encompassing presence, evoking a sense of the whole of what is.[47] Beauty itself appears in the *Republic* as occupying the region whose high point is the Good. Beyond essence and our knowledge thereof, "the Good is fairer than knowledge and truth" (claim 3). I would suggest that Beauty itself is the radiance of the Good, the splendor of its manifestness.[48] The perception thereof is an index of the degree to which we have come to dwell

---

44. Plato, *Symposium*, 206b–212c.   45. Plato, *Republic*, II, 372c.
46. Ibid., II, 398a.   47. Plato, *Phaedrus*, 250d.
48. Plotinus, *Enneads*, VI, 9. I developed this insight into the centrality of beauty in the speculative tradition in my *Placing Aesthetics* in the chapter on the Latin Middle Ages.

in the Good and not simply to think, speak, and argue about it. It is only when we reach a sense of that more absorbing, encompassing aesthetic sensibility manifest in its first anticipatory instance in erotic experience that we can enter into the inward dynamism and felt texture of the Platonic ascent. In the *Phaedrus*, Socrates says that, of all the Forms, Beauty alone has this privilege, that it is visible to the eyes, and that this is the basis for its intoxicating effect upon us. In Beauty, the gap or separation between the abstract universality of the concept and the perceptible singularity of the individual is healed as vision and desire become one. The *reditio completa subiecti in seipso* to which the Line is calculated to lead us is not *completa* until it becomes identical with the desire for the whole of being that constitutes the ground of human nature.

In book VII, Plato introduces the quadrivium overtly as a means for turning the soul through mathematics from becoming to being.[49] In the process of doing so, he initially omits stereometry to go on to astronomy. But then he backtracks: we cannot study solids in motion until we study solids. What we are lacking is the "depth dimension," and we must make every effort to find one who can teach that dimension. After that strange admonition, Socrates tells Glaucon that he must now choose between the good of the city and the good of the soul.[50] I have suggested elsewhere that Plato is engaged here in a series of symbolic moves to help us solve the central structural riddle of the dialogue, which is one with the riddle of human existence, that is, the delayed transition from what appeared to be "the height of the argument" at the end of book IV (445c) to the declining forms of order in book VIII. What was missing at the end of book IV, which wholly subordinated the soul to the city, was the dimension of the depth of the soul, its fundamental *eros*, which, in its relation to the overarching Good, essentially transcends the city.[51] Socrates goes on in book VII to add harmonics to astronomy, claiming that for this we need a new principle, no longer one of seeing but one of hearing.[52] Following the suggestion of a symbolic reading, this brings to mind the "musical and loving nature" required for philosophy in the *Phaedrus*.[53] It

49. Plato, *Republic*, VII, 521c.
50. Ibid., VII, 527e.
51. See my "Image, Structure, and Content: On a Passage in Plato's *Republic*," *The Review of Metaphysics* 40, no. 3 (March 1987): 495–514.
52. Plato, *Republic*, VII, 530d.
53. Plato, *Phaedrus*, 248d.

also recalls the Seventh Letter where philosophy is enkindled as a spark that leaps from one person to another in philosophical conversation.[54] Hearing (not reading) the word, and thus essential relation to the presence of another human being, coupled with the rhythmic sensitivity of *musike* by which order and harmony sink deeply into the soul,[55] together bring us to the dispositional state wherein philosophy alone can free itself from contentiousness and partiality and install us completely in a lived fashion into the overarching order of the cosmos, which is never wholly manifest but to which we can learn to be holistically attuned.

There is another aspect of the real presence of Beauty in the visible. It is not only there in the harmonic proportions that lead us into mathematics and beyond. It is there in a special way in the look of the human other. The eyes of the other are not simply measurable mechanisms. They are, in the words of the *Phaedrus*, "the windows of the soul,"[56] the real presence in the visible of the locus of the manifestation of the Beyond, desire for the Encompassing, mediated, and thus supported and/or hindered by culture and choice. Not only hearing the words of this other, but the real, living presence of the dialogical partner, is the vehicle of Platonic ascent, the source of the spark that leaps from soul to soul in conversation about the Ultimate.

The evoking of the sensibility to which we have referred can also be the result of another mode of reflection, one employed by the poets, the reflection that leads to the construction of images capable of speaking to the erotic center of the soul. A complete reflection learns this sensitivity to the power of images and thereby understands, in a more than abstract way, the passionate life of the soul. Plato understood this life in a more profound and concrete way than perhaps any other philosopher. He employed that understanding to construct images, parables, and myths of great power.

The *Republic* itself ends in book X, after having begun by relegating the poets to the lowest fringe of reality,[57] with the construction of just such a powerful myth.[58] In this way, Plato concretely makes the case for poetry, and indeed for all the arts, the door to which he had left open by calling for the case to be made.[59] (See figure 3-5 for a summary of the levels of expansive reflection presented here.)

---

54. Plato, *Seventh Letter*, 341d.
55. Plato, *Republic*, III, 401d.
56. Plato, *Phaedrus*, 255c.
57. Plato, *Republic*, X, 597e.
58. Ibid., 614a.
59. Ibid., 607d.

FIGURE 3-5   *Reditio Completa Subiecti in Seipso*

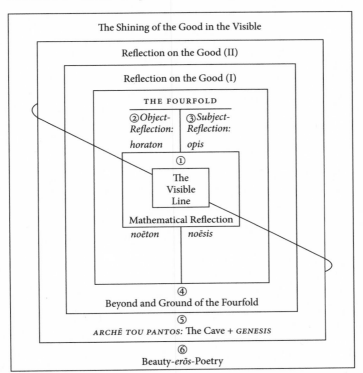

The Shining of the Good in the Visible

Reflection on the Good (II)

Reflection on the Good (I)

THE FOURFOLD

②*Object-Reflection:*   ③*Subject-Reflection:*

horaton   *opis*

①

The
Visible
Line

Mathematical Reflection

noēton   *noēsis*

④
Beyond and Ground of the Fourfold

⑤
ARCHĒ TOU PANTOS: The Cave + GENESIS

⑥
Beauty-*erōs*-Poetry

In the Line itself, Plato has constructed a pedagogical device of marvelous complexity and extraordinary power. It leads us beyond "Plato's opinions" to the most fundamental insights available in the field of experience. It lays out the whole panoply of types of evidence to which we have always to recur in carrying out our constructive explorations of the Whole. The exposition of the whole set of these types of evidence in their togetherness provides the fundamental inventory of things that have to be explained and of the tools we must employ in our attempted explanations. It sets the fundamental direction of human existence. It teaches us how to return from our relative self-absence in the culturally mediated world of *sensa* to our most fundamental selfhood in order to participate in that world more intelligently and more appreciatively.

4 ∾ Phenomenology and the Perennial Task of Philosophy

A Study of Plato and Aristotle

In his *Prolegomena to a History of the Concept of Time*, Martin Heidegger made what might seem an odd claim, namely, that phenomenology is a return to Plato and Aristotle.[1] But then that is not so odd when we consider that the practitioners of twentieth-century phenomenology and these two ancient founders were all initially after the eidetic or the essential forms given in experience. Plato is famous for his doctrine of Forms, of changeless eidetic features. He advises his readers, when carrying out eidetic analysis, to "carve along the joints" of what is given rather than hacking through like a clumsy butcher.[2] And for Aristotle, the intellect, as the capacity to apprehend the universal, is what he called *topos eidon*, "the place of the Forms."[3] Whatever argument one might make about any facet of experience or any explanation thereof, one has ultimately to test it by its coherence with the various eidetic features given in experience. That is precisely what Plato and Aristotle did. Whatever further ontological construals they might offer follow from questions that emerge from the relations between and implications of what is given in experience. But what follows can easily become an elaboration of problems far removed from that original givenness as the epigoni work intertexually and with sedimented concepts without recurring back to the origins in experience of the problems and concepts with which they concern themselves.

1. Martin Heidegger, *Prolegomena to a History of the Concept of Time*, trans. T. Kisiel (Bloomington: Indiana University Press, 1992), 136.
2. Plato, *Phaedrus*, 265e.
3. Aristotle, *On the Soul*, 429a 27.

The first phenomenological inventory of the field of experience is found in Plato's Line of Knowledge in the *Republic*.[4] It presents a stratified analysis of the field of awareness that invites its prolongation into various subsets of that field. Aristotle continued that analysis. We will rehearse our interpretation of the Line that compresses and develops our treatment in the preceding chapter and follow out an analysis of some of the subsets that moves in the direction of Aristotle. We will carry out our analysis, not simply by way of exposition of how these ancient thinkers used to think but by way of following out Husserl's motto and attending "to the things themselves," the eidetic features given in our own experience.

PLATO

Plato has Socrates envision the human condition as that of prisoners chained from birth to viewing only shadows several steps removed from "the real things" outside the Cave.[5] In the parallel Line of Knowledge, the initial state is one of sensation, specifically the relation of sight to the seeable. This is contrasted with the relation of intellect to the intelligible without any initial determination of what the full cash value of those by now overly familiar terms might mean. To begin with, the Line is a visible line divided according to any given proportion and subdivided by the same proportion to yield four segments. One sees it, but, by the peculiar way it is constructed, one is also invited to reflect upon it. When one does so, one discovers that, no matter what proportion is employed, the central segments are always equal. Not just *looking* at what one sees here but *reflecting* upon it as well yields a theorem, an intelligible. At a second level of reflection, the Line so drawn is used metaphorically to stand for a hierarchy of relations between awareness and its various objects.

Two modes of reflection are thus evoked here: mathematical reflection and metaphorical reflection. Mathematics, instantiated in the original Line and the theorem it in turn instantiates is placed metaphorically on the third level after the first great cut. It illustrates the distinction be-

---

4. Plato, *Republic*, 509d. For a further elaboration of what follows, see my "Plato's Line Revisited: The Pedagogy of Complete Reflection," in *The Review of Metaphysics* 45, no. 3 (March 1991): 525–47, reprinted in chapter 3.

5. Plato, *Republic*, 514a.

tween the visible and the intelligible, whose contrasting characteristics invite further reflection that extends beyond mathematics to all intelligible and visible objects. Indeed, if we reflect still further, we see that it extends to all sensible objects and even to the underlying things that sensory features both reveal and conceal.

Beyond that, and crucially important for a dialogue set in motion by concern for justice in the soul, we are led to see the distinction and relation between the powers of intellection and sensation and thus discover something of the character of our own soul as it engages in these reflections. Such metamathematical reflection is the domain of philosophy and occupies the fourth level of the Line beyond mathematics: the level of eidetic features, better known as the Forms.

If one confines attention to the focal Forms of the various virtues in the *Republic* and reinforces that by appeal to the same type of Form identified initially in the *Parmenides*,[6] one easily loses sight of what is at stake on the fourth level of the Line. Immediately, the concern expressed by the Line is epistemological, but it also turns out to be ultimately cosmological and ontological. Penultimately, the concern is anthropological, and, in the more general context of the *Republic*, it is ethicopolitical. The Forms of the virtues are underpinned by the Forms of anthropological structure and are related to the overall Form of the cosmos and its Source. By the way the Line is structured, one is pointed in the direction of eidetic analysis of the field of experience as the key to everything else.

Now the Line of Knowledge appears after a declaration of the peculiar study that makes a philosopher a philosopher: Socrates says that it is the study of the Good, about which, like a poet, he makes a series of unverified proclamations.[7] It is in the region of the intelligible, like the sun in the region of the visible: it provides *aletheia*, truth as the unconcealment that makes possible the relation of manifestness between intellect and the intelligible. Further, parallel to the sun as cause of the becoming of the living, the Good is said to be the source of the existence and beingness (*einai* and *ousia*) of intellect and the intelligible, though it is itself *epekeina tes ousias*, beyond beingness. Finally, an incomparable beauty, the Good creates the sun as an image of itself, providing not only light

6. Plato, *Parmenides*, 130b.
7. Plato, *Republic*, 508e.

for seeing but also warmth and light for the growth and sustenance of living things. After these claims, Glaucon says, "By Apollo, what a monstrous excess!" The Line is meant to cash in on these enthusiastically excessive proclamations.

Geometry is the pivot. The interlocutors from the very beginning of the dialogue are looking for what is "up" and what is "down" in human life. Socrates "went down" with Glaucon to the Piraeus, the seaport of Athens, and was about to "go up" to the city itself.[8] Applying the same metaphor here, geometry involves an "upward" way and a "downward" way.[9] There is first of all the remarkable movement of axiomatization, an *upward way* from a scattered plurality of metric regularities, initially discovered in hit-and-miss fashion through the building process, up to the few axioms that they implicitly presuppose. Then there is a *downward way*, a deductive way, from the fewness of the axioms to the plurality of known and even as yet unknown metric regularities linked to the axioms. Here, we cut loose from the trial-and-error method that discovered the metric regularities involved in the building process. Astonishingly, we no longer have to look and measure things to discover the regularities: we deduce them from the axioms. But Socrates points to a further "upward" way: from the fewness of the axioms metaphorically "upward." This invites us to consider the possibility of unifying the axioms by finding a single higher axiom—and indeed, to consider the possibility of finding a single higher principle not only for the geometric region but for all the regions of our experience. This principle would be "the One," the principle of unification, that which we seek, a final cause, therefore called "the Good." It is the true "Up," the Top of the cosmos.

In seeking unity in any scattered multiplicity, we move in the light of that Good/One. One who knows no English would hear a reading of this chapter as a scattered plurality of unintelligible sounds. One who knows English would hear a scattered plurality of English sentences. One who understands what I am saying *might* grasp a coherent presentation. In the light of our searching for unity, we find whatever intelligibility we find. The translation of the Good's being "*epekeina tes ousias*" as "beyond being" has generated a long history of what I consider a misunder-

8. Ibid., 327a.
9. Ibid., 510b.

standing.[10] What the Good is "beyond" is the plurality of the eidetic as correlate to intellect and therefore beyond intellect itself considered as the correlate to the Forms. That it is not "beyond being" is indicated by the fact that Plato also has Socrates refer to it as *tou ontos to phanotaton*, the most manifest aspect *of being*.[11]

The Forms are mirrored in the realm of the sensible display of what, along with and underlying that display, is designated comprehensively as the realm of *genesis* or becoming. It is the region of what Plato called a "mixture of being and nonbeing" or what Whitehead called the "ingression of the Forms into the flux."[12] Things are instances of types, but each such thing at one time was not and at another time will not be. And while it is, it moves from what it no longer is to what it is not yet. So we have three ontological regions: *genesis* or becoming as a mixture of being and nonbeing, *ousia* or what Heidegger more accurately called *die Seiendheit* or "beingness"[13] as the region of the Forms participation in which constitutes the beingness of beings in the realm of becoming, and the Good as the most manifest region of being, providing, metaphorically speaking, "light" for all the rest. There is a further reason why the Good is beyond the Forms: it is "the principle of the Whole" (*arche tou pantos*).[14] The Whole is not simply the whole of the intelligible but the cosmic Whole constituted by the interplay of the intelligible region and the region of individuals present in the sensible under the principle of unity for the Whole. By reason of the Good, the Whole is gathered together into unity displayed in the underlying kinship of all things: it is a uni-verse.

Geometry shows in the metric domain the "kinship of all things" proclaimed by Socrates in the *Meno* just before he took the slave-boy through the geometric exercise.[15] However, the isolated insight into the solution

10. Cf. Scotus Eriugena: being is the object of cognition, but there is something that transcends intellect as its ground: the Good "beyond being." Cf. Etienne Gilson, *History of Christian Philosophy in the Middle Ages* (New York: Random House, 1955), 116. Something can be viewed "beyond being" only if being is defined as something other than what is the case. For something to *be* beyond what is the case is not to be at all.

11. Plato, *Republic*, 509b.

12. Plato, *Republic*, 477a–479c; cf. Alfred North Whitehead, *Process and Reality: An Essay in Cosmology* (New York: Harper, 1957), 34.

13. *Einführung in die Metaphysik* (Tübingen: Max Niemeyer, 1966), 24.

14. Plato, *Republic*, 511b.

15. Plato, *Meno*, 81c.

to the problem posed to the slave-boy Socrates relegates to the realm of what he calls, both here and in the *Republic*, *doxa*. In the Cave allegory, the state of mind that possesses one who, chained or unchained, operates in the Cave is called *doxa*.[16] What the slave-boy achieves is designated further to be *alethes doxa*, as distinct from *orthe doxa*, *manifest* as distinct from *correct* appearance. *Doxa* thus has in this context at least three meanings: (1) *mere* opinion or what people happen to hold, true or false; (2) *correct* opinion or what happens to be true and not simply a matter of opinion; and (3) *manifest* opinion or genuine insight such as the slave-boy achieved. If the slave-boy told his conclusion to others and they repeated it without the insight and thus as a matter of hearsay, they would have *orthe doxa*, "orthodoxy," correct but not intellectually apprehended judgment. In the *Meno*, Socrates distinguishes this from *episteme* that "tethers" the insight through reasoning.[17] This points toward the development of an axiomatic system that would tie the insight into a web of demonstrably necessary relations, displaying the underlying kinship of all things metric. Yet all this is an apparent roundabout route to discussing the main topic of the *Meno*: the nature and teachability of virtue.

Socrates is after the same thing in the *Republic*, which deals with justice as the ground of the virtues. His Line of Knowledge uses mathematics to instantiate the difference between the sensible and the intelligible and thus to lead to a clear understanding of the difference between sense and intellect. Inquiry into those differences is a metamathematical inquiry into what mathematics presupposes but does not inquire into, namely, the eidetic framework of the fourfold relation of intelligible to sensible, intellect to intelligible, intellect to sense, and sense to sensible. If geometry is the first rationally demonstrable science and thus a matter of necessary insight, what it presupposes is even more necessary: the interplay of the fourfold and the formal logic that Aristotle will make explicit. This teaches us something significant about the soul as the locus of the virtues and presupposes certain virtues in its pursuit. The soul has a temporal and eternal aspect. In the latter, it is oriented toward that which, if attained, would both theoretically and practically unify the whole field of experience and what it entails.

In the *Republic*, Socrates follows his treatment of the Line with the

16. Plato, *Republic*, 534a.
17. Plato, *Meno*, 85d.

Allegory of the Cave. As we noted earlier, the human condition is envisioned as one of being chained from birth to looking at shadows of
things projected by a fire from behind the prisoners. One prisoner is unchained and forced to turn completely around and look at the fire. He is
then dragged up out of the Cave into the sunlight of the so-called "*ontos
on*," "the really real world." As I also said before, the overall state of mind
characteristic of the Cave situation is termed *doxa*. This is usually translated as "opinion," but as describing the overall situation it has a wider
sense. It is how things *seem* (*doxa* is cognate to *dokein*, to seem). Seeming
is first of all sensory appearance that does not occur *inside* a perceiving
organism but is a relation *between* a perceiving organism and a physical
object. It is a limited mode of manifestation tied in with the character of
our organs and our organic needs. It gives us organically dependent images of things, the first level of objects on the Line. But sensing is taken
up in terms of our understanding, especially of what is of import to us.
Socrates speaks of contending over "images of justice" in the courts.[18]
Providing the grounds of the community *doxa* in its most overarching
aspects is the work of the poetic tradition, of those who shine in glory
and celebrate the glory of their heroes. "Glory" is a further meaning of
doxa as the maximum of appearance. *Doxa* as the showing of the lifeworld is the residue of those long dead whose glory lingers on. In the allegory, the shadows are projected by puppet forms of natural and artificial things carried in front of the fire. The puppets are themselves images
of the originals outside the Cave.

The Cave allegory suggests that we can learn something of "the real
things" from the shadows, but in order to do so we have to be forced into
an *epistrophe*, a complete reflective about-face, a backing off from our
spontaneous assessments. We have to be forced further into an ascent
from the particulars of everyday life to the eidetic features they instantiate,
and on toward the ultimate presupposition, the always sought-after Principle of the Whole that makes everything into a cosmos, a universe, a plurality turned toward unity. It is in the light of the ever-sought-after One that a
seeker comes to understand anything of the scattered, flowing multiplicity
found in experience. Once understood as a term (though not necessarily

---

18. Plato, *Republic*, 493a. For an exploration of the importance of the notion of *doxa* in Plato, see my "*Doxa and Eros*, Speech and Writing, with Special Attention to Plato's *Symposium*,"
Existentia 17, fascs. 3–4 (2008): 247–61.

possessed), the Good as a Principle of the Whole intelligible-sensible cosmos brings us back into the Cave to sort out the truths dimly reflected in the shadowy opinions generated by tradition, some "orthodox," some not. One turns "inward," then "upward," and then "back down" through the practice of what I have elsewhere called "complete reflection," or what the medievals called the *reditio completa subiecti in seipso*.[19] In Plato, the soul's conscious movement among the Forms is called "dialectic," and the aim is *synoptic dialectical vision*, seeing in their interrelatedness the distinct forms involved in experience.[20] In the *Sophist*, the Eleatic Stranger identifies dialectic as the ability to see which Forms blend with which within the all-encompassing Form of Being.[21]

Now all of this is not simply a matter of juiceless abstraction. Plato not only identified the term of the search for the Whole in the Good as principle of the whole, but he indicated the peculiar disposition that propelled the search: *thaumazein*, awe linked to the sublimation of Eros in the appreciation of beautiful things.[22] *Thaumazein* has something divine about it: it lifts us out of our ordinary relation to things and is thus said to be a gift of the god Thaumas. It is a species of divine madness, a sublimation of Eros awakened by the presence of Beauty itself in beautiful things.[23] Indeed, in the *Republic* the philosopher is initially presented as a lover of the vision of Beauty itself, as distinguished from the cultivated denizens of the purged city as lovers of sights and sounds.[24] The Good is beyond the beingness of the Forms as correlate to intellect because it is correlate to Eros as the desire of the whole person for the Source of unity in the cosmos that evokes love for the Whole.

While much of this sounds very much like a private Plotinian retreat within and upward in order to be "alone with the Alone,"[25] the complete reflection that returns us to the lifeworld returns us to the dialogical situation, to the meeting of I and You as a permanent feature of the lifeworld.

---

19. See "Plato's Line Revisited" (chapter 3 of this volume) and Aquinas, *Summa Theologiae*, I, 84, 6.

20. Plato, *Republic*, 511b, 532a, 534b, 537c.

21. Plato, *Sophist*, 552e ff.

22. Plato, *Theaetetus*, 155d; *Symposium*, 206b ff.

23. Plato, *Phaedrus*, 245a ff.

24. Plato, *Republic*, 476b. For a further treatment of Plato's "aesthetics," see my *Placing Aesthetics*.

25. Plotinus, *Enneads*, V, 1, 6; VI, 7, 34; and VI, 9, 11.

FROM PLATO TO ARISTOTLE

Thus far, Plato. Let us follow out phenomenologically the direction indicated on the Line of Knowledge by reflection upon the visible and the tactual as the sensory fields within which experimental science operates, observing and manipulating things. I do this because in our age empirical science is the paradigm of knowing as in Plato's age it was geometry; and the originator of empirical science was Plato's pupil Aristotle, who developed further the eidetic inventory of the lifeworld begun by his master. As Plato's Line begins with the visible, Aristotle's treatment of the soul ends with the tactual. What are the eidetic features of the visible and the tactual?

Consider a visible object, for example, this piece of paper with rows of black figures on a white field, instances of the generic object of every act of seeing, namely, color. Even the so-called colorblind see shades of black, gray, and white. Secondly, the white and black colors adhere in the extended surface of the paper that stands within its own boundaries. In fact, so closely is color linked to extension that any color is not even imaginable apart from extension, necessarily co-present with it as the surface in which it inheres. Further, color appears not only within the extended space of a body but in light suffusing an encompassing space that separates the object from other bodies, most importantly, from the body of the viewer: this piece of paper stands over against my body and your body. Only thus can it appear. But such space is only phenomenally empty. A little reflection shows that it is itself suffused with nonvisually appearing sound, dust motes, radio and TV waves—indeed, all the irradiations of the electromagnetic spectrum.

Further, were we outside this room in open space, such space would be limited by the horizon. The horizon is a kind of psychic hoopskirt that goes ahead of us and surrounds us as we move. Neither wholly objective nor wholly subjective, it is a feature of the relational realm of manifestation, the subjective-objective togetherness that constitutes visual appearance. As Aristotle noted, "The sensible in act is the sense in act." It is a leading aspect in the space of manifestness we call sensation. Color exists as a mode of appearance of what we have come to call "bodies" in relation both to seeable eyeballs linked to nervous systems within organic systems and to the nonseeable power and act of seeing.

Again, the visible object only appears when light fills the encompassing, intrahorizonal phenomenal space. Turn out the lights in the audito-
rium and nothing is visible. Further still, the three-dimensional bodies
on which color appears in the light possess a depth that perceptually con-
tracts toward the horizon of each viewer, creating regular perspectival
distortion, as in railroad tracks that appear to converge in the distance.
Such perspectives cohere as I move in relation to any visually given body.
Through the sedimentation of past experience, our sensory system automatically discounts the distortion, so we rarely notice it. Finally, dis-
tributed throughout that visual space, extended colored things appear as
successively focal and marginal objects of our visual attention. In sum,
the elements that constitute the necessary eidetic features of any visible
object are: color, inhering in extension, appearing to visual awareness in
light across phenomenally empty space, within a horizon relative to the
viewer, in spatial separation from the viewer and from other surrounding bodies, involving perspectival distortion of the bodies on which it
appears, in relation to the coherence of the perspectives of each body,
appearing focally and marginally to an attentive viewer. Such analysis, I
would claim, is not a matter of opinion, of mere *doxa*, but of ever-present
givenness, verifiable every time we look at things in the light. It is part of
the pregiven world about which we form our opinions.

Consider again another sensory object: the tactual object. Unlike the
objects of seeing, there seems to be not one but several aspects presented,
each capable of being arranged on a correlative continuum. I grab the
podium: it is hard and smooth; it is slightly cool and slightly sticky. I attempt to move it: it is rather heavy. Resistance (hard and soft), texture
(rough and smooth), thermal quality (hot and cold), moisture content
(moist and dry), and weight (heavy and light): such are the eidetic features of the tactual object. Resistance, texture, and weight are constant
features; thermal quality and moisture content are variables dependent
upon context. The members of each pair appear as relative to one another and to the condition of the tactual perceiver. If I previously had my
hands in a bucket of ice, the podium would seem warmer; if I had them
near a heater, it would seem cooler. One acquainted with Plato's *Theaetetus* will recognize the evidential basis for the skeptical argument as to
the relativity of knowing, but also Plato's appeal to the eidetic constants
that constitute, self-contradictorily, the evidence for the relativist argu-

ment.[26] I might add, as a variation on the tactual theme, that taste presents all the aspects that touching does—hard-soft, heavy-light, rough-smooth, hot-cold, dry-moist—but adds flavor as its peculiar object.

Tactility has this peculiarity that, unlike the other senses, it has no single organ but is spread over the whole surface of the alert organism, the manifestation of the diffusion throughout the organism of the principle of unity that Aristotle called the *psyche* or soul. Presenting the resistant other, it presupposes the diffuse self-presence of the perceiver being in immediate touch with its whole organism. The condition for the possibility for otherness to be manifest is self-presence nonfocally manifest to itself in touch as other than the manifest other.[27] This can be correlated to Aristotle's observation that all animals have at least the sense of touch; I add that this is the basis in the perceiving organism for any appearing to occur.

Such observations of the eidetic features of the visual and tactual fields are not subject to falsification because they are verified every time we open our eyes and see or reach out and touch or are touched by something. They are the enduring basis for falsification and verification of claims we might make about the things they present to us. Popperian falsifiability applies, if it properly applies, only to scientific statements made *within* the ever-verified frameworks of seeing and manipulating things.[28]

Now such presentations are not given in discrete packets but are spontaneously retained and correlated with one another so that the past enters into the constitution of the present through recognition or re-cognition. The basis for the recognition of unified thinghood has as its ground temporally unified subjectivity, temporally enduring self-presence whose underlying system gathers into the present the differing modes of sensory presentation that have appeared at differing times—a point Plato's Socrates makes in the *Theaetetus*.[29] The togetherness of these modes fills the space of sensory manifestness with what the Greeks called *phantasmata* and the medievals *species*, both referring to modes of appearance relative to organically situated consciousness. Of great significance for understanding

26. Plato, *Theaetetus* 152a.

27. See my "Tactility: An Essay in Phenomenological Description," *Southwest Philosophy Review* 17, no. 1 (January 2000): 19–26.

28. Karl Popper, *Conjectures and Refutations: The Growth of Scientific Knowledge* (New York: Harper, 1963), 228ff.

29. Plato, *Theaetetus*, 184c ff.

animal awareness is the fact that these coordinated presentations are tied to the evocation of appetite in the form of desire. To begin with, the senses are not instruments for detached cognition; they are practical instruments that serve the needs of the organism. They allow it to identify opportunities and threats to its well-being.

Retention brings the past into present recognition; desire anticipates the future of satisfaction. Both past and future thus enter into the internal constitution of the way a sensing being is related to what appears to it in the present. Anticipation of future satisfaction sets the animal being in motion toward the desired object that culminates in tactual apprehension either by eating or copulating, fighting or caring for the object. The lived end product of the process is either pleasure, which is a sign that organic purpose is being fulfilled, or pain, which signifies that it is frustrated.

This is a compressed presentation of the observations offered by Aristotle whose treatment of the living being in *Peri psyches* begins with an account of his predecessors, provides his own general definition of *psyche*, examines the external senses, the internal senses, and intellectual operations, follows with a treatment of locomotion, and concludes by returning to a consideration of tactility. As Aristotle understood, before being theoretical instruments, the senses are practical instruments for the adjustment of the organism to its environment. They continue as modes of insertion of theoretically capable intelligence into the world in which it belongs, the world of physical processes.

EXPERIENTIAL EIDETICS

What we have been doing in the previous section is beginning to fill in the initially empty level of the Forms on Plato's Line of Knowledge by a phenomenological inventory that finds itself largely instantiated in Aristotle's *Peri Psyches*. Now let us proceed further at the same level by moving to a more abstract, and thus more comprehensive, mode of reflection.

Consider the general features of *any* sensory object and not simply of the particular objects of seeing and touching. There are five features upon which I want to focus attention. Any sensory object is always (1) individual; (2) actual; (3) immediately present here-and-now; (4) circumscribed, in an especially clear way in the case of organisms, by its own boundaries; and (5) set in observable sequences of antecedence and consequence. Such an object, adhering in extension, is what we spontaneously mean by a material thing or a body. Taking sensory evidence as the only securely knowable evidence, we have the underpinnings for the philosophy called *mechanistic materialism* that has understandably but unnecessarily dogged modern natural science. Taking such evidence as the only form of evidence, epistemologists become nominalists, considering universal claims to be only as valid as the number of single sensory experiences used to ground them. My claim is that while sensory evidence safely leads us on pragmatically, it systematically misleads us speculatively regarding the nature both of the sensed and especially of the sensing awareness.[30]

At this point, I will examine each of the general features of a sensory object in turn, comparing them with what emerges through a consideration of the act of sensing. Consider first the evident feature of *spatial circumscription* for organisms. Observing a human organism and the verifiable causal sequence requisite for seeing, we naturally conclude that its awareness is something inside its skull, in the visual center at the back of the brain. As the Nobel neurophysiologist Sir John Eccles used to say: the seeing consciousness looking at images in the back of the brain is like a person watching the screen of a television set.[31] What is most important is to explain what *watching* means—something which Sir John's and, indeed, anybody's neurophysiology by itself fails to do. To be able to make claims about the sequence of light sources, wave propagation, absorption, reflection, and refraction of light impinging upon the rods and cones of the retina and setting up electrical impulses that induce chemical changes so that the impulse is carried by a set of electrochemical switches on the optic nerve to the visual center at the back of the cortex, physicists and physiologists must see each of these features precisely *outside* the observable inside of their own organisms.

Awareness, I would claim, is *sui generis*; it is a way not directly observable from without in which a sensing organism exceeds its own ob-

30. See my "Individuals, Universals, and Capacity," *The Review of Metaphysics* 54, no. 3 (March 2001): 507–28.
31. Cf. John Eccles, in Karl Popper and John Eccles, *The Self and Its Brain* (Berlin, New York: Springer International, 1977), 367ff. In an oral presentation at the University of Dallas, Professor Eccles used a familiar image: consciousness inside is scanning the brain like we scan a television set.

servably circumscribed body to be *with* the object of awareness, "with" in the peculiar mode of manifestness that involves simultaneous self-presence. The diffuse self-presence of the alert perceiving organism to its organ system as a functioning whole that is exhibited in its entire bodily surface as the instrument of touch is the basis for any appearance of what is other. Typical in everyday life and in the sciences, it is what appears that is focal, not its very *appearance*. As Plato noted, that is a distinct kind of relation *metaxu*, between perceiving organism and perceived object,[32] or, as Aristotle put it, "the sensible in act is the sense power in act."[33] Or, in Hegel's terms, there is cognitive identity-in-difference between perceiver and perceived.[34] Once again, the basis for the manifestation of what is "out there" is the implicit self-presence of the perceiver in touch with its own organ system as a functioning whole. So, taking sensory features as the only kind of evidence systematically misleads us regarding the nature of awareness as transcendent of organic circumscription by being present both to what appears outside and to itself as the locus of such appearance.

Consider then the second generic feature of the sense object, the *immediate presence here-and-now* of all sensory evidence. An observation can be made regarding the relation of awareness to immediate presence similar to what we made earlier. Just as visual awareness exceeds the observable circumscription of the organism of the perceiver, so sensory awareness in general transcends the now of its focal attention by spontaneously bringing to bear past experience from all the senses in recognizing or re-cognizing what is seen. And because all sensory awareness occurs in function of desire anticipating future satisfaction, the future also enters into the constitution of the perceived object. So, as Heidegger would put it, sensory awareness is triply "ecstatic": its *ekstasis* involves its "standing out" of the present circumscribed organism to bring the past and the future into the now, where awareness stands out of its own circumscribed body in relation to the visual object perceived at a distance.[35] So a sensing organism inhabits space and time in a radically different

32. Plato, *Theaetetus*, 153d.
33. Aristotle, *On the Soul* III, 425b 27.
34. G. W. F. Hegel, *Hegel's Philosophy of Mind*, trans. W. Wallace and A. Miller (Oxford: Clarendon Press, 1971), §438.
35. Martin Heidegger, *Being and Time*, 377.

way than beings that are not aware. It occupies a living present articulated and focused outside of one's organic inside on objects in the environment by retention of the relevant past and protention of the immediate future. Indeed, for appearance to happen at all there has to be an inward temporal extension such that, for example in the case of hearing a melody, the first moment of appearance endures through the last in ever-flowing relation to the constant anticipation of further sounds until the last note sounds and the whole is heard. It can then be rehearsed in a second-order memory.

In the third place, consider the *actuality* of any sensed object. Actual seeing is an individual act of an individual organism grasping outside itself an individual color on an individual object. However, consider the potentialities involved on both sides of the relation: the active power to see and the passive power to be seen. The powers of seeing and being seen are also individual features of individual seers and individual visible bodies. But *they are not only individual*; they are *universal* orientations, having as their correlates *kinds* of objects. It is most important to underscore this insight.

On the part of the seer, the power of seeing is oriented toward *all* that can be seen, that is, toward the generic object "color," though it is activated only by the individual colors appearing on individual bodies. On the part of the seen, its visibility is open to *all* those who can see, that is, toward the generic subject "seer," whether humans, horses, cows, or mice. Powers are *concrete universals* whose nature overcomes the alleged dichotomy between universal and individual. Visual power requires universalizable features of seeing and of things seen as generic objects. And whereas cognitive sensory powers require kinds of *aspects* of things (color, sound, resistance, etc.), the appetites served by those powers require kinds of *things* in the environment, namely those that can actually nourish the organism. Distinguish here aspects and things. The *aspects* of sensorily appearing things are, in a sense, phenomenal and thus relative; the *things* themselves are transphenomenal. Eating transcends the phenomenal in a way that seeing does not. And since each of these entails other specified kinds of things that can sustain them, the capacity to see involves a whole ecosystem containing kinds of things related in the food chain (carnivores, herbivores, and plant life), together with the kinds of things in the nonliving environment (light, air, along with mineral elements and compounds) required to sustain that chain. Furthermore, seers as organisms can only come into being by reproduction and are themselves able to reproduce. Hence, seers can only exist as members of a specific reproductive species. Seers come not only in the *generic* type from insect to ape to human but also in the *specific* type of organism constituted out of its own reproductive line. The upshot of this analysis is that powers and kinds, not appearing at all directly in the actual individual bodies sensorily observable in the environment, are necessarily ingredients in the fact of sensory experience as the concrete conditions in sensible objects related to sensing subjects for the possibility of existent seers and manifest objects.

Now, all this is not simply the result of sensory observation, although sensory observation is the starting point for the analysis. We are not dealing simply with the actual individuals immediately given here-and-now in sensory observation but with the eidetic features exhibited by and implied in the powers of the objects and the subjects of such observation. The ability to arrive at the eidetic features is what we have come to call "intellect." It operates, not simply with this or that particular observable object here and there but with features that obtain *any time* and *any place* the conditions for their observation are realized. The "any time" and "any place" transcend the here-and-now, the past, and the future of sensory experience and relate to the whole of the spatiotemporal universe by reason of the underlying powers of interrelated things. Intellect is thus related to time and space in a way radically different than either sensation or sensorily observable things. As Kant noted, time and space, as essential projections of the human mind, are given as emptily encompassing any particular filling we might experience or infer.[36]

These considerations furnish the basis for Plato's initial discrimination between the visible and the intelligible, and for Aristotle's observation that the senses deal with the individual and the actual, the intellect with the universal (and—we might add—the possible, manifest as such).[37] The universality apprehensible by intellect is not only the ab-

36. Immanuel Kant, *Critique of Pure Reason*, trans. N. K. Smith (New York: St. Martin's Press, 1965), B27/A23–B73, 67–91.

37. Aristotle, *On the Soul* II, 417b 24. The very important term "actual" (*ton kath' hekaston he kat' energeian aisthesis*) is shockingly omitted by William Hett, the translator of the Loeb edition of *Peri Psyches* (Cambridge, Mass.: Harvard University Press, 1975), 99.

stract universality of kinds but the concrete universality of individual powers, active and passive. These considerations also ground Aristotle's claim that "the human soul is, in a way, all things: all things intelligible by intellect, and all things sensible by sense."[38] Following Plato's focus upon the notion of Being that interplays with the four other basic kinds—motion and rest, sameness and difference—as the overarching Forms, we would claim that it is the notion of Being that grounds everything distinctively human, for it refers ahead of time to all things. Appearing together with the principle of noncontradiction, the notion of Being has unrestricted generality.

The considerations we have presented likewise develop the suggestion Plato offered in the *Sophist* that the "definition" of being is the capacity of acting and being acted upon.[39] This means that each thing, through its active and passive capacities as universal orientations toward specific kinds of objects, is not an isolated atomic entity picturable as an actual individual by the visually based imagination but is necessarily interrelated with a cosmos of kinds of things that would answer to its peculiar cluster of active and passive powers.[40] This moves in the direction of Leibniz who insisted that the least complex entity involves an internal linkage with the cosmic system with which it is compossible.[41] While denying Leibniz's claim that each thing precontains in an unconscious mode all of the *individuals* it might encounter within the Whole, I would maintain that it precontains, as its active and passive powers, relation to the *kinds* of things it might encounter. And it is intellect that, in a way, precontains all things and all kinds within the whole opened up by the notion of Being.

Finally, it is the distance afforded by intellect's "being, in a way, all things"[42] that pries us loose from determination within the sensory circle comprised by cognitive specification, appetitive arousal, movement toward the desired object, tactual apprehension of it, and the satisfaction of the appetite with it. By reason of our reference to the Whole of what is via

38. Aristotle, *On the Soul* III, 8, 431b 21.
39. Plato, *Sophist*, 247e.
40. See my "Individuals, Universals, and Capacity," *The Review of Metaphysics* (March 2001).
41. Cf. Leibniz's notion of the compossibility of each thing with all the rest. *Monadology* 56, in *Leibniz: The Monadology and Other Philosophical Writings*, ed. and trans. R. Latta (London: Oxford University Press, 1951), 248.
42. Aristotle, *On the Soul* III, 8, 431b 22.

the notion of Being, we are free in relation to the animal field of awareness and hence able to grasp its eidetic features, take up different attitudes, project alternative futures, and make different choices than those afforded by sensory appetite. So, the initiation of free action breaks through the seamless continuity of the sensory, observed in its antecedent and consequent states, to introduce new lines of causality.

Let me add that, among the different attitudes humans might take, there is the distinctively aesthetic attitude. As Aristotle again observed, the hound loves the look of the rabbit, not because, like us, he is able to appreciate the beauty of the rabbit, but because he sees it as food.[43] Hence, Kant's observation that the detachment from organic need involved in intellectual apprehension allows us to give what he calls "unconstrained favoring" to the beautiful object. Not being constrained by need to assimilate it to our organic or culturally pragmatic systems, we are able to "let it be" before us as it is perceptually, shining in its pure appearance.[44] Distance from the causal network of the externally observable actuality of physical processes and inwardly generated desirous processes condemns us to distinctively human freedom as responsible self-determination grounded in the ability to let things be manifest, as Aquinas put it, "for their own sake.[45]

So awareness in general, both sensory and intellectual, takes the perceiving organism outside of its observable outside as well as outside of the immediate in gathering the past and anticipating the future. At the intellectual level, it transcends the actuality and individuality of the sensorily presented to grasp potentiality and universality. And, by reason of its reference to the Whole via the notion of Being, it is free to introduce new lines of causality into the seamless continuity of the immediately perceived with its antecedents and consequents. As I said earlier, seeing (and sensing in general) systematically leads us pragmatically in coming to terms with the environment, but it also systematically misleads us speculatively. Thinking in the direction of Plato and Aristotle allows us to enter properly the space of speculative knowing.

43. Aristotle, *Nicomachean Ethics*, 1118a 21–23.

44. Immanuel Kant, *Critique of Judgment*, trans. W. Pluhar (Indianapolis: Hackett, 1987), §2, 204 (Akademie 45). Cf. my "Kant's 'Antinomic' Aesthetics," in *Immanuel Kant*, ed. Rossi and J. Treloar, special issue of the *American Catholic Philosophical Quarterly* 75, no. 2 (June 2001): 271–95. This essay is reprinted in this book.

45. Aquinas, *Summa Theologiae*, I, 5, 6.

Finally, we might note that Aristotle's treatment of the soul brings the loftiness of intellect back into the world of everyday experience by concluding with a treatment of locomotion and tactility. The hand, "the tool of tools,"[46] is the means whereby we come to adjust to and tactually transform the world we inhabit through intelligent activity: creating tools, refashioning the environment in terms of utility and beauty, writing, lending a hand, embracing, and, in general, inhabiting the earth.

Plato's notion of soul tended in the direction of a dualism in which embodiment is a hindrance to the intellectual soul, like the Pythagorean notion of *soma* as *sema*, the body as tomb of the rational soul. In the *Republic*, "the mind's eye is, at it were, buried in a deep bog of mud."[47] It is like the sea-god Glaucus covered with barnacles and seaweed so that he is not recognizable.[48] In the *Phaedo*, philosophy is the practice of dying, separating the concentrated intellect from the flowing distractions of embodiment.[49] Nonetheless, in the *Timaeus* Plato has Timaeus, employing etymological relatives of *oikadzo*, identify the body as the *house* of the soul.[50] The two lines are resolvable by distinguishing psychological experience from ontological underpinning. Concentration is hindered by appetites and imaginings and the intrusion of others presented in sensation. Bodily existence distracts the one intent upon prolonged intellectual concentration. Nonetheless, ontologically, the body is the house of the soul. But the soul intent upon understanding has to put its house in order.

This is the direction Aristotle took, only adding significantly that the soul builds its own house through its nutritive power that creates the conditions in sense organs for the coming into actuality of the sensient power required for providing the information needed by the intellectual power, for knowing and acting in the realm of *phusis*. The *psyche* is the formal, efficient, and final cause or the organized body.[51] In the ontogenesis of the individual human being, the ability to exercise intellectual power is the *telos* of the process.

46. Aristotle, *On the Soul*, III, 8, 431a.

47. Plato, *Phaedo*, trans. W. Lamb (Cambridge: Harvard University Press, 1977), 62b, 82e; Plato, *Republic* X, 611d.

48. *Ibid.*, X, 611.

49. Plato, *Phaedo*, 80e.

50. In the *Timaeus*, Plato uses various terms indicating a "housing" of the soul in the body: *prosoikodomoun* (69c), *katoikoun* (70e), *oikisthe* (72d), *katoikisthai*, and *oikein* (89e).

51. Aristotle, *On the Soul* II, 412a 29.

Plato set in motion the project of philosophy as a design upon the Whole, attempting to grasp the whole nature of each within the Whole and, in doing so, carving eidetically along the joints of experience. He identified the notion of Being as the guiding notion encompassing the Whole and the highest term of the search as the Good, principle of the Whole. And he indicated the peculiar disposition that propelled the search: *thaumazein*, awe linked to the sublimation of Eros in the appreciation of beautiful things. His pupil Aristotle continued in the direction indicated by the eidetic analysis. Together, they laid out the inescapable universal features constituting the field of human experience and grounding all distinctively human ventures. The given features of that field furnish a direction for philosophic and scientific search along with the evidential materials that set us off on the way of ongoing inquiry and that, in their togetherness, furnish the bases for testing the adequacy of larger speculative claims. As we go in search of wider horizons and proceed to test those larger claims, the phenomenology taught to us by Plato and Aristotle furnishes a perennial task for philosophy to return attentively and comprehensively to the lifeworld.

5 ∽ Recollection and Two Banquets

Plato's and Kierkegaard's

In *The Concept of Irony*, Kierkegaard's dissertation, Socrates is the key figure. Developing the concept of irony around Socrates, Kierkegaard spends some pages giving an account of Socrates in Plato's *Symposium*.[1] That dialogue between a group of homosexuals takes place at a banquet following a banquet celebrating Agathon's having received the equivalent of the Academy Award for the best tragedy of the year. Several years after his dissertation, in the first part of *Stages on Life's Way*, "In Vino Veritas," Kierkegaard produced his own imitation of Plato's *Symposium* about another banquet some twenty-three hundred years later. The occasion is a sumptuous banquet, replete with wine, for five aesthetes, not, as their ancient Greek counterparts, clearly homosexual, but rather preoccupied with the nature of women.

In this chapter, I will compare the main features of the two dialogues, centering attention upon the several meanings of recollection basic to each dialogue. Recollection is linked up to the use of wine, a background theme in Plato's work but the central metaphor for recollection in Kierkegaard's work. In Kierkegaard's piece, there is a contrast between recollection as simple memory and as transformative vision; in Plato's, there is a distinction between recollection as the linking together of eternal truths and as the attempt to gather the past of memorable events or venerable opinions. In each case, "the erotic" is closely tied to certain types of recollection. In keeping with the pseudonymous author of Ki-

---

1. Kierkegaard first gives a sort of overview with a focus upon irony (*The Concept of Irony*, 41–52); later (*The Concept of Irony*, 78–79), he returns for a few paragraphs to Diotima. *The Concept of Irony*, trans. L. Cape (Bloomington: Indiana University Press, 1965). All internal references to the *Symposium* are to the standard Stephanus numbers only; references to the other dialogues are indicated by name.

erkegaard's dialogue, William Afham, for whom recollection is a matter of getting one's life as a whole into focus by grasping what is essential (*SLW*, 11), my own recollection will first attempt to survey each dialogue in terms of what is essential.

PLATO

Both dialogues deal with love: Plato's focally, but not exclusively, with homosexual love and Kierkegaard's with heterosexual love and with a special focus on the nature of women. Both dialogues consist of a series of speeches, both by men in the absence of women; but in both, a woman appears late and with terminal significance in the work. In both works, there are seven speakers. In Plato's they are, in order, Phaedrus, Pausanias, Eryximachus, Aristophanes, Agathon, Socrates, and Alcibiades, with Aristodemos as first, Apollodoros as second oral narrator of the event, and Plato himself a third narrator in writing. In Kierkegaard's work, there are also seven speakers: the Young Man, Constantin Constantius, Victor Eremita, the Ladies' Tailor, and Johannes the Seducer, each of whom gives a speech, followed by Judge William and his wife, whose conversation is observed by the group. There is one mediator, the writer William Afham, who, in addition to recording the event, offers a preface on recollection, with Kierkegaard himself as the author behind the pseudonym.

Plato's work presents a kind of ascending order to the speakers, the first two recollecting traditional views, with Phaedrus presenting a lower and Pausanias offering a higher view. Eryximachus, Aristophanes, and Agathon create new traditions as cosmologist, comic, and tragic writer, respectively. Socrates functions as critic of the previous speakers and mediator of *doxa*[2] (here "opinion") about a Ladder of Ascent out of the

---

2. In classical Greek, *doxa* carried a set of related meanings central to my interpretation of the dialogue. Lidell-Scott's dictionary of classical Greek usage roots *doxa* in *dokeo*, I seem. It has the following meanings: I. (1) notion, opinion, expectation; (2) sentiment, judgment; (3) mere opinion; (4) fancy, vision; II. (1) opinion others have of one, one's reputation; (2) glory, splendor. Plato's Ring of Gyges has as its function to "do away with the *doxa*" (*Republic*, II, 367b), understood here not simply as opinion but as one's appearance both to other men and to the gods. Further, the Cave in which we live our lives is referred to as the realm of *doxa*, which should thus be taken in a larger sense than simply "opinion" (*Republic*, VII, 534a). I am currently working on an attempt to show in some detail "*Doxa* as a Key to Plato's *Symposium*" by working out the relations between Eros as the love of the mortal for the immortal, the relative

Cave of *doxa* (as comprehensive lifeworld) to the highest object of Eros taught to him by Diotima the prophetess. Alcibiades locates the highest in his recollection of the life of Socrates, bringing it back down to the Cave of everyday encounters.

Phaedrus and Pausanias recall traditional thought and homosexual practice. Phaedrus recollects the teaching of philosophers and poets to support his absolutizing of Eros as a god, an assumption shared by all the speakers prior to Socrates. He proposes an army of homosexual lovers whose Eros motivates courage in battle inspired by the presence of the beloved whose *doxa* governs the lover (178a–180b). From Pausianias, we have a recollection of the customs of various Greek cities regarding the sexual relationship of men and boys, culminating in a distinction between heavenly and earthly love based upon love of the mind versus love of the body (180–185c).

Eryximachus the physician gives the discussion cosmic extension by seeing the duality of Eros in all things, recollecting and refocusing the medical tradition (186a–189b). As poets, Aristophanes and Agathon help form a new tradition. From Aristophanes, we get a view of three original natures, heterosexual and homosexual (the latter both male and female), and also the notion of Eros as the striving for wholeness, bodily and psychic, caused by a primordial split in the original natures (189c–193d). From Agathon, we get a focus upon creativity and the governing power of Eros (195a–197e).

Socrates functions as critic of the old and new traditions, attacking the notion that Eros is a god by getting the interlocutors to recollect from their own experience the essential lack that belongs to Eros by nature (198b–201c). He goes on to relate what he was taught by Diotima, a woman who intruded into the hitherto all-male discussion from which the women had deliberately been excluded. Mythically expressed, Eros was born on Aphrodite's feast-day from *Poros* as craftiness seeking fulfillment because of his linkage with *Penia* or emptiness, on account of which Eros, their offspring, is simultaneously always lacking and always seeking fulfillment. Eros is in all the living as the striving of the mortal for the immortal through reproduction. In addition, because human be-

---

immortality of famous men, events, and opinions secured by recollection as well as the peculiar recollection of the immortal eidetic features involved in the lifeworld. We will pick this up later in this chapter.

ings have minds that can deliberately recollect the past and anticipate the future, they seek to live on in *doxa*, in the glory realized in the eyes of others who recollect "immortal" works and deeds. More deeply still, minds can arise from the Cave of *doxa* through the Ladder of Ascent from the beauty of an attractive body to the beauty of soul, of customs shaping souls, and of the sciences of cosmic and human order that permit the assessment of customs and bodily beauty, culminating in the vision of Beauty itself. In his recollection of Diotima's teaching, Socrates builds up the *doxa* of his interlocutors regarding Diotima's teaching but thereby puts them and us as readers in the position to recollect the essential truths from our own experience (201d–212c).

Finally, Alcibiades recollects the stories of his own personal erotic experiences with Socrates, which help to establish the basis for Socrates's glory (215a–222b). And, of course, Plato writes the dialogue to aid in keeping the glory of Socrates as immortal as temporal transmission will allow. The dialogue is built as a series of recollections that produce the subsequent *doxa*, ultimately for us, regarding the banquet event and regarding Eros, and providing, in Diotima's account, a way from the Cave of *doxa* to *episteme* through another mode of recollection.

KIERKEGAARD

"In Vino Veritas" is also a recollection of an event; in fact, it is subtitled "A Recollection." Like the *Symposium*, the characters recollect famous opinions, the later speakers those of the earlier as well, and recollect their own experience in order to develop their opinions. Afham as narrator reflects upon recollection in the beginning of the work, and at the end Judge William's wife raises a question that provokes the judge's recollection about marriage in the essay following the dialogue in *Stages on Life's Way* (or at least that is how I interpret the origin of the second piece). The core of the dialogue recounts how five unmarried male aesthetes gathered at a banquet to enjoy a sumptuous feast and each other's company. Contrary to the *Symposium*, there seems to be no order of progression in the speakers. Paralleling in Plato's dialogue the common view of all but Socrates that Eros is a god, Victor, as a consummate aesthete, represents the view common to the five symposiasts that the aim of nature is to be taken up in the service of the senses and arranged into an integral whole.

Their "god" is their own refined enjoyment. For Victor the event has to be unique and the whole beautiful setting must be destroyed after the banquet is over (*SLW*, 22–25). Flux is king: what is important is to enjoy the immediate. The traces of the past are erased as the aesthetes look for ever new occasions for enjoyment.

The first speaker is a Young Man (presumably not named because he has not yet made a name for himself), who has deliberately kept himself from being involved with women.[3] This, he claims, gives him a relation in thought to all and not simply to one or a few women (*SLW*, 32). He is able to recollect all that he has been able to observe of women in a purely detached mode. As Phaedrus bases his opinions of Eros upon recollection of the opinions of famous men, so the Young Man, in explicit recollection of Plato's *Symposium*, praises Plato's exaltation of "Eros in the Greek sense," which is not that between man and woman—a possible discreetly ambiguous praise of homosexuality and/or of "Platonic love" (33). He also recollects Aristophanes's division of the sexes, a comic state that amused the gods (35). Love itself is a comedy. He finds it humorous that the matter of falling in love, taken to be so important by an epoch that requires reflectiveness before action, renders a man blind and unable to give reasons why one particular woman would be the object of his being so attracted (36, 41). Thus, women, for whom reflection is impossible, entice men to become ridiculous (46). Furthermore, rendering the whole matter contradictory, the egoism of pleasure leads to a total regard for another, only to establish a mutual egoism, itself overcome in reproduction (42–43).

Constantin Constantius is a detached psychological observer.[4] In his view, man expresses the absolute, that is, what is self-subsistent and thus at base absolved from all relation; woman can only exist in relationship

---

3. Compare the nameless young man of *Repetition*.

4. Perkins sees him, consistent with his name, as one who is so locked into his egoism that he is unable to undergo the changes required by existence. See Robert Perkins, "Woman Bashing in 'In Vino Veritas,'" in *Feminist Interpretations of Søren Kierkegaard*, ed. C. Léon and S. Walsh (University Park: Pennsylvania State University Press, 1997), 93–94. In the piece following "In Vino Veritas," that is, "Reflections on Marriage," the anonymous author refers to one who does not view marriage as a higher expression of love and remains unmarried as "a scoffer, a seducer, a hermit," or one who remains thoughtless in marriage. "In Vino Veritas: A Recollection," in *Stages on Life's Way*, trans. W. Lowrie (New York: Schocken, 1967), 100. The page numbers located in the body of the text refer to this work and are indicated by *SLW*. The three speakers who have names are Johannes the Seducer, Victor Emerita, and Constantin. One could suppose, then, that Constantin is the scoffer, as his speech also indicates.

(*SLW*, 48). He recollects the opinions of Plato and Aristotle (and in this they are followed by Aquinas),[5] that woman is incomplete man (55). She is the weaker sex who lives in imaginary illusion (48, 52). She regularly dies of love and then is reborn with the next love (55). Since she continually falls into contradiction, she needs to be corrected by the man (52). To become, like Othello, jealous of her falling to another man makes a man comic, something one cannot imagine in the case of Socrates (49–50).

Victor Eremita is the consummate aesthete: he describes the aesthetic conditions for the banquet; he is thrilled at the music of Mozart.[6] He has achieved the victory of a life of enjoyment of the senses and stands in an ultimate eremetical solitude, for his supreme joy does not presuppose the presence of others. He continues the snowballing denigration of woman, whose value he sees as inflated through gallantry (*SLW*, 56–57), and whose higher function, totally subservient, consists in inspiring the works of the spirit in the creative man. Ideality comes into the world, and poets receive their inspiration through woman (59). However, it is not the girl he gets but the girl he does not get that inspires the genius, the hero, the poet, and the saint, a privilege secured by a wife only through early death (61). Through recollecting his relation to her, a man produces inspired work. She inspires the striving and yearning that leads a man to the consciousness of immortality (60).

The Ladies' Tailor, like the Young Man, also nameless except in his special functional relation to women, experiences women everyday closeby in their vainest moments. Recollecting his experiences, he concludes that woman lives by her nature in an unreflective mode of the aesthetic life, immersed in the immediacy of relation to other likewise immersed females, caught up in the flow of novelty and addicted to fashion in all things (*SLW*, 66–71).

Johannes the Seducer plays a role similar to that of Diotima: he recollects, corrects, and grounds the views expressed in the previous speeches. In contrast to the Young Man, he knows firsthand and intimately an ever-increasing number of women. He detaches himself from the familial function (and thus has no surname). He is simultaneously the

5. Plato, *Timaeus*, 91a and see also *Laws*, XII, 944d; Aristotle, *On the Generation of Animals*, IV, 2; Aquinas, *Summa Theologiae*, I, q. 91, ad 1.

6. Croxall sees Victor as one who stands ironically apart from life. See T. H. Croxall, *Kierkegaard Commentary* (New York: Harper, 1956), 108.

most egoistically manipulative and the most philosophic of the group, suggesting that philosophy itself is a kind of aesthetic seduction.[7] Like Aristophanes and Diotima, he creates a myth: originally there was only man; but the gods became envious and, desiring to weaken him, created woman in order to trap him into the complexities of the finite through marriage (*SLW*, 75, 79). Recollecting the two bases of Western thought, he claims that creation of woman occurred either in the Hebrew way by removing a part from man as in *Genesis* or in the Greek way, as in Plato's Aristophantic view, by slicing man in two (*Symposium*, 190d). In his pithy, densely expressed Hegelian view and relating back to Constantin's speech, Johannes presents woman as the finite, which involves both "living in the genus" as reproductive and being accidental, that is, dependent upon the male. Conversely, the man is the infinite, detached from the finite and thus a free and substantial individual.[8] In the man, the essence of the species is found as an individual. Relating back to Victor's view, Johannes sees woman's inspiration cynically as the source of "the delusive infinity of all divine and human illusions" (*SLW*, 76). Seeing through the trap set by the gods (SLW, 75), Johannes understands that he can relate to an inexhaustible number of women and thus learns to maximize his gratification. He knows how to break off relationships at their consummation in order to go on to still further conquests (75–79). Both he and Victor transcend the masses who pursue sensuous immediacy. The two aesthetes seek the reflective cultivation of the senses. Victor Eremita lives the life of quiet and ultimately private aesthetic cultivation, while Johannes pursues the most intense of all sensual pleasures, sexual enjoyment. They live the height of the aesthetic life, mediated by reflection, one in the quiet, solitary mode and the other in the more intense pleasurable mode of sexual relation to members of the opposite sex.[9]

At dawn, Constantin brings the event to a close by commanding one

7. See "Reflections on Marriage," in *Stages on Life's Way*, 170–71 for a confirmation of this view from the anonymous author.

8. Hegel sees the infinity of the human to lie in the ability to detach oneself from every finite content, say "I" as over-against everything finite, even within oneself, and thus to be able to choose freely among the finite options. The System thus situates rather than absorbs the individual precisely in his/her subjectivity. See Hegel, *Hegel's Philosophy of Mind*, trans. William Wallace and A. Miller (Oxford: Clarendon Press, 1971), §381, *Zusatz*, 21.

9. Cf. "The Seducer's Diary," *Either/Or*, trans. D. Swenson and L. Swenson (Garden City, N.Y.: Doubleday, 1959), 1.

last libation followed by the breaking of the glasses as the crew arrives to dismantle the banquet setting, leaving no trace of the event (*SLW*, 80–81). This parallels Johannes's requirement of breaking off relationships at their consummation. The past is destroyed so that a new immediate, a new occasion for enjoyment, can come to be.

The banqueters are driven together some distance where they await their individual carriages. In the interim, they stroll through the woods and happen upon Judge William and his wife taking morning tea in their garden. The line of Afham's recollection culminates in Judge William and his wife, the former named by his function and the latter only by her functional relation to him, thus without any personal name at all. Of all the males in the dialogue, the judge has the most intimate knowledge of what a woman can be. As detached observers who have no personal knowledge of marital relations, the group observes the couple in secret, the judge and his wife oblivious of their presence (*SLW*, 82). Contrary to the insecure clinging that characterizes lovers, the married people move securely in each other's presence. The wife remarks to her husband that if he had not married her, he would have become a much greater person in the world, confirming Johannes's view of woman as the occasion for the fall of man (84). The judge does not reply directly but playfully hums the tune to a ballad about a husband cutting a cudgel for his wife, indicating the essentially subservient role of women in Danish practice and establishing the background for the negative view of women expressed by the symposiasts. After she complains that he never takes her seriously, playfully again he tells her to forget her remark. In effect, she should not bother her pretty little head about it but simply live in the immediacy of her functional relationship to him.[10]

The dialogue ends with Victor Eremita pilfering a manuscript from the judge's study, only to have it taken from him, in turn, by Afham. The manuscript is presumably the piece that follows, "Reflections on Marriage," the result of the judge's having recollected the question posed to him, no doubt several times before, by his wife.

Having sketched the most general content and progression of the speeches in each dialogue, I will go on to consider the theme of wine,

---

10. Perkins suggests that the morning tea of the judge and his wife and not the evening wine is the source of truth about woman ("Woman Bashing in 'In Vino Veritas,'" 100).

contained in the title of Kierkegaard's work. He explicitly ties it to the theme of recollection, which I will then consider in each of the dialogues.

WINE

Kierkegaard's title "In Vino Veritas" indicates the special role of what may seem to be a purely accidental theme, namely wine. In Plato's work, it serves to distinguish the Dionysian element, focally present in the discussion of Eros, from the Apollonian, ironically setting up, by the intrusion of nature in the form of hiccups, an accidental but measured and perfect Apollonian alternation in the arranged order of those present at the banquet between Dionysiac drinkers and Apollonian nondrinkers. And on this occasion, the initial deliberate Apollonian abstinence of all the speakers, drinkers and nondrinkers alike, is overcome by the entry of the drunken Alcibiades and the heavy imbibing that follows. Socrates rises above it all, drinking them under the table in Dionysian darkness and rising with the sun to bathe in the grove of Apollo, god of light. This is the setting for the proclamation of Dionysian ascent of Eros up the Ladder to Apollonian contemplation of the order of the cosmos and beyond to its Source in Beauty itself, the occasion for the highest level of intoxication.

In Kierkegaard's work, wine is present as a feature of the banquet, but it serves a more important function in the preface as the fundamental metaphor of the work. The password to the banquet is *In vino veritas*, "In wine there is truth," an adage that recalls a statement by Alcibiades in the *Symposium* (217e). Contrary to stipulation for the speakers in Plato's piece, the speakers in Kierkegaard's work *must* feel the power of wine in order to speak, just as the culmination of the whole of the *Symposium* comes in the testimony of the drunken Alcibiades. But, much more important, the preface to Kierkegaard's work first introduces wine as a metaphor for the theme of the subtitle, *recollection*. Recollection transforms the grapes of experience into wine (*SLW*, 9), grapes raised to a higher power, as it were.[11] The work aims to provoke recollection in the special

---

11. Schopenhauer uses the same metaphor for philosophy: philosophy transforms the grapes of experience into wine. See *The World as Will and Representation*, II, Supplement to Book 3, ch. 34, 407.

sense in which Kierkegaard employs it. Wine thus serves as symbol for transformed consciousness.

Following out the clue in Kierkegaard's title, what I want especially to attend to is the claim that, although the focal topic of each dialogue concerns sexual relations, the key to each lies in the notion of recollection and the "erotic understanding" it entails. The immediate theme of Plato's dialogue is Eros, the Dionysiac element *par excellence* and object of the after-dinner speeches. However, one often gains a clue for reflection upon the inner significance of a Platonic dialogue by attending to the first words.[12] The *Symposium* begins with *Doko moi*, "It seems to me," employing a cognate to the term *doxa* that is a constant in Plato's dialogues. *Doxa* is usually translated as "opinion," but its meaning is much broader. In addition to "seeming" and "opinion," it also means "glory," as in the liturgical doxology. As glory, it is the maximum state of how one seems to others and how one secures a measure of immortality by living on in the memory of others. The banquet is a celebration of the glory of Agathon's victory; the *Symposium* itself as a literary work is a celebration of the glory of Socrates. The *doxa* of Diotima's account notes how doing great deeds and producing great works is a way to achieve the glory of living on in the memory of others, one of the "minor mysteries" of Eros as the desire of the mortal for immortality. Alcibiades's concluding speech helps establish the immortal *doxa* of Socrates.

Plato uses *doxa* as the comprehensive term for the state of mind we are constantly in before the discovery of *episteme*. Comprehensively taken, it means "opining/appearing," or how things are present to us in ordinary life as appearing through the senses and mediated both by others and by the intrusion of the past into the present. In response to an inquiry about an event that took place many years ago, the very beginning of the dialogue asks for a recollection. It goes on to construct a path of recollection about the famous banquet. The process terminates in the building up of *doxa*, the seeming that constitutes a community, both with regard to past events generally and with regard to the theme of Eros. The

12. The *Republic*, for example, begins with *kateben*: "I went down," giving us the central metaphoric opposition of down and up linked to the opposition of darkness and light initiating the search for what is "up" or "down" in human experience and finding it in ascending from the darkness of the Cave to the sunlight of the Good. See my "Image, Structure and Content," 495–514.

dialogue shows the workings of *doxa* as the residue of recollection regarding that theme. From the dialogue as a whole, we gain some insight into the way *doxa* operates.

Apollodoros ("the gift of Apollo") recollects to an unnamed group of people (including us as readers) what he had narrated yesterday to Glaucon about what happened at a banquet when he and Glaucon were infants. Glaucon had asked Apollodoros to fill in what he had heard from an unnamed source who got it from Phoenix who, in turn, got it from the eyewitness Aristodemos, the same who had recounted it to Apollodoros. The initial focus of the dialogue is upon weaving the web of *doxa* within which members of a community live. The narrator, Apollodoros, recollects the process of the transmission of the *doxa* about the banquet held a long time ago. The dialogue itself fixes the transmission in writing, and both *Phaedrus* and *Theaetetus* reflect upon writing and reading as vehicles of building up *doxa*.[13] Seeming is dependent upon recollection and fixation either in memory or in writing, passed on by various pathways to constitute what Quine has called "the web of belief."[14]

Apollodoros tells us that Aristodemos cannot recall everything but only the memorable (178a). Memory is not a neutral recorder but operates in function of interest. What is important remains, and much that occurs is not judged as important and is thus forgotten. Memory works automatically, but it can also be deliberately cultivated. And language can be employed to actively seek to reconstruct the past through the aid of others as well as, with the rise of literate culture, through fixation on the page. Interest sustains the past by helping to weave the web of *doxa*. Plato is reflecting upon the construction of the Cave of human dwelling. The dialogue is thus in a significant way about recollection as the building up of a community's *doxa*.

Kierkegaard's subtitle indicates that the work itself is a recollection (*Erdringung*). And his preface is really a prerecollection (*Vor-erdringung*), or a recollection about recollection.[15] This shows that he has grasped what is at the center of Plato's work generally: the notion of recollection. The distinctively human does not consist in living in immediacy like an

13. See my treatment of this in "Self-Reflexivity in the *Theaetetus*: On the Life-world of a Platonic Dialogue," *The Review of Metaphysics* (January 1999).

14. W. Quine, *The Web of Belief* (New York: McGraw-Hill, 1978).

15. See Walter Lowrie's note to his translation of *Stages on Life's Way*, 27.

animal; it lives off of recollection. For Kierkegaard, the truth attained through the wine of recollection is what the *Concluding Unscientific Postscript* calls "subjective truth," truth held in the passion of inwardness.[16] The narrator aims at promoting what he calls "recollection's erotic understanding" (*SLW*, 15). Although he does not explain what he means by that expression, the qualification of understanding as "erotic" suggests a kind of heightened awareness and thus something more than clear insight into essential connections. It is a matter of intensified presence parallel to Diotima's description of the sudden epiphany of Beauty itself.

In "In Vino Veritas," William Afham is the reporter who subsequently relates the incident. How is he able to relate it? He is not described as an eyewitness the way Aristodemos, the original reporter of the *Symposium*, was. In the preface, Afham says that he sometimes feels as though he had not experienced it but had poetically invented it (*SLW*, 15). In this way, he participated in the banquet without being a participant: he made it up. Of course, we should not forget that the author is Søren Kierkegaard, who knows nothing of that secret, being himself unmarried. In this case, he is underscoring the need for experience to understand the depths of subjectivity by pointing to something he himself could not fully understand: the secret mentioned in the very first sentence of the work (27)—although, as real author of the anonymously authored "Reflections on Marriage," he presents himself indirectly as understanding matrimonial intimacy.

Having indicated the central notion of recollection in both thinkers, what I want to do from this point on is to examine that notion in greater detail, beginning with Plato.

RECOLLECTION I

Platonic recollection, the notion of *anamnesis*, is part of philosophic *doxa*, of the opinions passed on in the academic community. However, what it really entails may not be so well known. Baldly put, according to conventional *doxa*, Plato is said to handle "the problem of universals" by claiming that the Forms, the ground of language in the universals whereby we

16. Søren Kierkegaard, *Concluding Unscientific Postscript to Philosophical Fragments*, trans. D. Swenson (Princeton, N.J.: Princeton University Press, 1941), 1:203, 242.

come to identify individuals as being of a certain type, are innate in the soul from a previous existence. Experience of individuals in the sensory world reminds one of the preexistent Forms appropriate to understanding the specific individuals involved.

The "doctrine" is introduced in the *Meno* in conjunction with an exploration in geometry, which is itself introduced in a *prima facie* improbable attempt to ground Pindar's poetic proclamation that the soul is immortal.[17] Socrates leads a slave-boy to a geometric insight that is the solution to the problem of squaring a given square while retaining the square figure. However, Socrates claims that the boy only has *alethes doxa*, or manifest opinion or insight. This is a step higher than *orthe doxa*, or correct opinion guessed at or memorized without insight. But it is lower than *anamnesis*, which consists, Socrates says, in tethering the insight by reasoning. Such tethering (*desei* from *deo*, I bind) would consist in developing the axiomatic system within which the insight could be demonstrated. Reflected upon, this furnishes a basic insight into the distinction between *episteme* and *doxa*, which Socrates, who claimed in the *Apology* that his wisdom consisted in knowing that he does not know, claims in the *Meno* to be among the things he knows.[18]

Anamnesis is clearly distinguished from *mneme*, or simple memory, by its ability to gather together, axiomatize, deduce, and thus systematize what appears haphazard in experience. The geometric example is meant to be a regional demonstration of this ability. It begins the verification of Socrates's first introduction of the notion of *anamnesis* in the *Meno* by his proclamation that all nature is akin, and that, this being so, if one could recollect one universal truth, one could go on to recollect all.[19] *Anamnesis* is tied in with our ability to gather the whole of Being together in a unified way, to recollect it at the level of the togetherness of the eidetic features found in experience.

In the treatment of the Line of Knowledge in the *Republic*, Socrates uses a geometric theorem again, this time in order to lead us to a metareflection upon the eidetic features of the "play of the fourfold"—sensible and intelligible, sense and intellect—presupposed in all wakeful life. And that, in turn, leads us by "the upward way" to consider the Good as the

---

17. Plato, *Meno*, 81b–d.   18. Plato, *Apology*, 23b; *Meno*, 98b.
19. Plato, *Meno*, 81b–d.

source of unity and as the term of aspiration for intellect, which operates in the light of a sought-after unity. Ultimately, what we recollect is our founding reference to the whole of Being, and this leads us to recollect experience into a systematic eidetic whole.[20]

What is crucial to notice is that the Platonic dialogues deal with recollection on two levels: the active recollection of things past (retained in a more fixed and universally available way in writing), especially those connected with glory, and the active recollection of our place in the cosmos. Both operations are moved by a kind of Eros as the desire of the mortal for immortality, the desire to fix forever what perishes. Before it is tied into a theoretical claim to a recollection of previous existence or an anticipation of an afterlife, the *anamnesis* Plato is after is a matter of experience: it has to do with gathering the eidetic features of the eternal order of the cosmic whole in relation to the things we experience in the Cave of *doxa*, the communally based recollections of concrete events and judgments about things-in-general. But it also has to do with what Kierkegaard would call "the How" of that recollection. For Plato, it is suffused by an erotic intoxication with what Diotima calls "Beauty itself," linked to the Good as the origin and end of the cosmos.[21]

RECOLLECTION II

"In Vino Veritas" presents a substantial retrieval of the notion of recollection, adding a new dimension to it.[22] William Afham's *Forerindring* to the *Erindring*, his prerecollection to the recollection, begins by focusing upon the recollection of an unnamed secret which requires total recollection as a matter of obligation. One wonders immediately what the secret is. It turns out to be any true recollection that can only happen in the

---

20. Plato, *Republic*, VI, 509d. See my "Plato's Line Revisited: The Pedagogy of Complete Reflection," 525–47.

21. Plato, *Republic*, VI, 506e.

22. There seems to be a change of meaning for "recollection" here from that in *Repetition*. There, it is set in contrast with the title word and indicates a fixation that closes the openness of the future emphasized in repetition. See John Caputo, "Kierkegaard, Heidegger, and the Foundering of Metaphysics," 201–24, and Stephen Crites, "'The Blissful Security of the Moment': Recollection, Repetition, and Eternal Recurrence," in *Fear and Trembling and Repetition*, International Kierkegaard Commentary, ed. Robert L. Perkins (Atlanta: Mercer University Press, 1993), 225–46.

secrecy of one's own subjectivity (*SLW*, 14). One wonders also what "total recollection" is. It appears to be a grasping of what is essential to holding one's life together as a whole in the mode of "passionate inwardness." That is, it involves concern for the whole of one's life in a mode that involves the whole of one's awareness and not simply some recognitional or intellectually explanatory mode.

The wine theme of the title appears in the second paragraph: "the bottling of the recollection must have preserved the fragrance of the experience before it is sealed" (*SLW*, 9). This is immediately followed by a distinction between recollection and remembrance. Remembrance is only a minimal condition. Mere memory leaves one unconcerned (10) and what is merely memorized or what might float up in reverie might easily be forgotten subsequently. But what is truly recollected cannot be forgotten because it is a matter of concern (13).

Recollection "consecrates" the experience. The wine metaphor is significant here: it indicates a transformation in the how of our relation to things. According to Afham, an old man has poor memory, but recollection is his best faculty, giving him poetic farsight. The opposite is the case for the child: good memory, poor ability to recollect, and thus no "poetic far-sightedness" (*SLW*, 10). Furthermore, "the grape must not be pressed at every season" (10); a certain ripening of experience is required. For the child, both spontaneous experience and memory are matters of "immediacy." Memory itself only recalls immediately (12); recollection is reflection that produces a relation mediated by distance. This allows the old man to see things near at hand, whereas the child sees them from afar. This last turn in the metaphor should not be taken to mean that the child sees farther, for Kierkegaard has just said the opposite: it is the old man who has poetic farsight. Too close to life at the level of immediacy, one is unable to see it properly. In fact, living in immediacy, one is *not* close to things; living through recollection, one can in fact draw nearer to existent things. We see the former exhibited in the Young Man who has had no experience whatsoever with women in the erotic sense. But we see it also in each of the speakers who have not had the inner experience of marriage. They remain outside the experience within which alone one can understand woman at her best.[23] Their disposition looks

---

23. "Reflections on Marriage" is based upon a shift in perspective. See especially *Stages on Life's Way*, 124–25 and 143–44. One must not remain a mere connoisseur.

only to the present and the future of enjoyment with no attempt to hold it in continuity with the recollected past.

In a strange turn, Afham says that recollection is indifferent to past and present. One would have thought that it is concerned only with the past. Memory of the past is a necessary condition. The work of recording here is a setting free for recollection of what has been lying perfected in memory (*SLW*, 15). Drawing upon past experience through memory, one is able "to conjure away the present for the sake of recollection" (13). The nearness here is the nearness of familiarity, of what Heidegger would call "average everydayness" (*Alltäglichkeit*).[24] There is a deeper sort of nearness grounded in the achievement of the distance of reflection, which presupposes memory's gathering as its precondition. It requires a second or "double reflection."[25] The symposiasts recollect both their past experience and the opinions of others, but they do not practice the requisite reflection upon the recollection that deepens the experience. The deepening occurs by way of a kind of Heraclitean law of opposites: according to Afham, it requires acquaintance with contrast in moods, situations, and environments. What is at stake is an appreciative awareness involved in nearness. Thus, Heraclitus claimed that by sickness we know health, by hunger and thirst satiety; both Heidegger and Buber claimed that by anticipation of death we know the preciousness of life.[26]

But what is at stake is not simply the appreciation of some particular. Recollection, Afham further says, gives continuity to life. It is also not lost on Kierkegaard that the *Symposium* teaches a flux cosmology through the *doxa* Socrates hands on from Diotima (207d ff). Knowledge itself is in flux and has to be replaced by caring, by exercise, and by study (*meletan*). Knowledge as recollection is the struggle to hold one's life together as a whole as time flows by, and one, like a child, is immersed in the present moment. The distance provided by old age is what allows one to bind one's life together in recollection and to bring the relevant past

---

24. Heidegger, *Being and Time*, 149ff.

25. Kierkegaard, *Concluding Unscientific Postscript to Philosophical Fragments*, 73. See Gabriel Marcel's parallel distinction in *The Mystery of Being*, trans. G. Fraser (Chicago: Regnery, 1960), vol. 1, 95–126, between first reflection as abstractive and second as "recuperative," recovering the concreteness of existence at a deeper level.

26. On Heraclitus, see Kirk and Raven, *The Presocratic Philosophers*, 189, §204; on Heidegger, *Being and Time*, 278–311; on Martin Buber, *Daniel: Dialogues on Realization*, trans. Maurice Friedman (New York: McGraw-Hill, 1965), 91.

to bear upon the deepening of our relation to what is present. "Actually, only the essential can be recollected" (*SLW*, 12). A mass of detail distracts recollection (13). Here, Kierkegaard's character joins Plato in focusing upon the essential, which Afham explicitly connects with the idea. The question of the dialogue, then, is what is the essential matter with respect to a man and a woman and to the relation between them for the whole of their existence (30)? Grasping the essential through recollection allows one distance from the flow of immediacy to bring it to significant presence and to give continuity to one's life as a whole. However, the characters in the dialogue do not undertake the requisite reflection. It is what his wife requires of Judge William, the conditions for which are given by Afham. One has to go on to the next piece in *Stages on Life's Way* (presumably the piece pilfered from the judge at the end of the dialogue) to secure the proper perspective for the actual recollection.

Afham lays out the conditions for recollection. He says that the sounds and tastes are recollected best in a place "quiet, remote and forgotten"—the solitude of the forest in the peace of late afternoon, in "the infinite sea of silence," in the holy quietness of solitude (*SLW*, 18). Quietness, remoteness, forgottenness, solitude, silence: all involve being set at a distance from others, not hearing their addresses, not receiving their attention. In a forest far removed from the city, in late afternoon when the tasks of the day are finished, the shadows lengthen, and darkness begins to descend. They all create external preconditions for the sense of the infinite that can open up in inner silence. Max Picard's wonderful little work *The World of Silence* ends with a quote from Kierkegaard: the cities are factories for generating omnipresent noise; if he were a physician and were asked to cure the sickness of the age, he would have one prescription: create silence.[27]

In the light of the early morning sun, the judge's wife poses the question about his life without her. At that time, the judge is silent. Presumably the process of recollection is setting in. Just as Diotima's teaching on the ladder of erotic ascent may have provoked Socrates's own erotic recollection as he stood in rapt attention, so the judge's wife as a kind of second Diotima provokes his recollection.[28] Presumably, as a good wife,

---

27. Max Picard, *The World of Silence* (Chicago: Regnery, 1954).
28. I owe this most helpful insight to a suggestion by Robert Perkins.

she had asked the same question of him before, probably several times. Perhaps he found the full and requisite silence of solitude in the evening darkness where he composed his "Reflections on Marriage."

Afham attaches the notion of the holy to that silence found in solitude. One is reminded here of Kierkegaard's frequent remark that "we float on waters seventy thousand fathoms deep" and are scarcely aware of it.[29] The depth dimension to be attained by recollection is a secret growing in complete solitude, inaccessible from the outside. "The winepress of recollection every man must tread alone" (SLW, 15). One understands now why the first line of the work focuses upon the secret. There is a clear parallel in the Symposium that highlights in the beginning and in Alcibiades's speech at the end the frequent lapse of Socrates into prolonged periods of withdrawn silence and physical fixity (174d–175b, 220c).

Afham finds his retreat at the Nook of Eight Paths, located at the convergence of eight solitary paths upon which no one travels (SLW, 16). I suggest that the Eight Paths are the ways of life followed by each of the seven characters and by the narrator. No one really travels upon them because they are Kierkegaard's fictions, although they name essential possibilities. They are solitary because ultimately everyone travels alone in her/his heart of hearts. Quiet solitude is holy. This allows experience to be "consecrated" in recollection.

A long and very confusing penultimate paragraph (SLW, 17–19) parallels the intrusion of someone upon the quiet of an individual in solitude with the intrusion of someone upon lovers in solitude, seeing without being seen. It prefigures the penultimate scene of the dialogue when the group of aesthetes, seeing but unseen, comes upon a married couple in their solitary country home.

The prefatory remarks on recollection end thus: "anyone who has once understood what recollection is has been captured for all eternity and is captured in it; and anyone who possesses one recollection is richer than if he possessed the whole world; and not only the one about to give birth but above all the one who is recollecting is in blessed circumstances" (SLW, 19).

---

29. Kierkegaard, *Concluding Unscientific Postscript to Philosophical Fragments*, I:232.

RECOLLECTION III

As I have attempted to show, both dialogues, Plato's and Kierkegaard's, deal centrally with recollection. Both play on a distinction between memory, which is a precondition, and recollection technically taken. For Plato's Socrates, recollection (*anamnesis*) at its deepest consists in recollecting the eidetic features of the cosmic order from the contingencies of experience by seeking the single principle of order for the whole in order to deduce the whole eidetic realm there from. Plato's own focus sets the theoretical cosmological, scientific, and theological project within the context of a lifeworld in encounter with other individuals—hence, the dialogue form that his thought takes. To that extent, Plato's "essentialism," his focus upon essential Forms, plays in counterpoint with an "existentialism" in the dual sense of involving encounter with individual human existents and in calling for a peculiar modality of subjective inwardness—hence, the focus upon Socrates. But Plato also explores another sense of recollection, that which establishes the *doxa* in which a community lives, both spontaneously and in terms of the deliberate attempt to recollect the past. It is out of that web of *doxa* and back in relation to it that the erotic ascent takes place, which lays bare the underlying kinship of things within the cosmos.

For Kierkegaard's Afham, recollection consists in gaining distance from the flowing immediacy of the surface of life in order to draw near to what underlies that surface through bringing forward what is essential, drawn from the past into the present. This occurs in the secrecy of one's own subjectivity and has to do with the ineffability of the individual and the "erotic understanding," the transformation of awareness into passionate inwardness through the double reflection of recollection, fixing in memory and allowing what is thus fixed to draw near so as to affect one's life as a whole.

All the speakers in Kierkegaard's banquet live in a world from which the gods and the cosmic concern are absent. That would also seem to include the author Afham for whom "the holy" in the dialogue is not explicitly the divine. One has to go on to the next piece in *Stages on Life's Way*, "Reflections on Marriage," to find the religious dimension to marriage and perhaps the hidden secret behind the loving relation between the judge and his wife: "If the individual has not in faith placed himself in the relationship with God as spirit, paganism haunts his brain as a fantastic reminiscence and he cannot enter into any marriage" (*SLW*, 100). Certainly, in the dialogue in question, despite the parallels with and the deliberate invocation of Plato's *Symposium*, Diotima's cosmic interest is entirely absent. The world of "In Vino Veritas" is the narrow world of bourgeois individualism and aesthetic enjoyment with no cosmic sensibility whatsoever. William Afham has achieved a higher level of reflection than all the others as one who comprehensively reflects upon all the others. The judge, however, is one who exhibits in his marriage and profession a form of life higher than the speakers and also higher, through his lifelong commitment, than the higher aesthetic of William Afham.

But at least as important in attending to what is present in the dialogue is what is absent from it. One has to look to *Stages on Life's Way* as a whole and beyond. There, the equivalent of the cosmic and theological features of the *Symposium* lie in the stage of religion represented initially by the married author of "Reflections on Marriage," hence in all probability the judge displaying his deeper side. And one has to look to Kierkegaard's work as a whole to see the extent to which the cosmic extension of the human quest for eternity enters into his work. It certainly takes center stage in relation to Christ as the Paradox, the Absurd, as the Infinite made finite.[30]

In an age increasingly dominated by specialized scientific and technical thinking, it is crucially important to recover the dimension of religious sensibility to which Kierkegaard constantly points. But it is also crucially important to recover the ability exhibited by Plato to recover the whole context of human existence and thus find a place both for scientific and philosophic discipline. Plato simultaneously leads us to reflection upon the building up of *doxa* as the tradition within which a given community lives. Kierkegaard and Plato can thus be put into complementary relation with each other. And both together underscore the central import of "erotic understanding" in the recollective transformation of consciousness. Our reflection upon their two dialogues only opens up the beginning of a more comprehensive reflection, which will learn to mine both thinkers simultaneously.

30. Ibid., I:209ff.

6 ∽ Plato, Descartes, and Heidegger

An Inquiry into the Paths of Inquiry

The three figures Plato, Descartes, and Heidegger provide us with three anchors that allow us to look over the history of Western thought and compare the differing modes of inquiry and the differing (but also similar) things uncovered through the different modes.[1]

René Descartes attempted a bracketing of tradition in order to arrive at radical responsibility for the evidential grounding of whatever claims he might make and thus to secure the foundations of science. In this, he has a parallel in Plato's attempted ascent from the Cave of traditional *doxa* into the evidential grounds constituting *episteme*.[2] Descartes envisioned the Tree of Knowledge with roots in metaphysics, out of which grew the trunk of physics from which came the main branches of mechanics, medicine, and morals that culminated in our ability to pluck the fruit from the tree,[3] becoming "masters and possessors of nature" in order to improve the human estate.[4]

Heidegger, following the same metaphor of the tree, inquired into "the ground of metaphysics," the soil in which the tree of knowledge is planted.[5] He goes back to Plato as the historical source of the tradition

1. This chapter is connected with two previous papers that appeared in *Existentia*: "The Fugal Lines of Heidegger's *Beiträge*," 11 (2001): fasc. 3–4, 253–66 and "Phenomenology and the Perennial Task of Philosophy: A Study of Plato and Aristotle," 2 (2002): fasc. 3–4, 253–63. This study focuses upon method, situating the treatment of Plato's Line in the second paper and Heidegger's *Beiträge* in the first, both within the larger framework of their respective corpus and in relation to Descartes.

2. Plato, *Republic*, VII.

3. "Letter to Picot," in *Principles of Philosophy, in The Philosophical Works of Descartes*, vol. I, trans. E. Haldane and G. Ross (New York: Dover, 1955), 211. All references to Descartes's works will be to this collection.

4. René Descartes, *Discourse on Method*, VI, 119.

5. "Introduction to 'What Is Metaphysics?': The Way Back into the Ground of Metaphysics," in *Pathmarks*, trans. W. McNeill (Cambridge: Cambridge University Press, 1998), 206–21.

and examines his Allegory of the Cave and the corresponding Line of Knowledge.[6] He traces the transformation of the notion of truth from "uncovering" to correspondence to certitude and to the technological essence that completes the history of metaphysics.[7]

We will begin with Plato, go on to show certain parallels, developments, and delimitations of the modes of inquiry in Descartes, and conclude with an examination of Heidegger's "step back" from the history of metaphysics into its ground in the historical lifeworld. Indeed, in Heidegger we have a peculiar revisiting of the relation between philosophy and the lifeworld that situates the historical project of philosophy in a novel way.

PLATO

In a previous chapter, I sketched out an interpretation of Plato's Line of Knowledge.[8] It presented a connected series of more encompassing forms of reflection. A proportionately divided line, subdivided by the same proportion, invited reflection upon the theorem it instantiates: no matter what the chosen proportion, its central segments will always be equal. Plato used it to illustrate the wider distinction, covering the whole field of awareness, between the visible (the drawn line) and the intelligible (the theorem it instantiates). He used the relation between vision, the visible, and the sun as the source of light as a metaphor for the relation between intellect, the intelligible, and what he calls the "Good" as source of intelligible "light."[9]

The Line was to occupy the "space" between these two triplets. It, too, becomes a metaphor for the hierarchy of relations between awareness and its objects. In this way, he links a metaphor with a metaphor. The

6. Heidegger commented on the Cave allegory twice: first in a course on Plato's Cave and *Theaetetus* in 1931–32, *The Essence of Truth*, trans. T. Sadler (London: Continuum, 2002) and in less detail in "Plato's Doctrine of Truth," in *Philosophy in the Twentieth Century*, vol. III, ed. E. Barrett and H. Aiken (New York: Random House, 1962), 251–70.

7. Martin Heidegger, "On the Essence of Truth," in *Martin Heidegger: Basic Writings*, ed. D. Krell (New York: Harper and Row, 1977), 117–41; "Metaphysics as History of Being," in *The End of Philosophy*, trans. J. Stambaugh (New York: Harper and Row, 1973) 19–26; "The Question Concerning Technology," in *The Question Concerning Technology and Other Essays*, trans. W. Lovitt (New York: Harper and Row, 1977), 11–20.

8. Plato, *Republic*, VI, 509d.

9. Ibid., 506e ff.

lower two levels of the Line taken metaphorically stand for relations in the visual field: images and things. The upper two levels stand for relations in the intelligible field: mathematics and philosophy. What is going on in the case of the literal line is the occasion for exhibition of the distinction between visible and intelligible presupposed in mathematics. Illustrated by mathematics, that distinction goes beyond mathematics. So, we have the literal line inviting geometric reflection—the same line subject to metaphorical reflection and leading to a metamathematical reflection upon the basic distinction of objects of awareness involved in mathematics and, indeed, in all wakeful human life. But the wider context of the *Republic* is the order of the soul. Hence, the next move is a "transcendental reflection" upon the structures of awareness correlative to the visible and the intelligible, namely, the distinction between vision and intellect. However, the overarching aim of the dialogue is to find when the soul is going "up" and when it is going "down." Mathematics goes "up" to attend from the changing visible to the changeless intelligible. But it goes "down" in moving by deduction from idealized visibles and axioms to the theorems.[10] The fewness of the axioms unifies the plurality of metric relations discovered in the process of building. The movement "up" grasps the "ones" and shows unity in the plurality of axioms. But in geometry, it proceeds from idealized images mixed with a few basic intelligible relations. One can move "up" from there toward purely intelligible relations and finally toward that One in the light of which intellectual development occurs. Intellectual movement seeks unity in what would otherwise be scattered multiplicity. Intellect moves in the light of the deep desire for unification correlate to Eros moved by beauty. Oneness is what it seeks—hence, the Good as the One is its "illuminating" source. It is beyond the correlation between the intellect and the intelligible that yields the Forms, here the Forms of the nature of and relations between the fourfold of intellect and intelligible, sense and sensible. There are two reasons for the "beyondness" of the Good: it is the object of "the whole soul" expressed in Eros and it is principle of the Whole, that is, of the relation between the atemporality of the intelligible realm and the temporal realm shown in the sensory.[11] That it is "beyond" is

10. Plato, *Republic*, VII, 525b ff.
11. Plato, *Republic*, VI, 511b.

suggested metaphorically by the image of the sun, which cannot be seen without blinding us but in whose light we see.

Movement toward the One/Good as principle of the Whole involves a reflection that links the intelligible realm with the visible realm. It is a complete reflection that includes the complete situatedness of oneself in the lifeworld allegorically presented in the Cave story.[12] Here, our relation to the visible is complicated by reference to the situation as one of *doxa*, that is, to the state of mind that has not sorted out the eidetic from the opinions advanced about our situation. One tends to think exclusively, even about our own awareness, in terms of sensory objects, especially seen objects. So, we are represented as chained to images: to image-thinking and to "images of justice in the lawcourts."[13] One has to experience a complete *periagoge*, a one-hundred-and-eighty-degree turn to understand what produces the chained state of mind: biologically based sensations-*cum*-desires and tradition-bound interpretations. And one has to be dragged up out of the Cave—perhaps by the practical necessities that led to the development of mathematics—until mathematics could be developed purely for the sake of turning the soul "up." Once above, one can come to see the whole intelligible context.

Plato uses metaphors (the sun and the Line) and allegory (the Cave) to guide reflection to evermore encompassing awareness. The line metaphor operates within the sun metaphor, and the latter is picked up as the summit of the Cave allegory. The metaphors link the intelligible to more focal experiences. The allegory chosen resituates our everyday awareness so as to make the taken-for-granted strange and to help us to think about what lies hidden behind it.

Further still, the dialogue is structured from its first paragraphs by the binary metaphoric oppositions, ingredient in our embodied consciousness, of up/down and darkness/light. When the sun goes down at night (at least before the invention of artificial lighting), we go down to a prone position and fall into the darkness of the unconscious. And when it rises, we awake to the light of day and rise to an upright position. In speaking evaluatively about our situation, we spontaneously employ these metaphors. Ascending, going higher, being at the top as well as see-

12. Ibid., 514a ff.
13. Ibid., 493a.

ing the light are positive evaluative terms; descending, going down, being down at the bottom as well as being in the dark are negative. Plato has chosen the metaphors that spontaneously structure our value talk to structure a dialogue dedicated to finding what is "up" and "down" in human life and when we are "in the light" or "in the dark." What is at stake is not only correct conceptualization but also proper disposition, the "feel" we have for things. The very first word, *Kateben*, "I went down," announces the down/up metaphors.[14] The situation into which Socrates descended, the port of Athens, was celebrating for the first time the feast of Bendis, a goddess of the dark underworld. The dialogue proper takes place at night as they seek an understanding of justice as the height of humanness. The image of the spinning top that Socrates employs at the end of his first ascent (book IV) indicates what is involved in the finding of "the upright position" for humans sought in the dialogue: the support of that position by the revolutions at the periphery of the gyroscopic device, the sensations and desires that flow through our lives. The image of the spinning top also involves contrast with the situation where the peripheral movements lead to deviation from the upright, to progressive wobbling, and then, when the periphery touches the ground, to being carried erratically.[15] Finally, at the very end of the dialogue, the construction of the eschatological myth of descent into Hades sets inquiry itself into the largest possible framework, transcending the grasp of *episteme* by relating it to the unknown ultimates to which we are by nature referred, and again providing a proper disposition.[16] So metaphors, myths, and allegories structure the inquiry, but they play in tandem with "strictly intellectual" procedures to set them within our "feel" for the lifeworld.

For the starting point of inquiry, Socrates's interlocutors advance opinions on the nature of justice floating around in the community as part of the general *doxa*.[17] They are the "images of justice" contending in the law courts[18] to which Socrates later refers as he locates them at the lowest level of the Line, that of images to which we are chained. Socrates uses the dialectical/dialogical method of question and answer to show the inadequacy of the interlocutors' understanding of the common opinions. Yet, since shadows or images refer, however inadequately, to that

14. Plato, *Republic*, I, 327a.   15. Plato, *Republic*, IV, 436d.
16. Plato, *Republic*, X, 614b.   17. This is the content of *Republic*, I, 331c ff.
18. Plato, *Republic*, VII, 520c.

which they profile or reflect, once the largest framework of reflection is set by the Line, we are invited to return to the common opinions to sort them out in relation to that framework. Furthermore, the whole process of dialogic/dialectic is set within the encompassing framework of the Whole by narrative and description and by appeal to and struggle with the previous poetic tradition that provided the criteria of significance for the community.

The dialectical procedure has a fundamentally negative conclusion that clears the ground for the intellectual methods employed in the pedagogy of the Line: preliminary mathematical insight, idealization, axiomatization, and deduction; metareflection involving eidetic inventory, "transcendental reflection" and projection, and "complete reflection" that understands and employs metaphors to situate the intellectual project within the whole lifeworld. But that does not give us the whole battery of methods Plato employs. We have to move to other dialogues.

In the *Statesman*, the Eleatic Stranger, who carries the dialogue, announces that his intent is to show how to think about *all things*, and not simply political matters.[19] In this connection, he uses the polysemic metaphor of weaving to distinguish and relate the warp and the woof of coming to know our situation: the hard fibers of the vertical warp and the soft fibers of the horizontal woof represent *episteme* and the use of imagery, respectively.[20] Intellectual weaving has to combine the "hard-headed" analytical warp that shows from the top down (*apodeixis*) through *diairesis* or dividing (but also through demonstrative geometry) and the "soft-headed" showing alongside (*paradeigma*) in the employment of metaphors and myths. Their weaving together is the syncritical moment, the moment of synthesis and of comprehensive insight into the whole human situation.[21]

In the process of division that the *Statesman* takes over from its preceding companion dialogue, the *Sophist*, Plato shows how metaphors work by locating the analogue and its analogate within a hierarchy of genera and species. The generic samenesses allow for the linkage in spite of specific differences.

In the *Statesman*, the image of weaving is set within a larger frame-

19. Plato, *Statesman*, 285c.   20. Ibid., 282b.
21. Ibid., 383b.

work of ways of transforming nature distinctive of human existence. (We will return to that shortly.) But the whole process of inquiry and indeed of human culture is set within the largest framework by the myth of cosmic reversal.[22] Our epoch is one in which the god who steers all things has retired from his function as divine shepherd and turned over control to men while he sits on a perch observing the whole process. The myth not only situates the discussion cosmically but also provides the first paradigm of the statesman as shepherd of men. (The Stranger appeals to several paradigms of the statesman: in addition to the shepherd, there is the ship's captain, the weaver, the physician, and the trainer.)[23] The absence of the divine shepherd makes room for human self-determination involved in state-craft and places it under the watchful eye of the distant divine shepherd seated high on his cosmic perch. This allows Plato to assimilate and transform the previous poetic constructions.

The "hard weaving" on the epistemic side involves three methods: bifurcatory diaeresis, measurement, and what we might call "functional anatomy." The former was introduced in the *Sophist* and the second work in the trilogy *Theaetetus-Sophist-Statesman*. The *Sophist* and the *Statesman* are linked by a hierarchically arranged umbrella of divisions, beginning in the *Sophist* with the notion of Being as all-encompassing. The *Theaetetus* announced the distinguishing feature of the philosopher as having his eyes always fixed on the Whole and on the whole nature of each thing within the Whole.[24] In the *Sophist*, that occurs through the notion of Being, "defined" as the power of acting and being acted upon.[25]

If we reflect upon that, we discover that "power" (*dunamis*) is not directly experienced, since what we experience is always actual and individual. It is rather discovered through reflection upon what actual experience of individuals involves: the capacity to experience and the capacity to be experienced—for example, to see and to be seen. Now, the capacity to see is an individual power of an individual seer, but as a power it is a *universal* orientation toward a *kind* of object. And the same with the seen: it is the activation of a visibility open to all instances of the kind we call seers. This situates the notorious "problem of universals" in an inter-

---

22. Ibid., 268d–274e.
23. Shepherd, 274e ff; weaver, 277a ff; trainer, 294d; physician, 295d; captain, 2197e.
24. Plato, *Theaetetus*, 174a and 175a.
25. Plato, *Sophist*, 247e.

esting way. Individual seers and individuals seen anchor perception, but their powers present us with universals ingredient in their very individuality as beings with powers to act and be acted upon that require correspondent types of aspects and things in the environment. To be is thus not to be isolated but to be related, via the cluster of powers constituting a given nature, toward all the kinds of things that can act upon and be acted upon by the thing that has that nature, wherever and whenever they are encountered.[26]

The first division of the notion of Being so conceived is between what comes into being by *techne* and what does not.[27] The latter is found in nature or *physis*. *Techne* or human art is a developed power of individual humans, a universal orientation toward the kind of problems solved by the *techne* in question. It is in turn divided between the art of taking possession and the art of production, with the former divided into exchange and conquest and the latter into divine and human production.[28] The Stranger introduces another set of divisions that involve a kind of metareflection locating the process of division itself: the division of *the art of discrimination*.[29] He divides it into the discrimination of like from like and of better from worse. We should note that no place is provided for this set of divisions in the overall umbrella of divisions presented in the *Sophist*. We have to look to the *Statesman* to discover the larger framework for positioning the tree of discrimination.

In the latter dialogue, the basic distinctions are located under the heading of *episteme/techne*. It is divided into the critical and the gnostic, with the latter divided in its turn into the diacritical and the syncritical.[30] The former is equivalent to the discriminatory category of the *Sophist* that had no category above it to locate it. That dialogue divided power as the overarching category into things that come into being by nature and things that do not. We are invited to consider the first divisions under those things that do not come into being by nature to be the practicoproductive and the gnostic. This provides the larger framework for discrimination, especially since the diacritical is divided into the separation of like from like and of better from worse, the very same division provided by the *Sophist* for the art of discrimination. The *Statesman* pro-

26. See my "Individuals, Universals, and Capacity."
27. Plato, *Sophist*, 219a.
28. Ibid., 219a, 265c.
29. Ibid., 226c.
30. Plato, *Statesman*, 282b.

ceeds to locate the ones exercising the various arts that were anatomized in the *Sophist*.

These divisions exhibit bifurcatory diaeresis, a cutting in the middle of the category to be divided. The Stranger distinguishes arbitrary divisions, such as that of humans between redheads and nonredheads, from natural divisions, such as that between male and female.[31] But he points out that not everything admits of bisection and advises that, when we cannot bifurcate, we should divide the topic like a sacrificial animal along the joints and as near bisection as possible.[32] This leads him to an anatomy of functions in the state that are divided into arts providing instruments, those providing services, those providing leadership aid, and those providing oversight.[33] Instruments begin with extraction of raw materials, developing tools from them, and then providing security, culture, and health. Services are divided into subalterns and higher-level leaders. The former includes those who operate in the fields of labor, commerce, religion, and lower levels of government. The leadership group includes rhetors, generals, and judges. Oversight is provided by the statesman. Falling outside the classification are both teachers and sophists. Presumably the former are the philosophers who are transpolitical and the latter are pretenders. The Stranger thus lays out the functional aspects of the polis.

The dialogue itself is cut in the physical middle, which turns out to be also the logical middle, by the introduction of qualitative measure as the mean between extremes in everything that comes into being—whether natural or artificial.[34] This center cuts the dialogue between nonvalue and value considerations. It asks us to use the art of qualitative measurement to judge the excesses and defects of the previous presentations.

The elaborate divisions of *Sophist* and *Statesman* were exercises oriented toward the philosophic *habitus* described in the middle of the *Theaetetus*: to come to know the whole nature of each with eyes fixed on the Whole. To do that, one must learn analysis and synthesis, separation and combining, displaying networks of sameness and difference so as to see how each thing fits into the Whole. One must also learn to weave together the hard and the soft, *apodeixis* and *paradeigma*, "showing from the

31. Plato, *Sophist*, 226c.
32. Plato, *Statesman*; cf. Plato, *Phaedrus*, 265e.
33. Plato, *Statesman*, 287c–305d.
34. Ibid., 383b.

top down" in terms of hierarchies of Forms and geometric demonstration but also "showing alongside" in terms of metaphors, myths, and allegories. And that Whole is not only the network of Forms; it is also the changing sets of things and circumstances where the Good, principle of the Whole and not just of the intelligible, can be instantiated. This requires the art of qualitative assessment. The *Sophist* points to the highest level of Forms involved: Being, motion, rest, sameness, and difference.[35] Being is the whole that is to be divided. Sensation presents us with things in flux, the Forms with things absolutely at rest. Sameness and difference appear throughout, both at the level of Forms and at the level of things in flux, that allows for the hierarchical dissection of Forms.

Through it all, one should also not lose sight of *thaumazein* as the divine gift of awe (the principle of the philosophic life) that deepens if inquiry proceeds properly.[36] The latter entails a growing awareness of ignorance brought about precisely by the twofold advancement of knowing: grasping the multiple ways in which Forms or types can be interrelated and learning to recognize the measure in each situation. In addition to *apodeixis* and *paradeigma*, the latter applies *phronesis* as the ability to recognize what the situation requires.[37] When one advances in these ways, one recognizes just how limited we humans are in both respects. It is precisely this awareness that provokes greater attentiveness and further inquiry at both levels. It is that which makes us an inquiring and practicing community exhibited in the dialogues and not the divine solitaries suggested by the Cave Allegory, nor the divinely omniscient shepherds invoked in the *Statesman*.

DESCARTES

It is my contention that Descartes follows the same path as the Line of Knowledge, though with a significantly different twist and with a significant narrowing of method. In his time, the overarching *doxa* of the European community had been fractured by the Reformation directed against a corrupt religious establishment and generating the bitterly fought wars that followed. Thinkers began scrambling for sources of legitimation of

35. Plato, *Sophist*, 254d.   36. Plato, *Theaetetus*, 155c.
37. Plato, *Statesman*, 283c.

their common coexistence other than the religious that was tearing them apart. One direction was suggested by mathematics, to which Descartes contributed analytical geometry.

Descartes attempted to consider all thought on the model of mathematics, beginning with clear and distinct axioms and proceeding deductively from there. Remember that Plato's Line of Knowledge moves up from the realm of Becoming to that of Being through the fixity of mathematical knowledge. Remember, too, that the Allegory of the Cave transfers attention from the limited state of sensory seeing to the total state of mind afflicting preepistemic awareness, the state of *doxa*.

Descartes, too, turns about in the Cave: he observes that we are determined by appetites within and teachers without.[38] We are creatures of biologically based desire and socially conditioned thought. He also moved from the comprehensive state of *doxa* toward the level of *episteme*, from the flux of sensation and tradition to the fixity of science whose paradigm is mathematics. Again following the path Plato trod, Descartes attempted to move to a higher level than mathematics itself but by a new method that sought a certitude even more basic than mathematics. And he hit upon a method for sorting out levels of certitude: methodic doubt.[39] It involved setting aside previous teaching, "razing" the old buildings and using some of their materials to build anew.[40] It involved putting out of play, at least until the new foundations could be secured, everything that was not *absolutely certain*. He attempted to ignore what he had learned from others and turned to the evidences available in experience. Armed with his new method, he began his examination with what is immediate in experience, the world of the senses.

As with Plato, the sensory world is the first to undergo criticism. Copernicanism cast doubt about the reliability of the senses for theoretical purposes. The readily verifiable movement of the sun around the earth is only apparent. Furthermore, studies in physics and physiology showed that seeing, for example, required a causal series initiated from light sources, with light partially absorbed and partially reflected by objects passing through the lens in the eyeball to the retina and on to the visual center in the back of the brain. It seemed obvious that color sensation was

38. Descartes, *Discourse on Method*, II, 88.
39. Ibid., IV, 101ff.
40. Ibid., II, 89.

a psychic effect produced inside the head of the observer by that causal series. So color, sound, smell, and the like are not "in" or "on" things as they appear, but are only "in" the awareness spatially inside the observer. The world of sensory experience is only apparent. This is a conclusion Descartes will draw at the end of his reflections.[41] He begins with the observation that there are perspectival distortions, optical illusions, hallucinations, and dreams. There is the phenomenon of "the phantom limb," where patients with a severed leg still feel sensations where their foot used to be.[42] And in the dream state in particular, the objects presented are every bit as charged with the index of "reality" as in the wakeful world. Descartes's conclusion is that for theoretical purposes, the sense world was not *absolutely* reliable. So, he begins his ascent out of the Cave.

Plato turned from the sensory world because it is in flux and thus seemingly cannot afford the stability involved in the kind of knowing of which mathematics is the paradigm. Descartes also makes the turn to mathematics. He, too, sees it as paradigmatic, not simply in its stability, which especially impressed Plato, but in its method: beginning with clearly and distinctly defined principles and proceeding step by step from there. That is the reason why it has gone on progressing over the ages, securing stable knowledge in one region after another, while metaphysical systems continue to battle one another. At this point, the method turns bizarre, shaking the foundations of mathematics itself by invoking the possibility of an "evil genius" manipulating our minds to make us *think* we have carried out necessary deductions.[43] Descartes admits that nobody in their right mind would "really" doubt "the world out there," much less think there really is an evil genius; the point is methodological.[44] The wildness of the hypothesis has a sober point: to force us to examine whether there is something even more certain than mathematical proof. And it is here that Descartes brings to the fore the famous *Cogito ergo sum*, the co-implication of awareness and existence as an unshatterable evidence, the self-presence of the thinker in any conscious state.[45] Descartes here is not reporting upon a particular episode in his private life: he is presenting us with an eidetic necessity. Any awareness

41. Descartes, *Meditations on First Philosophy*, VI, 191.
42. Ibid., I, 145; VI, 189.   43. *Ibid.*, 148.
44. Ibid., VI, 198–99.
45. Descartes, *Discourse on Method*, IV, 101.

capable of reflection is such that its own existence is necessarily co-given in any conscious state, no matter what the focus of awareness. The self-presence of awareness to itself is absolutely indubitable since even doubting it instantiates it.

Plato did not focus upon this self-presence directly but did so indirectly. For him, the point of attending to mathematics in developing the Line was to provide us with an example of the difference and relation between the intelligible theorem and the visible instances that instantiate it but also, correspondingly and most importantly, to provide us with the structures of the field of awareness on the side of the knower, namely, intellect and sense. The aim is to get to a clearer and more articulated grasp of "the soul." In this case, soul and awareness are identical—at least initially.

Descartes's "turn to the subject" focused more directly upon the subject that uses sense and intellect. He took a step back from Plato's focus upon "faculties" in order to attend to the self that employs them. Having anchored certitude in the conscious subject, he presented, without exploring, an inventory of the levels of its experience: sensing, feeling, desiring, imagining, remembering, understanding, judging, inferring, and choosing.[46] Whatever the status of the objects of these various acts, one cannot also doubt that things *seem* in these various ways. He thus delineated the field for phenomenological inquiry without pursuing it systematically, for his aim was to ground the certitude achieved in a still deeper ground.[47] The former was undertaken in the last century by Edmund Husserl.

Descartes noted that doubting involves imperfection and thus a contrast with perfection. As he saw it, the notion of a perfect being implicates such a being as the only adequate cause of the idea.[48] Furthermore, a perfect being is such that its essence includes existence.[49] We might try to reconstruct that a bit by considering the presupposition of the *Cogito ergo sum*, namely, the *sum*.

"I am" is a contraction of the notion of Being that contains a refer-

46. Descartes, *Meditations on First Philosophy*, I, 153.

47. Ibid., II, 153. Cf. Husserl's *Cartesian Meditations*, trans. D. Cairns (The Hague: Martinus Nijhoff, 1960), 1–6.

48. Descartes, *Meditations on First Philosophy*, III, 171.

49. Ibid., V, 180–82.

ence to all that is or can be: to everything and to everything about everything. If we ask whether Being can be limited, we move beyond any putative limit, so that the notion of Being presents itself as absolutely unlimited. I do not *possess* the infinite in the notion of Being, but I am *referred to* it and thus can recognize myself as finite. Nothing finite could cause the notion of infinite being in me, so that the only adequate cause of this idea is the Infinite Being itself. This notion of infinitely perfect Being is a development of Plato's notion of the Good as principle of the Whole.

This notion of Being is equivalent to the notion of "natural light" to which Descartes appealed as "the sign of the creator in the creature."[50] He claimed not to have included it in his methodic doubt.[51] It has a long history going back to Parmenides, Plato, Aristotle, and Aquinas. Aquinas considered "Being" to be the first thing that occurs in the intellect along with the principle of noncontradiction as having unrestricted generality.[52] Formal logic follows from the application of that principle. In Plato, the light of the mind was "the light of the Good," which, though "beyond *ousia* (beingness)," is "the most manifest region *of being (to tou ontos phanotaton)*" as the Principle of the Whole. Descartes claimed that Infinite Being is "the most manifest," even more certain than the *cogito*. This is so, I would claim, because we have to have "the natural light" as the condition for the possibility of recognizing the eidetic necessity of the *cogito*. Indeed, we have to have such "light" in order to carry out methodical inquiry, being clear on the meaning of the terms and the inferences we employ to question the various aspects of our psychic life.

From the perfection of the absolutely Infinite Being, Descartes concludes to its nondeceiving character and thus exculpates God as a possible candidate for the "evil genius."[53] Everywhere subjected to error and doubt, we could not be created by a perfect God unless two things held true: that this subjection had a purpose and that we had the ability to work our way through it to arrive at the truth. The clear and distinct recognition of both the *cogito* and the perfect God indicates that clar-

50. Ibid., III, 170.
51. Ibid., 162, and "The Second Set of Objections" in *The Philosophical Works of Descartes*, vol. II, 34–35.
52. Aquinas, *Summa Contra Gentiles*, II, ch. 83; III, ch. 2.
53. Descartes, *Meditations on First Philosophy*, III, 171.

ity and distinctness of ideas are criteria of certitude.[54] This is what we find in mathematics. Even though, like the *cogito*, mathematics needs grounding in the natural light, unlike the *cogito* it is initially subjectible to doubt. Descartes concludes that whenever we proceed methodically, beginning with clear and distinct ideas, as always in mathematics and now in the recognition of the *cogito* and of the perfect God, we can be secure in the progress of our knowing. He then proceeds to apply mathematics to the knowledge of the physical world.

That world initially makes itself known to us in sensation. And sensory appearance itself turns out on examination to be the result of measurable processes outside our bodies impinging upon our bodies, setting up the measurable physiological reactions that terminate inside the brain and there effect the states of mind we call "sensations." Such appearance happens the way it does because of the need to identify things in the environment as objects of organic need.[55] Things themselves are not sensory. When we abstract from the appearances all sensory features as events occurring in us, what is left over, so to speak, are the measurable properties. Here, Descartes is, in one sense, in the line of Aristotle, who distinguished between the proper and the common sensibles. The former are "proper" to a given sense—for example, color is the proper object of seeing and sound of hearing; they belong to things only as related to a perceiver in a distinctive mode of appearance. The common sensibles are independent of any particular sense and are common to all: motion and rest, number, dimensionality.[56] Descartes considered the Aristotelian common sensibles together under the general heading of *extension*, and he considered extension to be not, as with Aristotle, a basic property rooted in the deeper recesses of physical substance but the very essence of that substance.[57]

Similar to Plato, Descartes thus ends up with a fundamental dualism. There is the inward privacy of the *cogito* as awareness with all its modalities, beginning with the passive affects we call sensations and culminating in the activities of intellectual comprehension and choice, and there is the public character of extension wholly treatable in a mathemat-

54. Ibid., 158.
55. Ibid., VI, 194.
56. Aristotle, *On the Soul* III, 1, 425a, 15.
57. Descartes, *Meditations on First Philosophy*, V, 179.

ical manner.[58] The equality of the central segments of Plato's Line that deal with things on the lower level and mathematics on the next higher can be read as indicating that the proper intelligibility of physical things as being physical is mathematical—an insight Plato followed in the *Timaeus*.[59] Descartes carried the insight so far that he eliminated Aristotle's substantial forms and presented physical reality as a field of universal mechanism. The clear and distinct mathematization of the physical makes that world subjectible to our manipulations once we understand the mechanisms. In this way, we can become "lords and masters of nature" for the relief of the human estate. Through understanding the mechanisms, we could lessen the burden of labor by the invention of machinery, and we can improve our health through medicine, thus plucking the fruits from the Tree of Knowledge.

Descartes viewed previous tradition as a set of haphazardly constructed buildings that had to be razed before we could secure the field of methodically controlled knowledge. But he considered the possibility of using isolated materials of the tradition here and there in building the new edifice.[60] In this, he also followed Plato, who considered previous claims to know as shadows that had to be seen in relation to the fuller, more stable realities shadowed forth. But Plato developed multiple ways to that end: not only the way of mathematics or the way of diairesis, bifurcatory or otherwise but the way of dialectic. The latter was not a solitary exercise but a dialogical exercise, taking the common opinions held by the interlocutors, most often on questions of ethics—though also regarding the nature of knowing—and proceeding to question them in order to show their limits and errors. And the testing of the presuppositions and consequences of such opinions took place by appealing to certain eidetic constants present within the lifeworld. Furthermore, Plato understood well the constitutive role of metaphor in the lifeworld and the essential limitation of philosophy that called for the significant role of myth in coming to terms with the ultimate implications of our experience: death, the afterlife, and final reality. Philosophy for him remained *philosophia*, love and therefore pursuit of wisdom as knowledge of the Whole that escapes all our attempts even as it lures us on to an

58. Ibid., VI, 191.
59. Plato, *Timaeus*, see esp. 53b ff.
60. Descartes, *Discourse on Method*, II, 89.

ever more comprehensive hold on our experience and what it entails. Plato's concern was not simply with reconstructing experience through the abstract isolation of certain theoretically privileged aspects but with experience as a whole. And philosophy itself, though it contained a measure of doubt regarding traditional opinion, nonetheless was sustained by awe that increased as inquiry went forward. Such increase was tied to a knowledge of ignorance—not absolute ignorance but ignorance regarding the fullness into which one inquired, ignorance regarding what might lie beyond human limitation. Such a disposition seems poles removed from the attempt to become lords and masters of nature. Nonetheless, the project launched by Descartes led to the triumphant march of science coupled with modern technology both as the tool and fruit of modern science. It also pointed in the direction of a phenomenology that would resituate Descartes's project in the ever-encompassing lifeworld.

HEIDEGGER

As Husserl pointed out, Descartes's methodic doubt initially put out of play any affirmation of extramental existence but left open the field of experience where things *seemed* to be in a certain way.[61] Descartes himself presented us with an initial anatomical labeling of the capacities of awareness involved in the field of experience: sensing, feeling, desiring, imagining, remembering, understanding, judging, inferring, and choosing. He was following Aristotle's articulation of the field of experience further than the simple Fourfold opened up in Plato's Line.

Husserl launched phenomenology in the direction indicated but not pursued by Descartes: describing the essential features, not only of the acts and capacities involved in the field of human awareness but also and initially of their necessary correlative objects. Eventually, under the impetus of Heidegger, Husserl came to recognize the priority of the lifeworld, the Cave of *doxa* that all theoretical work presupposes.[62]

As we indicated earlier, Heidegger questioned Descartes's image of the Tree of Knowledge by asking what the soil is in which the tree is planted: what is the ground for the metaphysical roots? It turns out to

---

61. Husserl, *Cartesian Meditations*, 18–20.
62. Edmund Husserl, *The Crisis of European Sciences and Transcendental Phenomenology*, trans. D. Carr (Evanston, Ill.: Northwestern University Press, 1970), sec. 33–44.

be precisely that Cave of *doxa* out of which Plato, and after him Descartes, attempted their ascent: the historically different ways in which worlds open up for human dwelling. The Cave is precisely the fundamental mode of human reality as Being-in-the-World, beginning "outside" our putative Cartesian privacy, always involved with things in a common human world of meaning.[63]

Heidegger considered the eidetic region explored by Plato as that of the "beingness of beings," with Being as light beyond that. So, for him, we have three regions: beings, their beingness, and Being.[64] They parallel Plato's distinction between *genesis*, *ousia*, and the *agathon*, the Good as light of the intelligible world. However, in Heidegger the realm of beingness is no permanently lit stage but a function of the emergence of historical worlds of interpretation. Further, Heidegger's Being is not "the principle of the Whole" but of the revealing (and concealing) of the Whole.[65] This requires a move from eidetic inventory to hermeneutics, to interpretation of what is both revealed and concealed in differing perspectives. The turn in the hermeneutical direction takes us back into the Cave of *doxa* and into proximity with poetry.[66] As the history of philosophy demonstrates, there is no one philosophy but different modes of thinking about the Whole. (Hegel draws the opposite conclusion from that history: each philosopher, like one of the seven blind Indians in relation to the elephant, has a hold on one aspect; the task is to bring the several partial insights into one systematic whole.)[67]

Now, Husserl follows Plato's eidetic description within the framework of "seeming" presented by Descartes. Heidegger locates that move in the realm of the *Vorhanden*, the present at hand, which is a distillation out of a more primordial relationship. Before being objects of eidetic description, things are *chremata*, *pragmata*, *Zuhanden*, present-to-hand, available for our action and fitting into instrumental complexes.[68] Before

63. Heidegger, *Being and Time*, 78ff, 152.

64. Heidegger, "Plato's Doctrine of Truth," 262 and 268.

65. Martin Heidegger, *Time and Being*, trans. J. Stambaugh (New York: Harper and Row, 1972), 71.

66. See Martin Heidegger, *Poetry, Language, and Thought*, trans. A. Hofstadter (New York: Harper and Row, 1971).

67. G. W. F. Hegel, "On Philosophy," in *On Art, Religion, Philosophy*, ed. J. Glenn Gray (New York: Harper and Row, 1970), 236–55.

68. Heidegger, *Being and Time*, 95ff.

appearing focally as a distinguishable thing with describable properties, a hammer is linked to nails and lumber in the complex of relations constituting the building process and serving the purpose of providing shelter for certain human activities. A description of each of the components singly composing the hammer will not reveal what the thing is as functioning within that whole complex. Any thing is most fundamentally revealed in terms of how it fits into our inhabitance of the collective world.

For Heidegger, inhabitance is primarily a matter of disposition or mood (*Befindlichkeit*) presenting a certain attunement (*Stimmung*).[69] It has to do with how we are in time, how the past enters into the present in the light of how we project our future. Against the background of Kierkegaard's distinction between the objective thinker focused upon the what and the subjective thinker focused on the how,[70] Heidegger distinguished between appropriated (*eigentlich*) and unappropriated (*uneigentlich*) existence. The terms are usually translated by "authentic" and "inauthentic," suggesting that the latter is "phony"; however, that is not what he intends. The unappropriated is a necessary feature of human existence, an "existential." It refers to the way upbringing and tradition shape awareness even before we come to reflect and choose: we think and act as "they" think and act. It is evident in the fact that each of us spontaneously speaks his or her native language: we speak the language that "they" speak. One lives in "average everydayness" necessary for the coordinated existence of a people. This involves a mode of communication in which it is never clear what is truly manifest and what is just what "they" say." But it also involves a kind of personal drift. One moves into the future in a mode of curiosity, attracted now by this project, now by that, especially by what is "in."

By contrast, appropriated existence involves a kind of existential bracketing of this modality of inhabiting the common world. It is brought about by running ahead to the ultimate term of one's own being in the world: one's inevitable death. One opens oneself to being taken by this thought in a "moment of vision" where it becomes no longer a mere thought but a presence. This returns one to the present in a transformed way, allowing for projecting one's future with a sense of ultimate perspective, resolutely

---

69. Ibid., 134–42.
70. Kierkegaard, *Concluding Unscientific Postscript to Philosophical Fragments*, 181ff.

taking over direction of one's life by retrieving the possibilities afforded by one's tradition. For Heidegger, personally, that involves commitment to a life of philosophic reflection.

Such reflection is itself rooted in certain dispositions. What carries the philosophic tradition at its inception is wonder as awe that is deepened as inquiry proceeds.[71] But that is gradually replaced by methodic doubt and the development of certitude and then turned into making demands on nature to serve our projects.[72] However, the project of mastery was implicit in Plato. In the *Timaeus*, the Forms are viewed as archetypes for the demiurgic construction of the world within the chaotic Receptacle of space-time. Heidegger speaks here of the productive essence of traditional metaphysics.[73] Conceptual mastery is parallel to, antecedes, and portends technological mastery. Modern scientific methodology, rooted in Descartes's approach to nature, plays in tandem with experimental manipulation. The history of thought is the working out of that technological essence.

Heidegger himself seeks another beginning rooted in another disposition. It is the disposition of "startled dismay" (*Erschrecken*) at the "forgottenness of Being" from the very beginning and its progressive occlusion as time goes on.[74] Finally, we reach our own epoch where Being is not simply forgotten but is drained from our experience. Our very success in uncovering and inventing more and more through modern technological science has led to the view that only such uncovering is important. But scientific-technological uncovering is not only simply one mode of uncovering but is a mode that occludes the practitioner as a living person who operates out of a "sense of Being." Heidegger claims that such a sense develops in the "Play of the Fourfold"—a different play than that involved in Plato's Line. Heidegger's Fourfold brings together our belonging to the earth under the regular measure of the sky, aware of our essential mortality and open to "the Most High," whatever form that might take.[75] It is a sense sustained by a peculiar mode of thinking that

71. Martin Heidegger, *What Is Philosophy?*, trans. W. Klubach and J. Wilde (New York: Twayne, 1958), 78–85.

72. Heidegger, *The Question Concerning Technology and Other Essays*, 85.

73. Martin Heidegger, *The Basic Problems of Phenomenology*, trans. A. Hofstadter (Bloomington: Indiana University Press, 1982), 106ff.

74. Martin Heidegger, *Contributions to Philosophy: From Enowning*, trans. Parvis Emad and Kenneth Maly (Bloomington: Indiana University Press, 2000), 11.

75. Martin Heidegger, "Building, Dwelling, Thinking," 49–51.

Heidegger contraposes to the thinking that belongs to philosophy, mathematics, science, and scholastic (as distinct from monastic) theology. The latter inquires and arranges methodologically, aiming at mastery.[76] The former thinking does not follow a method but rather a way.[77] The way is "meditative" (*besinnliche Nachdenken*), aimed not, as with the predominant modes, at mastery, whether conceptual or technological, but at "letting things be" (*Gelassenheit*) and thus of being mastered. Its more widespread mode of articulation is poetry. But it also silently governs the great philosophers as well. It dwells in the sense of the Mystery of Being. The sense of this Mystery is the element in which we humans naturally live.

Since Being has been progressively drained from our experience, precisely under the influence of "productive metaphysics," we have become like fish out of water, floundering and gasping for air.[78] The metaphor is not unrelated to Nietzsche's announcement of the death of God when the madman asks, "Who has given us the sponge to soak up the sea?"[79] The metaphor of the sea as the element in which sea creatures live parallels St. Paul's notion of God "in whom we live and move and have our being." Though Being is not God, it is the element within which we draw near to the divine.[80] Today, we live in an epoch of the flight of the gods and the darkening of the earth.[81] It is an epoch that provokes "startled dismay" in those sensitively attuned.

In spite of the general oblivion of *Seyn* (Heidegger's archaic Being) throughout the philosophic and scientific traditions, in past times, having a place for the Holy put people in contact with the environing ground that philosophy both fed off of and disregarded. Even further today, not only is that environing ground unheeded philosophically but, because of the result of the tradition, our relation to it has virtually dried up. In the startling expression of the *Introduction to Metaphysics*, today things have "lost their being" and have become data standing as reserve for our projects.[82]

---

76. Martin Heidegger, "Memorial Address," in *Discourse on Thinking*, trans. J. Anderson and E. Freund (New York: Harper and Row, 1966), 45–47.

77. Martin Heidegger, *On the Way to Language*, trans. P. Hertz (New York: Harper and Row, 1971), 90ff.

78. Heidegger, "Letter on Humanism," 272.

79. Friedrich Nietzsche, *The Gay Science*, 3, #125, trans. W. Kaufmann (New York: Vintage, 1974), 181–82.

80. Heidegger, "Letter on Humanism," 293–94.

81. Martin Heidegger, *Introduction to Metaphysics*, trans. G. Fried and R. Polt (New Haven, Conn.: Yale University Press, 2000), 40.

82. Ibid., 66.

Obviously, that cannot mean that they have vanished. It means rather that they no longer rise up to meet us out of the unfathomable depths of their belonging to the all-encompassing.

The direction in which Heidegger moves reverses the direction of Western thought set in motion by Plato and pointed toward its culminating phase in Descartes. The dispositions that guide thought are explored in a work celebrated as his second great classic after *Being and Time: Contributions to Philosophy: On Enowning.*[83]

Heidegger calls the basic divisions of his *Beiträge* "Sechs Fügungen der Fuge," translated now as "six joinings of the jointure" (57). But *Fuge* can also be translated as "fugue," as in Bach's *Tocatta and Fugue*. Hence, we translate: "six articulations of the fugue." They are: playing forth (*Zuspiel*), echo (*Anklang*), leap (*Sprung*), ground (*Grund*), the ones to come (*Zukünftigen*), and the last God (*der letzte Gott*). The first four are metaphors. Playing forth and echo are musical terms. The first relates directly to the musical fugue as a matter of counterpoint. The counterpoint in Heidegger's thought concerns what he calls the "beginning" (*Anfang*), of which he identifies two that are to play in relation to one another: that which initiated Western thought and the "other beginning" that he claims to be initiating. The dispositional root of the first beginning—expressed in Plato's *Theaetetus*—is *thaumazein*, wonder as awe, a gift of the god Thaumas. The second is Heidegger's distinctive experience that he calls *Erschrecken*, translated as "startled dismay." What he means by "Being" is experienced as an echo, implying a sense both of emptiness and of something derivative. Both awe and startled dismay entail something negative. Awe involves the awareness of not-knowing, startled dismay of not being grounded or rooted. But awe seems to involve an awareness of plenitude, whereas startled dismay seems akin to despair.

Both dispositions are articulations of what Heidegger calls *Verhaltenheit*, translated as "reservedness" and that also is the ground of care.[84] There is a distinction between, on the one hand, a kind of native distance grounding the care that absorbs us in the everyday world against the background of the unsettledness of the question of one's being as a temporal whole[85] and, on the other hand, a peculiar sort of distance from

---

83. Wood, "The Fugal Lines of Heidegger's *Beiträge*."
84. Heidegger, *Contributions to Philosophy*, 25, 34.
85. Heidegger, *Being and Time*, 227–44.

that which can lead us to remain silently attuned to stillness. It involves a certain mode of reflectiveness, a withdrawal into a mode of listening in and to stillness. Reservedness involves a certain inward, reflective distance from our involvements in order to be taken up in a different way: the way of wonder or the way of dismay as dispositional grounds of the first and other beginning, respectively. The first beginning sets in motion the metaphysical tradition.

The other beginning that Heidegger sets in motion seeks a ground beneath the ground of the tradition of metaphysics: he calls it the *Abgr-und*.[86] It is correlate to the sense of unencompassable Mystery that surrounds our lives and exceeds all our conquests, speculative and practical. Like Kierkegaard's faith, it requires a leap (*Sprung*) assisted by a kind grace, a gift from above for which can only remain open.[87] Living in the silent sense of Mystery, we prepare the way for those who are to come and for the announcement of the ultimate God—presumably something like Paul Tillich's the "God beyond God."

However, we must underscore that all of this takes place within the counterpoint between the first and the other beginning. Both the following out of what has been correctly asserted in the metaphysical tradition and attention to its own "Abground" in the surrounding Mystery are required. The tradition is not repudiated but set into its ultimate context. As in music, the meaning is not something we see but something we hear—something to which we are attuned. And, as in music, it is our dispositions that are the key to understanding.

If I may quote my previous work:

The six fugal themes name encompassing features that we have to become attuned to, learn to inhabit, rather than to define. They interrelate as melodic themes to form the single whole that is the fugue of concrete Being-in-the-World. In music, each note and each line sets up harmonic reverberations with every other note and line. "Fugal hearing" is a matter, as it is in music, of allowing one to be carried by the interplay of the melodic lines and harmonic modulations into the set of felt dispositions evoked by the music; it is a matter of being carried into the felt unity of the whole fugue.

To play counterpoint to logic launched on its career by Plato and Aristotle,

---

86. Heidegger, *Contributions to Philosophy*, 23, 209, 271.
87. Ibid., 161ff.

Heidegger here coins the term "sigetic" from the Greek term for "silence," *sige*:[88] silence is set over against the clash of disputation and the clattering of the apparatus of inference whereby we come to master our experience—necessary as these may be. Silence opens us to being mastered, listening for the opportune moment and the right word like a stone dropped into the unrippled surface of a pond. Silence focuses upon the uniqueness of what opens up in the mode of letting things be[89] as opposed to the thrust of conceptual mastery. "Silent listening to the stillness flows from *Verhaltenheit*."[90]

The crucial distinction involved in all this is that between two modes of truth that Heidegger sees indicated by two Greek terms for truth: *aletheia* and *orthotes*, literally, unconcealment and correctness. The latter pertains to what can be verified within a given framework. Thus, Descartes's more focused methodological conquests and Plato's broader "phenomenological" and dialogical achievements as well as Husserl's more precise eidetic descriptions are each contained within certain horizons or modes of "unconcealment." Within such horizons, particular formulations can be developed that are verifiable, that correspond to what shows itself when we pay peculiar attention. But such horizons stand within the ultimate horizon of the lifeworld, what Plato had seemed to disparage as mere *doxa* over against the more reflectively verifiable domain of *episteme*. For Heidegger, the ground of such perspectival achievements lies in the uncovering of the framework that itself emerges out of concealment. But the latter, the *lethe*, remains permanently beyond any framework we can develop. Dwelling for humans has to do with how we retain a place for the *lethe*, the permanently hidden in our lifeworlds.

Heidegger thinks Being, the Abground or Ground of the ground of the tradition, in the direction indicated by Plato's notion of the Good as *to on* beyond *ousia*, as being beyond beingness and thus beyond intellect and its epistemic conquests. However, Heidegger challenges the underlying presupposition of permanent presence belonging both to the Good and to the intelligible that allegedly situates the whole region outside of time and becoming. For Plato, what we have at the level of beingness is a permanently lit stage. But for Heidegger, on the contrary, Being is time—

---

88. Ibid., 54–55.
89. Heidegger, "Memorial Address," 46–54.
90. Wood, "The Fugal Lines of Heidegger's *Beiträge*," 255.

or rather time-play-space that involves revealing *and* concealing in ever-differing ways.

If I may quote my previous work once more:

Heidegger's work involves a *Schritt zurück*, a step back from all this work of uncovering and systematizing to point to its deepest presupposition in the sense of Being, which remains essentially covered. What is uncovered in eidetic analysis, deduction, and systematization has its own necessity and we are called to follow it out; but it is not basic enough, does not go deeply enough to what we as humans fundamentally *are*. In Heidegger's terms, all this might be correct, that is, verifiable and masterable, but it leaves aside the question of the original opening, the *aletheia* that it necessarily presupposes. And it is not *representing* to ourselves this opening that is at stake; it is rather meditatively *dwelling* in it. This involves a leap into the grounding of the tradition. And such a leap entails a reversal of disposition: from mastering to being mastered, from transforming to letting be.[91]

Heidegger may be envisioned as moving from our world of scientific-technological mastery back to its grounds in Descartes's project of methodological mastery. But, he moves back further to Descartes's own grounding in the mode of unconcealment represented by Plato's Line of Knowledge. And he moves back beyond Plato to the ground of the Western rational-scientific project in the lifeworld as the *doxa* of a community. The trick is to find a place for the *lethe* in the world of omnivorous technology. And the way back to the ground draws close to the arts as "the saving grace" in an era of darkening and alienation.[92] But in this, Heidegger is also close to Plato's own practice as a literary master who employed metaphors, allegories, and myths and fed off of a sense of encompassing and pervading Beauty to reinvigorate the lifeworld and sustain a sense of encompassing Mystery implied in the notion of *philosophia* as a perpetual aspiration guided by a sense of lack.[93]

91. Ibid., 265.

92. Heidegger, *The Question Concerning Technology and Other Essays*, 35.

93. For a comparison of Plato with Heidegger and Nietzsche on art and truth, see my "Art and Truth: Plato, Nietzsche, Heidegger," in *On Truth: Studies of a Robust Presence*, ed. K. Pritzl (Washington, D.C.: The Catholic University of America Press, 2009). It is reprinted in this text.

7 ∽ Art and Truth

Plato, Nietzsche, and Heidegger

Plato and Heidegger stand at two ends of the philosophic tradition. Plato launched metaphysics as the search for the truth of the Whole; Heidegger attempted to get back to the ground of metaphysics after it reached its supposed end—in one sense in Hegel and in another sense in Nietzsche. Crucial to Plato is the struggle of philosophy with art over the basis of human existence. The infamous line in the tenth book of the *Republic* places art "three degrees removed from truth (*aletheia*)."[1] It provides images of images of things that are themselves images of the "beingly beings," the Forms. Artists decorate the Cave; they provide the basic *doxa* of a community regarding what is high and low in human existence. They filter and distort the intelligible realm, which alone can provide the true measure of human existence.

Contrasted to Plato, Heidegger claims that metaphysics is not the fundamental mode of thinking of Being. He finds a further ground for metaphysics itself: it lies precisely in the Cave, that is, in our prephilosophic mode of Being-in-the-World, our inhabiting a common way of understanding and acting formed out of a tradition determined essentially by the poets.[2]

Crucial for our purposes is Plato's view that the relation between philosophy and poetry is one of subordination of the latter to the former. Philosophy is the censor of poetry because it grasps Being, whereas poetry creates and is subject to appearance. For Heidegger, on the contrary, the relation between philosophy and poetry is one of coordination evoked in the image of the occupants of twin peaks equidistant from the valley

1. Plato, *Republic*, X, 597e.
2. Martin Heidegger, "The Way Back into the Ground of Metaphysics," in *Pathmarks*, ed. W. McNeill (Cambridge: Cambridge University Press, 1998), 277–90.

of everydayness. Poets and philosophers are both *deinoi, unheimlich,* uncanny, distant from being-at-home and thus able to create for the first
time a new or renewed mode of being-at-home. Both struggle with appearance for the sake of Being. The philosopher thinks "Being" while the
poets proclaim "the Holy."[3]

In between Plato and Heidegger is Nietzsche, who lashed out against
what he saw as the disparagement of temporal and bodily existence in
Platonism and Christianity, who attempted to get behind the tradition to
its motivational sources, and who substituted perspectivism for absolute
truth.[4] Nietzsche called for the study of knowing from the viewpoint of
art and the viewpoint of life.[5] For Nietzsche, we have art lest we perish of
truth, the supposed object of religion and traditional philosophy; indeed,
art is higher than truth.

In this chapter, we will examine the position of each thinker in turn
on the nature of and relation between truth and art. We will attempt to
point out the way in which each subsequent thinker is both critical of and
crucially assimilates what preceded them. But we do so not to perform
some antiquarian scholarly exercise but to come into an essential relation
to the matters considered. We will do that explicitly in the conclusion. We
begin with Plato.

PLATO

Plato's major treatment of art is in his *Republic,* and his major explicit
treatment of art and truth is in Book X of that dialogue. There, poetry
appears not as it did earlier in terms of its civic exemplarity but in terms
of its truth-content. It is measured against the hierarchy displayed in the
Cave and in the Line of Knowledge: images and things in the Cave surmounted by mathematicals, the Forms, and the Good outside the Cave.
It is here that the question of truth emerges—the truth that would allow
us to assess the civic.

In his Book X assessment, Socrates uses a very odd device, a dou-

---

3. Prologue to Heidegger, "The Way Back into the Ground of Metaphysics."
4. Friedrich Nietzsche, *Beyond Good and Evil,* trans. W. Kaufmann (New York: Vintage,
1966), 3.
5. Friedrich Nietzsche, "Attempt at a Self-Criticism," 1886 preface to 1872 *The Birth of Tragedy,* trans. W. Kaufmann (New York: Vintage, 1967), 2/19.

ble metaphor. His immediate target is poetry, but he relates poetry to claims about painting, indicating something of his attitude toward the arts beyond the poetic. He compares poetry with painting and painting with mirroring. Anticipating the invention of the camera, he says that one can become a painter of everything visible by simply holding up a mirror.[6] What one gets is an exact replica of the perspective afforded by the mirror: an image of a perspective, itself a subject-dependent image of a thing. But the thing whose perspective is mirrored is itself, in turn, metaphorically speaking, an image, since it is, ontologically speaking, a spatiotemporal instantiation of its Form. Without the accessibility of the Form, we can gawk at but not understand the true being of the thing. Hence, he says that painting, an image of a perspective of a thing, itself an image of a Form, is "three degrees removed from truth." Socrates applies the observation to poetry as a kind of verbal mirroring that exemplifies the same allegedly superficial relation to reality as painting.

In introducing his disparaging discussion of poetry in Book X, Socrates allows that a case might still be made for it—although he does not subsequently make it.[7] Instead, he concludes the work by practicing it, concocting the myth of Er, whose vision of the afterlife inspired Virgil, Dante, and Milton and through them the entire Christian tradition of thinking imaginatively about the afterlife.[8] The myth is a mode of fictional fantasy, creating a World that never was and never will be. Fantasy fiction removes us from the encrustations of everyday existence and creates a disposition evoked by the novel context in which certain features found otherwise in everyday existence become particularly prominent. In the myth in question, its working creates a disposition that calls for a decision with regard to life as a whole.[9] The same observation might be applied to art in general: it creates certain dispositions to behave that affect our life-conduct.

One might also note that when we come to the ultimate questions of human and cosmic origins and ends, Plato turns to myth. The myth of Er concerns human destiny as does the parallel myth of the judgment of the dead concluding the *Gorgias*.[10] The *mythos* of the *Timaeus* concerns

---

6. Plato, *Republic*, X, 596d. For a more comprehensive approach to the location of the aesthetic in Plato's thought, see my *Placing Aesthetics* (Athens: Ohio University Press, 1999), ch. 2.

7. Plato, *Republic*, X, 608a.   8. Ibid., 614b.

9. Ibid., 617e–619a.   10. Plato, *Gorgias*, 523a.

cosmic origin,[11] as does the myth of cosmic reversal in the *Statesman*.[12] Even the notion of the ultimate principle perennially intersecting time, the Good of the *Republic*, announced as beyond the impetus that carried the discussion, is presented in an image that itself suggests inaccessibility: the sun which, as the *Laws* reminds us, would blind us were we to attempt to stare at it.[13] All of this suggests a limit to conceptuality, a beyond in relation to which we move but that we can only hermeneutically explore though mythopoiesis.

In the *Republic*, the myth or Er is not the only place where Plato exhibits his poetic practice. Looking back at the *Republic* as a whole, we see that he functions throughout as a literary artist, not only in the way he draws his characters or the way he uses allegory and parable but also in his selection of the overarching metaphors that structure the entire work: up and down, light and darkness, culminating in their supreme employment in the allegory of the Cave. The very first word, *Kateben*, "I went down"—namely, to the Peiraeus—and its shortly appearing correlative, "going up"—namely, back to the city—announce the melodic theme.[14] The subsequent dialogue occurs in the darkness of night, with the passing of the torch of argument from interlocutor to interlocutor as a substitute for the promised torchlight procession on horseback. The main argument ascends from the city of simple need through the luxurious city to the purged city and up, beyond the city to the philosopher-king and the Cave allegory, illustrating the final ascent to the cosmic highpoint, the Good as illuminating source. Then the argument moves down from aristocratic monarchy through the declining correlative regime- and character-forms to tyranny. It concludes with a descent into the darkness of Hades in the myth of Er.

Here—and indeed in ordinary language—the metaphors up and down, light and darkness become value terms. Evaluation involves more than what we would rationally conclude. The metaphor draws upon the felt associations of the terms and thus makes more of an appeal to "the whole soul," to our spontaneous attractions and felt proclivity to behave. This observation helps to clarify the enigmatic question qualifying the procedure adopted at the end of the first major argument conclud-

11. Plato, *Timaeus*, 29d.
13. Plato, *Laws*, X, 897d.

12. Plato, *Statesman*, 269b.
14. Plato, *Republic*, I, 327a.

ing in Book IV of the *Republic*, where Socrates introduces the tripartite division of the soul: "What if there is something we do with the whole soul?"[15] (We will return to that later.)

However, more than the metaphor, aesthetic form, the configuration of the sensuous in *musike* or fine art in general, is said to reach most deeply into the soul.[16] The dispositional tuning brought about by literary art is accompanied and, indeed, we would maintain, deepened by the arts that feature the distinctive aesthetic qualities cultivated in the purged city. Socrates's analysis there works in terms of a distinction between the referents of poetry and its aesthetic form.[17] Though he spends by far the most time purging the content of poetic tales regarding gods and heroes, it is not truth that is at stake but civic exemplarity. It is not expedient, he says, to tell tales of gods and heroes doing unseemly things, "*even if they are true.*"[18] Furthermore, it is necessary to tell "noble lies" in order to hold the city together dispositionally.[19] And since the center of the dialogue transcends the city, progressively ascending and thus widening the view to consider all Greeks,[20] then all humankind,[21] then all time and being,[22] and finally the principle of the Whole announced as an incomparable Beauty,[23] since all this is so, we need to attend to those aspects of the purgation that allow an ascent from the city. We find these, I would claim, in the consideration of aesthetic form, something that Socrates completely ignores in his final disparagement of art.

In his discussion of purged art, Socrates contraposes what Nietzsche will later term the Apollonian and the Dionysian in his distinction between contrasting musical modes and instrumental timbres accompanying poetry. He considers them in terms of how they affect disposition. The Apollonian is characterized by order, restraint, good proportion, harmony, and gracefulness, and the Dionysian by wild abandon.[24] Each form imprints its respective characteristics on those who let it sink into their souls. Socrates advocates the Apollonian and discounts the Diony-

---

15. Ibid., IV, 436b.

16. Ibid., III, 401d.

17. Ibid., 398d.

18. Plato, *Republic*, II, 378a; emphasis added.

19. Ibid., III, 414c.

20. Ibid., V, 470a.

21. Ibid., 473d.

22. Ibid., VI, 486a.

23. Ibid., 509a.

24. Plato, *Republic*, III, 398d ff. Nietzsche's distinction appears in Nietzsche, *The Birth of Tragedy*, 1/33ff.

sian as preparing the ground for the emergence of reflective rationality.[25]

He adds to his discussion of music a significant extension of the Apollonian dimension and a most significant claim as to the role of art in human life that was taken up, among others, by the proponents of the International Style in modern architecture. The Apollonian features are extended to the whole of the visual ambiance. He says that the citizenry should be surrounded from birth to death by *visual* artifacts that have Apollonian properties. Here he lists buildings, clothing, utensils, furniture, and—most important for our purposes—*painting.*[26] According to Socrates, all these artifacts should have what today would be called good design properties. It is particularly important to underscore painting, for what is at stake here is not, as it was in Book X, what it represents but how it is organized, for that has a significant effect on disposition. Contrasted with Book X, here Socrates abstracts completely from the referents and focuses solely upon aesthetic form.

It is in relation to this that Socrates announces—somewhat surprisingly for the training of the military—that *paideia* at this level culminates in beautiful erotic objects (*eis ta tou kalou erotika*).[27] One could read this as a contrast with the luxurious city where the proliferating multiplicity of art forms is geared to appetitive pandering.[28] The soul is chained to subjectivistic wallowing in fine feelings, whether produced by music and painting or by wine and gourmet food—or today by electrode implants through which laboratory animals can give themselves pleasing sensations whenever they wish without engaging the normal objects evoking those feelings. Purged disposition is produced by a turning around of the soul, unchaining it from subjection to appetitive gratification, and focusing it outside upon beautiful objects. *Paideia* at this level evokes an Eros that is focused upon things rather than upon gratification—or perhaps better, gratification follows from focusing attention upon the beautiful objects rather than, as in the luxurious city, upon one's own gratification. As with Aristotle, the pleasure is "the bloom on activity," and not the ground of the activity.[29]

25. Plato, *Republic*, III, 402a. In the *Laws*, Plato has the Athenian Stranger back off the disparagement of the Dionysian, claiming that even such musical form gives some order to the chaos of emotions experienced by adolescents.

26. Plato, *Republic*, III, 401a.   27. Ibid., 403c.

28. Ibid., II, 372c ff.

29. Aristotle, *Nicomachean Ethics*, X, 1175b 33.

We should underscore the coupling of this aesthetic purgation with hard gymnastic exercise. The original basis offered for this is military, as is the purgation of the referents of traditional poetry. But the final ground lies in the counterpoint between dispositional traits: the softness of sensitivity produced by aesthetic training and the hardness of the courageous disposition produced by gymnastics. Too much *musike* makes one effete; too much gymnastics makes one brutish. The right blend of the two—and not simply *musike*—produces that disposition that, Socrates says, will welcome *nous* when it arises.[30] We might say that the body as a coherent whole is an existent rational system. But the emotions rising out of it tend in a chaos of directions (we suggest because they arise in an awareness that, being set at a distance from them, has to take over their organization). The tandem development of gymnastics and exposure to the Apollonian arts produce a harmonious disposition in what otherwise would be a chaos of emotions. Harmonic disposition arising out of a coherently functioning organism shaped by proper training, being rationality incarnate, that is, harmonic, coherently functioning, will allow us to recognize explicit reason when it arises.

Socrates compares the soul formed by such training with the image of the spinning top.[31] When the upright position is found, the motions on the bodily based emotional periphery support that position; but when it is lost, the soul tips and wobbles until the peripheral motions, touching the ground, drag the soul erratically, now this way, now that, without order. However, at the point in Book IV where this is introduced, what "upright" means is in accordance with civic exemplarity ruled over by merely calculative, logistical intelligence, intelligence that "looks down." But in this context, too, Socrates warns that, though they have reached an apparent highpoint in the argument, the entire approach has been defective.[32] Indeed, the tripartite division of the soul that guides the discussion at the conclusion to the exposition of the three cities is placed in question by raising the possibility of doing something with one's whole soul. That forecasts what is to come in the center of the dialogue.

Without the warning that the approach has been defective, the central books of the *Republic* seem at first blush to be an afterthought.[33] What

---

30. Plato, *Republic*, III, 410c.   31. Ibid., IV, 436e.

32. Ibid., 434d, 435d,437a.

33. See the discussion in Richard Lewis Nettleship, *Lectures on the Republic of Plato* (London: MacMillan, 1964), 162ff.

propels the inquiry is a feature of the psyche that was initially placed together with desire for food and drink as occupying the basement of the
soul but that the *Symposium* presents as the love of the mortal for the immortal, namely Eros.[34] In that dialogue, Eros both propels one to creativity in the city and transcends the city in the direction of the manifestation
of the deathless order governing the cosmos.[35] Socrates's interlocutors are
interested in his claim, made in passing, that in order to avoid the guard-
ians' favoring of their own families, they should not have nuclear families but should have women and children in common.[36] Understanding
the prurience of their interest, Socrates delays addressing the issue and
frames it between two other issues they did not expect: the equality of
women and men and the need for philosopher-kings. Regarding the first,
he tells them that women and men are equal in basic capacity and should
therefore be given equal education.[37] I take that to mean that women
are not simply the sexual playthings of men but their equals—though
Socrates panders to the prurient interest of the interlocutors by promising
sexual favors to those who perform most courageously right up to the introduction of the philosopher-king that alters the whole landscape.

Pertinent to our overall theme and leaning on the erotic interest,
Socrates introduces the philosopher as a peculiar kind of lover: in contrast to the lovers of beautiful things cultivated in the purged city, the
philosopher is a lover of the vision of Beauty itself.[38] An aesthetic feature
lies at the heart of the philosophic endeavor. He does not elaborate on his
claim at this point. However, anticipating the Line of Knowledge where
it will appear again, he goes on to distinguish opinion from knowledge.
When he presents the Good as the special object of philosophic study,
he says that it is an "incomparable Beauty," linking it back to the initial
characterization of the philosopher as a lover of Beauty itself.[39] I would
maintain that this, in turn, hearkens back to the discussion of the peculiar dispositional matrix balancing *musike* and gymnastics and finally
underpinning philosophy as a way of life.

---

34. Plato, *Republic*, IV 437b. Here, Eros is implicit as occupying the lowest level; it is made
explicit in IX, 573b.

35. The nature of Eros is announced in Diotima's speech in Plato, *Symposium*, 296b.

36. Plato, *Republic*, V, 449c, referring back to IV, 423e.

37. Ibid., 451c.   38. Ibid., 476b.

39. Ibid., VI, 509a.

Here we rejoin the first city—the healthy city deemed Pigsville by Glaucon, who ignores the dimension enunciated in the hymns to the gods.[40] Beyond biological need, the hymns involve the human reconstruction of sound according to discovered harmonic relations that produce dispositionally a way of interpreting the character of the Whole and the hierarchies that are taken to prevail within it. But at the center of the dialogue, the anthropomorphism involved is transformed. What articulates the umbrella of meaning is not the domain of some ethnically specific anthropomorphism; it is the realm of Forms, objects of eidetic insight.

Incomparable Beauty, the Good is also and centrally described as that which grants access to the Forms by furnishing the light of *aletheia* for the relation between intellect and the intelligible.[41] Translating *aletheia* simply as "truth" tells us little. Translating it according to Heidegger's perhaps specious etymology as "unconcealment" and, as Socrates does, linking it metaphorically to light as well as placing it beyond the intelligible as its source invites us to think of *aletheia* as a space of openness or manifestation.[42]

As the Good is identified with Beauty and the source of *aletheia*, it is also presented as *epekeina tes ousias*, beyond *ousia* as the realm of the correlation between *nous* and the *noeta*. I suggest at least two reasons for this "beyondness." First, as principle of the Whole,[43] the Good is beyond the intelligible because it binds together the Whole as the interplay of the intelligible and the sensible, the universal and the individual instance, the eternal and the temporal. Second, the Good is beyond as "incomparable Beauty" because it is the object, not of *nous* but of *Eros*. It is, I suggest, the activity of Eros that we perform "with our whole soul" according to Socrates's hesitation in his introduction of the tripartite division of the soul in the fourth book. Indeed, in the *Phaedrus* he makes that identification explicit.[44] One might say that the truth available to *nous* is exceeded by the erotic relationship to the Beauty that makes the truth

40. Ibid., II, 372b.

41. Ibid., VI, 508e.

42. Martin Heidegger, *The Essence of Truth*, trans. T. Sadler (London: Continuum, 2002), 9. Heidegger's etymology has been contested by philologists such as Friedlaender (*Plato*); but, as Hans Jonas notes (*The Phenomenon of Life*), the philosophic point remains. Cf. also John Caputo, *Demythologizing Heidegger* (Bloomington: Indiana University Press, 1993).

43. Plato, *Republic*, VI, 511b.

44. Plato, *Phaedrus*, 251c.

available in a way that draws upon our total dispositional state. This involves a kind of sublimated Dionysian. The erotic is not simply subrational as presented in the description of the three cities but is capable of transrational sublimation. This is so because it is the Eros of a soul whose higher power is *nous* but whose highest power is Eros itself aimed at the Principle of the Whole. It is only when the soul is harmonious—internally beautiful—and suffused with Eros that we can be in a position to let the sunlight of Beauty open to us the harmony of the cosmos, the great sea of beauty revealed in the togetherness of the sciences.[45]

I take that to mean that, though one might be able to discover piecemeal truths and achieve regional disclosures, one cannot understand the overall harmony of the cosmos unless one is dispositionally and simultaneously tuned to beauty and to courageous action over one's whole life. We would maintain that, insofar as *aletheia* is linked with beauty as the correlate to Eros, the arts play a significant role in turning Eros upward. We might call this the "truing" of our internal life. It involves a harmoniously tuned disposition of hardness and softness, of courage and acceptance, of resoluteness and letting-be, focused upon Apollonian properties suffused with Dionysian Eros. Such a focus mediates the presence of Beauty itself as the radiance of the Good that grounds the comprehensive rationality sought in philosophy. The relation between the hard and soft dispositions finds echo in the combination of philosophy and kingship. Socrates claims that such a combination is superior to the pursuit of either in isolation.[46] But whereas philosophy might lean more toward the receptive, kingship would lean more toward the aggressive: form-imposing rather than Form-viewing.

Such a vision inevitably clashes with the poetic proclamations that produced the anthropomorphic gods. For Plato, the tradition articulated and governed by poetic awareness is that upon which we are typically fixed or to which we are chained. He represents it by shadows on a cave wall projected by puppets carried by men and gods. He calls it the realm of *doxa*.[47] This is usually translated as "opinion," but it has a wider meaning. *Doxa* is etymologically related to *dokein*, "to seem." The main argument of the *Republic* is framed by the mental experiment of doing

---

45. Plato, *Symposium*, 210d.
47. Ibid., VII, 534a.

46. Plato, *Republic*, VI, 473d.

away with *doxa* and, after the main argument is concluded, restoring the *doxa*.[48] In this context, it is sometimes translated here as "reputation" but has a broader implication. When the experiment is introduced, Glaucon refers to the ring worn by the shepherd Gyges that caused him to disappear from the vision of others when he turned the signet inside the hand.[49] *Doxa* consequently means here the total realm of "appearance" in which we live, the *Lebenswelt*. The appearance of human beings within the lifeworld allows for the *reputation* one gains by having one's actions visible to others so they can form their *opinion* of them. Appearing in a way that solicits honor from others is standing in *glory*.[50] *Doxa* thus comes to mean—in an interconnected set of meanings—seeming, reputation, opinion, and glory. It is poets, masters of appearance, and those they hymn—gods and heroes—that, appearing in the sensuous, stand in the light of glory. Plato as the literary artist, through imagery and myth and through the defense of Apollonian art forms, glorifies Socrates and brings the truth that is beyond, here in the space of sensuousness. But he does so in such a way as to challenge traditional poetry in the light of the intellectual-erotic ascent.

Plato gives his extended treatment of Eros in the *Phaedrus* and the *Symposium*. In the latter, art is not the focus (nor in both dialogues, we might add, is the beauty of nonhuman nature focal, except in passing in the first part of the *Phaedrus*).[51] In their treatment of Eros, the dialogues are focused upon the beauty of the human body as the starting point for the erotic ascent.[52]

The *Phaedrus* is centrally about the art of rhetoric. The three speeches on Eros are introduced as illustrative of rhetorical practice, but one might also have it illustrated by exhortatory and forensic examples. In the view of the relation between art and Eros we are presenting, the example chosen is not indifferent. The deepest employment of rhetoric is to evoke the fundamental Eros of the human soul. Rhetoric, as *techne psychagogia*, "leads" the soul; but Socrates clearly places it in subordina-

48. Ibid., II, 367b; X, 612b ff.

49. Ibid., 359d.

50. Heidegger calls attention to this interrelation of meaning for *doxa* in *Introduction to Metaphysics*, trans. G. Fried and R. Polt (New Haven, Conn.: Yale University Press, 2000), 108–10.

51. Plato, *Phaedrus*, 230b–e.

52. Plato, *Symposium*, 210b; Plato, *Phaedrus*, 251a.

tion to philosophy as the depository of the true direction of the soul toward the truth itself. [53] However, the chief public locus for the practice of
rhetoric, the court, cares not for the truth but for what is convincing.[54] In
employing the poetic devices that move the soul, Plato's practice puts us
in the kind of dispositional state that opens out to the truth.

In the *Symposium*, art is treated only in passing. In Diotima's discussion of the so-called lesser mysteries of love, art is one of the forms that
eventuate from the erotic desire of the mortal for the immortal. Sublimated Eros leads to the creation of immortal works that live on in glory
through the appreciation of future generations.[55] In the so-called higher mysteries, on the ladder of ascent to Beauty itself we find character-
forming institutions and sciences that measure character, institutions,
and the World of bodies generally but with no explicit mention of art.[56]
Perhaps, however, in keeping with the role of purged art in the *Republic*,
we could locate it as one of the character-forming institutions. Generated by the Eros of the artist, in its Apollonian mode art aids in the harmonic tuning of the dispositions preparatory to the highest ascent that
suffuses the Apollonian with a Dionysian sense of eternal encompassment. If we take the Apollonian properties to present the characteristics
of beauty, Beauty itself adds the dimension of eternal encompassment to
those properties. This accords with the later Plotinian understanding of
two factors involved in the appearance of beautiful things: the togetherness of harmonic form and light, Apollonian properties illuminated
from Beyond.[57]

Along these lines, the *Phaedrus* adds a further significant dimension
to the discussion of beauty—and, by implication, to art as the production
of beauty. Socrates speaks of the beauty of things as the real presence of
Beauty itself in those things. Beauty itself is, he says, perceptible through
the eyes.[58] Following out in the opposite direction of his extension of the
Apollonian properties from the audile to the visual in purged art, we
could claim that Beauty itself is perceptible also through the ears. Here
the alleged gap between the realm of Forms and the sensible is healed
and what is Beyond is brought here. Attention to the beauty of sensory
form excites an Eros for the eternal that is not simply beyond but is also
immanent in the sensible.

53. Plato, *Phaedrus*, 259e ff.
55. Plato, *Symposium*, 209a–e.
57. Plotinus, *Enneads*, I, 6.
54. Ibid., 272d.
56. Ibid., 210a ff.
58. Plato, *Phaedrus*, 250d–e.

Let us go further. Truth focused upon content tends to deflect attention from its own ground in the peculiar radiance generated by the beautiful and the corresponding sublimation of Eros. The uncoveredness of things is provided by an incomparable Beauty beyond *ousia*. It empowers *nous* to comprehensive reflectiveness through the attunement to the overall order of things that it produces in the knower. Art in its Apollonian modes, in tandem with gymnastics, aids in that attunement, bringing Beauty itself "here" as a real presence in beautiful things found and fashioned. Plato in practice provides the basis for reflection to understand that the role of the arts is emotional tuning. Focus upon verisimilitude alone loses sight of the significance of this tuning. Plato's poetic practice works precisely at that tuning through the selection of the primordial metaphoric pairs up/down and light/dark to structure the dialogue, through the use of allegory and myth and through the recommendation of Apollonian art forms. Proper tuning both opens the soul upward toward the eternal and incarnates the eternal in sensuousness. This is meaningfully related to the image of the spinning top where the orientation toward the Top of the cosmos is reciprocally related to the motions rooted in the body. The Apollonian organization of the dispositions is reciprocally related to the Dionysian excess of Eros as the mortal's love for the immortal aimed at the Whole. The arts play a significant role in that ascent. They are not simply a mirroring of sensory surface but a transformation of surface that sinks deeply into the soul and enables it, as a whole and not simply as an intellect, to move upward toward the deathless principle of the Whole.

NIETZSCHE

Plato initiated the tradition of metaphysics and the location of aesthetic considerations within his metaphysical view. Heidegger claimed that Friedrich Nietzsche brings to a close the tradition that stems from Plato.[59] If for Plato truth stands higher than art, for Nietzsche, as a kind of inverse Platonist, the reverse is true. And if in Plato's case the relation between art and truth is more complex than it at first seems, in Nietzsche's case

---

59. Martin Heidegger, *Nietzsche*, II, trans. D. Krell (San Francisco: Harper, 1984), 205. For a more comprehensive treatment of Nietzsche's aesthetics within the overall framework of his thought, see my *Placing Aesthetics*, ch. 8.

the analysis of the relation reached a very high level of complexity indeed.

At first blush, Nietzsche's position would seem to be easy to discern by citing a number of aphoristic claims: "Belief in truth is something we have to overcome."[60] "The will to truth is rooted in the Will to Power."[61] "Truth is the kind of error without which a certain kind of living being could not live."[62] "Art is worth more than truth."[63] "We have art so as not to perish of truth."[64] But the matter is not so simple as it might appear: interpretation is complicated by the fact that "art" and "truth" are polyvalent terms in Nietzsche's works.

We have to set such declarations over against another line of claims: "How much truth can a spirit *endure*, how much truth does a spirit *dare?*—this became for me the real standard of value."[65] Again: ". . . [T]he service of truth is the hardest service. . . . Greatness of soul is needed for it."[66] Further, *Zarathustra*, he says, was "born out of the innermost wealth of truth." [67] "Zarathustra is more truthful than any other thinker. His teaching, and his alone, has truthfulness as the supreme virtue."[68] Finally, Nietzsche says of his own work that "this ultimate, most joyous, most wantonly extravagant Yes to life . . . is most strictly confirmed and supported by truth and science."[69] So, unless Nietzsche is simply incoherent—a gratuitous assumption that excuses one from having to take him seriously and blocks one from learning from him—we obviously need to make several distinctions.

We begin by attempting to sort out various meanings of the term "truth" in Nietzsche's work. Our starting point will be a declaration from his intellectual autobiography: "the truth speaks out of me. But my truth is *terrible*; for so far one has called *lies* truth. . . . I was the first to *discover*

---

60. Friedrich Nietzsche, "On the Genealogy of Morals," in *On the Genealogy of Morals and Ecce Homo*, trans. W. Kaufmann (New York: Vintage, 1967), III.24/150.

61. Friedrich Nietzsche, *Will to Power*, trans. W. Kaufmann and R. Hollingdale (New York: Vintage, 1967), 375/202; *Beyond Good and Evil*, 211/136; *The Gay Science*, trans. W. Kaufmann (New York: Vintage, 1974), I.13/87.

62. Nietzsche, *Will to Power*, §493/272.   63. Ibid., §853/453.

64. Ibid., §822/435.   65. Ibid., §1041/536.

66. Nietzsche, *The Anti-Christ*, 50/167 in *Twilight of the Idols and The Anti-Christ*, trans. R. Hollingdale (Baltimore: Penguin, 1968). For the knowledge of truth, see also "no sacrifice is too great." *Daybreak: Thoughts on the Prejudices of Morality*, trans. R. Hollingdale (Cambridge: Cambridge University Press, 1982), 33–34.

67. Nietzsche, *Ecce Homo*, preface, 4/219.

68. Ibid., IV, 3/328.

69. Ibid., III, in Nietzsche, *The Birth of Tragedy*, 2/272.

the truth by being the first to experience—to *smell lies as lies*."[70] Truth is, to begin with, what is taken for true in a tradition. It is what gives stability to the lives of those who believe it and repeat it without question. It is, secondly and dominating the Western tradition, the acceptance of another and better World beyond this one, ruled by a single Divinity. It is, thirdly, the set of fixed truths proclaimed by the metaphysical tradition: being, unity, purpose, subject, causality, freedom, and so on. It is, fourthly, what is uncovered by controlled methodological investigation linked to what presents itself in everyday existence. It is, finally, the positioning of all these within an ultimate framework—what Nietzsche himself claims to achieve. He sees the first three domains as a region of lies, of what is mendaciously willed into the foundation of things[71] that stands in the way of methodological inquiry and comprehensive knowing. Such "truth" has to be overcome by discerning the Will to Power that stands beneath it, by focusing what presents itself to everyday experience extended methodologically by science, and by providing a more comprehensive framework.

The term "art," too, is polyvalent in Nietzsche's usage. There is first of all the most obvious meaning: fine art as the fashioning of materials into something perfect.[72] There is also the broader meaning of art as the fashioning one's life by giving form to the potential chaos of passions and possibilities. Then, there is the more encompassing meaning: the art of forming a tradition that shapes human lives collectively. And there is, fourthly, the fashioning of a comprehensive framework within which all of the above occurs and wherein art and the search for truth coalesce. This is, finally, the vision of the cosmos as a work of art through the proclamation of Will to Power and Eternal Recurrence. Of that, the artist is the most perspicuous instance.

As Nietzsche sees it, the truth-intention, like all things human, has a genealogy of transformations and substitutions. It undergoes three metamorphoses in its history, exhibiting the stages of camel, lion, and child presented in *Thus Spoke Zarathustra*.[73] At first, the truth-intention is subjugated to other forces: it is the camel bearing the load of subservi-

---

70. Nietzsche, *Ecce Homo*, IV, 1/326.   71. Nietzsche, *Twilight of the Idols*, III, 2/36.
72. Ibid., IX, 9/72.

73. Nietzsche, "Thus Spoke Zarathustra," in *The Portable Nietzsche*, trans. W. Kaufmann (New York: Viking, 1954), I, 1\37.

ence of slaves to masters, of communities to tradition, of individuals to the passions. Then, in the rise of science it becomes the roaring lion going on the attack and achieving reactive independence. Finally, there is the active willing of truth itself, no holds barred. As John Richardson remarks, Nietzsche's "attacks really aim to refashion the goal of truth in such a way that that will come into its health and maturity."[74]

In Nietzsche's genealogical analysis, truthfulness has its origin in the severity of punishment meted out by masters to slaves in order to give them temporal extendedness over against the chaotic immediacy of subjection to spontaneous desires. This grounds the first meaning of "truthfulness" as the ability to make and keep promises.[75] Such holding oneself to promises is co-opted by the ascetic ideal where it becomes dedicated to truth conceived of as preservation and defense of what is proclaimed by the tradition. It eventuates in a revolt against this World, against the body and its passions in favor of a better and disembodied World of truth.[76] We arrive at Platonism and its mass adaptation in Christianity: "The 'true World' and the 'apparent World'—that means: the mendaciously invented World and reality."[77]

Passed on, truth here becomes the inertia that gives rise to contentment in simple belief.[78] Repetition and obedience take the place of truth.[79] One fights tooth and nail against any attempt at an independent evidential grounding of truth. Faith, indeed, becomes a veto on science.[80] "'Faith' means not wanting to know what is true."[81]

Nonetheless, the *cura minimorum*, self-control, and detachment from this-worldly consequences for oneself in the religious ascetic prepared the grounds for science.[82] Science itself arises out of challenge to the tradition but also requires a challenge to oneself and to those taken-for-granted truths dear to one's own heart.[83] Science had to fight the tradi-

74. John Richardson, *Nietzsche's System* (New York: Oxford University Press, 1992), 237–57. I owe my analysis of her to Richardson's work.
75. Nietzsche, *On the Genealogy of Morals*, I, 3/61.
76. Nietzsche, *Beyond Good and Evil*, preface, 3.
77. Nietzsche, *Ecce Homo*, 218; *Will to Power*, 572/308.
78. Nietzsche, *Will to Power*, #537/291.
79. Nietzsche, "Thus Spoke Zarathustra," III, 12, 7/312.
80. Nietzsche, *The Gay Science*, 48/163.
81. Ibid., 52/169.
82. Nietzsche, *Will to Power*, #469. Cf. Richardson, *Nietzsche's System*, 246.
83. Nietzsche, *The Anti-Christ*, 50/167.

tion of truth-claims every step of the way.[84] It requires what Nietzsche considers to be the characteristic modern virtue: honesty (*Redlichkeit*).[85] But it also requires careful methodology and acute observation to obtain the kinds of truth to which it is suited.[86] Nietzsche himself was what von Balthasar has called "this profoundly sincere soul."[87] He was intensely dedicated to whatever truths have been and can be uncovered by science as the necessary prerequisites for the philosophy of the future.

Conversely, as Nietzsche observes, science does not bestow meaning. A mathematical-physical, mechanical explanation of a musical piece leaves out what is most meaningful in it.[88] And the narrow view of the specialist combined with scientific conscience can leech out the lifeblood of the scientist. Here spirit becomes the life that cuts into life.[89] Flat on the ground, the specialized inquirer has a frog's-eye view.[90] What life requires is an eagle's-eye view, a view from the heights.

Now, we must understand that for Nietzsche all the way along, the will to truth is grounded in the Will to Power.[91] Once the will to truth gets launched historically, it is fed by something other than the will to truth purely and simply. In the priest and even too often in the philosopher, it is the will to defend the accepted.[92] In most people, it is the will to feel secure and in some to feel superior, to conquer, to belong, and to be recognized.[93] In scientists, it can be the will to overturn the accepted, trivial curiosity, vanity, desire for amusement, and boredom.[94] Each of us might profitably ask: In what is my will to truth rooted? Nietzsche remarks, "What one has forbidden so far as a matter of principle has always been—truth alone."[95] What has to be released is what Lonergan called the pure, unrestricted desire to know the truth. But that has to be seen in relation to the purported

84. Nietzsche, *The Gay Science*, 50/167.

85. Nietzsche, "Thus Spoke Zarathustra," I, 3/145.

86. Nietzsche, *Will to Power*, 469/261; *The Gay Science*, 13/123.

87. Hans Urs Von Balthasar, *The Glory of the Lord*, vol. I. *Seeing the Form*, trans. E. Leiva-Merikakis (San Francisco: Ignatius Press, 1982), 514.

88. Nietzsche, *The Gay Science*, V, 373/335–36.

89. Nietzsche, "Thus Spoke Zarathustra," IV, 4/360–63.

90. Nietzsche, *Beyond Good and Evil*, 2/10.

91. Ibid., 211/136.

92. Nietzsche, "Thus Spoke Zarathustra," II, 8/214.

93. Nietzsche, *The Gay Science*, 13/87; *Will to Power*, 423/227; 455/249.

94. Friedrich Nietzsche, *On the Uses and Disadvantages of History for Life*, in *Untimely Meditations*, trans. R. Hollingdale (Cambridge: Cambridge University Press, 1983), 6/89.

95. Nietzsche, *Ecce Homo*, preface, 219.

superiority of art: "Art," Nietzsche says, "is worth more than truth."[96]

Having worked through, however sketchily, the polyvalence of Nietzsche's notion of truth, let us do the same for his notion of art. In the *Will to Power*, he outlines the task for us: the artist-philosopher forming men is preceded by the hermit forming himself and the artist forming materials.[97] We proceed in inverse order.

Contrasted with the ascetic tradition, fine art has deep roots in the beauty available through the senses and linked to sexual desire.[98] But it involves a spiritualization of desire and a spiritualization of the senses.[99] In general, Nietzsche, before Freud and following Plato, sees all higher things as sublimations of sexuality. Aroused by beauty, sexuality as the essential self-transcendence of life bursts forth as art. Art is "an excess and overflow of blossoming bodily being into the World of images and desires."[100] The condition and effect of artworks, whether of a Dionysian or an Apollonian sort, is rapture, a being taken outside oneself.[101]

Rapturous spiritualization occurs as the "*compulsion* to transform into the perfect."[102] But perfection requires discipline and tradition. Far from viewing the artist as rooted in a bohemian flaunting of convention with unchained subjectivity and sexual indulgence, Nietzsche maintains first that the "most natural" state of the artist is far from "letting himself go."[103] Artistic genius indeed is "the greatest freedom under law."[104] Restraint is essential and subjective art is just bad art.[105] Nietzsche maintains further that convention is *not* an obstacle but the condition of great art. Great art, as anything great, emerges out of centuries-long discipline along a single line that brings that line to perfection in the Classical.[106] In the artist that involves the harmonization of all strong desires, the greatest feeling of power over opposites without tension.[107] "When power becomes gra-

96. Nietzsche, *Will to Power*, 822/435.
97. Ibid., 795-6/419.
98. Nietzsche, *Twilight of the Idols*, IX, 8–9/71–73.
99. Nietzsche, *Will to Power*, §820/434.
100. Ibid., §802/422.
101. Nietzsche, *Twilight of the Idols*, IX, 10/73.
102. Ibid., 9/72.
103. Nietzsche, *Beyond Good and Evil*, 188/100; *Will to Power*, 811/238.
104. Nietzsche, *Will to Power*, §834/439.
105. Nietzsche, *The Birth of Tragedy*, 5/48.
106. Nietzsche, *Will to Power*, §809. Cf. also Nietzsche, *The Anti-Christ*, 188/109; *Will to Power*, §799/420.
107. Nietzsche, *Will to Power*, §800/420 and §803/422.

cious and descends into the visible—such descent I call beauty."[108] Paralleling the Apollonian preference of Plato, Classical art becomes logical, it becomes law, even mathematical.[109] As the grand style found in Homer, Hafiz, Raphael, Rubens, and Goethe, artistic creativity expresses gratitude for existence, letting harmony sound from every conflict.[110]

At the same time, great art involves a sense of the background of Mystery involved in our belonging to the Whole. Art, Nietzsche says, is "what eternally compels us to life, to eternal life."[111] He saw this as aligned with the Dionysian sensibility that overcame the *principium individuationis* and was taken up in rapture with a sense of belonging to the Whole.[112] At the same time, anticipating Heidegger, the young Nietzsche remarked that, while theoreticians are interested in the cast-off veils, artists are interested in what still remains veiled, with the hidden Mystery brought to presence in the artwork.[113]

What he opposes in art is what stands opposite the Classical. It is the forgetting of the Whole in focusing upon the merely pretty, in Romanticist escape from life, and especially in the view of art for art's sake.[114] He speaks of the latter as "the croaking of frogs in a nihilistic swamp."[115] Nihilism emerged in the history of the West through the death of the power of the other-worldly to shape human existence.[116] One way of avoiding the issues involved is escape into the partial and narrow, whether through immersion in the everyday World of the Last Man, in scientific specialization, in the pursuit of the trivially beautiful, or in the production of art for art's sake. As an escapist from life, Schopenhauer thought of aesthetic contemplation as temporary relief from life; for Nietzsche, art is the great stimulant to life.[117] As far as art is concerned, the real issue for Nietzsche is whether it issues from a feeling of power and abundance and gratitude for existence as in the grand style or whether it issues from weakness and reaction.[118] Nietzsche sees Romanticism as rooted in reaction: it wants to be released from suffering or to destroy what currently exists.[119]

But art is not confined to so-called fine art. It is found more deep-

---

108. Nietzsche, "Thus Spoke Zarathustra," II, 13/230.
109. Nietzsche, *Will to Power*, §842/444.   110. Ibid., §844-6/445-6.
111. Cited in Heidegger, *Nietzsche*, I, 29.   112. Nietzsche, *The Birth of Tragedy*, 1/36.
113. Ibid., 15/94.   114. Nietzsche, *Twilight of the Idols*, 24/81.
115. Nietzsche, *Will to Power*, §808/427.   116. Ibid., §12/12ff.
117. Ibid., §812/430; §802/422; §853/452.   118. Ibid., §802/422; §853/452.
119. Ibid., §845–47/445–46.

ly in the comprehensive shaping of men through tradition: Nietzsche found the greatest works of art in the Roman Empire, the Prussian officers corps, and the Jesuit order.[120] These traditions involve discipline and obedience over centuries. The works of art here are traditions that foster individuals who themselves can become works of art by focusing their powers. The saints are exemplars of wholly concentrated existence.[121] As in the case of art proper, here in the case of shaped existence, the tradition functions as a magnifying glass that focuses the rays of the sun until the object focused upon bursts into flame. The religious traditions aid the individual in gaining power over himself, over the chaos within that is thus able to take on form.[122] But such religious heroes and their traditions are guided by "the ascetic ideal" that involves contempt for the Earth.[123] Their ultimate legitimation is a lie.

Nietzsche sees the essential role of ascetical practice in shaping the self as a center of creative power. But he wants to make asceticism natural again, without contempt for the earth and what it entails: the senses, the body, and sexuality.[124] He wants to help others become artists of their own lives,[125] achieve comprehensive self-formation, and "'live resolutely' in wholeness and fullness,"[126] compelling the chaos of differing directions to take on form and forming and being formed against the background of a sense of the Whole.[127] What he seeks is the "grand style, no longer merely art, but become reality, truth, *life*."[128] In this sense, "art is the real task of life, art as life's *metaphysical* activity."[129]

There is another facet to art. Early Nietzsche claimed that art is the will to illusion that overcomes truth. Truth, he said, is ugly: the World is pervaded by disease, war, struggle, deformity, suffering, and death. "We possess *art* lest we *perish of truth*."[130] Later, he focuses upon another di-

---

120. Ibid., §796/419; Nietzsche, *The Anti-Christ*, 39/93.
121. Nietzsche, *Beyond Good and Evil*, 59/71; *Daybreak*, 60.
122. Nietzsche, *Will to Power*, §915/483.
123. Nietzsche, *On the Genealogy of Morals* III, 27/160.
124. Nietzsche, *Will to Power*, §915/483; *The Gay Science*, 57/178; *On the Genealogy of Morals*, III, 8/108.
125. "You found me. . . . Now I bid you lose me and find yourselves." Nietzsche, "Thus Spoke Zarathustra," I, 22.3/190.
126. Nietzsche, "Attempt at a Self-Criticism," in *The Birth of Tragedy*, 7/26.
127. Nietzsche, *The Anti-Christ*, 58/180, esp. 59/182.
128. Ibid., 59/182 and 58/180.   129. Nietzsche, *Will to Power*, §853/453.
130. Ibid., §822/435.

mension of ugliness. Platonic truth as the realm of Forms and its allied Christian vision of eternal life beyond gives meaning by helping us cope with the horrors of existence; but they are lies: there is no eternal bliss, no eternal rest in an afterlife. Even the consolation of philosophy is a set of lies: no subject, substance, atoms, causality, freedom, being, purpose, unity.[131] These unmaskings are all ugly, discomforting truths, for they lead to nihilism.

But art is the overcoming of nihilism.[132] In all of its forms and in its widest and deepest extension, art exhibits the other side of existence. In spite of its destructive side, life is incredibly fertile and creative, forming as it destroys and destroying as it forms.[133] At the human level, the creative life at its deepest is measured by how much truth one can bear.[134] Eyes wide open to the horrors of existence and the threat of nihilism, the philosopher-artist as the Overman gives shape to his life in such a way as to bring into being a formative tradition, open to whatever truth can be found, open above all to the character of the Whole.[135] True philosophers depend upon scientific laborers, but they go beyond to create a horizon of meaning.[136] In this way, "when artistic energies and the practical wisdom of life will join with scientific thinking . . . a higher organic system will be formed."[137]

The issue of art and truth is linked to Nietzsche's fundamental commitment to perspectivity.[138] It involves the claim to an essential limit to conceptuality. What he calls "day wisdom," the sphere of Apollonian clarity, must be linked to "night wisdom," an awareness of the essentially hidden. This is correlated though not identical with his distinction between the little reason or reflective awareness and the greater reason of the organism.[139] Perspectivity also entails that truth-claims are founded upon "art" (i.e., the creation of a perspective). Science itself is rooted in perspective—that provided by the method and the paradigm. As such,

---

131. Nietzsche, *Beyond Good and Evil*, 12ff/19ff; *Will to Power*, §515ff/278ff; *Twilight of the Idols*, VI, 47ff.

132. Nietzsche, *Will to Power*, §853/452–53.

133. Nietzsche, *The Birth of Tragedy*, 15–16/103ff.

134. Nietzsche, *Will to Power*, §1041/536.

135. Nietzsche, *The Anti-Christ*, 211/136.

136. Nietzsche, *Beyond Good and Evil*, 211/136; *Will to Power*, §976/511.

137. Nietzsche, *The Gay Science*, 113/173.

138. Nietzsche, *Beyond Good and Evil*, 34/46.

139. Nietzsche, "Thus Spoke Zarathustra," I, 34/146.

its point of view is created. Hence, science is a form of art. But if, for
example, Newtonian physics is perspectival and not absolute, that does
not mean that one is free to think as one pleases or that nothing true is
manifest within it. Perspectivism entails a measurement of claims made
by what necessarily appears within the perspective. Occupying the perspective of Newtonian physics allows things to appear that would not
otherwise appear.

Yet in spite of his commitment to perspectivism, Nietzsche exhibits the design on the Whole characteristic of the metaphysical tradition:
the whole of what is, set within eternity. His fundamental truth-claim is
that being is Will-to-Power culminating in the Overman and linked to
the Eternal Recurrence of the Same.[140] Eternal Recurrence—Nietzsche's
most central thought—is his way of stamping being as permanence upon
becoming.[141] Affirmation of Eternal Recurrence is affirmation of creativity, formation, truth-seeking, and the Overman as the height of existence along with suffering, destruction, lies, and even the contemptible
Last Man.[142] Eternal Recurrence is the expression of the ultimate "yes" to
what is, loving it so much as to will all that is and was and will be to repeat itself forever.[143]

Will to Power has to be understood not only as capacity to coerce and
destroy but also and more fundamentally as a capacity to create, to give
form. The cosmos itself as the locus of the Will to Power is ultimately
viewed as art, as creation of form. "To the expanded concept of artist,
art is the basic occurrence of all beings; to the extent that they are, beings are self-creating, created."[144] The phenomenon of the artist is Will
to Power's most transparent form.[145] The artist is thus a means to what
Richardson has called "a truer truth."[146]

Life in general is based upon destroying and transforming aspects of

140. Cf. Heidegger, *Nietzsche*, III, 189.
141. Nietzsche, *Will to Power*, 617/330.
142. The prologue to "Thus Spoke Zarathustra" teaches both the Overman (3/124ff) and
his polar opposite, the contemporary Last Man (5/128ff). But the central concept of the work,
according to *Ecce Homo*, is Eternal Recurrence (*Ecce Homo*, III, in Nietzsche, "Thus Spoke
Zarathustra," 1/295). It appears in III, 2/267–72. Zarathustra's great nausea is caused by the difficulty in accepting the Last Man.
143. Nietzsche toyed with this notion as a truth claim grounded in science (*Will to Power*,
§1066/548–49), but basically it is a test for one's ability to say "yes!" to all being.
144. Heidegger, *Nietzsche*, I, 72; *Will to Power*, 796/419.
145. Nietzsche, *Will to Power*, §797/419.
146. Richardson, *Nietzsche's System*, 259n98.

the environment so that they contribute to the growth and sustenance of the organism.[147] Such destruction allows for the progressive emergence of the active powers of the adult organism that terminates in reproduction. Will to Power is the gathering of power to create beyond itself: to create its own organ system and its own offspring, the fundamental creation by the organic individual beyond the individual.

The notion of the Will to Power is linked to an evolutionary perspective that Nietzsche welcomes as definitively blocking the vision of a transcendent origin and destiny to human existence.[148] The transcendent vision acts as if our embodiment were a prison, an exile for the spiritual soul. The evolutionary view underscores our essentially belonging to the earth. It consecrates organic existence, the senses, sensory beauty, and art. It gives the lie to disembodiment and the contempt for the earth linked thereto. Humanness is the expression of the essential self-transcendence of the Will to Power operating from the earliest origins of life up to the expectation of the Overman.

Each instance of the Will to Power involves a perspective. A perspective is, in a sense, an illusion, a kind of "lie."[149] Animal perception is a perspective that simplifies and gives the illusion of fixity and stability serving organic need. In the human case, "truth" as the claim to ultimate meaning is the peculiar lie our species needs in order to live.[150] Truth in this sense involves the creation of a horizon of meaning by so-called Higher Men. These are the highest expression of the Will to Power thus far for they define the ultimate for those who come to exist under their vision.[151] Each poses itself as absolute and encompassing; and yet by the very nature of the case, each is only a perspective. Whatever it discloses, it thereby simultaneously closes other ways of ultimate conception and whatever is disclosable within those other ways. But such a lie is needed to allow people to grow up and adjust—a kind of second womb created by culture from which one has to be "born again." Indeed, for Nietzsche, "in art the lie becomes consecrated, the will to deception has good conscience at its back."[152]

147. Nietzsche, *Beyond Good and Evil*, 259/203.

148. Nietzsche, *Daybreak*, I, §49, 47.   149. Ibid., II, §117, 117.

150. Nietzsche, *Will to Power*, 493/272.

151. *Schopenhauer as Educator*, in Nietzsche, *On the Uses and Disadvantages of History for Life in Untimely Meditations*, 5/159.

152. Nietzsche, *On the Genealogy of Morals*, III, 25/153.

Throughout history, there have been multiple encompassing views that each bound a people together but simultaneously separated them from others.[153] Nietzsche sees the truth-lover's task as the multiplication of many perspectives, the development of many eyes.[154] He attempts to understand each perspective from within in terms of the Will to Power that supports it. But we are not simply stuck with multiple perspectives. His announced aim is to become "the circumference of circumferences," to create a perspective that will provide a place for each of the perspectives that have held sway throughout the history of humankind by explaining them, showing their partiality and the power they serve, and devising a view that will surpass them all. It is in this way that Nietzsche intends to become "the circumference of circumferences."[155] This view involves the combination of Will to Power, Eternal Recurrence, and the Overman.

On Nietzsche's own terms, the recognition of these related truth-claims would entail that together, as the creation of Nietzsche's art, they constitute one among many perspectives. But Nietzsche's claims recommend themselves by how they are able to encompass all other putative circumferences. Though the vision involved might itself be a perspective, it is not *merely* a perspective but one that challenges all other claims to outdo it if they can.[156]

For Nietzsche, the ultimate truth is the simultaneous destructive and creative character of existence. The truth of art is its creative triumph over the destructive forces, following the struggle that is life itself: to compel the chaos to take on form, shaping a life and shaping a tradition. In its highest form, it expresses and evokes a Dionysian sense of the encompassing Whole by willing the Eternal Recurrence of the Same as a matter of developed disposition, saying "yes" to life, to the totality it presupposes.

I should add that this view does not in principle entail atheism. What Nietzsche fights is a degenerate notion of God, God as "the *contradiction to life*, instead of being its transfiguration and eternal 'Yes'!"[157] Zarathus-

---

153. Nietzsche, "Thus Spoke Zarathustra," I, 15/170.
154. Nietzsche, *On the Genealogy of Morals*, III, 12; *Will to Power*, 540/291.
155. Nietzsche, "Thus Spoke Zarathustra," III, 14/334.
156. Cf. Richardson, *Nietzsche's System*, 290.
157. Nietzsche, *The Anti-Christ*, 18/128.

tra would accept a God who celebrates life by laughing and dancing.[158] It is a creative divinity who looks at His creation and finds it good—but who also created the crocodile.

I want to end this exposition by returning to Plato. Though Nietzsche generally and most fundamentally positions himself against Plato, in *Will to Power* he acknowledges that his exposition has been a caricature.[159] Plato is for Nietzsche an agonistic friend: one who stimulates and challenges him to surpass himself.[160] When Nietzsche glorifies the creative self-transcendence of life, he links himself with what he then calls "the divine Plato," the Plato of the *Symposium* with its vision of sublimated Eros aroused by beauty.[161] Indeed, much of Plato returns in Nietzsche: Eros as the origin of the attempt to mirror eternity in time by producing beauty in the sensible, the priority of Apollonian art forms as sublimated Dionysian in the grand classical style, the ideal harmonization of the self required for comprehensive vision, the hierarchy of types climaxed by the philosopher-king (but also by Plato himself), the philosopher-artist who creates out of an overflowing abundance of life and establishes a visionary tradition that shapes human life.[162] In this, Nietzsche is a modern descendent of Plato. A double relation to Plato also characterizes Martin Heidegger, to whom we now turn.

HEIDEGGER

Martin Heidegger pursued one thought throughout his whole career and through over one hundred volumes: the thought of Being.[163] Human reality as *Da-Sein*, is the *Da*, the place where *Sein* (Being), the meaning of the Whole, comes into question. Human beings exist as the question of Being.[164] However, the relation between truth and art lies at the heart

158. Nietzsche, *Thus Spoke Zarathustra*, I, 7/153.

159. Nietzsche, *Will to Power*, 374/202.

160. Nietzsche, *Daybreak*, §370/373. Cf. Richardson, *Nietzsche's System*, 116ff on Nietzsche's positive appropriation of Plato.

161. Nietzsche, *Twilight of the Idols*, IX, 22, 80; *The Birth of Tragedy*, 12/85.

162. Nietzsche, *Will to Power*, 973/511.

163. Cf. Martin Heidegger, "The Thinker as Poet," in *Poetry, Language, and Thought*, trans. A. Hofstadter (New York: Harper, 1971), 4. For a more comprehensive treatment of Heidegger's aesthetics within the overall framework of his thought, see my *Placing Aesthetics*, ch. 10.

164. Heidegger, *Being and Time*, 27.

of Heidegger's thought. His step back from metaphysics as putative thought of Being into its ground follows both Plato and Nietzsche. It follows Plato in his notion of the Good beyond *ousia* furnishing the light of *aletheia* to the relation of intellect to intelligible. The light is linked to the notion of the beautiful which, as we have seen, is in turn linked to the nature of art as productive of attunement. He follows Nietzsche in his attempt to think through the ground of the will to truth in the Will to Power understood as the will to create form. Against Plato and following Nietzsche's perspectivity, for Heidegger truth is not a permanent fixture but truth happens, and art is one fundamental way in which it happens.[165] Indeed, art is finally "the saving grace" in the contemporary epoch of Nietzsche's Last Man, who has lost all sense of transcendence.[166]

The fundamental experience that set Heidegger's life task is *Erschrecken*, startled dismay at what he calls the forgottenness of Being in the tradition and the withering up of the sense of Being in contemporary existence.[167] He shares Nietzsche's analysis that nihilism pervades our World without troubling the many who are contented with their technologically provided World of health, comfort, and entertainment.[168] For Heidegger, we are like fish out of water, fallen out of our element and gasping for air—though we are too dulled to realize it.[169] His key experience is closely linked to Heraclitus's claim: *phusis kriptesthai philei*, "nature loves to hide." This is what guides his interpretation of Plato's Cave allegory to which he twice gave extended attention (1931–1932 and 1946).[170]

In his interpretation of the Cave, he underscores the function of terms related to *aletheia* throughout the allegory: the shadows on the

165. Martin Heidegger, "Origin of the Work of Art," in *Philosophies of Art and Beauty*, trans. and ed. A. Hofstadter and R. Kuhns (Chicago: University of Chicago Press, 1964), a translation of *Der Ursprung des Kunstwerks* (Stuttgart: Reclam, 1960), 666/25. We will refer to the translation first, followed by the German original.

166. Martin Heidegger, *The Question Concerning Technology and Other Essays*, trans. W. Lovitt (New York: Harper, 1977), 25.

167. Martin Heidegger, *Contributions to Philosophy: From Enowning*, trans. P. Emad and K. Maly (Bloomington: Indiana University Press, 2000), 11.

168. Heidegger, *Introduction to Metaphysics*, 40.

169. Heidegger, "Letter on Humanism," in *Martin Heidegger: Basic Writings*, ed. D. Krell (New York: Harper and Row, 1977), 189–242.

170. In a course on Plato's Cave and *Theaetetus* in 1931–1932, see Heidegger, *The Essence of Truth*, 68. He also covered the same ground in less detail in "Plato's Doctrine of Truth," in Barrett and Aiken, 251–70.

cave wall, the figures and light inside the cave, the figures and light out-side.[171] The goal of the ascent is the Good that is the source of the light of *aletheia* for intellect and the intelligible. With Heraclitus's aphorism and his own fundamental experience as a guide, he takes the etymology of the term *aletheia* to lie in the privative *alpha* joined to *lethe* as the con-cealed. Founding truth is "un-concealment" that allows particular truths to arise in the correspondence of intellect to the intelligible.[172]

Heidegger accepts Plato's analysis: it is the presence of the eidetic that allows us to move from sensory gawking and emoting to understand-ing. The Forms open up the beingness of the beings encountered.[173] Hei-degger follows Plato up to the *aletheia* that makes the grasping of the Forms possible. He follows further the linkage of *aletheia* with beauty and Eros. He comments, "[O]nly what is held in . . . the most primordial yearning is authentically *there*."[174] Further, "The unhidden corresponds to the beautiful, for the essence of the beautiful lies in being *ekphanesta-ton* (the most manifest) (*Phaedrus*)."[175] And ultimately, he sees the pro-duction of unhiddenness to lie in the power of art—although not exclu-sively there.[176]

For Heidegger, Plato's focus upon truths as found in the Forms un-fortunately loses sight of what Heraclitus knew: the essential hiddenness from which unconcealment emerges. For Plato, the opposite of *aletheia* is not the hidden but the *pseudon*, the distorted or false, both of which occur within the manifest.[177] For Heidegger, on the contrary, the hidden is the Mystery of Being, the operation of the "not" that allows the "is" to step forward out of the matter-of-fact.[178]

In the analytic of Dasein preparatory to thinking Being, the realiza-tion of one's own mortality casts a new light upon everyday existence: one's own possible not-being challenges our everyday mode of awareness and the whole of our existence appears in a strange new light. *Heimlich-*

---

171. Heidegger, *The Essence of Truth*, 32ff.

172. Ibid., 26. "On the Essence of Truth," in *Martin Heidegger: Basic Writings*, trans. D. Krell (New York: Harper, 1977), 124.

173. Heidegger, *On the Essence of Truth*, 38.

174. Ibid., 171.

175. Heidegger, *Nietzsche*, I, 266.

176. Heidegger, "Origin of the Work of Art," 686/50.

177. Heidegger, *On the Essence of Truth*, 99.

178. Ibid., 96; "Origin of the Work of Art," 690/54.

keit, or being at home, becomes *unheimlich*, or uncanny.[179] Beyond the analytic of Dasein in the thinking of Being itself, the question "Why are there beings and not rather nothing?" functions similarly to the thought of death.[180] It sets off what is and the beingness of what is over against nothingness in such a way that the "is" of what is juts into prominence and a fundamental strangeness falls over the everyday. With Heraclitus, Heidegger moves beyond Plato into a sensitivity to the hidden. Heidegger's Being that is forgotten takes the place of Plato's Good as that which draws us on, for Plato's Good is *phanotaton tou ontos*, the most manifest of being;[181] Heidegger's *Sein*, by contrast, is the essentially hidden that empowers the unhidden.[182]

But there is a further feature. Heidegger maintains that one has to go beyond Plato to grasp the problem of ideas anew in terms of the relation between viewer and viewed and the disposition involved in that relation.[183] For Heidegger, the light of *aletheia* is not a permanent shining on a permanent stage; it is an historical occurrence.[184] Truths are available within an historically variable framework of truth as illuminated opening. It is likely this claim that leads Heidegger to translate *eidos* as "outward appearance," correlate to an historically situated viewer.[185] The *eidos* does not present the inner being of things but only the face they show to an intellectual viewer. Here, we see a parallel with Nietzsche's holding to the essential perspectivity of all truth claims. And with Nietzsche, Heidegger sees a hierarchy of perspectives. The "central task and methodological problem is to arrive at the *right* perspective."[186] The problem, obviously, is to find out what that is. Minimally and formally, one would have to say that which most comprehensively comes to terms with all the parameters of the peculiar historical situation in which we exist—and that would include the deep history of one's tradition as a whole.

One can observe the operation of perspectivity in the transformation of the meaning of nature in modern science. Over against the predom-

179. Nietzsche, *The Birth of Tragedy*, 229–47.
180. Heidegger, *Introduction to Metaphysics*, 1.
181. Plato, *Republic*, 509b.
182. Heidegger, *On the Essence of Truth*, 96.
183. Ibid., 52.
184. Heidegger, "Origin of the Work of Art," 680/42.
185. Heidegger, "On the Essence of Truth," in *Martin Heidegger: Basic Writings*, 261.
186. Heidegger, *On the Essence of Truth*, 203.

inant Aristotelian view of a complex of natures, each seeking their respective ends in the light of imitating the final end, nature for modern science is a single system of mass points of energy combining and separating according to fixed laws.[187] This allows truths to emerge that were not available under the Aristotelian view. But this also hides another transformation. Underlying modern science is its technological essence. Its essential experimentalism is transformative and serves the eventual taking of the whole of nature as standing reserve for human projects.[188] It is this that finally dries up the sense of Being that prevails in contemporary existence and leads to Nietzsche's Last Man. It is in this context that Heidegger speaks of art as the saving grace that allows a turning, an *epistrophe*, from the contemporary cave.[189] But he also follows out a direction indicated by the linkage of truth, beauty, and art in his Plato interpretation.

Heidegger defines art as "the setting to work of truth."[190] The view does not require some form of representation, the sole focus of attention in *Republic*'s Book X, for it is not about truths regarding some particular sorts of things. It is about truth as the opening of a region for human dwelling. In order for this to happen, the artist must already have stood in the openness brought to form in the art product.[191]

Great art sets the functional context of everyday life more deeply into the character of Earth and the character of World. It creates the sphere of World as openness and sets it upon the Earth as sensuous form. In the work of art, World is manifest as a *World of inhabitance* and Earth as *native soil*.[192] Native soil is not something a chemist could ever analyze but is revealed in the peculiar sense of being at home that opens up when we inhabit, that is, habitually dwell in a given geographical location pervaded by traditional practices incarnating ways of understanding. In the work of art, contrary to the character of everyday objects, Earth as the sphere of the sensuous is not subsidiary, disappearing in its function; it enters into the focal character of significant presence. Here, Heidegger

187. Martin Heidegger, *What Is a Thing?* trans. E. Gendlin (Chicago: Regnery, 1967), 66ff.
188. Heidegger, *The Question Concerning Technology and Other Essays*, 27.
189. Ibid., 34.
190. Heidegger, "Origin of the Work of Art," 666/25; 682/44; 697/62.
191. Ibid., 688/52.
192. Ibid., 672/33.

shows the fidelity to the earth called for by Nietzsche.[193] Sensuousness is doubly rooted in the Earth: in the bodiliness of what appears in sensation and in the correlative bodiliness of the one sensing. But, Heidegger notes, the openness of a World that corresponds to full dwelling includes releasement to the encompassing Mystery, and the rising up of Earth in sensuousness involves its fundamental falling back into closure.[194] The open occurs within the encompassing Mystery.

There is another Heraclitean element in Heidegger's thought. For Heraclitus, the deepest harmony arises only out of struggle: war is king.[195] In Heidegger, the tension between the openness of World and the closure of Earth creates a tear (*Riss*) within everyday appearance in the field of relation between Dasein and appearing things. The *Riss* as the breaking point of tension is the Gestalt, the form the work takes on.[196] Parallel to Nietzsche's "grand style," such form arises out of and produces a higher state of agitation that is simultaneously a state of repose. The Gestalt that brings about this agitated repose is the shining of the beautiful.[197]

In this whole context, there is a fourfold relationality involved between the artist, the art product, the audience, and the encompassing.[198] Heidegger rejects as inadequate the view of the work as an on-hand object with aesthetic properties producing an esthetic state of mind.[199] Artist and audience are not isolated subjects, the one expressing private subjectivity and the other having an isolated aesthetic experience brought about by the form of the object. Artist, audience, and art product necessarily occupy the space opened up by the tradition that shapes their Dasein as essentially Being-in-a-World with others.[200] Furthermore, the subjectivistic aesthetic view misses both the essential strangeness of the work and the Mystery of fundamental encompassing opened up in it.

Parallel to Dewey's distinction, for Heidegger the *work* is distinct from the *product* of art. For Heidegger, its work is the occurrence of *Be-*

193. Gadamer calls Heidegger's notion of Earth his fundamental contribution to the understanding of art. "Zur Einführung" to *Der Ursprung des Kunstwerks*, 98.

194. Heidegger, "Origin of the Work of Art," 681/43–44.

195. Martin Heidegger, "Heraclitus," in *Presocratic Philosophers*, ed. G. Kirk and J. Raven (Cambridge: Cambridge University Press, 1957), 53.

196. Heidegger, "Origin of the Work of Art," 688/52.

197. Ibid., 703/67.   198. Ibid., 692/56.

199. Heidegger, *Nietzsche*, I, 77ff.

200. Heidegger, "Origin of the Work of Art," 690/54; *Being and Time*, 49ff.

wahrung.[201] Translating the latter as "preservation" misses a crucial aspect of the term. It misses the *wahr*, the "true" in *Be-wahr-ung*, which we translate, albeit clumsily, as *be-truth-ing*. Be-truth-ing involves the coming out of concealment of the Whole. It occurs when one lets oneself be taken into the opening up that happens in the work. In average everydayness, the perceiver is in a world of tools and objects, the *Zuhanden* and the *Vorhanden*, among them art products.[202] The work of the work of art is to bring the art product out of its at-hand objectness as a work that was into a work that now, once again, "is."[203] While turning the art product into the work as a happening, it brings the perceiver into resolute openness and reveals the encompassing Mystery.

Resolute openness is a be-truth-ing as standing in the openness of beings.[204] Such standing admits of degrees of intensity. The more essentially it happens, the stranger and more singular the work becomes and the more one comes to realize "that it is." And the more this happens, the uncommon juts forth and the apparently matter-of-fact fades.[205] Not only the singular piece but all things are bathed in a new light. Heidegger claims that the work creates so much World space that in it even the ordinary appears extraordinary.[206]

The strangeness surrounding the everyday and the opening of the Whole recalls the early Nietzsche. While theoreticians are interested in the cast-off veils, artists are interested in what still remains veiled. Nietzsche saw this as the Dionysian sensibility that overcame the *principium individuationis* and was taken up rapturously with a sense of belonging to the Whole.[207]

The problem for Heidegger is the perennial flattening of everydayness and the peculiar closing of the horizon in contemporary life. His emphasis upon resoluteness is central here. As in Plato, what is invoked is no mere passive aestheticism. One has to enter into the *polemos*, to fight the battle to keep the horizon and everyday things with it from col-

---

201. Heidegger, "Origin of the Work of Art," 690/54.

202. Ibid., 653/9; 693/57.   203. Ibid., 669/30; 690/54.

204. Ibid., 691/55.   205. Ibid., 690/54.

206. Heidegger, *Introduction to Metaphysics*, 28. We note in passing Heidegger's remark that this may give us a new approach to understanding *esse*, something he had earlier understood merely as the positing of essence. ("The Way Back into the Ground of Metaphysics," 280).

207. Nietzsche, *The Birth of Tragedy*, 1/36.

lapsing into the merely matter-of-fact.²⁰⁸ As Kierkegaard put it, we forget that we float on waters seventy thousand fathoms deep.²⁰⁹ The *polemos* brings that realization center stage. And in this the work of art performs an essential service.

But art is only one of the ways in which truth happens as the creation of World space. Others include the action that grounds a political state, the experience of the nearness of the divine, essential sacrifice, and the thinker's questioning of Being.²¹⁰ The latter is Heidegger's own direction: making us see the hidden in what we think is clear and definitive, the Mystery that is involved in the everyday, and the antecedent decisions, most of which each of us has not made, that are involved in the way in which we come to think, act, and feel.

In the formation of world space, philosophy is a latecomer. Poetry comes first. Consider the Homeric books and the books of the Bible, the two roots of Western culture. Both come out of oral tradition and, among other things, record political founding. In the Bible, Abraham and Moses are the great founders, establishing the nation and the law, respectively. The Bible contains the words of the prophets who proclaim our relation to the divine. It also speaks of the intended sacrifice of Isaac and the actual sacrifice of Jesus. In each case, truth does not most fundamentally lie in what is represented but in the opening up of a world for dwelling through what is represented. But it is the artwork—in this case, that of the biblical books—that expresses and produces the tonality, disposition, and mood as well as the essential direction characteristic of a world as dwelling. In working through the historical character of the manifestation of Being, Heidegger follows Kierkegaard's distinction between thinking and dwelling by distinguishing two modes of thinking: one is "representative-calculative" (*das berechnende Denken*), and the other is "meditative," thinking as dwelling (*das besinnliche Nachdenken*).²¹¹ The former constructs and is ultimately governed by the will-to-power, to cognitive or practical mastery that emerged with Plato's focus upon the world of Forms. But meditative thinking "lets things be" in ap-

208. Heidegger, "Origin of the Work of Art," 677/38.
209. Søren Kierkegaard, *Concluding Unscientific Postscript to Philosophical Fragments*, trans. D. Seenson (Princeton, N.J.: Princeton University Press, 1941), 256.
210. Heidegger, "Origin of the Work of Art," 696–97/50.
211. Martin Heidegger, "Memorial Address," in *Discourse on Thinking*, trans. J. Anderson and E. Freund (New York: Harper, 1966).

preciatively dwelling on them. Representative-calculative thinking devises methods and makes progress. Meditative thinking follows a way and returns recollectively to where we always already are. The former operates in abstraction; the latter in coming to deepening presence. The former speaks to what we have come to call "the intellect," the concentrated point detached from our whole mode of indwelling; the latter speaks to "the heart," the core, the center of our being and ground of thinking, acting, and feeling that articulates our mode of indwelling.

In Heidegger's later thought, what gives rise to meditative thinking, the tension between Earth and World, is transformed into the Play of the Fourfold. It furnishes a template for all authentic dwelling and operates much like the square of opposition in logic where each corner of the square interplays with the others. World as world of inhabitance is that interplay, and Earth is one element within it. Earth plays in tandem with Sky and that relation is crossed by the tandem relation between Mortals and Immortals.[212] The sense of mortality still occupies center stage. It prevents things from falling back into the matter-of-fact. The "not" reveals the "is," but it is now tied to our relation to other mortals, to our inducting them into their own mortality. Mortality plays in tandem with a sense of measure bestowed from on high, from the Ground of the encompassing Whole, the dimension of the Immortals. The Immortals are "the messengers of the Most High," angels or muses, the sources of inspiration regarding what is high and low in human life and in the cosmos. This relation between the Mortals and Immortals is a relation whereby absence enhances presence. We approach everything differently when we carry with us the thought that death looks over our shoulder and differently still when we are aware of our relation to encompassing Mystery that lays claim on us. As Nietzsche noted, things exhibit a different face when the gods were thought to look at us through them.[213]

This relation between the Mortals and Immortals is sustained by *constant absence*: the absence of the ultimate term of one's future and the absence of the direct presence of the divinity. That relation is intersected by a relation of *constant presence* between Earth and Sky. Earth and Sky always surround us. We are rooted on the Earth, mortal because we are

212. Martin Heidegger, "Building, Dwelling, Thinking," in *Poetry, Language, and Thought*, 148–51.
213. Nietzsche, *The Gay Science*, 152/196–97.

human, made of humus and bound to return to the Earth. Earth rises up in sensation that is itself grounded in the earthiness of our own bodies and of the things sensed. Being made of Earth and belonging to the Earth comes to the fore in a special way in the work of art. Colors and sounds step out of their purely subsidiary function in everyday dealings. Earth rises up in sensation but falls back into an ultimate opaqueness.[214] But Heidegger stresses the appreciation of *sensa* qua *sensa*, sensory radiance as such—though tied to material opaqueness. The two, sensory radiance and material opaqueness, have to be experienced together. They are parallel to the dual awareness of manifestation and concealment in world-disclosure.

Sky, like Earth, is also a matter of presence. Its openness allows Earth to rise up to sensory presence. Its cycles are tied to the variations of day and night and the seasons of the year. They provide a fundamental measure of our existence on the Earth. But Sky as a measure combines its ever-present character with the need to retain no-longer-present past experience and anticipate not-yet-present future experience in order to discover its regular measures. In its measures, Sky also plays in relation to the Immortals as a metaphor for the measures of what is high and low in human life and in the cosmos.

The peculiar way in which this Fourfold happens—and thus how truth happens as an opening for inhabitance—has a history, depending upon how the Most High and the essential measures are taken as a gift from the past and as a challenge from the future. When the four regions play together in our silent listening, when we are not intent on mastery but are open, meditatively, thankfully letting things be manifest, the poetic word arises. With this word, things become significant presences, and with this play of things and word, World comes to hold sway.

"Things" in Heidegger's sense are what assemble and are assembled by the Play of the Fourfold. The German for "thing" (*Ding*) originally meant "assembly." Heidegger parallels that with the Greek term *logos*, especially as it appears in the fragments of Heraclitus. *Logos* is the origin of our

---

214. Heidegger here follows the tradition, at least in this respect, that matter in the thing and in the knower blocks intelligible presence and self-presence. One has to rise up above the sensations and desires that are rooted in the materiality of the body and tied to our own individuality in order to grasp the universal. He is also in the line of Aristotle and Aquinas that sensation and thus embodiment is an enduring feature of our access to things.

term for "logic," but it is ever so much richer. Logic cultivates the sphere of what is opened up and is thus derivative of that which opens up a region. *Logos* is related to *legein*, which means to read but also to gather; it also applies to that which is read, namely the word. (As is well known, *Logos* in the prologue to John's Gospel is translated as "Word.") According to Heidegger, for Heraclitus *logos* is primarily the gathering together of the Whole of things that occurs when the appropriate word arises. Such gathering is the opening out of a World for a people for which humanness as *Da-Sein*, as the "there" of Being, furnishes the locus. In one of Heidegger's most difficult yet more compressed and revealing statements: "Things thinging grant World. . . . World worlding grants things."[215] The disclosure of thing and World is reciprocal. It is not something we do but something done to us: things "thing" us by "thinging" (i.e., gathering, a World); World "worlds" by holding us and things together, presenting things in a way that has us in its grips. The play of thing and World in the clearing granted to *Da-Sein* comes to pass in and through the poetic word. And for Heidegger, such a word stands at the origin of every work of art.

Contrary to Plato, for Heidegger poets in particular and artists in general are not subordinate to philosophy. As we have noted in our general introduction to this chapter, in the image Heidegger employs, philosophers and poets occupy twin peaks and call out to one another above the valley of everyday existence.[216] At their best, they live off of a sense of encompassing Mystery that they bring to presence in differing ways. The later Heidegger shows a particular preference for poetry. But in general, for Heidegger, art, in revealing the fundamental character of the thing as an assembling of the Whole for dwelling, leads us back from the abstract one-sidedness of science, the all-sided abstractness of philosophy, and the partiality of all our particular interests to the wholeness of meaning as world-inhabitance. Art brings us from our various modes of absence and imposition to the presencing of the Whole in the sensuously present. It teaches us to "let things be"; it speaks directly to "the heart," the center of thought, action, and feeling; it teaches us meditative rather than simply calculative and representative thinking. It brings us back to the

215. Heidegger, *Poetry, Language, and Thought*, 179–81.
216. Martin Heidegger, "Postscript" to *Existence and Being*, trans. W. Brock (South Bend, Ind.: Regnery, 1949), 360.

ground of metaphysics: it articulates our sense of Being for the Whole within which we come to find our own wholeness.

Heidegger's appeal to the heart moves in the direction of Nietzsche where the will to truth is rooted in life, but the priority of meditative thinking as appreciative "letting-be" seems to reverse the priority of Will to Power in Nietzsche. This is in keeping with Heidegger's final assessment of Nietzsche, whom he judges to embody the contemporary view of Being as standing reserve.[217] But he is also close to Nietzsche in the several crucial respects we listed earlier. He follows Nietzsche in his attempt to think of the will to truth's groundedness in life as the will to create form. Against Plato and following Nietzsche's perspectivity, for Heidegger truth is not a permanent fixture but truth happens, and art is one fundamental way in which it happens. Indeed, art is finally "the saving grace" in the contemporary epoch of Nietzsche's Last Man, who has lost all sense of transcendence.

But the historical character of fundamental *aletheia* in some way is a return to Plato's notion of philosophy as *philosophia*, as a peculiar occupant of the *metaxu* between mere opinion and final truth, always on the way.[218] Heidegger's emphasis upon art and the radiance of beauty also reverberates with Plato. Heidegger even accepts the securing of truth in the eidetic, only he insists on the perspectival character of that securing. And he insists, most fundamentally, upon the developed sense that all of this is rafted upon ultimate encompassing Mystery, a sense deeply cultivated in the arts.

CONCLUSION

We have examined the relation between truth and art in Plato, Nietzsche, and Heidegger, as the later thinkers respond to the earlier. In each of the thinkers, the interest in truth is an interest not so much in particular truths or regions of truth as it is in what is most fundamental, what grounds and encompasses everything else. But in each of them art plays an important role in relation to truth, most fundamentally in Nietzsche and Heidegger

217. Heidegger, "The Word of Nietzsche: 'God Is Dead,'" in *The Question Concerning Technology and Other Essays*, 85 and 101.
218. Plato, *Symposium*, 202e; *Phaedrus*, 278d.

and less obviously so in Plato. What is central to each is art's providing dispositional attunement that will permeate the whole of life.

Plato's tracing the intelligibility of the Forms to the unconcealment provided by the Good and his correlation of Beauty itself with the ultimate level occupied by the Good is expressly linked to the elevation of Eros. His claim that Beauty itself is perceptible though the senses as a kind of real presence can be correlated with art's function as harmonizing the emotions. Emotional harmonization and erotic elevation provide formation and light, grounding the search for the intelligible in the life of the whole soul and not just in the development of a detached intellect.

In a similar direction, art takes on a deeper role in Nietzsche and Heidegger in the creation of the perspectives within which we can find truths. But the perspectives always concern how we stand with respect to the Whole. That Whole is what eternally encompasses us. The essential issues are how the eternal encompassment is thought and the "how" of our relation to it. In this respect, for Plato and Heidegger the notion of Being, peripheral in Nietzsche, takes center stage, though in different ways.

Plato's Eleatic Stranger identifies the notion of Being as one of the five great eternal kinds found throughout experience: Being, rest, motion, sameness, difference.[219] The notion of *Being* is the overarching notion, articulated into the two great regions of absolute *rest* (the region of the Forms as pure being) and ceaseless *motion* (the region of temporal things, as mixtures of being and nonbeing, participating in the Forms). The realms of absolute rest and ceaseless motion are cut across by *sameness* and *difference*. Sameness runs through all individuals of a type as well as through specific and generic types in a given logical line, while difference sets off one thing from another under a type and one type from another up its logical tree.

Nietzsche dismissed the notion of Being as "the last trailing cloud of evaporating reality."[220] For him, the fixity of Platonic forms was a perspectival illusion. However, the notion of the eternal still played a central role. According to his own assessment, his deepest thought was the thought of Eternal Recurrence.[221] Nietzsche's Zarathustra hymned eter-

219. Plato, *Sophist*, 254d.   220. Nietzsche, *Twilight of the Idols*, III, 4.
221. Nietzsche, *Ecce Homo*, 295.

nity in his great love song. The affirmation of each thing, willing its Eternal Recurrence as an exhibition of the will to create beyond itself, established his "circumference of circumferences," embracing each historical perspective and, at the same time, standing over each thing as its "azure bell and eternal security."

Heidegger fixed his attention upon the notion of Being as the single star that guided his way. In Heidegger's reading, Plato's distinction between the two great realms of eternal Forms and their temporal instances involved the distinction between beings (*die Seienden*) and their beingness (*die Seiendheit*). But, according to Heidegger, this involved the forgetting of what he calls Being itself (*Sein*). Being itself is not an object of intellectual apprehension. It is neither a concept nor the object of a judgment or of an inference. It is not what we apprehend but rather what apprehends us. Like Plato's Good, it provides the *aletheia*, the light that opens access to intelligible form. And like the Good, Being is correlative not to intellect but to the emotional attunement that Plato designates as Eros. However, for Heidegger the access to the eidetic is perspectival, so that the temporality of differing modes of access to truths is the way eternal encompassment shows itself. Indeed, like Nietzsche, Heidegger sees Plato's lighted region of the Forms as essentially tied to the *lethe*, the hidden, the Mystery of Being out of which the light emerges. (We might add that Plato's use of myths and images when it comes to ultimate things suggests as much.) No matter what the perspective, the quality of human existence is linked to the lived relation to Mystery lying at the center.

That which opens the living space for a tradition has a lived "sense" (Heidegger's *Sinn*) rather than a conceptual content. Indeed, while we have come to call "intellect" that through which we apprehend conceptual content, what apprehends us as "sense" takes place in what the tradition has come to call "the heart." It is in this direction that we can understand the importance of art as opening the space for dwelling, and thus for establishing the truth of human existence. "Being" names a direction and is correlate to the heart.

A line of thought in Plato that was significantly influential tends to disparage embodiment—and thus the world of the senses and also art—as an imprisoning of the human soul. Nietzsche sees in that form of Platonism a contempt for the earth. In vehement opposition, essential for Nietzsche is "fidelity to the earth," a love of the body as "the great reason," an appreciation of the senses and the pleasure derived there from, and the centrality of art. Nietzsche thought that the notion of evolution gave the *coup de grace* to otherworldly dualism and underscored our definitive belonging to the earth. Heidegger assimilated Nietzsche here in his notion of Earth as furnishing one pole for which the other is World. For Heidegger, both notions together articulate the sense of Being as the element of human dwelling.

(We should note in passing that in Plato there are countervailing texts to radical dualism and contempt for the body of which the spinning top is perhaps the most suggestive: the upright position of the soul, once found, is such that the outer motions from the body support rather than erratically mislead the soul. This gives harmony to the whole soul. In the *Timaeus*, the body is made to be the house of the soul, suggesting a psychological rather than an ontological reading of problems with the body.)[222]

In the case of each thinker we have examined, art has a significant role to play in coming into relation with encompassing truth. In Plato, it tunes the dispositions, rendering them harmonic so that they recognize reason when it arises. Reason here should be understood as that which uncovers the harmonic truth of the Whole as a cosmos, an ordered totality. Regional disciplines like mathematics find their place within the overarching region of the Forms rendered manifest by the light provided by the Good/One/Beautiful.

In Heidegger, art gathers the powers of human existence as it gathers the Whole into a place for human dwelling. It provides a "sense" of Being as the element in which we live. It is the work of the work of art to bring about the tension between Earth and World and prevent meaning from collapsing into the everyday. The work of art opens a World for dwelling and sets it upon the Earth. Conceptual thought has its own role to play, but it ultimately feeds off of the encompassing sense of Being expressed and induced by the arts. Art involves bringing to presence a sense of the hidden behind what is manifest.

In Nietzsche, art is the most perspicuous manifestation of the principle of the Whole: the Will to Power as the will to create beyond one's current state and beyond oneself within the encompassing horizon of Eternal

---

222. In the *Timaeus*, Plato uses various terms indicating a "housing" of the soul in the body: *prosoikodomoun* (69c), *katoikoun* (70e), *oikisthe* (72d), *katoikisthai,* and *oikein* (89e).

Recurrence. It is premised upon the traditions that give focus to the chaos of human possibilities. An artist brings to perfection a line of possibilities or opens new lines playing in tandem with the previous lines. An artist fuses the dynamic Dionysian with the ordering Apollonian, giving form to emotional upsurge, individuation to a sense of belonging to the Whole. But in the human being, such upsurge is tied essentially to the coming into focus of the eternal encompassing that involves a whole way of life. The deeper art is the formation of one's life, bringing unity to the potential chaos of directions, in relation to formative traditions. In Nietzsche, all of this mirrors the Whole as self-transcending form-bestowal in Eternal Recurrence.

I want to underscore that in all three thinkers what is at stake is "life" or "dwelling," not only *recognition* or correct assertion or systematic connection between correct assertions but the how of one's relation to the whole of experience. In Nietzsche's expression, it involves truth in service of life—or, one might say, it involves a true life. Heidegger's highlighting of the function of *aletheia* in Plato shows it as background. It operates through the evocation of Eros by the radiance of Beauty and is linked to *thaumazein* as enduring ground of philosophy.[223] Nietzsche appropriates the erotic dimension in the notion of the Dionysiac that preserves the sense of the cosmic Whole as ground and background for the Apollonian focus upon the clear and distinct. For Heidegger, what is involved is "the creation of world space" as space for dwelling. What for the most part articulates that space is art, especially poetry, that gathers the Fourfold. But philosophy also "creates world space," though it tends focally toward the objects clarified within that space, tending to forget the mode of dwelling within it and deflecting attention away from the immediate sensuously given. The ultimate term of that forgetting is the alliance between science and technology, each requiring the other. Such forgetting *empties* world space. Art recalls us to the sense of Being and sets it upon the Earth.

At this point, leaving behind exposition of the three thinkers, I want to follow especially the Heideggerian direction of the notion of Being articulated through the bipolarity of Earth and World—or the later Play of

223. See Martin Heidegger, *What Is Philosophy?* trans. W. Klubak and J. Wilde (New York: Twayne, 1958), 78–85.

the Fourfold. I do so in order to establish the enduring framework within which human existence and in it all thought-forms operate.

Human existence, I would maintain, is fundamentally bipolar as an organically rooted empty reference to the Whole of beings through the functioning of the notion of Being. The articulation of a world for human dwelling takes place in the space between the now of organic life and our reference to the encompassing Whole. This bipolarity constitutes the irremovable framework within which perspectives on the Whole come to exist. In fact, that structure explains why there has to be perspectives: because of the essential perspectivity of our biological grounding and the emptiness of our reference to the Whole. Such structure entails an imperative to enter into dialogue with the multiple perspectives present in the history of thought and in our contemporaries with a view toward gaining a more adequate understanding of our place in the whole scheme of things.[224]

Organic rootage is most obvious. In all wakeful life, we are confronted with the manifest actuality of individual bodies outside us in the environment of our own bodies. Our bodily organs mediate the manifestation and are supported by the metabolic activities going on under the surface. Initially, our whole attention—and, subsequently, a great deal of our attention—is taken up with such display operating in function of our bodily needs. So obvious is this mode of display that most people—including sophisticated scientists—are perennially tempted to take it as identical with, rather than being one mode of, the manifestation of what is. What is sensorily manifest are colored, sounding, extended actual individuals contained within their own boundaries and in observable causal sequence with their antecedents and consequents. This is what we commonsensically describe as a "body." One might cite here the early Augustine, who could conceive of nothing that was not a body.[225] One might also cite a plethora of reductionists working today in the sciences or influenced popularly by those who do so conceive of things. But sensory awareness itself, as a mode of self-presence grounding the manifestation of what is other and outside our own circumscribed bodies, goes beyond body in that sense of the term. We can easily overlook this self-

224. For a further development of this analysis, see my *Placing Aesthetics*, ch. 1. See also my "Nature, Culture, and the Dialogical Imperative," the first chapter in this collection.
225. Augustine, *Confessions*, VII, 1.

presence because we are preoccupied with the externally given and tend to model all our thinking upon that.[226]

What is even less obvious is the other pole of our being: initially empty reference to the Whole of beings. But it is the ground of the distinctively human: of religion, theoretical inquiry, art, justice. It is the ground of the questions: "What's it *all* about? How do we fit in *the whole scheme of things*? What is this scheme of things?" In Heidegger's phrase, humans exist as "the question of Being," directed toward the Whole but not in possession of it.

Articulated in any judgment that something *is* the case, the notion of Being encompasses everything because outside being there is nothing. As Aquinas would have it, Being is what first occurs within intellectual operation and with it the unrestricted principle of noncontradiction comes to light. The notion of Being gives us a scope that refers to absolutely everything, including God, but only initially in the form of a question.[227] Nietzsche was, indeed, right: the notion of Being is, by itself, sheer emptiness. But because the initial givenness is empty, we are drawn beyond empirical surface to the underlying powers and essences grounding the powers, and on to the ultimate ground. That surface is an appearance relative to the kind of filtering equipment provided by our own organs. We can reach toward the scope of the fullness of Being only by beginning at the other pole, the positive pole of organically grounded sensory experience.

The recognition of these general structural features involves an abstraction from the particularity of what is given in the sensory field. We grasp the eidetic structures as indefinitely repeatable wherever and whenever we might meet them. They involve a reference to space and time as a whole on the part of the mind that apprehends them. Such reference particularizes the overarching reference to beings as a whole that makes the mind a mind.

These observations, I would claim, are nonperspectival. They are as-

226. See my "Five Bodies and a Sixth: On the Place of Awareness in the Cosmos" later in this collection.

227. See Aquinas's distinction between the scope and power of intellect: its scope is all things, and its power is limited to knowing what is involved in knowing sensorily appearing things. But in the afterlife the power will be raised to the scope when, through the "light of glory," we shall see God, the Fullness of Being, face to face. Aquinas, *Summa Contra Gentiles*, III, ch. LIV.

pects of the reflective self-presence of mind. But they are founded upon and directed toward a Whole that indeterminately exceeds whatever is placed within our bipolar field. This, I would further claim, is exactly what is at stake in Plato's Line of Knowledge.[228] The nonperspectivity of the play of the fourfold of intelligible-sensible, intellect-intelligible, intellect-sense, and sense-sensible operating under the light of the Good is what founds *philosophia*. Love of wisdom involves an awareness of lack that propels us beyond where we might currently stand. It entails a dialogical imperative to criticize and appropriate light from any source, beginning with our own lights. Nonperspectival self-presence, with the manifest structural levels included therein, founds the construction and critique of perspectives aimed at the final truth of the Whole.

Nietzsche's assimilation of evolutionary theory in his notion of Will to Power as self-transcendence through form-bestowal underscores the essential belonging to the Earth of peculiarly human transcendence. It resituates the field of awareness within a broader framework that involves a transformation of our notion of matter as the locus of the active powers that lead to its own manifestation through the emergence of distinctively human awareness. Body is the locus of the epiphany of eternal encompassment. The organic, the senses, physical beauty, the arts: all underscore our essential belonging to the Earth. But it is still the belonging to the Earth of an awareness aimed at the encompassing Whole.[229]

It is that same reference to the Whole that pries us loose from the determinations that arise from the organic pole and condemns us each to be a unique "I," a responsible center of awareness forced to choose among the options available as we have come to understand them. Now, the options have been provided by the sedimented choices of others long dead that have come to fill the initially empty space with visions of the Whole as the arena for thought, action, and feeling. Such options do not simply lie outside us; they enter into the fabric of our own self-awareness. The freely self-determining and responsible I plays in tandem with the already determinate Me that establishes my concrete possibilities for responding to what is given from without in nature and in culture. The

---

228. See my "Plato's Line Revisited" in the present work.

229. See my "Potentiality, Creativity, and Relationality: Toward a 'New' Transcendental?" as an attempt to assimilate Nietzsche's views. *The Review of Metaphysics* 59, no. 2 (December 2005): 379–401.

determinate Me has a three-leveled structure. At the basic level is the genetic Me that contains the possibilities in the human gene pool focused in the peculiar way that is *my* distinctive set of possibilities. But since the genetically determined self arrives helpless, its peculiar possibilities are identified and focused through the mediations of others: parents, neighbors, friends, teachers, and the media generally. My parents taught me language and ways of behaving and understanding peculiar to our culture. Together with others, they provided to the initial stamp given by my genetic constitution a second stamp, narrowing but also focusing my possibilities. I did not ask to be born, to speak English, to be Catholic, lower-middle class, twentieth century, mid-Western American—indeed, to have the peculiar "feel" that comes with belonging to such a world. But with the emergence of the reflective I, I have chosen among the possibilities afforded by those two stamps within the limits of my own understanding and the mediations of others. All of this provides the habit structure that I currently have, with all the possibilities and limits that it imposes. All of this percolates down into a set of felt proclivities to behave, establishing in the environment a set of magnetic attractors that spontaneously solicit my attention. They appeal to what a long tradition has come to call "the heart," the aspect of Me closest to the I, the Me with which I spontaneously identify. That is, I would maintain, the region expressed and appealed to by art.[230]

Nonetheless, being projected toward the Whole via the notion of Being, I am perpetually pried loose from what I determinately am and condemned to choose how to shape it within the limits of my understanding of my concrete possibilities. I have to ask myself, "Where is my heart? Is it where it ought to be? And, further, where ought it to be?" It is the work of intellect to detach one from one's own heart, one's own deeply rooted subjectivity, one's own thoughts and preferences, in order to find the measures of human existence. Those measures lie in how we stand in relation to the Whole anticipated but not given in the very structure of human awareness. The basis for such measures has been exposed and discussed from multiple perspectives in the history of thought. And it is

230. This is one of the meanings of "placing aesthetics" in the title of my book *Placing Aesthetics*: placing aesthetics in the field of human experience. The other two meanings are placing it in the history of thought from Plato to Heidegger and placing it within the overall conceptual context of each thinker.

to that tradition that we go in order to guide our thoughts, even as we might venture beyond it.

I want to emphasize the fact that the antecedent filling of the space of meaning by tradition is what frees my possibilities—though it does so by chaining others. Furthermore, we have no current means of knowing what further possibilities lie hidden in the gene pool that could be identified, focused, and honed to perfection. History is the arena for the creation of institutions that carry that out.

How do such considerations aid in our understanding of the relation between art and truth? I would maintain that it is through the notion of the heart as the center of the self. Art expresses and effects human disposition. As the heart can sink down into the biological in pornographic art, it can rise to a mystical sensibility in religious art. Indeed, because human structure is a biologically grounded reference to the Whole, what comes out of the heart in expression and what addresses the heart from without carries in some way a sense of the Whole. Abstract thought, focused upon truths, may easily forget the rootage of the person in the sense of the Whole and may even take place in the context of a darkening of that sense. As Kierkegaard would have it, philosophers construct magnificent thought castles but dwell in miserable shacks nearby.[231] This is what provoked Heidegger's "startled dismay" at the forgottenness of Being. The sense of Being as the sense of the Mystery of eternal encompassment still operated, unthought, behind the tradition; but in modern times, it has dried up so that, in spite of all our conceptual and technological achievements, we are like fish out of water. The sense of Mystery no longer pervades our modes of thinking, acting, and feeling. Abstract thought, by itself, is insufficient. It has to be brought back to concrete dwelling, the intellect brought back to the heart. It is art's task to effect that return, that rootage of abstract meaning in the sense of Being.

But the heart does not exist in solitude and privacy. Human existence, as *Da-Sein*, as the place for the display of the sense of the Whole, is essentially Being-in-a-World. Its *Dasein* is essentially *Mit-Dasein*.[232] It has been initially shaped by the way the culture has been mediated by those who raised us in interplay with our own genetically based proclivi-

231. Kierkegaard, *Concluding Unscientific Postscript to Philosophical Fragments*, 181ff.
232. Heidegger, *Being and Time*, 153ff.

ties. It has been subsequently shaped by the way we have made our own choices from among the enlarged sense of our possibilities learned by experience and study, both of which bring a widened sense of culture into the picture. In this way, we have come to take our place within our collective world. The heart is the locus of inhabiting that world. Our own hearts are variations on themes provided by tradition.

Art arises out of attunement to the complex cultural world. It is more or less deep the more or less sensitive it is to the richness and depth of the strands contained therein. At its best, it expresses and solicits the sense of Mystery that surrounds the everyday. As the sensory exhibition of things gives us a sort of dashboard knowledge relevant to our biological mode of adjustment, so also with the cultural mode of taking up the sensory field.[233] We glance, categorize, and respond routinely to what appears. This aids practical functioning and collective adjustment. But in our own unreflectiveness, we tend to forget the depth that underlies our ordinary field of awareness. Inhabiting a world takes place against the background of being projected toward the encompassing Whole. Our small island of sensory and cultural light is surrounded by an encompassing darkness. But it is that to which we are essentially directed, to the Mystery out of which all manifestation emerges and into which it falls back.

Art is able to set the sense of Mystery upon the Earth of sensuousness, articulating the space of inhabitance for the human heart. Art presents the truth of the Whole for human dwelling that plays in dialectic with intellectual insight, construction, and critique. In Heidegger's image, philosophers stand over against the poets—the latter along with artists in general—on twin peaks equidistant from the world of everydayness. They call out to one another and together create so much world space that even the ordinary appears as it really is, extraordinary.

Whitehead said that the history of Western thought is a series of footnotes on Plato.[234] Our study has verified that in the cases of Nietzsche and Heidegger. Our own reflective response worked in relation to an understanding of the nonperspectivity of the Line of Knowledge as the self-presence of mind. The light of the Good underwent a transformation with

233. Cf. my *A Path into Metaphysics*, ch. 1.
234. Alfred North Whitehead, *Adventures of Ideas* (New York: Free Press, 1967), 228.

Heidegger's notion of Being as essentially hidden and Form-disclosure as essentially perspectival. Nietzsche's fidelity to the earth shed the negative understanding of bodiliness that dogged the Platonic tradition and pointed to a resituating of the field of awareness within an evolutionarily transformed notion of the cosmos and our place in it.

In each of the thinkers, art's role operated at the limits of conceptuality. And it operated in such a way as to bring the whole soul into relation with the ultimate, however that was conceived. Art is able to give articulation to the belonging of the whole soul to the character of the encompassing Whole. As such its task is not surface decoration "three degrees removed from reality." Its deepest task is to create a space for human dwelling, to bring the human heart into the truth of its belonging to the Whole, and to set that upon the Earth of sensibility. Its sensuousness is full of sense. Making full human sense is learning to inhabit the sensible, open to the eternal encompassing.

8 ∽ The Heart in/of Augustine's *Confessions*

A Contribution to Religious Phenomenology

The notion of *cor*, the heart, lies at the heart of Augustine's thought. It appears some 2,262 times in his works and some seventy-five times in his *Confessions*. It is its function in the latter work that I will examine in this chapter.

Cor appears at the beginning of the work in one of its most memorable lines: "You have made us for Yourself, O Lord; and our hearts are restless and will not rest until they rest in You" (I, i, I/2.).[1] The divine correlate appears at the end of Augustine's search in the vision of "Beauty ever ancient, ever new" as object of the heart's search, the beauty of God, Who, at the end of the volume, is announced as His own rest (X, xxvii II/146). In between, Augustine recounts the restlessness of his own life, the tumult of his heart, torn apart and tumbling through time.

Because Augustine describes his errant life, one might think that the *Confessions* is a confession of his sinfulness. However, the term *confessio*, as in *confessio fidei*, actually means "profession" or acknowledgment. Furthermore, the genre of the work is not simply autobiography, nor is it simply, in addition, philosophic and theological reflection that pres-

This chapter is a very belated follow-up on the sketch I gave in the introduction to my translation of Stephan Strasser's *Das Gemüt (Utrecht and Freiburg, 1956)* as *Phenomenology of Feeling: An Essay on the Phenomena of the Heart* (Pittsburgh: Duquesne University Press, 1977). It was presented at the Baylor University conference on Augustine's *Confessions*.

I want to acknowledge the helpful remarks made by Raymond deLorenzo, Kenneth Schmitz, and Roland Teske on an early version of this chapter.

1. "Fecisti nos ad te, Domine, et inquietum est cor nostrum, donec requiscat in te." St. Augustine's *Confessions*, trans. William Watt (Cambridge, Mass.: Harvard University Press, 1977). The translations are my own. I will use the translations in the body of the text and give the Latin original in the notes. I will refer to the *Confessions* with Roman capitals for the books and Roman lowercase for the sections, followed by the volume number of the Loeb edition in Roman capitals and the page number in Arabic separated from the volume number by a slash.

ents certain objective truths. It is all these within the context of speaking to God that arise out of dwelling from the bottom of one's heart in the presence of God. It acknowledges to others the work of God in Augustine's life and in the creation in which he had the privilege to share. It is a prime example of what Kierkegaard calls *subjective truth*: the speaking to our hearts, in passion and inwardness, of the Mystery surrounding every objective truth.[2] That is why we claim that the meaning-center, the heart of the *Confessions*, is the notion of the heart.

Books I–IX are a recapitulation of Augustine's personal journey from birth to his conversion. They begin with a personal address to God, an address that follows the liturgical command, "Lift up your hearts!": "You are great, Lord, and exceedingly praiseworthy" (I, i, I/2).[3] The *Confessions* is a prayer of praise to divine power and wisdom as displayed in Augustine's own life and, at the end of the work, in the cosmos itself as divine creation. After the autobiographical journey, he comes back reflectively into his own mind in Book X, specifically to examine its *memoria*, the pool from which the concrete individual proclivities of the heart arise, in order to search out the grounds for its ability to recapitulate its own journey and its cosmic locus in the temporality of the world both as gift of its Creator and as the place of exile.

The notion of heart is intimately linked to the notion of *anima* as distinct from *animus*, both of which are usually translated as "soul." I claim that *anima*, as animating principle, is, in its conscious phase, heart, while *animus* is judging and controlling ego. *Anima* appears throughout but in an especially illuminating way at the beginning of Book X, a privileged moment that follows the recapitulation of Augustine's wanderings.

Like Book I, Book X begins its reflections upon the grounds of the recollection in the first nine books with an address to God that focuses on the heart as linked to *anima*: "Let me know you, my knower, let me know you as I am known. Power of my soul, enter into it and take it over for yourself" (X, i, II/74).[4] What Augustine requests is not simply some intellectual insight, some "proof for the existence of God" carried

2. Søren Kierkegaard, *Concluding Unscientific Postscript to Philosophical Fragments*, trans. D. Senson (Princeton, N.J.: Princeton University Press, 1941), 267–322.

3. "Magnus es, domine, et laudabilis valde."

4. "Cognoscam te, cognitor meus, cognoscam, sicut et cognitus sum. Virtus animae meae, intra in eam et coapta tibi."

out through rational demonstration—though as a matter of *fides quae-rens intellectum*, of faith seeking understanding, he is not uninterested in such demonstration.[5] What he requests is that God enter into the *anima*. He asks that God establish in his *anima* a sense of nearness reciprocal to the nearness that God on His part always has to the soul—and, indeed, to all His creatures.

For Augustine, God is *interior intimo meo et superior superiori meo*, "interior to what is most intimate to me and superior to what is highest in me" (III, vi, I/120).[6] Noting of God that "He is intimate to the heart, but the heart strayed from Him," he declares and admonishes in Book IV (xii, I/180): "Return, sinners, to the heart, and cling to Him who made you."[7]

Augustine follows the typical neo-Platonic route: to find God we have to turn *within* to that interior and *above* to that height. So in Book X, in his treatment of *memoria*, Augustine turns within. We are reminded of the very end of Husserl's *Cartesian Meditations*, where he cites Augustine's words from *De vera religione*: "Do not go outside. Return into yourself. In the interior man dwells the truth."[8] We begin in animal extroversion: by a necessity of nature turned outside, magnetized by sensory forms that evoke biological resonances within our awareness. In Book X, Augustine writes: "And behold, You were within me and I without" (X, xxvii, II/126).[9] Precisely because our predominant extroversion is a function of bodily based desire, any encountered other is viewed in terms of one's own need, so that, as Augustine also says of this condition, "I was locked up within myself." Now from the point of view of physical existence, these statements are contradictory: I was outside myself; I was locked up inside myself. But from the point of view of psychic life, they reveal a truth, provided we understand what the "interior man" is.

---

5. The expression is Anselm's; Augustine himself says something similar: "*Crede ut intelligas*, I believe in order that I might understand." Anselm, *Proslogion*, edited and with an introduction by Thomas Williams (Indianapolis: Hackett, 2001), §1; Augustine, *Tractates on the Gospel of John*, trans. J. Rettig (Washington, D.C.: The Catholic University of America Press, 2002), 29.6.

6. "[I]nterior intimo meo et superior summo meo."

7. "[I]ntimus cordi est, sed cor erravit ab eo. Redite, praevaricatores, ad cor, et inhaerete illi, qui fecit vos."

8. "Noli foras ire. In te redi. In interiore homine habitat veritas." St. Augustine's *On True Religion*, trans. J. Burleigh and L. Mink (New York: Henri Regnery, 1991.), §39; Edmund Husserl, *Cartesian Meditations*, §64.

9. "Et ecce intus eras et ego foris."

To go "inside" in the sense in which Augustine is using this metaphor is not simply to retreat into some purely private subjective realm, even though that is an aspect of the retreat. In his discussion of *memoria* in Book X, Augustine uncovers various levels of so-called interiority. The deeper levels involve the apprehension of eidetic necessities, for example, in mathematics (X, xii, II/106), which stand above the mind.

God is "*interior intimo meo,* interior to my most intimate self," because He is my Creator and I am ultimately a mystery to myself. There is much in me to which I have no access: the memory, Augustine says, cannot contain itself; there is so much I am unable to retrieve (X, viii, II/98). And for whatever within me of which I am or have been or could be conscious, there is so much entailed of which I will never be aware. Not only am I for the most part caught in animal extroversion, I am for the most part oblivious of all that is within me, and even of what I most deeply desire. Further, what I desire I am not able to bring about because I find my will and my very desire divided. Augustine says, "I myself had become a great question to myself" (IV, iv. I/160).[10] Yet, while I am far from being transparent to myself, if God's Word draws me and all things from nothing, I am totally transparent to the gaze of God. Hence He is indeed, interior to my interior, closer to me than I am to myself. At the same time, as Augustine mounts up through the various levels of interiority and arrives at "*animi mei sedem,* the seat of my intellect"[11] (X, xxv, II/142) or "*caput animae meae,* the head of my soul" (X, vii, II/92), he notes that He Who made it still stands above it: immanent within and simultaneously transcendent of the soul that is made and continually grounded by and for Him.

So at the beginning of Book X (i, I/2), he asks God as the power of his soul (*virtus animae*) to enter into it. Later in Book X (xx, II/128), he clarifies what is involved in calling God "the power of my soul." He says, "For as my body lives by my soul (*anima*), so my *anima* lives by You."[12] There is a bi-level analysis here: *anima* animates, vivifies the body; God vivifies the *anima.* This bypasses the tri-level analysis one might expect: the body lives by

10. "Factus eram ipse mihi magna quaestio."
11. I translate *animus* as "intellect" and not as "soul" because the latter is captured by *anima* and because Augustine speaks of "*ego animus*" when addressing his *anima* and asking why it is sad.
12. "Vivit enim corpus meum de anima mea, et vivit anima mea de te."

the soul, the soul by the conscious mind, and the conscious mind by God. One would expect this because Augustine rather consistently uses the masculine term *animus* for the conscious, controlling self, the *ego-animus* that he counterposes to the *anima*. For example, in Book X (xvi, II/118) he says: "I am the one who remembers, I *animus*."[13] And he regularly uses the feminine *anima* for that which animates the body. The absence of *animus* in the passage where he says that the *anima* lives by God as the body by the *anima* suggests that *anima* here stands for both that which vivifies the body *and* for the conscious self. Yet, because of functions like *memoria*, which is a nonconscious repository of past experience (sometimes retrievable by consciousness, sometimes not), and the deep desire of the soul, *anima* may be not only wider than that which vivifies the body but also wider than the conscious self or *animus*. God empowers, gives life to the whole psycho-physical, conscious-unconscious self. So Augustine says, "I sought you so that my soul/*anima* might live" (X, vi, II/128).[14] The animation of the body occurs not as end but as basis for the seeking. The life of the *anima* he seeks is the stilling of the restless heart.

This interpretation is supported by the passage that follows and which, in effect, comments on the quotation already cited: "As the body lives by the soul, so the soul lives by God." Augustine noted that the beauty of things is their testimony to their creator and that, as he says— and with significant reduplication: "I the interior man knew these things, I, I the *animus*."[15] The use of the Latin term *ego* would already have been emphatic, since the verb *cognovi* (I knew) by itself would have included the I, but Augustine is not satisfied: he repeats the term "*ego*" two more times, the second time identifying it with *animus*. And then a few lines later, he goes on to say: "For, I say to you [and here he simply uses *dico* with no *ego* connected with it], you [*anima*] are better, because you enliven the mass of your body, offering it life—something which no body can give to another body. But your God also is to you the life of your life."[16] The interior ego is the *animus* that is capable of making intellectual inference from creature to Creator and of taking responsibility for deci-

13. "Ego sum, qui memini, ego animus."
14. "Quaeram te, ut vivat anima mea."
15. "Ego interior cognovi haec, ego, ego animus."
16. "Iam tu melior es, tibi dico, anima, quoniam tu vegetas molem corporis tui praebens ei vitam, quod nullum corpus praestat corpori. Deus autem tuus etiam tibi vitae vita est."

sions. And that ego speaks to the *anima* as both informing the body with life and being informed in turn, as ground of the whole psychophysical self, by God as its life.

But in the beginning of Book X, God is asked to "enter into" the *anima* in such a way as to take it over. If the *anima* is the life of the body and is, by nature, in its turn, vivified by God, the invocation makes no sense. So *anima* has to have a wider meaning. We see what that is when, upon the death of his friend, Augustine remarks on the pain that darkened his heart: "With what sorrow was my heart darkened. . . . And I asked my *anima* why it was sad." It could not afford a response (IV, iv, I/160).[17] Notice that he speaks of his *cor*/heart as darkened and then addresses his *anima*, indicating that the two are closely related and, in a sense, identical. Since the *anima* animates the body without the conscious ego being aware of it or understanding exactly how, *cor* would be the *anima* as it enters into the light of awareness. Augustine goes on: When he told his *anima* to hope in God—but at the stage of his life where he conceived of God erroneously—it rightly did not obey.[18] The resistance of the heart to command is here rooted in a dim recognition at the level of the *cor/anima* of the falsity of the command.

But even if the *cor/anima* and not the controlling ego is in error, the former cannot be directly commanded. Augustine wrestles with this at the death of his mother when he was bothered that his controlling *ego-animus* could not hold back the tears that welled up from his *cor/anima* (IX, xii). The conscious ego addresses its own self as affectively tuned: I as actively commanding ego address Me as being affected. Here *anima* is a feature of consciousness as the seat of affectivity. And it is just that involved in the notion of the *cor*, the heart. Heart is the seat of the emotions, the locus of the gravitational attraction experienced by the conscious self in relation to a desired object. Augustine finds a duality within his consciousness between his *cor* and his *animus*. He as controlling ego is not master in his own house. It is here that he goes on to say: "I myself have become a great question to myself" (IV, iv, I/160).[19]

The masculine *animus* and the feminine *anima* seem apt designa-

---

17. "Quo dolore contenebratum est cor meum. . . . Et interrogabam animam meam, quare tristis esset."

18. "Nihil noverat respondere mihi. Et si dicebam: 'spera in deum,' iuste non obtemperabat."

19. "Factus eram ipse mihi magna quaestio."

tions: viewed as analogous to the purely physical aspects of sexuality, the masculine is the active, giving principle, the feminine the passive, receiving principle. However, such receiving is not simply from the conscious *animus*; it is from whatever attracts the conscious aspect of the *anima*, whatever solicits the *cor*. And indeed, as in interpersonal relations, the feminine is not simply receptive, it is also supportive and controlling. The *cor* is the conscious part of the *anima* which, in its unconscious phase, also animates the body. As conscious it carries the *animus*, the self-directive center of judgment and responsibility. One chooses and thinks spontaneously in the direction of the heart, where one's dispositions tend to take one. The controlling *ego* is typically controlled by its *cor/anima*. Early in Book I (I, ii, I/4), he asks: "And what is the place within me by which my God comes into me?"[20] I propose that such locus is the *cor*, the conscious dimension of the *anima*, which is the principle of total life, unconscious-conscious, physiological, sensory, intellectual, which juts into consciousness as the locus of the conscious ego's gravitational attraction toward significant presences. In Book XIII (ix, II/390), he refers to the *pondus amoris*, the weight of love, the basic activity of the heart: "My weight is my love by which I am carried wherever I am carried."[21] The total self is not detached and fully self-directive, choosing arbitrarily and *ex nihilo* to change directions in the most fundamental character of its life. If I choose to abandon all that I have been, it would be because, as Augustine's account of his own history makes clear, the support for the fundamental direction of my life has been gradually shifting over a long period of time. The weight of my love would have to have been redirected little by little to another gravitational field. My heart would have to have been changed radically, converted. A gradual change of heart produces a struggle and then supports a culminating decision. Of course, it could also happen that the change of heart occurs suddenly by the intrusion of grace, as in St. Paul's being knocked from his high-horse.

The spontaneous directedness of the heart has a three—or perhaps fourfold origin. First are the inborn biological proclivities of our first nature boiling up from the animating principle into the field of awareness at the level of desire arising in the heart. At this level, Augustine was saddled with an overweening *libido*, which was the focal point of

---

20. "Et quis locus est in me, quo veniat in me deus meus?"
21. "Pondus meum amor meus; eo feror, quocumque feror."

his personal and intellectual struggles up to the time of the *Tolle, lege* experience that sparked his final conversion. A second formative influence upon the heart is the stamp of significant others, beginning with the ones who raised us, educated us, impacted and continue to impact us as friends and acquaintances or as the more pervasive forces of a given culture. This initially determines the further specification of the primordial set of directions made possible by our first nature. The third influence is the sedimented result of the decisions we have made within the context of the possibilities opened up by the interplay of nature and culture in our specific context as we understand those possibilities. This is what is proximately involved in the final determination of the *pondus amoris*, which provides the directive horizon of our everyday decisions.[22]

But there is another dimension to first nature: nature in us is not only biological; it is also spiritual, if we may use that term here. We are by nature referred to the Whole of what is, to all of being. In the Platonic tradition, this reference is fundamental human Eros aimed at the cosmic Good as the One, the end and origin, the omega and the alpha, the fullness of being of which everything else is an imitation and of which Beauty itself is the radiance.[23] That there is this reference to the Whole is clear from the fact that there are religions, that is, claims to tell the story of the Whole and how we humans fit into it. In Heidegger's way of putting it, human beings exist as the question (not as the possession) of Being, beyond any and all beings, which reference allows the question of beings as a whole to come to light.[24] It is precisely this reference to the Whole that affords us the distance from what we are and that condemns us to have to choose from among the concrete options available to us. This grounds the self-conscious and relatively self-directive ego, the I as a clearing supported by the Me, by the sum total of genetic, cultural, and historical-personal determinations concretely making me, Me. I am at a distance from the historically constituted Me because there is a dimension of Me that points beyond everything objectifiable to the Plenitude.[25] One might speak of the

22. This is what I call the I-Me relation. For a brief discussion, see the first chapter of my *Placing Aesthetics* (Athens: Ohio University Press, 1999).

23. *Republic*, VI. See *Placing Aesthetics*, ch. 2, for an exposition of these notions within the basic conceptual scheme involved in Plato's dialogues.

24. Heidegger, *Being and Time*, 27.

25. See my *Placing Aesthetics*, 11. I have addressed this in "Hegel on the Heart," *International Philosophical Quarterly* 41, no. 2 (June 2001): 131–44.

seat of the native desire for that Plenitude as *my heart of hearts.*[26] If the fundamental weight of my love, located in my heart that carries the weight of the past, does not coincide with the native direction toward the Plenitude, my heart is wounded, distracted, torn in two, even if it might be powerfully integrated around a consuming project. That weight constitutes the most fundamental functioning horizon of conscious life as the sedimented resultant of our whole history. To speak Heideggerian language, this gives us our basic *Bestimmung*, our *Befindlichkeit*, our fundamental attunement, the pervasive mood in which we find ourselves.[27] And that mood is characterized of necessity as a fundamental *Angst*, a permanent unsettledness because we are not in possession of the Whole to which we are directed.[28] Of that the *animus* might be entirely oblivious, focused as it is upon various kinds of objects, external or internal, low or high, rising to the consideration of the highest objects, existing in what we might call the space of exiled consciousness. The conscious self might not understand at all what underpins its own attention as its motivational source in its own heart.

Augustine speaks of *voluntas* or will as the origin of self-direction. But that is supported by what Aquinas called *voluntas ut secunda natura*, will as second nature, will as spontaneous directedness, as being carried by the *pondus amoris* in the heart.[29] It is that which is transformed by the intrusion of God's grace within the field of experience to enlighten and strengthen the divided will. The heart as *secunda natura* is the locus of the basic functioning horizon; the heart as *prima natura*, as every human being's "heart of hearts," is the source of the most basic horizon. The task of human life is to make the concretely functioning horizon of my action, the basic lived-through project of my heart, coincide with the native desire of the heart. "Our hearts are restless and shall not rest until they rest in Thee."

Our basic problem is one of the divided heart. In Book VIII, Augustine speaks several places of the *animus* commanding yet finding resistance within its own awareness (VIII, ix, I/446).[30] He says that it does not

26. I looked for this in Augustine and could not find it, continuous with his own thrust though it may be. So apposite is it that a computer search for the term in conjunction with Augustine turned up over 250 instances in passages that mention Augustine!
27. Heidegger, *Being and Time*, 72ff.
28. Ibid., 228–35.
29. Aquinas, *Summa Theologiae*, I-II, 10, 1, ad 1.
30. "Imperat animus sibi et resistitur."

command from its wholeness because it does not will from its wholeness (VIII, ix, I/448).[31] Here the *animus* is the source of command and thus functions as will. But Augustine speaks of two or more wills (VIII, v I/424 and x, I/454).

There are at least two levels of analysis here: chronologically, it may be a matter of contradictory choices whose bases set up a struggle within. And when we consider the bases, we are at the level of motivational sources, that is, at the level of the heart. Choice is not groundless but is based upon preference. And preference is not for the most part a matter of clearly analyzed reasons but a matter of habitual disposition. Further, it is not only a question of choice but also of the ability to carry through the choice; and not only carry through but also find delight therein, experiencing thereby the unity of the self in understanding, choosing, and feeling. One could make a decision and act it out but find no delight in it, so there is a distinction. But one decides on the basis of motives that may be more or less explicit. And one can weigh motives in terms of explicit criteria. So one could say that intellectually we weigh options, come up with the most rational, and choose accordingly—accompanied by delight or not. But this is not sufficient to explain choice, since one tends to invent reasons that support the direction in which one is already moving. That is the function of apologetics in any faith-community where the relation between reason and rationalization is difficult to determine. However, Augustine notes that even at our most rational in analyzing, assessing, choosing, and acting, we can be divided between our heart and our intellect. And even if we decide and act in terms of our rational assessment, we are divided if we find no relish in what we do.

Augustine found himself at the level of final assessment where one side of him wanted chastity, and so he prayed for it; but the other side relished intercourse. He reflected his ambiguity in prayer: "Lord, give me chastity and continence, but not just now!" (VIII, vii, I/440).[32] He understood his sorry state in being unable to secure the chastity he desired and was only able to do so through taking up of Scripture and being flooded with a different kind of light than that of intellectual recognition.[33]

31. "[S]ed non ex toto vult: non ergo ex toto imperat."
32. "Da mihi castitatem et continentiam, sed noli modo."
33. I worry about his final assessment regarding chastity. What he found wrong about sexual experience was his inability to exercise total control at the moment of orgasm: here he was

In the divided state, Augustine finds that the *animus* cannot operate *ex toto*, from its totality. This hearkens back to the Old Testament command to love God with one's whole heart, mind, and soul (Deuteronomy 6:5). One can *want* so to love God, but one might also find no particular relish in the effort. One lives in anguish at having one's heart divided. Its healing and thus its ability to fulfill the command is something only possible through the gift of God's presence inflaming the heart. Strange command, this: one is commanded to do something one cannot do on one's own: hence, the tendency to understand—and thus *mis*understand—it as a matter of willing alone.

The *ego animus* exists as a self-presence in the space of self-directive awareness, which is a kind of exile from the divine so deep that it is not usually felt as an exile, except insofar as a certain restlessness propels it on. That exile is time understood as the *distentio animi*, the "distention" of the ego-*animus*, judging and choosing awareness being dissipated, scattered, subjected to tumult in the heart as its polar opposite and ground. Augustine remarked, "Whence it seemed to me that time was nothing else than distention; but of what, I know not. And it is a wonder if it is not of the *animus* itself" (XI, xxvi, 268).[34]

Augustine further locates the three dimensions of time in the ego-*animus*: the future exists in the expectation of the *animus* now, the present itself in its attention, and the past in its remembrance (XI, xxviii, II/276).[35] This accounts for the three temporal dimensions, at least insofar as focal experience is concerned. But then he goes on to consider his whole life as a *distentio* that he describes as being dissolved in time, torn (*dilaniatur*) by a tumult of diverse attractions even to the intimate viscera of his *anima*, the depths of his heart and its desires, ignorant of their proper order. With this, he contrasts his life's being *extentus*, extended, broadened by following the deliberate intention of eternity. "Behold," he

---

being taken beyond his controlling *animus*. This is more a Stoic than a Christian notion. On Augustine's "nervousness" regarding sensory experience, see Hans Urs von Balthasar, *Studies in Theological Style: Clerical Styles*, trans. A. Louth, F. McDonagh, and B. McNeil, vol. 2 of *The Glory of the Lord* (San Francisco: Ignatius Press, 1984), 121. For a summary presentation of the seven volumes of this work, see my "Philosophy, Aesthetics, and Theology: A Review of Hans Urs von Balthasar's *The Glory of the Lord*," *American Catholic Philosophical Quarterly* 67, no. 3 (Fall 1993): 355–82.

34. "Inde mihi visum est nihil esse aliud tempus quam distentionem: sed cuius rei, nescio. Et mirum, si non ipsius animi."

35. "Animus expectat et adtendit et meminit."

says, "my life is a distention. . . . And I am dissolved in temporal things, of whose order I am ignorant, and my thoughts, the intimate viscera of my *anima* is torn with seething multitudes of things." However, "not distended, but extended, not according to distention, but according to intention, I follow to the palm of the supernal vocation" (XI, xxix, II/278).[36] What brings the soul to rest is the fire of divine love awakened within it, which purifies and liquefies the heart.

The notion of *distentio animi* is not simply a neutral analysis of the functions of expectation of the future, attention to the present, and memory of the past. Distention is distraction, being torn up, divided, being subjected to constant tumult, never being at rest, never being one. At the same time, by a metaphoric reversal, being subjected to the turbulence of time is becoming rigidified, locked into the mode of dispersion. In the most intimate viscera of the *cor/anima*, one is deeply restless. What brings the self to unity and peace is the intention of the future, the eternity that awaits us at the end. But this is not viewed here as a simple act of the iron will that stoically rises above all disturbance and maintains its *apatheia*, its lack of feeling. It is rather rooted in an experience Augustine describes of being both purged and liquefied in the fire of divine love so that one flows into God. He exists in tumult "Until I flow into You and am purged and liquefied in the fire of Your love."[37] Paradoxically, being caught within time is being rigidified *and* being in tumult; coming to intend the final eternal end at the level of the heart burning with divine love both fixes one on the future and renders one liquid. The metaphor of divine fire is significant: not only does it purify and liquefy, but it also illuminates so that one may flow, knowingly, into the divine.

There is a curious related text about the divine light in Book VII: "And thus admonished to return to myself, I entered into my most intimate parts. . . . I entered and saw with a kind of eye of my *anima* beyond that same eye, above my mind, an immutable light" (VII, x).[38] Here the *anima* is the ground and the eye belongs to the *anima*.

36. "Ecce distentio est vita mea . . . non distentus, sed extentus, non secundum distentionem, sed secundum intentionem sequor ad palmam supernae vocationis. . . . et ego in tempora dissilui, quorum ordinem nescio, et tumultuosis varietatibus dilaniantur cogitationes meae, intima viscera animae meae."

37. "Donec in te confluam purgatus et liquidus igne amoris tui."

38. "Et inde admonitus redire ad memet ipsum, intravi in intima mea. . . . Intravi et vidi qualicumque oculo animae meae supra eundem oculum animae meae, supra mentem meam, lucem incommutabilem."

Augustine goes on to say that it is *caritas* that knows this light. That would link it with the *pondus amoris* of the *cor*. Elsewhere, he complains that he sheds tears over fictitious presentations of the death of a beloved but none over the death of his soul. Here he invokes God as "light of my heart. . . . O power that marries my mind and the bosom of my thought" (I, xiii/I, 39).[39] "*Sinum cogitationis meae*" is an interesting expression: contrasted with *mens*, it indicates a personal appropriation process of what the *mens* would impersonally recognize. That throws a new "light" upon matters. It would seem then that there is a mode of seeing that belongs to the *anima* as *cor*, as the carrying, nurturing principle for the whole of human life. The light of the self-directing, reason-advancing, conscious self is linked to the unconscious encompassing self via the *cor* as the feeling phase of the whole self. The *cor* is the place where the unity and disunity of the whole self is displayed to the *animus*, which can reflect upon the attunement of consciousness. From the very beginning, Augustine prays that God enter into the *cor* and still its restlessness. In the opening paragraph of Book X, he goes on: "For behold You have loved truth, because one who does (makes) the truth comes to the light"—a citation from John's Gospel (3:21).[40] The term he uses here is *fac* from *facere*, which means both to make and to do. Here he notes that only one who makes/does the truth will enter into the light. The making/doing of the truth can only happen in the most fundamental sense when God enters into the heart and we learn to cooperate with the light. One makes oneself true by the action whereby one lets God enter into one's heart.

Following out the distinction between two kinds of light, Augustine in Book V contrasts and relates *animus* and *cor*: the words of Ambrose came into his *animus* and opened his *cor* (V, xv, I/256). Again, in Book VI (VI, xvi, I/326), accepting Epicurus into his *animus* meant accepting what Epicurus said as true, presumably based upon the ability to advance reasons; but Augustine had his reservations. So there is a difference between "intellectual acceptance" and opening the heart. Correspondingly, there are two sorts of discourse, argumentative discourse and persuasive discourse or eloquence.

Augustine also testifies to an experience of an enduring faith in Christ in the heart (VII, v, I/350) in spite of things tossing about in his "miserable

39. "[L]umen cordis mei. . . . virtus maritans mentem meam et sinum cognitationis meae."
40. "Ecce enim veritatem dilexisti, quoniam qui facit eam, venit ad lucem."

breast" (*in pectore misero*), which is physiologically the place of the heart. Here it would not seem to be a matter of the ability to advance reasons so much as it is an experience of the heart, an experience of a certain central stability that one experiences as a gift, in spite of the otherwise turbulent character of the heart. But in the crucial *Tolle lege* experience, reading Romans (xiii, 13), about making no provision for gratifying bodily lusts but putting on the Lord Jesus Christ, "a kind of light of security" was infused into his heart (VIII, xii, I/464).[41] Here again there is a "light" that is not something intellectual in which one can advance reasons and relate systematically to a whole region of coherently apprehended truths. There is a "light of security" for the heart, the dispositional center that can come through the persuasive power of Scripture. It is this that is apparently related to the most fundamental "doing/making of the truth." Here, in the reading of Romans, as distinguished from the stable faith in Christ that remained in his heart in spite of its turbulence, a new light dawned in the heart that allowed his *cor-anima-voluntas* to become one, whereas before, in spite of the stable faith, it was divided.

Let us return to the opening paragraph of Book I. The praise of God that Augustine here undertakes is not simply pronouncing the words of praise, intellectually understanding what they mean, and volitionally intending praise. That doesn't reach deeply enough. He prays for a gift of the heart, and the gift of which he speaks here is that of actually taking delight in that praise. It is in calling attention to the gift of delight that Augustine provides the setting for his famous words: "You have made us for Yourself and our heart is restless until it rests in You" (I, i, I/2).[42]

The *cor inquietum*, the restless heart, is the core of Augustine's *Confessions*. It takes center stage in Augustine's work, not only because it took center stage in his life but also because it is a central notion in the biblical tradition where God speaks to the heart and where the central commandment, cited in Book III of the *Confessions*, is: "Love God with your whole heart and with your whole soul and with your whole mind" (III, viii, I/126).[43] *Cor, anima, mens*, heart, soul, and mind could be taken here as equivalent.

In Book X, having recapitulated his life's journey, Augustine ex-

41. "[Q]uasi luce securitatis infusa cordi meo."
42. "[F]ecisti nos ad te et inquietum est cor nostrum, donec requiescat in te."
43. "Diligere deum ex toto corde et ex tota anima et ex tota mente."

claims in prayer: "You struck my heart with your word, and I loved you" (vi, II/86).[44] He goes on to contrast and relate what he loves in God with what he loved in seeking the embrace of a beloved: "Yet I love a kind of light, a kind of voice, a kind of fragrance, a kind of food and a kind of embrace ... of the man of my interior where it flashes forth to my *anima*." [45] When the heart is struck by the word of God, love is awakened, the *anima* receives light, and the equivalent of all the sensory modes of presence is evoked. The light of the *anima*, I would claim, is the sense of divine presence in the heart. The evocation of sensory modes other than seeing is significant—even though light finally takes center stage as that which flashes into the *anima*. It recalls the Psalmist's "Taste and see that the Lord is sweet" (Ps. 34: 8), but it adds embrace and fragrance and sound. It really invokes the image of sexual embrace as a total sensual experience that Augustine knew only too well in its forbidden form and later repudiated entirely. By that parallel one at least gets a sense of what total presence might mean and thus what loving God with one's whole heart, soul, mind, and strength might mean. But one must also recall Augustine's apt remarks upon his life of sexual indulgence when he was simultaneously outside himself and locked up inside himself. Sexuality involves a kind of ecstasy but one which might involve no real entry into the interior life of another but a kind of self-enjoyment, locking one inside of one's own feelings of gratification. But when the word of God strikes the heart, there is an embrace of love that simultaneously brings one outside of oneself and brings one into the holistic presence of the unfathomable interiority of the divine Other.

In Book X, as a kind of conclusion of his ascent, we find one of the most famous lines of the *Confessions*: "Late have I loved you, beauty ever ancient, ever new, late have I loved you. Behold you were within me and I without. There outside I sought you; and I, deformed as I was, rushed into those beautiful things which you have made. You were with me and I was not with you. The things which are not if they are not in you, held me captive at a great distance from you" (xxvii, II/146).[46]

44. "Percussisti cor meum verbo tuo, et amavi te."

45. "[T]amen amo quandam lucem et quandam vocem et quendam odorem et quendam cibum et quendam amplexum, cum amo deum meum, lucem, vocem, odorem, cibum, aplexum interioris homini mei, ubi fulget animae meae."

46. "Sero te amavi, pulchritudo tam antiqua et tam nova, sero te amavi! Et ecce intus eras

Augustine's experience of the *cor inquietum* indicates an underlying dynamism having by nature a final goal. Augustine sees it linked with the teleological dynamism of the inward-upward turning of the soul toward the Good as principle of the Whole in Platonism. But, as in Platonism, for the most part the conscious I (*animus*) is unaware of this teleology.

The *Confessions* closes with the words addressed to God: "But You as the Good lacking no good are always at rest, for You Yourself are Your rest" (XIII, xxxviii, II/474).[47] What man can teach another to understand this? But if one begs it of God and knocks at the divine door, it shall be opened. God is identical with his rest; man is restless until he rests in the divine Rest itself. If he but addresses the divine, the door will be opened that leads to that eternal rest for the restless heart.

---

et ego foris, et ibi te quaerebam, et in ista formosa, quae fecisti, deformis inruebam. Mecum es, et tecum non eram. Ea me tenebant longe a te, quae si in te non essent, non essent."

47. "Tu autem bonum nullo indigens bono semper quietus es, quoniam tua quies te ipse es."

9 ∞ The Self and the Other

Aquinas's List of Transcendentals

In the *De Veritate,*[1] Thomas Aquinas attempts a logical division of the transcendental properties of being according to the distinction between a being considered absolutely and considered in relation to another. Each division, in turn, is further divided into positive and negative properties. The positive relative properties, goodness and truth, have received extended treatment by the Scholastics, as has the negative absolute property, unity. However, the positive absolute property *res* (thing) and especially the negative relative property *aliquid* (other, i.e., *alium quid*) are generally given scant treatment.

This chapter will suggest the main lines of a reinterpretation of the transcendentals that will focus primarily upon *aliquid* as a relation in terms of which the absolute unity of a being and also its thinghood, intelligibility, and goodness are realized. We are going to suggest that any being "considered absolutely" *is* only as related to another. This is to be understood not simply in the sense that finite beings exist *as* relations to Infinite Being, but that any being proportionately shares in the perfection of being according to the extent and depth of its internal relatedness to another. Although we are considering notions presented to us initially by a text, our concern is not primarily textual but experiential. Hence, although suggestions will continue to be taken from texts, and at times some aspects of the Scholastic framework are assumed, this chapter should not be considered an example of Schulmetaphysik, except in the very broadest sense of the term. The appeal is basically *"zur Sache selbst."*

But as one attempts to pull out any slippery philosophic problem, he soon discovers that he has hold of the entire Medusa-head of philosophy.

---

1. The original hint came from Walter Kern, "Einheit-in-Mannigfaltigkeit," in *Geist in Welt, Festgabe für Karl Rahner,* vol. I (Freiburg i. Br. 1964), 207–39, especially 214 and 219.

Philosophy is an organism, each part of which is relation to the Whole. The more central the problem, the greater its involvement with the totality. As a consequence, when we deal here with the transcendentals, we have necessarily to paint with broad strokes. What we offer, therefore, is merely a related series of suggestions, an indication of lines for future reflection, any one of which may have to be altered or abandoned. We are moving *toward* a reinterpretation of the transcendentals: we have not yet fully arrived.

The facts with which we begin are the actual structures of human awareness. After a relatively brief investigation, we will attempt to show what these structures reveal of the other, then what they reveal of the self. After that, we will be in a position to suggest a generalized cosmic scheme on the basis of which we will, finally, sketch out the consequences of our investigations for a reinterpretation of the transcendentals.

Spontaneously, the famous man-on-the-street accepts immediate experience as empirically objective. Objects are "out there," other than myself, and just what they appear to be. But when asked to account for the way in which he comes to know things "out there" and the nature of his awareness, he tends to look for explanations along the lines of empirically objective factors. Proceeding further along the same lines, the scientist shows the basis for such knowledge in the registration of wave impulses upon receptor organs that electronically transmit these "messages" to the brain where they are interpreted and awareness occurs. But up to this point, nothing whatsoever is said of awareness. Some have concluded that awareness is nothing but the electronic activity of the nervous system.

Such an attempt, I submit, involves itself in a contradiction. To claim that there *really are* such things as waves coming from light sources and being reflected from visual objects, that there really are optic and cerebral structures, and simultaneously to claim that awareness is exclusively an intracerebral event leaves us with no basis for knowing whether there is even such a thing as a brain or visual objects or light waves, for the ground upon which we could know the reality status of such things is their givenness as other than the awareness that observes them. The knower must be endowed with a structure of transcendence, a leaping beyond what in himself is accessible to the pose of empirical objectivity, beyond what we are wont to call "the body."[2]

2. Cf. Sartre's penetrating remarks in *Being and Nothingness*, trans. H. Barnes (New York: Philosophical Library, 1956), pt. II ch. 3 on transcendence, 171–218 and on the body, pt. III, ch. 2, 303-359.

In more closely specifying the structure of transcendence, we might employ a tactic of the analysts and consider our usage of language. If one were to burst into the room crying, "I'm aware! I'm aware!" and then, to the excited query, "Of what? Tell us!," he were to reply, "Oh, of nothing: I'm just aware"—that would make little sense, and we would be left floundering. But likewise, if one were to ask what an empirically given object, such as a stone, is of or *about*, the would-be answerer is left suspended. Things appearing in the mode of empirical objectivity are, as such, just what they are and are not *of* or *about* something. Conversely, consciousness is always *of* or *about* something: it always intends an other to which it is intrinsically and necessarily related.[3] This is the basic structure of consciousness: its transcendence toward another, its intending another, in short, its *intentionality*.[4]

Because of the diversity of these two modes of experience (empirically objective and intentional), our natural tendency to think in the mode of empirical objectivity, and the huge success of the scientific method based upon such objectivity, we have to undertake constantly a reflective autotherapy in our usage of terms. In the Aristotelian tradition, for example, the usage of such terms as "reception" and "possession" of form "in" the mind to describe cognitive situations[5] has to be understood in terms of the basic structure of the mind as transcendence. Consciousness stands out and is *ecstatic* with respect to our empirically given structure; it is "out there," "in the world," so that something exists "in" the mind insofar as the mind exists and stands out of the empirical phase of the self.[6] On the basis of the fundamental structure of intentionally, Heidegger argues for the implementation of the Aristotelian categories, based as they are on the structure of empirical objects, with a set of "existentials" corresponding to the ecstatic structure of awareness.[7]

Now, the recognition of an irreducible distinction between the object as empirical and the act of empirical awareness as intentional implies the

---

3. Necessarily related, that is, to *an* other, not to *this* particular other.
4. Sartre, *Being and Nothingness*, lx–lxii et passim; Edmund Husserl, *Ideas: General Introduction to Pure Phenomenology*, trans. W. Boyce Gibson (London: Allen and Unwin; New York: Macmillan, 1952), 116ff and 241ff.
5. Cf. e.g. Aquinas, *Summa Theologiae*, I, 14, 1; *De Veritate*, II, 2, resp. and II, 5, ad 15.
6. Cf. Heidegger, *Being and Time*, 78ff and 377. Likewise, W. Richardson, *Heidegger, Through Phenomenology to Thought* (The Hague: Martinus Nijhoff, 1963), 102.
7. Heidegger, *Being and Time*,. 70.

introduction of an additional factor to awareness—for the awareness of an essential difference in kind implies the existence of a different kind of awareness.

To clarify: that by which we know empirical objects we term "sensation." As intentional, sensation is other than empirical objects. Hence that by which we know sensation cannot be sensation but some other factor. What is it? Let us look again to immediate experience

Immediate experience does not only involve ecstatic presence to things here-and-now. Things are not only sensed; they are interpreted as instances of meaning-patterns that extend far beyond the things interpreted. What I see here-and-now before me I interpret as paper, which meaning extends to all actual or possible papers, at all possible times and in all possible places. To fix nominalistically upon the words as another instance of a sensory entity in the here-and-now is to allow for no explanation of the intention of universality. Such an exclusion ends up in an inevitable "mysticism" that eventually reaches an impasse.[8] The significant fact of the matter is that the human knower constantly intends universality in and through every sensory individual it encounters, constantly stands ecstatically beyond not only its empirically observable structure in sensation but likewise beyond its own sensory field here-and-now.

In this latter ecstasy, we have, I think, the ground upon which the conceptual dissociation of immediate sensory consciousness from its empirical objects is possible. Standing beyond the immediate toward the universal, we can reflect upon the immediate. Thus, to stand beyond toward the universal and thereby to be able to reflect is what it means to have an intellect.[9]

But what makes possible universal knowledge of nonuniversal individuals? I suggest two factors: one objective, the other subjective—that is, one belonging to the known and the other to the knower. Granted the objectivity of universal knowledge, then the known object must be so con-

8. Cf. Bertrand Russell, who admits he *can* account for the objective basis for the universal through the similarity of stimuli but cannot offer explanation for the subjective basis in the conscious recognition of similarity itself. "Logic and Metaphysics," *An Inquiry into Meaning and Truth* (London: Allen and Unwin, 1940) excerpted in *Contemporary Philosophy*, ed. J. Jarett and S. McMurrin (New York: Holt, Rinehart, Winston, 1961) 102–6.

9. Cf. Aquinas, *Summa Contra Gentiles*, IV, 11.

stituted in reality that its actuality as an individual is distinguished from its given structure in such a way that the given structure is indifferent to being in the individual mode or in the mode of universality. If there were an identity between structure and mode of actuality (essence and existence), then a change in mode of actuality (from individual to universal) would result in a change in the structure, and hence there would be no identity between universal interpretative structure and the given individual that is being interpreted. But this is contrary to the fact, since we actually do interpret individuals in terms of universal structure.[10]

The second factor that makes universal knowledge possible lies within the structure of the subject who knows. In the Thomistic tradition, the securing of universal interpretative structures in individuals is said to take place by means of abstracting the structure from the individual by the illuminative action of the intellect upon sensory experience.[11] The notion of "illumination" here is metaphorical and, as such, nonexplanatory. In what could such illumination consist?

Let us return to the immediate situation: every sensory object interpreted as an instance of universal structure is simultaneously seen as an instance of being. For example, we see immediately that this upon which typing *is* paper—a seemingly innocuous but extremely consequential observation, for the meaning of "is," of being, is such as to extend not only beyond the individual or beyond the class (here "paper") but beyond any possible empirically given (because it is also applicable to the intentional order) and even beyond any limited class of being. The notion of being is absolutely unrestricted.[12] To question whether being is limited is to extend the questioning beyond any limitation and thus to intend the absolutely unlimited.[13]

Whence arises such a notion? Could the unrestricted as such derive from the limited experience we have of limited things? If the principle holds that effects do not exceed causes, hardly. The notion of being, I submit, must then be a priori. But its "apriority" must not be that of a

10. Aquinas, *On Being and Essence*, trans. and ed. A. Maurer (Toronto: Pontifical Institute of Medieval Studies, 1949), 40.

11. Aquinas, *Quaestiones Quodlibitales* (Turino: Marietti, 1949), VIII, 3.

12. B. J.` F. Lonergan, *Insight, A Study of Human Understanding* (London: Longmans, 1958), 348–75.

13. E. Coreth, "Die Gestalt einer Metaphysik Heute," *Phiosophisches Jahrbuch* 70, no. 2 (1963): 246ff.

content fully knowable in itself, since we obviously do not know the un-limited region of being, or else we would not (as we must) inquire.[14] The alternative is that we possess it as a tendency toward a term as yet unat-tained. Consequently, any specification of the mind moving toward the unrestricted is immediately seen in relation to the whole range of being and is thus seen as indefinitely repeatable wherever in that range the con-ditions for the peculiar specification in question are met.[15]

In moving beyond the sensorily present individual toward the whole realm of being, we necessarily view that individual in terms of a total metaphysics, no matter how primitive and vague. By thoughtfully follow-ing out this tendency as operative throughout our experience, we gradu-ally develop interpretative worlds of universal interrelatedness of greater or lesser adequacy. For example, the identification of this empirical object before us as an instance of universal paper finds meaning only insofar as paper in general is seen as related to writing implements in general, lan-guage in general, thought in general, person in general, and so forth; that is, paper finds meaning only as related to the world of communication as such. And each region of the world finds its significance in terms of a view of the world as such (i.e., a view of being).

Basically, then, the human mind exists as a twofold ecstasy: beyond its empirical structure toward the sensorily appearing object and beyond every possible finite object toward unrestricted being. In the interplay of these two ecstasies, human interpretative worlds arise in terms of which the human being finds his way in the world or loses it.[16]

Does this brief description of conscious structures tell us anything of the relation between the self and the other? We will next consider what it tells initially of the other, then what of the self. Following that, we will at-tempt to fit both the self and the other in a generalized cosmic scheme. Finally, we will suggest certain implications this has.

Prior to reflection, we find ourselves confronting sensorily present in-dividuals and are content with that. Asked for the nature of something, we point to sensory examples. But, since the mind is a drive toward un-restricted being, everything confronted is taken up into that drive. Thus, we move restlessly beyond the sensory presence toward the essential core

14. Ibid.
15. K. Rahner, *Geist in Welt* (Munich: Kösel, 1957), 129ff and 219–32.
16. Cf. Martin Heidegger, *Über den Humanismus* (Frankfurt a. M.: Klosterman, 1947), 25.

and full existential reality opened up by our relation to unrestricted being. Science in general arises precisely as the search for the essential core of things. And as it presses on in the investigation of empirical structures, it sees the content of initial presence as a filtered perspective made in view of biological adjustment. This piece of paper that statically appears approximately one foot apart from my eye, separated by an interval of apparently empty space, is in reality a swarm of particles separated by a less dense swarm from my visual organism. Were all this to be immediately and constantly manifest, biological adjustment would be impossible.[17] Sensory appearance thus has the ambiguity of the term we use to describe it: "sensory *appearance*." "Appearance" can mean either manifestation (as, "The president *appeared* before congress.") or illusion (as, "He gave the *appearance* of competence"). In sensory ecstasy, we stand outside our own empirical structure related to the other, not precisely in its otherness (as we shall see in more detail later) but as pragmatically related to our organism. Hence, if absolutized, sensory structure becomes illusory (i.e., misleading). The actual focus of attention is not upon the other but upon the self as a biological organism. Nonetheless, this is our root contact with the other. If properly conjoined with our fundamental intellectual dynamism, sensory presence becomes a progressive manifestation of the true reality of things.[18]

But our initial relation to things is not simply a matter of sensory presence. Things are not merely confronted; they are interpreted in terms of worlds of universal interrelation. Likewise, dangers lurk at this level. First, there is the insufficiency of any interpretation. Let us return to the fundamental structures of awareness: we initially confront sensory profiles through which we intend the being of the sensory things as related to unlimited being. Being is therefore given in awareness as conceptually unlimited, and it is given in the encountered objects as factually quite limited. Given this situation, there is possible proof for the existence of God that develops along the following line: only an actually existent unlimited Being could account for the existent limitation of being apparent in immediate experience and that in such a way things *are* only as relations to Infinite Being.[19] But to understand relations as such, one must

17. Cf. H. Bergson, *Time and Free Will: An Essay on the Immediate Data of Consciousness*, trans. F. Pogson (London: Allen and Unwin, 1950), 97.

18. Cf. Heidegger's commentary on Heraclitus in *Introduction to Metaphysics*, 98ff.

19. J. Donceel, *Natural Theology* (New York: Sheed and Ward, 1962), 57–92; Hermann Ebert,

understand the terms. If one term of the relation that is creation is infinite, the creatures as related to the infinite are never fully fathomable by finite intelligence.[20] All our knowledge is thus necessarily perspectival. But the mind is dynamic drive toward the unlimited. Hence, the history of thought, continually surpassing perspectives to secure new insights, which are, in turn, to be constantly surpassed in the direction of Infinite Being. The danger is constantly present of remaining stuck in mere perspectives and thus of failing to push on to the true otherness of the other. This is the general danger in any interpretation as such.

When we consider interpretations as socially operative, we see that the usual interpretations given to things are not thought out from the ground up but are accepted on the basis of what "they say" about what is "proper" for "one" to consider. Language is a set of signals for social adjustment, not, in the first place, a vehicle for the revelation of being. Common linguistic usage is not, in the first place, a vehicle for the revelation of being. Common linguistic usage thus creates an ambiguous film over the objects of experience, a literal appearance, but this time at the interpretative rather than the sensory level. There is a marked tendency to settle down, to be at home in *such* a world-as-appearance, the world Heidegger has so masterfully described as the world of *das Man*, where the dynamic orientation of the mind toward the essential core and fully actual in being is harnessed and the fundamental self is stamped with the image of conformity.[21]

But even granted the release of the mind from ordinary linguistic interpretation and its awareness of the limitation of any interpretation, the final danger has yet to be surmounted. The mind, on the hunt for universal essential structures, gives itself over to the object, allows it to be, and to be in a way transcending biological and social utility. However, at this stage, the other need not be allowed to be absolutely but only in its "to be" as an instance of some universal pattern. Since universal pattern exists as universal only "in" the mind, such a search becomes simply a higher mode of subjectivism where the other is revealed, again, only as

"Der Mensch als Weg zu Gott," *Hochland* 57, April 1965, 297–317. I translated the latter in *Philosophy Today* 10 (Summer 1966): 88–106; it furnishes the best introduction to contemporary German Scholasticism, the chief inspiration of paper.

20. J. Pieper, *The Silence of St. Thomas*, trans. J. Murray and D. O'Connor (New York: Pantheon, 1957), 57–67.

21. Heidegger, *Being and Time*, 163ff.

related-to-me, except that the "me" is the higher self of intelligence understood as the faculty of the universal.[22] The search for essences is only the halfway house in the mind's search for truth, which is a correspondence with the way things actually are, and things are not actually universal.[23] Be the conceptual netting ever so widely and intricately spread, what it fails to capture is the sea itself: being. For being is not capturable; it is best left be—not left alone, disinterestedly forgotten, for it is the very life of the mind, the goal of our search. Being must rather be left be in the sense of a concernful involvement that preserves for the other that vital space within which it can be, in and for itself, before us.[24]

Does that mean an openness in which new contents are progressively manifest? Partly, but not wholly. Content, after all, is something we can seize upon, master. What cannot be mastered is the primordial *presence* of things, their initial openness, accessibility. One can come away from beings with their data and laws: such favors can be seized: beings can be raped. But their being, their presence, must be left be, reverently, before their real secret is revealed.[25] This points to a line along which the Thomistic distinction between essence and existence could possibly be developed: essence, the graspable, manipulatable, calculable; existence, the inconceivable. There is more to our access to existence than the simple positing through judgment that existence is, after all, the most important principle, being the actuality of actualities.[26] What happens then? We go on juggling with concepts! What has to be more deeply pondered is the meaning of presence, both the original accessibility of the other and its deepening through "letting it be." This is the way back to the ground of metaphysics.[27]

But just because the drive of the mind is unlimited, letting be does

---

22. V. Vycinas, *Earth and Gods: An Introduction to the Philosophy of Martin Heidegger* (The Hague: Martinus Nijhoff, 1961), 94–100.

23. Cf. Aquinas, *Summa Theologiae*, I, 82, 7.

24. Heidegger, "The Essence of Truth," in *Existence and Being*, ed. Brock (Chicago: Regnery, 1949), 305ff.

25. G. Marcel, *The Mystery of Being*, vol. I (Chicago: Regnery, 1960), 242–70; W. Kern "Der Verhältnis von Erkenntnis and Liebe als philosophisches Grund-problem bei Thomas von Aquin," in *Scholastik*, 34, no. 3 (1959): 394–427, especially 397 and 423–27; Martin Buber, *I and Thou*, trans. R. G. Smith (New York. Scribners, 1958).

26. Aquinas, *De Potentia Dei*, VII, 2 and 9.

27. Cf. Heidegger's essay by the same title in *Existentialism from Dostoevsky to Sartre*, ed. and trans. W. Kaufmann (New York: Meridian Books, 1956), 207–21.

not concern just any other—this or that cherished individual, human or otherwise. Letting be must concern *the* other. And because any finite other—and indeed, my very self—is rooted creatively in the wholly Other, in Infinite Being, response to any other at the level where it receives the creative influx, at the level of its individual existence revealed in presence, opens a doorway to the Absolute. As Buber expresses it, response of an I to a Thou fills the heavens, bathes all in its light, and creates the indispensable condition without which God as Eternal Thou is not present to us.[28] Attachment to and identification with the other at the level of its being is detachment from the other *as* perspectively filtered, and attachment to that Other who *is* the ultimate Ground of all.

Much of the talk we hear about being revealing itself in silence and solitude—true though it may be—yet remains, it seems to me, locked up within cosmological categories where the peculiar angle of refraction, the *logos*, the gathering principle from which being is viewed is the empirical, objective *cosmos*. However, where being most deeply meets us in the other is in the encounter with a personal other, that other who does not simply bump into us or gaze at us in mute animal fashion but who speaks to us of the *logos* that he/she bears in every word and in every action. The human being is not simply there, but in being-there is bearer of a unique world of meaning. And as bearer of meaning, the human being is relation back to the Ground of being, the wholly Other: the human being is the image of God. In one person's meeting with another, the path is cleared for the person's relation to God. Silence indeed there will be before this, as before any other. It is that silence that appears in love, that silent richness out of which authentic speech arises.

Such a relation to the other is not to be conceived statically, as if we are relating to fully constituted objects, on our part; because of the filtered character of our immediate access to things, things are not fully constituted for us. Hence, science, art, philosophy, and religion arise, driving beyond immediate appearances, both sensory and interpretive, to the full thing-on-itself. On the part of the other to which we are related, there are two different types of non-self-fulfillment corresponding to the two levels of being in the universe of experience, the human and the nonhuman. The nonhuman (and, to the extent to which the human like-

28. Buber, *I and Thou* (1958), 75 and 78.

wise partakes of nonhuman factors, the human also) attains to a higher level of being by taking on the stamp of human intelligence through art and technology. But again, this must not occur conquestively. Before their being-there for *homo faber*, and even for *homo sapiens*, things *as existent* are there for the human being as *imago Dei*, and thus they are present as theophany. Further, there is the non-self-fulfillment of the human other who, *qua* human, is constantly in process toward or away from his/her own selfhood, as we shall see. Therefore, complete relation to the other, full "letting it be," implies acting upon the other to change it, stimulating it to attain to its own full unfolding—hence, the ambiguity of our situation and the danger of slipping into conquestive relations with the other, even under pretext of idealism. So, authentic action upon the other lies in the acceptance of a kind of independent third factor, subtending and overarching the beings that enter in relation to the realm of objective value in accordance with which the beings to be developed can do so authentically. Response to this realm of otherness is the basic presupposition for human development.

Empirically, with the development of the use of language, the self begins to take possession of itself. This refers back to the incipient mental grasp of worlds of universality, grounded in implicit reflection, bending back to recover oneself as the light of being,[29] which makes possible the development of universality. But to take possession of oneself in this way, however inchoately, is to provide the basis for the first recognition of otherness, to know that something *as other* than oneself implies an act of prereflectively conscious self-possession.[30] What is interpreted is the other; what *grounds* the interpretation is self-possession. The self takes possession of itself in internal relation to the other.

Owing to this relation, it is only when the otherness of the other is fully manifest that the selfhood of the self fully emerges. As Buber points out, the I of the I-It relation, where the other is considered only as object of cognitive or pragmatic conquest ("experience or use"), is a mere functional point. Only the I of the I-Thou relation is full and substantial.[31] The ground of this we have already suggested: the human being is a dynamic relation to being; only in relation to being is he/she fulfilled. But

29. Aquinas, *De veritate*, I, 9, corp.; X, 9 corp.; Rahner, *Geist in Welt*, 232.
30. Rahner, *Geist in Welt*, 59 and 134.
31. Buber, *I and Thou* (1958), 29.

sensory appearance and universal structure are not yet being: they are merely the means by which we have access to being. In internally distancing oneself from biological and even scientific *relatedness*, in holding oneself concernfully aloof from the other, one establishes his deepest bond with things; he identifies more fully with the other. Conversely, by totally absorbing oneself in biological or even scientific relatedness, one loosens his internal bond with the other. In either case, one gains or loses himself. However, we should distinguish sharply between biological and scientific absorption. Rooted in the explicit search for universals, scientific absorption implies a self-possession of a high sort, gathering oneself up from all sides out of the flowing distractions of the bodily senses.[32] But its height is its peril, for essence is not yet being. The good is often the greatest enemy of the better. Because there is only limited submission to the other, there is only limited self-gathering requisite: the totality of the self is *not yet* gathered up. Conversely, sensory absorption implies letting oneself go, letting oneself be driven by the nonfree forces that emerge from outside our free center. The ultimate term of such abandon is in orgiastic mysticism, where conscious self-possession is consumed in devouring the other.

The I-Thou relation implies a self-gathering that involves attitude, attunement, lived experience in which a unification of the traditional faculties of intellect, will, and feeling is achieved.[33] Underlying every deliberative act of intelligence and will is a more fundamental comportment, a primordial towardness (*ad-itudo*) through which every content—thought, willed, or felt—attains its presence. Since this is actually the basic "light" in terms of which we view things as ultimately worth our commitment or not, and since it gives us access to existence,[34] we conclude that this is the light of being in us. Since in it our totality is gathered, it is our most fundamental self. Since it is progressively achievable, self-identity must not be thought of as an abstract "A is A" that perdures throughout many changes but as a variable factor that is a function of our recognition of otherness. In the appreciative presence of beings, the human being pro-

32. Plato, *Phaedo*, 65–68.
33. Speculative mysticism in the Middle Ages speaks of the *apex mentis*, the single root of the soul's powers, which comes to light in *gustus experimentalis*. Bonaventure, *De Septem Donis Spiritus Sancti*, II, VII, 1, *Opera Omnia*, Peltier, vol. VII, 635b; *Itinerarium Mentis in Deum*, I, Peltier, vol. XII, 42.
34. Cf. *supra*, 11.

gressively achieves integral selfhood, gathered up from all sides out of his self-absence in sensory *and* scientific absorption.[35] As presence deepens, so does the human being.

Now, both the other at the level of its existence and the self as the light of being bear an intimate relation to Infinite Being. To respond to the other at the level of existence (i.e., to the other wholly as other) is to awaken and develop our own relation to Infinite Being.[36] But this is still implicit owing to our fundamental freedom from any particular finite other rooted in our fundamental ecstasy toward Infinite Being. We can reflectively explicitate both our own subjectivity through introspection and our relation to the wholly Other, scientifically in metaphysics, presentially in prayer.

The significance of an intuitive grasp of one's own subjectivity must be stressed. As Bergson observed, in the case of the self alone we have access to being "from the inside"; all other beings we only know from the outside through the pragmatic filter of sensory encounter.[37] Initially engaged with the other as object, we come to ourselves only gradually through reflection and begin to discover our own subjectivity. But this cannot be terminal. Any attempt to narcissistically contemplate one's own being cuts one off from relation to the other. And it is the progressively fuller recognition of the other that establishes our subjectivity more firmly in its depth and richness. Introspection must rather be one pole of a dialectical process: being appears initially from the outside in the other, then reflectively from the inside in introspection. One thus has the grounds for the recognition of the other as subject on analogy with what he discovers within the self.[38] This projection enables one to encounter the other more deeply, thereby to gain in richness and thus to be able to return to a fuller introspection, and so forth, setting up an endless spiral process of growth and development in depth.

We should note in this connection that there are various modes of

35. Kierkegaard, *Concluding Unscientific Postscript to Philosophical Fragments*, 267.

36. Cf. the development of this theme in J. B. Lotz, "*Sein* and *Existence* in Scholasticism and in Existence-Philosophy," *Philosophy Today* 8, no. 1 (1964): 19–34. Much of the interrelation of Scholastic and existential themes developed in this chapter is due to Fr. Lotz's stimulating article that I translated from German.

37. Bergson, *Creative Evolution*, trans. A. Mitchell (New York: Modem Library, 1944), 1.

38. I am aware of Scheler's dissenting position, but at present I am unconvinced of its cogency. Cf. *The Nature of Sympathy*, trans. P. Heath (New Haven, Conn.: Yale University Press, 1954).

introspection: first, a simple doting over one's peculiarities, which is scarcely worthwhile and easily degenerates into narcissism; secondly, an *objective self* accessed through reflection that ferrets out universal structures (such as we have employed in the first part of the paper), which easily rests content with a kind of "essentialism"; and thirdly, what might be called *subjective* self-reflection, whereby one becomes experientially identified with his own self. Bergson points out that the last mode requires an extraordinary effort against the normal projection of consciousness thrust outward through pragmatically filtered sensations. Such self-awareness occurs only in rare and fleeting moments.[39] Eric Fromm[40] suggested a technique for achieving this kind of self-identification that seems to parallel the Oriental quest for *moksha* wherein what is experienced is Atman, the Self.[41] This also has parallels in the Platonic-Augustinian tradition where one closes oneself to the outside sensory world and enters into himself and begins to achieve that *gnosce teipsum* without which there is no wisdom in the sense of *sapientia*, a tasting of the highest levels.[42]

But in that inward movement, what emerges is the gradual recognition that within oneself there is that which is above and beyond the self.[43] One discovers experientially the term of the mind's dynamic thrust that is likewise the ground out of which the human self emerges and within which the self is rooted. The peculiar tension between the self and the other reaches its climax here: the other is the wholly Other with which, nonetheless, the self is so intimately related that "God is more intimate to me than I to myself."[44]

Three factors, then, are always co-present in experience, mutually grounding each other, though at different levels: God, the self, and the finite other. In the conscious interplay of accentuating each factor at all possible levels and in maintaining a careful balance, a dialectical tension of opposite extremes, the human self comes to its fullness.

---

39. Bergson, *Time and Free Will*, 231; *Creative Mind*, trans. M. Andison (New York: Philosophical Library, 1946), 39; *Creative Evolution*, 260–61.

40. Eric Fromm, *The Art of Loving* (New York: Harper Colophon Books, 1956), 112.

41. J. Maritain, "The Natural Mystical Experience and the Void," in *Ransoming the Time*, trans. H. Binsee (New York: Scribners, 1941), 255–89.

42. Bonaventure, *In Hexaemeron*, XIX, *Opera Omnia*, Peltier, vol. IX, 125b.

43. Augustine, *Confessions*, VII, 10. Cf. R. Guardini, *The Conversion of St. Augustine*, trans. E. Briefs (Westminster, Md.: Newman Press, 1960), 212ff.

44. Augustine, *Confessions*, III, 6.

Otherness thus far has appeared solely in terms of one's relation with other centers of existence. The situation becomes rather peculiar when we begin to uncover layers of otherness *within* the self.

The first level appears in terms of what we call "bodiliness," which has a twofold aspect: the body as object and the body as subject. As object, the body is that which is accessible to the pose of empirical objectivity. And within that framework, my body appears just as any other body—even to me: it appears as alien, other. This *is* the body of anatomy and physiology.[45] Exclusive concentration within this framework leads to the traditional problems of dualism. But appearing in this way, the body is radically different than the body as I live it. In the latter case, there is a felt identity such that I actually *am* my body.[46] This is the body as subject.

And yet even within the context of the body as subject, there is a factor of otherness. The projects in which I engage are constantly threatened or at least impeded by the forces of inertia, passion, and distraction that specify the limits of my free activity and which, precisely because they pose a threat, stand. outside of my center of free projection. It is with these alien factors that the self is given to struggle in its battle to become itself.

Now there are two limits set to that struggle: birth and death, which appear, in the present moment of struggle, as likewise factors of otherness, with which one must come to grips, *as limits* of the past and future, respectively. This is the second level of otherness within the self: temporality. Birth confronts us with the mystery of our own origin and our own continuity with the otherness of the pair who gave us life, with the species, and beyond the species with the entire physical matrix from which all things living have emerged. The events since birth both burden and support us, taking their significance as we view them in terms of our basic projection into the other direction of temporal otherness: the future.[47] At least in the phenomenal order, the ultimate term of that projection is the moment of death, when the otherness of the universe claims us back, the moment when we shall be so radically other than what we have been. This is the shadow cast over our lives, from which we are so prone to flee as bodies clutching our own bodily existence. But as minds, the anticipative confrontation with our own dying releases us from that clutching grip,

45. Sartre, *Being and Nothingness*, 303ff.   46. Marcel, *Mystery of Being*, I, 113ff.
47. Heidegger, *Being and Time*, 385ff.

and through the contemplation of that shadow we begin to live in the light of existence. Through sickness, we know health; through hunger, satiety; through death, life. In facing up to what is other both within and without the self, the self comes to itself.

We are now at the point where we can begin to tie into a somewhat consistent fabric the various threads we have been spinning in order to supply the immediate basis for our suggestion of reinterpreting the transcendentals.

In our initial pose toward reality, we discover ourselves empirically to be what we term a "body" situated among other "bodies." Because of the natural thrust of awareness in the direction of such "bodiliness," there is an immediate temptation toward conceiving of all things in such a mode, including our very act of awareness. Any such attempt fails on at least three scores:

1. It fails to account for the *intentionality* of awareness, even on the sensory level, since things appearing in the empirical mode are what they are and are not *about* something.

2. It fails to account for objectivity, since objectivity (i.e., the recognition of otherness) is possible only on the score that the self has immediate possession of itself as a simple center of being distinct from the other and not a mere spatial center composed of externally conjoined molecular structures.

3. It fails to account for the *universality* intended by its own explanation that transcends the spatiotemporal immanence of the empirical object. "Materialism" fails.

But the concept of evolution likewise furnished a challenge to division of consciousness and matter, as if "bodiliness" were wholly other than consciousness. If evolution is a fact, it suggests very strongly that consciousness is produced by "matter" and that therefore "material" particles are not "mere matter" but are potentially aware—nor as if a stone could be aware, but the original elements at the base of the universe contain the potentiality to combine in such a way that awareness emerges out of them in highly complex and centralized organisms. But consciousness, because of its intentionality and universality, is other than that which appears in the mode empirical objectivity as apparently nonintentional and immanent in space and time. This again suggests very strongly that what we call "body" is as much a function of consciousness as it is the object; that it is one aspect of the total object, an external perspective upon that which, in reality, is at least potentially aware.[48] (And this would seem to hold even if specifically human consciousness is admitted as a special case.) We would do well then to approach reality simultaneously from the viewpoint of sensory empiricism and reflection upon the conditions of awareness.

We exist initially in a conscious state of outward projection, hypnotized by "bodiliness." The self becomes gradually aware of itself as self insofar as it gains the use of language, which points to an apprehension of universality and which is made possible by a bending back (reflection) upon the self as the light of being. Sensation thus appears initially as a mode of being-outside-oneself. Sensation, however, is a function of organic structure since (1) if any sensory organ is destroyed, the corresponding state of awareness is rendered impossible and (2) evidence of sensation appears only with the gradual emergence of complex centralized bodily structures. But curiously, this mode of being-outside-oneself involves a progressive lack of being-with-the-other, for any sensation is a filtered perspective ordered primarily to organic functioning, and therefore what is revealed is not the other as other but the other as related to the organic self. Now, if we examine sensation in ourselves, we discover that it can be hierarchically arranged according to decreasing levels of "objectivity" from vision to touch. In the case of vision, there is an experience of the other without any awareness of the organism in the normal visual conditions of neither excess nor defect of light; in the case of touch, experience of the organism goes hand in hand with experience of the other.[49] If we read the empirical data with this in mind, the further down the line we go in evolution, the lower the level of "objectivity" in sensation, until we reach the lower animal levels where only the sense of touch is apparent, owing to the lack of other complex perceptual organs. But simultaneous with this progressive decrease in objectivity, organic complexity and centralization likewise progressively disappear and the individual begins to dissolve in the "material" World-All, its freedom being essentially determined by the laws of nature. "Matter," or "bodili-

48. P. Teilhard de Chardin, *The Phenomenon of Man*, trans. B. Wall (New York: Harper Torchbook, 1961), 53–64.

49. Cf. Aquinas, *Summa Theologiae*, I, 78, 3.

ness," then appears as a mode of being-outside-oneself, dissolved in the other without the other appearing in itself.[50]

"Matter" then appears at the lower level of a continuum as sheer exteriority, without the inner dissociation of the self and the other. Through the increasing development of organic complexity and centralization (the dominance of "form" over "matter"), the self and the other become increasingly dissociated externally and more deeply associated internally. In the case of the human being, however, something like a leap to another genus occurs: rooted and grounded in the prereflective drive of the mind toward unlimited being, incipient conscious selfhood emerges and therefore the beginning of objectivity. Something can appear as other only to a self-presence as other than that other. And precisely because of that unlimited orientation, the mind is free to take up a relation to things. Basically, the directions open are two: either the dissolution of the self and the loss of the inner relation to the other through total surrender to sensory drive or possession of the self through inner relation to the other as other. Man is thus a sort of dialectical tension between self-possession and lack of self-possession, or what traditionally was termed "mind and body." But mind and body are no distinct entities; they are fluctuating poles within the dialectical tension that we are. And the self is no isolated ego but a relation to the other as such. However, as part of the World-All, emergent from it, man can encounter no other "material" being as wholly other, and consequently any sensorily encounterable other cannot fully ground his selfhood. But as he reflects upon the ground of this relation to the encounterable other, he discovers that he himself and every finite material other is rooted in the wholly other otherness of unlimited Being. Hence, only in relation to this wholly other Other can man come most fully to his selfhood. But since man is sprung from the World-All, such a relation has cosmic dimensions as the return of the cosmos to its Ground.

The universe then seems to be a totality which, in its initial stages, involves only external differentiation of parts with an inner unity devoid of inner differentiation of conscious centers. All things are internally outside themselves without being with themselves: exteriority dominates. Selfhood appears gradually emergent with the dominance of empirically

---

50. Rahner, *Geist in Welt*, 87 and 93ff.

patterned centers until in man it reaches the stage of conscious recognition of otherness and thus of the constitution of selfhood as such. This implies that the "material" universe has now turned back upon itself after the lengthy journey out from the original internally undifferentiated matrix. And the turning back is a *total* reorientation since the ground of selfhood and conscious otherness is precisely man's prereflective orientation toward the *whole* of being. All things as creatures are relations to God, projected out of the Ground of being. The human being as *Imago Dei* is a (prereflective) re-relation of itself and of all things with him back to God; and as such, the human being has the freedom to choose or not choose the reflective re-re-relation, the reflective return of the universe, from which man himself has sprung, back to the Ground.

The experienced hierarchy, viewed from the interiority of consciousness, reveals the progressive emergence of selfhood, not as blank self-identity to which accidental relations of consciousness may accrue (this substantialist view, we suggest, is based on absolutizing the misleading objectivity of sense-perception) but as a self-identity immediately based upon, as a function of, both the initial accessibility of, the freely developing access to the other as other.

Projecting this to the Ground of being, we might argue by analogy to Infinite Being who, as absolute Self, must not be conceived as self-identical after the manner of the lower levels experience but as self-identical in the manner of the highest levels of our experience in which selfhood is bound up with inner relation to the Other. *Infinite* Selfhood would thus seem to imply the most intimate union with other (i.e., identity) in the fully recognized difference of the other. The One in whose image man is made would thus seem to be a plurality-in-unity. Further reflection upon the self and the other as united through a ground would at least offer the *suggestion* of a Trinitarian Absolute.

We have reached the final section of the chapter, the point at which we have been aiming all along: the suggestion of a line along which a reinterpretation of the transcendentals may be effected, namely by using the analogy of the person. In Aquinas's logical division of the transcendentals, the particular attribute of being that seems rather curious is termed *aliquid* or *otherness*. Everything which is, insofar as the perfection of being is realized in it, is something other (*alium-quid*). One often gets the impression that otherness is a kind of external relation, as this page is other than those next to it, and other than those who read it, and so on. Considered in this way, the notion is understood in terms of a schematism derived from spatially perceptible objects and uncritically carried over to all realms. Our exploration has suggested that, at the level of awareness, otherness has to be understood as an internal relation to what is other, being other than what is other that is deepened insofar as otherness is more deeply displayed.

If what we have said holds true, then Aquinas's division of the transcendentals in terms of being considered in itself (*res* and *unum*) and of being considered in relation to another (*verum, bonum* and *aliquid*) has to be understood, if it is to accord with experience, in such a way that a being exists "in itself" insofar as it stands (internally) related to another—hence "outside" itself.

Being then is basically existence, a standing-out, present only potentially in the lower forms, hemmed in always by the kind of being in question. Transcendental *res* emphasizing kind or essence[51] appears as analogous but in an inverse sense: in the lower forms, kind dominates over individuality, essence over existence; in man, because of his ecstatic thrust toward unlimited Being, there appears the freedom of the individual existent to create his own essence.[52] Though still bound by the conditions of spirit in "matter," such freedom is indefinitely realizable and thus men differ *essentially,* in a very real though qualified sense, from each other. This advancement away from thinghood in the direction of the full realization of existence develops along the lines of *verum* and *bonum* that are functions of our inner recognition of *aliquid* as such. In the progressive inner relation to the other as *unum, verum, bonum,* and *aliquid*, one's own *unum, verum, bonum,* and *aliquid* are progressively achieved. All one's faculties are gathered up in progressively higher degrees of unity, being less and less dissolved in sensory being-outside-oneself. But in thus distancing oneself from his own nonbeing (as lack of self-possession), one actually establishes higher levels of intelligibility in oneself and thereby also higher levels of desirability. In this mode of self-possession, one's own distinctness from every other is truly established. Since this progressive otherness presupposes progressive identification

51. Aquinas, *De veritate*, I, 1.
52. Cf. Sartre, *Being and Nothingness*, 433–81.

with the other as such, one tends in the direction of self-realization as *Imago Dei*, mirror of that identity-in-difference that is God Himself.

Everything then hinges upon the internalization of relation, a transcategorical that grounds all the categories, but likewise a trans-transcendental that grounds all the transcendentals. And what is that which grounds everything but being itself? To say "being," we suggest, is to say "relation"; to say "being" fully is to say "internal relatedness of identity-in-difference." To work out the details of this sketch would required volumes. What we have provided here *is a provisional sketch.*

10 ⋙ Kant's "Antinomic" Aesthetics

Even a cursory glance at Kant's thought indicates that it revolves around "antinomies," literally "contrary laws" or the clash of different modes of legislation. In the *Critique of Pure Reason*, we find the famous *cosmological antinomies* setting the empirical against the rational: the limited or unlimited character of time, the divisible or indivisible character of the basic constituents of things, freedom or the laws of nature, and necessity or contingency as the basis of things.[1] In the *Critique of Practical Reason*, the rational nature, governed by duty, is set over against the animal nature of inclination, duty against happiness, deontology against teleology.[2] In the *Critique of Judgment*, each of the two parts, the aesthetic and the teleological, have their explicit antinomies. The teleological antinomy juxtaposes a mechanical and a teleological explanation of living phenomena,[3] while the aesthetic antinomy contrasts the adage *De gustibus non disputandum est* with the factual dispute that is ever present among those who are devoted to matters aesthetic.[4]

The basis for Kant's critical project is his analysis of the field of human awareness, the phenomenological field, as basically bipolar. At the one pole is the seemingly most obvious fact of sensory actuality: colors, sounds, smells, tastes, and tactual qualities that are effected in us by our being receptively related to the impact of the things around us. In their

1. Kant, *Critique of Pure Reason*, trans. N. K. Smith (New York: St. Martins, 1965), A409/B436-A567/B595 (386-484).

2. Kant, *Critique of Practical Reason*, trans. L. W. Beck (Indianapolis: Bobbs-Merill, 1956), II, I, 117-24.

3. Kant, *Critique of Judgment*, §§69-78, trans. W. Pluhar (Indianapolis: Hackett, 1987), 384-417 (265-301). Henceforth, we will refer to this work followed by the section number and the page number of the standard Akademie Edition, with the Pluhar page number in parenthesis.

4. Kant, *Critique of Judgment*, §56-57, 338-46 (210-20). I have given a comprehensive approach to Kant's thought twice: in *A Path into Metaphysics*, 237-62, focused more strongly on the first critique, and in *Placing Aesthetics*, 117-57, with the chief focus upon the third critique. This chapter is a further development of the analysis given in the latter work.

most primitive function, they evoke the appetites that serve the needs of the organism. At the opposite pole of the field of awareness is a directedness toward totality expressed in the encompassing Ideas of Reason: World, Soul, and God. These ideas are articulations of the drive toward totality in virtue of the outward directedness of sensation (World), the inwardness of our experience of that world (Soul), and the possible ground of both (God). Such ideas function theoretically as horizonal lures, ever receding, to bring our experience of things into ever more expansive unity.[5] They operate in relation to an everyday experience that has taken up the sensorily given in terms of certain principles, such as substance and accidents, cause and effect (*Categories of Understanding*),[6] locating them in space and time (*Forms of Sensibility*)[7] and stitching together what would otherwise be a chaos of sensations into an ordered sequence of distinguishable and relatively enduring things spread out and separated in space and succeeding one another in time. Such stitching is a function of judgment that operates over the bridge afforded by the imagination, unifying the manifold of sensory experiences and providing temporal schemata for applying the categories and also providing examples of empirical concepts of differing kinds of things.[8] The presence of the horizoning Ideas of Reason furnishes a permanent temptation to leap over the horizons beyond the sphere of ordered, extended, and unified experience. Yielding to that temptation has produced, and produced necessarily, the antinomies as conflicting and unresolvable claims about what might lie beyond all experience.

The peculiar way in which Kant understands causality links up with the way he considers the operation of the categories generally. The reduction of sensations to inner psychic effects of the impact of outer things and the imposition of categories upon these psychic contents locks us into our own human-all-too-human inner world—though it is in principle intersubjective by reason of the common forms of sensibility, categories of understanding, and ideas of reason that ground mathematics, physics, and logic, respectively.[9] The regularity of causal sequence is understood

---

5. Kant, *Critique of Pure Reason*, A674/B702 (552).

6. Ibid., A67/B92-B116 (104–19)   7. Ibid., A23/B38-B73 (67–91).

8. Ibid., A137/B167-A147/B187 (180–87).

9. This is the brunt of the *Prolegomena to Any Future Metaphysics*, trans. P. Carus, as revised by J. Ellington (Indianapolis: Hackett, 1977).

in such a way that the past wholly determines the future, leaving no room for the self-determining and thus responsible exercise of choice. But the mere phenomenality of things appearing under the limiting conditions of human awareness leaves open the possibility of choice emanating from beyond the phenomenal field. Kant thinks this shows that the ideas of World, Soul, and God have a function in the realm of action that is denied them in the realm of theoretical knowing.[10] Morality ultimately makes sense for Kant in virtue of free human self-disposal in relation to the deterministic world, the immortality of the self-determining soul in relation to the inevitable dissolution of the body, and a rewarding and punishing, all-just and all-knowing divinity. All this is the thrust of the first two critiques that splits experience in two: a phenomenal, deterministic world ordered by our categories and a free, self-determining but cognitively inaccessible noumenal world. So, in addition to the other antinomies within the theoretical project, there is an antinomy between the theoretical project and the practical project, between "metaphysics" and "morality," itself expressed in the theoretical antinomy of necessity and freedom. But this points to the fundamental antinomy: human existence itself, stretched between animality and totality. This tensive structure is negotiated in different ways in the aesthetic portion of the third critique, which we will examine more closely in this chapter.

THE THIRD CRITIQUE

The third critique is meant to help bridge the divide between the first two critiques by focusing upon phenomena that point beyond the mechanically deterministic outer world: aesthetic phenomena that display a peculiar togetherness suitable to our cognitive powers and the appearance of organisms that show how mechanisms can be subsumed under other principles, starting with our own ability to project and realize goals. Kant sees both aesthetic and organic phenomena as exhibiting "purposiveness" (*Zweckmässigkeit*).[11] They are both linked to the experience of our own ar-

---

10. Kant, *Critique of Practical Reason*, II, III–VIII, 124–51.

11. Kant considers the purposive unity of all things to be "the highest formal unity" (Kant, *Critique of Pure Reason*, A687/B715 [560]). For an approach to the third critique through the notion of purposiveness, see my "Aesthetics within the Kantian Project," in *Philosophy and Art*, ed. D. Dahlstrom (Washington, D.C.: The Catholic University of America Press, 1990), 175–92.

tifaction, organizing materials to reach goals we have projected.[12] Observers would thus understand both plows and paintings as products of the activities of goal-projecting agents. We further understand organic and natural aesthetic phenomena by projecting our own self-understanding as productive agents onto nature. Thus, organic forms, though appearing within the world of mechanisms, nonetheless cannot be understood unless we see them as operating in a manner analogous to our own artifactual activities: they are self-formative in terms of ends preestablished in the nature of incipient living form subsuming mechanisms under those ends.[13] Organisms are goal-seeking, though without deliberately projecting their goals and, in the case of plants, without being aware of their goals. Nature itself also exhibits an analogue of our experience in making and enjoying art: in its beautiful and sublime moments, it is as if it has been arranged to bring about aesthetic experience.

More than this, Kant sees the inner harmony we feel in aesthetic experience as linked to the suitability of organic phenomena, through the peculiarities of their regular sensory collocations, for cognitive arrangement into hierarchies of genera and species.[14] He understands aesthetic feeling as the experienced harmony between imagination and understanding involved in all judgment, a feeling that he sees coming to the fore as a consequence of distinctively aesthetic judgment. Indeed, this insight is the basis for Kant's understanding of aesthetics as rooted in something universally human.[15] In presenting itself through organisms and through aesthetic phenomena, nature, so to speak, comes to meet us, as if it were directed to our powers.

The beautiful is not the only object of Kantian aesthetics. His aesthetic treatment is actually divided into two parts, dealing with the beautiful and with the sublime. The experience of the sublime lies at the basis of Kant's entire critical project, involving the tension between the finitude of the sensorily dependent imagination and the infinitude of reason's native project as a design upon the totality of what is. The sublime is juxtaposed to the beautiful. The latter brings us to a sense of at-homeness in the world. But though the experience of the beautiful brings about har-

12. See Kant, *Critique of Judgment*, first introduction, 204 (393).
13. Ibid., §65, 372–76 (251–55).
14. Ibid., introduction, 185 (24) and, more developed, first introduction, VI, 217–18 (405–6).
15. Ibid., §38, 290 (155).

monious feeling, in Kant's treatment of the beautiful there is the constant evocation of "antinomic" features involved in the simultaneous sensory and intellectual character of experience. The antinomic comes to direct expression in the experience of the sublime, continually prying us loose from our at-homeness, giving emotional expression to the fundamental antinomy that is human existence itself and pointing beyond in a never-completed search for the fullness of being.

The properties that, for Kant, define the aesthetic are rooted in the same antinomy-generating structure: a satisfaction that is, nonetheless, "disinterested"; a universality that is "subjective"; a purposiveness "without a purpose"; and a necessity that is neither theoretically nor practically necessary.[16] We will treat each of these in some detail in the following discussion, but we note that contraries involved here are not posed as alternatives the way they are elsewhere. They are *synthesized in experience*. What thought puts asunder, aesthetic experience joins together. Nonetheless, there is a tension between individual taste and the ideal of consensus contained in the notion of an aesthetic *sensus communis* built up through the study of works that have stood the test of time. As he is a proponent of moral autonomy, Kant is also a proponent of aesthetic autonomy. Everyone must develop his/her own taste but must also stand open to being corrected by what emerges from aesthetic communication.[17]

Further, to continue with the list of tensions, the creative artist, the genius, stands in the tension between taste, developed from opening oneself to a canon of classic works, and originality that breaks with and thus contributes to the growth of that very canon.[18] Further still, the experience out of which the artist works involves what Kant calls "free lawfulness," following out the spontaneous and unaccountable upsurge of a personal and fully satisfying aesthetic idea and producing a work that, in its exemplarity, exhibits a lawfulness that others recognize as legislating a style or a genre.[19]

16. Francis X. Coleman sees these as having a thesis-antithesis-synthesis structure. *The Harmony of Reason: A Study in Kant's Aesthetics* (Pittsburgh: University of Pittsburgh Press, 1974), 32ff.

17. On aesthetic common sense, see Kant, *Critique of Judgment*, §20–22, 238–40 (87–90); on aesthetic autonomy, see Kant, *Critique of Judgment*, §8, 216 (59); §17, 232 (79); §32, 282 (145).

18. Kant, *Critique of Judgment*, §46, 308 (46); §50, 319–20 (188–89).

19. Ibid. §49, 318 (186–87).

THE BEAUTIFUL

Kant's entire descriptive enterprise here is replete with tensions, but they are tensions rooted in the tension that is human existence, which we said is strung between an animal sensibility rooted in the organism and a reference to the whole of what is. What we want to do from this point on is to look more closely at the tensions involved by following Kant's analyses of the beautiful and the sublime, respectively.

Kant's analysis of the beautiful depends upon a distinction between free and dependent beauty, which, unfortunately, he does not introduce until later in his analysis.[20] *Free beauty* is "pure," abstracted from all admixture of concepts; it involves the appearance of aesthetic form within the sensuous. *Dependent beauty*, again appearing within the sensuous, nonetheless involves a relation to concepts. Kant begins with an analysis of free or pure beauty, performing what Gadamer calls the act of "aesthetic differentiation,"[21] separating beauty from features with which it is, for the most part, mixed and therefore often confused. First, he removes from the experience of it both interest and concept and then eventually folds in both intellectual and empirical interest and links the beautiful with a concept. The initial abstractive focus gives us the entrance ticket into the realm of the beautiful: what is beautiful is form appearing in the sensory. This allows us to avoid certain confusions.

There is the empiricist confusion of beauty with what simply produces agreeable sensations, and there is the rationalist confusion of beauty with perfection, whether physical or moral, measured by some conceptual and therefore intellectual standard.[22] While, more often than not, agreeable sensations and concepts of what a given object ought to be accompany beautiful objects, for Kant these features do not constitute their beauty. However, free beauty is trivial beauty; it is literally super-ficial, yielding only aesthetic surface. Kant uses as examples of free beauty flowers, bird plumage, and seashells in the natural order and arabesque drawings (wallpaper design) as well as musical fantasias (without words) in the artistic order.[23] Nontrivial beauty is dependent beauty, requiring

20. Ibid. §16, 229 (76).

21. Hans-Georg Gadamer, *Truth and Method*, trans. G. Barden and J. Comming (New York: Crossroad, 1982).

22. Kant, *Critique of Judgment*, §13, 223 (68); §15, 226 (73).

23. Ibid., §4, 207(49); §16, 229f (76–77).

the unity of aesthetic surface with concepts expressing something more significant, especially in what Kant will term "the Ideal of Beauty" (of which we will discuss more later).[24]

He begins his treatment of the beautiful with a focus upon free beauty and arranges his analysis around the four basic genera of the table of twelve logical judgments: quality, quantity, relation, and mode. Schopenhauer considers this exercise a Procrustian bed where the given has to be either stretched or chopped off to get it to fit into the forms of the first critique.[25] Kant's appeal to the logical tables is rather his method of attempting to see a phenomenon from all logically possible angles. However, we must admit that the resultant organization seems like it is not too carefully thought out, since aspects that might, under certain rubrics, fall into one bin are found in another. Furthermore, Kant does not explain at all how in each case the appeal to the category helps the analysis. Guyer considers this "a remnant of the rationalist view of aesthetic perfection with which Kant grew up."[26] Lyotard suggests that the exercise is intended to show the uselessness of the direct application of the categories: the aesthetic given escapes the logic of the categories and produces "logical monsters."[27] It is dubious that this was Kant's intent. But perhaps the "logical monster" is human existence represented in Greek mythology by the image of the centaur whose tensive integration is revealed in the experience of the beautiful, but even more obviously in the experience of the sublime where it threatens to explode.

Kant focuses first upon the generic category of *quality*, wherein he locates the feature that he calls "disinterested satisfaction."[28] He connects up the experience with that category only through the name and gives no explanation. One has to speculate. The judgments listed under quality in logic are affirmative, negative, and infinite, where "infinite" combines the affirmative and the negative, negating the negation to arrive at a new affirmation.[29] An "infinite" judgment separates the object from all oth-

24. Ibid., §17, 231ff (79ff).

25. Arthur Schopenhauer, *The World as Will and Representation*, vol. I, trans. E. Payne (New York: Dover, 1966), appendix, 528.

26. Paul Guyer, *Kant and the Claims of Taste* (Cambridge, Mass.: Harvard University Press, 1979), 130.

27. Jean-François Lyotard, *Lessons on the Analytic of the Sublime*, trans. E. Rottenberg (Stanford, Calif.: Stanford University Press, 1994), 44–49.

28. Kant, *Critique of Judgment* §1–5, 203–11 (43–53).

29. Cf. Kant, *Critique of Pure Reason*, A72/B97 (108).

ers: to be any thing at all is *not to be* the indeterminate number of other things there are. As in Spinoza, *omnis determinatio est negatio*.[30] There seems to be a double separation of the aesthetic object here, both as a distinctive individual separated from all other objects and as separated from the needs of the observer. The latter is what disinterested satisfaction involves. The positivity of "interested" satisfaction from the point of view of the perceiver involves the negation of the object's independence: things are there to serve our appetites. But the aesthetic stance involved in disinterested satisfaction makes possible what Heidegger calls "unconstrained favoring" and thus negates that negation.[31] This allows the object to present itself "for its own sake" and not in its function of serving the appetites. It thus provides a higher level of positive subjective satisfaction, not limited by the object's subordination to need.

We are, in our animal base, guided by need. All our sensory experience arises from the organism and serves the needs of the organism. The cognitively very limited modality of sensory experience is for the sake of such service. What is given is precisely an *appearance* constructed by our system out of the meeting of our organism with things in the environment through the causal impact they make upon the sense organs. What appears is immediately tied to evoking those desires that set the animal in motion toward those things in the environment that would fulfill its needs and away from those things that would thwart them. Our bodily pleasures are thus what Kant calls "interested": feeling has to do here with how the object can be used.[32] As Aristotle noted, the hound loves the look of the hare but only because it is potential food.[33] Of course, what appears is not *merely apparent* since the appearance presents *real* food and mate, offspring and enemy. (This observation would seem to involve an understanding of phenomenality that does not chop it off from "noumenality" but which does restrict the mode of appearance to an organic subject-dependent mode.) But even whatever pleasure we might find in the good Kant claims to be likewise "interested," though in a different way.

---

30. Baruch Spinoza, *Ethics*, trans. R. Elwes (New York: Dover, 1955), I, VIII, 48.

31. Martin Heidegger, *Nietzsche: The Will to Power as Art*, vol. I, trans. D. Krell (San Francisco: Harper, 1991), 107–14.

32. Kant, *Critique of Judgment*, §2, 204 (45).

33. Aristotle, *Nicomachean Ethics*, 1118a, 21–23.

In the human case, it is the connection of organically based sensation with understanding or, even more basically, with the notion of an indeterminate Beyond, which lies at the base of our theoretical, practical, and aesthetic endeavors, that affords the distance from organically based desire involved in aesthetic appreciation as in theoretical and moral activity.[34] But even in relation to the distance afforded by mind, which can take a theoretical interest in those appearances, the focus is not upon the appearance as such but upon the expanding circle of what appears in regular causal interrelation where the individual functions as instance of the universal.

Kant seems to violate common usage by confining "interest" to the biological and the moral spheres. For common usage, there is also theoretical interest, which uses the sensory appearance to get at the universal; and there is aesthetic interest, which leads us to attend carefully to aesthetic objects and to linger in their contemplation. Kant doesn't deny this,[35] but his technical confinement of the term "interest" can lead to some initial confusion.

In focusing upon the kind of satisfaction, Kant notes that the judgment involved in the perception of the beautiful is based upon a feeling of pleasure and is thus subjective. Here we should note Kant's general claim that pleasure is a natural sign of the achievement of an end. Kant only mentions it in passing in his introduction, but it hovers over the whole work.[36] Pleasure is the experienced achievement of organic teleology, and in the aesthetic it is linked to the further feature, listed under the category of relation, of "purposiveness without a purpose."[37] An aesthetic object brings about the peculiar pleasure it does as if, in the case of natural objects, it were made to do so. There is a fit between the interplay of the faculties involved in judgment and the regularity of the way in which things affect us sensorily that rises to the level of a peculiar feeling in the experience of the beautiful. And since for Kant the ultimate purpose of human existence is moral, both the beautiful and the sublime ultimately serve the moral, but only if they are experienced "for their own sake."

The "disinterested satisfaction" involved in aesthetic pleasure is a fea-

34. Kant, *Critique of Judgment*, §59.
36. Ibid., introduction, VI, 187 (27).
35. Ibid., §12, 222 (68); §17, 236 (84).
37. Ibid., §10, 220 (65).

ture of a state of mind in which we attend, Kant says, not to "existence" but only to the sheer appearance of the object.[38] By the term "existence," Kant presumably here refers to such features as the process of the coming to be of the object or the causal consequences that follow from the reality of what appears as well as the real substructure of the object. In the case of food, one of the features of existence is that it will be consumed to nourish the body; in the case of an artwork, for example, a painting, there is the chemical composition of its components as well as the nature of the canvas and the support of the internal frame. None of this is a matter of direct aesthetic concern.

In the moral realm, one version of the categorical imperative "Treat humanity, whether in yourself or in others, as an end and never merely as a means" entails respecting that humanity "for its own sake" and would thus seem not to differ from aesthetic response in this regard.[39] Concerning our relation to the human other, morality too would be disinterested. But where it would differ from the aesthetic is that in respecting others, one does not abstract from "existence" to consider only appearance.

The feeling involved in the experience of the beautiful is variously described as one of harmony, enlivening, and free-play—all attributed to the peculiar relation between imagination and understanding.[40] "Harmony" by itself suggests something static—and this seems to be the way Schopenhauer was to understand it.[41] But "enlivening" and "free-play" suggest something more dynamic. Unfortunately, Kant does very little to elaborate on these features.

Enlivening is a feature Kant attends to, especially in connection with the work of art. When successful, it is described as live, fresh, organic; when not, it is described as dead and mechanical.[42] At its origin lies the aesthetic idea, fruit of the spirit that animates the faculties of the genius.[43] But in the experience of the beautiful, whether in nature or in art,

38. Ibid. §5, 209 (51).

39. Immanuel Kant, *Foundations of the Metaphysics of Morals*, trans. L. Beck (Indianapolis: Bobbs-Merrill, 1959), 429 (46).

40. Kant, *Critique of Judgment*, §1, 38; §12, 58; §23, 83.

41. Arthur Schopenhauer, *The World as Will and Representation*, vol. 1, trans. E. Payne (New York: Dover, 1966), I, 4, §68, 378ff.

42. Kant, *Critique of Judgment*, §9, 219 (63); §12, 222 (68); §35, 287 (151); §49, 313–17 (181–85); §53, 329 (199).

43. Ibid., §49, 314 (182).

Kant sees the enlivening as the promotion of the free-play between cognitive faculties.[44] This removes it from the kind of emotional stirring, the
being touched that one frequently experiences in encounter with aesthetic objects and that Kant finds a place for in his notion of awe before what
stimulates the experience of the sublime.

At least one aspect of the free-play would seem to lie in the freeing
of aesthetic judgment from the usual tasks of judgment that subordinate
the appearance either to practice or to theory. Judgment would then, as
it were, "go on a holiday." As with Schiller, aesthetic appreciation is like
play, free from everyday concerns by being free to give unconstrained favoring to the aesthetic object "for its own sake."[45]

Play is also involved in Kant's claim that an aesthetic idea gives rise
to much thought without being fully determined to one thought.[46] A
beautiful work, product of the aesthetic idea, is overdetermined: it sets
the cognitive faculties in peculiar motion to play within certain limits.
Furthermore, whatever symbols may appear in an artwork create an indeterminate set of associations governed by their harmonizing with the
disposition proper to a given form, so that the mind is set in motion to
move freely among these associated images and, presumably, among the
concepts that might be associated with them. There would then be a certain creative moment even in the reception of the beautiful object, so
that, as one commentator suggests, the meaning of free-play is creativity.[47] However, one could see in the case of music that allowing such a
free-play of associations might easily distract one from the music and
lead one to sink into subjectivist reverie. The music becomes only an occasion, establishing a certain background mood for such reverie and the
beautiful form does not come into focus.

This relation of harmony is the ground of the claim to universality in
the aesthetic judgment, for it is that which makes any knowing and any
distinctively human communication possible: that imagination as the
faculty of gathering up sensations harmonizes with our faculty of pro-

44. Ibid., §9, 62 (62).
45. Friedrich Schiller, "Fourteenth Letter," in *On the Aesthetic Education of Man* (New
York: Ungar, 1965), 74.
46. Kant, *Critique of Judgment*, §49, 314 (182).
47. Cf. John Zammito, *The Genesis of Kant's Critique of Judgment* (Chicago: University of
Chicago Press, 1990), 131.

viding universals fit for understanding such a gathering. It is the harmony, not the free-play, that is involved in all judgment. According to Kant,
the *feeling* of the a priori form of the judgment as the harmonic relation
between imagination and understanding is what is evoked by and reciprocally tied to the coming into focus of the form of the beautiful sensible
thing, produced in works of art through aesthetic ideas.[48] And just as
Kant speaks of the form as the play of figures in space or of sounds in
time,[49] so the form of the judgment to which it corresponds involves the
free-play of the cognitive faculties in aesthetic experience. Play, whether
of figures or of cognitive faculties, indicates a freedom from domination
by purposes, appetitive or moral. The aesthetic is a space of fully free
activity, though finally it is tied in several ways to our ultimately moral
destiny. But it is the reflective distance afforded by this relation between
the universal and the individual grounded in our relation to an indeterminate Beyond that pulls us out of the merely private subjectivity of
our sense-life and allows for the universal communicability of aesthetic
feelings.[50]

Here one needs to distinguish a focus upon one's own feelings from
a focus upon certain features of the object. Hence, even though distinctively aesthetic feeling is the first criterion of the presence of the beautiful,[51] Kant will swing attention from the peculiar pleasure involved in
aesthetic perception to the object of such perception and will attend to
what he calls the "form" of the object.[52] Though the analysis initially focuses upon the feeling, the feeling can only be had when the form, not
the feeling, of the object is the focus of attention. Focus upon the feeling
is first for the analysis, but it is nonfocal in the experience.

In connection with this, Kant distinguishes the *charm* of particular
sensory features and the *form* exhibited by the beautiful object. Consider
a melody played on the cello from the same played on a piccolo. The differing instrumental timbres might appeal differently to different people, depending upon what agrees with them. More, or even most, people
might prefer the cello. But it is not the sensory mode as such that, according to Kant, constitutes the beautiful; it is the *form* of the melody. To
prefer the sound of the piccolo to that of the cello is not a defect in the

48. Kant, *Critique of Judgment*, §40, 294 (160).
49. Ibid., §14, 225 (72).
50. Ibid., §39–40, 291ff (157ff).
51. Ibid., §1, 203 (44).
52. Ibid., §13, 223 (68–69).

perceiver, but to fail to appreciate the beauty of the form *is* considered a defect. The beautiful is such that all *ought* to appreciate it; and if one fails to do so, one is lacking. The sensory charms, which strike different persons differently, merely serve to bring into focus the form, which all should learn to appreciate as the sameness in the difference. Under the heading of quantity, Kant speaks of the judgment of taste as providing a satisfaction characterized by *subjective universality*.[53] The formal logical categories under the heading of quantity are: universal, particular, and individual, where, once more, the third synthesizes the first two.[54] A *particular* merely instantiates the type that is a universal over against the particulars that fall under it. An *individual* is such that in it the type is not only instantiated but fully realized. In the aesthetic object, the universality of beauty has a peculiar fulfillment, making the beautiful object a distinctive individuality. Here, the analysis joins up with our consideration of quality where the "infinite" judgment sets off the individual from the indeterminate number of other things. Furthermore, Kant focuses on the universality of the claim that the distinctive individuality of the aesthetic object makes: that all should respond to it appreciatively. This is the universality involved. Though the object is a distinctive individual, it makes a demand upon every human subject to give it its appreciative due—hence, the "subjective universality."

A satisfaction focused on the beautiful appearance for its own sake and not generated by any individual interest on the part of the viewing subject other than unconstrained favoring of the individual appearance raises one above the peculiarities of one's private subjectivity, but not in the way a concept does. The universality involved is not objective but subjective: it lays a claim upon all human subjects to respond to the beautiful object, which is itself not a universal but a distinctive individual.[55] Kant distinguishes the subjectivism involved in the claim that "I like it" from the in-principle objectivity involved in the claim that "it is beautiful."[56] The former has a kind of immediacy transcended through

53. Ibid., §6, 212 (54).

54. Kant, *Critique of Pure Reason*, A70/B95 (107). The corresponding pure concepts are unity, plurality, and totality (A80/B106 [113]), of which Kant does not seem to make even implicit use here.

55. Cf. Mikel Dufrenne, *The Phenomenology of Aesthetic Experience*, trans. E. Casey et al. (Evanston, Ill.: Northwestern University Press, 1993), 191.

56. Kant, *Critique of Judgment*, §8, 214 (57–58).

the mediation of judgment in the latter. That is, the experience of merely liking something that we find agreeable to our own peculiar constitution is distinct from the experience following the judgment of developed taste. Though both are "mediated immediacies," that is, both are focused by our past experience, the judgment claiming an object to be beautiful makes an appeal to something, in principle, universally human. However, though the claim is addressed to all humans, it does not mean that everyone would agree with such a judgment. One peculiarity here is that by appealing to all humans, one opens oneself up to being corrected. This involves the development of a community of taste based upon the exemplary individuality of a canon of works that have continually appealed to sensitive and reflective individuals through long periods of time.[57]

It is in the context of his treatment of subjective universality that Kant also disallows the entry of an explicit concept into the aesthetic judgment *qua* aesthetic. As we noted in the first moment, the judgment of taste with regard to the beautiful is based upon a peculiar feeling, not upon a concept, not even the concept of perfection, otherwise we would have an intellectual and not an aesthetic judgment.[58] In the case of dependent beauty, there is a concept of the perfection of the thing present with which the aesthetic form must harmonize. But the point is that it is not perfection as the completion of an object that is the criterion of beauty. Beauty lies in the form of the sensuous. One could then have a fully completed thing that is not beautiful. Consider here the ugliness of some insects.

But even in the case of free beauty, Kant claims that there is ultimately an *implicit* concept involved, since any judgment, including an aesthetic judgment, is an interplay of the universal and the particular.[59] This is the proximate ground for the transsubjective claim made in judgments of beauty. But there is a more ultimate ground. Understanding takes place within the horizon of the Whole provided by reason. This is the basis for a further ground in the indeterminate notion of a "super-sensuous beyond" underlying the appearance of nature and of ourselves as conscious

57. On the role of tradition in the development of taste, see Howard Caygill, *Art of Judgment* (Oxford: Blackwell, 1989), 348–66.

58. Kant, *Critique of Judgment*, §8, 213ff (57ff); §15, 226ff (73ff).

59. Ibid., introduction, IV, 179 (18). He later identifies the indeterminate concept as that of the supersensible ground. Kant, *Critique of Judgment*, §57, 339ff (211ff).

beings.[60] Indeed, it is this concept that gets differentiated, by reason of the relation of exterior and interior involved in all experience, into the ideas of World and Soul on the one hand and the idea of God as ground of their relationship on the other. There is, then, a reference to the noumenal that provides the peculiar attraction of the beautiful, though for Kant and contrary to Plato, this noumenal cannot itself appear. For Kant, beauty is not a "real presence" in beautiful things as it is for Plato.[61] And since our fundamental relation to the noumenal is moral, Kant ultimately aligns the beautiful with the moral, not as a means thereto but as a symbol thereof.[62] This is connected with the kind of automatic transfer whereby even colors come to take on the qualities of human action: we speak of them as bold, soft, stately, and so forth. This does not mean that the beautiful is mere means to the moral. The beautiful has its own constitution, and it is only when we attend to it as such that it can function as a symbol. Further still, Kant underscores our sole explicit link to that "Beyond" through the ideal of beauty in the human figure exhibiting moral ideality.[63]

The presence of the indeterminate concept of the supersensible as the horizon of all human wakefulness allows Kant to solve what he calls *the antinomy of taste* that arises when we reflect upon the aesthetic.[64] One side of that antinomy is attributed to Horace in the often-quoted *De gustibus non disputandum est*, "Regarding taste there ought not to be dispute."[65] The other side of the antinomy is the factual dispute that goes on throughout the ages. Insofar as the dispute claims to rest on determinate concepts from which one could rationally argue, for Kant dispute is beside the point, for the judgment of taste rests upon a feeling and not a determinate concept. Nonetheless, by reason of its alignment with the indeterminate concept of the supersensible, taste generates dispute because there is a universal claim made in the attribution of beauty. Horace's *de gustibus* claim applies to the agreeable, to our attention to sensuous charm rather than to beautiful form. Beautiful form evokes the

60. Kant, *Critique of Judgment*, §57, 339ff (211ff).
61. Plato, *Phaedrus*, 250d.
62. Kant, *Critique of Judgment*, §59, 351ff (225ff).
63. Donald Crawford in *Kant's Aesthetic Theory* (Madison: University of Wisconsin Press, 1974) sees this as the culmination of five stages to the "deduction" of the judgment of taste. He summarizes the stages, which he elaborates throughout the work, on 66–69.
64. Kant, *Critique of Judgment*, §57, 339ff (211ff).
65. Ibid. §56, 338 (210).

harmony of the cognitive faculties and refers, beyond this, to the indeterminate concept of the supersensuous Beyond that receives determination only through the moral order. So the link is not simply to a concept but to the indeterminate. This means we can never settle aesthetic disputes by appealing to conceptually articulatable rules. We have to cultivate our tastes by attending directly to the forms involved in works that have become canonical, allowing novel forms to work upon our developed taste, communicating with others so cultivated about a given work, and opening ourselves to being corrected. There is, then, a tension between one's own taste, the taste of the community both of cultivated and uncultivated judges, and that involved in the production and appreciation of the canon.

In connection with dependent beauty and with the idea of perfection, Kant introduces the so-called "ideal of beauty" that he locates in the depiction of the idealized form of the human being as morally expressive.[66] In discussing the expressive fusion of a moral state of mind with a species-norm, Kant suggests that one arrives at such a norm—remember it is a norm of *display*—by a kind of superimposition of experienced forms of the same kind until an average form is delineated. It suggests a type, an aesthetic idea with which nature itself can be thought to operate in producing the inexperienceable substructure in the thing that will display itself phenomenally in approximation to that norm.[67] Given Kant's description here, the art that carries the ideal most fully would be sculpture and, to a lesser extent, because of being limited to two-dimensional presentation, painting. The other art forms would seem to be excluded.

In the ideal, the beauty of the form is tied to its expression of something not directly sense-perceptible—a state of mind. When the moral state of mind finds a bodily display in a form that itself constitutes a norm for the human species, we have the ideal of beauty. State of mind

---

66. Ibid. §17, 231ff (79ff).

67. Ibid. §17, 234 (82–83). The Polycleitian Canon seems to involve another element, namely, a doctrine of harmonic proportions that need not necessarily be the kind of statistical average that Kant suggests. Here, we have a case of a kind of empirical-rational tension in arriving at a norm. Kant's seem to have had in mind the descriptions of Johann Joachim *Winckelmann* in *Reflections on the Imitation of Greek Works in Painting and Sculpture*, trans. E. Heyeer and R. Norton (LaSalle, Ill.: Open Court, 1987) and *History of Ancient Art*, 4 vols., trans. G. Lodge (Boston: Little Brown and Company, 1856–1873). Cf. the discussion of Winckelmann in Alex Potts, *Flesh and the Ideal: Winckelmann and the Origins of Art History* (New Haven, Conn.: Yale University Press, 1994), especially 155ff.

and state of sensory display have to be proportionate to each other for ideal beauty to be realized. However, for Kant as distinct from Plato, the moral state of mind is not itself beautiful but is only said to be so by metaphoric analogy. The ideal of beauty is the result of a conceptual amalgam of two distinct but related regions: sensory exteriority and moral inwardness.[68] There seems here to be a fusion between the sublime and the beautiful in the display of moral disposition.

In completing his round of the generic categories in the analysis of the judgment of the beautiful, under the genus of *relation* Kant refers to the feature of what he calls "purposiveness without a purpose," something we have already considered. Beautiful objects appear when the perception of their form brings about the free-play between imagination and understanding, *as if* nature had produced beautiful forms for that purpose.[69] It is helpful to recall the categories Kant located in the first critique under relation: substance-accidents, cause-effect, reciprocity.[70] The notion of purpose gathers up these categories in the notion of an organism, which, governed by purpose, is reciprocally the cause and effect of itself, and whose accidents, caused by the substance, cause the substance itself to become actual.[71] That notion locates the beautiful, together with the organic, in the larger view of purposiveness. That larger view is a moral worldview in which a divine moral Artisan arranges nature as an arena for the moral perfection of human beings. That, indeed, is what, for Kant, draws the critical project together.[72]

Under the genus of *mode*, Kant calls attention to the peculiar necessity attending the judgment of taste. Under the logical genus of mode are the categories of actuality, possibility, and necessity, together with their opposites.[73] For Kant, it is *possible* for any representation to be bound up with pleasure. A pleasant representation *actually* produces pleasure. But an aesthetic representation has a *necessary* reference to pleasure.[74] There is an appeal to a kind of necessity in the form of an obligation laid upon all humankind to attend appreciatively to what can be designated as

68. Cf. Kant, *Critique of Judgment*, general comment following §29, 270 (130).
69. Ibid. §10, 219ff (64ff).
70. Kant, *Critique of Pure Reason*, A 80/B 106 (113).
71. Kant, *Critique of Judgment*, §65, 372ff (251ff).
72. Ibid. §57, 344 (217).
73. Kant, *Critique of Pure Reason*, A 80/B 106 (113).
74. Kant, *Critique of Judgment*, §18, 236ff (85ff).

beautiful. Being able to do this involves the development of a *sensus communis*, a common aesthetic sense.[75] As contrasted with common sense understanding and Scholastic *sensus communis*,[76] an aesthetic "common sense" is a kind of ideal to be striven for: a capacity to judge beautiful objects built up through attention to the classical models that have emerged and stood the test of time by their continued ability to draw the attention of sensitive and reflective individuals throughout the ages.[77]

This does not mean that the past furnishes the unalterable set of rules for judgment and operation in the present, as certain neoclassical critics would have it. Proper attention to the classics involves the ability to contact the same sources of judgment and activity that the original geniuses contacted in the production of their works. They teach us how to see and, if we also are gifted with genius, create works that are both original and exemplary.[78]

For Kant, even though the canon guides the development of taste, there is no substitute for direct encounter with the beautiful, for direct experience of form without having to appeal to explicit criteria or authority. There is here a kind of aesthetic autonomy parallel to moral autonomy. One has to learn to see for oneself. Rules derived from past experience and/or from what others—especially the experts—tell us can get in the way of being open to the emergence of novelty in the work of genius. But though Kant tells us to stop up our ears when others speak of a given work and judge for ourselves when we focus upon the work, this does not mean that we cannot learn from other acute observers how to focus upon a given work and cannot test our own judgment against that of those observers.[79] The judgment of the beautiful operates against the horizon of an ideal consensus toward which we strive.

Overall, there is much ambiguity in Kant's formulations. On the one hand, in the initial moment, the judgment of the beautiful is based upon a feeling; on the other hand, the feeling is based upon a judgment. Judgment involves a certain detachment, a "holding one's own" in the face of the given, and yet the experience of the beautiful involves "being taken"

---

75. Ibid. §20–22, 238ff (87ff); §40, 293ff (159ff).
76. For the origin of this notion, see Aristotle, *On the Soul*, III, 2, 426b, 4ff.
77. Kant, *Critique of Judgment*, §32, 282ff (145ff).
78. Ibid. §32, 282ff (145ff); §46, 308 (175).
79. Ibid. §32–33, 282–85 (145–49).

by the form of the object that demands "unconstrained favoring." The experience involved is, on the one hand, that of the form of the judgment and, on the other, that of the form of the object. The genius produces originality whose exemplarity has to be tested against a previous canon.

As we are attempting to demonstrate, the whole region involves a certain tension of opposites. What is involved in each of the features indicated is the reciprocal emergence of judgment and feeling, of detachment and attachment, of the form of the judgment and the form of the beautiful thing, of originality and exemplarity. Kant gives a certain priority to the judgment because it alone gives us the distance that releases us from "constrained favoring" and allows us to let the object be itself. A genuine aesthetic feeling rivets our attention ever more carefully upon the form of the beautiful thing; a merely agreeable sensation brings our own feelings to the fore, and the object becomes the occasion for a focus upon oneself. In the experience of the beautiful, the tension that is human existence is brought to a kind of resolution, but one that threatens to slide into the merely agreeable or into the conceptual.

THE SUBLIME

We now have to consider the sublime, which has another ground than the beautiful. In a way, the experience of the sublime exhibits the same four moments as taste for the beautiful (disinterested satisfaction, subjective universality, purposiveness without a purpose, and necessary satisfaction) but with some difference.[80] Through the emergence of beautiful form within the space created by distancing oneself from the pressure of need-based perception and the search for conceptual clarification, we experience the harmonious relation between imagination and understanding providing a felt harmonic synthesis of opposing factors; we find ourselves at home in the world. Focused upon form, taste brings about a feeling of harmony. By contrast, the experience of the sublime occurs when we are overwhelmed by either formlessness or our incapacity to take in the form involved.[81] Further, if beauty involves loving something *without sensory* interest, sublimity involves esteeming something *against*

80. Ibid. §23, 244 (97ff).
81. Ibid. §23, 244 (98).

such interest.[82] The deep background surrounding psychic harmony in tune with the appearing environment lies in being pried loose from any being-at-home by reason's horizonal reference to the totality. Mind is directed to an unreachable Beyond. By bringing this directedness to the fore, the experience of the sublime threatens to break the fundamental tension that is human existence. The experience of the sublime displays emotionally, and not just conceptually, the fact that human existence itself is the fundamental antinomy.

Though in his precritical period Kant had written a book along Burkean lines, *Observations on the Feeling of the Sublime and the Beautiful* (1764),[83] the treatment of the sublime in the third critique was a kind of afterthought.[84] Nonetheless, we would maintain that such a feeling is the subjective ground of the whole critical project. Like Plato's, Kant's philosophy is carried by the aesthetic.[85] It is precisely because our fundamental structure is oriented toward the Whole that we are impelled to think about our existence as a whole and within the Whole. In Kant as well as in Plato, this is the function of the notion of Being that makes possible our having our eyes fixed on the Whole and the whole nature of each thing within the Whole.[86] It is the orientation toward Being that unsettles our tendency to settle into various limited and limiting modes of existence. The experience of the sublime awakens us to the sublimity of our own fundamental orientation as human beings.

Before Kant's original tombstone was replaced, there stood on it the words "The starry skies above, the moral law within."[87] Taken from the closing paragraphs of his *Critique of Practical Reason*, they appear within the full sentence: "Two things fill the heart with ever new and increas-

82. Ibid., general comment to §29, 267f (127f).
83. Immanuel Kant, *Observations on the Feeling of the Beautiful and the Sublime*, trans. J. Goldthwait (Berkeley: University of California Press, 1960).
84. Zammito, *The Genesis of Kant's Critique of Judgment*, 269 ff. Kant, *Critique of Judgment*, §23, 246 (100).
85. In Lyotard's reading, through the notion of the sublime, "the teleological machine [the attempted gathering together of reason in the notion of cosmic purpose] explodes." Rather than bringing reason into harmony, the sublime exposes the "spasmodic state" critical thought experiences when it reaches its limit, the "principle of fury" as the demand for the unconditioned that the critique restrains. This, however, seems to us extreme. Lyotard, *Lessons on the Analytic of the Sublime*, 54–56.
86. Kant, *Critique of Pure Reason*, B393/A336 (324). For Plato, see *Sophist*, 254a, and *Theaetetus*, 174a–175a.
87. Friedrick Paulsen, *Immanuel Kant: His Life and Doctrine*, trans. J. Creighton and A. Lefevre (New York: Ungar, 1972), 53.

ing admiration and awe (*Bewunderung und Ehrfurcht*)."[88] The subjective ground here is the heart and the experience is an emotional state attuned to a distinctive mode of presence. In his analysis of art, Kant called attention to the transformation of presence effected by attention to a work of art. Features of experience such as love, joy, and death are given a new mode of presence through art; they draw near and touch us.[89] And the unknowable Beyond is brought near by symbolic explorations, such as appear in Plato, Dante, and Milton, that extend the effects of our moral life into an afterlife. The correlate to the heart is charged presence, drawing near and touching us. In the experience of awe, the heart is filled because it intimates its own peculiar relation to the Whole.

Two special objects that bring about awe are the starry skies above and the moral law within, each functioning as a type of schema for the two distinctive modes of encompassment: World and Soul. The starry skies are the object and model for Newtonian mechanistic science; the laws that govern the stars govern all terrestrial motions as well. It was the mode of knowing involved in such science that furnished the exemplar of knowing analyzed in *The Critique of Pure Reason*. "The moral law within" is the object of the second critique. In *The Critique of Judgment*, one occasion for the feeling of the sublime arises when awe before the starry skies combines with awe before the moral law to produce the experience of the sublime.[90] In the presence of the overwhelming size of the starry skies, we experience the dual emotion of sensing our own insignificance (hence, the component of *Furcht* or fear) and overcoming it with a sense of the sublimity of our own minds and their moral destiny (hence, the component of *Ehre* or esteem in *Ehrfurcht* or awe). The cool feeling of *Achtung*, or respect, required by the moral law is turned in the direction of an emotional, stirring experience, especially on the occasion of encountering something overwhelming in the outer world. Checked initially by the sense of our own physical insignificance, powerful vital emotion bursts forth in the feeling of awe that entails an emotional uplift. Reference to the totality coupled with the notion of the *summum bonum* and of immortality introduces a principle of hope to which, in our reading, the experience of the sublime bears witness.

88. Kant, *Critique of Practical Reason*, II, 166.
89. Kant, *Critique of Judgment*, §49, 314 (182–83).
90. Ibid., §23–29, 244ff (97ff).

The experience of our own insignificance in this instance is linked to our ability to think beyond any given magnitude to the encompassing totality. From the point of view of understanding, this introduces us to a *progressus ad infinitum* that Hegel will later designate as "the spurious [or bad] infinite."[91] However, what is at stake in relation to reason is the ability to think of *the absolute totality* as the substrate underlying all experience. Reason runs ahead of the *progressus* of understanding to encompass it absolutely—though only in thought. As minds we can contain and exceed that which contains and exceeds our bodies. The empirically based experience of our being *abgestossen* (repelled) joins with the reflectively based experience of our relation to the totality to which we are simultaneously *angezogen* (attracted). This is the fundamental experience of the antinomic character, not simply of the *thinking* of the totality but of the *existence* of human reality manifest to itself experientially as held in the tension between the at-home and the Beyond.

This analysis lies at the background of Rudolph Otto's notion of the *Holy* as the *mysterium tremendum et fascinans*—the mystery that simultaneously repels and attracts us, that causes us to tremble in fear and to be bound to it in fascination.[92] Such an experience requires a certain level of mental cultivation to resist the purely negative feeling produced in us by nature's magnitude. The savage cowers in fear; one who has been awakened to the transcendent character of the human mind is in a position to experience the tensive state of awe before the sublime.

As Lyotard would have it: "The absolute is never there, never given in a presentation, but it is always 'present' as a call to think beyond the 'there.' Ungraspable, but unforgettable. Never restored, never abandoned."[93] This creates a fundamental tension within the human being, an irremovable *Widerstreit*.[94] It both wounds imagination as the faculty of presentation

91. G. W. F. Hegel, *The Encyclopaedia Logic*, trans. T. Geraets, W. Suchting, and H. Harris (Indianapolis: Hackett, 1991), §94, 149.

92. Rudolf Otto, *The Idea of the Holy*, trans. J. Harvey (New York: Oxford University Press, 1964), 12–40.

93. Lyotard, *Lessons on the Analytic of the Sublime*, 150.

94. Ibid., 123ff, 159, 214, 234; cf. also *The Differend: Phrases in Dispute* (Minneapolis: University of Minnesota Press, 1983), and *The Inhuman* (Stanford, Calif.: Stanford University Press, 1988). Paralleling Derrida, Lyotard speaks of it as the *differend*—that which is different than anything that falls within the field of our experience and must be permanently deferred in coming to presence. Lyotard makes this *differend* the center of his thought. For Derrida, see "Différance" in *Margins of Philosophy*, trans. A. Bass (Chicago: University of Chicago Press, 1982), 1–27.

by the essential nonpresentability of the encompassing Beyond and gives imagination an extension it would not otherwise have by luring it into the construction of symbols. The sublime, *das Erhaben*, performs an *Aufhebung* of imagination, both canceling it and taking it up.[95]

Kant actually refers to three types of sublime experience. The two that are focal in his exposition appear on the basis of nature in relation to cognition (the so-called *mathematical sublime*) and to desire (*the dynamical sublime*); the third appears in relation to persons. We have looked at the mathematical sublime, the sublime in relation to cognition. It has its higher finality in the dynamical sublime as related to the desire of reason, which is the will. For Kant, human reality does not culminate in the contemplative or theoretical but in the practical. The antinomies of theoretical reason block the way of theoretical completion but point to "the sole noumenal fact" of freedom under moral law that leads into the postulation of the immortality of the soul and the Divine as omniscient, omnipotent, and just Judge. The mathematical sublime is surmounted by the *dynamical sublime*, manifest in the encounter with the overpowering aspects of nature, nature under the aspect of causality.[96] In relation to the storm at sea or the tornado, what is threatened is not only the sense of one's significance in the massive order of space but one's very existence. One is reminded of Pascal's reflection upon the human being as a "thinking reed" that a mere vapor can destroy but whose whole dignity consists in thought.[97] For Kant, thought itself points to an awareness of the ultimate superiority of our moral vocation.[98] For Kant, then, nature in these displays is not sublime; sublime in the proper sense of the term is our vocation as possessors of reason. Nature's display only serves as a symbol of this distinctively human superiority.[99] Encounter with the sublime would seem to be another way, beyond the beauties of nature and art, in which we gain some indication that "we are meant" by the world process, that we are in some sense the purpose of what appears in the world. Only in this case, the tendency of the beautiful to make us feel at home in the world by surmounting the tensions involved in our relation to what appears is unsettled by our ever-unfulfilled reference to the

95. Lyotard, *Lessons on the Analytic of the Sublime*, 129.
96. Kant, *Critique of Judgment*, §24, 247 (101).
97. Blaise Pascal, *Pensées* (New York: Modern Library, 1941), VI, §347.
98. Kant, *Critique of Judgment*, general comment to §29, 269 (129).
99. Ibid. §26, 256 (113).

undisclosed totality. This makes the sublime appear not as purposive but as contrapurposive both to our vital existence and to our power of judgment. But this is only apparent, for it is the sublime that awakens us to our ultimate destiny and that fills the heart.[100]

However, in addition to his major focus upon objects occasioning the feeling of the sublime, Kant's discussion of the sublime in his general comment on aesthetic judgments also focuses upon persons and thus slides over into sublime dispositions. He includes *enthusiasm* as an affective straining of our forces by ideas that establish a powerful and permanent disposition. In the Jewish prohibition of graven images, that very negation in relation to the infinity of God produces a most exalted feeling of the sublime. But because enthusiasm deprives the mind of its ability to engage in free deliberation about principles, it falls prey to *fanaticism*, substituting emotional excitement for insight and easily sliding into *superstition*, involving uncritical acceptance of claims linked to our eternal destiny.

Further, for Kant, every vigorous affect is sublime. He mentions here anger and indignation, both of which lead us to overcome powerful resistance. But more sublime is the noble character pursuing its principles with vigor and without affect. Among the sublime dispositions, Kant also includes isolation from society, provided it rests not upon misanthropy or anthropophobia but upon ideas that resist sensible interest. Indeed, any case of setting aside our own needs for the sake of principle Kant regards as sublime.[101] It would seem that in art, the presentation of such a disposition in an ideal human form is what the ideal of beauty is all about.

For Kant, then, the beautiful, because it synthesizes the immediacy of animal-based sensation with the distance provided by understanding, comes to expression in the seeming incompatibility of a satisfaction that is disinterested, a universality that is subjective, a purposiveness without an explicit purpose, and a necessity that is neither theoretical nor practical. But in doing so, it generates the experienced harmony of imagination and understanding and thus manifests the suitability of our judgments to the sensory world in which we live. And yet, because it involves

---

100. Ibid. §23 (99).
101. Ibid., general comment to §29, 272ff (132ff).

the indeterminate concept of a supersensuous Beyond as the horizon of all our judgments, the experience of beauty points beyond itself to that which comes to emotional awareness in the experience of the sublime, our moral link to the noumenal. This link appears in the plane of the beautiful when the beautiful becomes a symbol of the morally good. At first, this link involves a kind of immediate transfer when sensory presentations are given moral features. It is explicitly represented in the ideal of beauty with the human form exhibiting moral sublimity. But it occurs most powerfully in the experience of the dynamical sublime. Here, the tension that is human existence, stretched between animal immediacy and empty reference to the totality, comes to its deepest emotional expression and fills the heart with awe. It is such experience that sustained the otherwise austere character of the Kantian project, providing a powerful, underlying emotional dynamism that gave expression to the newly emerging world of Romantic striving. Kantian aesthetics brings to emotional expression the antinomic character of human existence itself.

11 ∞ Hegel

From Misunderstanding to the
Beginning of Understanding

Hegel is without a doubt one of the most misunderstood thinkers in Western intellectual history, a history he claimed to sum up and bring to its maturity. This misunderstanding has several roots. One is the intrinsic difficulty of grasping Hegel's thought. It is dense, technical, dialectical, and arranged in such a way that, to understand anything in it, one has to understanding its linkage with the whole system of thought. This means that one could easily take any given statement out of context and find in it a meaning that on the surface sounds preposterous.

A second problem is the ideological fixation of many critics. An ideologist is dispositionally unable to enter sympathetically into a position he or she thinks is inimical to his or her own. Ideological thinking is defending what one already accepts rather than submitting oneself to critical assessment in the light of what might emerge from a careful and sympathetic reading of and/or dialogue with serious thinkers. One can expect very little insightful interpretation from such a disposition.

A third problem emerges from the first two: failure to comprehend because of intrinsic difficulty and because of ideological fixation combine to produce a tradition that excuses one from taking the pains to understand what Hegel has seen. One identifies with a "master" and follows his dismissal of or failure to attend to Hegel. One listens to Russell or Popper or certain followers of Strauss.[1] Hegel becomes a closed book, an ideological enemy.

---

1. The grandfather of all misunderstandings in the English-speaking world is Karl Popper in his *The Open Society and Its Enemies*, vol. 2: *Hegel and Marx* (Princeton, N.J.: Princeton University Press, 1962), chapter 12, "Hegel and the New Tribalism," especially 31–32, 35, 41, 49, 59–60, 78. Bertrand Russell, in his popular *History of Western Philosophy*, helped to turn the British world from neo-Hegelianism to logical positivism (New York: Simon and Schuster, 1945),

In the 1950s Maurice Merleau-Ponty observed that Hegel had spawned the major movements of thought that came after him. He was talking about continental thought; he mentioned Marx, Nietzsche, phenomenology, existentialism, and psychoanalysis.[2] One might add John Dewey to the list in the Anglo-American world. Dewey saw himself as a Hegelian minus the absolute standpoint, a Hegelianism turned experimental.[3] The decisive turning point on the continent was Alexander Kojéve's brilliantly one-sided lectures in the 1930s on Hegel's 1807 *Philosophy of Spirit*.[4] But Anglo-American thought in the final three-quarters of the twentieth century decisively repudiated Hegel, who had a strong presence during the first quarter in England in T. H. Green, Bernard Bosanquet, Ellis McTaggart, and F. H. Bradley.[5]

The two-hundredth anniversary in 1970 of Hegel's birth jumpstarted a Hegel Renaissance in the Anglo-Saxon world. Along with Errol Harris,[6] John Findlay was one of the leaders who anticipated it.[7] Charles Taylor turned from analytical philosophy to an extensive and systematic study of Hegel that put its stamp on Taylor's subsequent work.[8] In his review of Taylor's Hegel book, Richard Bernstein noted that the first part of Hegel's 1807 *Phenomenology of Spirit* was prophetic history of twentieth-century British philosophy, working out the logic of transition from sense-data positivism to the late Wittgenstein.[9]

In recent times, within the analytical tradition, Robert Brandom began a sympathetic reading of Hegel's phenomenology,[10] with Willem de

---

730–45. Leo Strauss has furnished the axis for the basic orientation of his followers in his "The Three Waves of Modernity," in *An Introduction to Political Philosophy: Ten Essays*, ed. Hilail Gildin (Detroit: Wayne State University Press, 1989), 81–98.

2. Maurice Merleau-Ponty, *Signs*, trans. H. and P. Dreyfus (Evanston, Ill.: Northwestern University Press, 1964), 63.

3. John Dewey, "From Absolutism to Experimentalism," in *On Experience, Nature, and Freedom*, ed. R. Bernstein (Indianapolis: Bobbs-Merrill, 1960).

4. Alexandre Kojéve, *Introduction to the Reading of Hegel*, ed. A. Bloom, trans. J. H. Nichols (New York: Basic Books, 1969).

5. Hiralal Haldar, *Neo-Hegelianism* (London: Heath, Cranton, 1927).

6. Errol Harris, *Nature, Mind, and Modern Science* (London: George Allen and Unwin, 1954), 228–55. Beginning with that work, Harris went on in several works to show the enduring relevance of Hegel's thought.

7. John Findlay, *Hegel: A Re-Examination* (New York: Collier Books, 1962).

8. Charles Taylor, *Hegel* (Cambridge: Cambridge University Press, 1975).

9. Richard Bernstein, "Why Hegel Now?" *The Review of Metaphysics* 31, no. 1 (1977): 29–60.

10. Robert Brandom, *Reasoning, Representing, and Discursive Commitment* (Cambridge, Mass.: Harvard University Press, 1994).

Vries following,[11] culminating in John MacDowell's *Mind and World*.[12] MacDowell traces the development of American thought from Quine through Sellars, Rorty and Davidson, to arrive at a position in which, as he says, we have finally caught up with Hegel.[13] So it seems times are ripe for revisiting Hegel, and it would be helpful to remove some of the commonest misinterpretations.[14]

For Hegel, history is the story of freedom.[15] But what is freedom? Hegel said that freedom is the recognition of necessity.[16] Spinoza said the same,[17] and Hegel further said that to philosophize is to think like Spinoza.[18] So in seeing history as the story of freedom, Hegel is simply placing Spinoza in historical perspective.

In Spinozistic fashion, the rule of absolute necessity is justification for any present arrangement, for Hegel said that "the rational is the actual and the actual is the rational."[19] This clearly underpins the practices of the Prussian monarchy of his time. Indeed, Hegel considered the state to be God on earth that has the absolute right to abrogate the right to life and property upon command.[20] In fact, Hegel was a closet atheist who deified humanity as found in the state.[21] Further, he thought of the

11. Willem de Vries, *Hegel's Theory of Mental Activity* (Ithaca, N.Y.: Cornell University Press, 1988).

12. John MacDowell, *Mind and World* (Cambridge, Mass.: Harvard University Press, 1994). MacDowell refers to Brandom's work on Hegel as "eye-opening."

13. Ibid., 111.

14. For a devastating critique of Popper's views, see Walter Kaufmann, "The Hegel Myth and Its Method," in *The Hegel Myths and Legends*, ed. Jon Stewart (Evanston, Ill.: Northwestern University Press, 1996), 82–103.

15. G. W. F. Hegel, *The Philosophy of History*, trans. J. Sibree (New York: Dover, 1956), 19.

16. Ibid., 50. This is also a reading of Hegel's claim (also in *The Philosophy of History*, 19) that "the essential nature of freedom," which involves in it absolute necessity, "is to be displayed as coming to a consciousness of itself . . ." as it is a reading of *The Encyclopaedia Logic* §48, trans. T. Geraets, W. Suchting, and H. Harris (Indianapolis: Hackett, 1991), 94.

17. Benedict de Spinoza, *Ethics: Ethica Ordine Geometrico Demonstrata*, trans. R. Elwes (New York: Dover, 1955), part I, XXVII, XXXI; part II, XLVIII; V, V.

18. G. W. F. Hegel, *Lectures on the History of Philosophy*, trans. P. Hodgson et al. (Berkeley: University of California Press, 1990), 154 and 155.

19. Preface to G. W. F. Hegel, *Philosophy of Right*, trans. T. Knox (London: Oxford University Press, 1952), 10.

20. Hegel, *Philosophy of Right*, §258, *Zusatz*/279. "The march of God in the world, that is what the State is." Again in the body of the same section: "[T]his final end has supreme right against the individual," 156. (In those works organized by section numbers, we will indicate the section number followed by a dash, after which we will indicate the page number of the translation.)

21. See, for example, Robert Solomon, *In the Spirit of Hegel* (New York: Oxford University Press, 1983), 5.

individual as an accident and the state as the substance that endures in and through the inevitable disappearance of the individual.[22] Hegel is thus the source of modern-day totalitarianisms. The Hegelian Left and the Hegelian Right met at Leningrad.[23]

Hegel further said that slavery is historically justified and is even now a necessary phase of human development. Historically, forced labor has been the key to freeing human skills as well as giving us a richer understanding of the nature upon which the slave works.[24] *Arbeit macht frei.* We know where that appeared.

In the long historical process leading to the coming into existence of the modern state, many an innocent flower had to be trampled underfoot.[25] So much for individual dignity. And indeed, in the historical process states themselves are used and discarded as are the great ones who lead history forward.[26] The *Weltgeist* is finally the only holder of rights within the Whole that is governed, by inexorable necessity, to reach its conclusion in the Hegelian System, which recognizes that necessity and is thus freed from the partiality that afflicts prior thought.

So much for all-too-common impressions of Hegel based upon citations taken out of context. But Hegel also said that the truth is the Whole.[27] It is only in relation to the Whole that any aspect can be understood. When we place all the aforementioned observations within the full context of his thought, an entirely different picture emerges. What emerges is a powerful defense of individual rights and a consequent political enlargement of the sphere of operation of individual choice.

During Hegel's own time, a certain Herr Krug first exhibited a misunderstanding that still persists. In reaction to Hegel's claim to be able to "deduce" "the Totality" in his "System" of so-called Absolute Knowing, Krug, holding up his pen, exclaimed triumphantly: "Let Hegel deduce *that!*" [28] He confused Hegel's thought with several claims that on

22. Hegel, *Philosophy of Right*, §145/105.

23. Review of Charles Taylor's *Hegel*, in *Political Theory* 4, no. 3 (August 1976): 377.

24. G. W. F. Hegel, *Phenomenology of Spirit*, trans. A. Miller (Oxford: Oxford University Press, 1977), §195, 118; *Hegel's Philosophy of Mind*, trans. W. Wallace and A. Miller (Oxford: Clarendon Press, 1971), §413, 153–54.

25. Intro to Hegel, *The Philosophy of History*, 32, 21.

26. Ibid., 31.

27. Hegel, *Phenomenology of Spirit*, §20/11.

28. G. W. F. Hegel, *Hegel's Philosophy of Nature*, trans. A. Miller (Oxford: Clarendon Press, 1970), introduction, 23, note. Herr Krug was probably Wilhelm Traugott Krug, a contemporary Romantic.

the surface seem identical. First is the appearance that Absolute Knowing is equivalent to divine omniscience. This is linked to Hegel's claim to be able to follow the thoughts of God before creation.[29] Second, Krug's misunderstanding is connected with the supposition that Hegel was attempting to fulfill in his own peculiar manner the ideal of the LaPlacean Mind. At the beginning of the nineteenth century, Pierre Simon LaPlace claimed that if one had a mind capacious enough to understand all the laws of nature and the position and velocity of all the particles at a given time, one could predict the whole of the future and "retrodict" the whole of the past.[30] This is not Hegel's view.

What we need to attend to is the fact that "the Totality" of which Hegel spoke was not the totality of all factual occurrences but the interconnection of all the categories required for there to be minds and the intelligibility of things. What are the systematic conditions for the possibility of the intelligibility of things and the existence and flourishing of intellectual beings? It is the System that, Hegel claims, eternally antecedes nature and history as the Logos through which all things were made.

The Krugian misunderstanding is further linked to the supposition that Hegel claimed to be able to find out the truth of nature or of history apart from the careful empirical inquiries undertaken by the natural and historical sciences. But the overarching intelligibility afforded by Hegel's System precisely leaves open the exploration of the vast multiplicity of species in nature and of ways of acting in history.[31]

Again, this is related to the misunderstanding that deduce-ability meant factual necessitation and that human beings simply played out a governing necessity in all the seeming contingencies of their lives. In fact, Hegel's "System" establishes a key role for contingency in general and the absolutely central role for free choice in particular.

The *Logic* deduces the necessity of contingency.[32] The *Philosophy of Nature* indicates that, though the general categories immanent in nature

29. G. W. F. Hegel, *Hegel's Science of Logic*, trans. A. Miller (London: George Allen and Unwin, 1969), 50.

30. Pierre Simon LaPlace, *The System of the World*, vol. 1, trans. J. Pond (London: Richard Philips, 1809).

31. Hegel, *Hegel's Philosophy of Nature*, §250, 22–23; *Lectures on the Philosophy of World History*, trans. H. Nisbet (Cambridge: Cambridge University Press, 1975), 66.

32. Hegel, *Hegel's Science of Logic*, 545.

are deducible, the vast variety of species and individual behaviors are not, but can only come to be known by patient empirical inquiry. Further, just because of the way things interact, the face of nature is the place where contingency "runs riot." Further still, because of the free and irremovable self-disposability of humans (as we discuss more in the following sections), each human introduces innumerable contingencies into his or her life and community by reason of the choices he or she makes. Through the human, the arbitrary and the counterrational appears. A fortiori, the interrelation of vast numbers of humans in context determined by the choices of those long dead, introduces a historical realm of vast contingencies.[33]

Another allied misunderstanding is linked to Hegel's metaphor—illuminating but even more misleading—that individual humans are "accidents" of the "Substance" of family and state.[34] What is illuminating about the metaphor is the fact that, like tanner skin in summer and paler skin in winter, individual humans come and go, while families and states endure, and that there is, indeed, something noble in the individual sacrificing himself or herself—for example, in child care or in war—for the good of the more enduring Whole. What is misleading is that this metaphor joins with the concept of deducibility and a related set of misunderstood concepts and leads to the common concept advanced by Kierkegaard that the individual human is swallowed up in "the System."[35]

History, Hegel maintains, is the playing out of a necessity, precisely the necessity of the realization of the human essence, and that freedom is the recognition of necessity. The latter derives from Spinoza, whose completely deductive system allows for no contingency whatsoever and whose unitary Substance does indeed contain all individuals as accidents ("modes") of the one divine (or natural) Substance.

Hegel said that "to philosophize one has to think like Spinoza."[36] But his assimilation of Spinoza has to be read in terms of Hegel's simultaneous critique of Spinoza. One moves beyond Spinoza by introducing

33. Hegel, *The Encyclopaedia Logic*, §145 *Zusatz*, 218.
34. G. W. F. Hegel, *Elements of the Philosophy of Right*, trans. H. Nisbet (Cambridge: Cambridge University Press, 1991), §163, 203.
35. Søren Kierkegaard, *Concluding Unscientific Postscript to Philosophical Fragments*, trans. D. Senson (Princeton, N.J.: Princeton University Press, 1941), 33, 107, 109, 117, 223, 240.
36. Hegel, *Hegel's Science of Logic*, 580ff; Hegel, *Lectures on the History of Philosophy*, trans. R. Brown, J. Stewart, and H. Harris (Berkeley: University of California Press, 1990), vol. 3, 154ff.

the Subject into Spinoza's Substance.[37] This can be seen in one of Hegel's central and continually repeated conceptions: that the ability to say "I" for each individual human involves an ability to back off freely at any moment from all determinants, interior and exterior, and to be able to be a new center of initiative in the causal networks, mechanical, teleological, and social, within which every "I" operates.[38] It is this, which he calls "formal, abstract, and negative freedom," that introduces the vast sphere of contingency, creative as well as irrational—and even evil—into human affairs.[39] It is the freedom to choose, to take responsibility in a radical way. But this formal freedom is rooted in being referred, via the concept of Being, to the totality that gives the basic *telos* for the process of the System. Formal freedom is fulfilled in "substantial" or "essential freedom," in coming to recognize clearly one's place in the overarching scheme of things—familial, social, historical, and cosmic—and coming to act in accordance with that recognition. The truly "free mind" is a mind free to be fully itself as a rational agency.[40]

History is the story of freedom, from Oriental empires in which one, the emperor, alone is free; through Greco-Roman societies in which some, the citizens, are free; to Germanic-Christian societies in which, in principle, all are free.[41] What "free" means here is minimally having formal freedom recognized by allowing scope for its operation. That plays out in Germanic-Christian societies in the development of "civil society," a bourgeois order (*bürgerliche Gesellschaft*) based upon an expansion of individual rights, basically to property, spelled out in a market system, and to conscience, developed in freedom of religion and thus separation of church and state, in freedom of inquiry, press, speech, assembly, choice in marriage partners, occupation, and the like.[42] Formal freedom is the principle of the bourgeois order. But to reach substantial freedom, it must be grounded in the encompassing orders of family and state and the all-encompassing cosmic-divine order. It is here that Hegel

37. Hegel, *Phenomenology of Spirit*, §17, 10.

38. Hegel, *The Encyclopaedia Logic*, §20, 49–51; *Hegel's Philosophy of Mind*, §381, *Zusatz*, 11.

39. Hegel, *Hegel's Philosophy of Mind*, §429, 268.

40. Ibid., §§481–82, 238–40. See my "The Free Spirit: Spinoza, Hegel, Nietzsche," *International Philosophical Quarterly* 51, no. 3 (Fall 2011).

41. Hegel, *Lectures on the Philosophy of World History*, 54.

42. Hegel, *Philosophy of Right*, on love, conscience, inquiry, §124, 151–52; further on conscience, §137, 164; on choice in marriage partners, §162, 201–2; on religion §270, 291ff; on speech and the press, §319, 356; on property, §41ff, 73ff; on occupation, §254, 272.

reintroduces the ancient concept of *pietas* as the sense of unpayable indebtedness to that which makes our concrete lives possible, a concept that stood in the way of modern freedoms but which now has to be counterbalance to them.[43]

The *Phenomenology of Spirit* presents "the ladder to the Absolute standpoint," that of the identity of Thought and Being within which the System develops.[44] Taking several runs at that standpoint, Hegel arrives successively, first, at the acting individual as the completion of rationality, second, at the fallibilistic dialogical community as the situation of action, and third, at revealed religion, Christianity, as the encompassing ground of such community. The acting community thus becomes the center, but the element of its action is the recognition of necessary fallibility, since no one can know the fullness of the circumstances within which we are called upon to act or therefore the full consequences of our action. One *must* act—the "beautiful soul," unwilling to act for fear of sullying one's purity, lives abstractly; but one must also attempt to justify one's actions before the community and be open to acknowledging mistakes in dialogue with others and thus to seek forgiveness.[45] What as a matter of fact historically grounds such community is revealed religion that proclaims the identity of the divine and the human in Christ, culminating in the Resurrection and Ascension as the grounds for the sending of the Spirit of truth into the community.[46] The element of the science of wisdom is precisely that element of the encompassing divine Spirit underpinning the fallibilistic, dialogical community of action. A free, dialogical community, incapable in principle of knowing all the contingencies of nature and history that will impinge upon its actions, is the teleological completion of the System.

This certainly indicates that "Absolute Knowing" does not mean "knowing absolutely everything about everything"; it does not mean omniscience. Inserted as a finite agent into a finite community, which, in turn, is inserted into the contingencies of nature, no one can know the full concrete context and actual consequences of his or her action. But one can

43. See Hegel, *Philosophy of Right*, §163, 112; also Aquinas, *Summa Theologiae*, II-II, 101, 1; Cicero, *On Invention et al.*, trans. H. Hubbel (Cambridge, Mass.: Harvard University Press, 1949), 2; Aristotle, *Nicomachean Ethics*, IX, 12, 1162a, 4ff.

44. Hegel, *Science of Logic*, 48–49.

45. Hegel, *Phenomenology of Spirit*, §666–70, 405–8.

46. Hegel, *Hegel's Philosophy of Mind*, §§564–71, 297–302.

come to know the pervading conditions of rationality in all contexts. That is what Absolute Knowing is all about.

These considerations should lay to rest the absurd notion that Hegel's System is totalitarian and that the individual is swallowed up in the System. Nothing could be further from the truth. The intrinsic dignity of each human being, announced by Christianity, is founded by Hegel upon the intrinsic rationality of the human subject.[47] And that, in turn, involves a reference to the totality of Being that grounds the ability to say "I," that is, to step back from all determinants and to determine oneself. Modern society, founded upon individual rights, carries out the consequences of that insight. Hegel's state is organized to protect those rights, creating a set of institutional buffers between the most encompassing power at the center or apex and the increasingly local levels down to the level of the individual. The state is structured according to the principle assimilated in the Catholic social encyclical tradition: the principle of subsidiarity. According to that principle, a state should not do at a higher level of organization what can be done at a lower level.[48] As much as possible, the conditions should be established for a maximum of individual and local decision making.

Hegel's statement that "many an innocent flower must be trampled in the march of the World Spirit" is a description, not a prescription. Factually, there will inevitably be "collateral damage" in any war. Similarly, that the "world-historical figures" such as Alexander, Caesar, and Napoleon were not moral paragons is a factual observance, not an element of praise.[49]

Linked to this is the claim that Hegel divinized the state. One source of this is his alleged statement that the state is God in the world. This is actually a mistranslation of "*Es ist der Gang Gottes in der Welt dass der Staat ist.*"[50] This should read: "It is God's way in the world that the state exists." And that is linked to his claim that God is active in the community as the Spirit binding the whole together. This is the wholly orthodox claim that providence guides the world and the Holy Spirit exists in His people. This is not saying that the state is "Creator of heaven and earth."

---

47. Hegel, *The Encyclopaedia Logic*, §147 addition, 223; *Lectures on the Philosophy of World History*, 54–55 and 131.
48. Hegel, *Philosophy of Right*, §290, 330–32 and §295, 334.
49. Hegel, *Lectures on the Philosophy of World History*, 82–89.
50. Ibid. §258, 269.

When Feuerbach and then thinkers like Kojéve see Hegel as reducing God to humanity, they ignore this last fundamental claim.[51]

And one must not fail to note that beyond Objective Spirit in the state, and as the final fruit of human existence, there is the realm of Absolute Spirit: of art, religion, and philosophy. The state is the *Dasein* of Spirit, not its *For itself*; its appearance, not its actuality. The state is the flower, but the fruit is what rises above the state.[52] Art speaks to all humankind; religion crosses state boundaries; and philosophy stands critically in relation to the Whole. Though religion lies at the foundation of the state, it must be separated, not only because it rises above the state to lie at the foundation of other states but also because religious belief cannot be compelled the way legal conduct can be.[53] Freedom of worship is essential. It involves not only the freedom of various religions to practice but the freedom of each citizen to choose her or his religious affiliation.[54]

Then there is the perennial misreading of his famous declaration that "[t]he real is the rational and the rational is the real." This is frequently taken to mean that whatever is, is rational and thus there is no room for social-political critique.[55] This is understood in relation to Hegel's claim that freedom is the recognition of necessity, and that is understood in relation to Spinoza's necessitarianism.[56] In addition, there is Hegel's parallel infamous declaration in his *Habilitationsschrift* that, "If the facts disagree with the Concept, so much the worse for the facts!"[57] Both the claim to the rationality of the real and the disagreement of facts with the Concept presuppose in Hegel's thought a teleological view of things. Agreement with the Concept is achieving the full actualization of the active potentialities implicit in the developing individual, as a fertilized ovum moving to a fully functional adult member of its species. Failure to reach that—through disease or destruction—is so much worse for the factual living being. Similarly, in a given society, what suits the overall

51. Ludwig Feuerbach, *The Essence of Christianity*, trans. G. Eliot (New York: Harper, 1957), see especially "The Essence of Religion Considered Generally," 12–32.

52. Hegel, *Philosophy of Right*, §360, 380.

53. Ibid., §§135–40, 163–84; *Hegel's Philosophy of Mind*, §552, 282ff.

54. Hegel, *Philosophy of Right*, §270, 290ff.

55. Ibid., preface, 20. See Nietzsche's "The Sheer Gaping at Success," in *The Use and Abuse of History*, trans. A. Collins (Indianapolis: Bobbs-Merill, 1949), 52.

56. Hegel, *The Encyclopaedia Logic*, §48 *Zusatz*, 94.

57. Ibid., §172; *Zusatz*, 250. Truth "is the agreement of an object with itself, i.e. with its concept." See also Hegel, *Science of Logic*, 657–58.

social context in such a way as to maximize individual possibilities for development consistent with the totality of existent factors in that society and in its given environment, social and natural, is rational and thus real (*wirklich* as realizing the fundamental potentialities of humanness). What hampers that development in that given context is to that extent "unreal," though fully factual (unfortunately, not for Hegel's System but for the factual failure in rationality). As "unreal" in this sense, there is crime, disfunctionality, and general irrationality.[58]

What is crucial here is the distinction between *Existenz* or *Dasein* and *Wirklichkeit* or actuality. *Dasein* is the more primitive category in the *Logic*. It refers to the relation of any entity to what it is not (i.e., to other entities and to its own prior and posterior conditions).[59] *Existenz* is a more developed category that refers to the same, but as coming out of a ground in what initially appears to be a hidden essence.[60] *Wirklichkeit* is the completion of such an essence by its "becoming what it is," by its reaching an identity of essence and existence or by its moving from its essential potentiality to full actuality in its kind.[61]

Consider more carefully the famous formula from the preface to *Philosophy of Right*: "*Was vernünftig ist, das ist wirklich* [What is rational, that is actual]; *und was wirklich ist, das ist vernünftig* [and what is actual, that is rational]."[62] The first statement emphasizes that rationality is not contained in some ideal Beyond but in what is actual and operative in life: that rational is actually operative in concrete existence. The second underscores the locus of rationality, not in any existent state but only in the mature situation: only what actualizes the essence of the thing is rational. Shot through with natural contingencies and with the contingencies set in motion by the interrelation of human choices past and present, there is nonetheless the operation of an underlying rational drive—the *List der Vernunft*, the cunning of reason—that cannot fail to be instantiated because there is a human essence striving to move from potentiality to actuality.[63]

58. Hegel, *Philosophy of Right*, §270, 302. See also a work that I did with intellectual historian Charles Sullivan, "Reason and Actuality in the Prussian Reform Movement," *Existentia* 21, fasc. 1–2 (2011).

59. Hegel, *The Encyclopaedia Logic*, §89–95, 145–52.

60. Hegel, *Science of Logic*, 484.

61. Hegel, *The Encyclopaedia Logic*, §§142ff, 213ff.

62. Hegel, *Philosophy of Right*, preface, 20; *The Encyclopaedia Logic*, §6, 29.

63. Hegel, *Lectures on the Philosophy of World History*, 89.

Here, as in many places, Hegel is actually Aristotelian. In Aristotle, the demands of human nature led to the gradual development of human organization until it reached the level of the *polis*, where the arts and sciences can flourish and reach their "natural" forms. In his own works, he often traces the development of the sciences in which he is inquiring out of their ground in myth and through the identification of various components needed to secure a rational account until they reach a certain highpoint in his own thought. For Aristotle, this natural development, though requiring human choice and effort, also necessarily dissolves back into less developed forms of organization and into mythical modes of conception, the latter of which preserve the central concepts but in inadequate because nonconceptual form. And, by reason of the eternal instantiation of natural species in the cosmos, the process repeats itself in an "Eternal Recurrence of the Same."[64] Hegel's difference from this view lies in his elimination of eternal cyclic repetition, introducing (and following the Hebrew-Christian view) a single linear development of the human essence without reinserting it, like Aristotle, into cyclic form.

We should note here Hegel's use of the term "essence" (*Wesen*) rather than "nature" (*Natur*). For Hegel, the latter is the subhuman. Both nature and spirit fall under the Logic and thus under the Logic of essence and Concept. Central to the former is the distinction of essence and existence and the notion of Actuality (*Wirklichkeit*) as the union of essence and existence. Central to the Concept is the notion of teleology that finds its progressively fuller instantiation in living form, in human cognition and choice, and in Absolute Knowing.[65]

The distinctively human is not nature but "spirit," though it is spirit requiring embodiment in nature. Just as in nature the essence of matter is gravity, so in the case of spirit, its essence is freedom.[66] That means that spirit has to produce itself through choice and the institutionalization of choice. However, not every choice—and, consequently, every institution—is rational; many fail to "measure up to the Concept."[67]

One should note further that "rationality" is a feature not simply of "thought" but of what is. "Rationality" is exhibited in the coherent func-

64. Aristotle, *On the Soul*, II, 415b 1.
65. On teleology, see Hegel, *Science of Logic*, 735ff.
66. Hegel, *Lectures on the Philosophy of World History*, 47–48.
67. Hegel, *Philosophy of Right*, §270, 302. On animal disease, see *Philosophy of Nature*, §§371–72.

tioning of the solar system, in a more intrinsic way in an organism and its ecosystem, and necessarily in a community that holds together over time—though the level of its rationality may be low because institutions of freedom are not developed in it. Consider Plato's observations on the criminal group who could not be "good" at what they do unless they exhibited some "justice" toward one another.[68] The rationality of human life "grows" through practice and is not simply a matter of abstract constructions. The task of philosophy is not to construct utopias or "systems" but to pay attention to the "kernel of rationality" already at work in things natural and historical.

There is, finally, the Kierkegaardian complaint that "passion and inwardness," the index of "the individual," disappears and the individual is "swallowed up" in "the System."[69] While that may have been true of the view propounded by the leaders of the Danish Lutheran Church in the first half of the nineteenth century, it is not true of Hegel. For Hegel, "he who does not have the experience of rising up in his heart in the midst of the everyday to the Eternal and All-encompassing does not have the experience, the comprehension of which is the task of the philosophy of religion."[70] The human being is a psycho-physical whole, with reason not only as the highest layer but as the pervading principle. In conscious life, "rational" living, participating in a "rational" community, sinks into the heart so that one can come to know intuitively what is the rational in action. Intuition here is immediate, but an immediacy mediated by rational patterns. Intuition is not self-certifying but is dependent upon past rationality—discovered on one's own or learned from others—that has sunk into one's felt life.[71]

Beyond this, there is passion as the ability to put the whole of oneself into a project. For Hegel, nothing great happens without such passion.[72] If rationality does not penetrate to the heart and culminate in passion, if it remains merely "in the head," then for Hegel we have a situation of inauthentic existence. "The possibility that, as they say, abstract, *Analytical Understanding* (*Verstand*) could be developed without the *Heart* and the

68. Plato, *Republic*, I, 352c.
69. Kierkegaard, *Concluding Unscientific Postscript*, 33, 107, 109, 117, 223, 240.
70. Hegel, *Lectures on the Philosophy of Religion*, trans. P. Hodgson et al. (Berkeley: University of California Press, 1988), 481–89.
71. Hegel, *Hegel's Philosophy of Mind*, §449, 199–200.
72. Hegel, *Lectures on the Philosophy of World History*, 73.

Heart without *Understanding*, that there are Hearts one-sidedly without Understanding and Heartless Understanding, indicates in any case only this, that there are bad existents, untrue in themselves."[73]

The human individual with its passion and inwardness is not "swallowed up" in "world-historical absentmindedness"; it is situated and in some cases can become the locus of world history. Far from swallowing up human subjectivity with its passion and inwardness, Hegel's System locates it within the Whole.

Hegel claims to complete the Platonic project by the systematic development of the central insights that have developed in the history of philosophy since Plato's time. Plato said that the philosopher "has his eyes fixed on the whole . . . and the whole character of each kind within the Whole." Today, the two warring camps of philosophers, analytical thinkers generating argument after argument regarding single issues and deconstructionist inveighing against "logo-centrism," have allowed the ability to think responsibly about the Whole to atrophy. Heidegger himself claimed that we are not at the level where we can encounter Hegel's thought.[74] It requires a change of philosophical disposition beyond the warring camps to begin to appreciate his thought.

Hegel's thought remains a permanent legacy of philosophic thought. With typical misunderstandings out of the way, we should be able to take in the rich harvest of his great work.[75]

73. Hegel, *Hegel's Philosophy of Mind*, §445, 188. The translation is mine.

74. "It is not that Hegel's philosophy has broken down. Rather, his contemporaries and successors have not ever yet stood up so that they can be measured against his greatness." Martin Heidegger, *Hegel's Phenomenology of Spirit*, trans. P. Emad and K. Maly (Bloomington: Indiana University Press, 1988), 40.

75. So as to assist in beginning to understand, I have devoted a book to Hegel: *Hegel's Introduction to the System* (Toronto: University of Toronto Press, 2014).

12 ∽ Hegel on the Heart

In a polemic typically aimed at Hegelians and in the name of religious piety, Kierkegaard complained that philosophers construct magnificent thought-castles and dwell in miserable shacks nearby. Dwelling is a matter of deepest individuality, of subjectivity, passion, and inwardness.[1] It is a matter of the heart, of which Pascal says that reason knows nothing.[2] And everyone knows that the individual with his precious heart is swallowed up in Hegelian panlogicism and ground under in the march of the Absolute through history.

What I intend to demonstrate is that none of these claims, which have become almost axiomatic in some quarters, apply to Hegel, who has a substantial and very positive teaching on the heart. He understood quite well the deficiencies of a merely abstract reason and equally well the conditions for the emergence of distinctively human individuality, with passion and inwardness, with a fully developed heart.[3] And he also

I want to thank Daniel Dahlstrom and Kenneth Schmitz as well as two anonymous reviewers for their helpful comments upon earlier drafts of this chapter.

1. Søren Kierkegaard, *Concluding Unscientific Postscript to Philosophical Fragments*, trans. D. Senson (Princeton, N.J.: Princeton University Press, 1941), 216 ff.

2. Blaise Pascal, *Pensées* (New York: Modern Library, 1941), IV, #277.

3. Hegel's reputation as master of the concept or, less adulatory, as supreme concept-monger has led to a neglect of what I regard as his central teaching on the heart. Charles Taylor's *Hegel* (Cambridge: Cambridge University Press, 1976), in commenting upon the System as a whole skips from the *Logic* to the treatment of ethical substance, using as transition "The Idea in Nature," saying nothing of subjective spirit, and *a fortiori* nothing about the heart. John Findlay's *Hegel: A Re-Examination* (New York: Collier, 1962), which touched off the Hegel renaissance, gives a brief account (291–311) of subjective spirit in the *Philosophy of Spirit* but says nothing of the notion of the heart. Sections §400 and §408 of *Hegel's Philosophy of Mind*, trans. W. Wallace and A. Miller (Oxford: Clarendon Press, 1971), contain some of the basic statements on the heart. Murray Greene in *Hegel on the Soul: A Speculative Anthropology* (The Hague: Martinus Nijhoff, 1972), though commenting upon the whole of the anthropology wherein these sections appear, does not even mention the term "heart." Willem de Vries in *Hegel's Theory of Mental Activity* (Ithaca, N.Y.: Cornell University Press, 1988) simply cites (62–63) a passage in which Hegel uses the notion, but de Vries himself does not comment upon it.

understood the non-self-certifying character of any appeal to the heart by itself, which may just as well be evil and obtuse as good and perceptive. Hence, one can find two lines of text regarding the heart: one negative and one positive.[4]

Throughout his writings, Hegel polemicizes against Romanticist emphasis upon the heart as the locus of intuition in opposition to the capacity for abstraction, inference, and construction. He speaks contemptuously of "the broth of heart, friendship, and inspiration."[5] For Hegel, at the level of religion the appeal to feeling and the heart reduces it to empty elevation to the eternal and bypasses the essential intellectual work of doctrinal development.[6] In philosophy, Hegel attacks the appeal to intuition, as if one could arrive at philosophical truth "shot from a pistol" over against "the labor of the notion."[7] He finds "the law of the heart" linked to "the frenzy of self conceit."[8] And he rejects the attempt of philosophy to be edifying, to appeal to the heart.[9] This provides fuel for the fire of Kierkegaard against Hegel as forgetting the passion and inwardness of the heart, characteristic of the existing individual in opposition to the abstract thinker.

It is the contention of this chapter that the notion of the heart and the implicit recovery of the notion of *pietas* in the development of the heart lie at the heart of Hegel's conception of reason. The heart is manifest at the level of objective spirit in family feeling and in patriotism, and at the level of absolute spirit in "the witness of the spirit" in the heart of

4. M. J. Petry calls attention to these two aspects and claims that in *Hegel's Philosophy of Spirit*, ed. and trans. M. J. Petry, 3 vols. (Dordrecht: D. Reidel, 1979), through his equation of *Herz* and *Gemüt*, or heart and disposition, Hegel corrected his earlier negative assessment. *Hegel's Philosophy of Spirit*, vol. 2, *Anthropology*, 484 and 496. Petry appends these comments in short notes and does nothing to develop them. Nor does he comment upon the several passages cited in our work.

5. G. W. F. Hegel, *Elements of the Philosophy of Right*, ed. E. Wood, trans. H. Nesbit (Cambridge: Cambridge University Press, 1991), preface, 6.

6. G. W. F. Hegel, *Lectures on the Philosophy of Religion*, trans. E. Speirs and J. Sanderson (London: Kegan Paul, Trench, Trübner, 1985), vol. I, 15; G. W. F. Hegel, *Hegel's Phenomenology of Spirit*, trans. A. Miller (Oxford: Oxford University Press, 1981), §10, 6. I am aware of the newer translation of the *Lectures on the Philosophy of Religion* by Peter Hodgson (Berkeley: University of California Press, 1988), which gives us the text of the 1827 edition prepared on the basis of the best critical edition. Speirs and Sanderson used the Marheineke edition of 1840. I have referred to their translation when the texts I cite are not in the Hodgson translation.

7. Hegel, *Hegel's Phenomenology of Spirit*, §27, 16 and §70, 43.

8. The two phrases form the title of the *Phenomenology*, C, (AA), B, b.

9. Ibid., §9, 6.

the individual believer, which Hegel also considers the principle of philo-sophical knowledge.[10] The first clear appearance of absolute knowing in the *Phenomenology of Spirit* is in conscience where "God is *immediately* present in its mind and heart, in its self."[11] The heart is grounded in and required by the structure of subjective spirit. The heart instantiates a pre-reflective reason that overcomes—at the level of *Sittlichkeit*—the abstrac-tions of Enlightenment rationalism. At the level of the logic, this is because logical completion involves "the singular," which is fully achieved at the level of the human who thinks fully rationally because he or she lives fully rationally.[12] But that means that concrete reason operative in life provides the basis for reflective or speculative reason and that speculative reason, precisely in order to be truly comprehensive, must return to the lifeworld.

In the first part of this chapter, I will examine Hegel's explicit treat-ment of the heart, focusing primarily upon the *Encyclopaedia Philosophy of Spirit*. In the second part, I will show how this functions in the *Phi-losophy of Right*. I will end with some remarks on the unity of the field of awareness involved at the level of absolute spirit.

PHILOSOPHY OF SPIRIT

The heart that interests Hegel is not the physiological pump in the center of the chest; it is the locus of feeling in the field of awareness. "The heart signifies the all-embracing unity of the feelings, both in their quantity and also as regards their duration in time. The heart is the ground or ba-sis which contains in itself and preserves the essential nature of feelings, independent of the fleeting nature of their succession in consciousness."[13]

Feeling arises out of the animal organism and is the expression of the "omnipresence of the unity of the animal in all its members." It presents at the level of rudimentary awareness the triumph by the organism over the tendency to dissolution involved in being material.[14] The heart is the resultant in felt attunement of all the internal and external adjustments

10. Hegel, *Lectures on the Philosophy of Religion*, I, 43.
11. Hegel, *Hegel's Phenomenology of Spirit*, §656, 398.
12. G. W. F. Hegel, *Science of Logic*, trans. A. Miller (New York: Humanities Press, 1969), 618–22.
13. Hegel, *Lectures on the Philosophy of Religion*, III, 181.
14. Hegel, *Hegel's Philosophy of Mind*, §381, 10, 13.

or maladjustments of the individual animal organism. The heart is "the form of particularity as such."[15] It is differentiated through the system of the senses but in function of the fundamentally desirous, needy character of the organism. As such, it reduces what is other than itself to its own needs. As a matter of animal immediacy, the heart is "natural and selfish." When humans revert to mere nature, what are freed are "the self-seeking affections of the heart, such as vanity, pride, and the rest of the passions— fancies and hopes—merely personal love and hatred."[16] The heart in the condition of nature, of immediacy, of mere being, thus stands as part to Whole over against what is spiritual, universal, and all-encompassing. So considered, the heart has to be overcome.

But one does not begin life with such a split. Experience in its early character is a matter of lived identity with one's own body wherein awareness of one's spiritual nature is merely implicit. The task of human existence is to "transform its identity with its body into an identity brought about or mediated by mind."[17] And that involves the emergence of spirit from the immediacy of nature and its feelings. Through the dialectic between upbringing, as the choices of others, and one's own choices based thereon, a second nature is produced that shapes and sublimates what is originally given by nature. The soul becomes an actualized soul, a being-for-self that encloses the plurality of habits formed out of the pool of potentialities provided immediately by nature. The habituated second nature provides the basic felt attunement of the heart out of which we spontaneously operate.

Habituation (*Gewohnheit*) negates feeling as it immediately rises from natural desire and makes it indifferent. In its positive form as skills, habituation frees the soul to be engaged in an other-than-immediate way. However, habit, "the mechanism of self-feeling," produces as a second nature a new level of feeling, a sense of being at home with oneself (*Beisichsein*).[18] Parallel to the English "inhabit," *wohnen* means to dwell; and where one dwells, what one inhabits, is one's home. Dwelling is thus a

---

15. Hegel, *Elements of the Philosophy of Right*, §126, 85.

16. Hegel, *Hegel's Philosophy of Mind*, §408, 124; cf. also §400, *Zusatz*, 75: "Feeling is the worst form of a mental or spiritual content and . . . can spoil the best content." It does not follow from this that the best forms are without feeling, as indicated by Hegel's frequent claims that the higher contents *must* find their culmination in "trained and sterling feeling" so as to establish a union of heart and heart.

17. Ibid., §410, *Zusatz*, 146.   18. Ibid., 144.

matter of self-feeling. Habituation is inhabitation as the formation of one's heart. Hegel here distinguishes feeling from the heart as the fleeting from the permanent. "The heart is what I am; not merely what I am at this moment, but what I am in general; it is my character."[19] Everything turns upon how character as second nature is formed and thus how feeling is transformed into a mediated immediacy. What is crucial is that this being at home with oneself be realized in being at home with others[20] and that both be governed by the assimilation of the universal into the heart. And of course, as we shall examine later, the first place this is realized is at home, in the family.

Minimally, conditions have to be established and are regularly established for the emergence of the ego, the concrete "I" that sets everything over against itself. Its *telos* is to have "filled the initially empty space of its inwardness with a content appropriate to its universality."[21] This constitutes healthiness of the soul.[22] "Healthiness" is defined in terms of the recognition and adjustment of what is merely mine, merely internal and idiosyncratic, to what is outside me. It involves the breaking of the merely subjective will and the rising up to the level of the universal. Here, "universal" does not only qualify abstract principle; it means "one over many" concretely; that is, it involves my identification with others who are different from me, who are allowed to invade my subjective space and place a demand upon me.[23] Children are the obvious example and through them one's sexual partner as demanding much more than momentary gratification of a natural urge, as demanding a shared life required for child-rearing. The major problem of the subjective will is its inclination to fill that "empty space of its inwardness" with the vanities of its own isolated self, to follow its undisciplined heart and thus to allow itself to be governed by the self-seeking vanities of mere nature. To begin with, the will is "the immediate or natural will" that is one with its "impulses, desire, inclinations, whereby the will finds itself determined in the course of nature."[24]

19. Hegel, *Lectures on the Philosophy of Religion*, I, 133. Conversely, Hegel seems to negate that when he says (*Hegel's Philosophy of Mind*, §400, 3), "It is with a quite different intensity and permanency that the will, the conscience, and the character, are our very own, than can ever be the true of feeling and of the group of feelings (the heart)." In the introduction, I have called attention to a line of countervailing texts that downplay the role of feeling, intuition, and the heart.

20. Hegel, *Hegel's Philosophy of Mind*, §413, *Zusatz*, 154.

21. Ibid., §412, *Zusatz*, 152.   22. Ibid., §408, *Zusatz*, 129.

23. Ibid., §436, 176.

24. Hegel, *Elements of the Philosophy of Right*, §11, 25.

So we see a tension between nature and spirit manifest in the felt proclivities of the human heart. But the general principle under which Hegel operates in the treatment of things human is that "in the human being there is only *one* reason in feeling, volition, and thought."[25] Where understanding (*Verstand*) operates in abstraction, reason (*Vernunft*) is not a separate faculty but precisely the "faculty" of unitary human life. Hegel even remarks, intriguingly but enigmatically, that "in feeling, there is present *the whole of reason*."[26] This spells out at the level of human operational capacities what the pervasive logical-ontological principle of identity-in-difference involves. Hence, Hegel claims that, after a sufficient process of development, "a lower and more abstract aspect of mind betrays the presence in it, even to experience, of a higher grade. Under the guise of sensation we may find the very highest mental life as its modification or its embodiment."[27] The higher ideas such as God and morality cannot only be thought; they can also be felt and, indeed, *must* be felt.[28] So higher-level operations, defined by their relation to more encompassing wholes, can penetrate into the lower levels of sensations and feelings. When they do so, they render the heart intuitive. There develops a "feeling intelligence" in which our higher operations are concentrated. It is ultimately necessary to speak from an intuitive grasp of the subject matter in any field. For Hegel, "this demands that a man should have his heart and soul, in short, his whole mind or spirit, in the subject matter."[29]

But then again, the higher ideas may fail to penetrate, and we have a split within our experience. Relatively autonomous regions of functioning can occur in quasi-separation from others. Hence, Hegel speaks of "the possibility of a culture of the intellect which leaves the heart untouched ... and of the *heart without the intellect*—of hearts which in a one-sided way want intellect, and *heartless intellects*—[which] only proves at most that bad and radically untrue existences occur."[30]

What is in my abstract ego can be kept away from my concrete subjectivity as "my very own." The I stands at an infinite distance from the Me.[31] By reason of reference to the Whole, which is emptily included in

25. Hegel, *Hegel's Philosophy of Mind*, §471, 231.
26. Ibid., §447, *Zusatz*, 194; emphasis added.
27. Ibid., §380, 7.
28. Ibid., §471, 231; *Lectures on the Philosophy of Religion*, I, 132.
29. Ibid., §449, *Zusatz*, 199.   30. Ibid., §445, 188; emphasis original.
31. Hegel, *Elements of the Philosophy of Right*, §5, *Zusatz*, 21.

the notion of Being, I can at any time abstract from everything, including the whole of what I am objectively and at the core of which stands the heart. I can ask myself: Where is my heart? Is it where it ought to be? Such a capacity founds the possibility of the emergence of relatively autonomous regions of human experience and thus of a split between head and heart. The model and basis of such capacity for splitting is the emergence of *Verstand*, or what most people call "reason," especially since the Enlightenment. It was this meaning of "reason" that was employed by Pascal and Kierkegaard in contrast to "the heart" and "subjectivity."

That heart and intellect can develop in relative separation to form a "bad and radically untrue existence" means that their unity is a matter of obligation. The truth of human existence lies in the unity of heart and head; their separation is a matter of moral failure. Hence, Hegel writes: "Let it not be enough to have principles and religion only in the head: they must also be in the heart, in the feeling."[32]

Furthermore, if a split occurs, the priority does not automatically go to "the head." Although Hegel remarks that feeling *may* be "one-sided, unessential and bad,"[33] he also says in his discussion of *das praktische Gefühl* that "when feeling is opposed to the logical understanding, it, and not the partial abstractions of the latter, *may* be the *totality*."[34] He even goes so far as to say that "there is more rationality in even the mere *feeling* of the *healthy* soul . . . since it contains the *actual* unity of the subjective and objective" than in abstract understanding.[35]

What one has to see here is the operation of the distinction between *Verstand*, or the capacity for abstraction and isolation of thought-objects (usually translated as "understanding"), and *Vernunft*, or the drive toward totality, which recognizes identity-in-difference (translated as "reason"). *Vernunft* involves the concrete totality. That is why Hegel speaks of one reason in feeling, volition, and thought. We cannot stress too strongly this notion of one pervasive reason as distinct from the highest level that a popular caricature of Hegel considers to act in abstraction from the lower levels that factually support it. *Verstand* is what most writers refer to as "reason." It is certainly what Kierkegaard and Pascal had in mind when they employ the term "reason." In the Hegelian project of rational comple-

32. Hegel, *Hegel's Philosophy of Mind*, §400, 73.
33. Ibid., §400, 74.   34. Ibid., §471, 230.
35. Ibid., §408, *Zusatz*, 129.

tion, the work of philosophy consists in reconciling the individual and the universal, and that translates at the level of inquiry itself into the heart and the head or the individual-personal and the encompassing universal. The heart is the moment of subjectivity in the positive sense. It is the region where the universal becomes mine; it is not simply the level of abstract attention. It is in the heart that what I grasp abstractly is assimilated into my own life. And that is part of the essential task of human existence.

When there is a real unity of head and heart, Hegel speaks of "trained and sterling feeling."[36] It is in this connection that he makes the remark that "in feeling, there is present the whole of reason." The examples he uses are drawn from the practice of the specialized sciences where one has been introduced to a tradition of intellectual practice in which the components have been rendered explicit—such is the nature of the practice. The trained eye of the biologist sees more in a given specimen than the causal onlooker or even the curious but untrained observer. The development of such intuitive ability is one of the goals of intellectual development. It is in direct intuitive attention to given objects that what has been abstracted comes to concrete awareness. Hegel says, "[N]ot until my cognition of the object developed in all its aspects has returned into the form of simple intuition does it confront my intelligence as an articulated, systematic totality."[37] So there is a reciprocity of abstraction and reversion to immediacy in all spiritual development. "All our representations, thought, and notions of the external world, of right, of morality, and of the content of religion develop from our feeling intelligence; just as, conversely, they are concentrated into the simple form of feeling after they have been fully explicated."[38]

But we might observe that "the owl of Minerva spreads its wings only with the falling of the dusk."[39] Explicit *Vernunft* is only retrospective. There are other practices where the work of *Vernunft* is not immediately evident: for example, in learning one's native language.[40] This occurs before the explicit development of grammar and lexicons. It is a rational practice of achieving social identity in the differences of individual sub-

---

36. Ibid., §447, 194.

37. Ibid., §449, *Zusatz*, 200.

38. Ibid., §447, *Zusatz*, 194.

39. Hegel, *Elements of the Philosophy of Right*, preface, 13.

40. Cf. Hegel, *Hegel's Phenomenology of Spirit*, §652, 395: "Language is self-consciousness existing for others."

jectivities through recognizing identities in the differences of the objects with which each person deals. Language is "an 'I' that is a 'We' and a 'We' that is an 'I.'"[41] Learning a native language renders intuitive innumerable subtle distinctions in experience. It is upon such rational practice that the explicit practices of reflective rationality and the work of abstract understanding are developed.

Abstract understanding and its practical equivalent, formal freedom or the freedom of individual choice, have a significance role to play. They are the motors of a higher development of reason itself. They carry out the articulations of the otherwise relatively unarticulated functional identity-in-difference realized at a lower level. At the theoretical level, there is no synthesis without analysis. At the practical level, there is no fully developed rational society without the autonomy of individuals and lower-level groups. Hence, there is both a theoretical and practical praxis that precedes the more encompassing theoretical advancement of reason. It is "the cunning of reason" that guides the development of human existence.[42]

In the realm of social practice generally, "world-historical figures" are not philosophically rational (i.e., rational in a comprehensively reflective way). Based upon their attunement to the comprehensive situation, they intuit the need for a new rational order: the move from polis to empire in Alexander, from the *ancien regime* to the beginnings of a more fully rational state through the legal, bureaucratic, and economic systematization introduced by Napoleon. Their hearts are so thoroughly involved in their projects that they rise to the level of passion. As Hegel remarks, "Nothing great is achieved without passion."[43] He further claims that pathos is "an essential part of the content of rationality and the free will." It "sets a string in motion, which vibrates through every human heart. . . . Pathos moves us because it is that which is essentially the vital force of our human existence."[44] Intuition interplays with passion in the hearts of such world-historical figures. Furthermore, in the securing of an articulated sense of the final encompassing Whole, religion takes the lead, rooted in the heart. Its expressions are the imagery of *Vorstellung.*

41. Ibid., §177, 110.
42. G. W. F. Hegel, *Philosophy of History*, trans. J. Sibree (New York: Dover, 1956), 33.
43. Ibid., 23.
44. G. W. F. Hegel, *Aesthetics: Lectures on Fine Art*, trans. T. Knox (Oxford: Clarendon Press, 1975), vol. I, 232–34.

Revealed religion, where the basic truth of the identity of the divine and the human is announced, is presented intuitively before it is developed in the form of explicit rationality.[45]

Philosophy itself has to take root in the lifeworld and especially in the relation to the eternal and encompassing found in religion and its tradition of doctrinal formation. For Hegel, the ancient adage holds true: *Primum vivere, deinde philosophari*, "Live first, then philosophize." But for Hegel, philosophy occurs in its breakthrough forms only at the end of an epoch in the life history of a community. There has to have been rational practice and thus intuition based upon the heart and fired by passion as there has also to have been the emergence of abstract *Verstand* before there can be fully reflective, explicit *Vernunft*. "The owl of Minerva takes wing only at dusk."

Yet in spite of the centrality of feeling, intuition, and the heart, Hegel also insists that it is with a quite different intensity and primacy that "the will, conscience and character, are our very own, than can ever be true of feeling and of the group of feelings (the heart)."[46] Hegel clings to the notion that feelings are something we share with the animals, even though in us the quality of those feelings is graduated through their association with explicit rationality in its various modes. However, we must not understand this sharing as something from which it is desirable to abstract ourselves in order to be "godlike," for in Hegel the divine itself requires the whole of the world and the whole of human experience for God's own completion.[47] The crucial thing is that feeling and the heart are not the *source of legitimation*.[48] It is thinking that distinguishes man from beast, while feeling he has in common with them. However, abstract thinking is only a halfway house to full humanness.

Since there is *one* reason in thought, volition, and feeling, the quality of feeling is elevated higher according to the height of the level of mental development that penetrates it. Moreover, that quality of feeling must penetrate it in order that, on the one hand, the higher levels have the sensory-based materials upon which to operate and, on the other, that one may achieve integral humanness. One who develops in a fully reflective man-

45. Hegel, *Hegel's Lectures on the Philosophy of Religion*, II, 327–48 and 391–404.
46. Hegel, *Hegel's Philosophy of Mind*, §400, 73.
47. Ibid., §564–71, 297–571.
48. Ibid., §400, 74.

ner sees and hears more intelligently and even feels more deeply.[49] When rationality penetrates one's heart, the heart becomes intuitive. As we have already noted, this is true at the level of scientific and philosophic work. One would have to say the same of a member of a functional family, of citizens in a state that holds the spontaneous allegiance of its citizens, and of a serious member of a religious community. By reason of participating in those communities, one intuitively apprehends the suitability or non-suitability of certain options for understanding and action. For Hegel, participation in objective spirit, in institutions that are inherently rational, gives one that "healthy sense" that may be truer than the claims of abstract thinkers. There is operative here what Aquinas called knowledge by connaturality.[50] Hegel underscores the social dimension of such capacity.

We might conclude our considerations up to this point by two significant quotations: "The notion which is aware of itself in its objectivity as a subjectivity identical with itself and for that reason universal—is the form of consciousness which lies at the root of all true mental or spiritual life—in family, fatherland, state, and all virtues, love, friendship, valour, honour, fame." And the accompanying *Zusatz* reads:

The speculative, or the rational and true, consists in the unity of the Notion or subjectivity, and objectivity. . . . It forms the substance of ethical life, namely, of the family, of sexual love. . . , of patriotism. . . , of love towards God, of bravery, too, when this is a risking of one's life in a universal cause, and lastly, also of honour, provided that this has for its content not some indifferent, particular interest of the individual but something substantial and truly universal.[51]

"Rationality" is thus something lived and felt before it is something explicitly articulated conceptually. "The Concept" is operative prior to reflection and even behind the backs of those wherein it is operative. Philosophy's task is to make that explicit.

PHILOSOPHY OF RIGHT

We are now in a position to explore further how this notion of the heart operates at the social level in the *Philosophy of Right*. Our general claim

49. Ibid., §448, *Zusatz*, 197.
50. Aquinas, *Summa Theologiae*, II-II, 45, 2; *Commentary on the Divine Names*, ch II.
51. Hegel, *Hegel's Philosophy of Mind*, §436 (176–77).

here is that Hegel is reinvigorating the ancient tradition of *pietas*. In the tradition going back from Aquinas through Cicero to Aristotle, *pietas* was a disposition, a sense of unpayable indebtedness to one's family, one's country, and God or the gods, for providing the concrete framework, and together the increasingly more comprehensive frameworks, for one's actual existence and real possibilities.[52] In Hegel, such *pietas* shows itself immediately in family feeling, in the feeling of patriotism, and in religious feeling, all of which have their locus in the heart.

The first such framework is the family.[53] It is, on the one hand, grounded in nature, in the differences of the sexes. Even in the crudest form of the sexual relation, one feels one's identity with species life, from which eventuates the emergence of new members of the species.[54] Hegel speaks here of the immediate foundation of the family in love, which goes beyond sexual attraction. In fact, he goes so far as to say that the feeling of love should rather follow than take the lead in entering the state of marriage. Attraction itself is not fully immediate—though the sexual element is closer to immediacy. Attraction is mediated by the recognition of the other as human, where both the self and the other have been formed by a community. The immediacy of feeling, which arises from nature, is shaped by institutions that are themselves sustained by the habit structures of individuals. Institutions arise when master-slave relations, which would be involved in a relation between the sexes based purely upon nature, are surmounted through the laws of a settled community. The naturally based, culturally mediated attraction of love takes on greater significance within the context of a freely chosen and permanently intended relation of marriage wherein the family capital is shared and children are produced and reared. Marriage is an essential social institution, grounded in custom and law and thus dependent upon an established society. Along with agriculture, it is the most basic of institutions.[55] After the question how we are to eat is settled, the next question posed to spirit but not settled by nature concerns our offspring. How are we to bring infants (the helpless results of following out our sexual attractions) to a state of

---

52. See Hegel, *Philosophy of Right*, §163, 112; also Aquinas, *Summa Theologiae*, II-II, 101, 1; Cicero, *De Inv. Rhet.*, 2; Aristotle, *Nicomachean Ethics*, IX, 12, 1162a, 4ff.

53. Hegel, *Philosophy of Right*, §158ff, 110ff.

54. Hegel, *Hegel's Philosophy of Mind*, §381, *Zusatz*, 10.

55. Hegel, *Philosophy of Right*, §167, 115; 203, 131; §350, 219.

adulthood minimally functional enough to sustain institutions of food production and/or food gathering and child-rearing as well as institutions of protection against threats from other reproductive and food producing and/or gathering units?

Provided we are speaking of a functional family, it is here that not only husband and wife but also their children are most free to be themselves because they identify with one another. Like the unity of all the parts of an organism, the family constitutes "a single substance" of which the individuals are the "accidents" who come and eventually, through the development of new families and through death, also go.[56] Here is a situation of functional rationality, an exhibition of identity-in-difference, where each finds his or her individual identity through promoting and identifying with the difference of the other family members. Here is home, "where the heart is." Here is love in its most fundamental sense. And here is rationality prereflectively operative, both at the biological level of individual and species life and at the distinctively human level of family membership. Such rationality is experienced integrally in family feeling, a state of the heart that makes one intuitive with regard to the dispositions, facial expressions, and gestural styles wherein the mind of the other family members is expressed.[57]

At the more encompassing level of the state (not as government but as the social-political whole), the parallel at the level of the heart to family feeling is the feeling of patriotism, a sense of belonging, of identification.[58] Such a sense makes one spontaneously willing to risk life and property for the sake of the larger whole which, under normal circumstances, protects just that life and that property.[59] Here, it is even more true that the state is the "substance" and the individuals are "accidents," insofar as individuals arrive and pass on while the state continues.[60] It is language like this, the language of substance and accidents, that has no doubt supported the unsupportable claim that Hegel has submerged the individual in the state. It is crucial to Hegel's view that the "accidents" must be seen as "I's," as rational centers of reflection and choice that not

---

56. Ibid., §145, 105.

57. I have not considered it part of what I was after here to indicate what today would be regarded as an unwarranted relegation to women to the household and to a situation of dependency. See Hegel, *Philosophy of Right*, §166 addition, 263.

58. Ibid., §268, 163–64.   59. Ibid., §323–24, 209; §328, 211.

60. Ibid., §145, 105.

only stand upon and within the state but can also stand over against it and against one another. Central to the functioning of a state is the promotion of free and rational subjects, where freedom includes a wide range for the exercise of individual choice.

The feeling the individuals have toward the state is the more solid, the more rationally constructed that state is.[61] Rational construction entails the functional divisions of the social whole requisite for the work of sustaining the national unit. It entails a principle of subsidiarity with a hierarchy of mediating institutions between the governmental center and the regional, local, and individual units.[62] It entails, in addition, protecting individual rights and creating a large sphere for individual choices compatible with the overall unity of the state. Here, the modern notions of abstract rights and freedom of conscience constitute a particular advance in rational articulation. Freedom in the choice of marriage partners, occupation, worship, inquiry, press, assembly, and enterprise entails recognition on the part of the state of the capacity of each individual to choose for himself or herself and to live by his or her own wits.[63] These are the distinctively modern features of *bürgerliche Gesellschaft*, bourgeois or civil society. Its freedoms are a working out institutionally of what is involved in Christianity's proclamation of the infinite dignity of the human individual. Concrete subjectivity is not submerged in and subsumed under a rational state; it is rather located, provided with an increasing range of options, and given wide birth.

But it is at the level of civil society that problems of social dissolution lie. Civil society is guided by the notion of self-interest, the dynamics of which create an increasing interdependence of free-market operators. But it produces also great disparities of distribution and an increasing and increasingly impoverished mass of unemployed and unemployable, whose enforced lifestyle creates a negative predisposition toward the larger whole within which they live. The hearts of such workers are immediately not in their work and the hearts of the unemployable not spontaneously identified with the society.

61. Ibid., 260, 161; §289, 189.
62. Ibid., §290 and 295, 190 and 192.
63. Ibid., on love, conscience, inquiry, §124, 84; further on conscience, §137, 91; on choice in marriage partners, §162, 111; on religion §270, 168; on speech and the press, §319, 205; on property, §41ff, 40ff; on occupation, §254, 154.

So strong is the emphasis on the freedom of the individual in civil society that it threatens the dissolution of the society itself unless it is counterbalanced by identification with the larger whole that rises up in the feeling of patriotism. But the dynamics of civil society also lead to emphasis upon free-entry associations that become second families—what Hegel calls *Korporationen*—which would include business associations, learned societies, churches, and the like. One's felt identity with such associations, the *esprit de corps* that animates them,[64] is midway between family piety and felt identity with the larger organized whole Hegel calls the state.[65]

RELIGION

Finally, surmounting the state and founded upon the orientation of each rational individual toward the whole of what is, there is the mode of *pietas* for which, in ordinary parlance today, the word "piety" is most frequently employed: that is the level of religion. At its center lies the feeling of the heart rising up out of the everyday to a sense of identification with the eternal and encompassing, to a sense of the pervasive divine that is expressed in everything, but most especially in human existence wherein rationality is not only functionally present but also reflectively manifest.[66] "In religion, the Idea is mind in the inwardness of the heart."[67] The locus of religion is in the heart where emotions are evoked through imagination.[68] Hegel goes so far as to say, as an imperative matter, that "religion *must* be felt, . . . otherwise it is not religion."[69]

It is this level that both underpins the state and, at the same time, transcends it.[70] It is the lived ground for interest in the Logos-logic, the onto-logic that exhibits the comprehensive categories within which not only a given state but also the encompassing character of the cosmic Whole appears and is operative. Religion precedes philosophy and gives expression, at first in a mythical mode, to the structural ground of all hu-

64. Ibid., §207, 133. Knox identifies such corporate units in his translator's notes to PR, §229, 360.

65. Ibid., §252–55, 152ff.

66. Hegel, *Lectures on the Philosophy of Religion*, I, 4.

67. Hegel, *Philosophy of Right*, §162, addition, 284.

68. Hegel, *Aesthetics: Lectures on Fine Art*, I, 103–4 and 234.

69. Hegel, *Lectures on the Philosophy of Religion*, III, 180; emphasis added.

70. Cf. the somewhat lengthy discussion in Hegel, *Philosophy of Right*, §270, 165–74.

man experience: the reference to totality. Such reference requires that we seek some answer to the question that defines human existence: What's it all about? Or: How do we humans fit in the whole scheme of things? Such a question is not merely a matter of curiosity; it is a matter of the meaning of human existence that supports and locates every regional interest. But it is at first lived, felt, gripping the heart religiously, before it is a matter of that detached reflection that generates the history of philosophy.

It is on the question of the role of doctrine and thus of reflective articulation that Hegel parts company with the Romantics in their appeal to intuition and the heart. Without the articulation of doctrine, religion becomes simply a matter of empty elevation rather than an elevation rich in content.[71] Hegel remarks regarding religious feeling that "if it is piety of the right sort, it sheds the form of this emotional region as soon as it leaves the inner life, enters upon the daylight of the Idea's development and revealed riches, and brings with it, out of its inner worship of God, reverence for law and for an absolute truth exalted above the subjective form of feeling."[72] In light of what we have remarked earlier, "shedding the form of this emotional region" cannot mean shedding feeling, because the unity of head and heart is a fundamental Hegelian principle. It can only mean that feeling has to become that "trained and sterling" feeling that has come into the daylight of reflective awareness and conceptual work. There has to be a dialectic between initial religious intuition and doctrinal development. Hegel maintains that it is typically through doctrine and teaching that the feelings become aroused and purified, cultivated and brought into the heart.[73] But doctrine and teaching, in turn, are based upon the life experience of a given community.

Philosophy presupposes such development since it presupposes the implicit rational development over time of communities that are ultimately rooted in religion. We should consider in this connection Hegel's intriguing but unexplained claim in the *Encyclopaedia* that philosophy is the unity of art and religion.[74] We should also consider his claim that the *perennial task* of art is to heal the rift that thought establishes between the sensuous immediate and the reference to the Beyond.[75] That

71. Hegel, *Lectures on the Philosophy of Religion*, I, 15.
72. Hegel, *Philosophy of Right*, preface, 6.
73. Hegel, *Lectures on the Philosophy of Religion*, I, 38 ff. and 151.
74. Hegel, *Hegel's Philosophy of Mind*, §572, 302.
75. Hegel, *Aesthetics: Lectures on Fine Art*, I, 8.

task is not superseded by art having been surpassed by revealed religion and philosophy in carrying out the highest mission of spirit to reveal the Absolute. Religion's perennial task is to rise through the inwardness of the heart to the eternal and encompassing. Philosophy's action in unifying art and religion must *include* these moments *sublated* within itself, and not simply in terms of adequate conceptualization. Conceptualization still establishes a rift between itself and the "here" of bodily presence to which we are intuitively attuned by the heart, for Hegel also speaks of philosophy's task to reconcile the universal and the heart as the ground of individuality.[76] If this does not occur, the resultant is a split existence that is, to that extent, "a bad and radically untrue existence."

Explicit rationality is, in a first abstractly reflective moment, the work of *Verstand*. It requires a second reflective moment of *conceptually* resituating the abstractions within the concrete matrix out of which they were abstracted: this is the philosophically reflective mode of rationality that Hegel calls "the speculative." But it also requires reinserting the conceptual identities-in-difference into the *concretely given* identities-in-difference that constitute lived life.

We should note the parallel here with Marcel's first and second, abstractive and recuperative, reflection.[77] The first abstractive moment releases differences and sets the basis for deepening life—provided one surmounts them by containing them, preserved, in a more encompassing framework. But Marcel's second reflection is not simply a matter of categorical correctness: it is a matter of indwelling, participation, and feeling through the practice of recollection that invokes significant presences—precisely a matter of the heart.[78] Perhaps we need to introduce the notion of a "third reflection" here in order to distinguish fuller categorization from further reflective, "meditative" participation. There is a mode of reflectiveness, a thoughtfulness that takes place *in* the lifeworld and that

76. Ibid., 97–98.

77. Gabriel Marcel, *The Mystery of Being*, trans. G. Fraser (Chicago: Regnery, 1960), vol. 1, 95 ff. The very language of first and second reflection is borrowed from that severe critic of Hegelianism, Søren Kierkegaard, *Concluding Unscientific Postscript to Philosophical Fragments*, 68ff.

78. *Recollection* is another central Kierkegaardian notion: see "In Vino Veritas: A Recollection," in *Stages on Life's Way*, trans. W. Lowrie (New York: Schocken, 1967), 27–36. For a treatment of the notion of recollection in this work in comparison to Plato's *Symposium*, see my "Recollection and Two Banquets: Plato's and Kierkegaard's," in the International Kierkegaard Commentary on *Stages on Life's Way*. It is reprinted in this volume.

gains expression in the arts.[79] Hegel views this kind of development as an imperative: philosophic reflection must penetrate the heart; it must become "mine" until it becomes a matter of "trained and sterling feeling."

So for Hegel, there is a dialectic not only in philosophy and between philosophies but a dialectic of the relation between philosophy and human life. Philosophy arises on the basis of lived life: out of a sense of family, association, patriotic belonging, and religious feeling, all tied to the practices of a given community and set back into transformed sensuousness by the arts that speak to the heart. But philosophy must also set *itself* back into that lived matrix by becoming finally and once again a matter of the heart. If higher intellectual development in principle makes one capable of deeper feeling and more intuitively alert to what is present in the sensory world, then comprehensive rational development is not a retreat within or above some detached region of abstractions.

It is precisely because we have to act in individual, bodily situations that we have to go beyond the level of abstract universality, even the abstract universality of conceptual identity-in-difference. So there is a peculiar dialectic set up by reason of our cosmic position: we have to transcend the immediacy of our bodily based life of feeling and allow that transcendence to permeate that life of feeling so that we become, in our totality, spontaneously rational. Reflective inhabitation is the task of philosophy as complete reflection, a mode of reflection that includes the wholeness of the thinker and thus also the inwardness of the heart.[80]

Hegel aims at human wholeness, hence at a reciprocal inclusion of reflective rationality and feeling. He resists both hearts without intellect and heartless intellects. Here we have to understand the surmounting of the opposition of theoretical and practical reason in the free spirit who contains their togetherness in the integrally functioning human being where reflective reason pervades the heart and guides the passion of human existence.[81]

79. This is central to Heidegger's thought. For a development of this, see my "Six Heideggerian Figures" in *Martin Heidegger*, ed. John Caputo, special edition of *American Catholic Philosophical Quarterly* 69 (1995) 311–31. For a fuller elaboration through the history of philosophic thought on aesthetics, including Hegel and Heidegger, see my *Placing Aesthetics* (Athens: Ohio University Press, 1999).

80. For a parallel within Plato, see my "Plato's Line Revisited: The Pedagogy of Complete Reflection." It is reprinted in this volume.

81. Hegel, *Hegel's Philosophy of Mind*, §481–82, 238–40.

Though we have to say that for Hegel there is an absolute, teleological priority of reflective reason, nonetheless, that is because reason is operative nonreflectively throughout the whole of reality. For Hegel, rationality is not simply a human operation: prior to its being reflectively displayed in philosophy, it is cosmically operative. Thus, an organism is itself a rational system, a developing, self-sustaining whole comprised of various elements in tension, in dialectical relation with its environment and unintelligible without it. In animals, life is raised to the level of immediate manifestness through the system of the senses in function of biologically based desire. The capacity for abstraction in humans sets all that at a distance but arises concretely in the struggle for mutual recognition that produces modes of coexistent functioning for large groups of humans over long periods of time. This is the working of reason in actuality, often behind the backs of the participants. It furnishes the basis for the leisure required to make reflectively explicit in philosophy the rationality involved in the cosmic and historical bases for human thought and action.

But the reason Hegel invokes is precisely *Vernunft* as the reason of the heart of which the so-called "reason," *Verstand* as the analytical, separating activity of the understanding, knows nothing. Far from "constructing magnificent thought-castles and dwelling in a miserable shack nearby," far from the practice of an abstract thinking divorced from life, far from forgetting what it means to be a subjective thinker, to dwell with passion and inwardness, Hegelian reason involves precisely the passion and inwardness of full human dwelling. However, the heart with its passion and subjectivity is not the measure: the measure is found in taking our place within the concretely encompassing social and cosmic Whole whose underlying conditions for intelligibility concrete reason comprehends.

But we have to add one last thought, which opens up the deepest question lying behind the poses of Kierkegaard and Pascal. It is the question not of the unity of reason and the heart or of the free choices of individuals within the Whole apprehended by reason. In my opinion, both of these are handled well by Hegel. Kierkegaard sees the deepest passion evoked by what is for his "reason" the Paradox, the Absurd, the proclaimed identity of God and man in Christ. This has several large presuppositions: *if* one recognizes the most basic need of humankind to establish relation to the eternal, and *if* one sees that as only available through Christ whose absurdity—as the infinite God becomes finite human—is an affront to reason, then the deepest possible passionate inwardness is evoked.[82] However, Hegel takes just that "absurdity" as the principle of *Vernunft* in a reformulated notion of reason. *Verstand*, operating with the principle of identity, naturally sees the proclamation of the identity of the infinite God and the finite human as irrational. *Vernunft*, operating with the principle of identity-in-difference *revealed in* Christian revelation, takes this as the paradigm of rationality. The passion and inwardness of the heart are thereby encompassed by Hegelian reason, which, nonetheless, maintains its dialectical identity with the heart.

However, the deepest question nagging behind the objections of Kierkegaard and Pascal is the question of what might lie beyond even this reformed notion of reason. That question also lies behind the contemporary rejection of "onto-theo-logy" and its search for what might lie "beyond being" in a negative theology. I can only suggest a direction here for the basis in Hegel himself for raising the question: his requirement of the world process for God's completion poses the vexing problem of the relation of time to eternity, as if God had to wait for time to be before His own completion. This leads to the suggestion that God exists "beyond being" conceived in conceptual terms (though perhaps not "beyond being" thought in terms of individual *esse*)[83] and that Hegel has developed the notion not of *God's* unfolding but of the unfolding of humankind as *imago Dei*. This would then open up the possibility of the more profoundly passionate inwardness that Kierkegaard and Pascal knew and would raise their objections anew from this new understanding of reason. Then the heart, enriched and illumined by Hegelian rationality, would still have its reasons that even Hegelian reason does not comprehend. But that is only a suggestion that we cannot further pursue here.

82. Kierkegaard, *Concluding Unscientific Postscript to Philosophical Fragments*, 192–200.
83. I note, with no apologetic purposes whatsoever, that this is the direction Thomas Aquinas has taken.

13 ❧ High and Low in Nietzsche's *Zarathustra*

Friedrich Nietzsche is often viewed as the thinker who contributed most powerfully to the destruction of values, rendering arbitrary all distinction between better and worse, between high and low, and substituting a voluntarist imposition of value for objectively grounded value. As diagnostician of value-nihilism, he is viewed also as its strongest proponent.[1] I want to argue in this chapter that, far from being a nihilist, Nietzsche has a definite and, above all, largely defensible set of criteria for determining high and low values.[2] And I want to examine those criteria as they appear in what he regarded as his—and indeed, the world's—greatest work: *Thus Spoke Zarathustra*.[3]

THE LAST MAN, THE HIGHER MEN, AND THE WILL TO POWER

We can begin to see what orients Zarathustra's quest for the criteria of high and low by looking to three types he profiles: one is the Overman; a second is his opposite, the so-called "Last Man"; and the third anticipates but does not yet reach the Overman, the type exhibited by the so-called "Higher Men" who would still be what he terms "inverse cripples."

1. For a prominent example, see Alasdair MacIntyre, *After Virtue* (Notre Dame, Ind.: University of Notre Dame Press, 1984), 109–20.

2. Here I agree with Stanley Rosen (*The Mask of Enlightenment: Nietzsche's Zarathustra* [Cambridge: Cambridge University Press, 1995]) that the Left has ignored Nietzsche's insistence upon rank and hierarchy (43) and with Laurence Lampert (*Nietzsche's Teaching: An Interpretation of Thus Spoke Zarathustra* [New Haven, Conn.: Yale University Press, 1986]), who says that to view this as permissive relativism is to misunderstand (202). For an approach to Nietzsche that situates his aesthetics within the overall context of his thought, see the chapter on Nietzsche in my *Placing Aesthetics* (Athens: Ohio University Press, 1999), 203–29.

3. Friedrich Nietzsche, *Ecce Homo*, trans. along with *On the Genealogy of Morals* by W. Kaufmann (New York: Vintage, 1967). References to the work on Zarathustra will be to *Also Sprach Zarathustra* (Stuttgart: Körner, 1975) and to the translation by Walter Kaufmann in *The Portable Nietzsche* (New York: Viking, 1954).

The Last Man emerged in Nietzsche's mind together with the Overman. The Last Man is the modern individual.[4] The "last" here represents the nadir, the low point of all the peoples who have existed thus far. The most recent creation of "the individual" is a paradoxical invention: conceived of as *apart* from the group, "the individual" is a peculiar product of recent Western culture—a significant observation, since many interpreters find Nietzsche exalting "the individual." The Last Man is a set of contradictions: the low point that considers itself the high point of evolution and a set of "individuals" who are really a herd.

What are the features of these modern individuals? Through the invention of scientific medicine, they possess health and a long life. They take the chill off the night of ultimate meaninglessness in which they live by meeting frequently (texting continually): Zarathustra describes them as rubbing up against others for warmth. They have learned to live without quarreling since nothing ultimately counts for them. They have invented work without drudgery, so pleasing that they consider it as entertainment, as diversion from universal boredom. And when neither work nor close proximity to each other stave off the darkness, they turn to sedatives or narcotics. What is perhaps the worst thing for Nietzsche is the cult of equality among such so-called individuals, for it allows no tall trees to grow. Their individuality is held within such strict limits that real difference is seen as madness. But since leadership requires distinctive difference in height between the leaders and the followers, they are a herd without a shepherd. Shepherding would involve their acknowledgment of the superiority of those who would shepherd them.

Later, in *Twilight of the Idols*, Nietzsche carried out a further diagnosis.[5] The men of today cannot acknowledge superiority because the conditions for its emergence are lacking: they lack a sense of tradition, without which one cannot have standards of measurement. The past they consider simply dead and gone. Their art is decadent because they deny standards, even admittedly conventional standards, since all great art rests upon conventions that give focus to creative powers. The lack of tradition goes hand in hand with the lack of reverence[6] and hence the

4. Nietzsche, *Thus Spoke Zarathustra*, I, "Prologue," 5, 13–15/128–31.

5. Friedrich Nietzsche, "Expeditions of an Untimely Man," in *Twilight of the Idols*, trans. with *The Anti-Christ* by R. Hollingdale (Baltimore: Penguin, 1968), §39, 93–94.

6. Also Nietzsche, *Thus Spoke Zarathustra*, IV, "Conversation with the Kings," 270–72/357–58.

inability to obey. Modest in virtue, they simply desire to be contented like cows—and the greatest danger is "wretched contentment."[7] Kindness, "justice," and pity abound; but these qualities are rooted in weakness because their practitioners don't want to get hurt. Mediocrity passes as moderation.[8] What is more, they lack the ability to despise themselves (according to the Latin derivative *despicere*, to look down from above) and thus have no desire to ascend. It is their very sense of superiority that is perhaps their most degenerate feature, for it gives them no motive to go beyond themselves.

On the other end of the scale of human types developed thus far, there are the Higher Men. Early in his work, Nietzsche recognized higher men in the artists, philosophers, and saints, denizens of Hegel's Absolute Spirit.[9] They are the ones who created the horizons of meaning, the ring of myths within which the many have come to dwell. Having bound together millions of people over thousands of years, they are the greatest exhibitions of the Will to Power.

Will to Power, along with the Eternal Recurrence of the Same, are Nietzsche's most fundamental thoughts. We will focus upon Eternal Recurrence later. Let us here focus upon Will to Power. As *Wille-zur-Macht*, it is in each thing the will to create (*machen*) beyond itself. It is clearly revealed in living things that overpower other things in the environment in order to move beyond their incipient stage to their full maturity, at which time they are able to reproduce others beyond themselves. As this applies to humans, in addition to biological violation of others for food, individuals are able to exercise power over themselves in order to create beyond themselves, especially in producing, sustaining, and developing the power of institutions. Will to Power is will to centuries-long obedience to traditions that shape the chaos of individual lives.

Come back now to the treatment of the Higher Men. Preceded by the Soothsayer who preaches nihilism,[10] they are all looking for Zarathustra because they were caught by one or the other of his sayings, each focused upon a different feature.[11] The kings seek him because of his teachings on

7. Ibid., IV, "On the Higher Man," 3, 319/399.

8. Ibid., III, "On Virtue That Makes Small," 2, 188/282.

9. Friedrich Nietzsche, "Schopenhauer as Educator," in *Untimely Meditations*, trans. R. Hollingdale (London: Cambridge University Press, 1983), 159ff.

10. Nietzsche, *Thus Spoke Zarathustra*, IV, "The Cry of Distress," 265–77/352–54.

11. For Kings, the right- and left-wing leaders of the ass as the mob, the focus is upon

war and courage; the leech because of his teachings on spirit cutting into life; the magician because of his reputation for honesty; the Pope because of his piety, in spite of his godlessness; the Ugliest Man because of his lack of pity; the Voluntary Beggar because of his overcoming nausea; the Shadow because he wanted to be like Zarathustra.

The lack of pity seems problematic, given his embracing of the beaten horse. But Nietzsche's downplaying of pity is connected with what he would regard as bad fiction: creating an afterlife that would console the suffering of the vast majority of people out of pity for their suffering. Nietzsche thinks that pity distracts the sufferer from coming to terms with his suffering in stoic fashion. One might say he advocates what today is called "tough love."

The Higher Men are higher because they strove in some way to transcend themselves and are thus in some way leaders, yet they are all "inverse cripples ... . who had too little of everything and too much of one thing."[12] In their one-sidedness, they have not fulfilled the conditions for highest existence. They come to the mountain because they aspire to be higher than they are. And they see in Zarathustra one who aspires even higher. Zarathustra, in turn, sees himself as a kind of John the Baptist, announcing the Overman.

ZARATHUSTRA

Nietzsche chose Zarathustra, another name for Zoroaster, founder of the ancient Persian religion, in order to announce the "transvaluation of values," the transformation of the way of evaluating set in motion by the ancient sage Zoroaster and guiding Western culture ever since. In his intellectual autobiography, Nietzsche explains the choice of the name:

I have not been asked, as I should have been asked, what the name of Zarathustra means in my mouth, the mouth of the first immoralist: for what constitutes

---

political leadership (Nietzsche, *Thus Spoke Zarathustra*, IV, 269–73/356–60). In "The Leech," the conscientious of spirit pursues science (IV, 274–77/360–63); "The Magician" poetry (IV, 277–85/363–70), the Last Pope religious leadership (IV, 285–90/370–75); "The Ugliest Man," the destruction of divinity (IV, 290–96/375–79); "The Voluntary Beggar," religious practice (IV, 296–301/380–84), and in "The Shadow," discipleship to Zarathustra (IV, 301–5/384–87). They are each dissatisfied but have heard something from Zarathustra that appeals to them because of what they themselves are.

12. Nietzsche, *Thus Spoke Zarathustra*, II, "On Redemption," 151/250.

the tremendous historical uniqueness of that Persian is just the opposite of this. Zarathustra was the first to consider the fight of good and evil the very wheel in the machinery of things: the transposition of morality into the metaphysical realm, as a force, cause, and end in itself, is *his* work. But this question itself is at bottom its own answer. Z created this most calamitous error, morality; consequently, he must also be the first to recognize it. . . . What is more important is that Z is more truthful than any other thinker. His doctrine, and his alone, posits truthfulness as the highest virtue. . . . The self-overcoming of morality out of truthfulness; the self-overcoming of the moralist into his opposite—into me— that is what the name of Z means in my mouth.[13]

One must be careful here not to misunderstand what Nietzsche means by an "immoralist." He definitely does not mean that in his teaching anything goes. In *Daybreak*, he explicitly denied this, claiming that some things are *always* forbidden; but he leaves us guessing as to just what those things might be.[14] We will return to that later. What Nietzsche seeks is a foundation for ethics different than what ruled the tradition—above all, one that does not presuppose a two-tiered vision of reality tied to reward and punishment in an afterlife and thus to a divinity concerned with judging human action. "Morality" in Nietzsche's eyes thus seems not simply to involve criteria of right and wrong but a specific linkage between such criteria and a view of the ultimate ground of things. Zarathustra even speaks of the highest good now as the highest evil.[15] And what that would seem to underscore is the ultimate import for the tradition of an afterlife where the highest Good would be realized in a disembodied existence, the ultimate sin against the earth.

Insofar as the pursuit of the Platonic Good involved contempt for the body and fulfillment only in an existence beyond this one, it is the primordial sin against the earth. In Plato's imagery, the body, its senses, and passions imprison the mind in darkness. Platonism and Christianity, as "Platonism for the masses," viewed the self as essentially soul, as fallen into the bodily world, and as belonging to an essentially disembodied realm fully accessible only in an afterlife.[16] Platonism and Christianity exhibit the

13. Nietzsche, "Why I Am a Destiny," in *Ecce Homo* §3, 327–28.
14. Friedrich Nietzsche, *Daybreak: Thoughts on the Prejudices of Morality*, trans. R. Hollingdale (Cambridge: Cambridge University Press, 1982), II, 103.
15. (II, "On Self-Overcoming," 126/228).
16. Friedrich Nietzsche, *Beyond Good and Evil: Prelude to a Philosophy of the Future*, trans. W. Kaufmann (New York: Vintage, 1966), 3.

greatest sin: contempt for the earth. Because of this contempt, man has felt too little joy: that is the original sin. For this leads to self-imposed sufferings and to persuading others to feel guilty about their pleasures. By way of contrast, for Nietzsche, being faithful to the earth was one of the most basic criteria for what is "up" in human life.[17]

Zarathustra was also chosen because of his exaltation of truthfulness as the highest virtue. In the work that bears his name, Zarathustra identifies honesty (*Redlichkeit*) as the distinctively modern virtue[18] that undermines the faith that sustained past tradition. And yet, because tradition is the basis for any significant formation, one needs a paradoxical synthesis of reverence and honesty. One virtue in Christianity was that it spawned a respect for truth; but respect for truth, followed out further, has now destroyed Christianity.[19]

One wonders what might be the difference between truthfulness and honesty. Perhaps they are identical. But what was distinctive of ancient Zarathustra has become widespread among modern intellectuals. In any case, this seems a startling claim, given such statements as "We have art so as not to perish of truth,"[20] "Truth is the kind of error without which a certain kind of living being could not live,"[21] and "their will to truth is—*will to power*."[22] One could understand the first to refer to a specific truth, namely, that of the true horrors ingredient in life. The creative powers of life overcome its horrors: because of its indescribably fertile creativity, we can then say "yes" to life in spite of its inherent destructiveness.[23] The second statement is linked to the claim that all life needs a horizon within which to live, and specifically human life has an open horizon that is factually always fixed by a ring of myths.[24] One here un-

17. Nietzsche, *Thus Spoke Zarathustra*, I, "Prologue," 3, 9/125; "On the Gift-Giving Virtue," 2, 82/188.

18. Ibid., I, "On the Afterworldly," 33/145.

19. Nietzsche, *On the Genealogy of Morals*, III, 27, 160–61.

20. Nietzsche, *The Will to Power*, trans. W. Kaufmann and R. Hollingdale (New York: Vintage, 1967), §822, 435. For a more comprehensive treatment of the relation between art and truth in Nietzsche, see my "Art and Truth: Plato, Nietzsche, Heidegger," in *On Truth: A Robust Presence*, ed. K. Pritzl (Washington, D.C.: The Catholic University of America Press, 2010). It is reprinted in this volume.

21. Nietzsche, *The Will to Power*, §492, 272.

22. Nietzsche, *Beyond Good and Evil*, §211, 136.

23. Nietzsche, *Ecce Homo*, 272–73.

24. Nietzsche, "On the Uses and Disadvantages of History for Life," in *Untimely Meditations*, 63; *The Birth of Tragedy*, trans. with *The Case of Wagner* by W. Kaufmann (New York: Vantage, 1967), §23, 135.

derstands truth Platonically as absolute fixity, whereas one who really knows understands truth perspectivally. The third involves seeing truth as in the service of life. In Nietzsche's late (1886) prologue to his first published work, *The Birth of Tragedy* (1872), he announces his project as understanding *Wissenschaft* from the perspective of art and art from the perspective of life.[25] The honesty of modernity, become ruthless in Nietzsche, carries out to its final conclusion Zarathustra's original positing of truthfulness as the highest virtue. This leads to a position "beyond good and evil," where morality is no longer the fundamental aim of the ground of things. Parallel to Heraclitus's view, the divine as creative and destructive Dionysus is indifferent to "good and evil."[26] And yet there is still high and low in human life.

What emerge as our first criteria of what is "up" and, correspondingly, allow us to judge what is "down" in human existence are two: fidelity to the earth and truthfulness, the latter in service to the former. We will find them deepened and supplemented by our further inquiry.

WISDOM AND THE DEATH OF GOD

At the beginning of *Thus Spoke Zarathustra*, we find that, in order to overcome his former teaching, Zarathustra had gone up to live on the mountain for ten years, "carrying his ashes," the dying remnants of the dreams of which men had robbed him.[27] Presumably his dreams have to do with his moral project of installing good and evil as the motor of the universe and its corollary linkage with a disembodied afterlife to compensate for the obvious injustices in this life. Up on the mountain and inside his cave, Zarathustra was the first to discover solitude.[28] Religious hermits had for centuries gone into the wilderness to find solitude as removal from commerce with other humans, from their views and practices, in order to discover the presence of God. That, however, was not solitude but community of a different order. Being higher up the mountain than the hermit, Zarathustra had diagnosed the death of God. On

---

25. Nietzsche, "Attempt at Self-Criticism," in *The Birth of Tragedy*, §2, 19.

26. Heidegger, "Heraclitus," *The Presocratic Philosophers*, §102. 193.

27. Nietzsche, *Thus Spoke Zarathustra*, Prologue 2, 6/122; II, "The Tomb Song," 118–22/222–25.

28. Friedrich Nietzsche, *The Gay Science*, trans. W. Kaufmann (New York: Vantage, 1974), §367, 324.

the very top of the mountain, he had therefore found ultimate solitude, apart even from community with God, the greatest dream to come out of the tradition he launched.

When the time came for him to go back down to the city, he is astonished that the first person he encounters, an old hermit, has not yet heard that God is dead.[29] This, of course, hearkens back to *The Gay Science*, to the Parable of the Madman who announces and mourns that death. In the "Parable of the Madman," the speaker asks: "What did we do when we unchained this earth from its sun? . . . Is there any up or down left? Are we not straying as through an infinite nothing? . . . Is not night and more night coming on all the while?"[30] The death of God is the ineffectiveness of the Platonic Good, onto-theo-logically linked up with the Hebrew Yahweh, as light-bringing source, as unifying principle, as highest end of the cosmos. Outside of the orbit of this sun, we earth-bound creatures move in darkness without any sense of direction. Employing another metaphor, the madman asks: "How could we drink up the sea?" The all-pervasive divine plenitude, "in Whom we live and move and have our being," has drained away, and we are left in complete emptiness, like fish out of water, as Heidegger would later put it.[31]

Thus Spoke Zarathustra begins with the hero on his mountaintop, stepping out from his cave before the sun, which he addresses as "You, great star. . . ." No god, this sun, and no symbol of permanent fixture in a Platonic heaven of abstractions, for it rises and sets. Zarathustra's aim is the creative overcoming of the fixed and separate Platonic Good. But he begins "up" on the mountain and not "down" in the city below. And yet, in a curious inversion of Plato's allegory, there also, high on the mountaintop and not down below, Zarathustra has his cave. In fact, the combination of the mountaintop and the cave draws upon the symbolic equivalence of "deep" thought and "elevated" thought, a metaphorical *coincidentia oppositorum*. As with Plato, the darkness of the cave contrasts with the sunlight outside. But darkness is not, as it is in Plato, simply the negativity of ignorance in contrast to the positivity of wisdom.[32]

29. Nietzsche, *Thus Spoke Zarathustra*, I, Prologue, 2, 6–8/122–24.

30. Nietzsche, *The Gay Science*, §125, 181–82.

31. Martin Heidegger, "Letter on Humanism," in *Martin Heidegger: Basic Writings*, ed. D. Krell (New York: Harper and Row, 1977), 195.

32. See Heidegger, "Letter on Humanism," 71–74; Lampert, *Nietzsche's Teaching*, 16.

For Zarathustra, there is both a "day wisdom" of light and a "night wisdom" of darkness; and the night wisdom is the highest.[33] This would seem to be aligned with his distinction between the "little reason" of consciousness and the "great reason" of the body.[34]

As Nietzsche would have it in his youthful *The Birth of Tragedy*, the attempt to sever Apollonian clarity from Dionysian darkness has been a fundamental mistake of Western intellectual tradition.[35] As Kant would have it (I paraphrase): since birds discovered that they could move more freely in the ethereal region than, like worms, in the heaviness of earth or, like fish, in the relative density of water, it is as if they then said to themselves: Think how much better we could fly if we had nothing at all to resist our flight![36] Hence, Zarathustra's contrary claim that he who would ascend to the heavens must have his roots deep in the earth.[37] Heights and depths, the Apollonian and the Dionysian, are bound together. The Platonic attempt to sever them is the disaster that afflicted Western culture.

As in Plato, so in *Zarathustra*, height and synoptic vision are linked to sensitivity to beauty. We might suggest one reason for the conjunction: beauty might be described as harmonic togetherness, and comprehensive vision seeks the harmonic unity of all things. The perception of beauty elevates human experience and impels us to the wider vision that wisdom entails. At the same time, beauty seems to announce something more, something "beyond essence" (beyond *ousia* as correlate to *nous* but not "beyond being"), beyond the grasping power of intellect and correlate to fundamental Eros.[38] The erotic character of life underpins and encompasses the light of awareness. Nietzsche admits that his treatment of Plato had been largely a caricature: there is also "the divine Plato," the teacher of Eros.[39]

On the mountaintop, Zarathustra lives away from all men and to-

33. Nietzsche, *Thus Spoke Zarathustra*, II, "The Dancing Song," 117/221; III, "The Other Dancing Song," 2 and 3, 251–53/338–40; IV, "The Drunken Song," 251–59/429–36 See Lampert, *Nietzsche's Teaching*, 191–96.
34. Nietzsche, *Thus Spoke Zarathustra*, I, "On the Despisers of the Body," 34/146.
35. Nietzsche, *The Birth of Tragedy*, see especially §15, 93–98.
36. I want to thank John Richardson who found this Nietzsche-like passage in Kant.
37. Nietzsche, *Thus Spoke Zarathustra*, I, "On the Tree on the Mountainside," 43/154.
38. Plato, *Republic*, VI, 509b.
39. Nietzsche, *The Will to Power*, §374.

gether with his animals, an eagle and a snake, denizens of sky and earth. The one rises and can see far with its eagle eye"; the other clings closely to the earth. Zarathustra sees the combination of serpent's wisdom with the courage of the eagle as distinctive of humans.[40] There is a curious crossover of characteristics here: clinging to the earth narrows the horizon and yields wisdom; rising to the heights entails courage and yields far-sightedness. Wisdom is not the same as knowledge. Wisdom distinguishes trivial from humanly important truths. Wisdom is knowing how to live and that involves alignment with the instinctual, with the unconscious processes of life. But far-sightedness involves a courageous resistance to the merely instinctual or traditional. In *On the Genealogy of Morals*, Nietzsche speaks of keeping the dogs chained in the basement of one's life as the condition for "clear air at the top," that is, for clarity of mind.[41] In *The Will to Power*, he says that his aim was to make asceticism natural again.[42]

As we noted earlier, Nietzsche's being a so-called immoralist does not consist in his doing whatever he feels like. As he says, many of the practices associated hitherto with being moral are not cancelled out by his "immoralism" but rather given a new basis, polar opposite to contempt for bodily existence and yearning for an afterlife. In fact, In Zarathustra's teaching, poverty, chastity, and obedience—hitherto the supreme expression of contempt for the earth—are reinstated. Chastity is a requirement in certain natures for achieving an elevation of life itself. And Zarathustra says that he who thinks that lying with a woman is the greatest thing in life has mud in his soul.[43] He advised that one not marry out of lust or out of loneliness or discontent with oneself but out of mutual reverence and out of the desire to produce in one's offspring something higher than oneself.[44] To that end, one must first learn to conquer himself and become free of "the bitch sensuality" that even enters into the spirituality of the monk.[45] Regarding poverty, Zarathustra observed that one is possessed by greater and greater possession;[46] and about obedience, he

---

40. Nietzsche, *Thus Spoke Zarathustra*, IV, On Science," 336/415.

41. Nietzsche, *On the Genealogy of Morals and Ecce Homo*, III, 8, 108.

42. Nietzsche, *The Will to Power*, §914, 483.

43. Nietzsche, *Thus Spoke Zarathustra*, "On Chastity," 58/166.

44. Ibid., I, "On Child and Marriage," 74/181.

45. Ibid., I, "On Chastity," 58/167.

46. Ibid., I, "On the New Idol," 53/163.

said that he who would command must first learn to obey.[47] Making asceticism natural again is practicing restriction and sublimation of natural impulses in order to bring about the unity of ascending life. That involves "compelling the chaos within to take on form"[48] in order to seek the highest mountaintop that affords the most comprehensive vision and the broadest possible affirmation that extends to all beings.[49]

What Nietzsche seeks combines two directions: a synoptic vision that does not cut its ties with the instinctual. Wise and courageous, clinging to the earth like the snake and rising to the heights like the eagle, Zarathustra himself represents the foreshadowing of full humanity. As he sees it, life itself wants to build itself to heights so it can "look into vast distances and out toward stirring beauties"[50] as a dimension of "fidelity to the earth." But, as we noted, if the tree is to ascend to the sky, it must sink its roots deeply into the earth.

Actually, Zarathustra says it must sink its roots into "evil." There are *Three Evils* upon which he focuses special attention: sex, desire of ruling, and selfishness. But each has to be reinterpreted in the light of his teaching about the Overman.

The first refers to the common view of sexuality as "dirty." Some Church Fathers considered it a result of the Fall. Zarathustra considered it as both oriented toward reproduction and a matter of warrior's recreation. However, he retained the notion of dirtiness as he observed that those who think lying with a woman is the greatest thing "have mud in their souls," for they are blinded to the higher reaches of human activity. His discussion of marriage could be profitably read by any religious person. Marriage should not be a matter of two animals finding each other. As we already noted, for Nietzsche one should not marry out of loneliness or lust but out of respect for one another and out of desire to produce a higher life. One has to bring to marriage a disciplined self so he can raise offspring that can ascend beyond the level of the parents and prepare the way for the Overman.

---

47. Ibid., II, "On Self-Overcoming," 123/226.

48. Nietzsche, *The Will to Power*, §842, 444.

49. Nietzsche, *Thus Spoke Zarathustra*, III, "The Wanderer," 168/264–65. See my "Monasticism, Eternity, and the Heart: Hegel, Nietzsche, and Dostoyevsky." It is reprinted in this volume.

50. Ibid., II, "On the Tarantulas," 109/213.

The desire of ruling is correlated with the reinterpretation of selfishness. True love of self is tricky since it is full of traps and false surrogates. One should be concerned with reaching the highest level possible and bending every effort to "go under" as the self one currently is in order to ascend to a higher level. Only a disciplined self who has compelled his chaos to take on form and is overflowing with wisdom that involves comprehensive vision united with instinct, the union of the eagle and the snake, should allow the release of the desire of ruling as a dispensing of the gifts of wisdom.

Zarathustra reaches a stage of wisdom that overflows so that he "goes under" to dispense it to others. He is characterized by his "gift-giving virtue."[51] This has to be understood first in terms of his clear contempt for the Last Man. Zarathustra's ape is full of such contempt. But Zarathustra admonishes him that contempt should be linked to his actual love.[52] His gift-giving virtue has to be understood also in relation to his mighty struggle with pity throughout part IV. Pity and love are not equivalent. Overcoming pity is rather a matter of "tough love" that opens the subject that one would pity to the self-overcoming appropriate to his condition. Nietzsche himself said that "whatever does not kill me makes me strong."[53]

The togetherness of the eagle and the snake suggests a union of day wisdom and night wisdom. Nietzsche even depicts the eagle carrying the snake and circling above the mountain. Synoptic vision sees better when it leaves place for awareness of what exceeds conscious mastery. "The world is deeper than day ever thought."[54] Day wisdom is linked to the foreground, night wisdom to the background. Zarathustra wants to see the ground and background, whereas the practitioner of day wisdom, "the lover of knowledge who is obtrusive with his eyes," sees only foreground.[55] This is tied to reversing the Platonic victory of the theoretical man over the artist, philosophy understood Platonically over art.

From the beginning, Nietzsche contrasted the theoretical man with the artist. In *The Birth of Tragedy*, he claimed that the artist is interest-

51. Ibid., I, 186.
52. Ibid., III, "On Passing By," 287.
53. Nietzsche, *Twilight of the Idols*, §1, 8, 23.
54. Nietzsche, *Thus Spoke Zarathustra*, III, 183/278.
55. Ibid., III, "The Wanderer," 168/265.

ed in what remains veiled while the theoretical man, the invention of Socrates, is interested in the cast-off veils. The artist is the practitioner of "night wisdom." The rationalist spirit pursues what can be subjected to complete visual verification, whether that is understood literally in an empiricist mode or metaphorically in a rationalist manner. If Hegel claimed that one could render the fundamental principles of intelligibility fully explicit, bringing them all into the light of day, such explicitation could at best reveal the principles constituting the circumference of a limited horizon, no matter how embracing it might be. Beyond it lies that which encompasses all projected circumferences. Night wisdom would be learning how to relate to the dark encompassing mystery. In no way repudiating what can be brought to the light of day—indeed, pursuing it with all his power[56]—Nietzsche nonetheless sought a relation to that which exceeds, encompasses, and grounds all day wisdom.

In common with Plato, for Zarathustra both day wisdom and night wisdom involve a sense of eternity encompassing time. At the end of part III,[57] the song at midnight ends each of its verses with the refrain "For I love thee, O eternity!" And again, "All joy loves eternity, loves deep, loves deep eternity." However, this is not, as in Plato, an eternity beyond time; it is the eternity of time itself that repeats itself forever.

In the tradition following from Plato, eternity lies in a superior realm compared to which life on earth is a situation of darkness and exile. Christianity aligns itself with such a view, considering this life worthwhile only as a place of transition to "our true home." Baruch Spinoza, whom Nietzsche appreciated, considered the eternity of *natura naturans*, or the region of the laws of nature, to be inseparable from *natura naturata*, or the region of changing particulars. The physical world is the outside of mind that is the inside of human beings.[58] John Locke also gave witness to the necessary relation to eternity when he noted that if something comes to be, there is something eternal anteceding it.[59] Thinking *sub specie aeternitatis* is distinctive of humanness. The only question would be whether eternity is in or outside time.

56. Nietzsche, *Ecce Homo*, 328.

57. Nietzsche, *Thus Spoke Zarathustra*, "The Seven Seals," 253–55/340–43.

58. Benedict de Spinoza, *On the Improvement of the Understanding, The Ethics, Correspondence*, trans. R. Elwes (New York: Dover, 1955), part I, scholion.

59. John Locke, *An Essay Concerning Human Understanding* (Baltimore: Penguin, 1998).

Eternity in time is also in Plato. It is what is involved in all forms of life as expressed in Eros. Eros is the love of the mortal for the immortal.[60] As explicitly conscious sexual desire, it is the expression of the organism's unconscious striving to reproduce itself, to keep its kind of form going throughout the generations. At the human level, this is sublimated into the work of culture, keeping the tradition of understanding and corresponding practices going beyond the death of the individuals who initiated it. Just as animals spontaneously risk their lives and sacrifice themselves for the sake of their offspring, so also human beings spontaneously tend to sacrifice themselves to protect their way of life, to keep it going beyond their own demise. Nietzsche clearly assimilates that, but denies that which, for Plato, underpins it: a mirroring of an eternity *beyond* time. And Plato is ambiguous regarding that. As one ascends the ladder to higher levels, one tends to despise the lower levels and even to see them as hindrances to the higher aspirations, eventually looking upon the lower as a result of some kind of fall from the higher: reason is chained or entombed in the body with its senses and passions.[61] That is what Nietzsche categorically rejects.

The linkage of past traditions with an afterlife supported the imposition of ways of acting and evaluating that held the instinctive life, the life of the body, in chains. Nietzsche would overcome the dualism of reason and body that afflicts the tradition. Everything human is "physiological," not in the sense of everything being "body" but in the sense of undercutting the dichotomy of body and mind and underscoring "reason's" belonging to the earth.[62] Zarathustra sets himself resolutely against those who would despise the body, those preachers of the afterlife.[63]

The union of the eagle and the snake, of day wisdom and night wisdom, is aligned with the relation between the "greater reason" of the body and the "lesser reason" of what we would ordinarily call reason.[64] Reason I would take as the drive toward the comprehensively coherent. That is an expression in the field of awareness of the encompassingly co-

---

60. Plato, *Symposium*, 207d.

61. Plato, *Phaedo*, 62b, 82e.

62. See Martin Heidegger, *Nietzsche: The Will-to-Power as Art*, vol. 1, trans. D. Krell (San Francisco: Harper, 1979), 96.

63. Nietzsche, *Thus Spoke Zarathustra*, I, "On the Preachers of Death," 46–48/156–58.

64. Ibid., I, 34/146.

herent functioning of the body in the darkness of its own processes. The term "reason" would seem to involve, as it does in Kant and Hegel, the coherence of the Whole. Although Nietzsche speaks of the Whole as containing "pockets of rationality," nonetheless, the reference to the body as "the great reason" suggests that underlying what we are able to uncover as islands of light within an overarching darkness is the coherence of what lies in the darkness, that is, the coherent functioning of the organic whole we call a living being that supports the life of consciousness. And yet, granted the coherent "rationality" of the organic body, what underlies it is not "rational" in either a traditional or modern sense. Traditional forms of rationality involve purpose and necessity; modern forms deny purpose and underscore necessity. Zarathustra delivers things from purpose and necessity to the play of chance.[65] This element of play hearkens back to the Old Testament's notion of wisdom playing in the presence of God before creation and to Heraclitus's notion that the production of the world order is like a child playing dice.[66] Into this randomly organized whole rationality is mixed in as leaven. It keeps the Whole from flattening out into a one-leveled universe. And this leaven I would understand as the presence of life in coherently functioning organisms within the vastness of the nonliving universe.

So in reassessing what is "up" and "down" in human life, in addition to faithfulness to the earth, truthfulness, broad vision, and sensitivity to beauty, we have the unity of conscious and unconscious, of rational and irrational, of mind and body brought about by a natural ascetical organization of one's powers and a corresponding affirmation of eternity in time.

GATHERING INTO UNITY

As conditions for developing our humanness under these criteria, early in the work Zarathustra presents "three metamorphoses": that of the camel, the lion, and the child;[67] he returns to these in part II.[68] The camel is a beast of burden and would seem to represent the traditions with

---

65. Ibid., III, "Before Sunrise," 183/278.
66. Heidegger, "Heraclitus," §102, 93.
67. Nietzsche, *Thus Spoke Zarathustra*, I, "On the Three Metamorphoses," 25–27/137–40.
68. Ibid., "The Stillest Hour," 160–63/258–2591.

which peoples have been weighed down—although, for any lasting creation to occur, a sense of tradition is a prerequisite; the camel is indispensable. The lion would seem to represent the power and courage to attack the traditions as absolutely binding. And the child would then look to the future, rediscovering "the innocence of becoming," trusting in instinctive life, creating in fidelity to the earth. Beethoven would be a perfect example of all three: he wholly absorbed and revered the musical tradition into which he was inducted and which he had to assimilate before he could go on the attack and introduce new musical form.[69]

When Zarathustra went up to the mountain, he went up away from "The 1,000 Goals" that oriented peoples thus far.[70] A people gathers around the goals it collectively projects; it strives to attain what it considers to be a state higher than where it presently stands. It creates the criteria for up and down expressed in "the ring of myths" that determine a people's ultimate horizon. It thus forms a tradition that binds together the group vertically or synchronically at a given time and horizontally or diachronically across the generations that precede and follow it. But thus far, in uniting a given people, its goals separated it from other peoples. Zarathustra seeks an "up" that would unite *all* of humankind and not just some particular ethnic group. So another criterion for what is "up" in human life would be what could, in principle, unite all humankind as the 1,001st goal.

Further, previous projection of collective goals, besides dividing one people from all others, has succeeded in creating mere fragments of humanity and no complete human beings. Zarathustra claimed, "I create and carry together into One what is fragment and riddle and dreadful accident."[71] Past projections produced only "inverse cripples"—specialists without wholeness, represented in the image of a tiny man with one huge ear.

Nietzsche represents the specialized scientist through the imagery connected with the leech.[72] Specialized science produces a life form with the life sucked out of it; it provides a worm's-eye view, crawling upon the earth in order to ferret out one perspectively limited truth. Nonethe-

69. This follows Kaufmann's comments in his translation of *Thus Spoke Zarathustra*, 116.
70. Ibid., I, "On the Thousand and One Goals," 61–64/170.
71. Ibid., II, "On Redemption," 153/250–51.
72. Ibid., IV, "The Leach," 276/362.

less, Nietzsche is fiercely dedicated to seeking knowledge in every way possible. In his intellectual autobiography, he claims that affirmation of life yields insight that "is most strictly confirmed and supported by truth and science."[73] Further, "in the lover of knowledge all instincts become holy."[74] More recently, Michael Polanyi spoke of a scientist as having a kind of "tacit knowledge" that provides the hints and hunches through which science advances, based upon the scientist having been assimilated to his subject matter and become connatural with it.[75] Zarathustra has a tremendous sense of knowledge yet to be gained: there are a thousand paths never trodden.[76] And yet, they require an umbrella of overarching meaning and a corresponding set of instincts. In his preface to *The Birth of Tragedy*, Nietzsche quotes Goethe, his lifelong model, proposing "to dwell resolutely in wholeness and fullness."[77]

Let us return to the statement: "I create and carry together into One what is fragment and riddle and dreadful accident."[78] The way in which a people came to project what it considered "high" and thus also "low" is a matter of historical accident: it occurs over time by an almost blind process of accumulated tradition. The "dreadfulness" Zarathustra attaches to the accident might be seen to lie in the contempt for the earth that underlies the dominant tradition, in the fragmentary human beings the differing visions have produced, and in the fracturing of humanity into mutually exclusive warring groupings that resulted from the differences.

We might conjecture that the things that are always forbidden to "the immoralist" would have to do with what violates the conditions for the possibility of the coexistence of large groups of people over long periods of time—but which would also allow for the emergence of "higher men" as their leaders. Nietzsche sees as the supreme "works of art" the Roman Empire, the Prussian Officers Corp, and the Jesuit Order, each involving long tradition, reverence, obedience, and power over oneself.[79] But it

73. Nietzsche, *Ecce Homo*, 272.
74. Ibid., I, "On the Gift-Giving Virtue," 2, 82/189.
75. Michael Polanyi, *The Tacit Dimension* (Garden City, N.Y.: Doubleday, 1966).
76. Nietzsche, *Thus Spoke Zarathustra*, I, 22, 2.
77. Nietzsche, *The Birth of Tragedy*, 1886 Postscript, "Attempt at Self-Criticism," §7, 26.
78. Nietzsche, *Thus Spoke Zarathustra*, II, 153/250.
79. On the Roman Empire, see "Expeditions," in *Twilight of the Idols*, §39, 93, and *The Anti-Christ*, §§58–59, 179–83; on the Jesuit Order and the Prussian Officers Corps, see *Will to Power*, IV, §796, 419.

would also have to involve each individual finding what he or she is best suited for, cultivating his or her special virtue.[80] Zarathustra admonishes his followers: "Now I bid you lose me and find yourselves."[81] Finding and cultivating one's special virtue will, however, have to avoid becoming one huge ear attached to a diminished person. It would have to involve a *life* that has become form.

When Zarathustra gives his new tablets, they are only "half filled in."[82] That could mean two things: no single command is completed or the list remains incomplete.[83] In either case, the new legislation would allow for its own transformation both in overall development and in application to contingent circumstances. The second recalls Aristotle's judicial prudence. The second could be read as what America's Founding Fathers built into the Constitution: the possibility for its own amendment, but only with difficulty. The rule of law is necessary for developing a tradition, and for Nietzsche, contrary to individualistic interpretations, tradition is central: "the will to tradition, to authority, to centuries-long responsibility, to *solidarity* between succeeding generations backwards and forwards *ad infinitum*."[84] As such, the law should not be easily changed. But then circumstances change, and the laws have to be changed accordingly.

We have, then, further criteria to which Nietzsche's Zarathustra appeals, supplementing fidelity to the earth, truthfulness, broad vision, the unity of conscious and unconscious, sensitivity to beauty, and the love of eternity: we have the unity of humankind over centuries and the "well-roundedness" of the individual that allows each individual to find his/her own distinctive development within that unity.

RELATION TO THE WHOLE

But there is a deeper dimension to all this. What Zarathustra aims at involves being the locus through which all being and all becoming strive to become word. He says, "All being wants to become word; here all be-

---

80. Nietzsche, *Thus Spoke Zarathustra*, I, "On Enjoying and Suffering the Passions," 148 and II, "On the Virtuous," 206.
81. Ibid., I, "On the Gift-Giving Virtue," 3, 84/190.
82. Ibid., III, "On Old and New Tablets," 217/308.
83. See Lampert, *Nietzsche's Teaching*, 203.
84. Nietzsche, "Expeditions," in *Twilight of the Idols*, §39, 93.

coming wants to learn from me how to speak."[85] Not only is the human being referred to the Whole of what is but everything within that Whole is, in its turn, referred back to the human being through whom it takes on meaning. This is significantly harder to ground than our own verifiable reference to the Whole—even though that itself is difficult for most people to grasp. (We will return to this matter in our final section.)

Zarathustra says, "He who would grasp everything human would have to grapple with everything," since humanness is referred to the Whole.[86] He speaks of "this creating, willing, valuing ego, which is the measure and value of all things."[87] This could be given a Protagorean read, but it has to be taken in conjunction with the statement that all being seeks to become word in man. He says further: "The belly of being does not speak to humans at all, except as a human."[88] And again he says: there is nothing outside oneself.[89] Might that not be because being a self involves a reference to all things? (We will return to this in our final section.)

Nietzsche here is recurring back to Plato in a positive way: as Socrates would have it in the *Theaetetus*, the philosopher, the paradigmatic human being, has his eyes always fixed on the Whole and the whole character of each within the Whole.[90] To be human is not just to occupy an ecological niche, relating only to the functional circle carved out by sensation. The human being is directed toward the Whole.

We should consider this in relation to Zarathustra's complaint: "There is too much foreground in all men: what good are far-sighted, far-seeking eyes?"[91] Whereas essential humanness is related, beyond that functional circle, to the Whole of what is, what is typically focal is some particular feature revealed in function of some limited interest. But even in our ordinary limited focus, there is always a background articulation of the meaning of the Whole that holds our ordinary selective attention in place. Typically, it is a view of the Whole in which the gods function as ultimate sanctions of the way the circle of possible choices is limited and oriented

85. Nietzsche, *Thus Spoke Zarathustra*, III, "The Return Home," 204/296.
86. Ibid.
87. Ibid., I, "On the Afterworldly, 32/144.
88. Ibid., 32/144.
89. Ibid., III, "The Convalescent," 2, 241/329.
90. Plato, *Theaetetus*, 175a.
91. Nietzsche, *Thus Spoke Zarathustra*, III, "The Return Home," 205/297.

in a given culture. Typically, in Western culture it entails an afterlife of rewards and punishments for doing and foregoing or failing to do and forego the things dictated or forbidden by the culture. Given the focal attention, we are prone to forget about the background that holds that attention in place. And we are inclined to dismiss as useless any direct attention to the speculative possibilities afforded by our human condition.

In a telling description of his project, Zarathustra called his soul "destiny," "circumference of circumferences," "umbilical cord of time," and "azure bell."[92] Let us consider each of these descriptions, beginning with "the circumference of circumferences." This neatly describes both the historical necessity involved in all cultures and the desire to transcend all hitherto known cultures because of their divisive, fragmentary, and life-contemning elements. Humanness is founded upon reference to the Whole of what is. The Whole is given as a term of questioning, not as a secure presence. Nietzsche had said that the senses lie, but the lie is necessary for life.[93] The senses produce a selective distortion, creating, for example, the illusion of empty space in order to show at a distance what is beneficial and harmful to the animal being. But humans are distinguished by reference to the Whole. By reason of that reference, one must locate the givens of biologically relative sensory appearance in a view of the Whole that endows ordinary life with ultimate value. Each culture is thus compelled to create a horizon of meaning that holds in place everything else in terms of meaning. Literally, a horizon is relative to the position of the viewer but forms a circumference for everything that appears within that horizon. Metaphorically, every individual and every culture operates within a horizon of meaning that constitutes its circumference. As we noted earlier, Nietzsche claimed that all life needs a horizon within which to live and that humans need "a ring of myths" that define the horizon of meaning. Zarathustra desires to become "the circumference of circumferences." Zarathustra desires to encompass all the horizoning circumferences created by differing peoples.

92. Ibid., III, "On the Great Longing," 247/334. I agree with Heidegger in seeing this as "the climax of the work."

93. Friedrich Nietzsche, "On Truth and Lies in an Extra-moral Sense," in *The Portable Nietzsche*, 42–47. Nietzsche elsewhere said that the senses "do not lie at all. It is what we *make* of their evidence that first introduces the lie into it," *Twilight of the Idols*, 36. Yet in that same work (71), he says that nature exaggerates and distorts.

The second expression, "azure dome," suggests the experientially given dome of the heavens, the fixed limit, the final horizon of human visual experience. Here it becomes the image of Zarathustra's longing to encompass all things. Elsewhere he sings: "This is my blessing: to stand over every single thing as its own heaven, as its round roof, its azure bell, and eternal security."[94] Note that the relation to the Whole is here linked to careful attention to each individual thing, affirming it, preserving it. Nietzsche's last lucid act, the embracing of a horse that was being beaten by its owner, spells out this intent. But that Zarathustra might become each single thing's "eternal security" involves relating it to the encompassing Whole that includes all time within it.

The third expression, "the umbilical cord of time," is an enigmatic expression. The umbilicum is the source of nourishment for the growing fetus. Here it is time that is the umbilicum. It would seem that this is related to the sense of tradition that binds together past, present, and future. How a people projects the ultimate horizon of meaning determines how it takes up its past and thus illuminates its tasks in the present. Such vision nourishes that culture. Zarathustra claims to give all the old and new wines to drink.[95] He boasts that there is no soul more loving and comprehensive who brings past and future together better than himself.[96]

The fourth expression is "destiny." In what way is Zarathustra's soul "destiny"?[97] In being the first to tell the truth about the lies that passed as truths hitherto, about God and the afterlife that underpinned morality, in being the first psychologist of truth, he functions as the dividing line between past and future the way the first Olympiad did for the ancient Greeks, the founding of Rome did for the ancient Romans, and the birth of Christ did for the West thus far.[98] In his autobiographical retrospective, Nietzsche wrote regarding "Why I am a Destiny" that *Thus Spoke Zarathustra* is "not only the highest book there is, . . . [it is] also the *deepest*."[99] It establishes the beginning of the new great dividing line in history.

94. Nietzsche, *Thus Spoke Zarathustra*, III, "Before Sunrise," 182/277.

95. Ibid., III, "On the Great Longing," 247/334.

96. Ibid.

97. See Nietzsche, "Why I Am a Destiny" in *Ecce Homo*, 226–335.

98. A.D., *Anno Domini*, or the year of our Lord, is projected by Aldous Huxley in *Brave New World* (New York: Harper, 2006) as being superseded by "the year of our Ford."

99. Nietzsche, *Ecce Homo*, 219.

ETERNAL RECURRENCE

Relation to the Whole is tied in with Nietzsche's affirmation of the Eternal Recurrence of the Same.[100] That affirmation is the most difficult to see as a real option for thought. In the working notes collected in *The Will to Power*, he plays with a physicist interpretation: given a finite number of particles in the universe—however vast the actual number may be— and an infinite amount of time, the same patterns should have repeated themselves again and again, however long the epochs between the repetitions.[101] This, of course, means that nothing at all is at stake in Nietzsche's appeal to us to affirm life, to reject the Last Man and strive for the Overman. Whatever we do—living according to the "high" or the "low"—we have done it all endless times in the past and are fated to do it now and to repeat it forever.

Now there is a version of this held by the ever-sober Aristotle: it is that the *species* repeat themselves again and again forever—indeed, that the emergence of the polis as the center of the development of the arts, useful and fine, as well as the movement from mythology to philosophy would be repeated and has been repeated in an eternity of time.[102] But Zarathustra claims that the individuality of events—he himself with the dwarf before him and the spider in the corner—are subjected to the Eternal Recurrence *in their individual specificity.*[103]

One way of understanding this is an appeal to the will to affirm life, to accept it all, sufferings as well as joys. Saying "yes" to one's entire life, with everything present as the horizon of all our dealings, would involve accepting all of it just as it has been and will be. That there be an actual, literal recurrence of identically the same individual things and events seems too absurd to have been considered by this most acute thinker as a literal claim and, indeed, as his most profound thought. It is an appeal to us to will life as it is—to the ultimate yea-saying.

100. Lampert, *Nietzsche's Teaching* (81) claims this is the teaching for the sake of which this Zarathustra exists. Before Heidegger, it teaches us to "let beings be" (176).

101. Nietzsche, *The Will to Power*, §1066, 549.

102. Aristotle, *On the Soul*, II, 415b 1. Of course, for Aristotle, an antecedent eternity of a world, each element of which is in process and is able not to be, required an eternal ground outside of time in *Self-thinking Thought*. See *Metaphysics*, XII. 1074b 15 to 1075a 11.

103. Nietzsche, *Thus Spoke Zarathustra*, III, "On the Vision and the Riddle," 173-74/ 269-70.

This could also be understood as being tied to a kind of categorical imperative that would curtail pure arbitrariness: whatever you choose, consider beforehand whether you could live with its recurrence forever. This is Nietzsche's secular equivalence to the thought of heaven and hell in an afterlife. Eternity here is installed into time.

Zarathustra's song at the end of part III recovers the central insight of Plato's *Symposium* that Eros in all living things is the mortal's desire for the immortal: "But all joy wants eternity— . . . wants deep, wants deep eternity."[104] Each verse of "The Yes and Amen Song" that concludes part III ends with "*For I love you, O eternity!*"[105] Joy is the expression of the Will to Power as self-transcendence. In the human case, it is tied to the creation and passing on of tradition. But here it is tied to the awareness of beginning a tradition that will give us the final divide in history. All the previous criteria of high and low are underpinned by the notion of eternity beyond time. That is superseded by eternity in time, the Eternal Recurrence of the Same.

THE OVERMAN

As the source for the vision that would produce the great divide, Zarathustra announces the Overman, for whom he is John the Baptist. The Higher Men, though standing above the herd and especially above the Last Men, are still inferior to Zarathustra. He sees the criterion that would characterize one who would be gifted with the greatest power: possessing the most encompassing vision. He sets himself against the limitations of the past as he gathers from it the perspectives it affords. He attempts to secure multiple "pairs of eyes," providing as many perspectives as possible, to see as no one hitherto has seen.[106]

Humankind he sees as "a rope tied from ape to Overman"[107] following the tendency of all life to create beyond itself as the deepest expression of the Will to Power. Darwinism had cut off all appeal to some "divine origin" for human beings: an ape bars that entrance.[108] But Darwin

104. Ibid., "The Other Song," 253/339–40.

105. Ibid., 253–55/340–43.

106. Nietzsche, *On the Genealogy of Morals and Ecce Homo*, III, 12, 119; *The Will to Power*, §540, 201.

107. Nietzsche, *Thus Spoke Zarathustra*, I, "Prologue," 4, 11/126.

108. Nietzsche, *Daybreak*, §49, 47.

failed to discern the point of the struggle of each living thing to maintain itself in existence: that is, to create beyond itself—and he forgot mind.[109] Life is exhibited first in an organism's overpowering the things around it, assimilating them to itself in order to grow. But it grows as accumulation of power to create further, first as the power of reproduction but, even higher, as the power to create ever higher life forms. In humankind, there emerges the kind of being endowed with mind through whom all being strives to become word.

The vision is in many respects close to Hegel's. For Hegel, the *telos* of the world process is to have the main lines of the Whole, the interlocking set of concepts that determine the conditions for the possibility of rational existence, to have that come to clear expression.[110] But the crucial differences are, first of all, the dominance of chance in Nietzsche's view and, secondly, the superiority of "night wisdom" over Hegelian "day wisdom."[111] The latter distinction is most important. The poetic word is able to bring us into relation with encompassing mystery. We do not turn our backs on the encompassing darkness that surrounds the sea of light, the world of our senses and what is logically entailed by it. Through the poet, we can gain a sense of the continuity of the manifest and the hidden, and the sheltering of the former in the latter. We can live out of a sense of encompassing mystery. In Hegel, that is only a moment to be overcome in "day wisdom," the science of wisdom that reveals the ultimate Logos.[112]

As we noted, Nietzsche explicitly rejects purpose and delivers everything over to the play of chance and necessity. This clearly reverses Hegel's claim of ultimate purpose as the manifestation of the order of the Whole and the creation of a form of togetherness that allows rational creativity full leash. And yet Nietzsche at the same time holds that in man all being seeks to become word. Is this simple incoherence?

The Higher Men, driven by the Will to Power as the will to create beyond themselves the ring of myths within which the many come to live, succeed only in producing limited visions and truncated human beings. The Overman is the expression of the myth of transcendence: exhibit-

109. Nietzsche, *The Gay Science*, §349, 292.

110. G. W. F. Hegel, "The Absolute Idea," in *Science of Logic*, trans. A. Miller (London: George Allen and Unwin, 1969), 824–44.

111. See the discussion in Lampert, *Nietzsche's Teaching*, 103, 191ff.

112. See how this works in my comparison of Hegel and Heidegger in "Heidegger's *In-der-Welt-Sein* and Hegel's *Sittlichkeit*," in *Existentia* 21, fasc. 3–4 (2011): 255–74.

ing fidelity to the earth, truthfulness, broad vision grounding the unity of humankind and the "well-roundedness" of the individual, the unity of conscious and unconscious, sensitivity to beauty, self-affirmation in self-overcoming and the love of eternity, establishing a vision that could unite all humankind and in which each individual can pursue his or her highest potential. The Overman encompasses the limited circumferences of the Higher Men, organizing the chaos of human life into the possibility of "living resolutely in wholeness and fullness of being" and of doing so in utter fidelity to the earth.

The Overman would be the supreme artist. Art is worth more than truth insofar as truth obtains within perspectives.[113] If truth is the locus of day wisdom, art gives articulation to the night wisdom that creates a place for the mystery of encompassment. Art is the overcoming of nihilism[114]—not only the nihilism of the loss of orientation following the disappearance of God but the deeper nihilism of the place of value occupied by God.[115]

But finally for Nietzsche there is a god like the god Shiva: Dionysus, the simultaneous creative and destructive power of being, the underlying Will to Power. He is a god who dances and laughs, who celebrates the goodness of creation.[116]

DEFENSE OF THE PRINCIPLES

I have tried to show that Nietzsche's overcoming of nihilism involves an articulation of principles for determining the high and the low, and I have said that such principles were themselves eminently defensible. It is time to defend them. But I do so by overturning one of Nietzsche's basic pronouncements: that the notion of Being is the last trailing cloud of evaporating reality—or I should say that I assimilate and transform that view. "Being" applies to all because it abstracts from each and every being and therefore is, as Hegel saw it before Nietzsche, a pure emptiness; but it abstracts from every being *because it is referred to all.* "Being" names the horizon of distinctively human existence. It names the term of

113. Nietzsche, *The Will to Power*, §853, 453.
114. Ibid.
115. For a discussion of the forms of nihilism, see my *Placing Aesthetics*, 203–7.
116. Nietzsche, *The Will to Power*, §1049–52, 539–43.

our reference to everything and to everything about everything. It thus has an erotic structure in the Platonic sense: it is an oriented emptiness, an emptiness aimed at plenitude.

The notion of Being plays in tandem with our rootage in the sensorily given, itself necessarily grounded in an articulated organism. Genetically, the sensory field emerges out of a set of organs for perception that carve out a limited field of manifestness in function of organic need. The senses do not give things as they absolutely *are* but as they *appear* relative to the perceiving organism. The sensory field itself prepares the way for the emergence of reflective intelligence whose horizon is the notion of Being. Reflective intelligence is by nature pried loose from the limitations of the sensorily given by being referred—though emptily—to the encompassing Whole of what is. It situates the sensorily given in reference to that Whole by grasping the indefinitely repeatable regularities given within the sensory field and by adjusting its actions accordingly. But its reference to the Whole makes necessary the question of the ultimate why of all our knowings and doings. "Only if we possess our *why* of life can we put up with almost any *how*."[117] Hence, the need for giving some articulation to the empty encompassment afforded by the notion of Being. Hence, the need for limiting the horizon by providing a "ring of myths."

Each culture creates a different set of myths within which the ultimate why is given expression. But the founding notion of Being presses us beyond each differing mode of encompassment toward what would finally encompass them all. It calls us to enter into each of the perspectives in order to secure many "sets of eyes," putting us in a position to look for what would encompass them all.[118]

Crucial to the whole enterprise is sustaining a relation between what is manifest and what stands beyond. For Hegel, the Beyond is brought to presence in the final set of categories in which he claims to do justice—and I would claim to a large extent cashes in on that claim—to what has been seen in each of the perspectives generated by the history of thought.[119] For Nietzsche, what is crucial is maintaining a sense of

117. Nietzsche, *Twilight of the Idols*, 12.

118. See my "Nature, Culture, and the Dialogical Imperative." It is reprinted as the first essay in this collection.

119. See my *Hegel's Introduction to the System*, a translation, introduction, and commen-

what always lies beyond, provided the Beyond is an eternally ongoing temporal Beyond and does not entail the invidious distinction between the temporal and the detached eternal and thus between the body and the soul. By reason of the notion of Being, what we know is always referred beyond itself to what we do not know. "Day wisdom" is always encompassed by "night wisdom." The latter is related both to the unity of what is known and what remains hidden and to the unity of conscious and unconscious, of the reflective and the instinctive involved in the distinction between knowing and dwelling. The aim is "to dwell resolutely in wholeness and fullness of being."

As I indicated earlier, the human body is itself both ground and model of a rational system: a coherently functioning whole playing in tandem with the coherence of the ecosystem but sunk in the darkness of unconscious functioning. The organismic whole is not a mere agglutination of parts but rather involves the governance of the parts by the whole. As Hegel put it, the soul as principle of life is related to the body, not as part to part or as whole to whole but as encompassing concrete universal to its particulars.[120] The field of human awareness, as openness to the Whole via the notion of Being, translates that relation of the principle of organic wholeness to all that is. Human awareness as explicit reason seeks the coherence of *the* Whole grounded in that coherence that is organic existence.

The notion of Being directs us to the Whole via the togetherness of the categories whereby we locate ourselves within the Whole. In Plato's imagery, we move out of the cave of bodily, temporal, sensory, and individual existence by moving up the ladder of knowledge to the universal interrelatedness of eidetic features toward the Good as principle of the Whole. But one tends to forget that, as principle *of the Whole*, the Good is not only principle of the intelligible but of the relation between the intelligible and the sensible.[121]

The relation between intelligible and sensible, universals and particulars, functions in any natural power.[122] Any natural power is an orienta-

---

tary on the phenomenology and psychology from the *Encyclopaedia Philosophy of Spirit* (Toronto: University of Toronto Press, 2014).

120. G. W. F. Hegel, *Philosophy of Mind*, trans. W. Wallace and A. Miller (Oxford: Clarendon Press, 1971), 33.

121. Plato, *Republic*, VI, 511B.

122. See my "Universals, Particulars, and Capacity," *The Review of Metaphysics* (2001).

tion toward individuals of a definite *type*, the type suitable to that power's peculiar horizon of functioning. Thus, the power of seeing is oriented toward the kind of aspect called color, hearing toward sound, and so forth. But seeing and hearing in act only reveal *individual instances* of their respective *types* of objects. The awareness of types as such entails the activation of a kind of power oriented toward types as types. Cutting through the peculiarities of instances, intellectual power grasps the horizon of a given organic power in its generic object, as, for example, color for seeing. Intellectual activity involves the apprehension of the immanent powers of nature as concrete universals. Once we can exercise that, we can also develop new powers, the skills that allow us to find our way through the particulars, transforming them to suit our given and chosen ends.

However, as with any native power, orientation toward Being is not only orientation toward the universal but also toward the individual and indeed toward the fullness of any given thing. That fullness lies both in its being an instance of a type and its being a unique variation on the type. Nietzsche pushes so far in the direction of the individual that he falls into a purely nominalist reading of our awareness of types.[123] In so doing, he calls attention to the way an organic power disregards the particularity of a given individual in focusing only on its generic suitability for nourishment. One should note here that this is, indeed, the ground for the reflective emergence of universals. Seeing is a universal orientation toward its generic object, color, but is activated only by individuals who fall under the type. It is recognizable through distinctively intellectual activity that involves the capacity to apprehend the universal as universal. Nonetheless, Nietzsche's emphasis upon the individual, for each of which he would form its "azure bell, its eternal security," is essential to our relation to the being of things. Essential structures are found in and subordinate to existential individuals. It is how we deal with individuals that is crucial to human fulfillment.

Essence subserves existence. Reference to Being, finally, necessarily relates us to eternity. Being encompasses everything and thus all of time. If anything happens, eternity is its necessary horizon for us: eternal antecedence and eternal consequence. The only question is where to locate that eternity: in the eternity of the changing universe, that is, in time

123. "On Truth and Lie in an Extramoral Sense," in *The Portable Nietzsche*, ed. and trans. W. Kaufmann (New York: Viking Press, 1954), 46.

itself as endless, or in an eternity beyond time. Aristotle holds both; Nietzsche holds only the former. Platonic myth[124] and Abrahamic monotheism hold the limitation of time by reason of an absolute beginning and an absolute end. This view of limited temporality then entails an eternal Beyond, a God as cause of the beginning and as final end, the Alpha and the Omega. God encompasses time by being beyond it. Repudiating limited temporality, Nietzsche grounds all things in the immanent causality of the Dionysian Will to Power, the desire for eternity within time expressed in the creative joy experienced by sensitive beings.

I would relate "the wholeness and fullness of being" with the notion of the heart. Zarathustra constantly speaks to his heart.[125] And he will allow no one to philosophize who does not philosophize with his blood.[126] Thought which is whole and full reaches to the heart, the center of the individual. It is the heart that is involved in Zarathustra's frequent poetic outbursts. The completion of relation to Being lies not only in having one's eyes fixed on the Whole but in relating with the wholeness of oneself—with one's heart—to the wholeness of things, beyond what we can fully apprehend of their underlying mystery.

The separation of soul and body has its origins in the intellectual ability to abstract from the here-and-now and consider the encompassing eternal. It leads to an abstract theory of the body and of matter in general as an absolute other to soul and mind. But evolutionary theory suggests that body and matter are only relatively other than mind or soul. So-called "matter" is rather the locus of potentialities that can actualize themselves only under certain determinate conditions of systematic combination. As in the case of the fertilized ovum, an exhaustive empirical inspection will not display the powers it contains for the successive emergence of conscious and reflectively conscious activity. So in the case of the evolving universe, empirical inspection of its manifest actualities does not display the powers for the appearance of self-replicating wholes that result in conscious and then reflectively conscious individuals. "Matter" is the first level of actuality of a universe eventuating in "spirit." This view both spiritualizes "matter" and materializes "spirit." Mind is

---

124. Plato, *Timaeus*, 28b and 37d.

125. See my "Monasticism, Eternity, and the Heart: Hegel, Nietzsche, and Dostoevsky." It is reprinted in this volume.

126. Nietzsche, *Thus Spoke Zarathustra*, I, "On Reading and Writing," 152.

thus no stranger in a strange land but belongs essentially to the earth. In a Christian view, Christ's Incarnation and Resurrection underscores the goodness of embodiment and presages the resurrection of the body for all humankind. Unfortunately, this always has played in tandem with a view of the body as foreign to the spirit and life on earth as an exile for "our true home in heaven."[127] Hence, Nietzsche's polemic against Christianity as life-denying otherworldliness, as "Platonism for the masses."

In summary, "high" in Nietzsche's evaluation involves fidelity to the earth (as respect for embodiment, sexuality, sensory beauty, and pleasure), truthfulness, broad vision, the unity of conscious and unconscious, of bodily "reason" and explicit reason, and the love of eternity in tandem with affirmation of even the least thing as the "speculative" side of the artist-philosopher who, on his "practical" side, seeks to form his life in the proverbial "well-rounded" manner—compelling the chaos to take on form—in order to lay the basis for the unity of humankind where each could find that for which he or she is best suited. "High" would involve "the gift-giving virtue" that despises the low out of love and forsakes pity as "tough love" aimed at fostering the self-overcoming of those who would evoke pity. "Low" would be everything that stands opposite or blocks the attainment of these dispositions. We have attempted to provide the basis for the claim that such criteria are eminently defensible: it lies in the peculiarity of the structure of human experience, rooted in the notion of Being.

127. See my "Potentiality, Creativity, and Relationality: Creative Empowerment as a "New Transcendental?" *The Review of Metaphysics*, no. 59 (June 2005).

14 ∞ Monasticism, Eternity, and the Heart
Hegel, Nietzsche, and Dostoevsky

There is a sense in which Hegel summed up the philosophic tradition. And he did so by focusing attention upon the eternal encompassment present in life itself. Nietzsche carried on that movement "to install eternity in time." In both cases, the enemy was monasticism, whose focus on eternity beyond this life led to a genuine contempt for this life. Dostoevsky was sensitive to both sides in this encounter: ancient monasticism and the Hegel-Nietzsche attack on it. In his *Brothers Karamazov*, he realized a kind of *Aufhebung* of the antinomies in the figures of Fr. Zosima and his protégé, Alyosha Karamazov. In all three thinkers, the notion of the heart plays a central role. In this chapter, I will explore the relations between these three thinkers centered around the question of monasticism.

I will proceed in three stages. First, I will examine the grounds for the attack Hegel and Nietzsche level against monasticism and Dostoevsky's position as a kind of response. Then, I will consider their respective notions of eternity. Finally, I will examine what I consider to be central both to the monastic life and to the thought of Hegel and Nietzsche as well: the notion of the heart and its purification and elevation. In Hegel in particular, the function of the heart stands against "the Euclidean intellect" of Ivan Karamazov and presents at the level of lived life the functioning of what Hegel means by "rationality": the achievement of identity-in-difference. In the *Brothers Karamazov*, Fr. Ferapont's heartless contempt for this life has its parallel in Ivan's intellectualism: both exhibit the spirit of abstract separation from the heart, which Hegel's thought overcomes.

MONASTICISM

Hegel and Nietzsche are allied in their attack on monasticism. In both his *Philosophy of Mind* and his *Lectures on the Philosophy of Religion*, Hegel links his consideration of monasticism to a discussion of the contrast between Lutheranism and Catholicism that hinges upon a contrast between the inner witness of the spirit in Luther and external imposition in Catholicism.[1] Luther's witness of the spirit is continued in "the very different power" of philosophy begun anew with Descartes's demand for apodictic evidence. "The witness of the spirit" that is philosophy focuses upon what is rational in human experience as a whole, giving another shape to the content of religious experience and doctrine. For Hegel, in monasticism we have a development of Catholicism's externalist, impositional mentality: a life external to the world, a life of "sanctity" governed by the vows of chastity, poverty, and obedience. In the realization of human freedom through the modern state, the phases of *Sittlichkeit* (family, civil society, and state) supersede monastic separation. In place of renouncing sexual activity through the vow of chastity, one harnesses it to the development of the family, the permanent anchor of ethical life. In place of the vow of poverty, giving up property to others (and thus paradoxically enriching them), one takes on the duty to acquire and manage property as mediate relation to others. In this way, one is able to develop the intelligence, industry, and honesty entailed in economic life, in contrast to the temptation to laziness and lack of appreciation of the prerequisites of ordinary life too often attendant upon monastic existence. And in place of giving up responsibility for one's choices to the will of one's superiors through the vow of obedience, one accepts freedom under law rationally organized. Thus, instead of renouncing these crucial aspects of human existence—sexuality, property, and self-determination—for Hegel, fully rational existence involves organizing them into a coherent whole governed by reflective intelligence and inserted into meaningful institutions. In Hegel, what has to be achieved is a unification and hierarchization of our

---

1. G. W. F. Hegel, *Philosophy of Mind*, trans. W. Wallace (Oxford: Clarendon, 1971), §562; *Lectures on the Philosophy of Religion*, ed. and trans. P. Hodgson (Berkeley: University of California Press, 1988), 87, 137, 161, 396–400, 487–88. I use two translations of the same work because, derived from different earlier editions, there is pertinent material in one version that is not in the other. For a general approach to Hegel, see my *Placing Aesthetics*, ch. VI.

various powers brought about by the commitments involved in marriage, business, friendship, and civic obligations generally, in the creation and appreciation of art, in religion, and in scientific and philosophic inquiry.[2] One must learn to focus one's powers on the matters at hand and not flee in unhappy consciousness to the thought of a life beyond.[3]

In the *Brothers Karamazov*, Ivan, when discussing the relation of church and state, presented two alternatives: either collapsing the state into the church or vice versa.[4] In Hegel's view, these alternatives are undercut. In the Protestant state, religion entails the inner witness of the spirit and must therefore be a matter of free election and not Catholic imposition.[5] The proper articulation of common life follows the inherent rationality of each of the institutional arrangements and their interrelation. This involves a distinction of church and state but does not entail their separation, for all the practices are anchored in a sense of the eternal, encompassing Divine as the fully rational ground of the Whole and not just of the political. One needs no separately existing, world-renouncing ascetics. In the Protestant state, Christianity develops in the workaday world the consequences of its central doctrine of Incarnation.

Nietzsche's criticism of monasticism attacks the basic attitude to life itself, which he sees in Christianity, especially as guided by the ascetic ideal epitomized in monasticism.[6] Christianity is Platonism for the masses, a mythical surrogate for the intellectual ascent out of the Cave of temporal existence, the body, and its passions, into the eternal domain of separate, purely spiritual existence promoted by Platonism.[7] Fallen existence is bodily existence in this vale of tears, the condition of exile from our true and eternal, purely spiritual, disembodied home. Fear and hatred of sexuality in particular saturate Christian tradition. One can look to Origen, Gregory of Nyssa, John Cassian, and Augustine to verify this

2. Hegel, *Philosophy of Mind*, §552, 284–88.

3. On the notion of "unhappy consciousness," see Hegel's Phenomenology of Spirit, §206–7, 126–27.

4. Fyodor Dostoyevsky, *The Brothers Karamazov*, trans. C. Garnett, revised by R. Matlaw (New York: W. W. Norton, 1976), 52–58.

5. G. W. F. Hegel, *Philosophy of Right*, trans. T. Knox (London: Oxford University Press, 1952), §270, 165–74.

6. For a comprehensive approach to Nietzsche, see Robert Wood, *Placing Aesthetics* (Athens: Ohio University Press, 1999), ch. VIII.

7. Friedrich Nietzsche, *Beyond Good and Evil: Prelude to a Philosophy of the Future*, trans. W. Kaufmann (New York: Vintage, 1966), 3.

judgment.[8] Our religious culture still maintains the notion that sexual thoughts are "dirty thoughts" and sexual jokes are "dirty jokes." At the level of a kind of lived metaphorics, the notion of the Virgin, "pure and undefiled," involves a felt association with the inverse, one who is not a virgin being "impure and defiled." This is not so much a matter of "official teaching" as it is of the lived metaphorics lying at the ground of explicit claims. Some time long ago, I read a summary of the kind of attitude toward sex that perfectly captures my own Catholic upbringing: "Sex is dirty; save it for the one you love!" A few years ago, I heard, from a university pulpit, a reference to humankind as "conceived in the stench of bodily lust"—a statement I had read before, uttered by one or the other saint. What a far cry from John Paul II's *Theology of the Body* and his talk of "the beauty of human sexuality." Nietzsche was sensitive to these matters and saw in Christianity, especially in its attitude toward sex, a vindictive hatred of life itself.[9]

Nietzsche, the self-styled "immoralist,"[10] has Zarathustra say of *"sex, the lust to rule, (and) selfishness"* that "these three have so far been best cursed and worst reputed and lied about; these three I will weigh humanly well."[11] But for Nietzsche, being a so-called "immoralist" does not consist in doing whatever one feels like doing. As he says, many of the practices associated hitherto with being moral are not canceled out by his "immoralism" but rather given a new basis, polar opposite to the contempt for bodily existence underlying Christian culture.[12] In fact, in Zarathustra's teaching, poverty, chastity, and obedience are reinstated. Chastity is a functional requirement in certain natures for achieving an elevation of life itself.[13] And Zarusthstra says that he who thinks that lying with a woman is the greatest thing in life has mud in his soul.[14] He

8. Friedrich Nietzsche, *Twilight of the Idols*, trans. W. Hollingdale (Baltimore: Penguin, 1968), 8, 101, 110; for Gregory of Nyssa, see his *Hexaemeron* in *Patrologia Graeca*, 44, 189b–192a; see Peter Brown, *Body and Society: Men, Women, and Sexual Renunciation in Early Christianity* (New York: Columbia University Press, 1988).

9. Friedrich Nietzsche, *The Will to Power*, trans. W. Kaufmann and R. Hollingdale (New York: Vintage, 1967), §5, 21.

10. Nietzsche, *Beyond Good and Evil*, 226.

11. Friedrich Nietzsche, *Thus Spoke Zarathustra*, in *The Portable Nietzsche*, trans. W. Kaufmann (New York: Viking, 1954), III.10, 298–303.

12. Nietzsche, *Twilight of the Idols*, 101.

13. Nietzsche, *The Will to Power*, 76.

14. Nietzsche, *Thus Spoke Zarathustra*, I.13, 166.

advised that, if one is to marry, one not marry out of lust or loneliness or discontent with oneself but out of mutual reverence and out of the desire to produce in one's offspring something higher than oneself.[15] To that end, one must first learn to conquer himself and become free of what he called "the bitch sensuality" that enters even into the spirituality of the monk.[16] Regarding poverty, Zarathustra observed that one is possessed by greater and greater possession,[17] and about obedience, that he who would command must first learn to obey.[18]

One of Nietzsche's dominant aims is to make asceticism natural again, that is, to practice restriction and sublimation of natural impulses in order to bring about the unity of ascending life.[19] That involves not extirpating the passions but dominating them to the extent that they themselves gain more freedom.[20] That involves "compelling the chaos within to take on form"[21] in order to seek the highest mountaintop that affords the most comprehensive vision and the broadest possible affirmation that extends to all beings. *Thus Spoke Zarathustra* begins with reference to Zarathustra's ten-year stay on the mountaintop to which he returns again and again throughout the work. The second part begins with Zarathustra once more returned to his mountain. The third part opens with the wanderer standing before "his final peak," his "ultimate peak" where he can look down even upon the stars.[22] Finally, in part IV we find Zarathustra once again returned to the mountain. Corresponding to the ascent is the breadth of aspiration that seeks to be "the circumference of circumferences,"[23] to encompass thinkingly (and Hegel-like) all the limited horizons that define and separate different peoples.[24]

As opposed to the gnostic infiltration that longs for removal from the body and its desires, for both Hegel and Nietzsche, embodiment belongs to the nature of reason itself. For Hegel, spirit as such—and that means not only the human spirit but even the overarching, grounding divine Spirit—requires embodiment: the Word made flesh.[25] Flesh is the spirit's

---

15. Ibid., I.20, 181–83.   16. Ibid., I.13, 167.
17. Ibid., I.11, 163.   18. Ibid., II.12, 226.
19. Nietzsche, *The Will to Power*, IV, §915, 483–84; §921, 487.
20. Ibid., IV, §93, 492.   21. Ibid., III, §842, 444; §868, 465.
22. Nietzsche, *Thus Spoke Zarathustra*, III.1, 264–65.
23. Ibid., III.14, 334.
24. Ibid., I.15, 170–72.
25. Hegel, *Lectures on the Philosophy of Religion*, 452–58.

own otherness through which it comes to itself, penetrating and assimilating the body through habituation in order to be situated and able to function in the world.[26] For Nietzsche, the body is "the greater reason," the functionally coherent whole, greater in relation to "the lesser reason," or what we ordinarily call reason that is tempted—and vainly tempted—to declare its independence of its own embodiment.[27] Of course, though Nietzsche claims that there are "pockets of reason" within the Whole, against the "day wisdom" of Hegel he maintains the "night wisdom" that the Whole is not grounded in reason but is ultimately encompassing mystery.[28]

In the *Brothers Karamazov*, the target of Nietzsche's attack is epitomized in Fr. Ferapont: the grim ascetic, suspicious of—no, *contemptuous* of—anything that involves pleasure. Ferapont holds firmly to the view that life is "the vale of tears" and makes sure it is nothing but a vale of tears unrelieved by even simple pleasures.[29] He is witness to the fact that, as the narrator says, monasticism "may be a two-edged weapon and it may lead some not to humility and complete self-control but to the most Satanic pride, that is, to bondage and not to freedom."[30] It is from the position of contempt for this life that Ferapont passes harsh judgment upon Fr. Zosima, who explicitly refuses to consider this life a vale of tears, in spite of the suffering ingredient in it.[31]

From Dostoevsky's letters, we learn that the chapter on Fr. Zosima was "the culminating point of the novel."[32] So the monastic life he exhibits is crucially important. Zosima is not far from the claim of Dmitri Karamazov, which is exactly the same claim as Nietzsche: a lifetime of suffering is not too high a price to pay for the preciousness of one moment of existence.[33] And Nietzsche knew only too well how high a price one might be asked to pay. Stephan Zweig described Nietzsche's room as a chamber of suffering containing "unnumerable bottles and jars and potions: against the migraines, which often render him all but senseless for hours, against spasmodic vomiting, against the slothful intestines,

26. Hegel, *Philosophy of Mind*, §389, 32–34.
27. Nietzsche, *Thus Spoke Zarathustra*, I.4, 146.
28. Ibid. [1954], III.4.
29. Dostoyevsky, *The Brothers Karamazov*, 151–52.
30. Ibid., 22.   31. Ibid., 312.
32. Ibid., 757.
33. Ibid., 561; Nietzsche, *Thus Spoke Zarathustra*.

and above all the dreadful sedatives against his insomnia, chloral hydrate and Veronal. A frightful arsenal of poisons and drugs, yet the only helpers in the empty silence of this strange room in which he never rests except in brief and artificially conquered sleep. . . . [H]is fingers freezing, his double glasses pressed close to the paper, his hurried hand writes for hours—words the dim eyes can hardly decipher. For hours, he sits like this and writes until his eyes burn."[34]

Like Fr. Zosima, Nietzsche's suffering affirmed the preciousness of this life, its indescribably fertile and creative power and beauty, against Christianity and its paternal Platonism and gnosticism that would demean it. Nietzsche's Zarathustra preaches fidelity to the earth.[35] But in this he has not an enemy but a kindred spirit in Fr. Zosima. Fr. Zosima loves Mother Earth. That is at least part of the meaning of the polysemic epigram to the work: "Unless a grain of wheat fall to the earth and die, it abides alone; but if it dies, it brings forth much fruit."[36] It has a literal application in Alyosha's passionate embracing of the earth and in Fr. Zosima's kissing of the ground immediately before his death.[37] For both, it is a gesture of embracing Mother Earth, the fertile source of existence, of saying "yes" to life in spite of suffering and death. It is a countergesture to the proud contempt for this life in the attempt at wholly disembodied existence found in Fr. Ferapont. In the case of Fr. Zosima, falling to the earth also involves acceptance of his own return to the earth in death. The fruit brought forth through this final falling to the earth is, from the viewpoint of earthly existence, the fruit of example for others. Such is also the case with the death and burial of Ilyusha.[38] The child's suffering and death, his falling to the earth, gathers into community the children who had previously been his enemies, a gathering promoted by Alyosha as a follower of Fr. Zosima, the teacher of universal love.

Alyosha's literal falling to the earth occurs in the chapter "Cana of Galilee."[39] In his letters, Dostoevsky says that this chapter "is the most significant in the whole book, perhaps even in the whole novel. With this posting," he says, "I am finished with the monastery."[40] The scene opens

34. Kaufmann's introduction to Nietzsche, *Thus Spoke Zarathustra*, 104.
35. Nietzsche, *Thus Spoke Zarathustra*, I.2.2, 188.
36. John 12:24.
37. Dostoyevsky, *The Brothers Karamazov*, 340 and 303.
38. Ibid., 727ff.   39. Ibid., 337ff.
40. Ibid., 763.

with Alyosha kneeling in prayer before the coffin of Fr. Zosima. The narrator repeats what was said in the prologue: "There was reigning in his soul a sense of the wholeness of things."[41] During Fr. Paissy's reading of the Gospel describing the wedding feast, Alyosha had a vision of Fr. Zosima. The dead monk emphasized the fact that Christ worked his first miracle to further men's celebration of life. Zosima then sent Alyosha out from the monastery where he was to marry and live a life in the world. As Alyosha went out under "the vault of the heaven, full of soft, shining stars, stretching vast and fathomless above him" while "the fresh, motionless, still night enfolded the earth," "the silence of earth seemed to melt into the silence of the heavens. The mystery of earth was one with the mystery of the stars. . . . Alyosha stood, gazed, and suddenly threw himself down on the earth. . . . He did not know why he embraced it. He could not have told why he longed so irresistibly to kiss it, to kiss it all. But he kissed it weeping, sobbing and watering it with his tears, and vowed passionately to love it, to love it forever and ever."[42]

Here certainly is a gesture Nietzsche could only applaud. Embracing the earth is a gesture of love for all creation, as Zosima had preached: "Love all God's creation," he said: "The whole and every grain of sand in it. Love every leaf, every ray of God's light. Love the animals, love the plants, love everything. If you love everything, you will perceive the divine mystery in all things."[43]

Nietzsche was indeed one who exhibited such love. Contrary to what one might think from certain things he says about will to power, Nietzsche was no fire-breathing dragon. The people of Sils Maria, his favorite alpine summer residence, called him "their little St. Francis." As we have noted previously, his last lucid act was his embracing a horse who was being beaten by his owner.[44] Zarathustra, Nietzsche's surrogate, loves his animals and strives to affirm all things. His love for the earth was no mere abstraction, like revolutionary killers' "love for humanity." It was rooted in closeness to the least of things: "This is my blessing: to stand over every single thing as its own heaven, as its round roof, its

41. Ibid., 337.

42. Ibid., 340.

43. Ibid., 298.

44. Walter Kaufmann, *Friedrich Nietzsche: Philosophy, Psychologist, Antichrist* (New York: Meridian Books, 1956), 57.

azure bell, and eternal security."[45] In their fidelity to the earth, Nietzsche and Fr. Zosima were kindred spirits. Hegel joins them in holding the essentially incarnate character of human existence.

ETERNITY

The deepest dimension of relation to the earth in Nietzsche and in *Brothers Karamazov* as well as in Hegel has to do with a simultaneous relation to eternity. With them, Fr. Zosima affirms that our lives are even now anchored in eternity and the task is to learn to live out of that anchorage. But for him, we do so while awaiting life on the other side of the grave,[46] while Hegel and Nietzsche explicitly deny any personal afterlife. In the teaching of the afterlife, there is a danger involved for full human existence: not only contempt for this life but a disposition that will stay in line morally this side of the grave *only* because one believes in an afterlife with a rewarding and punishing God. Nietzsche's Zarathustra observed that the virtuous want to be paid: "They have lied reward and punishment into the foundation of things."[47] That is central to Ivan Karamazov's intellectual struggles: if there is no God who rewards and punishes and no afterlife where that can take place, everything is permitted and the human community falls prey to absolute selfishness and arbitrariness.[48] But of course that is absolutely false. One has only to look to the central argument of Plato's *Republic* and Aristotle's *Ethics* to see that. The function of the Ring of Gyges in the *Republic* is to render the agent invisible not only to other humans but also to the gods, so that the only consequences that follow concern the internal order of the soul in this life.[49] The afterlife of reward and punishment is tacked on to the main argument as that which, if true, is all the better for the just man but not at all the motive for his justice.[50] And for Aristotle, the possibility of the afterlife is so problematic that it serves no function at all in his ethical analysis. Aristotle refers to immortality as one of those impossible things we might wish for.[51] Elsewhere, he says that if anything is

45. Nietzsche, *Thus Spoke Zarathustra*, III.4, 277.
46. Dostoyevsky, *The Brothers Karamazov*, 299.
47. Nietzsche, *Thus Spoke Zarathustra*, II.5, 205.
48. Dostoyevsky, *The Brothers Karamazov*, 244 and 599.
49. Plato, *Republic*, II, 359d ff.   50. Plato, *Republic*, X, 612b.
51. Aristotle, *On the Soul*, III, 2, 1111b 25.

immortal, it is the intellect, and in the same work[52] he says that the active intellect, which is separate, is immortal; but he also says that if we as individuals are likewise immortal, we will be without any memory. This led Islamic thinkers to the famous doctrine of the one, separate Agent Intellect for all humans.[53] For Plato and Aristotle, God exists but only as a first principle, not as judge providing reward and punishment. During more modern times, we have the example of David Hume, in Peter Gay's characterization, "the complete modern pagan"[54] who deliberately cut out belief in God and immortality as foundations of morality. Of him, his friend Adam Smith said that he never met a man more virtuous.[55] Other thinkers of the Enlightenment thought that this was possible for the enlightened few but not for the many. Voltaire sent his servants out of the room when the talk turned to atheism; for he was afraid that if *they* believed there was no God they would slit his throat![56] He said further that if God does not exist, He would have to be invented as the only way to keep the many in line.

Nietzsche saw in the teachers of the afterlife the corrupters of true virtue for whom one acts virtuously because one wants to secure a reward or at least wants to avoid punishment.[57] One can see the danger to moral life in this way of viewing things: one offers aid to others because she wants to save her soul. It's like an airline stewardess smilingly taking care of you in order to win the Stewardess of the Month award. Response to need becomes a purely instrumental value. Conversely, Nietzsche also saw, as did Socrates's Diotima, that "all joy wants eternity, wants deep, deep eternity."[58] For Nietzsche, as for the tradition of speculative thought generally, the human spirit is related to the Whole: as Zarathustra says (paralleling Hegel), all being, all becoming seeks word

52. Ibid., III.5, 430a 23.
53. Aquinas, *Summa Theologiae*, I.76.6.
54. Peter Gay, *The Enlightenment: An Interpretation*, vol. 1, *The Rise of Modern Paganism* (New York: Vintage Books, 1966), 401–22. See David Hume, *Dialogues Concerning Natural Religion* (Indianapolis: Bobbs-Merrill, 1947) for a devastating attack on arguments for the existence of God, and *Enquiry Concerning Human Understanding* (Indianapolis: Hackett, 1977), VIII, 53–69 for a dismissal of human freedom. In *Enquiry Concerning the Principles of Morals* (Indianapolis: Hackett, 1983), 73–74 and 50 he rejects "monkish virtues" and founds morality on utility and benevolence.
55. Hume, *Dialogues Concerning Natural Religion*, appendix, 243–48.
56. Gay, *The Enlightenment*, 526.
57. Nietzsche, *Thus Spoke Zarathustra*, II.5, 205.
58. Ibid., III.15.3, 339–40; Plato, *Symposium*, 206b.

in the human being.[59] And Nietzsche's own teaching of Eternal Recurrence has to do with affirmation of all things. One who so affirms steps back from immersion in the limited and attends to the eternality of being that encompasses all becoming. But it encompasses as the whole of becoming and not as some eternally fixed and frozen region beyond.[60]

In Hegel, the eternal Logos encompasses everything, and human existence is the locus of the manifestation of the Logos.[61] But eternity finds its completion in time, in the temporal unfolding of human history. Our own participation in eternity requires our identification with the actualization of the human essence as the meaning of the Whole comes to progressive manifestation over time.[62] Religion is the permanent anchor of human existence in the eternal encompassing. As reference to Being, to the all-encompassing, the human spirit is naturally and perpetually religious. Such reference grounds the capacity of each I to step back from the finitude of its involvements and take responsibility for its actions.[63] Such actions are meaningful insofar as they are linked to the manifestation of the underlying rationality of the universe as embodied in rational institutions.[64] Philosophers from Parmenides onward have each apprehended an aspect of the eternal Logos; but it is only over time that we are put in a position to be able to overcome the one-sidedness involved in the articulations of these aspects and bring them into harmony with each other.[65] It is the eternal Logos, manifest in Jesus and operative in history, that guides it toward its full actuality. Familial, contractual, civic, and religious obligations have their own proximate grounds in the structure of the human being, in the structure of the interrelations of human beings we call institutions, and in the specific practices belonging to a given community, but they have their ultimate ground in the relation of the human spirit to the eternal encompassment articulated in religion and rendered conceptually in philosophy. Hegel expressed his disbelief

---

59. Nietzsche, *Thus Spoke Zarathustra*, III.9, 296.

60. Ibid., III.2.2, 269–70.

61. G. W. F. Hegel, *Science of Logic*, trans. A. Miller (Oxford: Oxford University Press, 1969), 50.

62. G. W. F. Hegel, *Philosophy of History*, trans. J. Sibree (New York: Dover, 1956), 53 and 457.

63. Hegel, *Philosophy of Mind*, §381, 11; 1952, §429, 20–33.

64. See Hegel, *Elements of the Philosophy of Right*, trans R. Nisbet (Cambridge: Cambridge University Press, 1991).

65. Hegel, *Lectures on the History of Philosophy*, I, 9; III 545ff.

in an afterlife of reward and punishment.[66] In response to the poet Heinrich Heine, Hegel's pupil, who remarked on the heavens as the abode of the blessed, Hegel is said to have remarked: "So you want to get a tip for having nursed your sick mother and for not having poisoned your dear brother?"[67]

In Fr. Zosima, anchorage in the afterlife adds a depth dimension to our appreciation of this life and does not cancel out its beauty and glory. Life is worthwhile in itself and is all the more wonderful because, according to Christian belief, we are perpetually anchored in the eternal dimension in which we will share forever. Fr. Zosima's ascetical practice is not rooted in contempt for simple pleasures and beauty: among other things for which Fr. Ferapont indicts him, he eats jam and collects beautiful art. Fr. Zosima's ascetical practice is rooted in subordinating the variety of human passions to our relation to the Whole. Self-conquest and self-mastery as well as freedom from the tyranny of possessions and passions are the fruits of the ascetical life for Fr. Zosima and Friedrich Nietzsche.[68] But that is not because one holds the life and the body in contempt; it is because one must learn to integrate them into a hymn to creation in Nietzsche and to creation and the Creator in Fr. Zosima. That integration takes place in the heart.

The treatment of the heart moves us into a dimension of relation to the eternal that is central to all three thinkers, even, and especially (most people will be surprised to know), in Hegel.

THE HEART

In Hegel's view, "monkish withdrawal means that the heart is not concretely developed, that it exists as something undeveloped."[69] As we have seen, Dostoevsky's work frees monasticism from Hegel's and Nietzsche's criticisms by freeing it from the kind of otherworldliness represented by Fr. Ferapont. This allows for a certain convergence of the three thinkers on the notion of the heart whose development is a central task of human

---

66. Hegel, *Lectures on the Philosophy of Religion*, 446; Benedict de Spinoza, *Ethics: Ethica Ordine Geometrico Demonstrata*, trans. R. Elwes (New York: Dover, 1955), V, Prop. XXXI, XLI.

67. Robert Solomon, *In the Spirit of Hegel* (New York: Oxford University Press, 1983), 3, 583.

68. Dostoyevsky, *The Brothers Karamazov*, 21.

69. Hegel, *Lectures on the Philosophy of Religion*, 482.

existence. Hegel's view is especially helpful in overcoming the tension expressed in medieval times between early monasticism with its emphasis upon the heart, as instanced in Augustine's famous teaching on the restless heart coming to rest in God,[70] and the emerging scholastic rationalism held in suspicion by followers of Francis of Assisi, the heartfelt lover of all creatures great and small.

According to Dostoevsky's prefatory note, the hero of *Brothers Karamazov* is Alyosha, who "carries within himself the very heart of the whole" while "the rest of the men of his epoch have for some reason been temporarily torn from it."[71] The notion of heart here is important. In this context, it would seem to refer to something apart from the human, but, of course, the Whole includes the human. And indeed, "the heart of the whole" has as its subjective correlate the heart of the human being. As it appears in *Brothers Karamazov*, the heart is the whole man.[72] It is the source of creativity and the locus of prizing.[73] It is capable of "infinite, universal, inexhaustible love."[74] The notion of the heart appears crucially in the lives of each of the three Karamazov brothers. Fr. Zosima says that God's gift to Ivan is a lofty heart capable of suffering because of the sufferings of the innocent.[75] For Dmitri, the heart is the battlefield where God and the devil fight over the character of beauty. And, of course, what is characteristic of Alyosha is his native good heart that is elevated and simultaneously concretized through the instruction of the monk, Fr. Zosima.

In Nietzsche's *Thus Spoke Zarathustra*, the notion of heart appears again and again as one of the great leitmotifs of the work. Zarathustra continually speaks to his heart, and he wants friends with overflowing hearts, broad and full.[76] Heart is the center of the emotions: of fright, anguish, joy, nausea, astonishment, melancholy, love, generosity, relief, reverence, weariness, attraction, refreshment, giddiness, elevation, longing, pain, and brokenness.[77] The heart is capable of being awakened[78] and is

70. Dostoyevsky, *The Brothers Karamazov* [1976], xvii.

71. Ibid.

72. Dostoyevsky, *The Brothers Karamazov*, 69.

73. Ibid., 156 and 211.

74. Ibid., 149.

75. Ibid., 61.

76. Nietzsche, *Thus Spoke Zarathustra* [1954], I. 16, 171; I.22, 188.

77. One can find these references scattered throughout the work. Since they are so frequent, it would be tedious to cite them all.

78. Nietzsche, *Thus Spoke Zarathustra*, III.11.1, 304.

the source both of a kind of knowledge[79] and of darkness.[80] It is the center of resolve, the locus of courage.[81] It is that which is touched[82] and draws one on.[83] It is connected with Zarathustra's demand that one philosophizes with one's blood and with the claim that one's little reason is grounded in the greater reason of the body.

That the heart furnishes a kind of knowledge is quite significant. It recalls Pascal's dictum that "the heart has its reasons of which 'reason' knows nothing."[84] I would suggest we connect it with the distinction between "day wisdom" and "night wisdom" in *Zarathustra*: "The world is deep—and deeper than day had ever been aware."[85] Though for Zarathustra, there are pockets of rationality in the cosmos; rationality itself is subordinate to chance, to the unpredictable. It is the heart's affirmation of the transrational encompassing that allows it to dance within the cosmic play.

Contrary to a common caricature, in Hegel the notion of the heart plays a central role.[86] In the beginning of the *Philosophy of Religion*, he says that one who does not know the rising of his heart from the quotidian to a sense of the eternal and encompassing does not have the experience, the clarification of which is the task of the philosophy of religion.[87] Religion has its locus in the heart, the region of deep subjectivity in the sense of distinctive individuality. The heart is the region of my unique personal self, that whereby I am most individual and most different from all others. But, of course, for Hegel there is a deeper subjectivity, that of reason, identical in all and correlate to the universal structures embracing all things. That is why for him philosophy rises above religion.[88]

For Hegel, the heart is the residue of all one's experiences and the ground of one's spontaneous tendencies to think and behave in certain ways. Formed within a family and a community whose institutions exhibit a high level of Hegelian rationality, the heart may be intuitively more rational than the rationality of abstractive intelligence.

79. Ibid., II.5, 207.
80. Ibid., III.3.2, 358.
81. Ibid., III.8, 291.
82. Ibid., III.8, 291.
83. Ibid., II.14, 233.
84. Blaise Pascal, *Pensèes*, trans. W. Trotter (New York: Modern Library, 1941), IV, §277.
85. Nietzsche, *Thus Spoke Zarathustra*, III.4, 278.
86. See my "Hegel on the Heart," *International Philosophical Quarterly* 41, no. 2 (2001): 131–144, chap. 12 in this book.
87. Hegel, *Lectures on the Philosophy of Religion* [1895], I, 4.
88. Hegel, *Philosophy of Mind*, §572–73, 302–3.

For Hegel, it is a fundamental requirement of authentic human existence that there be a union of heart and intellect. "The higher ideas such as God and morality cannot only be thought, they can also be felt, and indeed, *must* be felt."[89] There is thus "the possibility of a culture of the intellect which leaves the heart untouched . . . and of the *heart without the intellect*—of hearts which in a one-sided way want intellect, and *heartless intellects*—[but this] only proves at most that bad and radically untrue existences occur."[90] Through our intellectual activity, each of us ultimately has the responsibility of judgment and direction, but its criteria are derived from the prior functioning of prereflective rationality generally. Its culmination lies in sinking back into the life of the heart out of which we spontaneously live.

Let me explore for a bit this notion of prereflective rationality, following Hegel's lead. The living body in its coherent functioning, both within itself and in relation to its environment, is already prereflective rationality in action.[91] As Hegel would have it, the inherent rationality of the psyche as informing the body to give it total coherence overreaches the material assunderness of the components and is related to these components, not as one thing to another but as universal to particular.[92] Further, the species overreaches the individual to call it to its species-work of reproduction and to call it back to the ground in death. In cognition, attentive to the appearing other, one overreaches the isolated particularity of one's own inwardness to grasp the immanent rationality of any appearing other. In love, one overreaches one's own privacy to identify with one's wife, one's children, one's friends. In patriotism, one overreaches one's subjectivity in order to identify with the good of one's country, again at the level of the heart (i.e., of spontaneous feeling and proclivity to respond), even to the point of self-sacrifice. And finally, in religion one is drawn outward and upward in the heart to a sense of the eternal and encompassing. Reflective rationality makes explicit the rationality involved in all these movements of the heart.[93]

Here one must understand that the Euclidean mind prized by Ivan

89. Ibid., §471, 231; 1895, I, 132.
90. Ibid., §445, 188.
91. Recall that Nietzsche claimed the little rationality of wakeful life rests upon the larger rationality of the body. Nietzsche, *Thus Spoke Zarathustra*, I.4, 146.
92. Hegel, *Philosophy of Mind*, §388–89.
93. Ibid., §436, 176–77.

Karamazov is precisely that which Hegelian rationality overcomes. And it does so by resituating the abstractions that are based on the principle of identity governing this strictly subordinate "rationality of the Enlightenment." Hegelian reason resituates them in the concrete intelligibility involved in the functional rationality of identity-in-difference revealed in the Word made flesh.[94] Enlightenment rationality, with its principle of identity, thinks deistically of a single separate Watchmaker of the universe; of a separation of mind and body, if not the reduction of the former to the latter; of body itself as composed of externally related atoms; and of society as composed of external related individuals as atoms of self-interest calculating pleasures and pains. But for Hegel, Christian revelation gives a lie to all that and shows the centrality not of identity but of identity-in-difference. Jesus is not simply an individual; as the Word, He is the overarching principle of all Being. He is the manifest Other than the Father, in absolute union with the Father, before all things with the Father as that through whom the otherness of creation outside God is possible, and who, as principle of otherness within God, entered into the otherness of creation. What for Kierkegaard's understanding of understanding was the Paradox and the Absurd—namely, the infinite become finite, God become man[95]—was for Hegel the paradigm of rationality. We have to think everything in Hegel from that point. For him, the old adage *Primum vivere, deinde philosophari*, "First live, then philosophize," takes center stage. *Vivere* occurs in the authentic heart overreaching its mere private inwardness to identify with increasingly wider circles of concern; *philosophari* follows that by making explicit the identity-in-difference operative in and underpinning all experience, only to sink back, necessarily and by way of completion, into the spontaneously functioning heart in fully integrated human experience.

The Euclidean intellect of Dostoevsky's Ivan is overcome in a living way by the heart of Fr. Zosima, carried over into Alyosha, a heart that learns identification with others, with the earth, with all creation, and with the living God. But in many ways that moves close to Zarathustra, who strives for a vision of the Whole, a rising above the mud in his soul, simultaneously sinking into the earth of desire and sublimating that into

94. Wood, *Placing Aesthetics*, 159–63.

95. Søren Kierkegaard, *Concluding Unscientific Postscript to Philosophical Fragments*, trans. D. Swenson (Princeton, N.J.: Princeton University Press, 1941), 192–200.

a love of the Whole that includes even an affirmation of the disgusting selfishness and nonholistic, blinking vision of the Last Man.[96] Out of such piety emerges the notion of the god Dionysus, the god of simultaneous destruction and creation, a god who saw creation and proclaimed it good.[97] However, such affirmations are made possible by what Hegel uncovers in his analysis of the structural features of the human subject, their objectification in institutions that last beyond the lifetime of their originators, and their completion in the subject's rising to the eternal and encompassing, with one's heart in religion and with one's mind in philosophy simultaneously.

There are, nonetheless, major points of difference between the three thinkers that we should highlight. Nietzsche would side with Dostoevsky and with monasticism against Hegel in affirming the priority of "night wisdom," of the sense of encompassing mystery over the "day wisdom" of encompassing rationality. But Nietzsche would oppose both of them in their affirmation of the centrality of the God-man in human history. And Dostoevsky would stand over against Hegel and Nietzsche in their denying a life after death, stances linked to their rejection and Dostoevsky's acceptance of monasticism.

But what I have tried to show is that in spite of their significant differences, there are deep inner affinities between these three thinkers, a fact that reminds one of Heidegger's observation that philosophers and poets are kindred spirits, calling out to one another throughout the ages from mountain peaks that surmount the valleys of everyday existence.[98] Seeing that depends upon a sympathetic entry into the differing perspectives afforded by great thinkers, an activity I take to be an essential part of the central discipline involved in philosophic studies.

96. Nietzsche, *Thus Spoke Zarathustra*, I.5, 128–31; II.6, 208–11.

97. Nietzsche, *Will to Power*, §1051, 539.

98. Martin Heidegger, *What Is Called Thinking?* trans. Fred D. Weick and J. Glenn Gray (New York: Harper and Row, 1968), 134.

15 ✌ The Free Spirit

Spinoza, Hegel, and Nietzsche

One hears in Hegel that freedom is the recognition of necessity;[1] one reads in Nietzsche that the free spirit is characterized by *amor fati* as the will to the Eternal Recurrence of the Same.[2] It seems that we have identical, if paradoxical, claims. Both of them find affinities in Spinoza, for whom everything follows with rigid necessity, and the free man is one who is privileged by the working of necessity to recognize that fact by rising above the appetites that cloud the mind.[3] Awareness of belonging to the Whole and accepting the necessity of fate link Nietzsche to Spinoza and to Hegel, except on the pivotal last point: the issue of fate or at least a way of understanding fate that precludes any but illusory choices. But in all three thinkers, the claims have different systematic loci and thus different meanings. We will look at each of them in turn and then draw some conclusions.

SPINOZA

Spinoza claims that approaches to philosophy hitherto are never complete because of an abstract starting point, beginning with sensing or ordinary opinion or some regional science and so abstracting from the wholeness of things. Spinoza begins with the only concrete notion, that of Being, of which we see immediately that it is all-inclusive: outside of

---

1. G. W. F. Hegel, *The Encyclopaedia Logic*, trans. T. Geraets, W. Suchting, and H. Harris (Indianapolis: Hackett, 1991), §158.

2. For *amor fati*, see Friedrich Nietzsche, *The Gay Science*, trans. W. Kaufmann (New York: Vintage, 1974), §276, 223; for Eternal Recurrence, *Thus Spoke Zarathustra*, trans. W. Kaufmann in *The Portable Nietzsche* (New York: Vintage Books, 1954), 269–70.

3. Baruch Spinoza, *Ethics*, in *On the Improvement of the Understanding, The Ethics, Correspondence*, trans. R. Elwes (New York: Dover, 1955), part I, proposition XXIX.

Being there is nothing.[4] But if we ask for its outer limits, we see that we are beyond the limits in raising the question. And that is true of any putative limits, so that what corresponds to the notion of Being is absolute infinity. The notion of Being is thus absolutely unlimited. For Spinoza, Being is a total System, call it Nature, or call it God.[5] It is a single overarching Substance, which, as absolutely unlimited, must have an unlimited number of *attributes*.[6] Two of them we know: as in Descartes, we know *thought* by direct experience and *extension* by inference from sensation. For Descartes, thought is found in multiple substances, but extension is a single Substance, and individual bodies are "vortices" within the overarching extensive matrix—a historical antecedent to the space-time-energy matrix of contemporary physics. Real individuals are the consciousnesses using their particular segment of substantial extension. However, rather than there being, as with Descartes, two kinds of creaturely substance, with Spinoza thought and extension are related within the single Substance as inside to outside.[7] Spinoza thus appears as the father of contemporary dual aspect theory on the mind-body relation. The single Substance corresponds to Descartes's notion of God as Infinite Being and is parallel to Descartes's notion of extension. But in the largest framework, for Spinoza there are not, as with Descartes, three sorts of substance: finite thought with its multiple instances, a single substantial extension, and God as absolute, infinite thought. For Spinoza, there is only a single Substance that includes the others, known and unknowable. Things, rather than being individual substances—or, as in the case of Cartesian extension, vortices or enfoldings within a single substantial matrix—are *modes* or, in traditional language, accidents of that single Substance within which they are embedded.[8]

There are two levels to Substance: the level that governs and the level that is governed, *Natura naturans* and *Natura naturata*, or the level that gives birth and the level born, or the eternal laws of Nature and the temporal things of Nature.[9] Everything occurs because of eternally antecedent laws, so that there is no room for contingency. Everything follows by inexorable necessity.

4. Baruch Spinoza, *On the Improvement of the Understanding*, 15 and 29.
5. Spinoza, *Ethics*, preface to part IV and proposition XI.
6. Ibid., part I, definition VI.   7. Ibid., proposition X.
8. Ibid., definition V and proposition XV.   9. Ibid., proposition XXIX.

Human beings are for the most part driven by their passions that trap them into focusing upon a limited object or set of objects. Most men think that following their passions is true freedom, but the passions function to narrow intellectual vision. The more one understands his passions, the freer the mind is to pursue the wider vision. The free man is focused upon the character of the Whole; he is one who is drawn by the intellectual love of God as love of the Whole.[10] However, this is no merely abstract focus. The more one understands individuals within the Whole, and, as a condition for such understanding, the more one understands his own passions and thus gains clarity of mind, the more one loves God.

Yet because everything has an antecedent cause, "in the mind there is no absolute free will."[11] So the freedom of the rational man is of the same general type as the free flight of a bird, wholly explainable by antecedent laws. Its specificity lies in the coming to clarity of the causes of things that entails mastery over the limiting focus provided while under the sway of the passions.[12] Those who rise above the emotions through clarity of thought are, as it were, the elect of the cosmos. They are able to consider everything within that divine Substance *more geometrico*, viewing people as one views line, planes, and solids.[13] Ultimately, there is no teleological explanation and thus no failure or success, only factual sequence.[14] When one understands how necessity governs the totality, one should neither laugh nor weep but simply acknowledge. Einstein said that Spinoza's metaphysics is *the* metaphysics most in keeping with twentieth-century physics.

There is another aspect to Spinoza's view of freedom—action in a free state: "the true aim of government," he says, "is liberty."[15] The rational state provides the security to develop minds and bodies and employ reason unshackled. Such can occur when religion, which confines the work of reason, is made a matter of choice and its public exercise confined to the practice of charity and justice.[16] Entering such a state, "the individual justly cedes the right of free action, though not of free reason and judg-

---

10. Spinoza, *Ethics*, part V, propositions XV–XX and XXXII.
11. Ibid., part II, proposition XLVIII.   12. Ibid., part V, proposition XLI, note.
13. Ibid., preface to part III.   14. Ibid., part I, appendix.
15. Benedictus de Spinoza, *A Theological-Political Treatise*, trans. R. Elwes (New York: Dover, 1951), 259.
16. Spinoza, *A Theological-Political Treatise*, 265.

ment."[17] "In a free state every man may think what he likes, and say what he thinks." This leads to progress in science and the liberal arts.[18] Living in such a state allows for the free development of the rational man that is greater than in independent solitude. Free men are most useful to each other because they are rational.[19]

In spite of all this talk of freedom from the passions and free action in a free state, one has to keep in mind the overall context. There is no free will, no teleology; everything flows by inexorable necessity. Having a clear mind by being freed from entrapment by the passions and living in a state that promotes rational development is a matter of being one of the elect, in whom the necessity of Nature produces such freedom.

HEGEL

For Hegel, thinking like Spinoza is a requirement of speculative thought.[20] That means, first of all, beginning with the notion of Being as all-inclusive in orientation but factually empty as a starting point. Spinoza's starting point in a fully articulated Whole is Hegel's endpoint. For Hegel, the notion of Being is identical with the self as the *Begriff*, the grasping toward the totality that employs *Begriffen*, concepts in the ordinary sense of the term.[21] Thinking like Spinoza also means thinking in terms of the totality as a single Substance with individuals as modes or accidents of that substance. For Hegel, too, freedom is recognizing and submitting to the rational in it as one has been privileged to see. But for Hegel, Spinozist Substance must become Subject, and that means that the inexorable necessity of the natural Whole must leave room for free choice.[22]

The basic characteristic of Subject as spirit is freedom, just as the basic characteristic of matter is gravity.[23] Distinctive human freedom is grounded in the initially empty notion of Being that grants to the I, to

17. Spinoza, *Ethics*, part IV, proposition LXXIII. 235; *A Theological-Political Treatise*, ch. XX.
18. Spinoza, *A Theological-Political Treatise*, 261.
19. Ibid., 234.
20. Hegel, *Science of Logic*, 583.
21. Ibid., 536.
22. G. W. F. Hegel, *Phenomenology of Spirit*, trans. A. Miller (Oxford: Oxford University Press, 1977), §17, 10.
23. G. W. F. Hegel, *The Philosophy of History*, trans. J. Sibree (New York: Dover, 1956), 17; G. W. F. Hegel, *Elements of the Philosophy of Right*, ed. Allen W. Wood, trans. H. B. Nisbet (Cambridge: Cambridge University Press, 1991).

the self, primordial distance from all determination and gives it over to itself to decide upon what to make of itself. The notion of Being makes possible freedom of choice as *negative* or *formal freedom*.[24] Abstracted from any part by being referred to the encompassing Whole, the self is negative in relation to everything else, both outside and inside itself as a psycho-physical whole. If the human individual is an accident of the overarching Substance, it is an accident that can talk back and choose contrary to the goals immanent in that Substance; it can do evil as well as good. Evil is the choice of subjectivity *over* rather than *within* objectivity; it is choosing one's own preferences over what is true and good in itself. Doing good is exercising *essential* or *substantial freedom*, filling empty formal freedom with rational content, both theoretically and practically.[25]

Free choice entails the necessity of contingency—and, as Hegel sees it, contingency is also a necessity in Nature as Spirit's other.[26] There, as with Thomas Aquinas, complexity entails contingency. Hegel's view of rational necessity in things human is similar to that of Aristotle. There is a human nature (Hegel would say "human essence" since the term "nature" is usually restricted to what is other than spirit). Human nature or essence develops through generations. For Hegel, that does not preclude but requires human choice.

All this is linked to another fundamental difference between Hegel and Spinoza. Where Spinoza's Substance is mechanical, Hegel's is teleological. Hegel's System involves organisms and ecosystems. Ecosystems are understood in terms of systems of organisms that, in turn, are understood as systems of organic instruments. Thus teleology is a central notion in Hegel's System.[27] In fact, the Whole is directed toward the human being who, in turn, is directed toward the totality through the notions of truth and goodness.[28] This means that both theoretical and practical reason have optimal conditions toward which reason itself moves. Theoretical reason is free when it recognizes the rationality of the Whole and

24. Hegel, *Hegel's Philosophy of Mind*, trans. W. Wallace (Oxford: Clarendon Press, 1971), §469.

25. Hegel, *Hegel's Philosophy of Mind*, §469, 228; §5, 37–39, and Hegel, *Elements of the Philosophy of Right*, §149, 192–93.

26. Hegel, *The Encyclopaedia Logic*, §144–45, 217–19.

27. Hegel, *Science of Logic*, vol. II, sec. 2, ch. 3.

28. Hegel, *The Encyclopaedia Logic*, §§223–35, 294–303.

of each part within the Whole; practical reason is free when it lives and makes choices within the bounds of rationally constructed institutions. The latter occur in the state as overarching community that is organically articulated in terms of various functions and various levels of functioning—from the state government, through the provincial, to the municipal, and on to the individual. This entails what would later be called the principle of subsidiarity. Negatively expressed, it is: Do not do at a higher level of organization what can be done at a lower and, ultimately, at an individual level.[29] That creates a system of buffers between the power center and the individual, whose free initiative is central to the *telos* of the state.

Both theoretical and practical reason have a history of their own unfolding. Though both are always required for the long-range survival of communities, the types of communities undergo development over time. One condition for developing rationality is the emergence of institutions of free inquiry and publicity. This entails the recognition of the intrinsic dignity and freedom of individual human beings. Both are achievements of modernity. And here freedom involves the right of individuals to exercise their *Willkür*, their freedom of choice to move creatively and responsibly in all directions compatible with a like freedom for all others and in relation to organizing one's life as a consistent whole.[30] One of the problems here is the translation of *Willkür* as "arbitrariness." This suggests something out of line; but all it means in this context is *choice*. A rationally organized state allows maximum latitude for individual initiative and creativity in what Hegel called *civil society*.[31]

Emphasis upon individual initiative and creativity and the rights this involved led Hegel to adopt principles of the laissez-faire economics advocated by Adam Smith, whom Hegel greatly admired. Smith displayed *the cunning of reason* in the order of the economy as "the invisible hand" behind free economic development.[32] But Hegel also saw this level of civil society as necessarily operating within the larger encompassing framework of the state that provided infrastructure, a safety net for those who fell through the cracks in the inevitable booms and busts of the economic cycle, and an overall monitoring to ensure fair play.[33] It is the modern

29. Hegel, *Elements of the Philosophy of Right*, §§290, 295, 331, and 335.
30. Ibid., §§182–85, 220–23.   31. Ibid., §§182–256, 220–74.
32. Hegel, *The Philosophy of History*, 33.
33. Hegel, *Elements of the Philosophy of Right*, §§231–49, 260–70.

world that unleashed the power of individual initiative that has raised the standard of living for everyone.

Though civil society focused upon the individual atoms of society, fully rational freedom presupposes being "educated to universality," that is, to the point of view of the Whole, cosmic and sociopolitical. That entails surmounting *natural freedom*, the freedom of a child that is one with its appetites, and arbitrary freedom, the whims of the adult (both involving, in different ways, enslavement to desires without a rational framework within which to operate).[34] Education to universality involves exchanging arbitrariness as ultimate principle for rational freedom. The latter involves breaking the natural will and handing over the individual to itself as able to master his/her appetites, project and sustain long-range goals, and bring the lines of one's action into coherent form. It involves respect for other humans as such and for institutions that empower individuals; it also involves the ability to sacrifice for the common good. Such a society is one in which the various functions have been fully articulated in a hierarchical system, like an organism.[35] But the principle of the human sociopolitical system is the growth in rational creativity: empowering individuals to continually search out the order of nature in natural science and create variations in interhuman relations and in the artistic and technological transformation of nature. The general principles of a rational state that have finally come into view through developments in modern politics admit of an indeterminate number of instantiation in different traditions.[36]

At its deepest level, freedom involves the raising of the heart from the everyday to the eternal and encompassing in religion and even further to the comprehension of the main lines of the Whole in philosophy.[37] Without the latter move, religion can smother and has smothered legitimate levels of free operation, especially freedom of inquiry and the general rights for individuals that include freedom of choice in religion. Religion has functioned as, or underpinned, states that denied basic hu-

34. Ibid., §10, 44–45; Hegel, *Hegel's Philosophy of Mind*, §73, 234; Hegel, *Elements of the Philosophy of Right*, §15, 48–49.

35. Hegel, *Elements of the Philosophy of Right*, §259.

36. Ibid., §§214, 245–46.

37. G. W. F. Hegel, *Lectures on the Philosophy of Religion*, trans. P. Hodgson et al. (Berkeley: University of California Press, 1988), 481–89.

man rights. For Hegel, Catholicism is the Western version of such denial. Protestantism, with its appeal to the inner witness of the spirit, has opened up the possibility of full freedom in a rational state.[38]

One can fail to recognize rational necessity, but seeing it does not necessarily entail forming one's life as a life of rational freedom. Saying "yes!" to the rationality of the Whole involves shaping one's own life rationally. And that allows for an indeterminate number of possible choices. One cannot emphasize too much the wide range for individual choice central to, and a necessary ingredient in the rational state and for alternate sociopolitical instantiations of the rational state in different national traditions. In Hegel, Spinozist Substance has become Subject, and the free society Spinoza advocated is given its ground in a universe in which necessity and contingency are mixed and a central place is provided for individual free choice.

NIETZSCHE

Move then, in the third place, to Nietzsche. His image of the free man was Goethe. Of him, Nietzsche remarked: "What he aspired to was *totality*; he strove against the separation of reason, sensuality, feeling, will. . . . he disciplined himself to a whole, he *created* himself." His emancipated spirit "stands in the midst of the universe with a joyful and trusting fatalism . . . a faith baptized with the name Dionysus." Nietzsche further remarked that "Hegel's way of thinking isn't far from Goethe's when one listens to Goethe about Spinoza: Only in the totality everything redeems itself and appears good and justified."[39] This establishes a basic link between our three figures from Nietzsche's point of view.

In a letter to Overbeck in 1881, in the year he conceived of Zarathustra, Nietzsche said: "I have a *precursor*, and what a wonderful precursor! I hardly knew Spinoza. . . . In five main points of his doctrine I recognize myself. . . . He denies the freedom of the will, teleology, the moral world-order, the unegoistic, and evil."[40] As in Spinoza, for Nietzsche emancipa-

---

38. Hegel, *Hegel's Philosophy of Mind*, §552, 284–88.
39. Friedrich Nietzsche, *Will to Power*, trans. W. Kaufmann and R. Hollingdale (New York: Vintage, 1967), 9ff; §95, 60.
40. Walter Kaufmann, *Friedrich Nietzsche: Philosopher, Psychologist, Anti-Christ* (New York: Meridian Books, 1956), 119.

tion goes along with determinism. And as in Hegel, redemption involves a relation to the totality.[41]

We have noted that for Spinoza, as for Hegel, the notion of Being is pivotal, for it indicates a relation to totality. Nietzsche, however, claims that it is a completely empty notion, "the last trailing cloud of evaporating reality" (*den letzten Rauch der verdünstender Realität*).[42] It is a projection from the notion of the ego, itself a grammatical fiction. Nonetheless, he has Zarathustra announce that, through him, "all being strives to become word."[43] He would be "the circumference of circumferences," creating a vision that, as in Hegel, would surpass and include the encompassing views hitherto presented. And, as in Spinoza, love for the Whole is rooted in love for a knowledge of the individual; Zarathustra would "be for each thing its azure bell and eternal security."[44]

As in Spinoza, love for the Whole deepens through understanding and accepting individuals. Nietzsche was known in Sils Maria as "the

41. Hegel wrote to Goethe saying that everywhere in his own thought he finds Goethe's thought. Nietzsche's lifelong exemplar was Goethe. From 1872 in *The Birth of Tragedy*, trans. F. Golfing (New York: Doubleday, 1956), where Nietzsche features Goethe's adage: to live resolutely in wholeness and fullness, to 1886, where he repeats it in his "Attempt at Self-Criticism" (*The Birth of Tragedy*, 26), through *The Gay Science* (trans. W. Kaufmann [New York: Vintage Books, 1974]), in which Goethe is presented as a supreme representative of authentic culture (§103, 159), on to 1889 in *Twilight of the Idols*, trans. R. Hollingdale (Baltimore: Penguin Books, 1968), where he refers to Goethe as the last German before whom he feels reverence (104) and as one who aspires to totality against the separation of reason, sensuality, feeling, and will (102), and on, finally, to the posthumous *Will to Power* where Goethe is the spiritualizer of the senses (§118, 70), an exemplar of "the grand style," of giving form to one's chaos (§842, 444).

Nietzsche called Spinoza "the purest philosopher" (*Human All Too Human: A Book for Free Spirits*, trans. M. Farber and S. Lehmann [Lincoln: University of Nebraska Press, 1984], §475, 229), spoke of his thought as "a passionate soul-history" (*Daybreak: Thoughts on the Prejudices of Morality*, trans. R. Hollingdale [Cambridge: Cambridge University Press, 1982], §481, 198), named him with Plato and Goethe as a prototype of genius (*Daybreak*, §497, 203), designated his manner as "simple and sublime" (Nietzsche, *The Gay Science*, §333, 261), and honored him as one of his own spiritual ancestors.

But as with many things in Nietzsche, one can trace lines of text that move in opposite directions: Nietzsche called him one of the "sophisticated vengeance-seekers and poison-brewers" (*Beyond Good and Evil*, trans. W. Kaufmann [New York: Vintage Books, 1966], §25), who clad his philosophy with "the hocus-pocus of mathematical form." His philosophy was "the masquerade of a sick hermit" (*Beyond Good and Evil*, §5). He speaks of "that laughing-no-more and weeping-no-more of Spinoza, his so naively advocated destruction of the affects through their analysis and vivisection" (*Beyond Good and Evil*, §198).

42. Nietzsche, *Twilight of the Idols*, III, 4.

43. Nietzsche, *Thus Spoke Zarathustra*, III, 9, 296.

44. Ibid., 14, 334.

little St. Francis" because of his love for the things of nature. His last lucid act before he collapsed into insanity was embracing a horse that was
being beaten by its owner.[45]

How one stands within the Whole is indicated in *The Gay Science* in
verses by the fictitious Prince Vogelfrei: Prince Free-as-a-Bird.[46] As the
title suggests, Nietzsche promotes laughing, singing, and dancing to the
highest levels of existence. He says of his first work, *The Birth of Tragedy*,
which announces the Dionysian as the unity of conscious and unconscious, that, instead of describing it, he should have sung. Being free as a
bird, laughing, singing, and dancing would seem to involve the rejection
of traditional ways of acting and thinking that hamper spontaneity. It
would go hand in glove with Nietzsche's self-styled "immoralism." However, such a view is completely misleading.

For Nietzsche, tradition is the condition for the possibility of creating beyond tradition—centuries-long tradition, realized in the great art
forms that are the Roman Empire, the Jesuit Order, and the Prussian Officers' Corp.[47] In each, one learns to take oneself in hand, to subordinate
oneself within a hierarchy of functions, and to contribute to a project
that lasts for hundreds of years. In the process, more and more creative
powers come into play. Not only the political art but every great art form
rests upon a host of conventions. Subjective art is just bad art.[48] Yet society develops as individuals emerge who can create beyond the current state. They would be not bomb-throwing anarchists but men like
Beethoven, who mastered a tradition and went on to develop new musical forms on its basis.

Nietzsche sees that what follows from wallowing in the free flow of
appetites is chaos; hence he advises, with Goethe as his model, compelling this chaos to take on form. As in Spinoza, one needs the dogs
chained in the basement of one's life so one can have clear air at the top.
Nietzsche wants to make asceticism natural again, as something functional, like athletic training, rather than rooted in contempt for the body
and its sensory delights.[49] Previously, asceticism was linked to rejection

45. Kaufmann, *Friedrich Nietzsche*, 57.
46. Nietzsche, *The Gay Science*, appendix, 349–75.
47. Nietzsche, *Will to Power*, §796, 419.
48. Nietzsche, *The Birth of Tragedy*, §5, 48.
49. Nietzsche, *Will to Power*, §842, 444; *Genealogy of Morals*, III, VIII, 243; Nietzsche, *Will to Power*, IV, §915, 483.

of this world as a place of exile and not the place where we belong. Nietzsche's project that he designates as "immoral" does not involve the wholesale repudiation of tradition. It is not as if everything is permitted.[50] It involves the regrounding of tradition, taking over practices within a new overall framework.

Nietzsche promotes fidelity to the earth and love for this life, for embodiment and the enjoyment of the senses. Those who renounced this world through vows of poverty, chastity, and obedience were considered higher than those who lived in and loved the world because the vows detached them from the world. But over time, the ground crumbled and gave way to the offspring of Christianity, democratic socialism. It follows the condemnation of the rich and the exaltation of the poor preached by Christ. Such a view is rooted in the *ressentiment* of the rich and famous by those at the bottom, according to whom the former are evil and they themselves are good. Nietzsche's two greatest opponents are the preachers of the afterlife and the preachers of equality, both fueled by *ressentiment*.[51]

The latter also appear in the so-called freethinkers whom Nietzsche considers levelers, "slaves of the democratic taste and its 'modern ideas,'" "without solitude," "unfree and ridiculously superficial." The latter is especially the case when they consider old institutions alone as the cause of all misery.[52] They are the proponents of what Zarathustra called "the Last Man": secure, healthy, and fed, whose work is pleasant diversion, huddling together, escaping with drugs, wallowing in "wretched contentment."[53] The Last Man lives for today. Nietzsche says, in the modern world "one lives very fast—one lives very irresponsibly: it is precisely this which one calls 'freedom.'"[54] Further, "*modern* freedom is degeneration; it doesn't know how to prune," that is, to order the chaos of appetites.[55] And "modern liberalism is reduction to the herd animal."[56] It has lost the instincts out of which institutions grow: "the will to tradition,

50. Nietzsche, *Daybreak*, II, 103.
51. Nietzsche, *Thus Spoke Zarathustra*, I, 9, 156–58; II, 7, 156–58; *Genealogy of Morals*, I, VII, 166–76.
52. Nietzsche, *Beyond Good and Evil*, §44, 54–55.
53. Nietzsche, *Thus Spoke Zarathustra*, I, 5, 128–31.
54. Nietzsche, *Twilight of the Idols*, IX, 39.
55. Ibid., XI, 41.
56. Ibid., IX, 38.

to authority, to centuries-long responsibility, to *solidarity* between succeeding generations backwards and forwards *in infinitum*. Roman Empire and Russia."[57] Maturity of free spirit is "self-mastery and discipline of the heart."[58]

What the image of *Prince Vogelfrei*, Prince Free-as-a-Bird, suggests is thus poles removed from Nietzsche's conception of the free spirit. Freedom of spirit can only be won through continual self-overcoming, through "going under." For Nietzsche, the nature of life is Will to Power, gathering power from the environment in order to create beyond the current state of things.[59] The current state has to "go under" so that something higher might appear. This is realized both in natural evolution and in human development, individually and socially. Freedom is not a given but an attainment, the result of hardness, discipline, and refinement. Freedom is the will to self-responsibility.[60] Freedom is measured "by the resistance which has to be overcome, by the effort it costs to stay *aloft*."[61]

Standing above what has appeared hitherto in history, at the antipodes of the Last Man, is the Overman. He would in many ways look like Goethe, the emancipated man: disciplined, self-possessed, integrated, from whose mouth wisdom flows. He would create a vision of the Whole that could encompass every view that ever appeared. Man as we know him, man as he has been, is a rope stretched from ape to this Overman.[62]

As Nietzsche sees it, reaching this height of freedom involves detachment from persons, fatherland, pity, science, and from one's own virtues, even from detachment itself.[63] Why the latter? Because detachment is only the negative side to attachment, attachment to the drive to create beyond oneself in such a way as to be aware of and to affirm the Whole. Striving in this way opens the path to the heights of the Overman.

Affirmation of the Whole is the function of Nietzsche's central notion of Eternal Recurrence of the Same. He focuses upon the present moment of choice aimed at the future and gives it infinite weight by pro-

57. Ibid., IV, 39.
58. Nietzsche, *Human All Too Human*, 7.
59. Nietzsche, *Beyond Good and Evil*, §259, 203.
60. But cf. Nietzsche, *Twilight of the Idols*, VI, 7: Free will is posited in order to produce guilt and for one to be able to judge and punish.
61. Nietzsche, *Twilight of the Idols*, IX, 38.
62. Nietzsche, *Thus Spoke Zarathustra*, I, 4, 126–27.
63. Nietzsche, *Beyond Good and Evil*, §41, 52; *Human All Too Human*, 6–10.

claiming the Eternal Recurrence of the Same. Standing at the moment, one chooses; but in choosing, one thinks of the same choice and its consequences reoccurring forever and ever: could one live with that? The thought of Eternal Return saves the chooser from recklessness. With regard to the past, one affirms that also, since the past is the future replayed and vice versa. One is free from the burden of the past by willing it.[64] For Nietzsche, Eternal Recurrence is a way of saying "yes" to being, "yes" to all, to suffering and exultation, to the Overman and even, in spite of nausea, to the Last Man.[65] In the vision of the Eternal Recurrence of the Same, every individual is a piece of fate, for nothing exists apart from the Whole.

Nietzsche's *amor fati* is directly parallel to Spinoza's intellectual love of the divine totality. The difference lies in the cool stoic resignation of Spinoza versus the ecstatic proclamations of Nietzsche. And the parallel is exhibited by the language: mathematical and precise in Spinoza, imagistic and celebratory in Nietzsche. Nietzsche's view finally involves a union of awareness with spontaneity expressed in dancing. Going under and going beyond is going up to secure a broader vision that will evoke celebratory singing and dancing. It will involve the unity of day wisdom with night wisdom, an alignment of control with spontaneity, of awareness with the unconscious wisdom of the body.[66]

ASSESSMENT

At this point, I want to append a few remarks by way of assessment. Nietzsche's Eternal Recurrence means that the sense of our choices as initiating something new is an illusion, release from which is recognition of one's choices having been made an infinite number of times in the past and destined to be made an infinite number of times in the future. The thought of Eternal Recurrence would not *really*, but only *seem* to, make a difference in how we choose. Whatever we do, it is only a repetition of an infinite past where our choice has appeared an infinite number of times. And here we meet Nietzsche's Spinozistic *amor fati*. Freedom, as in Spi-

64. Within a stoic view of a necessitated universe, Epictetus advises one to *will* the necessity.

65. Nietzsche, *Thus Spoke Zarathustra*, III, 13, 329–33.

66. Ibid., 15, 338–39; IV, 20, 433; I, 4, 146.

noza, requires the recognition of necessity, and recognition is the gift of necessity.

Both Spinoza and Hegel, for all their rationalism, have a place for that which exceeds our rational hold. For Spinoza, the infinite number of attributes beyond thought and extension creates an opening beyond the closure of his system. Nonetheless, it plays no role in the rest of his thought. For Hegel, so-called "Absolute Knowing" frees its possessor of partiality, but it is not omniscience; it is awareness of the coherent universal framework within which everything happens, an awareness of the conditions of possibility—psychological, historical, logical, and cosmic—for rational existence and flourishing. Not known is the future of scientific discovery, the creativity of human willing in the development of institutions and the creation of works of art, as well as the contingency that results from the interplay of all existent factors. The Beyond in both systems answers to Nietzsche's "night wisdom" that in him is rendered focal. It is a wisdom that puts one in relation to the totality beyond our rational hold. I suggest it is aligned with Nietzsche's union of our "little reason" with the "greater reason" of the body, a union of conscious and unconscious in the spontaneity of celebratory singing and dancing. Here one is indeed "free as a bird"—though it involves a freedom found through the shaping of appetites into an integral whole. But again, it is a freedom swallowed up in necessity, just as in Spinoza.

Hegel's advantage is that he grounds the freedom of choice as a real and not an illusory feature of our lives in precisely that relation to totality that is central in Spinoza and in Nietzsche. It lies in the function of that notion Nietzsche saw as irrelevant emptiness: the notion of Being central to the philosophic views of both Spinoza and Hegel, and, indeed, to the speculative tradition as such. Hegel shows the basis for taking over the potential chaos of one's life and giving it coherent shape: it lies in the self that can step back from its determinants and choose to give them rational form. Hegel shows the basis for a rational society centered upon full human freedom that Spinoza too envisioned but did not ground. Hegel shows the basis for the religious ascent to the eternal and encompassing as the realm of final freedom comprehended by philosophy.

As I said, for Hegel, what Absolute Knowing does not encompass is all that empirical science has and will uncover, all that individuals have and will choose to introduce. As correlate to the whole realm of individuals and species, it would seem to require not only Absolute Knowing but omniscience that Hegel ascribes to God. Here would be the Mystery that exceeds all rationality. Here would be that correlate to night knowledge that leads Nietzsche to the celebration of being.

But you do not find such celebration in Hegel or Spinoza. As his writing indicates, Spinoza is stone-cold sober. And even in his youth, Hegel was known as "the old man." They could use Nietzsche's enthusiasm, his alignment with the Dionysian that follows from having a central place for laughing, singing, and dancing, free as a bird, because one has aligned oneself—or finds oneself privileged to be aligned, in a disciplined way, with the overall order of things. Such is the truly free spirit.

16 ∾ Five Bodies and a Sixth

Awareness in an Evolutionary Universe

WHAT IS A BODY?

Nothing seems more evident than the nature of body. We apply the term "body" to what presents itself through the five senses: what can be seen, touched, smelt, heard, and tasted. It is what is extended, mobile, and resistant, appearing in various shapes and exhibiting the properties correlative to each of the senses. We ourselves are evidently bodies and we have to do always with bodies in our wakeful lives. But that does not settle the question of their nature—only how we ordinarily use the term and how we identify instances of it.

If we look over the history of thought, we can distinguish at least six different answers to the question "What is a body?" each taking its point of departure from identification of what we have come to call "bodies" within the sensory field. We can thus speak of a Hobbesian body, a Berkeleyan body, a Cartesian body, a Platonic body, an Aristotelian body, and a Leibnizian-Whiteheadian body. It is our contention that the sixth trumps the other five, while incorporating aspects of each of them.

Each of the views takes its point of departure from sensory experience in which we are given a distinction between what appears to sensing and sensing itself, which does not so appear. One can see colored objects, but one cannot *see* seeing, though one *knows* that one is seeing. Furthermore, recognition of an essential difference between, for example, seeing and hearing and between the objects and acts of seeing and hearing involves a capacity other than sensing, for sensing yields individual objects, but grasping essential differences yields features true of all objects that meet the respective definitions. That cognitive activity other than sensing is rooted in what we have come to call "intellect."

In raising the question "What is a body?" we are then involved in a necessary comparison between what appears to our sensory experience—an extended, mobile, resistant object identified as "body"—and what does not so appear, namely, the sensory and intellectual awareness of bodies. The various views of "body" are governed by how we construe the relation of our awareness to what we call "body."

FIVE BODIES

A Hobbesian Body

In his *De Corpore*, Thomas Hobbes presented a view of body that claimed to cover all of experience, the inner subject side and the outer object side.[1] Experience itself involves a *fantasm*, an appearance that in reality is a motion in the nervous system caused by the causal impact of effluents from other bodies upon that system, provoking the countermovement we call sensation. The brain acts as a kind of computing system, functioning, among other things, to arrange interior motions to produce the fantasms.[2] The fantasm is at best an epiphenomenon, a secondary phenomenon produced by motion in the nervous system—or identical with such motion (the status of the fantasm is not at all clear in Hobbes). Hobbes's position is out and out reductionism, recommending we consider the difference between awareness and sensorily given objects and between the levels of awareness distinguishable as sensation and intellection to be simply combinations of what is viewed in terms of the character of sensory objectivity.

Hobbes's reductionism is linked to a frequently accompanying thesis: universal mechanism. Bodies are explicable in terms of their component parts, and the combination of these parts is explicable through universal mechanical laws. The upshot is that there can be no taking over of causal mechanisms by a self-determining consciousness. Our self-direction as conscious agents is only apparent. In principle, it is wholly explicable by antecedent conditions.[3] Such a position underlies very much of what goes

1. See, for example, Thomas Hobbes, *Leviathan*, ed. Michael Oakeshott (New York: Collier, 1973), I, 4, 38: "A thing may enter into account for *matter* or *body*; as *living, sensible, rational, hot, cold, moved quiet*; with all such names the word *matter* or *body* is understood; all such being names of matter."
2. Thomas Hobbes, *Elementa philosophiae: De Corpore* (London: Crook, 1655), IV, 2; *Leviathan*, I, 1, 21 and 5, 41.
3. Hobbes, *Leviathan*, I, 6, 54. Human choice does not escape universal determinism: no action is voluntary; choice is simply "the last appetite in deliberating."

on in contemporary cognitive science. Observable brain mechanisms in principle can explain all of conscious life.[4]

A Berkeleyan Body

Berkeley stands at the pole opposite Hobbes: there is no body in Hobbes's sense, only minds and their relations.[5] When average persons think of a body, they think of a unity of colors, shapes, tastes, sounds, odors, and tactual properties. But what are these outside of relations to a perceiver? The being of the body lies in its relation to perception: its *esse* is *percipi*.[6] A Hobbesian or an Aristotelian would say that what underlies the perceptual relations is a material substratum. Berkeley asks for the evidence and claims that any evidence produced would be a relation to a perceiver, and that this constitutes the reality of what we call "matter" or "body." Besides this, there is *percipere et velle*, the passive perceiving and active willing by a subject of awareness.[7] Perceptual objects as relations to perceivers provide the field of operation for willing subjects. Far from being "peeping Toms," "strangers in a strange land" of foreign "matter," or isolated subject-brains receiving impressions from an indifferent outside world, perceivers and "willers" are in their world, that which is there expressly for them. Body is simply appearance to mind. Ultimately, bodies are God's addresses to human beings—or human beings addresses to one another.[8]

A Cartesian Body

At one level, René Descartes (d. 1650) is like Hobbes: underlying the *fantasms* of sensory experience is material substance. Basing himself upon the public exteriority of the body to all perception and upon the descriptive difference between such exteriority and the private interiority of awareness, Descartes considered awareness to be a substance in itself,

4. The vast majority of the papers assembled by David Rosenthal in *The Nature of Mind* (New York: Oxford University Press, 1991) make this assumption.

5. George Berkeley, *Three Dialogues Between Hylas and Philonous* (LaSalle: Open Court, 1945), I, 9, appeared in conjunction with his *The Principles of Human Knowledge* (Gloucester: Peter Smith, 1978).

6. Berkeley, *Three Dialogues Between Hylas and Philonous*, I, 154; III, 220.

7. George Berkeley, *Philosophical Commentaries, in The Works of George Berkeley, Bishop of Cloyne*, ed. A. Luce and T. Jessop, vol. 1 (London: Nelson, 1948), 429.

8. Berkeley, *Three Dialogues Between Hylas and Philonous*, II, 198.

clearly both distinguished and separated from—though intimately connected with—the body.[9] The essence of the body for Descartes is extension, mathematical measurability.[10] The sensory properties we observe
are really effects in consciousness of the impact of the extensive properties of outside bodies upon our nervous system. Such effects in consciousness bear no necessary resemblance to the actual things.[11] Bodies
are drained of the features we observe through each of the senses, and
these features are then relocated in the interiority of awareness where
the illusion of exteriority is produced. Our own bodies produce in us
various kinds of desires—hunger, thirst, sexual desire—and the pleasure
and pain associated with them, which are evoked by peculiar patterns of
the inwardly experienced effects we call color, sound, taste, smell, and
tactual properties (heat, hardness, heaviness, roughness, wetness, and
their opposites) as well as the imaginings derived from these. The production of the sensory field serves the needs of the organism.[12] Besides,
this awareness entails the ability to imagine, recognize clear and distinct
ideas, judge, choose, and remember both those regions of experience derived from association with the body and those not so derived.[13] Where
Hobbes's materialism leaves no possibility of the human awareness lasting beyond the dissolution of the body, both Berkeley's and Descartes'
views open up that possibility.

A Platonic Body

For Plato (d. ca. 348 B.C.), the term "body" included the exteriority of
what we might call "meat" and the interiority of sensation and bodily
based desire. The *Phaedo* speaks of the mind being imprisoned in the
body and the *Republic* refers to the mind's being buried in the body as
in a bog of mud that Plato associates here with the physiologically based
passions.[14] "Body" thus had a kind of interior dimension beyond the
overtness of sensory observation. "Soul" in this context was mind (*nous*)
as the power of reflection that is capable of backing off from sensation

9. René Descartes, *Meditations on First Philosophy*, in *The Philosophical Works of Descartes*, trans. E. Haldane and G. Ross, vol. II (New York: Dover, 1955), II, 153; VI, 192 and 196.
All references are to the *Meditations on First Philosophy*.

10. Ibid., I, 146–47; II, 154–55; VI, 185.   11. Ibid., VI, 191.
12. Ibid., VI, 194.   13. Ibid., II, 153.
14. Plato, *Phaedo*, 62b, 82e; *Republic*, X, 611d.

and biological desire, laying hold of the *eide*, the Forms or essential features involved in our situation, and thus capable of reorganizing our interior and exterior lives. While embodied, soul is not recognizable, like the sea-god Glaucus covered by barnacles and seaweed.

Whereas in the *Phaedo* and the *Republic* Plato has Socrates present the body as foreign to the soul, in the *Timaeus* he has Timaeus present it as the *house* of the soul, a place made for the soul in which the soul is meant to live.[15] Nonetheless, as with Berkeley and Descartes, the split between mind and body—even though differently conceived—opens up the possibility of immortality.[16]

An Aristotelian Body

For Aristotle (d. ca. 323 B.C.), "body" was a relative term, correlative to the kind of organizing principle operative in it. "Soul" is the basic formal, efficient, and final cause determining the kind of process that a living being is and organizing the elements for the sake of reaching the immanent ends of the process.[17] What is involved in living processes are not two things, a body and a soul, but a single psycho-physical process related as organized to organizer and user. If in Plato's *Timaeus* the body is the house of the soul, for Aristotle through its nutritive power the soul builds and sustains its own house for the sake of the release of its higher powers through the provision of organic instruments. In commenting upon Aristotle's view here, Hegel said that soul is related to body, not as one thing to another but as a universal to its particulars.[18] Hegel used the expression "concrete universal" here to designate the pervasion of the individual organic parts by the soul, in contrast to the "abstract universal" involved in the grasp of essential distinctions.

The psychical is differentiated into three types, graduated from lower to higher in accordance with degrees of "remotion from matter": a vegetative, a sensient, and a rational type. In successively higher types of life,

---

15. Plato, *Timaeus*, 69d, 70e, and 72d.

16. Plato, *Phaedo*, 64c ff; synopsis to *Meditations on First Philosophy*, 141, where Descartes claims he will establish the bases from which immortality may be deduced; Berkeley, *The Principles of Human Knowledge*, §141, 136f.

17. Aristotle, *On the Soul*, II, 415b 10.

18. G. W. F Hegel, *Philosophy of Mind*, trans. W. Wallace and A. Miller (Oxford: Clarendon Press, 1971), §389, *Zusatz*, 33.

the higher presupposes the lower as the "material" for its functioning.[19] What we are observing when we see the body of a living being is the operation of its soul in forming and sustaining the elements as a functioning organic system or in perceiving, desiring, and moving toward an object of desire; or in automatically expressing one's disposition through one's habitual comportment; or in expressing one's understanding and deliberate intentions. Nonetheless, there is a lower level of elements from which living processes derive the materials of their self-formation. They are simply "matter" and "mere body."[20]

THE SIXTH BODY

A Leibnizian Body

Leibniz's view of body is derived by arguing from two directions: on the one hand from the notion of complex bodies and on the other from the nature of awareness. First, then, what we observe are complex bodies, but the complex presupposes the simple. However, one can always divide any alleged extended simple—at least theoretically, so that the ultimate theoretical simples would no longer be extended but pure qualitative points— "ones" or what he called "monads."[21] Secondly, sensory awareness involves *petites perceptions*, "little perceptions" that are no longer even matters of awareness. *Petites perceptions* entail what might seem to be paradoxical: unconscious perception. The sound of each drop of water, though imperceptible in itself at a distance, combines with others to produce the roar of the waterfall.[22] The notion reappears in contemporary psychology in the concept of subliminal perception. Awareness involves "apperception" as co-awareness of things and of awareness itself. In reflective knowers, it also involves "comprehension," as the ability to grasp eternal truths. Leibniz extends the notion of perception downward to

19. Aristotle, *On the Soul*, II, 415a 1.

20. Aristotle, *Metaphysics*, 1028b 10, 1044a 15. For a comprehensive sketch of Aristotle's thought, see chapter 8 in my *A Path into Metaphysics: Phenomenological, Hermeneutical, and Dialogical Studies* (Albany: State University of New York Press, 1991).

21. *Monadology*, §1–3, in Leibniz, *The Monadology and Other Philosophical Writings*, ed. R. Latta (London: Oxford University Press, 1951), 217–18. Unless otherwise indicated, references are to the *Monadology*.

22. Ibid., §21, 9. 230; "New Essays on Human Understanding," in *The Monadology and Other Philosophical Writings*, 371 ff.

318 Awareness in an Evolutionary Universe

the ultimate simples of his "exterior" analysis, so that, considered "from within," the monad is comprised of "perceptions and appetitions."[23]

He further argues that in order that each thing be, it must be com-possible with all the rest, and that this compossibility constitutes its very being. Hence, each monad mirrors the Whole from its perspective.[24] Further, it passes through differing relations to the Whole, driven by its innate appetites.[25] Each monad is thus constituted internally as percep-tion and appetition, that is, as modeled, in a way diametrically oppo-site to Hobbes, on awareness. Those who either reduce all to matter or view matter in the form it takes in sensory appearance are dealing with *phenomena bene fundata*, with well-founded, that is, empirically verifi-able *appearances*; but appearances have to be understood as correlative to the kind of awareness to which they appear. What we have in immedi-ate sensory experience are not "things in themselves" but things as exter-nally related to organic percipients with eyeballs, eardrums, and tactual sensors.[26] However, underlying all external appearance is the inner real-ity of things as perception and appetition.[27]

A Whiteheadian Body

These Leibnizian notions appear again in Alfred North Whitehead but against the background of evolutionary theory where, as a result of em-pirical inquiry rather than a priori argumentation, they gain anoth-er ground. We begin with a distinction between awareness and its ob-jects, which we call "material" objects. But, granted evolution, what is called "material" is an early stage of a developmental process that sup-plies factual conditions for the emergence of different functional capaci-ties, including awareness. We know what something is when we discover what comes out of it (e.g., a fertilized ovum shows what it is in potential-ity when we watch it actually grow into a functional adult). An exhaus-tive empirical inspection of the fertilized ovum will yield nothing of its potentialities for future development into a reflectively conscious adult

23. Leibniz, *Monadology*, §14–15, 224–26.
24. Ibid., §56–57, 248.
25. Ibid., §60, 250.
26. "De modo distinguendi phenomena realia ab imaginariis," in *The Monadology and Other Philosophical Writings*, 99.
27. See chapter 12 on Leibniz in my *Path into Metaphysics*.

(which makes it easy to treat it as on a par with other low-level functioning individuals).[28]

Evolutionary theory maintains that ontogeny recapitulates phylogeny: the development of the individual organism recapitulates the chronological phases of the development of the phylum or the general biological class to which it belongs. But since we have no means of knowing whether the phylogenetic process is at an end, we cannot say for sure what "matter" and thus "body" ultimately are except the potentiality to produce what comes out of them combined with what is observable.[29] If awareness emerges from so-called "matter," then "matter" is not simply nonliving and nonconscious but *preliving* and *preconscious*. Hence, Whitehead speaks not only of "apprehension" and "comprehension" as conscious acts but of "prehension" as the ultimate character of the "material" base from which awareness emerges. The basic particles "prehend" the objects of their specific powers.[30] The variations in the character of consciousness are emergent properties that require certain empirically discernible conditions for their emergence, just as the developed eyeball and nervous system are the empirically discernible conditions for the emergence of actual seeing.

This view does not entail the absurd position that an atom or a rock or a bone could think. The potentiality for the higher levels does not inhere in the individuals as individuals but in the relational systems, the interlocking combinations of individuals. The individuals have the innate potentialities for combination—chemical valence bonds—from which the new properties emerge. The early stages of the cosmos exhibit random mixings of elements until the sequence is met that unlocks the latent potentialities for progressively higher emergent properties.

Whitehead remarks that, since we have no means of knowing whether there will be still higher levels of emergence in the future, our inferential knowledge of "matter" is never completed and we are always "in between." This requires a simultaneous modification of what we mean by "mind" and what we mean by "matter." On the one hand, one might say

28. Alfred North Whitehead, *Science and the Modern World* (New York: Free Press, 1957), 39–55 and 100ff.
29. Alfred North Whitehead, *Process and Reality: An Essay in Cosmology* (New York: Harper, 1957), II, IV, V, 181–82.
30. Whitehead, *Process and Reality*, I, I, 28–29, developed in III, 329 ff.

that this view "materializes" mind, but on the other hand, we could say that it "spiritualizes" or "re-minds" matter. Thus spirit "matters."[31]

REFLECTIONS

There are three different sets of emergent properties ontogenetically and phylogenetically.[32] The first are those proper to a self-formative, self-sustaining, self-repairing, and self-reproducing organism. First, there has to emerge systematically functional wholes that replicate themselves. At the levels beyond the one-celled forms, such replication occurs both inside itself in the form of cells and organs, and outside itself in the form of others like itself. The potentiality for the initial formation of such controlling wholes lies in the relational properties of the elements. No element exists simply "in itself" as one might imaginatively picture a single atom. Each has a set of potentialities for acting and being acted upon that entail specific relations to the kinds of things that answer to those powers. Each exists as part of a system. What the potentialities are can only be discerned, not by an immediate empirical inspection but by inference from observing the kinds of relations into which a given element can enter and the kinds of behavior that follow from that.[33]

The second level of emergent properties clusters around sensory awareness as a correlation of awareness and desire, focused upon a correlation of various manifest aspects of things over time. This is tied to self-propulsion in the direction of what appears as the beneficial and away from what appears as harmful to the organism.

The third level of emergence is that of reflective awareness that is able to discern essential distinctions and thus to abstract from the here and now, the particular time and place, of what is given in sensation as such. It is able to combine such abstractions, make inferences, and choose from among the possibilities presented through inference. Whereas sensation always delivers the individual and actual, reflection discerns the

31. See chapter 15 on Whitehead in my *Path into Metaphysics*.
32. For a further development of these notions, see my "Potentiality, Creativity, and Relationality: Creative Power of a 'New' Transcendental?" *The Review of Metaphysics* 59, no. 2 (December 2005): 379–401.
33. See my "Individuals, Universals, and Capacity," *The Review of Metaphysics* 54, no. 3 (March 2001).

universal and possible and opens the possibilities for choice. Both intellection and choice are made possible by the reflective distance from
the immediately given environment, a distance provided by the notion
of Being. That notion makes the human mind a mind by referring us to
the encompassing Whole, to the cosmos and its ground, for all that is
is contained within Being and outside Being there is nothing.[34] Such reference grounds the questions lying at the background of all our experience: What's it *all* about? What is the place of human existence in the
whole scheme of things? What is the whole scheme of things? Religious
and philosophical cosmologies are attempts to answer these questions.

It is the irreducibility of these three sets of properties exhibited by
organic life, sensory awareness, and reflective awareness upon which the
Aristotelian view is based. Each requires soul as the principle of controlling wholeness, and each requires a different kind of soul than the others, though the higher presuppose and subsume the lower. Aristotle em-
phatically rejects evolution, even though it was proposed by Empedocles,
based upon his observations of fossil levels in the quarries at Syracuse.
Aristotle's basis is the claim that like only produces like and that devia-
tions die out rather than reproduce their like.[35] "Mere bodies" remain
as the elemental basis from which organic bodies are produced by the
offspring of adult organisms. Evolutionary theory, based upon a vastly
wider range of empirical evidence than Aristotle was able to command,
pushes the potentialities of the soul back into "mere bodies," elevating
them to the level of the psychic *in potentia*. If we have to modify our view
of mind by seeing it as emergent from so-called "matter," we have no less
to modify our view of mere matter by seeing it as potentially minded.[36]

Hobbesian reductionism is based upon explaining away our own
self-conscious activity. The Cartesian view accepts the phenomenology
of consciousness but explains away the empirical presentation of animal
awareness and organic holism as mere external combinations within na-

34. On the notion of Being, see Bernard Lonergan, *Insight: A Study of Human Understanding* (London: Longman, Green, 1957), 348 ff.

35. Aristotle, *Physics*, trans. P. Wicksteed and F. Cornford (Cambridge, Mass.: Harvard
University Press, 1980), II, 8. On Empedocles, see G. Kirk and J. Raven, *The Presocratic Philosophers* (Cambridge: Cambridge University Press, 1966), 336 ff.

36. One of the most comprehensive treatments of this view is in Errol Harris, *The Foundations of Metaphysics in Science* (Lanham, Md.: University Press of America, c. 1983).

ture as an overall extended matrix of mindless, nonliving material with the potentiality only for mechanical combinations.

We need to come to terms with a common claim that the effect can be no greater than the cause. Well, in evolution we have evidence that, in the way it is too often understood, the claim is false. But in evolution, the cause is not any individual type of entity but peculiar and specific kinds of *relations* to sets of individuals operative at a lower level, through which relations the powers latent in the earlier phases emerge into actuality as selves of various hierarchically scaled sorts.

What we need is a quasi-Aristotelian potency-act view, with souls as emergent powers from a low level of preliving and preconscious, not simply nonliving and nonconscious functioning. The difference between ontogeny and phylogeny is that the former begins with an already-formed whole separated from other things, whereas the latter begins with a vast multiplicity from which such ontogenetic individuals are to emerge. The potencies for such emergence lie in the whole system rather than in a given individual.

Emergent out of animal awareness, human awareness is able to grasp eidetic distinctions because it is referred to the encompassing whole of Being beyond the organic needs that sustain its lower levels of operation. It is that reference that leads it to inquire into the conditions for the possibility of there being a universe with the properties observed in it. But human awareness can develop its inquiry only on the basis of the relationality of social systems, beginning with language that allows the passing on of discoveries over generations. As the potentialities immanent in the earliest phases of the universe can only emerge through the peculiarities of relational systems, so the potentialities immanent in the human gene pool can only emerge through the peculiarities of the relational systems proper to human beings: linguistic, social, economic, political, artistic, religious, scientific, and philosophic.

In an evolutionary universe, body and soul, matter and mind have to be understood as dialectical poles in a hierarchically developing set of systems. Mind is no stranger in a strange land, a Peeping Tom in an alien universe, but the self-presence of the evolutionary whole given over to itself as the creator of cognitive systems that display and practical systems that transform what is present to an essentially embodied awareness.

On an evolutionary view of things, our understanding of body and of awareness has each to be modified in relation to the other. They are always given as other—as subject and as object, each with radically different modes of appearance. But they are not different *things*; rather they are different sequentially appearing phases. Being is that which underpins both body and awareness as its two aspects. Body is a lower phase of a developmental process of which sensory and reflective awareness are the higher and highest phases. Body in its lowest and earliest phases is not nonliving and nonconscious but preliving and preconscious. As Schelling would have it, Being splits into the outwardness of body and the inwardness of awareness so that Being not only can *be* but can also be *manifest.*[37] Reflective awareness, exhibited especially by the scientist, is the self-manifestation of the evolving universe. The whole of nature involves an at least implicit inwardness directed toward the self-presence of the Whole in developing human awareness as the cutting edge of an evolving universe.

What is a body? Something more than the appearance in which it shows itself through the selective filters of sensation, something whose essence we are tempted to view as identical with its mode of appearance. To use the language of German idealism, body and the matter that comprise it are implicitly spirit.

37. Friedrich Wilhelm Joseph von Schelling, *System des transzendentalen Idealismus, Schriften von 1799–1801* (Darmstadt: Wissenschaftliche Buchgesellschaft, 1982), 607.

17 ∽ The Phenomenologists

What is Phenomenology? Externally considered, it is a philosophical movement that originated in Germany at the turn of the nineteenth into the twentieth century, found its classic inspiration in the sustained work of Edmund Husserl, and developed in differing ways in thinkers like Max Scheler, Martin Heidegger, Jean-Paul Sartre, and Merleau-Ponty, more recently in Paul Ricoeur and Hans-Georg Gadamer and most recently in figures like Jean-Luc Marion. It continues to have wide impact in such diverse areas as the philosophy of physical science and mathematics, psychology, psychiatry, sociology, legal theory, economics, history, literature, political science, linguistics, anthropology, aesthetics, and religion.

A consideration of the etymology or root meanings of the term used to describe the movement will provide preliminary orientation with respect to its internal meaning. Its two components are the Greek derivatives *phainomenon* and *logos*, which mean, roughly, "appearance" and "essence," respectively. Etymologically considered, then, phenomenology is an attempt to focus upon the essential features of the way in which things appear. Phenomena or appearances have to be understood in contrast to realities or things-in-themselves. The focus here is on things making their appearance before consciousness, that is, entering into the light of awareness. Thus, phenomenology attends to the relation between things and consciousness. The focus on *logos*, or essence, has to be understood in contrast to a focus on individuals. As any science, phenomenology searches out the universal, essential features that apply to all individuals of a given kind. Just as science is interested in individuals only as specimens of the general laws of structure and functioning that apply to the species in question, to its subspecies, higher genera and beyond, so also phenomenology as a science is interested in individuals only insofar as they afford insight into essence, or *eidos* (Greek for essence but emphasizing "that which is seen").

EDMUND HUSSERL (1859–1938)

These considerations can be amplified by considering the situation in philosophy that Husserl confronted when he first set out on his phenomenological journey. Alternative speculative theories about the ultimate nature of reality and man's place in it had been warring for ages but were divided in a particularly sharp way at the turn of the century. The starkest contrast among these alternatives was between so-called "materialism" and so-called "idealism"—so-called because there are variations upon each of these themes, from the naive to the sophisticated. Again, for purposes of orientation, we might say that materialisms tend to claim that reality is ultimately what we can perceive through our senses, and that so-called mental and spiritual dimensions are to be explained in terms of this. Conversely, idealisms rest on the fact that what we know is, after all, what we know and is thus part of our field of awareness. They then claim that perceptible objects are ultimately to be explained in terms of the reality of knowledge and of the mind that knows and feels and wills.

A third development, strong at the turn of the century and significant for phenomenology's beginning, was a kind of irrational protest against both materialistic and idealistic claims. The movement, called *Lebensphilosophie*, or life philosophy, had its historical roots in Arthur Schopenhauer (1788–1860) and Friedrich Nietzsche (1844–1900) and its turn-of-the-century expression in thinkers like Henri Bergson (1859–1941) in France and Wilhelm Dilthey (1833–1911) in Germany. According to these thinkers, all rational forms—whether materialistically or idealistically conceived—are secondary expressions of the underlying vitality that generates them. "Life" calls forth different expressions at different historical times and places and in different individuals, but there are no ultimate rational forms. Life itself is the unfathomable abyss that mysteriously produces individuals and cultures. When the focus is on the individual, this position involves what is often referred to as psychologism; when the focus upon cultures, it is called historicism or cultural relativism.

Husserl stood opposed both to the "ultimate claim" theories of materialism and idealism, and to the dissolution of rational forms in historical and psychological processes by life philosophy. Against the former, he called for a suspension or bracketing or *epoche* of ultimate claims in order to attend to the common ground in which all claims are rooted.

This common ground is the way in which things present themselves in consciousness, the way they appear in experience. Whatever reality ultimately is, since no consensus is forthcoming on that question, let us pay closer attention to "the facts themselves," to the actual modes of presentation that we can describe, to the "phenomena."

But if we can hold in abeyance the tendency toward speculation—no longer so difficult today since its roots in religion and general culture have largely withered—we still have to contend with the movement, which today is more powerful than ever, toward the relativism and subjectivism involved in life philosophy. Description of the immediately given might appeal to its proponents, but for Husserl more was required. Life philosophy repudiates the roots of the great rational tradition that lies at the base of Western philosophy and science alike. Life philosophy gives up on an objectively discernible structure to reality that is common to all disinterested observers. Life philosophy gives up on the *logos*, the essential structure of reality.

In a preliminary way, then, phenomenology might be defined as a method of describing the common essential features (not the subjective, individual peculiarities) of reality as it presents itself in experience (not of "ultimate reality"). But one of the interesting things about Husserl's development is that attending to the essence of phenomena will generate a position that will decisively repudiate materialism and reinstate idealism, and that will ultimately show the primacy of the *Lebenswelt*, or lifeworld, over all the rational structures we perceive and/or construct on its basis.

Before he developed his phenomenology, Husserl had been a student of mathematics and an assistant to the great mathematician Karl Weierstrass. Husserl wrote his first book, *Philosophy of Arithmetic*, in 1891. But under the criticism of the logician Gottlob Frege, he began to see that his approach, common in the late nineteenth century when he wrote and very much alive today, did not actually allow for the objectivity of mathematical science but reduced it to a set of psychological acts. His next work, *Logical Investigations* (1900–1901), was considered by Bertrand Russell, one of the fathers of contemporary analytical philosophy, to be one of the great classics in logic. Husserl spent two large volumes showing, among other things, the objectivity of logical and mathematical principles, their "objection" to being explained in terms of individual psychological acts. The problem here is the failure of an individual-psychological explanation to account for the universality and necessity that impose themselves upon the mind in mathematics and in logic. Psychologism is one variation on the general tendency of empiricism (from the Greek *empeiria*, "experience") to claim that reality is the sum total of individual facts. The classic paradox of such a position is its inability to account for itself, for as a universal claim, it itself is more than an individual fact and bears witness to universal meaning. From an exploration of the objectivity of mathematical and logical structures, Husserl went on, especially in the three volumes of his *Ideas* (only one volume of which was published in his lifetime, in 1913), to extend his investigations to the whole field of the ways different types of objects present themselves to consciousness and the differing ways in which consciousness is correlated to these objects.

But being a philosopher who was drawn into philosophy through his mathematical studies, Husserl placed himself in the line of thinking stemming from René Descartes (1596–1650), the discoverer of analytical geometry (recall the Cartesian coordinates) and the father of modern philosophy. One of Husserl's later attempts at clarifying the nature of phenomenology explicitly dealt with meditations modeled on Descartes, appropriately titled *Cartesian Meditations* (1929). Comparison with Descartes will lead us to clarify certain significant aspects of Husserl's thought.

Like Husserl, Descartes was concerned with a fresh start vis-à-vis the competing speculative claims of his time. Inspired by the rigorous evidence of mathematics, Descartes sought a similar evidentiality for philosophy. To see if he could find absolutely indubitable evidences, his initial methodological move was *radical doubt*, deliberately putting out of play everything but what could survive the wildest possible supposition, such as the existence of an "evil genius" giving me my experiences or "painting them on the dome of my intelligence," to employ Emerson's graphic image. What survived such doubt was thinking itself. I might be deceived about the hand in front of my face: perhaps I am dreaming or pathologically deluded. But even supposing this to be the case, I am necessarily present to myself in my very thinking of that hand: "I think, therefore I am" (*Cogito ergo sum*). And there is no conceivable act of thinking that could fail to show forth that necessary self-presence.

Husserl was convinced that in the *cogito* Descartes had discovered something essential to the development of philosophy as a strict science, beyond speculative constructions. But Descartes had likewise confused the issue with his own speculative constructions as to the ultimate nature of God, the world, and the self, which thinks and acts. The recognition of the imperfection of his own fallible thinking implied the notion of perfection. And from the presence of the notion of perfection in the *cogito*, Descartes thought he could deduce the existence of God as a nondeceptive guarantor of responsible thinking. Responsible thinking, however, turned out to be the mathematical physical thinking that Descartes himself, together with contemporaries such as Galileo, was developing: a science that reduced the physical world to pure measurability. Descartes drained the objects in ordinary experience of their apparent sensible qualities and made these qualities part of the study of mind. Colors, for example, are not "outside" as aspects of real things; what is "real" is only wavelengths, only regular, measurable motions. Perceived color is an effect produced in the mind by "reality." The human body having been submitted to a similar interpretation, the human person is then split into an extended, measurable mechanism on the one hand and a mind externally conjoined to the body mechanism on the other. Such considerations have very much affected thought in physics, physiology, and psychology, even to this day.

Husserl refused to follow such constructive substitutes for experience. In the search for rigorous evidence, Descartes had made a significant move through his methodic doubt. He had attained an indubitable evidence through intuition, through immediate presence, responsibly arrived at, in the *cogito*. But he immediately proceeded to muddy the waters with his speculative constructions. With a modification of the doubt and an extended employment of intuition, Husserl claimed to enter a new mental landscape that Descartes saw only confusedly.

My hand in front of my face—for which practically nothing is more evident for common sense—may be a phantom created in my mind by an evil genius. But it still has a clearly discernible structure of appearance, a mode of presenting itself to consciousness that exhibits certain necessary features. Were we to employ the *epoche* and bracket or put out of play not only speculative constructions but also what Husserl calls "the thesis of the natural standpoint" (the spontaneous belief in the reality of the normal deliverances of awareness), we could then rigorously attend to the essential features of the presence to consciousness even of ordinary objects. The thesis of the natural standpoint itself could then become the object of reflective investigation. Then necessary givenness would attach not only to the bare *cogito* but also to the necessary features of the differing types of objects present to the *cogito*. Phenomenology will seek to confront intuitively both the object-types and the differing modes of adhesion of consciousness to its objects. With the natural standpoint put out of play, the content attended to is reduced to the mode of its appearing before consciousness. Hence, the move here is called the *phenomenological reduction*.

As we have previously indicated, Husserl is seeking to establish philosophy as a strict science, and every science is on the hunt for essences. But we must distinguish between, on the one hand, empirical laws or factual connections that are repeatedly verified in experience but are open to falsification by further experience and, on the other hand, a priori laws or universal structures that are presupposed by and revealed in the very character of the experience. It is these universal structures, necessarily given, that are the objects of phenomenological investigation. For example, that red succeeds green regularly in the leaf of one species of oak during autumn is a kind of empirical law, at least thinkable as not being confirmed in all instances. But that color can only be given as adhering in some kind of extension, and as exhibiting a certain hue, brightness, and saturation, that the leaf can be given only in perspectives that call out in their mode of being given for supplementation by other perspectives, and that all this can be given only in some sort of temporal order, are eidetic invariants, necessary, essential, given as true in all instances without any thinkable falsifiability. Husserl sees a parallel here with the mathematical and logical forms that were the objects of his initial attention as a philosopher. The properties of a triangle in geometry, the square of opposition, and the law of excluded middle in logic are not given through empirical generalization and are not open to falsification through further experience. They are immediately present in an eidetic intuition as both universal and necessary. The Cartesian *cogito* is another such evidence, for its indubitability is not merely another particular fact about my consciousness but a necessary truth about any conceivable consciousness.

The move here from individual objects to essences is called *eidetic reduction*, and the path to the essences is through imaginative variation. The empirical individual, either given in sense experience or constructed in the imagination, is considered as one possible instance of the *eidos* in question. One imaginatively varies the different features of this instance to discover what remains necessarily present through all the instances. He will discover in this way those variations that will lead to a change in the *eidos* as distinct from those that lead simply to another possible typical instance within the limits of the *eidos*. In this way, what pertains to this essence is brought to immediate evidence in intuition. Admission of the intuitive presence of essential evidences implies a broader notion of experience than some of the traditional forms of empiricism were willing to admit. Husserl speaks here of a *radical empiricism*.

Husserl's intuitive method should not be confused with the common connection of the term "intuition" as some extraordinary or even mystical capacity. The clue for intuitive procedure is rather the way we arrive at definitions in geometry or logic. "Intuitive" here has the meaning of immediate, direct, or evidential and is to be contrasted with the indirect, the inferred, or the supposed. Every claim must rest ultimately on some immediate presentation that is itself certain and from which one might proceed by way of inference or construction to the nonevidential. Even the structure of inference by means of which one attempts to move beyond the immediately present is open to evidential intuition. Those who object to the priority of intuition in this sense by reason of the claim that every "given" is mediated by language either have evidence in their favor or they do not. If they do not, then they need not be taken seriously; if they do, they are on Husserl's side and have implicitly rejected their own claim. The truth-value of such intuitive deliverances is rooted in the fundamental character of consciousness, which reveals the eidetic structure of objects as they necessarily present themselves. The whole phenomenological region involves a self-gathered subject standing at a certain "inward distance" from its objects, which are thereby opened up to the subject. Every act of awareness is of or about something, or, technically expressed, is *intentional*. That is to say that the subject, at least in an implicit way, becomes aware of itself in the very act wherein it reveals the other. We might see this by considering a set of contrasts.

Spontaneously, the famous man on the street accepts immediate experience as objective, that is, objects are "out there," other than himself, and are just what they appear to be. But when asked to account for the way in which he comes to know things "out there" and the nature of his awareness, he tends to look for explanations along the lines of factors that can be displayed as sensory objects. Proceeding further along the same lines, the scientist shows the basis for such knowledge in the registration of wave impulses upon receptor organs that electronically transmit these "messages" to the brain where "at point X" they are interpreted by the brain and awareness occurs.

Up to this point, nothing whatsoever has been said of awareness. What is this awareness that allegedly occurs "at point X" in the brain? Some have maintained that awareness is nothing but an electronic activity of the nervous system. Such an attempt involves itself in a contradiction and reveals another case, following the lines laid down by Descartes, of a construction imposed upon, not given in experience. To claim that there really are such things as waves coming from light sources and being reflected from visual objects, that there really are optic and cerebral structures, and simultaneously to claim that awareness is exclusively an intracerebral event leaves us with no basis for knowing whether there is even such a thing as a brain or visual objects or light waves, for the ground upon which we could know the reality-status of such things is their givenness as other than the awareness that observes them. Therefore, the knower must be endowed with a structure of transcendence, that is, an ability to "leap beyond" that in himself which is accessible to sensory observation and which we are wont to call "the body."

Ordinary language usage reveals that we do implicitly grasp this situation. Suppose someone were to burst into the room crying, "I'm aware! I'm aware!" but when asked "Of what?" were to reply, "Oh, of nothing. I'm just aware!" That would make little sense and we would be left floundering. Similarly, to claim to see but to see nothing, to have an idea but not an idea about anything, makes no linguistic sense. Likewise, if one were to ask what a sensorily given object, such as a stone, is of or about, the would-be respondent is left suspended. Things appearing as objects of the senses are, as such, just what they are; they are not of or about anything. Consciousness, by contrast, is not what it is unless it is of or about something; it always intends another to which it is intrinsically and necessarily related. This is so to such a degree that consciousness is inclined to overlook its own nature and even to fall into the trap of conceiving itself on the model of sensory objects.

That the sensorily appearing other be revealed as other, consciousness must be implicitly manifest to itself as the term contrasted to that other. What appears sensorily is other than the consciousness that makes it manifest. But the self-manifestation of consciousness is in an entirely different mode than its manifestation of a sensory other. If the sensory object is the theme of attention, the conscious self is given in a prethematic mode: hence, its inclination to overlook its own nature. Consciousness, then, does not reveal itself as a container into which experiences are poured or a machine that processes information, or even as an observable brain that performs functions described by such images. As far as clarifying the nature of consciousness is concerned, these images are constructions, useful for certain purposes but self-contradictory and misleading if taken for anything but useful fictions in this regard.

When we try to probe further the nature of consciousness as it now presents itself, we find a kind of flowing stream, moving out of the past and into the future, a stream in which all sorts of contents advance and recede, struggle and disappear. As I now attempt to write, my attention is drawn by a fan droning in the background. A tree toad buzzes annoyingly outside. My attention is further drawn to a still-warm coffee cup on my desk, in the midst of a large variety of somewhat cluttered odds and ends. I feel a slight sticky, itchy discomfort from the heat. I remember that I was up early this morning with hay fever, and I am reminded of the hollow feeling in my sinus cavities several minutes after taking medication. Dreams of a placid few hours of fishing this coming evening play around invitingly in the back of my mind, along with an anxious anticipation of some galley proofs a month overdue that might be in the mail today. But a sense of quiet pervades it all as I think by contrast of my children who will burst in on me from school in two short hours. The variety of sounds, the multiplicity of visual objects, the recollections and anticipations, the discomforts, the anxieties and satisfactions: all flow and tumble together, jostling for attention in the stream that is my conscious life.

And yet what pulls consciousness out of its confusion and temptation to self-absorption, giving some solidity and direction and order to the stream, is the hard structure of objects. In spite of the confused flow of the stream of awareness, I can return again and again to the varying objects in relation to which my awareness flows. Each time a given object yields a perspective, a profile is set up by the interplay between the object and my position. But each profile points to still others that are related in a systematic way so that I can pass from one to the other and return again and again to the same object after many differing experiences have flowed by. Visual experience confirms, corrects, and extends visual experience; audile and tactile images gradually cohere with one another, grow, and supplement the expanding visual experiences.

Guiding the differing ways in which the objects cohere one with another are the differing types of poses consciousness can take in revealing the object modalities. A pragmatic pose yields one set of profiles on the object; an aesthetic pose yields another; a scientific pose reveals yet other aspects; a philosophic approach shows something further, while a religious attitude displays still another dimension. But all perspectives coalesce in the object, and all approaches cohere in the system of possibilities for the conscious subject—though each coherence occurs in an open way. The object presents itself in each of its given aspects as exceeding each of them and containing aspects yet to be revealed. Consciousness thus *constitutes* its objects, builds them up through the process of coalescing aspects that continues throughout the temporal span of conscious life. But this building up of the object-for-consciousness points to the thing itself as what Husserl terms the "internal horizon" of the object, ever receding before the constitutive power of consciousness. Thus, in intending a given object, consciousness has both an "empty intention" of the whole of the thing itself and a partially and progressively "filled intention" constituted from its past and present experience.

In addition to the givenness of the internal horizon, there is also the presence of an external horizon. As a visual object, the oak tree whose leaves we alluded to earlier only appears as an object of focus against the background that surrounds it and is related for consciousness to the object as fringe to focus. The background fades out into the distance of the spatial horizon that itself recedes as we approach it, pointing beyond itself to the indeterminate spread of space within which all objects are embedded. Further, the object, its environing objects, the perceiver, and the spatial horizon conjointly appear within a time spread that points to a double horizon: the indeterminately receding past and the indeterminately approaching future. Perceptual objects then necessarily appear within both internal and external horizons.

But the notion of horizon also extends beyond the various aspects of the perceptual situation to the interpretative frameworks within which the perceptual object is understood. At this moment, the perceptual object before you is seen as a page in a book. But page and book are concepts whose intentional structure points, on the one hand, beyond this particular page and book to all actual and possible pages and books, and, on the other hand, to the interrelated set of meanings that comprise the thematic field or world of communication within which pages and books and you and I, as now indirectly communicating, fit and can be understood. Beyond that world is the world as such, not only as the sum total of all possible entities in space and time but also as the relation between all of this and the set of actual and possible meanings within which everything is or can be interpreted. Husserl uses the expression *intentional analysis* for the following out of the massive complexity afforded by these directions and the making explicit of all the various strands of experience that go into the constitution of the various objects of experience.

Exploration that develops along these lines is situated in the "between," in the relation between consciousness and its objects. But there is the further consideration of our awareness of both consciousness and its objects. How is awareness aware of awareness and of the relationship between awareness and its objects? The upshot of moving in this direction for Husserl is the notion of the *transcendental ego*, that deepest dimension of the self upon which we ultimately rest for reflection and for which everything else, reflection included, is an object. To it is correlated the world as a whole.

Perhaps we might best approach this dimension in terms of a consideration of the truth-intention. If the sphere of the truth-intention is reality as a whole, that from which the intention stems, as a relation to reality as a whole, is a deep dimension of myself, but not of myself as a finite, conditioned, psycho-physical individual, limited in so many obvious ways. It is the depth-dimension of myself as intending the unconditioned, the ultimate truth of reality as a whole and of myself within it. It is in this very direction that we might find the roots of traditional doctrines seemingly so foreign to minds conditioned to think in terms of sensorily observable objects: doctrines like Aristotle's agent intellect,

Plotinus's world-intelligence, Augustine's divine illumination, German idealism's Absolute Spirit, and India's Atman-Brahman—in all of which the self and the All are somehow necessarily related. Husserl used the expression *transcendental reduction* for this attending to the total field of the truth-intention as referred to the transcendental ego, where all aspects of experience are viewed in terms of their reference to the total truth-intention. Reflection on the eidetic character of transcendental subjectivity leads on to the notion of *transcendental intersubjectivity*. This is correlated to the systems of eidetic intuitions, which begin with the laws of logic or the theorems of geometry and extend to the entire field of phenomenology, providing, in principle, convincing evidence to any properly attending subject.

However, whatever is made explicit always rests upon a foundation that is not explicitated. The reflective disengagement of differing aspects of the situation is always performed on the basis of what Husserl calls *operative intentionality*, which involves the ultimate foundations of subjectivity itself as intending absolute totality. Furthermore, the methodical attempt at intentional analysis rests likewise upon the preestablished life of the psycho-physical individual as a member of some community, for it is the underlying structure of the person and the sum total of his or her culturally mediated experiences that make possible both the experience of the object and the intention and activity of explicitating that experience. Both the experience and the reflective analysis thereof involve selective attention that is a function of the interrelation of personal and cultural history. The *Lebenswelt*, or lifeworld, which is also and necessarily a cultural world, always precedes and founds the methodical analysis thereof. All the reductions—phenomenological, eidetic, transcendental, and others not treated here—are ways of focusing attention, ways of causing to stand out certain features of the *Lebenswelt* otherwise hidden within our ordinary preoccupations. Thus, we are led back to some affinities with the *Lebensphilosophie* against which Husserl earlier had protested—but with a difference, for now the rational forms are appreciated as the very forms of that lifeworld. Heidegger and Merleau-Ponty will follow in this direction.

MAX SCHELER (1874–1928)

The highpoint of the first phase of phenomenology was Husserl's *Logical Investigations*. The beginning of a second great phase was the publication in 1913 of the first volume of the major review of phenomenology as a more broadly based movement: the *Jahrbuch für Philosophie und Phänomenologische Forschung* (*Annual for Philosophy and Phenomenological Research*, or *Jahrbuch* for short). That volume contained the first installment both of Husserl's *Ideas* and of Max Scheler's central work, *Formalism in Ethics and Ethics of Value-Content.*[1] The relation between these two men and their relation, in turn, to philosophy in contemporary culture might be clarified by looking back to one of the pivotal texts of Western philosophy: Plato's *Republic*.

In the famous allegory of the Cave and, correlated with it, the diagram of the Line at the very center of the work,[2] Plato asks us to visualize the human condition as that of people being collectively chained in a deep, dimly lit Cave. They attend to shadows on a wall, flickering and shifting projections of those in control behind the scenes. Plato here gives us, so to speak, the charter for the discipline of the sociology of knowledge, a discipline that Scheler was to revive in our own times. The one who is unchained first surveys the total factual situation in the Cave. The line diagram describes these two states as (socially based) conjecture followed by (factually based) belief.

For Plato, the move out of the Cave is begun with the recognition of the eidetic invariants of mathematics. Husserl began the ascent from the Cave of subjectivism (psychologism, cultural relativism) through the investigation of the objectivity of the foundations of mathematics and

---

1. Manfred Frings's translation of *Der Formalismus in der Ethik und materiale Wert-Ethik* as *Formalism in Ethics and Non-Formal Ethics of Value* is strange. The contrast is between form and matter or content. *Materiale Wert-Ethik* is best translated as *Ethics of Value-Content*. One significant approach to the study of Husserl would be to begin where he ended, with the *Lebenswelt* writings. The most significant work in this regard is *The Crisis of European Sciences and Transcendental Phenomenology* of 1937, trans. D. Carr (Evanston, Ill.: Northwestern University Press, 1970). A readable approach to this is the Vienna Lecture of 1935, "Philosophy and Crisis of European Humanity," reprinted as an appendix to the English edition of the larger Crisis volume (269–99). It would provide a transition to the later developments of the existential phenomenologists, a refocused attention to Husserl's entire life's work, and an orientation toward Western culture as a whole.

2. The Cave and the Line are contained in books VI and VII of the *Republic*.

logic. He went on to extend it to the foundations of science in the eidetic structures of the lifeworld.

But Plato's main concern, like Scheler's, was with values, specifically with those virtues that lie at the base of social order. In his magnificently brief dialogue *Meno*, Plato has Socrates discuss the teachability of virtue with the subject of the dialogue, whose personal, socially reinforced set of values (wealth, power, fame) so block his insight that he can offer only memorized, socially acceptable answers to the basic questions of value. Meno is, indeed, chained in the Cave. So Plato turns to a "value-free" example from mathematics (a variation on the Pythagorean theorem) to get Meno to see that there are truths that exceed his shallow views, that there is an objectivity here that imposes itself upon psychological and sociological conditions. But this is only a first step out of the Cave: the real question is that of values, specifically of the Good. It is this level that Scheler, following upon the mathematical, logical, and foundations-of-science investigations of Husserl, is most intent upon exploring. Scheler is the theoretician of values par excellence. But because he is so concerned with values, he is simultaneously concerned with the social conditions that inhibit and foster them.

Scheler's basic distinction in this regard is between "real" and "ideal" factors. The real conditions—physiological, psychological, sociological—of men in any particular epoch constitute a kind of filter that permits only certain values to be realized or even to be seen. Scheler broadens the Marxist notion of social infrastructure beyond the narrow Marxist consideration of the means and relations of technical production to the broader foundations in political, racial, and even sexual and general biological conditions. Indeed, "real factors" extend also to the Marxist notion of superstructure as the ideology or system of ideals not only legitimating the social structure but reciprocally determining the infrastructure. This total infrastructure-superstructure situation at any given time functions as a selective agency in relation to "ideal factors" or eidetic necessities that completely transcend the society.

For example, the eidetic invariants of the visual field, which transcend this visual experience at this particular point in space-time, require as foundation that one have here-and-now visual experience (directly given or given in memory or imagination), so that one born blind could never grasp the peculiar eidetic structures of this region. Similarly, the eidetic structures of the region of value require as foundation the appropriate mode of feeling that discloses value. Scheler vigorously opposes the subjectivization of feeling and carries out many descriptive analyses of differing types of feeling that disclose value: sympathy, shame, modesty, *ressentiment*, repentance, and so forth. He distinguishes feeling-states of various levels of the self: from localized somatic feelings, such as an itch on the back of my hand; through generalized somatic states, such as a sense of vigor; to psychic states, such as an angry mood; and on to spiritual states of joy and despair. He further distinguishes such states from intentional acts of feeling that disclose value related to what is other than our states (e.g., an angry mood reveals our own psyche, but being-angry about something reveals that "something" as well).

The objectivity of the modes of cognition investigated by Husserl found its parallel for Scheler in St. Augustine's (354–430) order of love (*ordo amoris*) and Blaise Pascal's (1623–1662) logic of the heart (*logique de coeur*), which Scheler attempted to revive and develop. A person's or a society's *ordo amoris* may produce the phenomenon of value-blindness in certain domains.

And just as it is vain to attempt to explain the perception of color to one born blind, it is the same in dealing with one blind to certain values. Following Plato, Scheler holds that one who would aspire toward a vision of the whole of being and value (i.e., the would-be philosopher) must be inspired by a love (*eros*) for the totality, must humble himself before the truth, and must exercise discipline in his life so that the order of love might lead to the cognition proportionate to the object of philosophy's search.

Values are distinguished from their bearers as all eidetic structures are distinguished from their empirical embodiments. Values likewise are disclosed in appropriate modes of intentional feeling and given in an intrinsic hierarchy of higher and lower. Scheler presents five basic criteria of intrinsic preferability that determine that hierarchy. First, the enduring values are preferable to the transient. Second, the less divisible are superior because they can be participated by many without loss. For example, if I share my money, what someone else takes I cannot at the same time retain; but if I share what I know with another, my knowledge not only is not lost but, in proportion to the depth at which I share, my knowledge actually is deepened. Third, a founding value is higher than one founded; for example, an instrument's value is founded on the value it serves to realize. Fourth, the higher the value, the greater the depth of satisfaction it supplies. And fifth, the higher the value, the greater the independence of our organic condition.

According to these criteria, Scheler distinguishes four basic levels of value, arranged from lower to highest: (1) values of the agreeable and the disagreeable revealed in feelings of pleasure and pain; (2) vital values, such as vigor or health, revealed in vital feelings of our somatic totality; (3) spiritual values independent of the body and the environment, corresponding to the old transcendental properties of beauty, goodness, and truth; and (4) values of the holy and the unholy encompassing our totality and the totality of our relations.[3]

The forms of human groupings exhibit some parallels with this hierarchy and thus found various possibilities of value-blindness and value-disclosure. At the lowest level is *the crowd*, where each individual loses its identity in the infectious mass emotion. A second form is the life community (*Lebensgemeinschaft*), rooted in blood, spatial proximity, and tradition. This is contrasted with the rational, contractual society (*Gesellschaft*) that has become more common as economic and industrial systems become more complex and face-to-face relations increasingly are pervaded and somewhat superseded by deliberately planned structures. Scheler here appropriates the distinction made famous by Ferdinand Tönnies's work, *Gemeinschaft und Gesellschaft* (1887). But Scheler adds a fourth significant form of relatedness: *Persongemeinschaft*, the community of persons founded in common tendencies directed toward spiritual values and values of the holy. Scheler places these forms within the broader framework of relationships that include one-to-one relationships between human individuals and communion with nature in his work *Sympathy* (1913).

Scheler sees the modern world, for all its vaunted progress, as blind to many of the higher realms of value by reason of a persuasive sense of *ressentiment*. He borrowed, in significantly modified form, the term and much of the analysis from Friedrich Nietzsche, but he gave it a twist which was favorable to Christianity (which Nietzsche considered one of the great sustainers of *ressentiment*) in a work titled *On Ressentiment* (1912). Though not a pure analysis of eidetic structures, the work does ex-

---

3. Scheler gave special attention to the Holy in *On the Eternal in Man*, trans. B. Noble (New York: Harper, 1960). The range of materials considered in this work would provide significant information for one interested in further pursuit of Scheler's work.

hibit a sensitive and quite plausible interpretation of the aspects of degeneration of values by one who has become sensitized to their hierarchy. The French Revolution's "Liberty, Equality and Fraternity" is a prime exhibition of *ressentiment* directed toward the earlier life communities and the intrinsic hierarchy of persons on the basis of differing excellences (as it was also based upon justified revolt against pseudo-hierarchy and decayed community). Equality tends to flatten out intrinsic rank. Socialist fraternity that is based on such flattened egalitarianism (Scheler himself argued for a Christian form of socialism early in his career) destroys true brotherhood founded in rejoicing at my brother's excellences. And liberty as dissolution of ties corrodes all organically based community and leads to widespread breakdown of discipline and to the all-too-common conception of the subjectivity of values. "Love of Humanity" emerges out of hatred of face-to-face relations, "altruism" out of flight from interiority.

Just as Scheler had no difficulty going beyond strict phenomenological procedure to an interpretation of modern history, so also he was never averse to engaging in metaphysical speculation. In his last work, *The Place of Man in the Cosmos* (1927), he combined anthropological and metaphysical speculations in his view of man's place as at the intersection of the blind drive (*Drang*) of nature and the aspiration of spirit (*Geist*). Spirit discloses the higher regions of value but only by being able to say "no" to the lower region's claim to absoluteness. In the process of ascending to the higher, spirit, which is powerless in itself, must enlist the aid of the driving forces of nature. The result is the progressive emergence of deity as the goal rather than the traditionally conceived cause of the cosmic process.

MARTIN HEIDEGGER (1889–1976)

The line of succession in the phenomenological movement passed from Husserl and Scheler to Martin Heidegger. Heidegger was first a student, then a secretarial assistant, and eventually a colleague of Husserl. Heidegger's first major work, *Being and Time*, the third of the phenomenological classics to appear in the *Jahrbuch*, was published in 1927 and dedicated to Husserl. In that work, Heidegger announced the project of a series of historical studies on time, only one of which was published—*Kant and the Problem of Metaphysics* in 1929. This second of Heidegger's major publications was dedicated to Scheler. His immediate antecedents were clearly established.

At the same time, Heidegger was deeply influenced by the widespread interest after World War I in the work of the Danish thinker Søren Kierkegaard (1813–1855) and the German Friedrich Nietzsche. Approaching their contemporary situation from differing ultimate concerns, Kierkegaard the Christian and Nietzsche the atheist saw that "the System" was threatening to swallow the individual and that men were in danger of forgetting "what it means to be an existing individual." In the name of individual human existence, Kierkegaard protested against "Christian civilization," which had been elaborately rationalized in the massive theoretical system of G. W. F. Hegel (1770–1831). In the name of the essential superiority of the highest creative types—artists, philosophers and saints—Nietzsche protested against the leveling tendencies in the growing confluence of democracy, socialism, and modern scientific technology. Together, Kierkegaard and Nietzsche became the fathers of contemporary existentialism. In Heidegger, the confluence of the existentialist influence with the phenomenological orientation of Husserl and Scheler gave rise to existential phenomenology, that is, phenomenology focused upon the structure of the existence of the human person.

If we stay with our parallelism between the phenomenologists and the development of Plato's Cave and Line, we might say that Heidegger radicalized phenomenology by attending not simply to the eidetic structures of knowledge and value and to the varying social-historical contexts in which they appear and operate but to the direction indicated in Plato's Cave allegory as the Good, the source of being and light for knowledge of the Ideas. That light makes possible the manifestation of the entire human situation at all its levels. Heidegger calls it "the light of Being," which appears through man in the midst of the multiplicity of beings and enables them to be manifest as beings. Accordingly, Heidegger calls the human being *Da-Sein*, the "there" (*Da*) of Being (*Sein*), the place where the light of Being appears. Thus, the questions of the nature of Being and of human being are intrinsically bound together.[4]

4. A concise approach to the central problem of Being in Heidegger is provided in his "What Is Metaphysics?" of 1927, to which he added an important introduction, "The Way Back into the Ground of Metaphysics," in 1949. Will McNeil has retranslated them and put them together with other essays in chronological order in *Pathmarks* (Cambridge: Cambridge University Press, 1998).

What is the meaning of Being as found in all its instances—from the material, through the living and the conscious, to the personal and even the Divine? Particular disciplines investigate each of these regions: physics, biology, psychology, sociology, and theology; each discipline is concerned with the methods and evidences proper to its own sphere of interest—and, beyond this, with nothing else. But what about this "nothing"? It shows that human awareness always thinks the particular beings and regions with which it is concerned against a background that exceeds these beings and regions. Every judgment about any determinate being is made in terms of the meaning of Being. A preliminary analysis of the structure of the judgment directs attention to this dimension of Heidegger's concern.

Following our investigations of Husserl, in the judgment "this is paper," the "this" points to the perceptually present individual perceived as paper. The "is" opens up the realm of the peculiarly human, for it involves a kind of implicit reflection, a coming to the individual in the environment from a mode of being that is beyond the individual and the environment. As a concept, "paper" is a universal intention that is understandable only in terms of an interrelated set of universal intentions that constitute a world of meaning.

The various worlds of meaning that we might bring into play appear within the "space" referred to by the "is" of the judgment "this is paper." The "is," displaying the meaning of Being, has an unrestrictedly universal intentionality: it refers to all actual or possible instances, of whatever kind, including in its intentionality the total universe of things judged and judgeable, as well as the one judging. The totality of beings and meanings—"the world" as such—appears in the light of a projection beyond the totality of what is. Contrary to Nietzsche, the meaning of Being is not "the last trailing cloud of evaporating reality" but the deepest, most central feature of human reality. Indeed, that Being could so appear to Nietzsche at the end of the Western metaphysical tradition only because this tradition was born out of the "forgottenness of Being." Preoccupied with the presentation of sensory or intelligible objects over against the attentive cognitive subject, the West has forgotten the space within which such encounter can occur.

The founding structure of human existence lies in relation to the "space" or "clearing" or "light" wherein things not only are but also appear or are manifest; and wherein simultaneously the subject to whom the appearance of things occurs not only is but likewise (prethematically) is self-manifest. This appearance is not only the here-and-now manifest sensory individuality of things but also their simultaneous appearance *as* something, that is, as instances of meanings within worlds of meaning. The human existent comes to the here-and-now individual from being beyond the individual and the here-and-now, from being with Being as a whole. Heidegger calls attention to this transcendence of the here-and-now by speaking of Dasein's existence, literally its "standing-out"; this is its freedom from the now and from the weight of the past and its freedom for the future.

Because Dasein stands out, transcends, exists in reference to Being as a whole, "in the light of Being" there occurs the peculiar process of revealing-concealing. Every "filled intention," every revealing takes place against the background of the internal horizon of the thing. The revealed perspective, or the sum total of sedimented perspectives, always stands in relation to the concealed wholeness of the thing, its "being." Every revealed field of meaning, every holistic interpretative structure set up from the "angle" afforded in a given epoch, always settles into the space of the concealed totality. Thus, Being appears as "nothing," as a "not," with respect to what is manifest. In this way, phenomenology becomes not simply intuitive presence of the evidential but also hermeneutics (i.e., interpretation) structured from differing perspectives, of beings and of Being that are revealed and concealed in the interpretative process. In this way, when it is pushed to its ultimate descriptive horizon phenomenology becomes ontology, that is, theory (*logos*) of being (Greek *on*, genitive *ontos*).

More crucially, projected toward Being as a whole, we are simultaneously opened up to the wholeness of our own being, so that one's most basic concern is about the meaning of one's own being as a whole: what do I make out of my life as a whole? That whole is simultaneously revealed and concealed. It appears in an underlying anxiety about our wholeness. Contrasted with fear that is related to some specific object (e.g., a fear of failing a test), anxiety, as related to that not-manifest wholeness of our life, is without a specific object. Because of the structural (prethematic, horizonal) directedness toward the Whole, anxiety is a perennial feature of human existence; it becomes thematic only in certain moments—generally when our ordinary meaning-structures tend to collapse. It surfaces most clearly in our being grasped by our own mortality.

One of the crucial features of our existence is that this deep concern is covered over by our physiological, psychological, and sociological conditions. Heidegger calls this the situation of an impersonal individual, of *das Man*, of "one" (as in "One must die," "One must do his duty," etc.) or "they" (as in "They say . . ."). We are "thrown" into a pregiven world, raised in it, given modes of interpretation, values, and even feelings with their own orientations before we reflect upon them or make fundamental choices. Though fashioned by our past, we consider ourselves "self-made." We project our futures in the mode of what Heidegger calls "curiosity," in which we are not at all aware of the full seriousness of our situation. Above all, in the impersonal mode of *das Man*, we flee from our mortality. The result of our past and future orientations is a mode of dwelling in the present, which Heidegger terms "chatter" or noncommunion posing as communion.

Such a mode of existence is "inauthentic." This is a somewhat misleading expression, for Heidegger insists that he is not speaking here in moral terms. Literally, the term means "not to be one's own" (*uneigentlich*). A less misleading term might be "unappropriated," rooted in the Latin *proprius*, also meaning "one's own." In the impersonal situation of *das Man*, one has not yet deeply made one's own the conditions determining himself, even to the intimacy of feelings. "Authentic" existence begins to emerge when one is "appropriated" by one's own mortality. Death is not merely our biological term, out there in the future; it is the condition here and now raising the question of the meaning of my being as a whole in more than a cognitive way. As being-toward-death, we are able to determine the way in which we will appropriate and thus shape the past as included in the fact that we are already oriented in a peculiar way. Our orientation toward death functions as a kind of *epoche* freeing us from preoccupation regarding our ordinary condition. Rebounding from the ultimate future of our own death, the present opens in its true preciousness and genuine communion becomes possible. Nevertheless, appropriation is possible only on the basis of the unappropriated, just as we employ language to speak about language: the impersonal aspect of *das Man* is an essential feature of even the most "authentic" individual.

Being open to appropriation by death as a real condition of our being from which we are inclined to flee enables us to be opened to the full being of things. More basically, we are opened to appropriation by Being itself—the sense of the Whole, which is beyond beings but in the light of which beings come to be more or less meaningfully present to us. Being is not only event but appropriation (*Ereignis*). Besides and grounding knowledge that assimilates its objects, there is "knowledge" as being assimilated to or appropriated by beings and Being. Beyond the superficiality of the impersonal *das Man*, there is also that fundamental "sense" or "light" of Being that undergoes deep changes from culture to culture and from epoch to epoch. One who is tuned deeply to that sense, just as to one's own being toward death, opens oneself to being apprehended and thus to a distinctive way of selecting interpretative perspectives for dwelling with others.

Being then is not an ever-present idea, occupying an eternal now, as Platonism is inclined to affirm. The now is only one dimension of the temporal process. Being is a presencing, a movement out of the past and into the future that determines the sense of our dwelling in the present. But presencing changes as we change and are changed by our gathering of the past in view of the way in which we project the future and hence is like an event.

Heidegger finds this gathering into presence as early as 500 B.C.E. in the *logos*-doctrine of Heraclitus (which was to be expressed secondarily in the development of logic as a kind of atemporal set of valid linkages among ideas). Being as the logos is a gathering or interrelating of beings, which allows them to be seen as something. However, this logos is not the subjective process "in us"; it is rather the cosmic process to which we are to be attuned. Heidegger sees this as closely related to the understanding of *noein* ("to know") in Parmenides (who also lived around 500 B.C.E.) as "the event which apprehends man." Before we set about mastering things, we are in the grips of a way of revealing that makes mastery and submission possible. Western metaphysics progressively fell away from those understandings; beginning with Plato, it focused upon those aspects that can be objectified and thus also mastered, used, or controlled. Truth became correspondence between concepts and things and then between models and data. But correspondence can occur only in terms of the openness of both concepts and things against the background of the hiddenness of the Whole. Primordial truth is unhiddenness (*a-letheia*) that is essentially tied in with hiddenness (*lethe*) and thus with the sense of mystery. To focus exclusively upon truth as correspondence is to forget this more primordial notion of truth and thus fall into forgetfulness of the light of Being. At the end of the process of Western metaphysics, Nietzsche makes clear the underlying sense of Being that guided the entire development and terminated in the omnivorous character of Western technology: Being is the will to power. Instead of attuning oneself to being apprehended by the underlying *logos*, people have become increasingly concerned with cognitive and practical mastery. Thinking that presses beyond such mastery to ponder the light of Being is essentially appreciative, essentially thanking. For Heidegger, thinking primordially is thanking (*Denken ist danken*), which implies a closeness to things (*Dingen*). *Ding* is originally the term for an assembly: for one appreciatively attuned, things assemble or gather into themselves the cosmic *logos*. Thankfulness takes place in the *thanc*, an old Anglo-Saxon term related to the heart as the center that founds our differing modes of interpretation. Such thankful thinking is capable of "letting things be," letting them speak on their own terms, and letting them open out to the mystery of Being, which not only exceeds their perspectival manifestations but also transcends the realm of beings entirely. Such thinking parallels the Chinese meditation on the Tao, terminating in a "nonaction" (*wu-wei*) that produces the right action as ripe fruit falling from the tree. Such thinking is on the way toward the Holy, only in proximity to which can the question of God be raised authentically in an era that has darkened the light of Being, standardized existing human beings, and led to the death of God.

JEAN-PAUL SARTRE (1905–1980)

Phenomenology moved into France after Jean-Paul Sartre's studies of Husserl and Heidegger in Germany during the mid-1930s. It attained its first classic French expression in Sartre's *Being and Nothingness* in 1943 and in Maurice Merleau-Ponty's *Phenomenology of Perception* in 1945. The influence of Hegel and eventually also of Marx (1818–1883) was added to the influence of Husserl, Scheler, and Heidegger and of Kierkegaard and Nietzsche: social structure and social action increasingly became objects of attention. Under the influence of Husserl and especially of Heidegger, Sartre began with a phenomenological approach. But under the influence of Hegel, Sartre's philosophy was built up by dialectics, that is, the struggle of opposites that mutually require one another. In *Being and Nothingness*, this phenomenological-dialectical approach was developed from the point of view of the individual human existent.

Following Heidegger, Sartre removed the Husserlian brackets from phenomenology so that it concerned not only essence but especially existence. Phenomenology became ontology, the revelation of Being. For Sartre, Being is appearance—though not the mere appearance of the here and now. The being of phenomena is the sum total of possible perspectives systematically related. The revelation of Being and the perspectivity thereof is grounded in consciousness as pure emptiness situated by being the awareness owning a body. Hence, the fundamental dialectical tensions are between the fullness of Being and the emptiness of consciousness, and between consciousness and its own embodiment. However, contrary to Hegel, dialectics does not lead to a synthesis of opposing tensions but to continual struggle.

The emptiness of consciousness enables it to be intentional, that is, to reveal what is other, to reveal Being. As pure emptiness, consciousness likewise does not itself appear: consciousness is the nothingness of *Being and Nothingness*. But this very no-thingness, this nonobject status of consciousness is its freedom; and above everything else freedom is Sartre's chief concern. Where Heidegger ponders the human being (*Dasein*) for its openness to Being, Sartre focuses upon consciousness for the sake of its freedom. Heidegger is ontocentric, Sartre egocentric (in a sense that would have to be qualified in a fuller study than we can present here).

Returning to our guiding image of Plato's Cave and Line, Sartre's major concern is with the unchaining. But the purpose of unchaining is not for the sake of theoretical contemplation or being beholden to objective value or being apprehended by Being. It is in order to be the origin of one's own values: it is for the sake of the freedom to create one's own essence. For the sake of freedom, Sartre reengages in the speculative endeavors that Husserl's brackets were intended to eliminate. Speculation emerges with a vengeance. To sustain the otherness of consciousness in reference to Being, Sartre tries to locate all negativity in consciousness. The basic operations of awareness are all reduced to negations: affirmation is possible because consciousness is *not* the other, negative judgment because consciousness finds *not* present what it expects, questioning because consciousness does *not* know, and evaluation because values are *not* factual states of affairs but human choices. The aspects of negativity that seem to inhere in things are repositioned in consciousness. Potentiality, for example, is not a datum. Whatever we experience is actual: we see actuality, feel actuality, smell, hear, and taste actuality. Reality, Sartre says, is full, like an egg. Potentiality as nonactual comes through consciousness reflecting back upon itself.

Allied with potentiality is temporality, since both involve change. Time involves the synthesis of the past, present, and future. But the past is the no-longer and the future the not-yet. Neither is present "in-person"; both are given through consciousness reflecting on itself. The present in which such reflection occurs is itself a flight from the no-longer to the not-yet in which the nonbeing of consciousness reveals the actuality of the nonconscious. And even the multiplicity of things is located in one's not being the other, fringed by the indeterminately spread emptiness of space that consciousness as nothingness once more introduces. Somewhat like Immanuel Kant (1724–1804), who claimed that the indeterminate spread of time and space were not immediate deliverances of the senses but forms of the mind like a pair of internal spectacles through which we focus on things, Sartre similarly claims that the elements of negativity in experience are provided by the nonbeing of consciousness. And in many ways reminiscent of Parmenides whom Heidegger revered, Sartre envisioned Being in itself as a massive, unitary, changeless whole, totally indifferent to the "disease" of negativity it has contracted with the birth of consciousness.

The nothingness of consciousness, paradoxically, does have a kind of structure. It is aware of itself as not being the objects it reveals. This is the "con-" of "consciousness," literally a "co-knowing" or a "knowing-with." Co-present with the objects, though never in the mode of the object, consciousness is the nothingness of the object. Consciousness, then, does not exist "in itself" (*en soi*, derived from Hegel's *an sich*) like a thing but "for itself" (*pour soi* for Hegel's *für sich*), present to itself. This is "unreflected" or "prereflective" consciousness (*cogito*). Subsequently, there do emerge phenomena that we call "me" or "I" or "ego," but these are all constructions, reflective objects founded on the prereflective consciousness' relations with what is other, out there, in the world. Consciousness for Sartre has no essence but has to construct through its choices what it is to be.

Consciousness is free from objects in being aware of them and (prereflectively) aware of being aware. But it is inclined to hide its freedom from itself, to exist in the "bad faith" of pretending it cannot do other than it does because of "environment," "upbringing," "innate tendencies," "God's will," "the moral law," and so forth. It tries to identify wholly with its roles, to become a waiter-thing, a soldier-thing, a professor-thing, a homosexual-thing, a husband-thing, and so on. But being aware of them, the person is "condemned to be free." One is solely responsible for what one becomes. One's choice alone is responsible for sustaining or breaking from the roles and the multiplicity of the meanings one chooses to project for one's life.

Consciousness, however, is founded upon the body, co-implicated with the body. This provides the perspective through which being is revealed. It provides, in addition, an element of "facticity" or brute fact, without which freedom or "transcendence"—surpassing, going beyond, being other than facticity—would have no field of operation. Freedom can be exercised only in a situation that provides invitations for choice, materials to shape, occasions for choosing our attitude. Our physiological, psychological, and sociological facticities are the artist's material to shape according to our choice.

But the body through which the elements of facticity confront awareness is ambiguous. The body as object is the body of the sciences, available to public inspection but equivalent to a nonpersonal mechanism; this is an abstract body. The body as subject is the body as I live it: the body suffused with my projects, alive with my sensibility, embodying my awareness. Ever since the radical dualism that accompanies the rise of modern science in the philosophy of Descartes, the body-subject has been largely neglected.

Through the look of the other person, the body-object is surpassed and we are introduced into the world of the struggle of consciousnesses introduced by Hegel in his master/slave relation. I, the body-subject, am exposed through the look of that other. Prior to the experience of the look of the other, the world was my world, a set of objects built around me as the center that allows them to be revealed in terms of my interests, my projects, and my values. But as freely projected meaning, the meaning of my world is not that of the world of a conscious other. Others see and judge me from their total perspective, just as I see them from mine. Our basic relations are matters of struggle, matters of who can succeed in subsuming whom under their world. As the play *No Exit* has it: "Hell is other people." The only resolution lies in the ideal possibility of a "sado-masochistic" relation, where one surrenders to the other under the bad faith that he or she can do no other and is a "captive"—perhaps of love.

One significant aspect of Sartre's thought—contrary to the phenomenological thinkers so far considered—is his denial of the existence of God. In one place, he speaks of his work as one of drawing the consistent implications from a "postulatory atheism"; that is, on the assumption of the nonexistence of God, what follows? Ultimately, Sartre answers, what follows is our own total responsibility for the meaning of our lives. The way Sartre sets up the basic contrast of in-itself (*en soi*) and for-oneself (*pour soi*) leads him to two proofs for the nonexistence of God. First, if there is a God who thought-creates all things, consciousness would be His object and therefore not free. But consciousness is not an object, cannot be an object, and is free; hence, there can be no God. The second proof develops from the idea of God as complete being-in-itself, that is, at the same time, total self-transparency or complete being-for-itself. But as being aware is always being other, always distance from being-in-itself, the idea of God that as both being-for-itself and being-in-itself is internally self-contradictory. Actually, it is a fundamental projection from the situation of man and the source of the perennial temptation to bad faith. As one's basic passion is to be an in-itself-for-itself, one is prone to pretend to be identified with one's biology, past, roles, the will of God, and so forth. But being aware of all this, one is beyond it: "Man is a futile passion to become God."

The publication of the *Critique of Dialectical Reason* in 1961 exhibited a notable turn of thought. It had a significantly different focus but retained continuity with the preceding. Here Sartre sees existentialism as a parasite existing on the fringes of the only philosophy adequate for our epoch, namely, Marxism. Throughout his career, Sartre fought with the Communist Party in France, not because of its Marxism but because of its betrayal of Marxism. "Orthodox" Marxism had rigidified; having become overly impressed by the objectivism of science and technology, it had turned the existing person into a function of a vast and repressive bureaucratic system. Sartre felt that the bourgeoisie privatization of existential freedom, impotent by itself, had to be brought into relation with a Marxian analysis of institutions and historical development, of classes and oppression.[5]

---

5. A 1946 essay titled "Materialism and Revolution" significantly engaged "orthodox" Marxism and presaged the transition to Sartre's later neo-Marxism. It is found in Barrett and

MAURICE MERLEAU-PONTY (1908–1961)

In Maurice Merleau-Ponty, we find an integration of the previous thinkers but expanded to take careful account of experimental work in psychology, ongoing dialogue with Marxist social theory, and a kind of renewed Hegelianism. Whatever tendencies there may have been in Husserl and in Scheler to fix upon essence, as one mode of Platonism would have it, Merleau-Ponty returns, in a sense, to the actual practice of Socrates, the one who has been unchained and speaks in the dialogues of Plato. His wisdom, Socrates said, consisted in knowing that he did not know. Philosophy, for Socrates, was not *sophia*, the possession of wisdom, but love and pursuit of wisdom, *philosophia*. This led to an ongoing critique of those positions that would lay claim to the title of wisdom. Merleau-Ponty followed this Socratic way in an ongoing dialectic rooted in the *Lebenswelt*, or lifeworld, in which the crucial roles are played by the self and the human other as embedded in nature through the body and in history through the community of consciousnesses. Everything is rendered incomplete except the indubitability of the self-present-to-the-world. This sets the task for phenomenology as a constant attempt to return everything to its own beginnings, to practice a genetic phenomenology in order to awaken wonder at the mystery of existence.

In a general way, Merleau-Ponty exhibited a movement paralleling Hegel's central notion of *Aufhebung*, which means—alternatively in ordinary German but simultaneously in Hegel—cancellation, preservation, and elevation. In Hegel, opposing positions are cancelled out in their one-sided form, preserved in the truth they each exhibit and elevated to compatibility with their contending opposites by being raised to a new level. This style of attempting to resolve counterpositions was followed by Merleau-Ponty, not in the direction of some terminal Absolute Spirit, as in Hegel, but in the direction of tracing each position back to its origins in the lifeworld. In particular, he attempted to show both the value and the one-sidedness of empiricism, on the one hand, and of intellectualism, on the other.[6]

Aiken, vol. 3, 387–429. It is suggested as one of the better first readings in Sartre himself and much more helpful than the essay "Existentialism Is a Humanism," which often is used as introductory reading in Sartre.

6. Perhaps one of the less difficult places to begin reading Merleau-Ponty is the last chap-

Empiricism sought to establish causal connections by diverting attention from meaningful wholes at the biological level and from the presence of a conscious subject in behavior, particularly at the human level. In a way reminiscent of Aristotle, Merleau-Ponty describes the functioning of controlling wholes at the organic level, which establish and maintain the overall "style" or "form" of behavior. Along these lines, he shows the limitation of the dogmas of cerebral localization and of rigidly conditioned reflexes. Cerebral lesions often lead to the allegedly localized functions being "relocated" in other aspects of the brain or to a general lessening of the intensity of the functions without destroying their form. Destruction of a limb often leads to the transfer of the style of behavior to other limbs. The rule here is not set responses to identical stimuli but "systems of equivalences" establishing an overall style of behavior. Rigidly conditioned reflexes are the real anthropomorphism, since they are artificially induced by man for a purpose and appear as pathological in relation to the harmonious style of normal organic behavior. The human equivalent would be addictions that disturb and eventually also disintegrate holistic performance.

On the other side of the picture, intellectualism tends to abstract from the "operative intentionality" of our bodily presence to the world in terms of our awareness both of other persons and of our own self. Thus, according to Merleau-Ponty, Sartre's description of the look of the human other, which is used to support his contentions regarding the mutual alienation and struggle of consciousness, is actually based upon a detached, judgmental, intellectualist analysis of consciousness. Sartre fails, as Scheler before him did not, to consider the prejudgmental reciprocity of consciousnesses that goes on in many differing situations but most clearly in love and sympathy. The other's consciousness can be met in his/her behavior; it does not have to be inferred from the behavior behind which in some way it is hidden.

Thus, in the behavior of the other, I see his anger; I do not infer it. Anger is not a state of mind that is expressed outwardly but is simultaneously and indissolubly state of mind and overt behavior. For certain reasons and in certain contexts, one might abstract from the fuller reality to focus on one aspect of behavior. The ophthalmologist, for example, ab-

ter of *The Structure of Behavior*, trans. A. Fisher (Boston: Beacon Press, 1963), which deals with the classical alternatives.

stracts from the living presence of the person in his/her look in order to focus on the eye-as-mechanism with a view toward correcting abnormal visual functioning. In actual practice, the ophthalmologist often shifts back and forth from the abstract, purpose-oriented and therefore filtered phenomena to the personal presence of the human other in carrying on conversation about family, politics, weather, sports, fees, and so forth. The eye mechanism recedes from attention, and a more complete human presence manifests itself. However, behavior is not wholly transparent or wholly unambiguous; even in verbal behavior, it is not wholly expressive of the full intentional life of the other person, even for the other person.

Though the person of the other can be met (though not comprehended, encompassed, exhausted) in his/her behavior, one's own self-presence, on the other hand, can be achieved only by being embodied in one's bodily behavior. In terms of access to one's own consciousness, thought finds itself when it finds the words to express itself. Prior to the words, thought is but a groping or sense of direction. As the words come and thought is made "incarnate," thought comes clear—at least clearer—regarding its own direction. But as there is always a surplus of direction of thought, the mind moves on. So also with states like "being in love": one does not discover this by introspecting the peculiar texture of one's consciousness here and now but by the course of behavior sustaining genuine consideration for the other that might issue from that state. In general, one discovers one's own potentialities only in actual performance as they are externalized in actual behavior.

All this is founded upon the operative intentionality of bodily "knowings"—for example, how to focus in order to perceive; how to coordinate limbs in order to move about; how to position tongue, teeth, lips, and palate in order to speak; how to construct sentences, and so forth. Founded upon a primary set of such bodily "knowings," the human subject builds up, in and through acts of significant others, a "second body" of habits— motor, perceptual, linguistic, and so on—characterized by both structure and openness toward being appropriated and shaped anew by the conscious subject who establishes relationships and takes up responsibility. This second body is not simply "in me" but is a mode of relation to what is "outside me." There is, for example, a very real sense in which the artist dwells in his brush as in his own hand, so that his awareness "flows through" the brush to its tip and onto the canvas. Thought itself becomes embedded in this second body and in the world of nature and history through the "internalization" of language—which is simultaneously the "externalization" of consciousness. But all this occurs in such a way that, just as one cannot take an inventory of all that one knows how to do in moving, writing, and speaking, so one cannot inventory the sum total of linguistic and perceptual habits that found a particular level or act of insight. (Hence, the immense problem of really teaching!)

In all of this, the freedom of the conscious subject is engaged not simply, as Sartre would have it, in breaking away from all relations but, more positively expressed, in the establishment of meaningful relations. Merleau-Ponty comes to see the value for the significant freedom of the human subject of the institution of personal and cultural habits. Whereas Sartre is more preoccupied with rebellion in order to be free from the institution and in order to allow the new to be born, Merleau-Ponty is more appreciative of the tradition as the condition for the incarnation of the person in his/her socially founded and sustained habits.

The interplay between freedom and "institution" can be seen as the source of some of the crucial problems of the human sciences and as a means for their resolution. For example, in the study of language, the primary social institution, one can abstractly study the structure of the language that we bring into play in clarifying our thought. But language as a structure, the object of the science of linguistics, is actualized only when it is taken up and thereby recast in the actual act of speaking, to the other or to oneself.

A similar relation obtains between the act of choice and psychophysical causation. Choosing always rests upon motives, but motives only come to be motives, that is, become actual moving forces in the exercise of our choices, when we make them motives by choosing them as the basis for our decisions. In deterministic forms of thought, the distinction between cause and motive is not attended to: human behavior is reduced to a complex series of causal connections, and freedom is explained away as illusion. But in phenomenological analysis in this case, causes are, at best, solicitations for choice, "temptations" for freedom to take them up and make them actual motives. However, freedom is not as absolute for Merleau-Ponty as it is for Sartre. It can fall prey to mechanical causation, and the task of therapy—chemical, behavioral, psychoanalytic, and so forth—is to bring the conscious subject back into control.

Along such lines, Merleau-Ponty leads the one-sided considerations of differing sciences and philosophies back to their origin and hence to their fundamental compatibility in the original lifeworld (*Lebenswelt*) from which they emerged—basically back to the incarnate situation. All the machinery of the phenomenological method—the phenomenological, eidetic, and transcendental reductions—are means for prying us loose from our incarnate condition in order to allow us to see its inexhaustible mystery.

CONCLUSION

Phenomenological investigation has led in many directions. In contemporary thought, it has been a protest against the "deexperientialization" of thought and the substitution of aspects of experience for its fullness. Philosophy itself, originally conceived and traditionally sustained as concern for the wholeness of experience, often has fallen into abstractly moving from text to text or from one technical problem to another until its experiential root all but disappears. Phenomenology recalls thought to its roots in experience. In so doing, it also recalls philosophy to its historical sources. Thus, throughout this chapter, we called attention to the way in which phenomenological philosophers continually refer back to Parmenides and Heraclitus, to Plato and Aristotle, to Augustine, Pascal, Descartes, Kant, Hegel, Marx, Kierkegaard, and Nietzsche. Other historical sources that might have been mentioned: Husserl himself greatly appreciated one of the giants of modern empiricism, David Hume (1711–1776); Heidegger wrote an early dissertation on a work attributed to the late medieval thinker Duns Scotus (c. 1266–1308); and Husserl's assistant, Edith Stein, wrote on Thomas Aquinas, the prince of medieval philosophers (1225–1274). Following out these connections would fill in the general outline of the whole history of Western philosophy. More recently, thinkers like Paul Ricoeur have joined the dialogue with contemporary analytical thought, while John Wild has worked on the similarities between Husserl and William James (1842–1910), one of the fathers of American pragmatism. Capping off the movement of historical retrieval, Hans-Georg Gadamer, a pupil of Heidegger, has developed rich, historically grounded reflections on hermeneutics and has given special attention to applying these reflections in his studies on Plato and Hegel.

Broadly based in experience and in the history of thought, phenomenology has continued to address itself to all of the disciplines and to the
competing options on the philosophic scene.[7] By far the most broadly
ranging, open movement in philosophy, it deserves serious consideration
as one of the most significant approaches to philosophizing in our age.

7. Two collections show the breadth of disciplines engaged by phenomenologists: J. Kockelmans and T. Kisiel, eds., *Phenomenology and Physical Science* (Evanston, Ill.: Northwestern
University Press, 1970); and Maurice Natanson, ed., *Phenomenology and the Social Sciences*, 2
vols. (Evanston, Ill.: Northwestern University Press, 1973).

18 ✑ Six Heideggerian Figures

INTRODUCTION

Throughout Heidegger's works, six figures, exhibiting six different ways of life, emerge, the exposition and comparison of which might help to bring his thought into focus. I will call them the ways of the peasant, the artist-poet, the philosopher, the scientist, the man on the street, and the thinker. The peasant and the contemporary man on the street exhibit ways of life that have to be constructed out of Heidegger's concerns, but they throw light on the other ways. They help illuminate what Being-in-the-world entails. The first two ways, that of the peasant and that of the artist-poet, antedate the emergence of philosophy as a design upon the Whole and continue as possible ways thereafter. The way of the scientist as specialist follows the emergence of philosophy and that of the contemporary man on the street follows from the technological impact of science upon society as a whole. The way of the thinker is poised somewhat ambiguously between philosophy and poetry. The peasant, the artist-poet, and the thinker operate in the medium of the lifeworld. The philosopher, the scientist, and even the man on the street suffer from a certain abstraction from the full medium of experience. We will treat them in what is, for the most part, a kind of chronological order and conclude with some comparisons between them.

Underlying them all is the notion of human existence as *Da-Sein*, as the *Da*, the "there" of "here" of Being, the locus of concern for the whole of what is and thus also for the whole of its own existence.[1] The distinctive character of human existence is this standing out from other entities by standing toward the Whole and having to understand itself in terms of how the Whole discloses itself. This underlying concern sur-

---

1. Martin Heidegger, *Being and Time*, trans. J. Maquarrie and E. Robinson (New York: Harper and Row, 1962), 34.

faces in situations of great disappointment where we are inclined to ask the strange question "What's it *all* about?" But it is also present implicitly in the answers to the question how we fit in the whole scheme of things offered by various religions and philosophies. For Heidegger, everything human turns upon how we live and think in relation to that whole.

THE PEASANT

I use that term "peasant" to refer to those like Heidegger's Schwartzwald neighbors for whom he exhibits the greatest respect. The peasant world is the world of Heidegger's own origins and the chosen milieu within which he primarily thought. So respectful was he of those who dwelt in this world that he even claimed to have asked and followed the advice of one old farm neighbor when he received a call to come to teach in Berlin in the early days of the Nazi regime.[2] The peasant represents a mode of Being-in-the-world largely untouched by philosophy, science, and modern technology.

The peasant (in German, *Bauer*) lives in an order of building (*bauen*)—in other words, both cultivating and constructing—for the sake dwelling or inhabiting (becoming habituated to and familiar with) his world. At his best, he treasures things through thinking meditatively (i.e., recollectively), appreciatively. He learns to let things be present, to make their claim upon him.[3] He is engaged in his daily tasks where things appear in equipmental contexts.[4]

Undertaking those tasks, he dwells on the earth as his native soil, under the sky. He allows the alternation of night and day and the cycles of the seasons to govern his life. He entrusts his crops and cattle to the earth and cultivates them.[5] He has a place in his home for a reminder of death, the *Totenbaum*, the niche awaiting the corpse of the next family member to die.[6] There is also a place near the common table, the *Her-*

2. Martin Heidegger, "Why Do I Stay in the Provinces," trans. T. Sheehan, *Listening* 12, no. 3 (Fall 1977): 124.

3. Martin Heidegger, "Building, Dwelling, Thinking," in *Poetry, Language and Thought*, trans. A. Hofstadter (New York: Harper and Row, 1971), 146ff.

4. Heidegger, *Being and Time*, 95ff.

5. Martin Heidegger, *The Question Concerning Technology and Other Essays*, trans. W. Lovitt (New York: Harper and Row, 1977), 15.

6. Martin Heidegger, "Hebel—Friend of the House," trans. B. Foltz and M. Heim, *Contemporary German Philosophy*, vol. 3, 93. Cf. also Heidegger, "Building, Dwelling, Thinking," 160.

rgottswinkel, the Lord God's corner, surmounted by a religious symbol.[7] The peasant heeds the announcements of the Most High, the inspirations that give him fundamental orientation in life, mediated by his own religious tradition.[8] He walks over the bridge that blends into the banks and is surmounted by a statue of a saint, a bridge that becomes a living image of his own transition from mortal to immortal shores.[9] He respects the ways passed down to him from ancestral times into which he initiates his own children.

Solitude is an essential part of this life. It affords the power of "projecting our whole existence into the vast uncommonness of the presence of all things."[10] The *Bauer* lives out a sense of the environing Mystery from which everything arises into his field of awareness.[11] One who lives thoughtfully in this element knows how "to receive the blessing of the earth and to become at home in the law of this reception in order to shepherd the mystery of Being and watch over the inviolability of the possible."[12] He comes to know the ancient *phusis* as "the arising and receding of all that is present in its presencing and absencing."[13] He gathers things into his heart in respectful repose.

The key notion here is *the heart*, related to the old Anglo-Saxon word *thanc*.[14] It is not a merely emotional but an essentially dispositional notion. It is the region of our basic stance toward what is, inclining us habitually to attend and act in certain directions. It is tied essentially to gratitude, appreciation, and thankfulness. It treasures past blessings and hence is essentially linked to memory. Memory, in turn, is originally tied to the holy and the gracious, the inviolable that grants.

7. Heidegger, "Why Do I Stay in the Provinces," 123.

8. Heidegger, "Building, Dwelling, Thinking," 149.

9. Heidegger, *The Question Concerning Technology and Other Essays*, 153.

10. Heidegger, "Why Do I Stay in the Provinces," 123.

11. Martin Heidegger, "Memorial Address," in *Discourse on Thinking*, trans. J. Anderson and H. Freund (New York: Harper and Row), 1966, 55.

12. Martin Heidegger, *The End of Philosophy*, trans. J. Stambaugh (New York: Harper and Row, 1973), 109.

13. Heidegger, "Hebel—Friend of the House," 97.

14. Cf. Martin Heidegger, *What Is Called Thinking?* trans. F. Wieck and J. Glenn Gray (New York: Harper and Row, 1968), 139–48 for what follows. Cf. Also Martin Heidegger, "What Are Poets For?" in *Poetry, Language and Thought*, 127ff. For a development of the notion of the heart in the line of Heidegger, see Stephan Strasser, *Phenomenology of Feeling: An Essay on the Phenomena of the Heart*. Translated and introduced by Robert E. Wood. Preface to the English edition by Paul Ricoeur. Humanities Press, 1977.

Heidegger refers to the characteristic activity of the heart so conceived as *das andenkende Denken*, thinking that recalls, or meditative thinking.[15] Such recollective thinking is the supreme thanks. It evokes devotion.[16] Recollection and devotion, turned in gratitude toward what has been granted and devoted to acting in accordance with it gathers time together and in so doing deepens present being by providing it with the ultimate lived context of the Mystery. Since it rests upon the structure of Dasein as relation to the Whole, it reaches out most fully to the outermost limits as well as to the most inward (i.e., it develops a sense of the encompassing Whole of what is, which simultaneously reaches inward to what is deepest in Dasein).[17]

Meditative thinking is not given to abstraction and logical arrangement. It thinks in the medium of the lifeworld, in the mode of dwelling, of inhabitance. Such meditative dwelling is a mode of thinking that belongs to humankind as such and is distinguished from the modes of thinking characteristic of specially talented types: mathematicians, scientists, philosophers, theologians.[18] Heidegger attests that his own philosophic work "belongs right in the midst of the peasants' work," rooted in the Alemannian-Swabian soil.[19] So much is that the case that he reported in a letter to Gadamer that the *Kehre*, the turn in his thought from Dasein to Being, "came to me in a rush"—*Ereignis*-like—as he returned home to Freiburg and the Black Forest and began "to feel the energy of his old stomping ground."[20] We should take that claim with the utmost seriousness.

Among contemporary intellectuals, it is precisely this that has been the object of resistance, even ridicule. Heidegger's background and chosen milieu incline him toward what is regarded as the closed society of the peasant, an anti-intellectual society suspicious of strangers, resistant to the other, the outsider, opposed to the city, to democracy, debate, com-

15. Martin Heidegger, "The Thing," in *Poetry, Language and Thought*, 181.

16. Hans-Georg Gadamer suggests the relation between *Andenken*, or remembrance, and *Andacht*, or devotion, though etymologically dubious, may have been intended to convey the proximity of such thinking to religious experience: see *Heidegger's Ways*, trans. J. Stanley (Albany: State University of New York Press, 1994), 27.

17. Martin Heidegger, "The Origin of the Work of Art," in *Poetry, Language and Thought*, 36.

18. Heidegger, "Memorial Address," 47.

19. Heidegger, "Why Do I Stay in the Provinces," 123.

20. Gadamer, *Heidegger's Ways*, 117.

promise, to technological and scientific advance, the components of the chosen milieu of modern intellectuals. What surfaces here is an essential tension between freedom and *pietas* reflected respectively in modern society and its intellectual apologists on the one hand and, on the other, in Heidegger's peasant society and the apologetic ingredient in his own thought. *Denken als Danken* is the reinvocation of ancient *pietas* (given expression in Aristotle, Cicero, and in Aquinas)[21] as an attitude of gratitude for gifts that is rooted in a sense of an indebtedness that cannot be repaid, for the gift provided is the whole context of one's life. *Pietas*, exercised toward one's family, toward the tradition, and toward God, involves the recognition of the origin of all of one's real possibilities: the family brings one into being and provides one's fundamental stamp, one's *karakter*, mediating the ways of one's community that afford the concrete possibilities for any effective action, suffused with a sense that the whole context—one's own being included—is provided by the Divine. Modern freedom had to fight an uphill battle against such *pietas*, which tended quite naturally to hold one in thrall to the given economic-social-political order. Hegel's work may be viewed as an attempt to establish ancient *pietas* within modern civil society based upon individual freedom of inquiry and operation.[22] Heidegger's work—at least at a fundamental level—reinvokes such *pietas* against the civil society of his contemporary critics.

THE ARTIST-POET

Even living in the way described, the peasant, like everyone, falls into a mode of everydayness, into the "they," the anonymous "one."[23] Mystery tends to disappear. Routine and surface come to dominate as things become flattened out. It is the artist, and especially the poet, who provides what Heidegger refers to as a "world space" in which the mysterious

21. Cf. Thomas Aquinas, *Summa Theologiae*, II-II, q. 101, a. 1. As antecedents, he cites Aristotle, *Nicomachaean Ethics*, IX, 12, 1162a4ff, and Cicero, *De Inv. Rhet*, ii.

22. Cf. Hegel's *Philosophy of Right*, trans. T. Knox (Oxford: Oxford University Press, 1952). The section on ethical life is divided into sections on family, civil society, and state (§§142–340, 105–216), in which the flanking notions—the loci of "substantial freedom"—set the limiting frame for the central section that deals with modern freedoms—market, marriage, press, occupation, assembly, and the like.

23. Heidegger, *Being and Time*, 149ff.

depth of the thing announces itself as emerging from and as sheltered within that which encompasses everything.[24] Indeed, the peasant moves in a world opened up by the creative ones, basically the poets and the founders.[25] One should think here of the role the biblical authors play in providing for the West the ultimate framework and feeling for the world. In the light of the poetically achieved world-space, everything is taken out of the commonplace; in Heidegger's terms, it receives its "being."[26]

The artist-poet struggles with everyday appearance, fights the battle between world and earth, establishes figure in the rift between the two and thus opens up the "inwardness of things."[27] In the 1930s especially, the *polemos* of Heraclitus tends to take center stage: struggle, battle, the praise of the strong.[28] But it is not the physical strength exhibited in overpowering others that is involved here; it is the spiritual strength to win back a sense of the depth that surrounds us from the tendency toward superficiality in everyday appearance. The struggle is essentially with such a fallen appearance for the sake of "Being" as depth and as encompassing in relation to the everyday surface.[29]

24. Martin Heidegger, *Introduction to Metaphysics*, trans. G. Fried and R. Polt (New Haven, Conn.: Yale University Press, 2000), 26.

25. Cf. Heidegger, "The Origin of the Work of Art," in *Poetry, Language and Thought*, 74 and 62. Jacques Taminiaux points to a fundamental shift from the first version of the lecture "The Origin of the Work of Art" in November of 1935 to the third one year later. In the first two, he was still in continuity with the contempt for everydayness evidenced in *Being and Time* and in *Introduction to Metaphysics*; in the third, he shows a renewed appreciation for the strangeness of the familiar. See "The Origin of 'The Origin of the Work of Art,'" in *Reading Heidegger: Commemorations*, ed. J. Sallis (Bloomington: Indiana University Press, 1993), 392–404. This may dovetail with Gadamer's report (see *Heidegger's Ways*) on the transformation Heidegger experienced upon his return to the Black Forest.

26. Heidegger, *Introduction to Metaphysics*, 11, 63.

27. Heidegger, "The Origin of the Work of Art," 63. On innerness, see Heidegger, "What Are Poets For?" 126–30. Cf. Michael Zimmermann, *Heidegger's Confrontation with Modernity: Technology, Politics, Art* (Bloomington: Indiana University Press, 1990), 123; cf. 117 on the connection of Heidegger with *Innerlichkeit* as the center of Hölderlin's thought.

28. For a treatment of the notion of *Kampf* in Heidegger, cf. John D. Caputo, *Demythologizing Heidegger*, (Bloomington: Indiana University Press, 1993), 39–59.

29. Heidegger, *Introduction to Metaphysics*, 61ff. Caputo (*Demythologizing Heidegger*, 6 and 39ff) claims that Heidegger moved from an early concern with the thematics of New Testament *kardia* or the heart to the *Kampf* of faith and thus to *polemos* as central orientation. Need the two be incompatible? It seems to me that for Heidegger it is only through struggle with the tendency to settle down in surface appearances that beings draw near. In such drawing near, they speak to the heart. At any rate, it is clear that for later Heidegger, the heart again becomes a focal notion (cf. Heidegger, *What Is Called Thinking*, 139–48; "What Are Poets For?" 127ff; Strasser, *Phenomenology of Feeling: An Essay on the Phenomena of the Heart*).

We said that for Heidegger the struggle with appearance consists in fighting the battle between World and Earth.[30] Earth as counterposed here to World is not primarily a chemical mass in the solar system. It is the unpurposed bearer of our lives and of the things that surround us. It rises up in sensuousness but falls back in essential resistance to any attempt to penetrate it completely. It is a kind of final opacity.[31] In art, it shows itself in its sensuous appearance as what it is unreflectively in the peasant's experience: as native soil, as that to which he belongs essentially. But in art, the sensuousness is not simply subsidiary as it is in our ordinary functional relations with things; it is focal. In everyday relatedness, the sensuous is assimilated into our focus on function, as are the visual appearance of this page in relation to the meanings I am attempting to convey. But in art, the sensuous medium is part of the message: in Heidegger's terms, it makes focal a sense of *native soil* (*heimatliche Grund*). In poetic language, "Earth" rises up in sound.[32]

At the same time as it sets us on the Earth, art opens up World—again not as the cosmological whole but as a world of meaning. Meaning here entails not simply conceptually unpackable relations but a space of holistic dwelling, opening up paths for thinking, acting, and feeling characteristic of a people, as in the *world* of the ancient Greeks, the *world* of primitive Christianity, the *world* of the medieval Chinese, and so forth.[33] Meaning is essentially a sense of direction for life, fundamental orientation.[34] It is such a world, we might add, that is most immediately accessible in art, so that we can gain our first access to a foreign world through its artworks. Being in such a world is the distinguishing characteristic of *Dasein*.[35] Art reveals the lived world, but in so doing it deepens

---

30. Heidegger, "The Origin of the Work of Art," 55, 63, 75f.

31. Gadamer (*Heidegger's Ways*, 100, 106–7, 190–1) claimed that the notion of "earth" is the basic contribution in Heidegger's treatment of art. It establishes the tension between revealing and concealing, sheltering entailed in every display of truth. Heidegger thus transformed phenomenology from concern with the given to concern with the hidden (123).

32. Martin Heidegger, *On the Way to Language*, trans. P. Hertz (San Francisco: Harper and Row, 1971), 99–101.

33. Heidegger, "The Origin of the Work of Art," 42ff.

34. From *sinnan*: cf. Heidegger, *The Question Concerning Technology and Other Essays*, 180. Derrida links the term to Indo-European *sent* and *set* in relation to the direction of a road in *Of Spirit: Heidegger and the Question*, trans. G. Bennington and R. Bowlby (Chicago: University of Chicago Press), 90.

35. Heidegger, *Being and Time*, 78ff.

the manifestness of that world and even reorients it, in content and direction as well as in the mode of manifestness. Art—and especially poetry—creates the space of lived directedness within a community.

In Heidegger's later work, the tension between Earth and World is transformed: Earth is a component within World that is constituted by what Heidegger calls "the play of the fourfold": Earth and Sky, Mortals and Immortals.[36] The fourfold (*das Geviert*) is like the logical square of opposition. *Earth*—which still carries the functions it did in the earlier dyad—here stands opposite Sky and is essentially related to the *Mortals* who come from and return to Earth, as humans from the humus. Mortals stand opposite *Immortals* as messengers of the Most High, of that which gives the essential measure for human life. Immortals are related to *Sky* as the unreachable above that measures our days and seasons. Humans learn to dwell when they liberate Earth from domination, welcome the Sky that guides the seasons, hold themselves ready for the announcements of the Immortals, and lead other humans toward their authentic death.[37] Things *are* in Heidegger's sense; they have their *being*, they appear charged with significance, as they gather a world of inhabitance. In so doing, they "thing" us (i.e., they lay hold of us and gather us together

36. Heidegger, "Building, Dwelling, Thinking," 149ff; "The Thing," in *Poetry, Language and Thought*, 172ff. Jean-François Mattéi relates the fourfold not only to Hölderlin but also to Plato's *Republic, Gorgias, Symposium,* and *Phaedrus* in "The Heideggerian Chiasmus," in *Heidegger from Metaphysic to Thought* by Dominque Janicaud and Jean-François Mattéi, trans. M. Gendre (Albany: State University of New York Press, 1994), 101, 105, 114, 124, 136. This invites a rereading of Plato's alleged "contempt for the earth." Zimmermann (*Heidegger's Confrontation with Modernity,* 239) suggests that Heidegger may also have been indebted to Rilke's reflections on Cezanne. Reiner Schürmann, in his in many ways excellent interpretation of Heidegger, makes the unpersuasive association of earth and sky with *eon,* and mortals and immortals with *logos* in Heidegger's expositions of Parmenides and Heraclitus: cf. *Heidegger on Being and Acting: From Anarchy to Principles* (Bloomington: Indiana University Press, 1990), 224. Caputo (*Demythologizing Heidegger,* 165) appropriates Véronique Fóti's attack (*Heidegger and the Poets*) on Heidegger's claim to find the fourfold as the essence of poetry. One would at least have to ask for the display of what necessity governs his laying out of these parameters as essential to poetic dwelling. Heidegger links the *Geviert* with the crossing out of the term "being" in *On the Question of Being,* trans. W. Kluback and J. Wilde (London: Vision, 1959), 83.

37. Mattéi, "The Heideggerian Chiasmus," 112. Leading humans in this way seems to be the sole locus, scarcely focused and developed, of *Mitdasein* in later Heidegger. Essentially following Levinas, Caputo notes Heidegger's predominant concern for things and not so predominant concern for people, and especially not for those other than fully functional adults (Caputo, *Demythologizing Heidegger,* 65). But he notes further that what is required is more than an extension of "letting things be" from things to people but a more radical openness to what is other (146).

insofar as we are available to "let them be"). Heidegger plays here on the German word for thing, *Ding*, which originally meant assembly. Things are not simply passive to our projects; they can also take hold of us, absorb us, magnetize our attention. And they can so "thing" us insofar as world "worlds" (i.e., insofar as an encompassing way of thinking, acting, and feeling has us in its grips, for things appear meaningfully present as they stand in webs of meaning relations that ultimately stretch to the Whole. It is paradigmatically in art that things come to "thing" and world comes to "world" us.[38]

The artist as shaper of materials—of paint and of glass, of stone and wood, clay and bronze—depends upon the most primordial of artists, the poet who gives shape to language that opens up the Whole. Language gives expression to the *logos* that gathers a community over time as it gathers together the coming to presence of the Whole for the community.[39] Poetry creates the primary music that sets linguistic meaning upon the earth of sonority. Within the space of its meanings, all other art forms come into being.[40]

Art in general operates in the same medium as meditative dwelling characteristic of the peasant who takes things to heart, who is thoughtful. *Mnemosune*, memory as devotion, is the mother of the Muses but also the daughter of Sky and Earth.[41] Thinking that recalls is the origin of poetry.[42] It proclaims the Holy, which, for Heidegger, is ancillary to consideration of the divine. The Holy, announced by the poet, is a dimension of encompassment and demand that calls for devotion. Only in letting things be, devotedly, thoughtfully, can the true sense of the divine dawn.[43] Great art occasions such thinking for a community. Great art is grateful letting be.

38. Heidegger, "Language," in *Poetry, Language and Thought*, 199 and 203.

39. Cf. my "Heidegger on the Way to Language," in *Semiotics 1984*, ed. J. Deely (Lanham, Md.: University Press of America, 1986), 611–20.

40. Heidegger, "The Origin of the Work of Art," 73–4.

41. Mattéi, "The Heideggerian Chiasmus," 133.

42. Heidegger, *What Is Called Thinking?* 11.

43. Martin Heidegger, "Letter on Humanism," in *Martin Heidegger: Basic Writings*, ed. D. F. Krell (New York: Harper and Row, 1977), 230.

THE PHILOSOPHER

Philosophy is a distinctively Greek phenomenon. For Heidegger as for Hegel, there is no non-Western philosophy but only a certain family resemblance to philosophy *stricto sensu*.[44] Philosophy emerges in the West in the train of Anaximander, Parmenides, and Heraclitus, who were primordial thinkers and not yet philosophers—indeed, at least for the Heidegger of 1951, they were too great to be philosophers.[45]

Philosophy has what we might call its proto-origin in a poetic-intellectual experience of Being in Heraclitus and Parmenides as emerging into presence that they termed *phusis*, whose stems stress emergence (*phuo*) and manifestness (*phainomenon*).[46] Plato and Aristotle focus on the "what" in what emerges into presence, and the coming to presence is itself unfocused.[47] The "what" is *idea* or *eidos*, the intelligible look, the face things present to intellectual looking, the ever-now, always already there, perpetually standing intelligible.[48] Here we see what Janicaud has described as "the transition in metaphysics from Being-present to Being-essential."[49] In the peculiarity of philosophy's emergence, Being so conceived is placed in contrast with becoming, with appearance, with thought, and with the ought to create a set of related dyads: being and becoming, being and appearance, being and thought, being and the ought.[50] Among the Greeks, what sets up the contrast is the notion of Being as always present, as occupying a standing now, so that the ever-present must appear as contrasted with the changing, with the appearing and disappearing, with thought as that which views it over against itself, with the term of aspiration that grants the viewing.[51] And yet, becoming, appearance, thought, and the ought "are," each in their own way, so

44. Heidegger, *What Is Called Thinking?* 224; *What Is Philosophy?* trans. W. Kluback and J. Wilde (New York: Twayne, 1958), 31.

45. Heidegger, *What Is Philosophy?* 53.

46. Heidegger, *Introduction to Metaphysics*, 14, 101. I find little ground for Zimmermann's contention that Heidegger did not adequately emphasize the first stem (Zimmermann, *Heidegger's Confrontation with Modernity*, 225). The text cited seems to me to make that transparent.

47. Heidegger, *What Is Philosophy?* 53.

48. Heidegger, *Introduction to Metaphysics*, 180ff; Heidegger, *What Is Called Thinking?* 233, 238.

49. Dominque Janicaud, "Heideggeriana," in *Heidegger From Metaphysic to Thought*, 16.

50. Heidegger, *Introduction to Metaphysics*, 93ff.

51. Heidegger, *What Is Called Thinking?* 102.

that Being conceived of as their opposite cannot encompass the way they themselves also are. Western philosophy in its fundamental character as metaphysics operates out of that conception of Being but fails to consider what holds sway in it. The distinction between Being so conceived and beings who appear as its instances still occupies, in Heidegger's view, the level of beings (*Seienden* as things and principles) and does not rise to the level of Being (*Sein*) as that which grants the distinction.

However, in his reading of Plato and Aristotle, Heidegger claims that for them, as the first philosophers, philosophy still plants its roots in awe; it feeds on astonishment before the mystery of the Whole and grows in such astonishment as it carries on its essential questioning.[52] It is led to ask about the most fundamental things, to unsettle all the settled so as to get to the roots of things. Like art, philosophy too creates so much world space that in its light even the ordinary appears extraordinary.[53]

But just as in art what comes to be is subjectible to the everydayness that flattens out all appearance, so also with philosophy. The astonishment allied with the peculiar coming to presence of that which is given for thought disappears, and one falls into argumentation and construction far removed from fundamental awe. The passing on of problems within a given horizon fails to think the unconcealed horizon in relation to the concealed encompassing out of which it comes.[54] Philosophic problems are subject to what Heidegger—perhaps thinking originally of the Sophists but not only of them—calls "the cheap acid of a merely logical intelligence."[55]

The history of philosophy, precisely as metaphysics, becomes the history of the forgottenness of Being as mysterious encompassment coming to presence in what it grants for thought. Truth migrates from *aletheia* or coming out of concealment (in which awareness of the *lethe*, the con-

---

52. *What Is Philosophy?* 79. There is much in the Platonic dialogues that supports this way of reading *thaumazein*. However, when Aristotle explicitly treats it in his *Metaphysics* (I, 1, 982b 12), it is not awe but curiosity as that which disappears when one can offer an explanation. I suspect Heidegger reads this into Aristotle because he had even greater respect for him than for Plato, whom, Gadamer suggests, Heidegger never really understood (*Heidegger's Ways*, 144). In general, Heidegger read Plato in the light of Aristotle, as is clearly indicated by his spending the first 237 pages of his 668-page *Platon: Sophistes* in *Gesamtausgabe*, II (Frankfurt am Main: Vittorio Klostermann, 1992) on Aristotle.
53. Heidegger, *Introduction to Metaphysics*, 26.
54. Ibid.
55. Ibid. See also 120–1.

cealed, provokes recurrent astonishment) to *orthotes*, correctness or correspondence of propositions, formulated within the unconcealed sphere of meanings, to things revealed in terms of that unconcealed sphere of meanings.[56] As Heidegger put it in *Being and Time*, "Assertion is not the primary 'locus' of truth. *On the contrary*, . . . the most primordial 'truth' is the 'locus' of assertion."[57] From truth as grounded in correctness of assertion, truth is transformed at the beginning of modern times into *certitudo*, into the methodic certification of things under terms set up by a controlling subject.[58] And from there we arrive at truth as "enframing," whereby things appear as standing reserve for our projects.[59] The latter explicitly surfaces in Nietzsche, who, in Heidegger's view, has developed the ultimate possibility of metaphysics,[60] since Plato's original view of the Being of things as the ever-present intelligible look was essentially tied to the view of things as products of intelligence, instanced in the *Timaeus* where the divinity fashions things by looking to the Ideas.[61]

Though there is a reigning forgetfulness from the very inception of philosophy as metaphysics, nonetheless, metaphysics is not false or wrong.[62] But unless it is led back to its own ground, what is essential to Dasein is lost.

THE SCIENTIST

For Heidegger, science operates in the conceptual space opened up by philosophy.[63] Scientific thinking is derivative from philosophy.[64] But the development of the sciences is their separation from and completion of philosophy.[65] Science always and necessarily operates on the basis of

56. Heidegger, "On the Essence of Truth," in *Martin Heidegger: Basic Writings*, 122ff.

57. Heidegger, *Being and Time*, 269.

58. Heidegger, "The Age of the World-Picture," in *The Question Concerning Technology and Other Essays*, 148.

59. Heidegger, *What Is Called Thinking?* 17.

60. Heidegger, *The End of Philosophy*, 95; *Time and Being*, trans. J. Stambaugh (New York: Harper and Row, 1969), 56–57; cf. Schürmann (*Heidegger on Being and Acting*, especially 112ff) for one of the most plausible cases for the comprehensiveness of Heidegger's seemingly implausible claim to the exhaustion of possibilities.

61. Plato, *Timaeus*, 28, on the *demiourgos*.

62. Heidegger, *What Is Called Thinking?* 103, 211.

63. Ibid., 131; *What Is Philosophy?* 31–33.

64. Heidegger, *Introduction to Metaphysics*, 26.

65. Heidegger, *Time and Being*, 57.

what is manifest in the lifeworld but only insofar as that has been transformed by conceptual transcription. After distinctions have been conceptually inventoried, specializations can be cultivated that are no longer concerned with their origins or their relations with one another. Just as one can operate within the functional circle of the everyday world, unaware that, as Kierkegaard put it, "we float on waters 70,000 fathoms deep," so in science, we can master cybernetic functions without ontological meaning, without questioning the framework of manifestness within which science itself occurs.[66]

Scientific specializations emerge in the wake of Plato and Aristotle.[67] But distinctively modern science emerges through a distinctive projection of the ground plan of nature that sets it in decisive contrast to the Aristotelian view that it supplanted. For Heidegger, this is not necessarily a progression *tout court*—although there is clearly a progressive manifestation of features of nature under the modern paradigm. What holds sway in modern science is the essence of technology, a view made thematic in Nietzsche for whom Being itself is Will to Power.[68] Nature is made over into what it has to be in order to be progressively controlled and assimilated into our projects. In the Galilean-Newtonian view, there are no longer natures seeking to actualize their forms; there is only nature, a single system of colorless, odorless, tasteless, soundless, valueless, irreducible elements located in an empty container space and, simultaneously, in a flowing, river-like time, combining and separating according to invariant laws.[69] As a consequence, from the point of view of science natures can thus no longer be violated. Aristotelian natures, substantial forms each seeking their respective *tele*, are considered mere phenomenal appearances of what has been called "the dance of the atoms." And learning how they dance without us enables us to become conductors of the dance. In this way, for Heidegger things lose their "being" and become data.[70] But for Heidegger also, this was already prepared for when Plato thought the Being of beings as intelligible looks functioning as archetypes for divine production.[71]

66. Ibid., 58.
67. Heidegger, "Letter on Humanism," 232f.
68. Heidegger, *The Question Concerning Technology and Other Essays*, 75ff.
69. Heidegger, *What Is a Thing?* trans. W. Barton and V. Deutsch (Chicago: Regnery, 1967), 80ff.
70. Heidegger, *Introduction to Metaphysics*, 62–63.
71. Cf. Schürmann, *Heidegger on Being and Acting*, 75: philosophy had its roots in Greek

In the first emergence of science, we have the age of the world picture: nature is the in-principle viewable. But then, with twentieth-century physics, nature disappears into the objectlessness of standing reserve: *Gegenstand* becomes *Bestand*.[72] In contrast with nature for the peasant, modern nature is placed under demand, no longer entrusted with sustaining us and our works. Standing within nature, attuned to its essential rhythms and fitting human projects within it, the peasant is disposed by a basic *pietas* for the nature the god has provided. In contrast, in the modern disposition, humanness stands over against nature, which it summons to appear in such a way as to provide maximum yield for humanity's projects: nature is a field for the operation of unbounded human freedom. Rather than the shepherd of Being, modern man seeks to become the lord and master of nature.[73] Held in the grips of the scientific-technological way of viewing, we allow no other view of nature to stand. People look to science to decide upon the place of human being in the Whole and to set the standards for human decision.[74] Much is revealed, but what is concealed is the fact of *revealing itself* and thus Dasein as the locus of manifestness.[75]

Though a scientist may, as a reflective person, shift into the philosophic mode, science does not, as science—indeed *cannot* as science—think its own presuppositions, its own rootedness in the structure of Dasein; hence, science is in the dark regarding its own nature.[76] In Heidegger's not too rhetorically wise way of putting it: "Science does not think."[77] Its thoughtlessness regarding its own encompassment is rooted

---

astonishment before things produced by man. This accounts for the dominance of "teleocracy" in all Western thinking (83). Metaphysics then becomes "the generalization of modes of thought appropriate to only *one* region of phenomena—artifacts" (105). For a critique of the Platonic origins of this notion, see Stanley Rosen, *The Question of Being: A Reversal of Heidegger* (New Haven, Conn.: Yale University Press, 1993), 10–21, 43. Rosen thinks that, among other things, Heidegger fails to deal adequately with Platonic Eros, which operates in the crucial relation between mythos and logos (29). We noted previously Gadamer's claim (*Heidegger's Ways*, 144) regarding Heidegger that the Platonic dialogues "remained inaccessible to this impatient questioner."

72. Heidegger, *The Question Concerning Technology and Other Essays*, 17.
73. René Descartes, *Discourse on Method*, trans. D. Cress (Indianapolis: Hackett, 1980), 33 (Adam Tannery, 62).
74. Heidegger, *What Is Called Thinking?* 43.
75. Heidegger, *The Question Concerning Technology and Other Essays*, 27.
76. Heidegger, *What Is Called Thinking?* 43.
77. Ibid., 8. Schürmann (*Heidegger on Being and Acting*, 291) suggests that this parallels Kant's distinction between thinking and knowing. This would seem to imply that science does

in its essential one-sidedness.[78] And the great danger that attends this movement is that Dasein itself will disappear into the standing reserve: human beings will themselves become simply on-hand for the projects of some Overman.[79]

THE MAN ON THE STREET

Human reality as Dasein is thrown Being-in-the-World, on account of which we are always inauthentic in the sense of not being fully self-possessed but being in the grips of a world articulated long before we entered on the scene.[80] But there is a massive difference between the world of the peasant and the world of the contemporary man on the street. The inauthenticity of the peasant was still the expression of a world that had a place for the essential things that he could thinkingly take to heart. An essential part of his world was the heeding of the poets—again, consider here the biblical authors.

The contemporary man on the street is held in the grips of the same mode of revealing characteristic of modern science as its technological essence has come to clearer focus. Scientific technology holds sway, and for it there is no longer any room for that which falls outside the scope of its methods, for action not guided by its attitude of dominance, hence, for the Holy that places its demands upon us.

In lines reminiscent of Nietzsche's *Last Man*,[81] Heidegger speaks of the devastation of the earth as the condition for a guaranteed high standard of living and happiness for all, leading to the "high-velocity expulsion of Mnemosyne,"[82] of meditative thinking, of thoughtful recollection attuned to the Holy. For Heidegger, we live in a time of "the darkening of the world, the flight of the gods, the destruction of the earth, the trans-

---

not think because it knows—though it does not know what exceeds, situates, and makes itself possible.

78. Heidegger, *What Is Called Thinking?* 32ff.

79. Cf. Zimmermann (*Heidegger's Confrontation with Modernity*, 58–59) on Heidegger's relation to Jünger: human beings are viewed as standing reserve to be stamped with the Gestalt of the worker. Meditation on Hölderlin led to the opposite view of drawing out of forms that are already there (76).

80. Heidegger, *Being and Time*, 219.

81. Cf. Heidegger, *What Is Called Thinking?* 57ff.

82. Ibid., 30.

formation of men into a mass, the hatred and suspicion of everything free and creative."[83] The sense of history vanishes (one recalls Henry Ford's famous remark: "History is bunk!") and the boxer (or, today, the multi-million-dollar athlete) is hero. Devotees of speed and of time-saving devices, we seem to have no time.[84] If we think of the whole at all, we think of it in scientific-technological terms. The arts are pleasant diversion, entertainment, prettification, not manifestations of the fundamental. The Holy that great art proclaims has disappeared from our purview. For Heidegger, "perhaps what is distinctive about this world-epoch consists in the closure of the dimension of the hale [*das Heiligen*]."[85]

Modern humanity is essentially homeless.[86] It has lost the element in which Dasein by nature lives. Even the contemporary farmer no longer lives in nature as the ever-environing whole, unencompassable by science. Technology in the form of radio and television invades his silence and prevents his meditative thought.[87] Language as simultaneously the home of Being and the dwelling place of humankind degenerates into an instrument for communicative purposes[88] and further into "a mere container for their sundry preoccupations."[89] Without the sense of Being, humankind is like a fish out of water.[90]

THE THINKER

Given what Heidegger understands by thinking, logic is not, as logicians claim, the requisite thinking on thinking.[91] In fact, if we cannot think beyond logic, we are left with the previously designated "cheap acid of a merely logical intelligence." And science does not think. Both science and logic cultivate a domain already open. Thinking is concerned with coming back reflectively upon that opening.

Heidegger regularly refers to philosophers as thinkers, in contrast to

83. Heidegger, *Introduction to Metaphysics*, 38.
84. Heidegger, *What Is Called Thinking?* 101.
85. Heidegger, "Letter on Humanism," 230.
86. Ibid., 218.
87. Heidegger, "Memorial Address," 48.
88. Heidegger, *On the Way to Language*, 58.
89. Heidegger, "Letter on Humanism," 239.
90. Ibid., 195.
91. Heidegger, *What Is Called Thinking?* 21.

scientists who are said not to think insofar as philosophy deals with the frameworks presupposed by science. For example, Socrates is the purest thinker of the West,[92] and Nietzsche is a great thinker.[93] Aristotle, Plato, and Kant are thinkers.[94] Presumably, philosophy has to do with conceptual elaboration, construction, and argumentation as a means of working out that thought. But Heidegger also distinguishes *philosophy*, which is in essence metaphysics, from *thinking*, which concerns the ground of metaphysics.[95] As we have noted earlier, for Heidegger Heraclitus and Parmenides were thinkers but were too great in stature to be philosophers. Here, from Socrates to Nietzsche, something essential loses focus. Metaphysics is the ultimate conceptual framework presupposed in all our dealings, scientific and otherwise; but it does not think that which it itself presupposes, the way Being itself comes to presence. Metaphysics thus contributes to the forgottenness of Being—indeed, because it considers itself the most fundamental form of thought, it is the major culprit in the occlusion of Being that holds sway in Western philosophy and science.[96]

Metaphysics, Heidegger claims, thinks of beings as beings, entities in terms of their principles. It operates within the framework opened up by the early Greeks, who viewed the being of entities in a specific way: in terms of the enduring presence of their principles. Given that framework, propositions can be formed whose correspondence with things can be checked and from which, by the use of logic, inferences can be drawn. But what remains unthought is the coming into presence of the framework. And within that framework, there is a history to how the being of things is thought. What is overlooked is the original coming out of concealment that founds truth so conceived. And correlative with the coming out of concealment is concealment itself. Heidegger refers here to the mystery of the hidden to which we are nonetheless essentially related.

Because philosophy, observing and inferring, operates from out of the perspectives granted in each case but does not think the granting of the perspectives, the history of philosophy calls for a "destruction,"[97]

92. Ibid., 17.   93. Ibid., 50.
94. Ibid., 77.
95. Cf. "The Way Back into the Ground of Metaphysics," in *Existentialism from Dostoyevsky to Sartre*, trans. and ed. W. Kaufmann (Cleveland: World, 1956), 206ff.
96. Ibid., 276.
97. Heidegger, *Being and Time*, 44.

a dismantling (*Abbau*) of "representations that have become banal and vacuous,"[98] a desedimentation that leads back to the ground of original givenness, originary coming to presence. This allows one to stake out the positive possibilities of the tradition. Such a process involves an overcoming (*Überwindung*) of metaphysics. Heidegger insists that the destruction or overcoming of the history of metaphysics is not its elimination because metaphysics is not false or wrong.[99] He later admitted that the term "destruction" had lent itself to a misunderstanding "of insuperable grotesqueness."[100] He rejects as superficial those interpretations that would "consist in setting oneself against metaphysics, in rejecting it as an opinion, or else in dismissing it as a discipline now obsolete. . . . Metaphysics is less overcome than assigned to limits."[101] In fact, for Heidegger metaphysics belongs to the nature of humanness—presumably, like science, available in principle to any human.[102] "For metaphysics overcome in this way does not disappear. It returns transformed and remains in dominance as the continuing difference of Being and beings."[103] "Overcoming" metaphysics signifies not elimination but incorporation.[104] Heidegger says that what is involved is "neither a destruction nor even a denial of metaphysics. To intend anything else would be childish presumption and a demeaning of history."[105] In this sense, overcoming is related to authenticity in which, instead of taking for granted and going along, we each appropriate and thus take radical responsibility for the "inauthentic" that is our irremovable ground as the prior genetic and cultural shaping we have and must

98. Heidegger, *The Question of Being*, 92.

99. Heidegger, *What Is Called Thinking?* 103, 211.

100. Heidegger, *The Question of Being*, 92.

101. Dominique Janicaud "Overcoming Metaphysics," in *Heidegger From Metaphysic to Thought*, 5, 7. I agree completely with Mattéi's judgment that Heidegger is concerned with "displacing the metaphysical *point of view* on Being—not in order to cancel it but to show its essential insufficiency in the absence of a premetaphysical *counterpoint*" (*Heidegger from Metaphysic to Thought*, 74). Janicaud correctly remarks that "at stake is the question of taking metaphysics upon oneself, and not leaving it aside" ("Overcoming Metaphysics, 197). I think then that Derrida is way off the mark in claiming that Heidegger dealt with metaphysics in order to "send it packing" (*Of Spirit*, 75).

102. Heidegger, *The End of Philosophy*, 87; cf. "The Way Back into the Ground of Metaphysics," 267.

103. Heidegger, "Overcoming Metaphysics," in *The End of Philosophy*, 85.

104. Heidegger, *The End of Philosophy*, 84ff. Cf. Stambaugh's note 1. It seems to me that Gadamer (82, 184–85) is on firm ground when he claims that Heidegger's work gave metaphysics new strength and was calculated to do so.

105. Heidegger, *On the Way to Language*, 20.

have received. Deconstruction is "the *return* toward the original site of metaphysics in order to appropriate it within its own limits and to prepare a new beginning."[106] Thought climbs back down from metaphysical abstraction into the nearness of the near.[107]

Furthermore, in Heidegger's view, each philosophy, which is at base metaphysics, is inexhaustible. "Overcoming" metaphysics is transforming it by replanting it in the soil in which it originated, the soil of fundamental awe.[108] But this requires a loosening up of the soil. In what does this "loosening up" consist? Heidegger uses another metaphor here: it involves attempting to "get into the draft" that draws the thinker, guiding him in his conceptual articulations.[109] Concepts have to be brought back to their origins in the lifeworld. Rootless elaboration of problems that follow from previous formulations, argumentation of positions pro and con, construction of explanations, elaboration of systematic connections: all this philosophic work has to be led back to its origins, not simply in specialized experiences but in the encompassing field of the lifeworld that, above all, includes our orientation toward the Whole.[110]

We accomplish this leading back by thinking the unthought, presumably the lifeworld payoff, the deepening of the sense of real presences, for thinking takes place in the medium of the lifeworld,[111] as Heidegger identifies the locus of his own thinking in the lifeworld of the Swabian peasant. In leading the conceptual apparatus back to the lifeworld, we see that, primordially considered, philosophy is lived correspondence with the Being of beings.[112] But then, without some form of

---

106. Mattéi, *Heidegger From Metaphysic to Thought*, 54.

107. Heidegger, "Letter on Humanism," 231.

108. Heidegger, *The End of Philosophy*, 85.

109. Cf. Heidegger, "What Are Poets For?" 105ff.

110. On the notion of "sedimentation of concepts," cf. Edmund Husserl, *Crisis in European Science and Transcendental Phenomenology*, trans. D. Carr (Evanston, Ill.: Northwestern University Press, 1970). Gadamer (*Heidegger's Ways*, 61–62, 70, and 141) notes the astonishment of himself and his fellow students as Heidegger demonstrated that, instead of charting out relations and formally linking judgments, thinking is showing and getting things to show themselves in and through the thinkers he examined, with whose horizons he fused his own. He thus showed that the break with the tradition was "just as much an incomparable renewal of the tradition" (70).

111. Heidegger, *What Is Called Thinking?* 31.

112. In view of everything we have pointed out, I find it mind-boggling for Rosen (*The Question of Being*, 272) to claim that Heidegger has detached philosophy from everyday life, except insofar as Rosen might understand that as not providing any guidance for living our lives except for "listening to the voice of Being," which Rosen regards as vacuous (217, 263).

such correspondence we would not be able to speak: the Whole has to be opened up in a certain way through language. However, for Heidegger, philosophy—adequately understood—is *fulfilled* correspondence.[113] Presumably, in maintaining some distinction between philosophy and primordial thinking, the fulfilled correspondence is not simply the demonstrable circle of concepts but the experiential filling of that circle, the rising up and return of conceptualization to the sense of holistic attunement to the Whole, revealed and concealed in and through the peculiarity of a given philosophic circle of concepts.[114]

The thinker's task is to make clear the perspectives we occupy in relation to the encompassing Mystery. In so doing, he operates within the element thematized by the artist-poet but also implicitly constituting the lifeworld of the peasant. Thinking, Heidegger says, is "memory, devotion and thanks," features that characterized the meditative taking to heart of his peasant friends.[115] "Thinking" operates prereflectively in the peasant, the artist-poet, and, indeed, even in the philosopher. But it is not attended to explicitly in any of them. That is the task for what Heidegger comes to call *the thinker*. He is ultimately "the shepherd of Being,"[116] one who cares for the presencing in what is present. Heidegger uses another metaphor: he is the one who "works at building the house of Being," the house that is language.[117] He builds linguistically by setting language into the element in which it lives.[118]

In this regard, Heidegger's understanding of Parmenides is central. He focuses particularly upon two Parmenidean dicta: *to gar auto estin noein te kai einai*, usually translated as "thought and being are one,"[119] and *chre to legein te noien t'eon emmenai*, often rendered as "one should both say and think that being is."[120] Thought in its primordial sense is

113. Heidegger, *What Is Philosophy?* 75, 79.

114. If this interpretation is correct, Heidegger already circumvents Janicaud's objection that Heidegger creates a solidified dichotomy between metaphysics and the thought of Being, which disallows a "rational dwelling" in terms of a "non-techno-logical-scientific rational thinking . . . [which] reigned freely in the Medievals' theory of *analogia*." (*Heidegger From Metaphysic to Thought*, 35 and 29).

115. Heidegger, *What Is Called Thinking?* 163.

116. Heidegger, "Letter on Humanism," 221.

117. Ibid., 192, 236.

118. Heidegger, *On the Way to Language*, 98ff.

119. Heidegger, *What Is Called Thinking?* 241.

120. Ibid., 174. Heidegger spends the rest of the book (-244) explicating this and the following sentences.

the place where the sense of the Whole opens up. It *is* this opening up. Early Heidegger calls this place *Dasein*, human reality as the "there" of the dawning of the meaning of Being (*Sein*). The thought of Being is the being-taken by that meaning, being attuned to it, living in it. *Noein*, thinking, is taking to heart, which is letting be; *nous* is related to the *thanc*.[121] Taking to heart allows the presence of what is present to make its claim.[122] Taking to heart presupposes the gathering (*legein*) performed by language that lets things be present in the way they are present. Linguistically mediated manifestness precedes taking to heart as letting lie before. But it also follows as safeguarding in the gathering of what is taken to heart.[123] The two together, *legein* and *noein*, rooted in language and the heart, show what thinking is.[124] "Letting lie before" corresponds to the theoretical moment, but taking to heart fulfills our belonging to Being. Philosophy as fulfilled attunement to Being sets the conceptually elaborated within the framework of fundamental awe attuned to the encompassing Mystery out of which all that comes to presence comes to presence.

Contrary to what it might seem, from very much that Heidegger says and from much that his readers draw from him, he is not calling for a repudiation of technology, science, or metaphysics.[125] They are part of the history of what has been granted to us. What is needed is a "friend of the house of Being," who, as he says, "in equal manner and with equal force is inclined toward both the technologically constructed world-ediface *and* the world as a house for a more original dwelling," one who is able "to re-entrust the calculability and technicity of nature to the open mystery of a newly experienced naturalness of nature."[126]

121. Heidegger, *What Is Called Thinking?* 202, 207; "What Are Poets For?" 127ff.
122. Heidegger, *What Is Called Thinking?* 241.
123. Ibid., 208.
124. Ibid., 209.
125. There's always been a problem with Heidegger's rhetoric, which may go deeper than rhetoric. For example, in the use of terms like "authentic" and "inauthentic," surrounded in his own usage with high moral tone, Heidegger still denies any moral features to the notions involved. He seems to attack metaphysics and then to reinstate it; he does the same with technology.
126. Heidegger, "Hebel—Friend of the House," 98.

CONCLUSION

The thinker, the artist-poet, and the peasant operate out of meditative thinking. Each has a peculiar sense of the environing Mystery to which we essentially belong—belong, in other words, as called upon to be aware of it and to listen for the essential claims it makes upon us. But each operates with a different vehicle: the thinker operates negatively in the sphere of concepts, loosening them to get a sense of the unsaid draft that draws on the philosopher; the artist-poet operates in the sphere of what is most immediately insistent in the lifeworld, sensory manifestness, within the context of a lived sense of the Whole. The artist-poet, by bringing sensuousness and earthiness to focal presence, works to win back the sense of the Whole and thus the depth of each least thing from the flattening out that tends to constitute everyday appearance. The paradigmatic peasant occupies the sphere of everyday experience pervaded by tasks but knows the nearness of the environing Mystery that he takes to heart. They are all friends of the simple who have experienced its quiet force.

In a sense counterpoised to these are the philosopher, the scientist, and the contemporary man on the street. The former operates constructively in the sphere of the concept, feeding off of fundamental generative intuitions that produce encompassing frameworks. The modern scientist operates out of a peculiar framework that transforms nature into what it has to be in order for us to manipulate it. The contemporary man on the street is the recipient of the scientific-technological framework that tends to drive out of consideration other modes of revealing. The latter two types—scientist and man on the street—are in principle, insofar as they think exclusively in the dominant framework, alienated from the element proper to humankind, the element of meditative thinking. The philosopher seems to be a transitional figure. He thinks in terms of the presuppositions of science and the lifeworld, but he fails to think the Mystery in the element proper to it because he is dominated by the thought of Being as standing now. Insofar as he is an essential thinker, he is sustained by fundamental awe and lives in a deepened presence of the Whole appearing in all things, but apparently, *qua* philosopher, he does not *think* that off of which he lives. In attending questioningly to the ground of metaphysics, Heidegger has performed an essential service: in the words of Dominique Janicaud, he "has altered the light in which the landscape was bathed."[127]

Getting back behind what holds sway in Western thought from its inception leads to the possibility of a second beginning. It leads into the element in which the arts operate. It could provide, in the darkened era in which we now live, the "saving grace," for the reinvoking of a lifeworld, like the lifeworld of the peasant, which has a place for the Holy. However, such a reinvocation can occur only in relation to the context of scientific-technological orientation, which is the dominant mode of revealing granted to us today. In the element of the lifeworld, we can relearn how to correspond to the Mystery that surrounds us. In this element, we can learn a mode of thinking other than the representative-calculative mode that currently dominates us. We can learn again meditatively taking to heart.

127. Janicaud, *Heidegger From Metaphysic to Thought*, 22. I have tried to approach select highpoints in the history of metaphysics by leaning especially upon Heidegger's notion of *aletheia* and developing a set of "secular meditations" that follow that lead in *A Path into Metaphysics*. Cf. especially chapter 1 on meditation and chapter 16 on Heidegger. I have also linked Heidegger with the poet-essayist Max Picard and with Martin Buber in "Silence, Being and the Between: Picard, Heidegger and Buber," *Man and World* 27 (1994): 121–34. It is reprinted as the last chapter in this volume.

19 ✑ Weiss on Adumbration

Paul Weiss, founder of the Metaphysical Society of America and of *The Review of Metaphysics*, had a special knack for attending to items that other philosophers tend to ignore. Shakespeare's line, "There are more things in heaven and on earth than are dreamt of in your philosophy," though applicable to many thinkers, seems inappropriate when applied to Weiss. In his own way, Weiss is even more ample than the omnivorous Hegel, who, after all, never elaborated a philosophy of sport. But then again, many seem inclined to reverse Shakespeare's line in Weiss's case: "There are more things in Weiss's philosophy than there are in heaven or on earth."[1]

Where many thinkers—by no means most—are comfortable with the encountered actualities of Weiss's first book, *Reality*, and many too are also comfortable with one transcendent addition to such actualities—a God frequently thought of as the highest actuality—people in general, and the generality of philosophic people as well, get extremely uncomfortable with four, not to mention five, transcendents *or* modes of being or finalities, including, and in some sense co-equal with, God.[2]

Now one of the items ignored by many other philosophers, especially those attracted by logic, is what Weiss calls "adumbration." It appears in almost all his works, beginning with *Reality* and continuing to *First Considerations* and *I, You and the Others*. The exploration of this notion may give us some access to at least one of the routes that could make Weiss's finalities more palatable to at least some contemporary thinkers. In the process, it may also reopen access in a fresh way to the history of speculative thought in the West.

1. See, for example, Andrew Reck's reply in Paul Weiss, *First Considerations* (Carbondale: Southern Illinois University Press, 1977).

2. In his central work, *Modes of Being* (Carbondale: Southern Illinois University Press, 1958), Weiss distinguishes, in addition to God, Actuality, Ideality, and Existence (*Reality*, 58). In *Beyond All Appearances* (Carbondale: Southern Illinois University Press, 1974), Actuality is split into Substance and Being.

Adumbration appears initially and centrally in Weiss's first book, and there its use itself adumbrates his later move to transcendent finalities. It appears first in the midst of a discussion of the components of a simple perceptual judgment, such as "this is paper." "This" names what Weiss calls "the indicated," the locatable, the particular, the here-and-now sensorily present, the ostensive object. "Paper" names "the contemplated," the universal meaning, detached from the particular yet oriented toward it as an instance of the contemplated meaning. But the "is" has several functions: first, a synthetic, propositional function joining the indicated and the contemplated and, second, a judgmental function referring the propositional synthesis to the encountered object. Weiss detects a third function: adumbration. Adumbration refers to the in-itself-ness of the encountered, standing beyond the reach of the indicated-contemplated surface. Verification that the contemplated fits the indicated is not enough, for we know of the "not" and the more than what fits within the clearly articulated elements of the judgment. But knowledge of that more is a kind of nonknowledge, a knowing ignorance.[3]

Weiss claims to stand in this matter somewhere between Kant and Hegel. Kant restricts knowledge to a phenomenal circle mirroring back the constructive power of the mind but cut off from the noumenal order of the things-in-themselves. Reference to the object is thus reference to what has been constituted by the mind. But having restricted knowing to the phenomenal order within which alone categories such as existence, causality, and substance operate, Kant nonetheless claims to know that the thing-in-itself (1) *exists*, (2) *causes* the sensory material, and (3) *substands* the phenomena that stand "on our side" as verifiable sensory-intelligible content. Kant thus violates his own restrictions. To avoid this violation, Weiss accordingly distinguishes two modes of knowing, one dealing with the verifiable indicated-contemplated surface jutting into our side and another—knowing in a broader sense of the term—*knowledge by adumbration*.[4] "We are" he says, "phenomenalists who are aware that there is a truth beyond phenomenalism making it possible."[5]

Adumbration at this phase of Weiss's thought has two facets: a per-

3. Paul Weiss, *Reality*, 32ff, 57, 69; *Philosophy in Process*, vol. II (Carbondale: Southern Illinois University Press, 1962) (January 14, 1962), 22.

4. Paul Weiss, *Nature and Man* (Carbondale: Southern Illinois University Press, 1947), 50.

5. Weiss, *Reality*, 142. Weiss acknowledges his special debt to Kant (together with Aristotle and Whitehead) in the preface.

382 Weiss on Adumbration

ceptual and a recessive facet. The elliptical presentation of a plate seen from an angle declining from frontality involves a perceptual adumbration of the circularity of the plate.[6] Presumably, the outer and macro-observation of the body involves perceptual adumbration of the future penetration of physiology, microbiology, and microphysics. The perceptual adumbrative makes possible a move from where we are, within the phenomenal circle of the public common sense world, to an extended phenomenal circle. But the recessive adumbrative refers to the ultimate private substantiality of the existing thing, beyond even the extended circle.[7]

Contrary to Kant, Hegel claims to "overreach" the phenomena and eventually stand completely in the place of the *Ding-an-sich*. For Weiss, this errs in the other extreme, though Weiss has great sympathy for Hegel, considering *The Phenomenology of Spirit* to be perhaps the greatest work in the history of thought.[8] However, Hegel's final claim to penetrate fully to the other side through the development of the Absolute System claims too much. Kant, Weiss claims, began in the wrong place, with articulate knowledge, not with that which antedates such knowledge and to which adumbration points. Hegel's *Phenomenology* seems to begin with articulate knowing but of the most impoverished sort: the here-and-now sensorily present. But the movement of the dialectic leads to a progressive broadening and enriching of the scope of the investigation to include desire as that upon which the initial knowing rests. So also does Weiss. We actually begin with what he calls the *insistence* of our being as desirously moving outside itself to the insistent being of the other.[9] For Weiss, the adumbrated is "correlated . . . with the unexpressed needs constituting our very privacy,"[10] with emotions, with "affective tone," and even, in one way of fulfillment, with mystical experience. All of these expressions refer to a prearticulate level of experience, which

---

6. Weiss, *Philosophy in Process*, I (April 24, 1959), 521.

7. Weiss, *Reality*, 58.

8. As an aside worth repeating, Weiss once confessed to the author that if (*per impossibile*) God had "in the beginning" taken him aside, shown him all the great works to come in the history of philosophy—"in all their glory"—and asked him of which work he would like to be the author, he would have replied, without hesitation, *The Phenomenology of Spirit*. Indeed, one could profitably read *Beyond All Appearances* as directly parallel with the *Phenomenology*.

9. See Paul Weiss, "Our Knowledge of What Is Real," *The Review of Metaphysics* 18, no. 1 (September 1964): 10.

10. Weiss, *Reality*, 282.

carries our being beyond itself. Adumbration thus constitutes the acknowledgment of what the irrationalists and the Romanticists have insisted upon and against which the logicians and the rationalists have fought.[11]

But the very obscurity of this move calls for clarification and is indeed made possible by the prime principle of the clarificatory move: the principle of noncontradiction that Weiss calls "the category."[12] Its evidentiality seems to be immediate and its scope unlimited. When we acknowledge the lowliest, most fleeting aspect of our experience to *be* (i.e., when we not only meet it but meet it "as being" and judge that it *is*), we recognize immediately that a thing cannot both be and not be at the same time and in the same respect. And since outside *being* there is nothing at all, "the category" refers us to what exists within and beyond the phenomenal circle: to the whole of what occurs and can occur within that circle, to the whole of what lies beyond it in each thing—ourselves included—and in the absolute totality.[13] But just for the very reason that it includes the totality in its reference, the category is a kind of emptiness that has to be filled in various ways with the encounterable and the inferable. The law of noncontradiction, Weiss observes, is "inseparable from a completely universalizable variable 'any adumbrated.'"[14] It involves a kind of Hegelian overreaching of the phenomena that are relative to my perceptual powers and a standing, though emptily, in the place of the other. Actually moving into the other occurs in artistic penetration, in love, in mystical experience, and in speculative inference.[15]

For Weiss, art has a special place in this matter. "It is the special task of art to express the perceptually adumbrated side of perceptual matters of fact in such a way as to embrace all other adumbrateds."[16] Art moves into the particular but in such a way as to open out "the whole of reality as substantial and inward."[17] "Substantial" here means underlying, grounding the phenomena, and "inward" expresses a privacy correlated with our own privacy, where the manifestation of the depth of the thing requires and evokes the deeper side of ourselves. Art gives articulation to

---

11. Ibid., 31.
12. Ibid, 144ff.
13. Ibid., 284.
14. Ibid., 147.
15. Ibid., 99, 261; *Philosophy in Process*, I (February 13, 1959), 403.
16. Weiss, *Reality*, 99.
17. Ibid., 116.

a special sense of, a "feel" for, the Beyond. But by reason of our structure, if not also the structure of things themselves, disclosure of the inwardness of any thing involves disclosure of the whole of things. Weiss seems quite close to Heidegger's view of the work of art here.[18] Art is more than the production of a pleasing surface, more also than an expression of my subjective reaction to things: art discloses the Whole in an inward and substantial way.

To adumbrate, then, is to foreshadow, to anticipate darkly, but to do so in a mode of feeling rather than in the mode of conceptualization. Speculation follows feeling here as an abstract, and to that extent, inferior mode of expression of the transphenomenal, revealed and concealed in the phenomena. But speculation has its own advantage in that it clarifies feeling to itself by bringing it into systematic relation with all the modes of experience and interference.

What appears within the phenomenal circle has then to be interpreted as showing or hiding what lies beneath. But the underlying has to be repeatedly rescued from the routinized interpretations that settle into a kind of "dashboard" relationship to the underlying.[19] The phenomenal circle becomes a pragmatic circle of knowing how to push, pull, and turn the surface to get the regularized responses required by a culturally mediated need-base.[20] This is the surface that I sometimes suspect is what many so-called realist philosophers mean by "reality." Not so Weiss— and rightly not so. Dashboard realism can at best be a starting point. It must be corrected and extended by the deeper realism of love, art, mysticism, and speculation that add the depth dimension to the pragmatic-phenomenal surface.

The rational and the nonrational, the clearly conceived and the lived, the articulated and the nonarticulated are brought together in a dialectical relation where the adumbratively lived, made possible by the clarity of the Category, leads on inquiry as the extension of that clarity. Logic, Weiss's own early preoccupation in the time before *Reality*, as a discipline of absolutely clear distinctions and relations, arises through cutting

18. See "Origin of the Work of Art," in *Philosophies of Art and Beauty*, ed. A. Hofstadter and R. Kuhns (Chicago: The University of Chicago Press, 1964), 649–701.

19. This very apt expression is Owen Barfield's in *Saving the Appearances: An Essay in Idolatry* (New York: Harcourt, Brace and World, n.d.).

20. Cf. Weiss, *Beyond all Appearances*, 9–11.

off the adumbrative component. When this mentality dominates, every-thing else tends to be pejoratively relegated to the nonrational realm, locked into the merely subjective. Weiss is more temperate here than Hei-degger who refers in this context to "the corrosive acid of a merely logi-cal intelligence."[21] Weiss would rather heavily underscore the "merely" and, characteristically, create ample place for logic. But like Heidegger, he would not only refer the logical to the verifiable surface of the indi-cated and the methodically controlled conceptuality of the contemplated that develops in relation to that surface but also to the hidden, the under-lying, the encompassing mystery of Being that suggests the framework for ontologically construing the indicated and the contemplated.

What is adumbrated is not only the substantial wholeness of actuali-ties but also the totality of all actualities. The adumbrated, Weiss repeat-edly affirms, is the correlate of the copula "is" in the judgment. But there is also, Weiss claims, a penumbra surrounding the nucleus of each of the elements in knowing—including both the indicated and the contemplat-ed.[22] In *Modes of Being*, Weiss attempts to move speculatively into the penumbra surrounding each of those elements, only to discover a corre-late for each that is not another actuality but rather a realm, self-existent, other than the actualities in which the actualities participate in various ways.

The adumbrated fringe surrounding a given contemplated universal is a region or mode of being called Ideality or Possibility. The adumbrat-ed fringe surrounding a given indicated is the realm termed—somewhat eccentrically, I think—Existence. And presumably the adumbrated that makes possible the unity of Ideality and Existence entering into any giv-en actuality is God as the ground of that unity. Exploration of each of the modes and their interplay with each other and with actualities allows us to clarify the pull that each mode of Being exerts within the fuller matrix of lived experience.

The Category or the notion of Being, articulated for actualities in the principle of noncontradiction, is not assigned to any mode or treated as a distinct mode in *Modes of Being*. Being is rather the interplay of all the modes. And by reason of possessing, or being possessed by, the Category

21. "What Is Metaphysics?," in *Pathmarks*, trans. Will McNeill (Cambridge: Cambridge University Press, 1998) 82–96.
22. Weiss, *Reality*, 78–79.

at the core of our consciousness, we are able to stand in that interplay and grasp it as such.[23]

In *Reality*, adumbration as linked to the Category was filled in concretely by art and abstractly by speculation—although love and mysticism also appear as means to concrete fulfillment. In *Modes of Being*, art is said to move into the realm of Existence that plays in the inwardness of the artist as feeling and displays itself in various ways. These ways of displaying are determined by the interplay of Existence with the other modes. Existence itself is basically an "othering," a dividedness.[24] Related to actualities, Existence is expressed as spatiality, the othering of spread-out-ness, the ontological root of varying types of space, from the abstract space of Euclidean geometry, through the tensed but extrinsic space of relativity physics, to the lived spaces of differing organisms and differing consciousnesses, entering profoundly into human experience in the articulation of the spatial arts of architecture, painting, and sculpture. Related to Ideality, Existence is expressed as temporality generated through reference to the possibilities to be realized in the future, articulated further as chronometric and lived time of various sorts, and brought to special articulation in the temporal arts of musical composition, story, and poetry. Related to God as the One, Existence is expressed as dynamism, energy, a restless movement out of what is at any given time and place, seeking in each case and in the universe as a whole a maximal unity and attaining special articulation in the arts of musical performance, drama, and dance. Though itself a tendency to dispersal, Existence is established as a single ground of a single spatial-temporal-dynamic realm also by relation to the Divine Unity. The arts thus establish and articulate a concrete feel for peculiar aspects of Existence but adumbrate as well, in their differing modes, a concrete feel for the underlying encompassing wholeness of Existence.[25] It is a feel directed at the wholeness that lures the theoretical physicist to elaborate a view of the total realm of space-time-energy and clues the cosmologist as to the ultimate mode grounding these pursuits. In Weiss's later work, *Beyond All Appearances*, the proper

23. Weiss, *Modes of Being*, sections 1.96 and 2.12. Cf. Weiss, *First Considerations*, 157ff.

24. Weiss, *Modes of Being*, 301. For what follows, cf. *Modes of Being*, 302 ff.

25. See Paul Weiss, *Nine Basic Arts* (Carbondale: Southern Illinois University Press, 1960) and *The World of Art* (Carbondale: Southern Illinois University Press, 1961) for a fuller development of these notions.

emotional attitude that both opens up and is evoked by the encompassing finality of Existence is awe.[26] The dwelt-in adumbrative move past the surface leads on toward speculative comprehension.

Weiss offers several novel approaches to the divine mode. The adumbrative relation to God is lived through in various ways as well as logically clarified. Weiss lays out the geography of nine differing sets of proofs (not nine proofs but nine *sets* of proofs), only *one* set of which involves traditional logical inferences.[27] There are other and richer vehicles whereby God is "proven" to men long before logical proof was thought of—"proofs" having to do with such things as prayer and work and institutional participation. "Proof" here means something like "the proof of the pudding is in the eating." It is the whole set of relations to God and the multiple ways to God that men live through that Weiss sets out to clarify. Weiss works persistently with the logic of possible relations between finalities in their interplay with actualities. If I understand the general lines of Weiss's analysis of the sets of proofs for the existence of God, there should be some 729 proofs possible within the modal philosophy (9 x 9 x 9: nine teleological beginnings, working through nine cosmological relations, terminating in nine ontological detachments). But again, the adumbratively lived is dialectically related to the logically articulated.

Weiss's later view of five finalities provides seemingly endless logically possible combinations; for example, in his treatment of the five basic dimensions of the self, (namely, psyche, reason, mind, sensibility, and spirit), Weiss sketches out five functions of mind, subdividing two of these functions into five differing acts, each division corresponding to the five finalities as they ricochet off one another within the interior of each differing type of actuality.[28] But the point for our purposes is that all this constructive work is not strung over an empty experiential void but is in constant interplay with an extraordinary alertness to the lived adumbration of each of these areas.

After *Modes of Being*, differing facets of adumbration continue to be unfolded, bringing together features to which we have already called attention: intensive adumbration, directed toward actualities; extensive

26. Cf. Weiss, *Beyond all Appearances*, 17.
27. Weiss, *Modes of Being*, 4.14–4.60.
28. Weiss, *Beyond all Appearances*, 342–48.

adumbration, directed toward the other modes of being; and cosmic adumbration, directed toward the interplay of both, leading to a sense of the absolute totality.[29] Again, he divides adumbration, from another perspective, into two types: a determinate and an indeterminate type. The *determinate* involves our lived-through, dwelt-in, concrete rootage. *Indeterminate* adumbration involves the possibility held open by the presence of "the Category" in us, of leaving our own rootage to enter sympathetically into the lifeworld of others, though never as richly as in the case of our own.[30]

Weiss comes to see the adumbrated as having its own sort of dynamism. Things and finalities do not merely stand beyond the circle of our penetration, resisting our complete entry; they also exert a positive pull.[31] The more we enter into them, the more they seem to take hold of us. We move from grasping and controlling to being apprehended. In *Beyond All Appearances*, this attracting power is linked up with the power of symbols, distinguished from but related to the function of signs. The latter are symbols that have lost their drawing power and are capable of being manipulated by us.[32]

The distinction seems remarkably close to Heidegger's description of the flattening-out process whereby beings "lose their Being" (i.e., their revealing-concealing power that draws us into intimate presence) and become mere data, equidistant from us and capable of being manipulated.[33]

But in that same work, Weiss distinguishes adumbration from lucidation—the former term now being reserved for our relation to actualities, the latter for our relation to finalities.[34] Because of the even stronger emotional pull exerted by finalities such as awe, wonder, reverence, and the sense of mystery that still surrounds finalities,[35] one wonders at this terminological shift. But it surely is connected with the fact that

29. Weiss, "Our Knowledge of What Is Real," 11.
30. Weiss, *Philosophy in Process*, II (July 10, 1964), 153.
31. Weiss, *Beyond all Appearances*, 97.
32. Ibid., 89ff.
33. Cf. "The Origin of the Work of Art." Though Weiss's speculative-constructive, systematic approach to philosophy is poles removed from Heidegger's ruminations, and though Weiss has little positive to say of Heidegger, these two thinkers share many central insights. The most essential difference between Heidegger and Weiss is Weiss's Platonic acceptance of ever-present, changeless truths-in-themselves.
34. Weiss, *Beyond all Appearances*, 89.
35. Cf. Weiss, *Philosophy in Process*, VI (October 15, 1970).

it is through the exploration of the finalities that one comes to recognize more clearly the character of the actualities into which we enter in our living experience of them. In *Reality*, the tension between the logical clarity of the Category and its essential linkage with adumbration foreshadows this later distinction between lucidation and adumbration.

In *Beyond All Appearances* as well, Weiss adds two new modes and renames them all "finalities." Being as the interplay of the modes in *Modes of Being* becomes a distinct finality and is distinguished from a new finality that he calls Substance.[36]

Substance, a finality in which all actualities participate as standing in themselves, stands also in itself. It is linked with Weiss's taking seriously the claim of certain mystical types to identity with an impersonal Encompassing reached within the innermost privacy of the self but linked to all other privacies. This is the kind of mysticism represented by Taoism.[37]

No longer the neutral point of the interplay between the modes, Being, too, now takes its place as a distinct finality. But though the finalities are coequal and coeternal for Weiss, Being would seem to play a pivotal role.[38] For Weiss, it is the greater equalizer—a univocal and apparently minimalist notion of being-outside-of-nothing common to absolutely everything. It is Being that man alone of all the actualities internalizes. It affects all his other relations by granting him access to all that is, enabling him to live his life in reference to the totality, enabling him to be drawn from the surface toward the depth of actualities and from actualities into the ultimate depth of finalities.

Weiss links mysticism with Being and Substance, as well as with God. His treatment of mysticism thus appears to move like the famous statues of Daedalus, shifting from union with God as a personal Evaluator, to the Taoist impersonal but inward identity, to a Parmenidean mysticism of the identity of thought and Being. Add to this awe in the face of the overwhelming character of power and spatiotemporal vastness and we have a list of the essential types of experience that are too often collapsed into relation to a single encompassing finality, to which many people are perhaps too quick to affix the name "God." Distinguishing different finalities allows us to distinguish different types of experiences

36. Weiss, *Beyond all Appearances*, 232, 267ff, 272.
37. Cf. Weiss, *First Considerations*, 114, #52.
38. Weiss, *Beyond all Appearances*, 275–77.

that seem to move beyond experience of actualities. Indeed, by reason of their dialectical relation, distinguishing different experiences aids in the clear discrimination of differing finalities.

But even for those for whom the experience of the personal Evaluator is the pivotal experience, by reason of the interplay of the different finalities one can begin to understand how each distinctive experience becomes for the religious man a symbol of God. Depth experience in each of the finalities can draw us into the others. But once again, just as symbols can flatten out into signs as empty reference when we lose the ability to enter into the drawing power of the symbols,[39] so also real experience of the finalities may be only conventionally referred to the presence of God in relation to whom we may not be truly dwelling. However, recovering the power of religious symbols would seem to be linked significantly to recovering the adumbrative-lucidative reverberances of finalities in relations of respect and love directed to other actualities, in the development of artistic sensibility, and in the various forms of mysticism directed to finalities.

Weiss's philosophy is essentially a revised Platonism with the *chorismos* between Being and Becoming, and correspondingly between soul and body, eliminated along somewhat Hegelian lines of mutual inclusion, and with the aristocratic hierarchy of hypostases reestablished in a democratic society joined by the lowly Receptacle as principle of the rabble of plurality. Weiss's democratization of the finalities has the advantage of breaking the grip of privilege accorded the rational realm of Forms in the history of Western philosophy that provoked periodic outbursts of irrationalist revolution (though Plato's own erotic relationship to the final Good actually anticipates and assimilates the protest). Relation to the World-Soul, recovered by Weiss as the Taoist inwardness of the encompassing Substance, is acknowledged to be as profound and as deserving of attention as the clarity of the Forms. Artistic sensitivity especially has led to a rich articulation of the Receptacle. Art, installing us firmly in this world, nonetheless opens us to a realm of Existence including the transcending actualities and allowing access to the interplay of the other finalities in it. The lowly Receptacle is elevated as Existence by being given its due respect in art and in theoretical physics.

39. Weiss, *Philosophy in Process*, VI (February 4, 1971), 642.

But in Weiss's case, breaking the grip of privilege accorded to the rationalist domain has resulted in a rich development of the rational itself—as if in humbling itself, the rational is all the more exalted. The tandem movement of adumbration and speculation across the finalities has resulted in a dialectical interpenetration of the speculative and the lived. It is this that constitutes the deeper lure of Platonism: its rootage in a more primordial lived relationship to the differing ways in which the phenomenal surface of the everyday world is girt about by encompassing, transcending regions that we cannot exhaust and whose inexhaustability is the reason why we can, at best, achieve *philosophia*, a loving pursuit of the final encompassing, why we can never—if we are wise—lay claim to final wisdom. Weiss, like Plato, and in many respects beyond Plato, is keenly aware of the soil in which the tree of metaphysics is planted.[40]

Of course, in relation to Weiss's variation on the themes of Platonism, a metaphysical creationist will have obvious difficulties locating the divine in a democratized pantheon—even as a *primus inter pares*. But viewing God as the creative ground of all the rest—and thus as other than the rest in a radical way—the creationist can still applaud the sensitive way in which Weiss does justice to the other transcending enterprises that have functioned and can still function as routes to God.

In Weiss's thought—and, I think, in fact—we humans can stand open to the presence of finalities as we stand open to the presence of the inwardness of actualities—our own included—by reason of our standing in the region of Being. Expressed in the humblest judgment, the presence of the category of Being in us opens us to the whole of what is, in the differing modes in which things are. But is this Being as empty as Weiss suggests? Is it merely the great equalizer, the lowest common denominator? Doesn't Being rather include the wholeness of each actuality and finality—partially filled, but emptily for the most part, from the side of our knowing-dwelling? And is it not then hierarchically realizable? Can it not then be realized in a single instance as a nature, not hemmed in by the various modalities of finitude? Can it not, then, like Weiss's Substance, stand over against the beings who, by participating in it, are en-

40. Cf. Martin Heidegger, "The Way Back into the Ground of Metaphysics," in *Existentialism from Dostoyevsky to Sartre*, trans. W. Kaufmann, 206–21 (Cleveland: World Publishing, 1956), 277–90.

abled to stand over against it as well? Might not, then, all our adumbrations and lucidations finally point to that, not as one among many but as the ultimate term of our heart's desire? Might it not, then, be identical with Being itself, which all others mirror in some way—as awesome power and vastness, as eminent intelligibility and enticing, prescriptive value, as inwardness and encompassment, as full actuality but, finally, as the mystery that all of this only adumbrates? Weissian thought, from a creationist perspective, has the great value of opening us to the experienced symbols that lead us first in a lived, adumbrative way, then by way of speculative comprehension and clarification, into encompassing regions other than God and other than actualities but pointing to their functioning, in turn, as symbols of God in the interplay of the finalities.

Kierkegaard complained that most philosophers construct magnificent thought-castles but dwell in miserable shacks nearby. Weiss has surely constructed magnificent thought-castles, but he has been able to do so because he has learned so deeply what it means to dwell in fullest humanness. Adumbration points to that. Weiss holds together the lived and the comprehended in a single system, the lived leading on comprehension, comprehension clarifying the lived and holding open, in a time when so many factors conspire to close it, the space of transcending life.

20 ∽ Buber's Use of Oriental Themes

In the East and in the West today, religious and philosophical traditions seem to be in a rapid state of decay brought about by the geometrical increase in the It-World of scientific and technical mastery that emerged out of the West since the time of the Renaissance. If such an It-World seemed overpowering in 1923 when Buber's classic *I and Thou* appeared, it has moved light-years beyond since then in its industrial-scientific component and in the social regimentation connected therewith.[1]

The religious ecumenical movement within the West and the developing dialogue between world religions today have infrastructural roots in this situation of scientific-technical development. Traditions that for centuries and even millennia viewed each other with attitudes ranging from lofty indifference through suspicion to outright hostility are now more inclined to accord to each other the respect and even reverence that their own traditions have taught, for they all have their backs to the wall before the common threat of their growing irrelevance.[2] But whatever its sociological roots, the dialogue of world religions is an important component on the contemporary scene.

Buber entered into dialogue with the East very early in his career and maintained contact with it to the end of his life, guided by his conception of the community of his birth. Buber was a Westerner, but he was a *Jewish* Westerner, and that meant for him one who stands at a peculiar confluence of Western and Eastern sources, for he saw Judaism as essentially Oriental and as the religion that brought the spirit of the Orient to the West.[3]

In this chapter, we will explore the presence of Oriental themes in

1. Cf. Peter Berger, Brigette Berger, and Hansfried Kellner, *The Homeless Mind, Modernization and Consciousness* (New York: Vintage, 1973).

2. Peter Berger, *The Sacred Canopy* (Garden City, N.Y.: Anchor Books, 1969), especially chapter 6.

3. Both during the period when he began writing *I and Thou* (in 1916, in his lecture on

Buber's thought. We will continually take our point of departure from the explicit citation of Oriental sources in the very center of Buber's work *I and Thou*. In the process, we will move on to consider some Oriental themes in *I and Thou* that have not been explicitly identified as such. We will consider, in turn, Buber's treatment of Hinduism, Buddhism, Taoism, and Zen. Implicated in all this is a form of the spirit[4] that Buber termed "teaching" *(Lehre)* and which we will treat in a penultimate section. Finally, we will deal with the question of how the philosophical conceptualization that has developed in the West and to which Buber contributed stands in relation to the basic teaching of the Orient to which Buber attended.

HINDUISM

The Hindu notion of *Brahman*, the ultimate reality underlying the multiplicity of appearances, manifest on one level as a personal God but at a deeper level as the impersonal absolute, Buber considers briefly in part I of *I and Thou* (section §23 in the numbering sequence I have adopted in my commentary)[5] in connection with the primitive notions of *mana* and *orenda*. Buber suggests the equivalence of these notions and uses them to illustrate his claim that "in the beginning is relation." These notions are rooted in the stirring of the whole psycho-physical person by what is met in primitive experience. Movement, interpenetration of inner and outer, and stirring of the whole person are characteristics of what Buber calls the "motor" type peculiarly cultivated, among the higher cultures, in the Orient.[6]

"Der Geist des Orients und das Judentum," originally in *Reden über das Judentum*, 1916, reprinted in the volume of Buber's collected works on Judaism, *Der Jude und sein Judentum* (Köln: Joseph Meizer, 1963), 46–65) and also several years after his mature thought had been formulated (in his 1934 lecture on "The Power of the Spirit," reprinted in translation in Martin Buber, *Israel and the World* [New York: Schocken, 1965], 173–82), Buber held that Judaism could only be understood by comparing it with the "reality systems" of the Orient because it was a product of Oriental thinking.

4. Cf. *Schriften Zur Chassidismus, Werke*, vol. 2 (München: Kösel, 1963), 991–98.

5. Buber, *I and Thou*, trans. Walter Kaufmann (New York: Scribner, 1970). The translation is a significant improvement over the older English translation, several problems with which I have pointed out in my *Martin Buber's Ontology: An Analysis of I and Thou* (Evanston, Ill.: Northwestern University Press, 1969). There is still one problem with Kaufmann's translation: cf. *The Origin and Meaning of Hasidism*, trans. M. Friedman (New York: Harper, 1960), 220–39.

6. Buber, "Geist des Orients," 47–50.

Buber cites the vedic *Brahamana of the Hundred Paths* in part II (§38) in the midst of a discussion of the alienated I who lives exclusively in the I-It relation and before the contrast between such an *Eigenwesen* and the authentic *Person*.[7] In the Brahamana, the gods and the demons are contrasted in terms of whether they offer sacrifices to one another or each to himself alone. Prajapati, the Lord of Creation, offers himself to those, gods indeed, who entered into relation with each other, the *persons* of the I-Thou relation, not the demonic *Eigenwesen*. Buber repeats the mythic tale without explanation but sets it in a context where an existential reading of the myth is possible.

Both the preceding citations are significant in showing Buber's contention that the great religions know the Thou, since he will later criticize the Oriental traditions for their tendency to remain within the self.

In part II (§36),[8] the Hindu doctrine that the results of our actions remain with us as we pass from existence to existence illustrates, in its historical transformation, the transition from a human cosmos, rooted in a relational event and developed into a house in which the spirit can live and grow, into the oppressive weight of the It-World where causality rules. *Karma* is originally, in pre-Buddhist times, the promise of a higher existence as the result of our good deeds in this existence. The negative result of *karma* as the weight of past misdeeds is relieved by sacrifice and meditation. But by the time of the Buddha, the negative has taken over: *karma* is the oppression of the wheel of rebirth, from which the Buddha offers liberation. The early function of *karma* formed part of a meaningful *cosmos* in which one could meet the Eternal Thou. But times change—that's part of the Way of God and man in history: the Thou disappears from the world and the forms that expressed it remain as empty shells and become oppressive to the spirit.

The three citations mentioned thus far Buber brings up by way of illustration and, as it were, in passing. Of greater significance and of greater substance is his lengthy encounter with Indian mysticism in part III (§50), by far the longest section of the book.[9] The section is anything but clear, though Buber later refers back to it as "the clearest statement of his position on mysticism."[10]

7. Buber, *I and Thou*, 110–11.   8. Ibid., 103–5.
9. Ibid., 134–43.
10. Letter to Will Herberg, 1/25/53 in Martin Buber, *Briefwechsel aus sieben Jahrzehnten*, vol. 3, Grete Schaeder ed. (Heidelberg: Lambert Schneider, 1975), 326.

The immediately preceding section (§49) rejected the positions of Schleiermacher and Rudolf Otto on the essential relation to God as one of the feeling of dependency or creaturehood. Buber rejected them because, in effect, they collapsed the human pole of the relationship. In the supreme relation, creature-feeling and the feeling of free creativeness unite in one, a case of the *coincidentia oppositorum* essential to all wholeness (which we will discuss more later). In the section in question here (§50), Indian mysticism is considered together with Christian mysticism as maintaining the opposite error: collapsing the divine pole in favor of the human. Buber calls them both doctrines of "immersion" (*Versenkung*, which can also mean meditation) or descent into the self. Though they seem to move in opposite directions, Buber sees them as identical at base. The Christian mystic is stripped of all I-ness, all subjectivity— which would seem rather to be an extreme version of the collapse of the "I" side of the relation. In ecstasy, standing outside himself, he is united with God, or God enters into the self. Buber chooses Eckhart for this version of Christian mysticism. According to this doctrine (and in contrast to the Indian), there is duality between Creator and creature, but it is overcome in the moment of ecstasy.[11]

Buber sees this mysticism as doubly mistaken. It is, first of all, a misreading of the Johannine Gospel, seeing Jesus as identical with, rather than in purest human relation to, the Father. Secondly, it is a misreading of authentic meeting with God where the actual relation seems but only *seems* to obliterate the poles of relation (and this would apply to the Indian doctrine itself, insofar as it is rooted in authentic meeting). Buber sometimes speaks as if such meeting with God can only occur in meeting with others in the world, but elsewhere he acknowledges such encounter apart from the world.[12] However, in these cases, meeting with God does not exclude the world and community with other men but rather involves mission to that world. Buber's basis for assessment is a combination of reference to the literature of worldwide testimony to such

11. This very aspect of Ekhart's mode of speaking, obliterating the distinction between God and creatures, thus suggesting pantheism rather than theism, was the reason Ekhart was regarded as suspect by his own church. Orthodox mystics use the language of union rather than *identity*.

12. Cf. John Caputo, "Fundamental Themes in Ekhart's Mysticism," *The Thomist* 42, no. 2 (1978): 197–225 for a different—and textually well-grounded— interpretation of Ekhart that is closer to Buber's own understanding of meeting with God.

meeting and also apparently to his own experience. It is, I think, important to note that the dialogue style appears here in the text (as it does
in several other places, breaking the normal flow of exposition). For authentic dialogue, one must speak from where he stands while attending
to the other where he stands. Buber listened to the mystical traditions
and spoke to them from out of his own experience.

The actual encounter with the Indian tradition speaks from the tradition as a single whole, from the *Upanishads* to their culmination in the
teaching of the Buddha. Throughout the *Upanishads*, it is repeated again
and again that *Atman is Brahman*, the Self is the All, an identity hidden
by *maya*, the veil of the appearance of otherness, of multiplicity.[13] The
famous "*Tat tvam asi*," "that art thou," said of any encounterable other, though suggesting genuine relation, actually precludes it according to
Buber, for the otherness of the other is proclaimed as deception.[14] Each
and every thing is, in fact, absorbed into the self. Contrary to the Christian mysticism of Eckhart, the real duality of things is not simply surmounted in the moment of identification with God; it is reduced to the
status of illusion.

In this context belongs the Upanishad's teaching of deep, dreamless sleep that annihilates the difference between the Self and the other.
The *Mandukya Upanishad* relates this to the mystical syllable OM (also
transliterated as AUM), where the *A* represents the waking world from
which we begin, the *U* the state of sleep and dream designated as "the
brilliant," and the *M* the culminating deep, dreamless sleep that is contact with "the source of all, the controller."[15] The latter is a state of no
consciousness or memory, yet it is an *experience* that Buber speaks of as
resembling, not *being*, actual sleep. For Buber, it is one of the phenomena
at the edge of real life, at its limit, and thus is confusing and difficult to
interpret in any satisfying way. He admits that there may be truth here,
but we have no means of knowing for sure in this life. It is, *at best*, an
object of living experience, but it is not something that can be lived (i.e.,

13. Cf., for example, the *Isa Upanishad*, 6 and 16; *Chandogya Upanishad*, VIII, xi, 1–3;
Brhadaranyaka Upanishad, III, iv, 1 and vii, 15 and 23, *A Sourcebook in Indian Philosophy*, ed.
Sarvepalli Ranakrishna and Charles Moore (Princeton, N.J.: Princeton University Press, 1957).

14. Cf., for example, *Chandogya Upanishad*, in *Sourcebook*, VI, ix–xiii.

15. *Mandukya Upanishad*, *A Sourcebook in Indian Philosophy*, 1–12. Actually, there is a
fourth state described here, beyond even the dreamless sleep and wherein the "cessation of becoming" occurs.

integrated into the whole of one's life, that is, after all, life in the midst of the multiplicity of beings). Later, Buber will be less cautious about mysticism in general: he declares it to be an experience whose "object" is the self. But because it takes place in a sphere apart from encounter and thus comparison with other creatures, the principle of individuation is lost sight of and one confuses the self with the All.[16]

In the context of his discussion of Eckhart, Buber appeals to his own experience. He speaks of the experience where all the soul's powers—sensual, emotional, volitional, intellectual, and spiritual—are united: this is an indispensible precondition for producing the works of the spirit, but it is an experience whose object is the self, not God. There is also an experience arising out of the meeting with any other where the relation seems, but only seems, to swallow up the partners. This latter is apparently what he understands by the claim of Christian mysticism. But the Hindu experience seems to be neither. It is a straining after the pure, the essential, and therefore a rejection of the sensual and emotional. Ultimately, it is a straining after the void, which for Buber has a demonic rather than a divine character.[17]

But what Buber regards as his most important testimony here is that God can be met in the everyday: "a streak of sunshine on a maple twig and an intimation of the Eternal Thou" is "for us"—in other words, for those who share his experience—"greater than all mysticism, all phenomena on the edge of life."[18] Mysticism for Buber is a gathering of the powers of the soul between encounters with other creatures and with God. It is "on the borderline of faith, where the soul draws its breath between word and word."[19]

Granted that confusion is more likely here than in other realms of experience, the curious thing is the temptation (if temptation it be) to identify the self with the "All." Why "All"? This is important for Oriental teaching—and it is critically important for philosophy as well. The aim of the teaching is to find reconciliation and unity not just with this or

16. Martin Buber, foreword to *Pointing the Way*, ed. and trans. Maurice Friedman (New York: Harper and Row, 1963), xv–xvi. Buber returned to this assessment of the dreamless sleep in "What is Common to All," in *Knowledge of Man*, trans. M. Friedman and R. Smith (New York: Harper and Row, 1965), 94–96.

17. Buber, *The Origin and Meaning of Hasidism*, 220–39.

18. Buber, *I and Thou*, 135–36.

19. Ibid., 239.

that, nor simply within oneself, but with the All. Philosophy itself emerges as a kind of design on the All, as Eros for the One, seeking a vision of the Whole that makes the multiplicity of things into a universe. There is a structural feature of humanness here, one to which much of the contemporary world seems blind. We will have occasion to attend to this again in the last section of this paper.

Buber dealt briefly with the Hindu position in *Daniel* where, in an apparently autobiographical section, he describes it as the beginning phase of a maturing process. It is a feeling of unity detached from appearances and thus from the rest of life. But it awakened a striving for unity in the whole of life, realized finally in *I and Thou*.[20]

BUDDHISM

Returning now to section 50 of *I and Thou*, Buber devotes several pages to a discussion of the Buddha as the culmination of the *Upanishad* tradition.[21] It is difficult to untangle the various observations and evaluations Buber makes here. However, the observations do fall into three parts: (1) the character of the teaching, (2) the nature of the goal of the teaching, and (3) the ultimately negative evaluation Buber attaches to it as the culmination of the Hindu tradition.

First, Buddha's teaching involves no theoretical account of the world. It rather shows a way, a path to walk toward salvation. A theoretical account belongs to the It-World, a world of division because it divides subject and object and because it involves a division of objects from one another. But walking the way involves indivision. The categories of thought neither can contain this nor are they relevant to the actual walking. For this reason, in an early essay (1913), "Buddha," where he claims a substantial agreement between the Buddha, Socrates, and Jesus on this point, Buber warns that the Buddha must not be approached in terms of a doctrine of "Buddhism."[22] Buddha indeed does not elaborate a metaphysics; rather by means of his Four Noble Truths, he points directly to life. Men suffer because of desire and can be liberated from such desire by follow-

---

20. Martin Buber, *Daniel: Dialogues on Realization*, trans. M. Freidman (New York: Harper and Row, 1960), 117ff.

21. Buber, *I and Thou*. 138–43.

22. Martin Buber, "Buddha," in *Neue Blätter* (Hellerau and Berlin: Erich Baron, 1913), 63–64.

ing the Eightfold Path.[23] As he remarked, we are like one shot with a poisoned arrow: the immediate task is to remove it, not seek the person who shot it or why he shot it.[24]

Second, as far as the goal is concerned, three things go together in Buber's account: expressed negatively, the goal is "the annulment of suffering"; expressed in terms of its effects, it is "salvation from the wheel of rebirth," from the necessity of returning to the disjointed world; and expressed positively in itself, the goal is, in Buber's reading, "to confront the undivided mystery undivided." And this seems to involve at least one theoretical claim, that "there is an Unborn, Unbecome, Uncreated, Unformed," the undivided Mystery as the goal.

Thirdly, as to the ultimate Hindu character of the Buddha's teaching, according to Buber the Buddha knows "Thou-saying" to this Mystery; and in the Buddha's dealings with his disciples, he shows that he knows "Thou-saying" to his fellow men, but he does not *teach* it. The claim is indeed confusing since Buber had just spoken of confrontation with the unborn, the undivided Mystery as the goal of the Way. Buddha does also teach a compassion that "includes in the heart all that becomes,"[25] a variation for Buber on the Hindu "*Tat tvam asi*" that takes place *in the self* and not in full encounter with what is over against the self. For the Buddha claims (another theoretical assertion that he is not supposed to make) that the world dwells in him when he passes beyond the deception of forms. Ultimately, then, the Buddha's teaching becomes a doctrine of immersion where the world is in the self, a position Buber himself had praised in his 1913 Buddha essay: Buddha, the Indian Prometheus of inwardness, stands above the gods and *is* the world.[26]

Buber thus claims, in effect, to discern the encounter with the Thou at the root of Hinduism in the primitive notion of Brahman and at the root of Buddhism in undivided encounter with undivided Mystery. Each tradition develops a way for its followers and brings the everyday world into contact with the Eternal Thou through the establishment of holy

23. *A Sourcebook in Indian Philosophy, Samyutta-ni Kaya*, v, 420; *Majjhima-nikaya*, iii, 248–52.

24. *A Sourcebook in Indian Philosophy, Majjhima-nikaya*, 63.

25. Buber, "Buddha," 65. Cf. my *Martin Buber's Ontology*, 5–15 for his early mystical phase.

26. Cf. Martin Buber, *The Eclipse of God: Studies in the Relation between Religion and Philosophy* (New York: Harper, 1957), 38–42.

times and places, holy practices and teachings, and a view of the cosmos in relation to the Holy. But their primal encounter is confused with certain experiences whose object is not the Eternal Thou but the self. For Buber, genuine encounter with the Eternal Thou is not so much the transmission of a *content* as it is a matter of a confirming *presence*. This position is apparently related to the burning bush revelation to Moses in which Jahweh said: "I will be there in the way I will be there." The relation between content and presence is one of basic problems of Buber's philosophy, since he is not inclined to abstract the universal from the situation—a move absolutely essential to *any*, including (by his own admission) Buber's own, philosophy.[27] The translation of encounter into a content depends upon the character of the culture and thus opens it to misrepresentation.

TAOISM

Returning once again to our point of departure in *I and Thou*, we find that the Chinese tradition appears in an immediately identifiable way only once, in part II, #32, in a discussion of art as one of the "forms of the spirit," one of the ways encounter with the Absolute expresses itself in the observable world. Buber recounts the tale of a Chinese poet who played his jade flute before the people and was rejected. He then played before the gods and was heard, and from then on, the people listened to his music. For Buber, all art that is more than decoration or amusing distraction speaks of relation to that which transcends the world of changing, relative values: true art speaks of the Absolute.

But in spite of this solitary explicit mention of Chinese things in *I and Thou*, Buber's thought was actually closer to the Chinese tradition than to the Indian. Recall his early publication of *Chinesische Geister und Liebesgeschichten* in 1911 and especially of *Reden und Gleichnisse des Tschuang-Tse* in 1910.[28] The latter contains an essay titled "The Teaching of the Tao" (written in 1909) that was one of the few early pieces Buber allowed to be published in his collected works. For Buber, it represents a stage he had to pass through, very close to the position represent-

---

27. Cf. *The Origin and Meaning of Hassidism*, 220–39.
28. "Vorwort" *Schriften zur Philosophie, Werke*, I (Heidelberg: Lambert Schneider, 1962), 8.

ed in 1913 in *Daniel*. It was a stage, he said, without which he could not have reached his final position.[29] And even after he reached his mature thought, in his 1928 lecture on "China and Us," he claimed that, while we of the West could no longer fully appropriate the Confucian side of the Chinese tradition, we could still learn much from the Taoist side.[30]

There are at least six interlocked Taoist notions that became important for Buber: (1) *Tao* itself as a way, discovered and traversed by (2) *nonaction*, that involves (3) the *coincidence of opposites*, and (4) the *realization* of what one already knows, terminating in (5) the *unity of one's life* as a whole, which establishes (6) the *unity of the world*.

Tao means essentially "the Way," the path on which to walk, and thus involves not so much seeing as doing. Tao is the path of oneness, holding together yin and yang, the basic opposites: male and female, light and darkness, active and passive. Tao is a path that can only be known if it is walked (i.e., knowing at this level is coincident with doing, for it is a knowing-how). Such know-how is taught, not by prescription but by example, and is learned by plunging in, muddling through, and gradually forgetting ourselves and our prescriptions in their verbal, conceptual form as we live them out.[31]

The essential reality here is termed *wu-wei*, or nonaction. It is one of the central notions of *I and Thou*.[32] It involves a fusion of activity and passivity, so different from what we ordinarily call activity as to be called nonaction. As in any graceful performance, there is a coincidence of opposites: conscious and unconscious, mind and body, where "it acts in me" as much as "I act." The attempt to force one's actions from the outside, as it were, by a detached picturing of one's actions ahead of time—like a batter paying explicit attention to the positions of his body—leads to ungraceful activity. "Grace" is a gift, the gift of instincts and situations. And only if one comes into contact with this gift, if one prepares its conditions in oneself, to "let things be," does a graceful performance follow.

At the same time, nonaction brings with it a parallel nonknowing according to which, as action binds itself to passivity, so knowing enters

---

29. Buber, "China and Us," *Pointing the Way*, 121–25.
30. Buber, "Die Lehre vom Tao," *Werke*, I, 1021–51.
31. Buber, *I and Thou*, §46, 125; §59, 157; §14, 62.
32. Buber, "Die Lehre vom Tao," 1043–45.

into a relation with love.[33] So knowing and doing, activity and passivity, conscious and unconscious, knowing and love are bound together in the essential act that follows the Tao. Such activity helps to establish the unity of one's life and at the same time gives it expression. Through this unity of one's life, there occurs to the Taoist the starkest change and the purest unity.[34] At the same time, this unity of life expresses the unity of the world and helps to establish it.[35]

This theme of establishing the unity of the world through one's own life is the decisive point that is truly difficult to make clear, since it is completely foreign to the atomism and faith in the senses of the last couple of centuries of Western thought. We understand entities as clearly circumscribed units that are identical in principle with sensorily presented form. Field theory, ecology, and sociological thought shake atomism, but we have not abandoned the consequences of our trust in the sensory world. That an individual can stand in cosmic relations that act upon the All—indeed, that it may present a dimension of the presence of the eternal in the spatially circumscribed and temporal that is in principle closed to observation as the true ground upon which religion rests— this lies far from the modern Western tradition, though not, of course, from its ancient roots, which lie beneath this tradition. In these ancient traditions, my most personal acts operate upon the All, which one must not think of simply as the direct or indirect effects of my public activities but of what is called "winning God's blessings for the world"—and which comprises the deepest theological motive for the contemplative life.

The unity of human life as a whole is *the* central object of Buber's thought. Unfortunately, what Buber said about that is exposed to serious misunderstanding, as if the best that man can attain consists in an alternation between a very shabby life and the It-world from which springs the sudden ecstatic episodes with the Thou. This interpretation—or better, false interpretation—overlooks Buber's awareness of the latency of the Thou in the It and his distinction between (momentary) "encounter"

---

33. Ibid., 1039.

34. Ibid., 1039–41. Cf. Buber, *Daniel*, 141.

35. "Die Lehre von Tao," 1043–45. On the notion of "latency," cf. Buber, *I and Thou*, 69; on *Beziehung* and *Begegnung*, cf. "Replies," *Philosophy of Martin Buber*, ed. Paul Schlipp (Lasalle, Ill.: Open Court, 1967), 105 and 712; on unity as the basic thrust of Buber's thought, see my *Martin Buber's Ontology*, especially 16–8. See also note 65.

and (lasting) "relation" that is understood in terms of the alternation between "inspiration" and "work." It misjudges the effective power of this
thought.[36]

In a letter to Max Brod in 1913,[37] Buber indicates affinities between his
recently published *Daniel* and the work of Tschuang-tse, who, after Lao-
tze himself, was the greatest of the Taoists. Buber contrasts both *Daniel*
and Taoism with the ecstatic experience of his own earlier preoccupations. Ecstasy has the soul as its object; its character is passive, receptive;
its time-relation is episodic. His own and the Taoist position, on the contrary, have the world as their object; the character of their central experience is active, their temporal relation lasting and binding. But in *Daniel*
itself, Taoism is apparently the third of the three levels, after Hinduism
and idealism, that "the faithful one" had to pass through,[38] for the Taoist dwells in the midst of life in the mode of indifference. According to
Tschuang-tse, the perfected one is essentially without direction; he leans
neither to the right nor to the left; for him, all things are equal.[39] But in
Daniel, one of the key notions is finding one's own direction in the midst
of things.[40]

Some aspects of *Daniel* can further aid us in understanding Buber's
assimilation of Taoism. That work closes with the observation that the
book had been basically a reflection on life and death, the basic polarity
of life itself for Taoism.[41] Reflection upon our awareness of this relation
will shed light on a second basic polarity in *Daniel*, that between knowledge by way of *orientation* and by way of *realization*,[42] which, in turn,
foreshadows the central polarity of Buber's mature thought: the polarity
between I-It and I-Thou.

Orientation is a mode of knowing that considers a given entity in

---

36. Letter of 6/12/13 in *Briefwechsel*, vol. I, 1972, 350–52.

37. Cf. *Chandogya Upanishad*, VI, ix–xiii. There is a problem here with Buber's own later
assessment of this phase. In the foreword to *Pointing the Way*, it was in reference to the essay
on Taoism, which Buber had reprinted there, that Buber spoke of his "mystical" phase, preoccupied with special ecstatic moments without relation to the much more frequent nonecstat-
ic moments of life as a whole. This would seem to be a lapse on Buber's part insofar as the essay itself calls attention to the perfected one who lives the Tao as combining unity and change
throughout his life (cf. LT, 1039).

38. Chuang-tzu, *A Chinese Classic: Chuang-tzu*, trans. Fung Yu-Lan (Foreign Languages
Press: Beijing, 1989), ch. 17, 6; 17b–21b.

39. Buber, *Daniel*, 49–59.   40. Buber, "Die Lehre vom Tao," 1040.
41. Buber, *Daniel*, 22–31   42. Ibid.

terms of its fitting into a scheme developed through past experience. This mode comes into *I and Thou* as the I-It relation characterized by pastness. Our orientational knowledge of the inevitability of our own death is merely one of the items of information within our repertoire of factual knowledge that we can repeat to ourselves at any moment and whose truth we can readily verify. But there are times when death takes hold of our life: we "see" it, or rather are apprehended by it, and are touched by it. And then it is as if we had really never seen it before: we *realize* it for the first time, or perhaps it would not be incorrect to say that we *believe* it for the first time. As Laotze said, "Everyone seeks to know what he does not yet know; but few seek to realize what they already know."[43] The "motor" type, the Eastern man, does not simply look detachedly but is moved in the whole of his being by realized thought. Orientational knowledge, knowledge in the usual sense of the term, is only one mode of truth. Buber, in effect, parallels Heidegger's distinction between truth as *orthotes* or correct representation and truth as *aletheia* or original emergence into presence.[44] Orientational knowledge affords a valid *object* of knowledge but not a real *presence*. And it is presence that is the key word in understanding I-Thou. When death becomes a presence for one who seeks reality and flees illusion, life itself is opened up in its strangeness and preciousness. As Daniel says, "The script of life is so unspeakably beautiful to read because death looks over our shoulder."[45]

Once more, however, the coincidence of opposites in the mode of realization has still to be brought into the whole of our life. For the "motor" type, following the Way is not simply a matter of experience (*Erlebnis*), no matter how "lively" and moving; it is a matter of life itself, for which the coincidence of opposite feelings is only a sign.[46] The realization of one's death brings life as a whole into focus—for that moment. But life itself is many moments. Realization enters the fabric of life and is fully "realized" in action.[47]

---

43. Buber, "Die Lehre vom Tao," 1037.

44. Martin Heidegger, "The Essence of Truth," in *Existence and Being*, trans. and ed. W. Brock (Chicago: Regnery, 1949), 292–324.

45. Buber, *Daniel*, 91.

46. Cf. Buber, *I and Thou*, §49, 130.

47. Throughout *Daniel*, Buber plays on variations of the verb *wirken*, to do, to effect, to produce, to act, in *Wirklichkeit*, reality, and *Verwirklichung*, realization.

ZEN

Zen does not enter into *I and Thou*, at least not explicitly. However, it has clear affinities with Buber's thought by reason of its own Buddhist and Taoist background. Buber published nothing on Zen until relatively late, and in each case it was in the context of a comparison with Hasidism: in the early 1940s in "The Place of Hasidism in the History of Religion"[48] and in 1963 in "Noch einiges zur Darstellung des Chassidismus."[49] In the latter, Zen, Hasidism, and Islamic Sufi are compared in terms of the basically oral character of the transmission of their teachings, which received written expression only later in their development. The relation of teacher to disciple in the lived context of total psycho-physical encounter is the way to teach "the one thing necessary."

In the earlier essay, Zen is presented as an originally Chinese synthesis of Buddhism and Taoism that traces its line of descent back to the Flower Sermon of the Buddha. Here the Buddha's speech was his deed: he simply held out a lotus before his companions. The one thing necessary is the silent unfolding of the Buddha nature, as in the flower. From this the way leads to the Mahayana *Lankavatara Sutra* and also to Lao-tze, for both of which the highest things do not admit of conceptual expression: "He who knows does not say; he who says does not know."[50] The truth is to be done rather than said. For this, silence is crucial, and yet it too can be deceptive. Silent unfolding terminates in concrete but not in conceptual expression: the Zenist paints as the Hasid dances.

The rejection of conceptual expression in Zen belongs together with the rejection of all mediation. So, for example, the enlightened one is depicted as he destroyed Buddhist writings or artworks. One excerpt reads: "If you meet the Buddha, destroy him." The Buddha nature can only be found if one indicates directly the soul of man, thus only in each one himself. All exterior things at their highest are a symbol.

For all the similarities in other relations, this is the point where Zen and Hasidism part company. They agree that unity must be reached in the world; in this, they agree with Taoism. Zen even gives to Taoism a new twist in that *Nirvana* goes together with *Samsara*, the blowing out

48. Buber, *The Origin and Meaning of Hasidism*, 220–39.
49. *Schriften Zur Chassidismus, Werke*, vol. 5, 991–98.
50. Lao Tzu, *Tao te Ching*, trans. D. Lau (Baltimore: Penguin Books, 1963), ch. 56.

of desire and being involved in the endless wheel of becoming. Different than Taoism, Hasidism and Zen treat the dream world as the least level and see the waking world as its measure. But the relation to the otherness in the world and the mediating role of tradition shows itself as the boundary line between Zen and Hasidism (with which Buber's thinking also agrees). The measure of the waking world is for Hasidism not personal experience, clothed with historicity, as for Zen it is characteristic, but the *Torah*, the teaching of the tradition, that is anchored in the decisive encounters of the Jewish people in its relation with JHWH, the wholly Other, which has drawn near. But also decisive ("also" here does not denote a purely external existence of one beside the other but a necessary implication) is the encounter with the Other in the world, the encounter with the Other as fully realized and not only as a symbol. As with Kant's "Humanity," for Hasidism and for Buber every Other is an end and not merely a means, not even a means in relation to the Unconditioned. A response to the complete otherness of the Other makes open the way to the Eternal Thou.

Tradition and encounter anchor the Hasid firmly in history and community. But similar to the compassionate Buddha to which the historical roots of Zen go back, the Zen adherents can pass on the teaching to others. Teaching itself does not necessarily include a relation to others. For the Buddhists, it is a choice: instead of going into Nirvana, he becomes a *Boddhisatva*, a savior for others. For Buber, encounter with God, with the Absolute, includes a mission to the world. Community with others opens the Between within which God speaks at various times and places, according to His will; and that is the way of history.

TEACHING (*LEHRE*)

In the middle of all these manifestations of the spirit of the Orient, as Buber sees it, stands the phenomenon of that which he calls "teaching" (*Lehre*). Teaching is the most fundamental of the *geistige Wesenheiten*, which I prefer to translate as "forms of the spirit."[51] Buber speaks of spir-

---

51. Kaufmann (57) follows the older translation in rendering this as "spiritual beings." In *Martin Buber's Ontology*, 43, I have argued for "forms of the spirit." Kaufmann's choice leads him to ignore some nuances in meaning elsewhere, for example, 126 where he conflates *Wesen* and *Wesenheit*, claiming that "in English the single word 'being' must serve for both terms." It

it in different ways: it is a relation between man and that which transcends the world; it is the Between and thus more than man; it is the Word into which man enters; it is closely related to *Urdistanz*; and it is that which timelessly envelopes nature.[52] Encounter with the spirit's forms along with encounter with things of nature and with other persons constitute the three regions of the I-Thou relation. The forms are the original inspirations, Thous that are not empirically "there" but which speak of the Unconditioned, Absolute, and Eternal and lay upon the inspired one a demand to give empirical shape to the Unconditioned out of the conditioned material available in the age. Though closely linked to man, spirit is more than man, for it "breathes into," it in-spires him: it appears through man in temporal conditions and yet timelessly envelops nature because its inspirations speak of the Eternal and Unconditioned.

There are three types of these forms of the spirit, in the three realms of what Hegel characterized as the region of Absolute Spirit: art, philosophy, and religion. Buber speaks of responding to the forms *bildend, denkend, handelnd*,[53] shaping in art, thinking in philosophy, and acting in religion, realized paradigmatically for the West in Goethe, Socrates, and Jesus, respectively.[54] Elsewhere, Buber speaks of responding to the same trinity of forms *bildhaft, gedankenhaft, traumhaft*: shapingly, thinkingly, dreamingly, where *traumhaft* appears in place of the former *handelnd*, as characteristic of religious *Lehre*.[55]

Traumhaft recalls the Hindu teaching of the dream state as on the way to the highest state of dreamless sleep; it likewise recalls Tschuang-tse's equating of waking and dreaming—perhaps indeed holding for the superiority of the latter that exhibits the Tao in us without our intervention. Buber rejects the claim of the nonwaking states to be the highest. He prefers rather the Heraclitean claim that the waking is superior because of the common world of the *Logos*, whereas the sleeping involves retreat into a private world. The Orientals retreat into the self and lose the abil-

---

shouldn't. This is the one expression that, I think, Kaufmann has not translated well—a rather minor flaw in an otherwise excellent translation.

52. Martin Buber, "On the Psychologizing of the World," in *A Believing Humanism*, trans. Maurice Friedman (New York: Simon and Schuster, 1967), 147; Buber, *I and Thou*, §32, 89; "Distance and Relation," in *Knowledge of Man*, 59–71; Buber, *I and Thou*, §25, 75, Cf. *Martin Buber's Ontology*, 38–40.

53. Buber, *I and Thou*, §9, 57.   54. Ibid., §40, 115–17.
55. Ibid., §28, 81.

ity, or rather consider as inferior the ability to dwell together with others in the struggle to build a common cosmos. Solitude has the primacy, and the dream state approaches absolute primacy.[56] However, dreaming does suggest, negatively, the nonintervention of the purpose-oriented waking self and positively, contact with the unconscious and with inspiration. It thus points to nonaction as centrally characteristic of the source of religious teaching.

The form of the spirit that lies at the source of "pure effective action" results in a life that is itself teaching, the showing of the Way.[57] The empirical shape given to the inspired form is the shape of a life and is thus far superior to the forms created outside the self in art and in philosophy, in shaping and in thinking. In an entirely secondary sense, teaching translates into words and works that lie at the base of a common cosmos, a shared world of meaning taking shape in the restructuring of time and space into holy days and holy places. Dwelling in such a cosmos leads to inspired works of the spirit in a growing number of followers: to the development of new forms of art and new developments in philosophy. It leads to the possibility of the life of the spirit becoming unified as religion, philosophy, and the arts embody and evoke the same spirit.[58]

The object of teaching, the one thing necessary, being truly one, being whole, may be realized in several ways. First is the unity of the simple people (*Einfaltigen*), the incomplex, those who maintain their peace and balance in the midst of change. Such simple ones live in a collective world created, in its original inspiration, by a second type: those who, out of the swirling multiplicity of their natures, have become one (*Einge-wordenen*)[59] and are thus able, as the simple are not so able, to create the works of the spirit in all three regions of the spirit. Buber speaks also of the becoming one of the soul as apparently identical with this type.[60] There is, in addition, a third type, associated with the becoming one of the spiritual life that involves the organic interplay of all the forms of the spirit in an individual and in a culture.[61] Beyond, but not above this, is

---

56. Martin Buber, "What is Common to All," in *Knowledge of Man*, 89–98 and 102–5.
57. Buber, *I and Thou*, §32, 91E.
58. Cf. Buber, *I and Thou*, §35, 98 and §36, 103.
59. Buber, "Die Lehre vom Tao, 1026.
60. Ibid.
61. Martin Buber, *Good and Evil*, trans. R. G. Smith (New York: Scribner, 1953), 129.

the experience of the void in Hinduism, at best an anticipation of unity, but not its possession.[62] But the highest type is one who has achieved unity throughout the whole of his life in relation to the primal mystery, the Eternal Thou: he is the holy man, the *arhat*, the *zaddik*, the saint who has himself become *Lehre*, who has become *Torah*, whose very existence opens up a Way for a community.

There is another type of unity, unity of thought or what we might call philosophic unity, the search for which has become characteristic of the West. Buber sets up a contrast between Eastern and Western types of ideal unities in terms of the "motor" East (which we have already met) and the "sensorial" West. Western man is primarily "sensorial," dominated especially by vision, the objective sense par excellence. Contrasted with touch, for example, that involves the reciprocal experience of the felt other and the feeling organism, vision, in its normal functioning, involves the disappearance of the organic self from the field of experience and the appearance of the detached other. Furthermore, the other appears in terms of relations of spatial exteriority to other visible individuals as well, and it manifests itself as relatively static. Such visually observed others are worked into a world picture through subordination to conceptual *eide* that are the objects of intellectual "seeing." Individuals so conceived are fit objects for mastery, the underlying aim that lies at the heart of Western man's orientation. At an early phase, the object of such a stance might be contemplative—though it is still object of conceptual or experiential mastery. But when this mode of knowing is conjoined to a peculiar mode of *praxis* in experimental science, it attains to an open-ended dynamism that transposes more and more from the unconscious and semiconscious and works at the refashioning things by a humanity bent on conquest and the imposition of its own order upon things.[63]

Oriental man, by contrast, is essentially "motor." Where static images and concepts guide Western *praxis*, movements and actions guide Oriental thought. Here Buber speaks of Laotze, the *Upanishads*, Zarathustra, and the prophets: the Chinese, Indians, Persians, and Jews. Indeed, the latter are the "motor type in its purest expression." For Oriental

62. Buber, "Philosophical and Religious Worldview," *A Believing Humanism* (New York: Simon and Schuster, 1967), 133.
63. Buber, "Geist des Orients," 47–50.

man, experience is essentially dynamic. The movements in the "outer" world reverberate through our "inner" world as well. As we are interconnected with others, so the others are linked with one another, and the movements within us act upon one another: all things interpenetrate in action; all the perceptual powers interpenetrate in the active life of a person. Oriental man, thinking in terms of movement, is thus more temporally than spatially oriented. The world is not primarily a set of things to be seen and comprehended in a conceptual system but a way to be walked, a path, the *Tao*. And walking the path is also, at the same time, finding response by "doing the truth," "the one thing necessary," realizing the One within which the split world is healed. The recognition of a split into opposites pervades all the Oriental cultures: a split between the knower and the world in Hinduism, within the world itself for Taoism, between the agent and the world in Zoroastrianism, and a split within the agent himself in Judaism. With the recognition of different dualities, different paths are proposed. But they all are part of the Way of the One. Teaching of the Way is the dominant characteristic of the religious teachings in each of the cultures.[64]

Overcoming the split is more than a conceptual-theoretical overcoming—in fact, the conceptual may constitute a fundamental obstacle to it. Hinduism, Buddhism, Taoism, Zen, and Hasidism all place conceptual expression in an inferior, if not a negative, position. Overcoming the split involves not so much a view as a path, and therefore not so much a knowing-that or a knowing-what, as a knowing-how. Such knowing is taught more by example than words.

In the Hindu-Buddhist-Zen line, such knowing is referred to variously as *moksha*, *nirvana*, *satori*, or "enlightenment," in the different nuances that term has in each tradition. Though often spoken of as a single experience, what it effects is a shift of level for the whole of one's life, which then attains its unity. Buber's equivalent is "the experience of faith," prepared for by encounter with many Thous but realized when the many are heard as messages from a single Voice.[65] But the unity of life is not simply meeting with the Thou, not even with the Eternal Thou. It is rather the coming and going from meeting with the Thou to mission

64. Ibid., 47–54.
65. Buber, "Replies," 689–90.

into the world of It; but the process now no longer loses its relation to the Center. For Buber, "the unity of life . . . once truly won, is no longer torn by any changes."[66]

Of great significance is the fact that achieving the unity of one's life is not simply something that occurs to and in an individual person but something that has cosmic repercussions. For Hinduism, the self is identical with the All; for Taoism as for Zen, the unity of the world is achieved through the unity of the self, and in Hasidism, the world gains its unity through the unified man.

The latter notion appears in the last part of *I and Thou* where the I-It and I-Thou relations are said to mirror a twofold movement in the cosmos: the movements of Being and Becoming.[67] Becoming is the unfolding of the potentialities of beings as they move out from their divine Source, whereas Being involves the return of these beings to that Source. Man can aid in the former through his activity in the world, but it is only through man that things are returned to their Source. In Hasidic terms, man is the cosmic mediator sent to release the holy sparks from things and to establish the carriage of God's majesty in the world.[68]

Teaching has come to the West from the East. Today, it is in the process of eclipse in the West and in the East, even though it shows "the one thing necessary," without which human life, and likewise the created world itself, is torn apart, unredeemed. Teaching differs from era to era, and yet it is the same. It is the same in that it displays an ultimately ineffable presence that heals, that makes whole. It is different because it finds different expression, different content at different times and places. When the content fits both the one who has become whole with his expression and the age to which he speaks as its message, a Way opens up for a people, a common *cosmos* that speaks of the Eternal Thou. Today, however, our situation is such that, for Buber, there is no common Way.[69] But there is the place where a Way may eventually show itself, the place where the Thou is met, the flashing forth of presence when we are open

66. Martin Buber, "Dialogue," in *Between Man and Man*, trans. R. G. Smith (Boston: Beacon, 1961), 25.

67. Buber, *I and Thou*, §54, 149.

68. Buber, *Hasidism and Modern Man*, ed. and trans. M. Friedman (New York: Harper and Row, 1958), 33 and 118.

69. Martin Buber, *For the Sake of Heaven*, trans. Ludwig Lewisohn (New York: Harper and Row, 1966).

to it and not closed within the well-trod paths of the It-World. Buber's task has been to ponder the traditions of teaching and point to the place. If these flashings-forth cohere in the experience of faith for many,[70] perhaps there will arise in our midst those who can teach a Way for us who now dwell in the age of the eclipse of God.

LEHRE AND PHILOSOPHY

Near the conclusion to *Daniel*, Buber refers to a progressive maturing of *Lehre* in him, from Hinduism through philosophic Idealism to Taoism and on to the position maintained in that work,[71] which was itself superseded and brought to full maturity in *I and Thou*. The level of philosophic Idealism was the level where he achieved the unity of life but only in thought, or, in Kierkegaard's terms, only as a possibility of existence. Buber returned to the level of philosophical comprehension in a significant way toward the end of his life in the essays collected in *The Knowledge of Man*. In this concluding section, I wish to clarify and extend Buber's reflections in terms of the relation between philosophy and religious teaching.

Buber sees philosophy and religion as fragmented into many traditions and thus each in some way relative to the historical conditions out of which they arose. But just as religion is a mixture of conditionality and unconditionality, of the age and the one thing necessary, so also with philosophy.[72] This relation to the unconditioned through the conditioned is what makes dialogue between differing traditions not only possible but obligatory. However, the anchorage of each in a historical context is not a superfluity from which one can abstract to achieve a pure, universal message. Anchorage in the concrete is where the truth is to be found.[73]

There are a number of philosophic claims involved in the above (i.e., claims to universal truth that transcend conditions). If we accept Buber's claims, then we are forced to distinguish two levels to the philosophic enterprise—both, I think, indispensable. There is first the level at which the aforementioned claims operate, the level of the conditions for the

70. Cf. Buber, "Replies," 693.
71. Cf. Buber, *Daniel*, 117ff.
72. Buber, "On the Situation in Philosophy," *A Believing Humanism*, 136–37.
73. Cf. Buber, "China and Us," in *Pointing the Way*, 122.

possibility of distinctively human existence as such. There is, secondly, a level concerned with the concrete unfolding of human existence. The two levels implicate each other, since the coming into light of the first level is part of the unfolding of the second and stands open itself to the development in the light of further concrete unfolding. One discovers the universal imperative of dialogue and the conditions that make it possible and necessary in the particularity and contingency of one's own concrete existence, and these conditions can be brought to greater clarity in the course of that existence.

Philosophical thought lays hold of individuals in terms of universals, principles, laws, but that is only following out in an explicit way the path laid out by language itself. This involves certain underlying structures both on the part of the knower and on the part of the known. On the part of the knower, this involves a reference beyond the individual to the broader context within which it fits. It involves a reference to all actual or possible instances of the kind dealt with in a given instance of knowing, a reference to a universal context, a network of universals within which the kind is understood, a world of meaning. But that itself is made possible by the human knower being, at base, reference to the whole of reality itself, to all actual or possible instances of Being, a reference that Buber termed *Urdistanz* or primordial distance.[74] Any sensorily encountered individual is taken up into this ultimate reference: the notion of all actual or possible instances of Being is contracted to all actual or possible instances of the kind in question in the empirical encounter, and the empirically given individual is displayed as an instance of its kind.

On the part of the known, since thought reveals it as what it is, it must be more than its empirical individuality; it must itself actually *be* an instance within a set of universal networks, ultimately an instance of being, a relation to the Whole. Particular networks are a combination of construction and discovery, and they develop in the light of the expansion of empirical encounters. But the existence of such networks displays certain necessary structures of thought and things upon which science itself rests.

What has this to do with the Orient and with its *Lehre*? The level of being in us is the level of our unconditional reference to the whole of real-

74. Buber, "Distance and Relation," in *Knowledge of Man*, 59–71.

ity and thus also to the wholeness both of ourselves and of any encounterable other. The level of being in things is the level of their reference to the Whole. Empirical encounter and conceptual interpretation afford us aspects of the wholeness of things—appearances revealing in part, concealing in part, pointing to the wholeness from differing positions, differing cultural angles, differing methodologies while never encompassing that wholeness. Yet there *is* the wholeness of each thing, the wholeness of ourselves, and the wholeness of reality, and we are referred to that in the depth of our being. This structural feature of our humanness points to the possibility of a mode of relation to things other than empirical and conceptual: thus, a relation beyond appearances (though not without them), a possible relation of the wholeness of ourselves to the wholeness of others, and a possible opening through that relation to the wholeness of reality itself. This would explain why, in certain modes of self-experience, "I and the All are one," for the self in its depth is a reference to the All. This would explain why meeting with the Thou is an intimation of the Eternal Thou and why the cosmos itself is implicated in any experience of such wholeness. This approach allows us to explain the foundations of *Lehre* without explaining it away.

But the philosophical explication of these conditions is not the living through of the one thing necessary. Philosophy here points to the possibility of that which *Lehre* lives. And in so doing, philosophy performs a service to *Lehre* by holding open the space of that possibility at a time when so many factors converge to close it. It heads off a now-popular psychologizing of Oriental teaching in which meditation is considered a mere intraorganic event of learning how to "relax" but having nothing essential to do with the ontological concern of relation to the whole of reality so central to all teaching. This psychologizing is itself expression of a doctrine that claims scientific sanction and reduces the self to its empirical inspectability, and thus, in effect, cuts off the roots of science itself. It is this, above all, that closes off the space of openness to the spirit. The experiential testimony of religious teaching is dialectically related to philosophical explication of the sort we have here indicated. The teaching points to such explication, and such explication points to the teaching. Western "enlightenment" eliminated both and now rules the world. A return to the relation between teaching and philosophy is a requirement of the age. Buber has set us on the way to such return.

Such structural analysis likewise supplies the conditions for the possibility of dialogue that moves from such analysis, on the basis of such analysis, to encounter with the concrete richness of the multiplicity of cultures and individuals. Dialogue would then be not merely a pragmatic matter of alienated cultures and individuals bound together by reason of a common threat standing over against them all. It would be dialogue rooted in the underlying structures of the human situation itself. To such structure and such dialogue Buber has led us, a dialogue of East and West, a dialogue between two forms of the spirit, a dialogue between religious teaching and philosophy, and a dialogue that is one of the urgent requirements of our age.

21 ∞ The Dialogical Principle

Buber and Marcel

Riding the crest of a wave of popularity in the 50s, 60s, and 70s, today Gabriel Marcel and Martin Buber are largely thinkers who have been forgotten—except perhaps for *I and Thou*, whose poetic character gives it the status of something like Kahil Gibron's *The Prophet*.[1] And yet the center of what they both touch upon—the center that they share in common with each other and with a still "live" thinker like Heidegger—is something essential to being human and thus carries an enduring relevance.

Though the terminology may differ, there is a remarkable parallelism between the basic principles—or should I say the basic direction—of the thought of Gabriel Marcel and that of Martin Buber. And there is little doubt in my mind that the basis lies in the fact that both are deeply religious thinkers. Marcel told Ricoeur that his work was a generalization of his Christian faith, developing it at a philosophic level prior to special religious faith and thus available to all humans, whatever their peculiar religious or nonreligious commitment.[2] Buber has been understood to have developed Jewish Hasidic mysticism of the everyday life into a similar general philosophy available to all humankind.[3] It is the religious

Address to the Gabriel Marcel Society, March, 1997. This work parallels my paper comparing Buber with Martin Heidegger and the poetic essayist Max Picard: "Silence, Being, and the Between: Picard, Heidegger, and Buber," *Man and World* 27 (1994): 121–34. This is reprinted as the last entry in this volume.

1. Martin Buber, *I and Thou*, trans. W. Kaufmann (New York: Scribners, 1970). For a general interpretation, see my *Martin Buber's Ontology: An Analysis of I and Thou* (Evanston, Ill.: Northwestern University Press, 1969).

2. Gabriel Marcel, *Tragic Wisdom and Beyond*, trans. Stephen Jolin and Peter McCormick (Evanston, Ill.: Northwestern University Press, 1973), 239.

3. Arno Anzenbacher, *Die Philosophie Martin Bubers* (Vienna: Schendl, 1965), 12–22. Buber's collected *Werke* divide into three volumes: vol. 1, *Schriften zur Philosophie* (München: Kö-

commitment that sustained an enduring interest by both thinkers in the *question of wholeness*, the wholeness of one's own being and one's relation to the wholeness of what is, over against the confinement of interest to regional problems or piecemeal treatment of conceptual puzzles, and, indeed, beyond the focus of traditional philosophy upon conceptual system. In both men, there is a return to a lived sense of the Whole itself from the abstract delineation of the encompassing framework of all our dealings in relation to that Whole. In Marcel, the question of wholeness takes the form of centering upon what he calls "the ontological mystery,"[4] or, as his Gifford Lectures would have it, *The Mystery of Being*.[5] In Buber, it has to do with what he terms the I-Thou relation, our doorway to the Eternal Thou.[6]

Marcel's notion of mystery is set off over against the notion of problem that parallels Buber's setting off I-Thou from I-It relations.[7] On the surface, Marcel's distinction would seem to be the more universal, while Buber's I-Thou would seem to be restricted to the interhuman. But this is only apparent, for I-Thou relations are possible with any entity. Such relations exhibit what he calls "the dialogical principle," the interchange of being with being.[8] Buber speaks of three regions of such relation: with men, with nature, and with so-called "forms of the Spirit."[9] Outside of human relations (that he curiously downplays in his major work, *I and Thou*), the examples he uses are: a piece of mica, a cat, his horse, a tree, a Doric pillar, and a book.[10] In fact, a piece of mica was the occasion for his discovery of the Between, the region of relation irreducible to subjective response. The Doric pillar and the book are examples of mediated relations with so-called forms of the spirit whose origins lie in an original meeting on the part of their authors with a nonempirically present form that demanded embodiment in a work. As in Hegel, such meetings

sel, 1962); vol. 2 *Schriften zur Bibel* (München: Kösel, 1963); vol. 3, *Schriften zum Chassidismus* (München: Kösel, 1963).

4. Gabriel Marcel, "The Ontological Mystery" in *The Philosophy of Existentialism*, trans. M. Harari (New York: Citadel, 1961), 9–46.

5. Gabriel Marcel, *The Mystery of Being*, 2 vols. (Chicago: Regnery, 1960).

6. Buber, *I and Thou*, I, 53.

7. On problem and mystery, see Marcel, *The Mystery of Being*, vol. 1, 251ff, and *Being and Having* (New York: Harper and Row, 1965), 100ff; on I-Thou as distinct from I-It, see n. 6.

8. Martin Buber, *Between Man and Man*, trans. R. G. Smith (Boston: Beacon, 1955), 19ff.

9. Buber, *I and Thou*, I, 60–71. Cf. Wood, *Martin Buber's Ontology*, 40–45 and 50–51.

10. Cf. Wood, *Martin Buber's Ontology*, 46, for the relevant texts.

announce something of the eternal and encompassing in three differing modes: in art, in philosophy, and in religion, culminating respectively in an external work, a system of thought presented in writing or in speech, and a form of life displayed in word and deed.[11] But the center of the three regions of relation lies in meeting with one's fellow humans that interplays with what lies below in relation to nature and above in relation to the forms of the spirit to establish a meaningful communal lifeworld. In Marcel, the central focus in the question of the mystery of being lies in relation to the Thou.[12] Hence, he called his philosophy "a metaphysics of *we are*" rather than, in the Cartesian line, a metaphysics of *I think*.[13]

For Buber, I-Thou relations are unique, unpredictable, immediate, and involve the whole of oneself "bound up in reciprocity" with the other. I-It relations are predictable, linked to the universal, mediated by past experience, and involve only a part of oneself that stands at a distance from the object. I-It relations are third-person relations, so that for "It" one could substitute also "He" or "She" or "They." An "It" is something or someone I talk about; a Thou is something or someone I talk to because the Thou addresses me. I-It relations, built up over time, constitute the firm world of everyday personal and communal inhabitance.[14]

As I said, Buber's contrast between I-It and I-Thou relations has its parallel in Marcel's distinction between problem and mystery. Crucial to Marcel's notion of problem is that one who considers a problem is capable of leaving himself out of consideration. This is underscored by the Greek etymological roots of the term "problem" in *pro* and *blema*, yielding "that which is thrown before one." Its exact Latin-derived equivalent is the term "object" from *ob* and *jectum*. I can disengage myself from a problem and set it over against me as an object. Mystery, by contrast, includes me as one who experiences and inquires.[15] The most obvious region where we deal with problems is in the realm of the sensorily given.

Marcel's favorite examples have to do with our own contrivances, the

11. G. W. F. Hegel, *Hegel's Philosophy of Mind*, trans. W. Wallace and A. Miller (Oxford: Clarendon, 1971), §§533–77, 292–316.

12. Gabriel Marcel, *The Existential Background of Human Dignity* (Cambridge, Mass.: Harvard University Press, 1963), 38–40; *Creative Fidelity*, trans. R. Rosthal (New York: Noonday, 1957), 35, 149ff.

13. Marcel, *The Mystery of Being*, II, 10.

14. Buber, *I and Thou*, I, 53ff and 61–68; Wood, *Martin Buber's Ontology*, 52–61.

15. Buber, *I and Thou*, I, 53.

realm of technology. But that rests upon the region of natural scientific inquiry that tries to figure out the mechanisms operative in the sensorily given. Linked with that in modern science is the whole region of mathematics that, though not appearing sensorily over against our act of observing it, does stand before our "mind's eye." Implied in mathematical procedure is the more abstract region of logical analysis. These are clearly regions of problems in Marcel's sense of the term. But even they involve as their foundation the sensing and thinking self, so that one has to take into consideration the involvement of the subject in knowing the objects. And here we enter the realm of mystery that includes the subject as well as the object. The direction of thought here follows at one level Plato's move up the Line of Knowledge where the metamathematical region would include not simply logic but also the eidetics of the relation of the sensed and the intellected to sensing and intellection.[16]

Marcel's development of the notion of mystery leads from sensation as participation in one's own body and through it in the material world to participation in the life of others in family, friendship, and community, to participation in God through faith, hope, and love developed in and through community with others.[17] Feeling is the sign of participation—beginning with somatic feelings that reveal to me my body that, from one point of view, presents itself as the other to my conscious self, and yet an other that I simultaneously *have* and *am*. But beyond that, sensory feeling reveals what is other than my psycho-physical self. Marcel even views sensation as a sharing in the other's obscure delight in existence—and here he is speaking of appreciating the smell of a flower.[18] This seems to parallel Buber's keen sensitivity for the Thou in things of nature. I as one sensing, as one who lives bodily in and through sensations, thereby participate in the external world. In fact, Marcel sees the lived body and the external world on the same footing: I participate in both.[19] There are also the modes of felt identity with significant others,

16. See my "Plato's Line Revisited: The Pedagogy of Complete Reflection," *The Review of Metaphysics* 44 (March 1991): 525–47. It is reprinted in this volume.

17. On participation generally, see Marcel, *The Mystery of Being*, I, 127ff; on feeling, sensation, embodiment, and participation in the sensed other, see Marcel, *Metaphysical Journal*, trans. B. Wall (Chicago: Regnery, 1952), 241–61; cf. also Marcel, *The Mystery of Being*, II, 119; Marcel, *Tragic Wisdom and Beyond*, 53, 222; "The Mystery of the Family," in *Homo Viator: Introduction to a Metaphysics of Hope*, trans. E. Craufurd (New York: Harper, 1962), 68ff.

18. Marcel, *The Existential Background of Human Dignity*, 44.

19. Ibid., 47.

beginning with the family and passing through friendships.[20] All this is sustained by a global sense of participating in Being as whole, culminating in the felt presence of the Absolute Thou.[21] The being of a human existent is thus not limited to the circumscribed locus of its sensorily inspectable body; it *is* that in which it participates. There is an overlap, an overreaching of my physical boundaries to share in the entities that surround me. Marcel's talk here seems to blur the lines of what we tend to think of as clearly circumscribed individual substances.

Buber too sees the self as essentially involved in what is other than itself. For him, there is no I taken in itself but only the I of relation.[22] But in the I-It relation, the other is a function of the experience and use of the I, whereas in the I-Thou relation the other rises up to appearance as receding to infinite depths. Adapting a Hasidic saying, Buber maintains that in lovingly meeting with other persons and things, one releases from them the holy sparks that lie in their depths and belong to the roots of one's own soul.[23] He maintains further that one's own soul is really the expression of the soul of one's people.[24] And he maintains finally that the relation between God and His creation is one of the rivers to the ocean where no clear line of separation is determinable—and all this in such a way that, for Buber, at the deepest level the principle of noncontradiction does not hold. We are both in God and stand over against Him in dialogue.[25]

In many ways, Buber and Marcel follow, at least conceptually, certain directions taken by Hegel. And as in Hegel, for Marcel it is feeling that reveals to me the modes of participation in the other.[26] The vision of our relation to the other entailed in the claims of both Buber and Marcel requires a transformation of categories along Hegelian lines. Our view of what an entity might be is haunted by visually circumscribed objects and a certain Greek understanding of the principle of identity realized ideally in the *atomos* or, alternatively, in its antecedent, Parmenidean *estin* or *it is*, completely one and changeless, apart from everything. But these are abstractions. The deeper categories are derived from reflection upon friendship,

20. Marcel, *The Mystery of Being*, I, 224.   21. Ibid., II, 141.

22. Buber, *I and Thou*, I, 54.

23. Martin Buber, *Hasidism and Modern Man*, trans. M. Friedmann (New York: Harper and Row, 1958), 32–33.

24. Martin Buber, "Das Judentum und die Juden," *Reden über das Judentum* (Köln: Melzer, 1963), 12–18.

25. Buber, *I and Thou*, III, 130, 141, 155–56.

26. Hegel, *Philosophy of Mind*, §381, Zusatz, 10; §518, 255.

perception, understanding, and their ground in life, reading the preliving forms downward from there. What emerges is a notion of identity-in-difference, where identity is deepened by the inclusion of difference. And of course the ultimate expression of such insight is the Christian doctrine of the Trinity. An entity *is* to the extent that it exceeds itself and includes otherness within itself or, perhaps better, allows itself to be taken up into otherness without losing its own identity—indeed, gaining precisely that identity through this donation to otherness. For Marcel, as for Hegel, the notion of identity in traditional logic has to be overcome.[27]

For Marcel, participation through feeling in the mystery of one's own body, of the sensorily given world, in the mystery of the lives of significant others, of relation to the larger community and, finally, in the mystery of relation to God, is set over against a first level of reflection that abstracts out certain features for consideration.[28] This leads to the development of philosophy, the sciences, and technical arts and consequently to a transformation of that first lived immediacy into a set of problems. What pervades that development, however, is what Marcel calls "the spirit of abstraction."[29] When that gets transferred into the first level of participation and becomes the ruling element, we reach the contemporary situation of "the broken world."[30]

Buber's parallel is the growth of the It-world over time, most especially with the rise of modern science and technology[31] but always dogging the development of an ordered communal lifeworld, for example, the lifeworld of the Jewish Pharisees. It is accompanied by a decline in the ability to say Thou.[32] Both thinkers see a new kind of pervasive attitude governing the way a scientific-technical world comes to presence. Both see a kind of necessity—even obligation—in this kind of development, "adding to the becoming of the world," in Buber's terms.[33] Near the end of his life, backtracking upon his early strong criticism of technolo-

27. Cf. Marcel, *The Mystery of Being*, I, 115; G. W. F. Hegel, *The Encyclopaedia Logic*, trans. T. Geraets, W. Suchting, and H. Harris (Indianapolis: Hackett, 1991), 179–81.

28. Marcel, *The Mystery of Being*, I, 95ff.

29. Gabriel Marcel, *Man Against Mass Society*, trans. G. Fraser (Chicago: Regnery, 1962), 153ff; Marcel, *Metaphysical Journal*, ix.

30. Marcel, *The Mystery of Being*, I, 22ff.

31. This is the thesis of Buber, *I and Thou*, II, 87–122.

32. Buber, *I and Thou*, 91.

33. Ibid., III, 149.

gy, Marcel claims that, though good in itself, without the countervailing disposition of attendance to the mystery, it leads to the most severe alienation from the element in that the human being naturally lives.[34] Buber speaks of an increasing sense of alienation that follows the development of the It-world. Early Franciscans detected it in the rise of scholasticism; Buber and Marcel find it especially rampant in the modern development of science and technology and share the Franciscan concern.

What Marcel calls "first reflection" abstracts from participation in the lifeworld. Whereas participation governed the lifeworlds of communities before the rise of what develops into the spirit of abstraction, paradoxically, participation in the contemporary world makes increasingly more rare what we might call, paralleling Marcel's coinage for the region of problem, "the spirit of participation." There is then need for another level of reflection, not abstractive but "recuperative," recovering the primary sense of participation from the dominant spirit of abstraction.[35] For Marcel, this is called *second reflection*. It is a matter of a recollection of oneself as a whole, the achievement of a certain inward grip, the deepening of a sense of presence, where "sense" stands for a certain feeling that allows me to participate in what is outside of myself. The term "recollection" is used religiously for a re-collection of ourselves from the scatteredness of everyday existence, but it is extended by Marcel to a recollection of ourselves from the abstractness introduced both at the level of abstract thought and at the level of the lived world insofar as it has been pervaded by the spirit of abstraction.[36] This is a level of reflection upon reflection, considering the global status of the first level of reflection. There is a negatively critical aspect that emerges here: a negation of the negation involved in the first level. But this depends upon recognizing the positive character of primary participation.[37]

Now there are two levels to second reflection that Marcel does not seem to distinguish clearly: a conceptual and a participatory. In this connection, Buber notes that philosophy aims at welding its concepts into a comprehensive whole, but it is a whole realized apart from life.[38] And for

34. Marcel, *Tragic Wisdom and Beyond*, 245.
35. Marcel, *The Mystery of Being*, I, 102–3.
36. Marcel, *The Existential Background of Human Dignity*, 86.
37. Marcel, *The Mystery of Being*, I, 95ff.
38. Martin Buber, *Daniel: Dialogues on Realization*, trans. M. Friedman (New York:

Buber even the realization of a certain lived unity of oneself achieved in solitude as a precondition for the works of the spirit is still apart from the real unity of life in connection with others.[39] But to my knowledge Buber does not speak of another mode of reflection here. Husserl called attention to another level of reflection in his attempt to lead all abstractions back to their origin in the lifeworld, but, as in Hegel, his "leading back" was at the conceptual level.[40] In the present context, this would involve the recognition of the status of the abstractions of first reflection and lead to the development of the categories requisite to clarify the status of primary participation. The latter, participatory level is the level of presence, lived directly and deepened through a mode of reflection that does not *comprehend* but *dwells* in deepened presence precisely through recollection. There is another feature of thoughtfulness involved in the taking to heart involved in recollection: it is displayed in actions on behalf of those whose life we share and that might invoke the exclamation from our beneficiaries: "How thoughtful!" Recollective presence—that can invoke presence even in physical absence—is what we might call *vocational* presence,[41] that which calls for thoughtful action, action that involves thinking the presence of the other person. That should lie at the base of thinking directed toward the means of being able to do for the other. Here first reflection is guided by second.

For Buber, all thought should lead back to the I-Thou relation that requires a meeting of will and grace.[42] Marcel refers to experiences that cannot be relived at will but require "disposability" or availability to respond to the requirements of the situation.[43] Buber speaks similarly of the side of will as that of responsibility in the sense of capacity to respond.[44] In this regard, Buber distinguishes an aesthetic experience from

McGraw-Hill, 1965), 137–40. I have explored the place of philosophy in Buber's thought in "Buber's Conception of Philosophy," *Thought* LIII (September 1979): 310–19.

39. Buber, *I and Thou*, III, 137 and 140.

40. Edmund Husserl, *Crisis of European Sciences and Transcendental Phenomenology*, trans. D. Carr (Evanston, Ill.: Northwestern University Press, 1970), 48ff and 123ff.

41. See Gabriel Marcel, "An Essay in Autobiography," in *Philosophy of Existentialism*, trans. M. Harari (New York: Citadel Press, 1961), 126–27, on the primacy of action and on "being as the place of fidelity," and Marcel, *Tragic Wisdom and Beyond*, 29, where Marcel notes approvingly that for Buber man is vocation and not simply nature.

42. Buber, *I and Thou*, I, 62.

43. Marcel, *Creative Fidelity*, 38–57; Marcel, *The Mystery of Being*, I, 262.

44. Buber, *Between Man and Man*, 16.

an I-Thou relation in that the former requires only an aspect of our-selves.[45] What is involved in the I-Thou relation is not an exquisite or an intense feeling on the one hand or simply the phenomenal surface of what appears on the other. The I-Thou relation is not an episodic experi-ence; it transforms one's whole sense of being. But one's wholeness does not simply lie in passivity to meeting; it entails a readiness to act: some-thing is not only experienced, it must be *done*.[46] It requires and consti-tutes the wholeness of ourselves in relation to the underlying wholeness of what is encountered. Though it occurs in the now of real presence, such presence gathers the past and opens the future. In meeting with God, meeting always entails mission to the community.[47] Meeting with a Thou is thus not an aesthetic but a *vocational* experience. It leads to the transformation of our lives.

In *I and Thou*, Buber's initial focus is upon the passing character of meeting with the Thou, the happy coming and the sad but inevitable go-ing of each Thou that is fated to become an It.[48] He emphasizes this to such extent that even his translator Walter Kaufmann reads Buber as holding to an overall drab everyday world of I-It relations punctuated by ecstatic episodes with the Thou.[49] At one level, the continuity between such episodes is established by bringing form into the I-It world—an ac-tivity that inevitably is accompanied by the downward drag drawing one from form to object.[50] But at another level, it is essential to hold one-self open for the transformation of the routinized world with the reemer-gence of the Thou whenever one is so graced, for the I-Thou relation is a matter of a meeting between will and grace.[51] Such pattern may repeat itself in different regions of our lives, not only in friendship and family but in work, politics, our dealings with art and thought, and in our reli-gious life. Meeting with the Thou leads to the development of the forms of communal life. Morality establishes the general framework of prin-

---

45. Buber, *I and Thou*, I, 54.
47. Ibid., III, 164.
46. Ibid., III, 159.
48. Ibid., I, 68.

49. In his address to the Buber Centennial in 1979 at Beer-sheva University, Buber himself explicitly says that "the unity of life, as that which is truly won, is no more torn by any changes, not ripped asunder into the everyday creaturely life and the 'deified' exalted hours; the unity of unbroken, raptureless perseverance in concreteness, in which the word is heard and a stam-mering answer dared." Buber, *Between Man and Man*, 25.

50. Buber, *I and Thou*, III, 167; cf. Buber, *I and Thou*, II, 90, also for the reverse process.
51. Buber, *I and Thou*, I, 62.

ciples for all our activities, while religion provides the ultimate grounds in the story it tells about the character of the Whole and about the place of humans within that Whole. But it is here, at these most fundamental levels, that the greatest and most hidden dangers lie. Buber said, "Just as there is nothing that can hide from us the face of our fellow man as morality can, so there is nothing that can hide from us the Face of God so much as religion can."[52] Through dogma especially—necessary and well-grounded though it may be—from age to age "we perfect the armor of invulnerability against revelation." He even speaks of one who is obsessed with possessing God as a "theomaniac" (*der gottsüchtige Mensch*).[53]

How does relation with a Thou become a disposition and not an episode? It is here that Marcel's notion of "creative fidelity" makes a significant contribution.[54] In marriage and in religion, the same disposition is required: fidelity on the one hand and creativity on the other. Through the vow or the pledge of faith, one establishes a constant self over against the fluctuations that might otherwise enter in because of changing circumstances. Those who would fail to pledge themselves because of the possibility of changed circumstances fail to realize that it is the pledge that first establishes a self.[55] But such fidelity might be indistinguishable from a stubborn closure. *Creative* fidelity involves a constant reinvocation of the presence of the other, a refusal to be lulled by routinized modes of response, as necessary as a certain measure of routine is for cooperative action. The solid self that must be established is one characterized by availability for new demands, attentive to the transforming presence of the other, the Thou.

In this regard, both Buber and Marcel distinguish between *presence* and *object*.[56] In his earlier work, for "presence" Buber used the more subjectivistic term "realization" (*Verwirklichung*)—as in moving from believing or knowing to realizing.[57] For Buber, "object" is the negative extreme of the I-It relation, a relation that includes, as its positive pole, what he calls *form* as the product of a response to meeting with a Thou. "Form" contains the Thou like a chrysalis the butterfly.[58] But then form

---

52. Buber, *Between Man and Man*, 18.   53. Buber, *I and Thou*, III, 164.
54. Marcel, *Creative Fidelity*, 157ff.   55. Ibid., 163.
56. Buber, *I and Thou*, I, 63; Marcel, *The Mystery of Being*, I, 251.
57. Cf. Wood, *Martin Buber's Ontology*, 54ff.
58. Buber, *I and Thou*, I, 69, III, 165.

becomes object when the ability of the form to speak of the Thou is lost. Religion is reduced to creed, code and cult, philosophy to a set of arguments and the history of opinions, art to the subject matter for biographers and sociologists, for students of styles and technique and chronological periods. Like Heidegger, for whom works in a museum are works that *were*, for Buber object is characterized by pastness.[59] We might say that they become presences when they "speak to us," "grab hold of us," "haunt us," and "master us." Like Heidegger, we can only learn to "let them be," for we cannot master presences, only objects.[60]

Presence is like a light, capable of intensification. Indeed, Marcel continually returns to the metaphor of light here.[61] However, he distinguishes between the light of presence and the light of the understanding that parallels his distinction between mystery and problem.[62] But the light of presence does not exclude; it rather nourishes understanding. Light, however, is a visual metaphor. Marcel claims that what carries his philosophy is an aural metaphor, namely that of music.[63] Music arises out of a global feeling that summarizes one's past. This is directly related to the point of departure of his thought from the notion of feeling as the sign of participation.[64] Music as the distillation of feeling, though embedded in the sensuous, is at the same time supersensuous; and though one's response arises out of one's own life, it is an expression of intersubjectivity that reveals the concrete *Thou* and establishes the concrete *we*. It expresses and evokes a suprarational unity beyond images, words, and concepts of the great symphony of Being.[65] Further, Marcel sees a certain music arising from philosophic success.[66] As in music, there is a felt sense of attunement, a sense, not a concept, of cohesion and plenitude that answers to our fundamental ontological exigency. Conceptualization is led by that sense. In looking back over his overall development, he sees hidden connections between his philosophy, his dramatic works, and his interest in

---

59. Buber, *I and Thou*, I, 63; cf. Heidegger, "The Origin of the Work of Art," in *Poetry, Language, and Thought*, trans. A. Hofstadter (New York: Harper, 1971), 41.

60. Martin Buber, "Memorial Address," in *Discourse on Thinking*, trans. J. Anderson and E. Freund (New York: Harper, 1966), 54–56.

61. Marcel, *Creative Fidelity*, 56, Marcel, *The Mystery of Being*, I, 16.

62. June 3, 1921, entry to Marcel, *Metaphysical Journal*, 276.

63. Marcel, *The Existential Background of Human Dignity*, 82–84.

64. Ibid., 21, 50, 82–83.   65. Ibid., 82–83.

66. Marcel, *The Mystery of Being*, I, 95.

music—connections that were hidden from him for some time. Using a geographic metaphor, he views his philosophy proper as the continent and his dramatic works as the islands that surround it; but the connecting element is music, that, he says, runs the deepest.[67] On the philosophic continent, he works through the categories required to comprehend the human situation. It requires supplement by reflection within the element of life itself that Marcel finds in drama. But human action and human thought live in the deeper element of the surrounding mystery, relation to which is a kind of feeling, a lived sense of plenitude and cohesion that guides the development of character as well as the categories of thought.

Buber too gravitates toward the aural rather than the optic—in fact, he thinks that the former is characteristic of religious thought as such.[68] This is closely linked to his notion of hearing the Word addressed to us in the everyday. The optical field is something I can command; the aural field is something dependent upon the initiative of the other addressing me.

Marcel contrasts an approach by way of language to an approach, such as his own, by way of the body and the relation of felt participation of our awareness in it.[69] This would seem to differ from Buber for whom the Word has a primacy. However, Buber has a peculiar notion of Word here, for what it delivers, in relation to the Eternal Thou, is not content but presence.[70] And so we are in the same region as Marcel's felt participation, for that music seems the most apt metaphor—or more than a metaphor: for Marcel, it is the clearest expression of our indwelling in the encompassing mystery.

Focus on presence in Marcel and Buber does not, I think, fall under the strictures of those who attack "the metaphysics of presence," since for both thinkers we are concerned with, the presence in question is the presence of the mystery, and hence the announcement of an absence in the kind of presence of which they speak.[71] Buber claims that in the I-Thou

---

67. Marcel, *Tragic Wisdom and Beyond*, 231. See Gabriel Marcel, *Music and Philosophy*, introduction by Robert E. Wood, trans. Steven Maddux (Milwaukee: Marquette University Press, 2005).

68. See my exploration of this in "Buber's Use of Oriental Themes," in *Martin Buber: A Centenary Volume*, ed. H. Gordon and J. Bloch (Beersheva: Ktav, 1984), 325–49. It is reprinted in this volume.

69. Marcel, *Tragic Wisdom and Beyond*, 222.

70. Buber, *I and Thou*, III, 158. See my "Martin Buber's Philosophy of the Word," *Philosophy Today* 30 (Winter 1986): 317–24.

71. Cf. Jacques Derrida, "Différance," in *Speech and Phenomena* (Evanston, Ill.: Northwestern University Press, 1973), 139, 147, 155–56.

relation, especially as that reaches a kind of culmination in "a glimpse through to the Eternal Thou," the Thou is met but not comprehended. He expressly refers to Kant here, holding to the essential unknowability of the thing-in-itself by reason of the finitude of our biologically rooted cognitive powers but maintaining, nonetheless, that the fullness of the other addresses us, expressing its own arising from incomprehensible depths in the field of finite appearance. Marcel claims that one cannot get outside of the encompassment in which we participate to make it a speculative object. The metaphysics of presence describes a position in which the totality is in some sense present-at-hand for the gaze of a speculative thinker; both Buber and Marcel claim that humans cannot occupy such a position.

For both thinkers, the center lies in how we are in time. Buber speaks of I-It as characterized by pastness, whereas presence is clearly related to the now that opens up a new future. I-It is a matter of becoming experienced, having been there before, knowing our way around, carrying within ourselves a kind of orientational grid, a conceptual map overlaid with a set of directions, developed out of past experience, for responding to what might appear on that map.[72] I-Thou culminates in the experience of the Eternal Thou who encompasses all of time. This possibility is structurally grounded in the distance of spirit as a relation between human existence and that which transcends the world as a whole.[73]

Marcel is particularly exercised with the development of science and technology that has a future-oriented character, repudiating the essential pastness of traditional lifeworlds and aimed, in an expansive and methodologically self-corrective manner, at the deep future when all the secrets will have been unlocked.[74] For him, presence, which has at its center living participatively in the now, harkens back to the deep past with which it is in essential continuity and looks to the deep future as a realm of possibility.[75] But dwelling in presence is, at the same time, characterized by a certain critical distance from being caught up in the latest.

Marcel's observations on the essentially future-oriented character of scientific research is not incompatible with Buber's claim to the essen-

72. Buber, *I and Thou*, I, 63; *Daniel*, 64.
73. Martin Buber, "On the Psychologizing of the World," in *A Believing Humanism*, trans. M. Friedman (New York: Simon and Schuster, 1967), 147.
74. Marcel, *The Mystery of Being*, I, 151.
75. Ibid., I, 238–39.

tial pastness of I-It relations. In spite of the future-oriented character involved in the spiral alternation between normal and revolutionary science, it is the general stance toward what is governing science as a whole that is itself governed by pastness insofar as the tradition that enters into that stance fails to recognize the more encompassing framework of the lifeworld wherein conversion of one's whole life and the life of an entire community is possible.

For Buber, the structural ground that makes distinctive humanness possible lies in *Urdistanz*, primordial distance, our basic being pried loose from the tendency toward immersion in animal immediacy or in various forms of cultural mediation by being referred to the Whole.[76] Marcel uses the same German term *Distanz* to refer to the same phenomena, but, following a tradition that goes back to Plato, he names the term of that reference "Being."[77] Reference to Being founds distinctively human capacities. In Buber, this primordial distance is what makes possible setting everything encountered over against ourselves as fitting into a world, thus establishing an intellectual I-It relation. But the encompassing whole of the It-world is precisely surface relative to the human being who inhabits that world and, indeed, for Buber relative to a given cultural epoch. *Urdistanz* also makes possible an entry into relation with the wholeness of an encountered other in a relationship that includes the I and that culminates in the experience of any other as a word spoken by the encompassing ground that Buber names the Eternal Thou. Marcel speaks here of two forms of distance: that of scientific-technical objectivation and that of the disposition of the saint. For the former, distance prevails in an impersonal approach, while for the latter detachment is a way of drawing near to things.[78]

For Buber, the origin of religion lies in the drawing near of the Thou that addresses us in extraordinary ways. Prior to what Jaspers called "the axial age," beginning around 600 B.C.E., most religions have been polytheistic.[79] For Buber, they are rooted in the encounter with what he calls "gods of the moment": the god of the brook, of the sacred grove or moun-

76. Martin Buber, *Knowledge of Man*, trans. M. Friedman (New York: Harper, 1965), 59ff.

77. Marcel, *The Mystery of Being*, I, 181; "On the Ontological Mystery," 13–17.

78. Marcel, *Creative Fidelity*, 56; Marcel, *Being and Having*, 20.

79. Karl Jaspers, *Way to Wisdom*, trans. R. Manheim (New Haven, Conn.: Yale University Press, 1954), 99.

tain, and the like. The Hebrew Bible bears witness to "an experience of faith" in that all of them are heard as words spoken by a single Voice.[80] In the beginning, Yahweh speaks and things are. The wholeness of each thing is expressed in that humanly relative surface appearance in such a way that each thing becomes in turn expression of the ineffable Speaker who utters it. Crucial to such utterance is the experience of the personal presence of that divine Speaker addressing precisely each person who is able to hear it. The aural metaphor here supersedes the visual metaphor. The divine presence cannot be seen, but it can be heard as coming from inexpressible depths. As we said, for Buber meetings with a Thou become a Thou-world only through such meeting with the Eternal Thou. This directly parallels Marcel's link between the Thou and the Absolute Presence. In both cases, it is a matter of moving from description to testimony. As we also said, such encounters are necessarily translated into form, both for oneself and for others: creed, code, and cult emerge. A community gathers, a world of faith is formed, and a tradition is established. But it hardens and comes to constitute a screen between those who live within it, those who live outside it, and the living God who speaks when and as He wills.[81]

Marcel is keenly aware of the difficulties pervading these regions of our experience. Like Buber, he is aware of the indispensability of creed, code, and cult but also of the perennial tendency to confuse the forms with the substance. This confusion shows up significantly in relations with those who do not share one's understanding of the forms when one remains closed to the relation to truth sustained by the other and violates charity in dealing with those "others." For Marcel, believers must enter into cooperative relations with others, especially in matters dealing with justice. Sharing a life in this way may open to deeper modes of sharing and unpredictable growth in our own religious understanding.[82] This underscores Marcel's basic view of the human condition as *homo viator*.[83]

The modern condition, dominated in our lifeworld by the spirit of

---

80. Buber, *Between Man and Man*, 15.

81. Buber, *I and Thou*, III, 160–68.

82. On the problems of faith, see "Orthodoxy versus Conformism," 184–94, in *Creative Fidelity*; on ecumenism, see "On the Fringe of the Ecumenical," in *Creative Fidelity*, 195–209, especially 203; cf. also Marcel, *The Mystery of Being*, I, 164.

83. Marcel has a whole book devoted to the theme: *Homo Viator*.

abstraction, has dried up the basis of religion. Nonetheless, as we said previously, the modern condition has also driven together religious traditions that treated each other from attitudes ranging from indifference to contempt, often spilling over into attempts at annihilation of the different. Buber speaks here of an unparalleled situation for religious dialogue, the possibility of learning really to listen to the Other.[84] He sees this as moving from I-It to I-Thou relations between peoples of differing faiths. In fact, he understands the I-Thou relation to be "the dialogical principle," a principle of reciprocity rooted in a sense of the encompassing wholeness of the Other that is met but not comprehended. Such dialogism is a requirement of *Urdistanz*, or of Marcel's relation to Being that refers us to the Whole without giving us ultimate possession. Buber finds it also linked to what he regards as the essential perspectivity of any mode of understanding.[85] Reference to Being, standing in tension with insertion into a biologically mediated environment of sensory appearance, demands that we attempt to understand how we are fitted into the encompassing Whole and make our choices opened up by that understanding. This generates differing human lifeworlds, each relative to their own histories. But the structural feature of reference to the Whole points to the overarching order that, if known, would situate and judge the limitations of each factual lifeworld. It poses a task of dialogue between traditions that was not recognized until pressed upon from without by the expansion of the scientific-technological approach that abstracts from the lifeworlds within which it has its point of departure. Buber sees this as part of the Way: the experience of alienation this entails invokes a deep longing for wholeness that puts the traditions into dialogue. One ought not, as did the Enlightenment thinkers, seek simply for some neutral natural religion that bypasses the various faith traditions—"heretics from natural religion," as Lessing somewhere put it. Entry into dialogue calls for each digging back into its own tradition to touch the vital religious root that generated the growth that appeared throughout the centuries and to bring that to the table as a contribution.[86] That root lies in relation to the Eternal Thou, the presence-in-absence that addresses us as Absolute Mystery in each of our encounters with the sensorily appearing

84. Buber, *Between Man and Man*, 7.
85. Marcel, "On the Situation of Philosophy," in *Being and Having*, 137.
86. Buber, *I and Thou*, III, 161.

Other. Our dialogue with one another is rooted in heeding the address of Absolute Mystery at the heart of the mystery of Being.

Marcel and Buber together have walked a remarkably similar path. Each was trying to recover the element in which humans live, the element of relation to the encompassing Mystery. They each laid hold of the structural ground of that relation in our fundamental reference to the Whole of being. Like Heidegger, they saw the fulfillment of that relation, not in the conceptual work of the intellect culminating in metaphysics but in a more holistic, lived sensibility that metaphysics forgets.[87]

However, unlike Heidegger, who focuses primary attention upon the recovery of relation to the thing, they find their primary focus in relation to other humans. And beyond Heidegger's focus upon the Mystery of Being, they bear witness to the epiphany of the Eternal or Absolute Thou as personal presence addressing us out of the heart of that Mystery. It is the sense of the presence of this Thou that gives a sense of plenitude and coherence, the only safe guide to the philosophic task of developing comprehensive categories. Philosophy thus points beyond itself and, in an era when so many factors converge to close it, holds open the space of genuine religious existence. It is in fully living life in the divine Presence addressing us in all our encounters that one can reach the root of one's own religious tradition and be in position to conduct a dialogue—demanded by the human condition itself—between religions as well as between religious existence and the world we occupy. Marcel and Buber remain significant guides in that project and thus, in spite of their momentary eclipse, retain their perennial relevance.

87. Martin Heidegger, "The Way Back into the Ground of Metaphysics," in *Existentialism from Dostoyevsky to Satre*, trans. W. Kaufmann (Cleveland: World Publishing, 1956), 209.

22 ∾ Silence, Being, and the Between

Picard, Heidegger, and Buber

Max Picard's notion of Silence,[1] Martin Heidegger's notion of Being,[2] and Martin Buber's notion of the Between[3] are not identical notions; but these three, I would suggest, stem from the same region of experience. It is a region whose loss all three thinkers bemoan as the ground of our modem unrest and rootlessness, for we are no longer planted in the soil, the relational context that is our proper element as human beings. When one thinks of rootedness, one thinks of family or of tradition, and, as significant regions of relatedness, these are not unrelated to the notions in question. But the notions go even deeper into the basic phenomena of humanness found in the region in which family and tradition are, in turn, rooted. The three notions—Silence, Being, and the Between—coming out of three different modes of linguistic formulation, will allow us to triangulate on the phenomena in question and thus bring them to some measure of clarity. It is crucially important to gain a sense of this region since philosophy in its traditional form, aimed at the Whole, can be measured by the degree to which it does justice to all the significant parameters of the field of experience. But if it is true that we have lost our sense of the region to which all three point and in which all three thinkers operate, critical assessment is impossible unless we regain some sense of that region. Further, if it is the case, as the three thinkers contend, that this region is the element in which distinctively human existence lives, failure to attend to it involves failure to understand ourselves.

1. Max Picard, *The World of Silence* (Chicago: Regnery, 1954).
2. The central focus of Heidegger's thought from his first and most influential major work, *Being and Time*.
3. Buber's central work is *I and Thou*. See my *Martin Buber's Ontology: An Analysis of I and Thou* (Evanston, Ill.: Northwestern University Press, 1969) for a selected commentary on the basic notions.

All three thinkers fall roughly in the category of phenomenological thinkers whose point of departure is descriptive adequacy in relation to the basic features of the field of experience. Phenomenology so understood is, if anything, the permanent prolegomenon to all philosophical argumentation and is implicit in all philosophic endeavors. It is to the phenomenological camp that the current attempt at exposition and appropriation belongs.

We will begin our exposition with Picard's notion of Silence since it speaks in terms of that without which access to the region is blocked. We will then pass on to Heidegger's notion of Being, which he sets off from the whole philosophic tradition as that which, though unthought, is the factual ground in which the tradition is rooted. Following that, we will discuss Buber's notion of the Between that can be considered a kind of fulfillment of the promise held out by the other two thinkers. After that, we will draw our own conclusions.

PICARD'S SILENCE

Picard is not a philosopher in the technical sense. His work is almost exclusively proclamatory and thus poetic. His most important work, *The World of Silence*, is pervaded by similes and the mode of "as if." But what he describes provides a significant approach to the region common to our three thinkers.

First of all, Picard distinguishes silence from the absence of sound. The silence to which Picard bears witness cuts across sound and its absence. There is speech that is both rooted in silence and able to bring about the appearance of silence.[4] Secondly, silence is not simply a subjective state. It is Picard's word for an all-encompassing region into which we enter. Entering into this silence is not sinking into ourselves but rather stepping out of ourselves into the region of the depth and togetherness of all things, ourselves included.[5]

Poetry especially is rooted in silence. Ordinary speech, particularly under the impetus of the development of modern means of communication, goes forth "horizontally," where words follow from other words

---

4. Picard, *World of Silence*, 129ff.
5. Ibid., 221.

and not from the silence. One thinks here of certain readings of deconstruction rooted in Saussure, where meaning is permanently deferred by passing through the sign-system as a system of differences and in which the presence of the thing spoken about evaporates. In contrast, for Picard poetry is rooted "vertically" in the perennial envelopment of silence that encircles every encounter.[6] It leaves room for a surplus in things beyond our usual modes of access.

Further, poetry stands at the confluence of beauty and truth. Truth is the systematic togetherness of things and is pregiven to us in the structure of language.[7] The word opens up Being (i.e., the Whole) and thus the whole of any given thing.[8] Language is therefore not, as some would have it, rooted in our gestures or our choices for self-expression, but it arises from the showings of things. For Picard, beauty as "the gleam of truth" prepares the way for truth.[9] Poetic language as the articulation of beauty gathers us together as a whole and has for its correlate a vision of the Whole of things. However, such vision is not a "world-picture" that we master. Rooted in silence, poetry prepares the way for mystery and thus opens up the possibility of genuine belief.

Poetry is not the only art form that makes silence present. Archaic sculptural figures are carved more out of silence than out of the earth.[10] Ancient statuary is like a door through which the gods are made present.[11] In the old cathedrals, silence is enclosed, though today they have become museums, places where we are detachedly curious onlookers or uncommitted aesthetes but scarcely full participants.[12] And of all the art forms, music, connected with but exceeding even poetry, is able to bring the silence itself to presence.[13] Think here of the difference in receptive stances and effects in the case of a symphony as distinct from a rock concert: the sounds of silence versus the sounds of noise.

Unified by silence,[14] one can receive the primary phenomena—love, life, fidelity, truth, faith, death.[15] Present in silence, the distance of death

6. Ibid., 58.

7. Ibid., 32. The English translation does not capture the claim that truth is *vorgegeben* in language. *Die Welt des Schweigens* (München: Piper, 1988), 28–29.

8. Picard, *World of Silence*, 53.

9. Ibid., 34

10. Ibid., 166.

11. Ibid., 134.

12. Ibid., 168.

13. Ibid., 27.

14. Ibid., 70

15. Ibid., 21, 207.

in particular makes the flowers, meadows, and trees more present.[16] But silence is even more primordial than such primary phenomena, as the matrix within which they come to presence. In fact, silence makes possible the unity of faith and knowledge, truth and beauty, life and spirit, past, present, and future, that has been separated in modern times.[17] According to Picard, even contemporary existentialism, while focusing attention upon crucial human phenomena like anxiety, care, unhiddenness, and death, only displays part of the phenomena that are absolutized and thus brought out of relation to the broader region of experience.[18]

The pervasive loss of silence in contemporary culture goes hand in hand with modem specialization.[19] Everything is torn out of the environing Whole and thereby subjected to our dominance. Modem cities, incarnating the principle of specialization, are factories that manufacture a world of constant, all-encompassing noise.[20] But since we belong primordially to the world of silence, we lose ourselves in the modem urbanized world where we are prisoners of the "world-noise" that is now omnipresent.

Together with our self-loss goes the loss of the Thou.[21] Indeed—and not unconnected with the loss of the Thou—the sense of the omnipresence of God likewise disappears in favor of the omnipresence of noise that the modem means of communication provide.[22] According to Picard, mystery is present in silence[23] and silence is the essence of the primordial mystery, God Himself.[24] Even the polytheists had a glimpse of this: according to Plutarch, "We learn silence from the gods, speech from men."[25] Today, we have lost silence, and thus we enter the era of the death of God.

Silence is then a primordial phenomenon that encompasses the Whole. In silence, one listens to the mystery of which things are the expression. Out of silence arises the authentic word, the word that places its hearers back into the mystery. In silence, all is healed, life is whole; there are distinctions but no splits. In silence, one can live, but in noise one flees endlessly and life is split. One goes forward, conquers, arranges without silence; but one is also simultaneously caught in endless flight.

16. Ibid., 218–19.
18. Ibid., 78
20. Ibid., 211.
22. Ibid., 206.
24. Ibid., 229

17. Ibid., 66–67, 73, 93.
19. Ibid., 72.
21. Ibid., 208
23. Ibid., 227.
25. Ibid., 154–55.

The World of Silence ends with a quote from Kierkegaard: "In the contemporary situation of the world, the whole of life is sick. If I were a physician and one asked me what I would advise, I would reply: Create silence!"[26]

HEIDEGGER'S BEING

"In alle Gipfeln gibst Ruhe, gibst stille, stille Ruhe. In all the peaks there is rest, there is silent, silent rest."[27] Heidegger loved to quote this line from Goethe on the silent repose that encompasses the mountain peaks; Heidegger loved his retreat in Todtnauberg, the ski hut in the wooded mountains. As he grew older, his thought attended more and more to language, and more and more to the poetic in language. His thought took on more and more the character of poetry itself.[28] He thought his way constantly back into the ground of the metaphysical tradition, which, driven by the Western Will to Power, sought to bring the Whole under conceptual and eventually, in modem technology, also under physical control.[29]

Heidegger's thought moves in the "ontological difference" between beings (*Seiende*) and Being (*Sein*), between things, persons, and their principles or "beingness" (*Seiendheit*) on the one hand and the openness of the Whole that makes access to things, persons, and their "beingness" possible.[30] For the metaphysical tradition, the beingness of things lies in their exhibiting themselves as instances of universal principles or forms. For Heidegger, what makes such exhibition possible is "the light of Being" that comes to light in human existence. Human reality is *Da-Sein* as Being-in-

---

26. Ibid., 231.

27. The notions of stillness and silence appear often in Heidegger's writings: cf., for example, "The End of Philosophy and the Task for Thinking," in *Basic Writings*, ed. D. Krell (New York: Harper and Row, 1971), 387; "Language," in *Poetry, Language, and Thought*, trans. A. Hofstadter (New York: Harper and Row, 1971), 206ff; "A Dialogue on Language," in *On the Way to Language*, trans. P. Hertz (San Francisco: Harper and Row, 1971), 44–45, 52–53; "The Nature of Language," *On the Way to Language*, 78, 106, 108.

28. Cf. the essays collected in *Poetry, Language, and Thought* and *On the Way to Language*. Cf. also my "Heidegger on the Way to Language," in *Semiotics: 1984*, ed. J. Deely (Lanham, Md.: University Press of America, 1985), 601–20.

29. Cf. Martin Heidegger, *The Question Concerning Technology and Other Essays*, trans. W. Lovitt (New York: Harper and Row, 1977).

30. Martin Heidegger, "The Way Back into the Ground of Metaphysics," in *Existentialism from Dostoyevsky to Sartre*, trans. W. Kaufmann (Cleveland: World Publishing, 1956), 217ff.

a-world, as the place where the Whole opens up, beyond the sealed-in inwardness of most versions of modern subjectivity. "World" here means cultural world, a meaningful articulation of the Whole of what is, an all-encompassing relational complex that opens paths for our thinking, feeling, and acting among the things we encounter.[31] World is an articulation of the space opened up when humanness happens, "a dimension that lies between the thing and man, which reaches out beyond things and back behind man."[32] It is the depth dimension, the dimension of Being, which, as dimension, furnishes the basic measure of our existence.[33]

The metaphysical tradition, though rooted in the soil of Being, is nonetheless governed by a forgottenness of Being,[34] by a restless movement away from Being in order to disclose more and more about beings and thus to conquer them, whether speculatively or practically. It operates in terms of calculation and representation, develops methods, and makes endless progress.[35] But its progress is always and necessarily one-sided. In it we lose our way as we become uprooted and alienated from the soil that grounds us. The way back into the ground is the way of meditative thinking, of learning to let things be (*Gelassenheit*), of silent attentiveness to what is not conceptually manifest but which factually grounds that mode of manifestness.[36]

All representative-calculative thinking moves within a framework that opens up aspects of things as it closes other aspects. It thinks of truth as the correspondence of our propositions to the antecedently open.[37] It fails to ponder that openness and the system of interrelated concepts embedded in the peculiarity of the language and corresponding life-forms that make possible both the formulation of propositions and the availability of beings within that openness. Openness happens only in and through

---

31. Martin Heidegger, *Being and Time*, trans. J. Maquarrie and E. Robinson (New York: Harper and Row, 1962).

32. Martin Heidegger, *What Is a Thing?* trans. W. Barton and V. Deutsch (Chicago: Regnery, 1967), 244.

33. Cf. Martin Heidegger, "What Are Poets For?" in *Poetry, Language, and Thought*, 128 and 130; "Language," in *Poetry, Language, and Thought*, 203; "Poetically Man Dwells," in *Poetry, Language, and Thought*, 220 and 227.

34. Heidegger, "The Way Back into the Ground of Metaphysics," 217ff.

35. Heidegger, *On the Way to Language*, 93.

36. Martin Heidegger, *Discourse on Thinking*, trans. J. Anderson and E. Freund (New York: Harper and Row, 1966), 54–56.

37. Heidegger, "On the Essence of Truth," in *Basic Writings*, 117ff.

the language in which we dwell without giving it a second thought. Above all, representative-calculative thinking fails to attend to the finitude of the openness that any method we might contrive and, indeed, that even the more encompassing phenomenon of natural language make possible. It thus fails to think the mystery of the concealed behind all manifestation.[38]

Heidegger uses the Greek term *orthotes* to refer to the notion of truth as propositional correctness, which corresponds to the already opened. *Orthotes* or truth as correctness appears in "orthodoxy" or correct opinion, in "orthodontia" or dental correction, and in "orthopedic" shoes, which correct problems with the feet. But truth as the opening-concealing of the Whole, grounded primordially in language and finding expression in various ways in the metaphysical tradition, Heidegger refers to by another Greek term for truth, *aletheia*, or truth as unconcealment, *a-letheia*. He stresses the *lethe* as what is concealed through the manifestation, as the dimension of mystery, of the undisclosed to which we are, nonetheless, essentially related.[39] For we are, at base, *Da-Sein*, the "there" of Being, the locus of the manifestation/concealment of the Whole. The phenomena of anxiety, care, unconcealment, and death to which Picard refers are, contrary to Picard's claim, precisely *not* torn out of the context of the Whole. However Heidegger's existentialist followers may have considered them (one thinks especially of Sartre in *Being and Nothingness*), for Heidegger they are features of the way in which we dwell in relation to the Whole.

Truth as correctness, through which, in representative-calculative thinking, we learn to master things, occurs by way of what we have come to call "intellect" or "reason." Truth as unconcealment, through which, in meditative thinking, we learn to "let things be" appreciatively there for us in their unfathomable mystery, occurs by way of what Heidegger, following a long tradition, calls "the heart." He evokes the old Anglo-Saxon term connected with heart: *thanc*, which carries the appreciative connotation of thanksgiving. If the mystery of Being is the "object" of meditative thinking, its "subjective correlate" is the depth-dimension of the heart.

The thoughtful relation of our heart to the mystery finds primordial expression in poetry and through poetry in all the arts.[40] Art for Hei-

38. On *lethe*, cf. Heidegger, "On the Essence of Truth," in *Basic Writings*, 132ff.
39. Ibid., 118–32.
40. The notion of the heart, like the notion of silence, appears throughout Heidegger' s works: cf. *What Is Called Thinking?*, trans. F. Wieck and J. Gray (New York: Harper and Row,

degger contains "the saving grace" in an era when everything, including ourselves, is taken up as material standing in reserve for someone's projects of control and manipulation, albeit in the interest of human well-being.[41] In one of Heidegger's earlier expressions, the art work stands in the rift between Earth and World. And here Earth does not mean a chemical mass located in the solar system. One has to hear it in the expression "native soil," which interplays with "World," not as the objective cosmos that science uncovers but as the dwelling place for a people, as the opening up of paths for thinking, acting, and feeling. When one truly dwells in a World, Earth becomes native soil and things and persons appear in a kind of nearness, even though—and perhaps especially when—one is objectively far away. Later, Heidegger articulated things in a slightly different way: things appear fully as things when they stand within the play of "the Fourfold," namely Earth and Sky, Mortals and Immortals, that constitutes a world of dwelling for a people.[42]

But that is a further articulation of the primordial "Between." It constitutes the way we dwell in relation to primordial mystery. Heidegger's thought then moves into the groundedness of metaphysics in the sense of the Whole, manifest in the way a people inhabits its native soil and articulated in the arts, but in a special way in the linguistic art of poetry. The arts create a world space within which things can recover their being, their nearness, in an era when they have been reduced to data standing at a distance in reserve for our projects.[43] In recovering nearness and world space, we come into contact with the primordial mystery.[44] Through this contact, the sacred appears and the question of God emerges in its full existential power.[45]

Together with Picard, Heidegger sees the modern era as "the era of the world as picture," as that whose being is taken to be identical with the

1968), 139ff.; "Memorial Address," in *Discourse on Thinking*; "What Are Poets For?" in *Poetry, Language, and Thought*, 127ff.

41. Heidegger, "The Origin of the Work of Art," in *Poetry, Language, and Thought*, 72ff .

42. Heidegger, "The Question Concerning Technology," in *The Question Concerning Technology and Other Essays*.

43. For the earlier statement (1935), see "The Origin of the Work of Art," in *Poetry, Language, and Thought*, 48ff; for the later treatment (1951), "Building, Dwelling, Thinking," in the same collection, 149ff.

44. Martin Heidegger, *Introduction to Metaphysics*, trans. G. Fried and R. Polt (New Haven, Conn.: Yale University Press, 2000), 23 and 66.

45. Cf. Heidegger, "Letter on Humanism," in *Basic Writings*, 229–30.

objective face it presents to us in scientific inquiry.[46] The sense of depth of the environing mystery of Being to which we humans as *Dasein* are essentially related is consequently closed off, forgotten, uncultivated. And it is this that leads us likewise into the epoch of the death of God, the darkening of the earth, and the standardization of humans.[47]

BUBER'S BETWEEN

Silence, in the depth dimension of Being, follows the articulation of the "Between" that surrounds the self and any encounterable other. Both Picard and Heidegger are aware of the phenomenon of the fracturing of modem existence and link it to the withering up of this region in which holistic existence can be found. Critics of Heidegger call attention to a preoccupation with the notion of the integrity of the thing and a lack of significant focus on the personal Other. Buber's thought is centered upon the personal Other and pivots about a distinction between what he calls I-Thou and I-It relations that establish the realm of "the Between."[48] As Picard's Silence suggests a distinction between sound and its lack, Buber's terminology suggests a difference between relation to a person and relation to a thing. But though relation to a person is the central instance of an I-Thou relation, I-Thou cuts across the distinction between persons and things, just as Silence cuts across the distinction between sound and its absence.

Recognizing, classifying, and using both things and persons—for example, in a purely commercial transaction—though necessary and not morally reprehensible, involve what Buber calls I-It relations.[49] What is crucial is that an aspect of ourselves relates to an aspect of things and per-

46. Heidegger, "The Age of the World Picture," in *The Question Concerning Technology and Other Essays*, 116–54.

47. Heidegger, *Introduction to Metaphysics*, 59.

48. "What Is Common to All," in *The Knowledge of Man*, trans. and ed. M. Friedman (New York: Harper and Row, 1960), 107. In several places, I have tried to clarify Buber's thought, which centers upon this distinction and this dimension: originally in *Martin Buber's Ontology*; further in "Buber's Conception of Philosophy," *Thought* 53, no. 210 (September 1978): 310–19; in "Oriental Themes in Buber's Work," in *Martin Buber: A Centenary Volume*, ed. H. Gordon and J. Bloch (Beer-Sheva: Ktav, 1981), 325–49; and in "Martin Buber's Philosophy of the Word," *Philosophy Today* (Winter 1986): 317–24. The essay on Oriental themes appears in this volume.

49. Buber, *I and Thou*, 68ff, 85.

sons insofar as they fit within a system of identification and of goal projection. Such a system is built up out of our past, which is also the past of our culture, mediating all immediate relation.[50] The Other is in fact if not in intention treated "in the third person" and thus outside the mutuality of I and You. The Other is he or she, not you—even when "you" is said with the mouth.[51] For Buber, he, she, and such a you are equivalent to It.

In an I-Thou relation, by contrast, we stand in a direct and mutual relation. The whole of ourselves is brought into play by meeting the wholeness of another.[52] To use the examples Buber himself employs, such meeting can be with a person, a thing of nature, living or not (a stone, a tree, a maple twig, a horse, a cat), or even a cultural product (a Doric pillar, a text—poetic or philosophic or religious).[53] Will, understanding, and sensibility are transformed and unified in relation to the wholeness—met but not comprehended—that speaks to us out of the partiality of sensory surface and culturally mediated interpretation in such meetings.[54] And the wholeness in ourselves that is touched and transformed is not the fleeting state of awareness with its experiences strung out over time but our deepseated, enduring *character*, the well-spring of our action, that which tunes our dispositions. Such a meeting transforms our whole sense of things and reorganizes our projects.[55] In doing so, however, it necessarily establishes the relational complexes that become the It-world where things are mastered in systems of identification and use. The generation of the It-world is part of the mission that stems from meeting with the Thou: the mission to reorganize our lifeworld.[56]

Buber introduced a scale in the It-world that extends from what he calls "form" to what he calls "object."[57] Form appears in the arts, which

---

50. Ibid., 63; Wood, *Martin Buber's Ontology*, 54ff.

51. Buber, *I and Thou*, 53.

52. Ibid., 62.

53. Cf. my "Martin Buber's Philosophy of the Word," note 12, 322b, for the references to these various encounters.

54. Cf. Martin Buber, "Man and His Image Work," in *The Knowledge of Man*, trans. M. Friedman (New York: Harper and Row, 1965), 157.

55. IT, 63, 56–57, 90–92, 115–17. Cf. also "Man and His Image Work," in *The Knowledge of Man*; Wood, *Martin Buber's Ontology*, 54ff. I have explored in some depth the religious form in "Oriental Themes in Buber's Work," 325–49; the philosophic form in "Buber's Conception of Philosophy," 310–19. "Oriental Themes" appears in the present volume.

56. Buber, *I and Thou*, 165.

57. Ibid., 160–68.

primarily articulate our relation to nature, in philosophy, which primarily articulates our relation to our fellow human beings, and in religion, which primarily articulates our relation to God.[58] Original form is rooted in meeting with a Thou, which lays a demand upon us to respond in ways that enter into public appearance in the interpersonal world. Form, as a shape given to our ways of responding, is closest to the Thou, indeed, in some ways it contains the Thou as the chrysalis contains the butterfly.[59] But by an inevitable kind of inertia, forms—philosophic, religious, and artistic—tend in the direction of what Buber calls "object," which is eventually sealed off from the Thou. Religion becomes creed, code, and cult; philosophy becomes argumentation and system-building; art is object for art historians who study techniques and styles as well as psychological and sociological influences. The Thou or the original inspiration disappears behind the work of epigoni. In this connection, Buber remarks, regarding the central regions of morality and religion: "Just as there is nothing that can hide from us the face of the Thou as morality can, so nothing can hide from us the face of God so much as religion can."[60]

In the case of both types of relation, I-Thou and I-It, what is involved is a way of articulating the whole of reality but with different emphasis in each case. The I-It relation emphasizes the Whole insofar as each individual is fitted into a classificatory system.[61] What you are now looking at is a page in a book. This page as a page is understood as an instance of a universal meaning that applies to all pages. "Page" is understood as a related set of such universals: paper, print, book, writing, reading, language, communication, instrumentality, persons, things, relations, existence, and the like. Each notion in turn has a set of "unpackers," notions entering into its definition, until the whole of being comes into particular focus as the prearticulated framework coming out of our specific linguistic tradition. Conversely, in the I-Thou relation, the individual is emphasized as it addresses us in its unencompassible wholeness apart from the universal nets of identification and use.[62] The alternation between these

58. Ibid., 56–57, 90–92, 115–17.

59. Ibid., 69 and 165.

60. Martin Buber, "Dialogue," *Between Man and Man*, trans. R. Smith (Boston: Beacon Press, 1961), 18.

61. Buber, *I and Thou*, 56–57; "The Word That Is Spoken," in *The Knowledge of Man*, 114.

62. Buber, *I and Thou*, 57–60.

two modes of relation, the coming and going between meeting and mission, is the Way of human beings. Meeting and the emergence of form contributes to the becoming of the world, but form inevitably becomes object and the world a screen between ourselves and the Thou. The unpredictable flashing forth of the Thou prepares the way for a deeper experience of faith that contributes to the Being of the world.[63]

The single condition for the possibility of both relations—I-Thou and I-It—is what Buber terms *Urdistanz*, or primordial distance. This is a relation between humanness and "what transcends the world."[64] Minimally, this means that humanness is projected beyond the whole of what is, so that what is can be considered as a whole in our networks of identification and use but also so that things and persons within the Whole can appear in their wholeness (partially revealed, partially concealed). Maximally, it means that the address that things make in the unpredictable occurrences of a Thou can coalesce into a Thou-world when we hear them as words addressed to us by a single Voice from that which eternally encompasses the whole as the Eternal Thou.[65] This, for Buber, is the core of biblical revelation: the world, displayed in the experience of wholeness, rooted in a life responsive to the Thou wherever it appears, is the speech of Yahweh.[66] The World is a Word addressed to us by Yahweh, who speaks to us ever anew in unpredictable ways in the flashing forth of the Thou, which breaks into our routinized world of identification and response, transforming and reorganizing it. "Hearing the Word" as Thou breaking into our ordinary world of relation to persons and things involves a meeting of will and grace,[67] both in the anticipatory encounter with a Thou and in "the experience of faith." We cannot call forth the Thou as we can the intelligibility and usability of things and persons. We can only be ready to turn, to reorganize our lives—or to let them be reorganized—when Thou addresses us. *Urdistanz*, developed in the region of

63. Ibid., 69, 149, and 165.
64. Buber, "Distance and Relation," in *The Knowledge of Man*, 96. This article is Buber's most philosophically significant work.
65. Buber, *I and Thou*, 122ff; "Dialogue," in *Between Man and Man*, 14–15. IT, 55; "The Word That Is Spoken," in *The Knowledge of Man*, 114.
66. Buber, *I and Thou*, 151; cf. also Martin Buber, *Moses and Revelation* (New York: Harper and Row, 1958), 39–55; "Replies to My Critics," in *The Philosophy of Martin Buber*, ed. M. Friedman and Schilpp (LaSalle, Ill.: Open Court, 1967), 689–90.
67. Buber, *I and Thou*, 62 and 124–26.

I-Thou, establishes the Between (*das Zwischen*) as the experienced binding together of the Whole. Buber refers to our entering into the Between
of I-Thou-encompassment (if I may so phrase it) as "entering into the
Word," the Logos, the Tao that gathers all together when we learn to let
it be in its unpredictable flashing forth.[68] For Buber, such happenings,
bound together in the experience of faith, not only accomplish our own
healing; they also redeem things.[69] But here, it seems, we pass beyond
phenomenological description to particular belief and proclamation.

The Between is a relational context, grounded on the one hand in
the basic structure of humanness as relation to that which transcends
the whole of what is, and on the other in the speech of Yahweh as Eternal Thou. It is actualized momentarily as the Between in meeting with
the Thou in any encounterable Other and more enduringly but partially
when living with the Thou establishes a relation; but it is actualized with
in-principle plenitude when meetings and relations with the finite Thou
become a world of Thou in hearing them all as divine speech.

CONCLUSION

My initial contention was that Picard's conception of Silence, Heidegger's
meditation on Being, and Buber's notion of the Between stem from the
same region of experience that provides the relational context for all human relations. We have given a brief exposition of each in turn. It is time
to conclude by attempting to draw the considerations together in order to
locate the phenomena involved within the field of human experience.[70]

Human nature has a double ground. On the one hand, there is the
obvious *biological ground*, jutting into the field of awareness as *sensa* correlated with the upsurge of desire for nourishment and sex and anchored
in the flowing now. On the other hand, there is, less obvious, what I call
the *ontological ground*. It is that whose articulation the three thinkers
together have attempted in their differing ways. Usually only prereflec-

68. "What Is Common to All," in *The Knowledge of Man*, 89–91, 96–98, 104–7; cf. also "The
Teaching of the Tao," in *Pointing the Way*, trans. M. Friedman (New York: Harper and Row,
1963), 31–58.

69. Martin Buber, *Hasidism and Modern Man*, ed. and trans. M. Friedman (New York:
Harper and Row, 1958), 33 and 118.

70. Cf. my *A Path into Metaphysics* for a larger framework and fuller development of the
notions advanced in this section.

tively present in the field of awareness as reference to the encompassing Whole, the ontological ground is evidenced in the unrestrictedness of the principle of noncontradiction, our first intuitive articulation of the notion of Being. Reference to the Whole is reference to the fullness of Being and includes within its fundamental intention the fullness of ourselves and the fullness of any encounterable other. Such encompassing reference indicates the essential nonclosure of our own selves, our being pried loose by nature from any putative sealed-in subjectivity: the self is a node in a relational system that opens out to the Whole. This opening indicates as well the essential excess in things beyond any objectification we may achieve. The distance from any particular, any limited presentation afforded by that reference forces upon us by our nature the necessity to choose how we are to settle the problems posed by our nature and situation. We are forced first of all to interpret what it is that confronts us in the field of sensory presentation and desire and who we are who are condemned to this task. We are confronted secondly with the necessity of choosing how we are to act in the light of those interpretive decisions. The sedimented results of such decisions fill the initially empty space between the full plenitude of the *sensa* and the empty totality of Being with institutions, beginning with language, which appear to those born into them as second nature. Hence, the feeling of the need for interpretive decision is blunted. Within this context, the reference to the Whole gets articulated in such a way as to establish a certain "feel," a "sense" of Being that constitutes the "heart," the "core" of our own being.[71] This sense is a dynamic sense that orients us in terms of significant presences that draw near as precious and in terms of at-hand objects that stand at a distance as hostile or indifferent. However, the process tends to settle into comfortable routines of stereotypical identification and routinized responses that constitute a commonsense "dashboard realism"[72] whereby we learn to push, pull, and turn what presents itself on the everyday surface of things in order to get the responses that help us to realize our preconceived ends. The thrust of our nature toward Being as a Whole is dulled by our presumptive achievement of adult experience. The empty inten-

71. For a full development of the notion of "the heart," cf. Stephen Strasser, *Phenomenology of Feeling*.

72. This felicitous expression is Owen Barfield's in *Saving the Appearances: An Essay in Idolatry* (New York: Harcourt, Brace and World, n.d.), 28–35.

tion of the wholeness of each being within the wholeness of Being is partially filled by the world of culture as we assimilate it and are assimilated to it in making our personal decisions. But this is largely a world of closure and insensitivity. This is "the world" that comes to stand before us, as a relatively closed relational system, as object of experience and use—the It- world, to employ Buber's expression. It comes to stand between us and Being as a screen, verifiable, correct, allowing us to make progress by constraining beings to our terms, as Heidegger observed.

Drawn by our ontological nature, we are impelled to enter into the struggle with biologically and culturally mediated appearance for the sake of Being, our own as well as that of any encounterable Other standing in itself as Thou. Openness to the Thou, the wholeness of a given being that gathers us into our wholeness, "letting things be," manifest before us in often unpredictable and uncontrollable ways—like the emergence of a friend or a beloved at the level of beings or the emergence of a vocation or a new sense of the Whole at the ontological level—depends upon our ability to enter into silence: indeed, to carry silence with us as a cushion, as Picard describes it. Developing the spirit of silence is a concrete entering into the full intentionality of our nature as referred, beyond all filling, to the mystery of wholeness. The spirit of silence holds off the noise of our desires and the chatter of the It-world. The spirit of silence holds open the space for heeding the not fully disclosed as it draws near. Our initially empty natural orientation toward the Whole is then filled in a way other than either the filling of everyday common sense or even the filling of an intellectual mastery of portions of the world within and beyond the common-sense world. It is filled by reason of openness to the mystery that we touch in every encounter but can never encompass. It is filled through alertness and appreciation, a thankful thinking perhaps best given expression in the arts. Silence alerts us to the ground of metaphysics but also to the essential insufficiency of any metaphysics for the encompassing mystery that lies at the heart of each thing.

Awe before the mystery of Being, silent heeding of the sacred as it speaks to us in all things constitutes the depth dimension of our own being. But this is a dimension obscured by our noisy busyness, our overweening desire to make progress in mastering the world and to fill our lives with novel experiences. Returning to silence prepares us to receive the unpredictable flashing forth of the Thou and to heed the call of the mystery of Being.

Viewed in this way—with the help of Picard's notion of Silence, Heidegger's notion of Being, and Buber's notion of the Between—the human being appears as no sealed-in monad but rather as related, in the mode of manifestness, to the whole of Being by being related, in and through sensory manifestness and cultural mediation, to the wholeness of each encounterable Other. The manifestness of Being is not something we can coerce with suitable methods, for methods set things within our networks of relation. The manifestness of Being is that which precedes all methods and allows us to return the methodologically captured to its own concealed fullness within the even more deeply concealed fullness of encompassing Being.[73]

73. For a development of this theme, see my "Being and Manifestness: Philosophy, Science and Poetry within an Evolutionary Worldview," *International Philosophical Quarterly* (December 1995): 437–47.

Bibliography

Anselm. *Proslogion*. Edited and with an introduction by Thomas Williams. Indianapolis: Hackett, 2001.

Anzenbacher, Arno. *Die Philosophie Martin Bubers*. Vienna: Schendl, 1965. St. Louis, Mo.: Aquinas Institute, 2012.

Aquinas, Thomas. *Summa Theologiae*.

———. *Summa Contra Gentiles*. Notre Dame, Ind.: University of Notre Dame Press, 1975.

———. *On Being and Essence*. Translated and edited by A. Maurer. Toronto: Pontifical Institute of Medieval Studies, 1949.

———. *Quaestiones Quodlibitales*. Turino: Marietti, 1949.

Aristotle. *Metaphysics*. 2 vols. Translated by H. Tredennick. Cambridge, Mass.: Harvard University Press, 1941.

———. *Sophistical Refutations*. Translated by E. Forster. Cambridge: Oxford University Press, 1955.

———. *Nicomachean Ethics*. Translated by H. Rackham. Cambridge, Mass.: Harvard University Press, 1975.

———. *On the Soul*. Translated by William Hett. *Peri Psyches*. Cambridge, Mass.: Harvard University Press, 1975.

———. *Physics*. Translated by P. Wicksteed and F. Cornford. Cambridge, Mass.: Harvard University Press, 1980.

Augustine, Aurelius. *Confessions*. Translated by William Watts. 2 vols. Cambridge, Mass.: Harvard University Press, 1974.

———. *On True Religion*. Translated by J. Burleigh and L. Mink. New York: Henri Regnery, 1991.

———. *Tractates on the Gospel of John*. Translated by J. Rettig. Washington, D.C.: The Catholic University of America Press, 2002.

Barfield, Owen. *Saving the Appearances: An Essay in Idolatry*. New York: Harcourt, Brace and World, n.d.

Baur, M., and R. Wood, eds. *Person, Being, and History: Essays in Honor of Kenneth Schmitz*. Washington, D.C.: The Catholic University of America Press, 2012.

Berger, Peter. *The Sacred Canopy*. Garden City, N.Y.: Anchor Books, 1969.

Berger, Peter, Brigette Berger, and Hansfried Kellner. *The Homeless Mind, Modernization and Consciousness*. New York: Vintage, 1973.

Bergson, Henri. *Creative Evolution*. Translated by A. Mitchell. New York: Modem Library, 1944.

————. *Creative Mind.* Translated by M. Andison. New York: Philosophical Library, 1946.

————. *Time and Free Will: An Essay on the Immediate Data of Consciousness.* Translated by F. Pogson. London: Allen and Unwin, 1950.

Berkeley, George. *Three Dialogues Between Hylas and Philonous.* LaSalle: Open Court, 1945.

————. *Philosophical Commentaries.* In *The Works of George Berkeley, Bishop of Cloyne*, ed. A. Luce and T. Jessop, vol. 1. London: Nelson, 1948.

————. *The Principles of Human Knowledge.* Gloucester: Peter Smith, 1978.

Bernstein, Richard. "Why Hegel Now?" *The Review of Metaphysics* 31, no. 1 (1977): 29–60.

Brandom, Robert. *Reasoning, Representing, and Discursive Commitment.* Cambridge, Mass.: Harvard University Press, 1994.

Brown, Peter. *Body and Society: Men, Women, and Sexual Renunciation in Early Christianity.* New York: Columbia University Press, 1988.

Buber, Martin. "Buddha." In *Neue Blätter.* Hellerau and Berlin: Erich Baron, 1913.

————. *Good and Evil.* Translated by R. G. Smith. New York: Scribner, 1953.

————. "Dialogue." In *Between Man and Man*, translated by R. G. Smith, 1–39. Boston: Beacon Press, 1955.

————. *The Eclipse of God: Studies in the Relation between Religion and Philosophy.* New York: Harper, 1957.

————. *Hasidism and Modern Man,* Edited and translated by M. Friedman. New York: Harper and Row, 1958.

————. *I and Thou.* Translated by R. G. Smith. New York: Scribners, 1958.

————. *The Origin and Meaning of Hasidism.* Translated by M. Friedman. New York: Harper, 1960.

————. "Vorwort." *Schriften zur Philosophie. Werke*, I. Heidelberg: Lambert Schneider und München: Kösel, 1962.

————. "Das Judentum und die Juden." In *Reden über das Judentum.* Köln: Melzer, 1963.

————. *Pointing the Way.* Edited and translated by Maurice Friedman. New York: Harper and Row, 1963.

————. *Schriften zum Chassidismus. Werke, vol. 2.* München: Kösel, 1963.

————. *Schriften zur Bibel. Werke, vol. 3.* München: Kösel, 1963.

————. *Daniel: Dialogues on Realization.* Translated by Maurice Friedman. New York: McGraw-Hill, 1965.

————. *Israel and the World.* New York: Schocken, 1965.

————. *Knowledge of Man.* Translated by M. Friedman. New York: Harper, 1965.

————. "What Is Common to All." In *Knowledge of Man*, translated by M. Friedman and R. Smith, 89–109. New York: Harper and Row, 1965.

————. *For the Sake of Heaven.* Translated by Ludwig Lewisohn. New York: Harper and Row, 1966.

————. *A Believing Humanism.* Translated by Maurice Friedman. New York: Simon and Schuster, 1967.

————. *I and Thou*. Translated by W. Kaufmann. New York: Scribners, 1970.

————. *Briefwechsel aus sieben Jahrzehnten*, vol. 3, edited by Grete Schaeder. Heidelberg: Lambert Schneider, 1975.

Caputo, John D. "Fundamental Themes in Ekhart's Mysticism." *The Thomist* 42, no. 2 (1978): 197–225.

————. *Demythologizing Heidegger*. Bloomington: Indiana University Press, 1993.

————. "Kierkegaard, Heidegger, and the Foundering of Metaphysics." In *Fear and Trembling and Repetition*, International Kierkegaard Commentary, ed. Robert L. Perkins, 201–24. Atlanta: Mercer University Press, 2014.

Caygill, Howard. *Art of Judgment*. Oxford: Blackwell, 1989.

Chuang-tzu. *A Chinese Classic: Chuang-tzu*. Translated by Fung Yu-Lan. Beijing: Foreign Languages Press, 1989.

Cicero. *Marcus Tullus. De Finibus*. Translated by H. Rackham. Cambridge, Mass.: Harvard University Press, 1931.

————. *On Invention et al.* Translated by H. Hubbell. Cambridge, Mass.: Harvard University Press, 1949.

Coleman, Francis X. *The Harmony of Reason: A Study in Kant's Aesthetics*. Pittsburgh: University of Pittsburgh Press, 1974.

Coreth, E. "Die Gestalt einer Metaphysik Heute." *Philosophisches Jahrbuch* 70, no. 2 (1963).

Cornman, James. "Philosophical Analysis and the Future of Metaphysics." In *The Future of Metaphysics*, edited by R. Wood. Chicago: Quadrangle, 1970.

Crawford, Donald. *Kant's Aesthetic Theory*. Madison: University of Wisconsin Press, 1974.

Crites, Stephen. "'The Blissful Security of the Moment': Recollection, Repetition, and Eternal Recurrence." In *Fear and Trembling and Repetition*, International Kierkegaard Commentary, ed. Robert L. Perkins. Atlanta: Mercer University Press, 1993, 225–46.

Croxall, T. H. *Kierkegaard Commentary*. New York: Harper, 1956.

de Chardin, P. Teilhard. *The Phenomenon of Man*. Translated by B. Wall. New York: Harper Torchbook, 1961.

de Vries, Willem. *Hegel's Theory of Mental Activity*. Ithaca, N.Y.: Cornell University Press, 1988.

Derrida, Jacques. "Différance." In *Speech and Phenomena and Other Essays*, translated by D. Allison, 149–52. Evanston, Ill.: Northwestern University Press, 1973.

————. *Of Grammatology*. Translated by G. Spivak. Baltimore: Johns Hopkins University Press, 1976.

————. "Violence and Metaphysics." In *Writing and Difference*, translated by Alan Bass, 79–102. Chicago: The University of Chicago Press, 1978.

————. "Différance." In *Margins of Philosophy*, translated by Alan Bass, 1–28. Chicago: The University of Chicago Press, 1982.

————. "The Supplement of the Copula: Philosophy before Linguistics." In *Margins of Philosophy*, translated by Alan Bass, 175–206. Chicago: The University of Chicago Press, 1982.

454   Bibliography

———. *Of Spirit: Heidegger and the Question*. Translated by G. Bennington and R. Bowlby. Chicago: The University of Chicago Press, 1989.

Descartes, René. *The Philosophical Works of Descartes*. Translated by E. Haldane and G. Ross, vol. I. New York: Dover, 1955.

———. *Discourse on Method*. Translated by D. Cress. Indianapolis: Hackett, 1980.

Dewey, John. "From Absolutism to Experimentalism." In *On Experience, Nature, and Freedom*, edited by R. Bernstein. Indianapolis: Bobbs-Merrill, 1960.

Donceel, J. *Natural Theology*. New York: Sheed and Ward, 1962.

Dostoyevsky, Fyodor. *The Brothers Karamazov*. Translated by C. Garnett and revised by R. Matlaw. New York: W. W. Norton, 1976.

Dufrenne, Mikel. *The Phenomenology of Aesthetic Experience*. Translated by E. Casey et al. Evanston, Ill.: Northwestern University Press, 1993.

Feuerbach, Ludwig. *The Essence of Christianity*. Translated by G. Eliot. New York: Harper, 1957.

Findlay, John. *Hegel: A Re-Examination*. New York: Collier Books, 1962.

Fromm, Eric. *The Art of Loving*. New York: Harper Colophon Books, 1956.

Gadamer, Hans-Georg. *Truth and Method*. New York: Crossroad, 1982.

———. *Heidegger's Ways*. Translated by J. Stanley. Albany: State University of New York Press, 1994.

Gay, Peter. *The Enlightenment: An Interpretation*, vol. 1. New York: Vintage Books, 1966.

Gilson, Etienne. *History of Christian Philosophy in the Middle Ages*. New York: Random House, 1955.

Greene, Murray. *Hegel on the Soul: A Speculative Anthropology*. The Hague: Martinus Nijhoff, 1972.

Gregory of Nyssa. *Hexaemeron*. In *Patrologia Graeca*, vol. 44.

Guardini, R. *The Conversion of St. Augustine*. Translated by E. Briefs. Westminster, Md.: Newman Press, 1960.

Guyer, Paul. *Kant and the Claims of Taste*. Cambridge, Mass.: Harvard University Press, 1979.

Habermas, Jürgen. "Discourse Ethics: Notes on a Program of Philosophical Justification." In *Moral Consciousness and Communicative Action*, translated by C. Lenhardt and S. Nicholsen, 43–115. Cambridge, Mass.: The MIT Press, 1990.

Haldar, Hiralal. *Neo-Hegelianism*. London: Heath, Cranton, 1927.

Harris, Errol. *Nature, Mind, and Modern Science*. London: George Allen and Unwin, 1954.

———. *The Foundations of Metaphysics in Science*. Lanham, Md.: University Press of America, 1983.

Hegel, G. W. F. *Philosophy of Right*. Translated by T. Knox. London: Oxford University Press, 1952.

———. *Philosophy of History*. Translated by J. Sibree. New York: Dover, 1956.

———. *The Science of Logic*. Translated by A. Miller. London: George Allen and Unwin, 1969.

———. *Philosophy of Nature*. Translated by A. Miller. Oxford: Clarendon Press, 1970.

———. *Philosophy of Mind*. Translated by W. Wallace and A. Miller. Oxford: Clarendon Press, 1971.

———. *Aesthetics: Lectures on Fine Art*. Translated by T. Knox. Oxford: Clarendon Press, 1975.

———. *Lectures on the Philosophy of World History*. Translated by H. Nisbet. Cambridge: Cambridge University Press, 1975.

———. *Phenomenology of Spirit*. Translated by A. Miller. Oxford: Oxford University Press, 1977.

———. *Hegel's Philosophy of Spirit*. 3 vols. Edited and translated by M. J. Petry. 3 vols. Dordrecht: D. Reidel, 1979.

———. *Lectures on the Philosophy of Religion*. Translated by P. Hodgson et al. Berkeley: University of California Press, 1988.

———. *Lectures on the History of Philosophy*. Translated by P. Hodgson et al. Berkeley: University of California Press, 1990.

———. *Elements of the Philosophy of Right*. Translated by H. Nisbet. Cambridge: Cambridge University Press, 1991.

———. *The Encyclopaedia Logic*. Translated by T. Geraets, W. Suchting, and H. Harris. Indianapolis: Hackett, 1991.

———. *Lectures on the History of Philosophy*. Translated by E. Haldane. Lincoln: University of Nebraska Press, 1995.

———. *Hegel's Introduction to the System*. Translated with an introduction and commentary by R. Wood. Toronto: University of Toronto Press, 2014.

Heidegger, Martin. *Über den Humanismus*. Frankfurt a.M.: Klosterman, 1947.

———. *What Is Philosophy?* Translated by W. Klubak and J. Wilde. New York: Twayne, 1958.

———. *On the Question of Being*. Translated by W. Kluback and J. Wilde. London: Vision, 1959.

———. *Being and Time*. Translated by J. Macquarrie and E. Robinson. New York: Harper and Row, 1962.

———. *Einführung in die Metaphysik*. Tübingen: Max Niemeyer, 1966.

———. "Memorial Address." In *Discourse on Thinking*, translated by J. Anderson and E. Freund, 43–57. New York: Harper, 1966.

———. *What Is a Thing?* Translated by E. Gendlin. Chicago: Regnery, 1967.

———. *What is Called Thinking?* Translated by F. Wieck and J. Gray. New York: Harper and Row, 1968.

———. *Time and Being*. Translated by J. Stambaugh. New York: Harper and Row, 1969.

———. "On the Essence of Truth." In *Basic Writings*, edited by D. Krell, 113–42. New York: Harper and Row, 1971.

———. *On the Way to Language*. Translated by P. Hertz. San Francisco: Harper and Row, 1971.

———. *Poetry, Language, and Thought*. Translated by A. Hofstadter. New York: Harper, 1971.

————. "Metaphysics as History of Being." In *The End of Philosophy*, translated by J. Stambaugh, 19–26. New York: Harper and Row, 1973.

————. "Logos." In *Early Greek Thinking*, translated by D. Krell and F. Capuzzi, 59–78. San Francisco: Harper, 1975.

————. "Letter on Humanism." In *Martin Heidegger: Basic Writings*, edited by D. Krell, 189–242. New York: Harper and Row, 1977.

————. *The Question Concerning Technology and Other Essays*. Translated by W. Lovitt. New York: Harper and Row, 1977.

————. "Why Do I Stay in the Provinces?" Translated by T. Sheehan. *Listening* XII, no. 3 (Fall 1977): 122–25.

————. *Nietzsche*. 2 vols. Translated by D. Krell. San Francisco: Harper, 1984.

————. *Platon: Sophistes*. In *Gesamtausgabe, II*. Frankfurt am Main: Vittorio Klostermann, 1992.

————. *Prolegomena to a History of the Concept of Time*. Translated by T. Kisiel. Bloomington: Indiana University Press, 1992.

————. *Contributions to Philosophy: From Enowning*. Translated by P. Emad and K. Maly. Bloomington: Indiana University Press, 2000.

————. *Introduction to Metaphysics*. Translated by G. Fried and R. Polt. New Haven, Conn.: Yale University Press, 2000.

————. *The Essence of Truth*. Translated by T. Sadler. London: Continuum, 2002.

Heidegger, Martin, and Eugen Fink. *Heraclitus Seminar*. Translated by C. Seibert. Evanston, Ill.: Northwestern University Press, 1993.

Hobbes, Thomas. *Elementa philosophiae: De Corpore*. London: Crook, 1655.

————. *Leviathan*. Edited by Michael Oakeshott. New York: Collier, 1973.

Hume, David. *Dialogues Concerning Natural Religion*. Indianapolis: Bobbs-Merrill, 1947.

————. *Enquiry Concerning Human Understanding*. Indianapolis: Hackett, 1977.

————. *Enquiry Concerning the Principles of Morals*. Indianapolis: Hackett, 1983.

Husserl, Edmund. *Ideas: General Introduction to Pure Phenomenology*. Translated by W. Boyce Gibson. London: Allen and Unwin; New York: Macmillan, 1952.

————. *Cartesian Meditations*. Translated by D. Cairns. The Hague: Martinus Nijhoff, 1960.

————. *The Crisis of European Sciences and Transcendental Phenomenology*. Translated by D. Carr. Evanston, Ill.: Northwestern University Press, 1970.

Huxley, Aldous. *Brave New World*. New York: Harper, 2006.

Jaeger, Werner. *Paideia: The Ideals of Greek Culture*. 3 vols. Translated by G. Highet. New York: Oxford, 1945.

————. *Theology of the Early Greeks*. Oxford: Clarendon Press, 1960.

Janicaud, Dominque, and Jean-François Mattéi. *Heidegger from Metaphysic to Thought*. Translated by M. Gendre. Albany: State University of New York Press, 1994.

Jaspers, Karl. *Way to Wisdom.* Translated by R. Manheim. New Haven, Conn.: Yale University Press, 1954.

Jonas, Hans. *The Phenomenon of Life: Toward a Philosophical Biology.* New York: Delta, 1966.

Kahn, Charles. *The Art and Thought of Heraclitus.* Cambridge: Cambridge University Press, 1979.

Kant, Immanuel. *Critique of Practical Reason.* Translated by L. W. Beck. Indianapolis: Bobbs-Merrill, 1956.

———. *Foundations of the Metaphysics of Morals.* Translated by L. W. Beck. Indianapolis: Bobbs-Merrill, 1959.

———. *Observations on the Feeling of the Beautiful and the Sublime.* Translated by J. Goldthwait. Berkeley: University of California Press, 1960.

———. *Critique of Pure Reason.* Translated by N. K. Smith. New York: St. Martins, 1965.

———. *Prolegomena to Any Future Metaphysics.* Translated by P. Carus and revised by J. Ellington. Indianapolis: Hackett, 1977.

———. *Critique of Judgment.* Translated by W. Pluhar. Indianapolis: Hackett, 1987.

Kaufmann, Walter. *Friedrich Nietzsche: Philosopher, Psychologist, Anti-Christ.* New York: Meridian Books, 1956.

———. "The Hegel Myth and Its Method." In *The Hegel Myths and Legends,* edited by Jon Stewart, 82–103. Evanston, Ill.: Northwestern University Press, 1996.

Kerferd, George. "Sophists." In *Encyclopaedia Britannica,* 15th ed. Macropaedia, vol. 17, 11a–14a.

Kern, Walter. "Einheit-in-Mannigfaltigkeit." In *Geist in Welt, Festgabe für Karl Rahner,* vol. I. Freiburg i. Br. 1964, 207–39.

Kierkegaard, Søren. *Concluding Unscientific Postscript to Philosophical Fragments.* Translated by D. Swenson. Princeton, N.J.: Princeton University Press, 1941.

———. *Either/Or.* Translated by D. Swenson and L. Swenson. Garden City, N.Y.: Doubleday, 1959.

———. *The Concept of Irony.* Translated by L. Capel. Bloomington: Indiana University Press, 1965.

———. "In Vino Veritas: A Recollection." In *Stages on Life's Way,* translated by W. Lowrie, 25–93. New York: Schocken, 1967.

Kirk, G. S., and J. E. Raven. *The Presocratic Philosophers.* Cambridge: Cambridge University Press, 1966.

Klein, Jacob. *Commentary on Plato's Meno.* Chapel Hill: University of North Carolina Press, 1965.

Kockelmans, J., and T. Kisiel, eds. *Phenomenology and Physical Science.* Evanston, Ill.: Northwestern University Press, 1970.

Kojéve, Alexandre. *Introduction to the Reading of Hegel.* Edited by A. Bloom and translated by J. H. Nichols. New York: Basic Books, 1969.

Lampert, Laurence. *Nietzsche's Teaching: An Interpretation of Thus Spoke Zarathustra.* New Haven, Conn.: Yale University Press, 1986.

Lao Tzu. *Tao te Ching*. Translated by D. Lau. Baltimore: Penguin Books, 1963.

LaPlace, Pierre Simon. *The System of the World*, vol. 1. Translated by J. Pond. London: Richard Philips, 1809.

Leibniz, Gottfried Wilhelm. *The Mondology and Other Philosophical Writings*. Edited and translated by R. Latta. London: Oxford University Press, 1951.

Levinas, Emmanuel. *Totality and Infinity*. Translated by A. Lingis. Pittsburgh: Duquesne University Press, 1969.

Locke, John. "An Essay Concerning Toleration." In *Political Writings of John Locke*, edited by D. Wooton, 186–210. London: Penguin, 1993.

———. "A Letter Concerning Toleration." In *Political Writings of John Locke*, edited by D. Wooton, 390–436. London: Penguin, 1993.

———. *An Essay Concerning Human Understanding*. Baltimore: Penguin, 1998.

Lonergan, B. J. F. *Insight, A Study of Human Understanding*. London: Longman, Green, 1958.

Lotz, J. B. "Being and Existence in Scholasticism and in Existence Philosophy." *Philosophy Today* 8 (Spring 1964): 19–34.

Lyotard, Jean-François. *The Differend: Phrases in Dispute*. Minneapolis: University of Minnesota Press, 1983.

———. *The Postmodern Condition: A Report on Knowledge*. Translated by G. Bennington and B. Massumi. Minneapolis: University of Minnesota Press, 1984.

———. *The Inhuman*. Stanford: Stanford University Press, 1988.

———. *Lessons on the Analytic of the Sublime*. Translated by E. Rottenberg. Stanford: Stanford University Press, 1994.

MacDowell, John. *Mind and World*. Cambridge, Mass.: Harvard University Press, 1994.

MacIntyre, Alasdair. *After Virtue*. Notre Dame: University of Notre Dame Press, 1984.

———. "The Rationality of Traditions." In *Whose Justice, Which Rationality?* 349–69. Notre Dame: University of Notre Dame Press, 1988.

Marcel, Gabriel. *Metaphysical Journal*. Translated by B. Wall. Chicago: Regnery, 1952.

———. *Creative Fidelity*. Translated by R. Rosthal. New York: Noonday, 1957.

———. *The Mystery of Being*. 2 vols. Chicago: Regnery, 1960.

———. "On the Ontological Mystery." In *The Philosophy of Existentialism*, translated by M. Harari, 9–46. New York: Citadel, 1961.

———. *Man Against Mass Society*. Translated by G. Fraser. Chicago: Regnery, 1962.

———. "The Mystery of the Family." In *Homo Viator: Introduction to a Metaphysics of Hope*, translated by E. Craufurd, 68–97. New York: Harper, 1962.

———. *The Existential Background of Human Dignity*. Cambridge, Mass.: Harvard University Press, 1963.

———. *Being and Having*. New York: Harper and Row, 1965.

———. *Tragic Wisdom and Beyond*. Translated by Stephen Jolin and Peter McCormick. Evanston, Ill.: Northwestern University Press, 1973.

———. "An Essay in Autobiography." *Philosophy of Existentialism*. New York: Citadel Press, 2002.

———. *Music and Philosophy*. Introduction by Robert E. Wood. Translated by Steven Maddux. Milwaukee: Marquette University Press, 2005.

Maritain, J. "The Natural Mystical Experience and the Void." In *Ransoming the Time*. Translated by H. Binsee. New York: Scribners, 1941.

Mattéi, Jean-François. "The Heideggerian Chiasmus." In *Heidegger from Metaphysic to Thought*, edited by Dominque Janicaud and Jean-François Mattéi and translated by M. Gendre, 39–150. Albany: State University of New York Press, 1994.

McNeil, Will, ed. *Pathmarks*. Cambridge: Cambridge University Press, 1998.

Merleau-Ponty, Maurice. *The Structure of Behavior*. Translated by A. Fisher. Boston: Beacon Press, 1963.

———. *Signs*. Translated by H. and P. Dreyfus. Evanston, Ill.: Northwestern University Press, 1964.

Michelfelder, D., and R. Palmer, eds. *Dialogue and Deconstruction: The Gadamer-Derrida Encounter*. Albany: State University of New York Press, 1989.

Mumford, Lewis. *The Myth of the Machine: Technics and Human Development*. New York: Harcourt, Brace, and World: 1976.

Natanson, Maurice, ed. *Phenomenology and the Social Sciences*, 2 vols. Evanston, Ill.: Northwestern University Press, 1973.

Nettleship, Richard Lewis. *Lectures on the Republic of Plato*. London: MacMillan, 1964.

Nietzsche, Friedrich. *The Use and Abuse of History*. Translated by A. Collins. Indianapolis: Bobbs-Merill, 1949.

———. *The Portable Nietzsche*. Translated by W. Kaufmann. New York: Viking, 1954.

———. *Philosophy in the Tragic Age of the Greeks*. Translated by M. Cowan. Chicago: Regnery, 1962.

———. *Beyond Good and Evil: Prelude to a Philosophy of the Future*. Translated by W. Kaufmann. New York: Vintage, 1966.

———. *The Birth of Tragedy*. Translated by W. Kaufmann. New York: Vintage, 1967.

———. *The Case of Wagner*. Translated by W. Kaufmann. New York: Vantage, 1967.

———. *On the Genealogy of Morals and Ecce Homo*. Translated by W. Kaufmann. New York: Vintage, 1967.

———. *Will to Power*. Translated by W. Kaufmann and R. Hollingdale. New York: Vintage, 1967.

———. *The Anti-Christ*. Translated by R. Hollingdale. Baltimore: Penguin, 1968.

———. *Twilight of the Idols*. Translated by R. Hollingdale. Baltimore: Penguin, 1968.

———. *The Gay Science*. Translated by W. Kaufmann. New York: Vintage, 1974.

———. *Also Sprach Zarathustra*. Stuttgart: Körner, 1975.

———. *Daybreak: Thoughts on the Prejudices of Morality*. Translated by R. Hollingdale. Cambridge: Cambridge University Press, 1982.

———.*Untimely Meditations*. Translated by R. Hollingdale. Cambridge: Cambridge University Press, 1983.

———. *Human All Too Human: A Book for Free Spirits*. Translated by M. Farber and S. Lehmann. Lincoln: University of Nebraska Press, 1984.

Otto, Rudolf. *The Idea of the Holy*. Translated by J. Harvey. New York: Oxford University Press, 1964.

Owens, Joseph. *A History of Ancient Western Philosophy*. New York: Appleton-Century-Crofts, 1959.

Pascal, Blaise. *Pensées*. New York: Modern Library, 1941.

Paulsen, Friedrick. *Immanuel Kant: His Life and Doctrine*. Translated by J. Creighton and A. Lefevre. New York: Ungar, 1972.

Peirce, Charles Sanders. "The Scientific Attitude and Fallibilism." In *Philosophical Writings of Peirce*, edited by J. Buchler, 42–59. New York: Dover, 1955.

Perkins, Robert. "Woman Bashing in 'In Vino Veritas.'" In *Feminist Interpretations of Søren Kierkegaard*, ed. C. Léon and S. Walsh, 93–94. University Park: Pennsylvania State University Press, 1997.

Picard, Max. *The World of Silence*. Chicago: Regnery, 1954.

———. *Die Welt des Schweigens*. München: Piper, 1988.

Pieper, Joseph. *The Silence of St. Thomas*. Translated by J. Murray and D. O'Connor. New York: Pantheon, 1957.

Pinkard, Terry. *Hegel: A Biography*. Cambridge: Cambridge University Press, 2000.

Pius IX. *Quanta Cura and the Syllabus of Errors*. Kansas City, Mo.: Angelus Press, 2006.

Plato. *Laws*. Translated by R. Bury. Cambridge, Mass.: Harvard University Press, 1926.

———. *Cratylus*. Translated by H. Fowler. Cambridge, Mass.: Harvard University Press, 1929.

———. *Seventh Letter*. Translated by J. Bury. Cambridge, Mass.: Harvard University Press, 1929.

———. *Meno*. Translated by W. Lamb. Cambridge, Mass.: Harvard University Press, 1962.

———. *The Republic of Plato*. Translated by Allan Bloom. New York: Basic Books, 1968.

———. *The Republic*. Translated by Paul Shorey. 2 vols. Cambridge, Mass.: Harvard University Press, 1969.

———. *Gorgias*. Translated by W. Lamb. Cambridge, Mass.: Harvard University Press, 1975.

———. *Politicus*. Translated by W. Lamb. Cambridge, Mass.: Harvard University Press, 1975.

———. *Symposium*. Translated by W. Lamb. Cambridge, Mass.: Harvard University Press, 1975.

————. *Apology*. Translated by W. Lamb. Cambridge, Mass.: Harvard University Press, 1977.

————. *Phaedo*. Translated by W. Lamb. Cambridge, Mass.: Harvard University Press, 1977.

————. *Phaedrus*. Translated by W. Lamb. Cambridge, Mass.: Harvard University Press, 1977.

————. *Sophist*. Translated by H. Fowler. Cambridge, Mass.: Harvard University Press, 1977.

————. *Theaetetus*. Translated by H. Fowler. Cambridge, Mass.: Harvard University Press, 1977.

Plotinus. *Enneads*. Translated by Stephen McKenna. New York: Larson, 1992.

Polanyi, Michael. *The Tacit Dimension*. Garden City, N.Y.: Doubleday, 1966.

Popper, Karl. *The Open Society and Its Enemies*, vol. 2. Princeton, N.J.: Princeton University Press, 1962.

————. *Conjectures and Refutations: The Growth of Scientific Knowledge*. New York: Harper, 1963.

Popper, Karl, and John Eccles. *The Self and Its Brain*. Berlin: Springer International, 1977.

Potts, Alex. *Flesh and the Ideal: Winckelmann and the Origins of Art History*. New Haven, Conn.: Yale University Press, 1994.

Pritzl, Kurt. *On Truth: A Robust Presence*. Washington, D.C.: The Catholic University of America Press, 2010.

Quine, Willard van Orman. *The Web of Belief*. New York: McGraw-Hill, 1978.

Ranakrishna, Sarvepalli, and Charles Moore, eds. *A Sourcebook in Indian Philosophy*. Princeton, N.J.: Princeton University Press, 1957.

Richardson, John. *Nietzsche's System*. New York: Oxford University Press, 1992.

Ricoeur, Paul. *Fallible Man*. Translated by C. Kelbley. Chicago: Regnery, 1965.

Rosen, Stanley. *The Question of Being: A Reversal of Heidegger*. New Haven, Conn.: Yale University Press, 1993.

————. *The Mask of Enlightenment: Nietzsche's Zarathustra*. Cambridge: Cambridge University Press, 1995.

Rosenthal, David. *The Nature of Mind*. New York: Oxford University Press, 1991.

Russell, Bertrand. *History of Western Philosophy*. New York: Simon and Schuster, 1945.

————. "Logic and Metaphysics." In *An Inquiry into Meaning and Truth*. London: Allen and Unwin, 1940. Excerpted in *Contemporary Philosophy*, edited by J. Jarett and S. McMurrin. New York: Holt, Rinehart, Winston, 1961.

Sartre, Jean-Paul. *Being and Nothingness*. Translated by H. Barnes. New York: Philosophical Library, 1956.

————. "Existentialism Is a Humanism." In *Existentialism from Dostoyevsky to Sartre*, edited and translated by W. Kaufmann, 287–311. New York: Meridian, 1956.

Scheler, Max Ferdinand. *The Nature of Sympathy*. Translated by P. Heath. New Haven, Conn.: Yale University Press, 1954.

————. *On the Eternal in Man*. Translated by B. Noble. New York: Harper, 1960.

Schiller, Friedrich. *On the Aesthetic Education of Man*. New York: Ungar, 1965.

Schlipp, Paul, ed. *Philosophy of Martin Buber*. Lasalle, Ill.: Open Court, 1967.

Schopenhauer, Arthur. *The World as Will and Representation*, vol. 1. Translated by E. Payne. New York: Dover, 1966.

Schürmann, Reiner. *Heidegger on Being and Acting: From Anarchy to Principles*. Bloomington: Indiana University Press, 1990.

Snell, Bruno. *The Discovery of the Mind*. Translated by T. Rosenmeyer. Cambridge, Mass.: Harvard University Press, 1953.

Solomon, Robert. *In the Spirit of Hegel*. New York: Oxford University Press, 1983.

Spiegelberg, Herbert. *The Phenomenological Movement: A Historical Introduction*. Phenomenologica 6. The Hague: Martinus Nijhoff, 1960.

Spinoza, Benedict de. *A Theological-Political Treatise*. Translated by R. Elwes. New York: Dover, 1951.

————. *On the Improvement of the Understanding, Ethics, and Correspondence*. Translated by R. Elwes. New York: Dover, 1955.

Strasser, Stephan. *Das Gemüt. Utrecht and Freiburg, 1956. Translated as Phenomenology of Feeling: An Essay on the Phenomena of the Heart*. Translated and introduced by Robert E. Wood. Preface to the English edition by Paul Ricoeur. Atlantic Highlands, N.J.: Humanities Press, 1977.

Strauss, Leo. "The Three Waves of Modernity." In *An Introduction to Political Philosophy: Ten Essays*, edited by Hilail Gildin, 81–98. Detroit: Wayne State University Press, 1989.

Taminiaux, Jacques. *Reading Heidegger: Commemorations*. Bloomington: Indiana University Press, 1993.

Taylor, Charles. *Hegel*. Cambridge: Cambridge University Press, 1975.

Tillich, Paul. *Systematic Theology*. 3 vols. Chicago: The University of Chicago Press, 1951–1963.

van Melsen, Adrian. *From Atomos to Atom*. New York: Harper, 1960.

Voltaire. *Candide*. Translated by T. G. Smollett. New York: Washington Square, 1962.

Von Balthasar, Hans Urs. *The Glory of the Lord. Vol. 1. Seeing the Form*. Translated by E. Leiva-Merikakis. San Francisco: Ignatius Press, 1982.

————. *Studies in Theological Style: Clerical Styles*. Translated by A. Louth, F. McDonagh, and B. McNeil. Vol. 2 of *The Glory of the Lord*. San Francisco: Ignatius Press, 1984.

von Schelling, Friedrich Wilhelm Joseph. *System des transzendentalen Idealismus, Schriften von 1799–1801*. Darmstadt: Wissenschaftliche Buchgesellschaft, 1982.

Vycinas, V. *Earth and Gods, An Introduction to the Philosophy of Martin Heidegger*. The Hague: Martinus Nijhoff, 1961.

Weiss, Paul. *Nature and Man*. Carbondale: Southern Illinois University Press, 1947.

———. *Modes of Being*. Carbondale: Southern Illinois University Press, 1958.

———. *Nine Basic Arts*. Carbondale: Southern Illinois University Press, 1960.

———. *The World of Art*. Carbondale: Southern Illinois University Press, 1961.

———. *Philosophy in Process, vol. II*. Carbondale: Southern Illinois University Press, 1962.

———. "Our Knowledge of What Is Real." *The Review of Metaphysics* 18, no. 1 (September 1964).

———. *Reality*. Carbondale: Southern Illinois University Press, 1966.

———. *Beyond All Appearances*. Carbondale: Southern Illinois University Press, 1974.

———. *First Considerations*. Carbondale: Southern Illinois University Press, 1977.

Wheelwright, Philip. *The Presocratics*. New York: Odyssey, 1966.

Whitehead, Alfred North. *Process and Reality: An Essay in Cosmology*. New York: Harper, 1957.

———. *Science and the Modern World*. New York: Free Press, 1957.

———. *Adventures of Ideas*. New York: Free Press, 1967.

Winckelmann, Johann Joachim. *History of Ancient Art*. 4 vols. Translated by G. Lodge. Boston: Little Brown and Company, 1856–1873.

———. *Reflections on the Imitation of Greek Works in Painting and Sculpture*. Translated by E. Heyeer and R. Norton. LaSalle, Ill.: Open Court, 1987.

Wood, Robert E. *Martin Buber's Ontology, An Analysis of I and Thou*. Evanston, Ill.: Northwestern University Press, 1969.

———. "Buber's Conception of Philosophy." *Thought* 53 (September 1979): 310–19.

———. "Oriental Themes in Buber's Work." In *Martin Buber: A Centenary Volume*, edited by H. Gordon and J. Bloch, 325–49. Beersheva: Ktav, 1984.

———. "Heidegger on the Way to Language." In *Semiotics 1984*, edited by J. Deely, 611–20. Lanham, Md.: University Press of America, 1986.

———. "Martin Buber's Philosophy of the Word." *Philosophy Today* 30 (Winter 1986): 317–24.

———. "Aesthetics within the Kantian Project." In *Philosophy and Art*, edited by D. Dahlstrom, 175–92. Washington, D.C.: The Catholic University of America Press, 1990.

———. *A Path into Metaphysics: Phenomenological, Hermeneutical, and Dialogical Studies*. Albany: State University of New York Press, 1991.

———. "Silence, Being and the Between: Picard, Heidegger and Buber." *Man and World* 27 (1994): 121–34.

———. *Placing Aesthetics: Reflections on the Philosophic Tradition*. Athens: Ohio University Press, 1999.

———. "Tactility: An Essay in Phenomenological Description." *Southwest Philosophy Review* 17, no. 1 (January 2000): 19–26.

———. "The Fugal Lines of Heidegger's *Beiträge*." *Existentia* 11 (2001): fasc. 3–4, 253–66.

———. "Hegel on the Heart." *International Philosophical Quarterly* (June 2001): 133–44.

———. "Individuals, Universals, and Capacity." *The Review of Metaphysics* 54, no. 3 (March 2001): 507–28.

———. "Phenomenology and the Perennial Task of Philosophy: A Study of Plato and Aristotle." *Existentia* 2 (2002): fasc. 3–4, 253–63.

———. "Potentiality, Creativity, and Relationality: Creative Power as a 'New' Transcendental?" *The Review of Metaphysics* 59 (December 2005): 379–401.

———. "Doxa and Eros, Speech and Writing, with Special Attention to Plato's *Symposium*." *Existentia* (2009): 247–61.

———. "Five Bodies and a Sixth: On the Place of Awareness in the Cosmos." *American Catholic Philosophical Quarterly* 93 (2009): 95–105.

———. "The Free Spirit: Spinoza, Hegel, Nietzsche." *International Philosophical Quarterly* 51, no. 3 (Fall 2011): 377–87.

———. "Heidegger's *In-der-Welt-Sein* and Hegel's *Sittlichkeit*." *Existentia* 21, fasc. 3–4 (2011): 255–74.

Wood, Robert, and Charles Sullivan. "Rationality and Actuality: Hegel and the Prussian Reform Movement." *Existentia* 21, fasc. 1–2 (2011): 57–78.

Zammito, John. *The Genesis of Kant's Critique of Judgment*. Chicago: The University of Chicago Press, 1990.

Zimmermann, Michael. *Heidegger's Confrontation with Modernity: Technology, Politics, Art*. Bloomington: Indiana University Press, 1990.

Index of Authors

Subject Index

The Beautiful, the True & the Good: Studies in the History of Thought was designed and typeset in Minion by Kachergis Book Design of Pittsboro, North Carolina. It was printed on 60-pound Natures Book Natural and bound by Thomson-Shore of Dexter, Michigan.